THE BEST OF
THE FUTURE OF BUSINESS

> **Lawrence J. Gitman**
San Diego State University

> **Carl McDaniel**
University of Texas, Arlington

THOMSON

™

SOUTH-WESTERN

Australia · Canada · Mexico · Singapore · Spain · United Kingdom · United States

THOMSON
SOUTH-WESTERN

The Best of the Future of Business
By Lawrence J. Gitman and Carl McDaniel

Vice President/Editor-in-Chief:
Jack Calhoun

Vice President/Team Leader:
Melissa Acuna

Acquisitions Editor:
Steve Hazelwood

Developmental Editor:
Mary Draper

Production Editor:
Kelly Keeler

Manufacturing Coordinator:
Diane Lohman

Compositor:
Pre-Press Company, Inc.

Printer:
Courier, Kendalville, IN

Design Project Manager:
Michael H. Stratton

Internal Designer:
Michael H. Stratton

Cover Designer:
Casey Gilbertson

Cover Images:
PhotoDisc, Inc.

Photography Manager:
Deanna Ettinger

Photo Researcher:
Darren Wright

Library of Congress Cataloging-in-
Publication Data

Gitman, Lawrence J.
The best of the future of business /
  Lawrence J. Gitman, Carl McDaniel.
  p. cm
  Includes bibliographical references
  and index.
  ISBN: 0-324-18374-7 (soft cover)
    1. Management—United States.
    2. Business enterprises—United
    States. I. McDaniel, Carl D.
    II. Title.

HD70.U5 G5295 2002
658—dc21   2002022762

Prologue   1

>PART 1 PARTICIPATING IN THE GLOBAL BUSINESS ENVIRONMENT
>1 Understanding Economic Systems and Competition   14
>2 Competing in the Global Marketplace   46
>3 Making Ethical Decisions and Managing a Socially Responsible Business   80

>PART 2 STARTING AND GROWING A BUSINESS
>4 Forms of Business Ownership   106
>5 Entrepreneurship: Starting and Growing a Business   138

>PART 3 MANAGING FOR COMPETITIVE SUCCESS
>6 Management and Leadership in Today's Organization   170
>7 Designing Organizational Structures   196
>8 Achieving World-Class Operations Management   222

>PART 4 MANAGING AND LEADING HUMAN RESOURCES
>9 Managing Human Resources   254
>10 Motivating Employees and Creating Self-Managed Teams   286

>PART 5 MARKETING: DELIVERING VALUE TO THE CUSTOMER
>11 Understanding the Customer and Creating Goods and
    Services That Satisfy   312
>12 Developing the Marketing Mix   340

>PART 6 USING TECHNOLOGY AND MANAGING FINANCIAL RESOURCES
>13 Using Technology to Manage Information   368
>14 Using Financial Information and Accounting   390
>15 Understanding Money and Financial Institutions   418
>16 Financial Management and Securities Markets   438

APPENDICES
>A Understanding the Legal and Tax Environment   466
>B Managing Risk and Insurance   477

ENRICHMENT CHAPTERS
>A Using the Internet for Business Success—find it on the Student Companion CD-ROM
>B Managing Your Personal Finances—find it on the Student Companion CD-ROM.

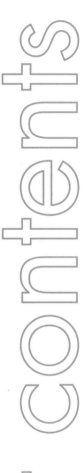

14

contents

PROLOGUE   1

Capitalizing on Trends in Business   2

Section 2

SOCIAL TRENDS   3
The Growth of Component Lifestyles   3
The Changing Role of Families and
Working Women   4
DEMOGRAPHIC TRENDS   4
Generation Y—Born to Shop   4
Generation X—Savvy and Cynical   5
Baby Boomers—America's Mass Market   5
Older Consumers—Not Just Grand-
parents   6   Americans on the Move   6
Growing Ethnic Markets   7
**EVOLVING GLOBAL ECONOMIC
SYSTEMS   7**
Capitalism   7   The Command
Economy   8   Socialism   9   Mixed
Economic Systems   9
TECHNOLOGICAL TRENDS   9
TRENDS IN GLOBAL COMPETITION   11
Technology and Communications   12
Improvements in Productivity   13

**>PART 1   PARTICIPATING IN THE GLOBAL
BUSINESS ENVIRONMENT**

**>1   UNDERSTANDING ECONOMIC SYSTEMS
AND COMPETITION   14**

Business in the 21st Century   16

Section 1

THE NATURE OF BUSINESS   16
Not-for-Profit Organizations   17
Factors of Production: The Building Blocks
of Business   17
**HOW BUSINESSES AND ECONOMIES
WORK   18**
Macroeconomics and Microeconomics   19
Economics as a Circular Flow   19
**MACROECONOMICS: THE BIG
PICTURE   20**
Striving for Economic Growth   21
Keeping People on the Job   22
Keeping Prices Steady   23
**ACHIEVING MACROECONOMIC
GOALS   24**
Monetary Policy   24
Fiscal Policy   25

**MICROECONOMICS: ZEROING IN ON
BUSINESSES AND CONSUMERS   28**
The Nature of Demand   28   The Nature
of Supply   29   How Demand and Supply
Interact to Determine Prices   29
COMPETING IN A FREE MARKET   31
Perfect Competition   32   Pure
Monopoly   32   Monopolistic
Competition   33   Oligopoly   34

Capitalizing on Trends in Business   34

Section 2

Delivering Value and Quality   34
Creating Long-Term Relationships   36
Creating a Competitive Workforce   37
Entrepreneurial Spirit in Former
Command Economies   37

Applying This Chapter's Topics   39

Section 3

SUMMARY OF LEARNING GOALS   40
PREPARING FOR TOMORROW'S
WORKPLACE   42
WORKING THE NET   42
CREATIVE THINKING CASE   43
VIDEO CASE   44
E-COMMERCE CASE   45

**>2   COMPETING IN THE GLOBAL
MARKETPLACE   46**

Business in the 21st Century   48

Section 1

AMERICA GOES GLOBAL   48
The Importance of Global Business to the
United States   49
**MEASURING TRADE BETWEEN
NATIONS   49**
Exports and Imports   49   Balance of
Trade   50   Balance of Payments   50
The Changing Value of Currencies   51
WHY NATIONS TRADE   52
Absolute Advantage   52   Comparative
Advantage   52
BARRIERS TO TRADE   52
Natural Barriers   53   Tariff Barriers   54
Nontariff Barriers   55
FOSTERING GLOBAL TRADE   56
Antidumping Laws   56   The Uruguay
Round and the World Trade Organi-
zation   56   The World Bank and
International Monetary Fund   58
**INTERNATIONAL ECONOMIC
COMMUNITIES   59**
North American Free Trade Agreement
(NAFTA)   59   The European Union   60
The Euro   62

PARTICIPATING IN THE GLOBAL
MARKETPLACE 62
  Exporting 63   Licensing 63
  Contract Manufacturing 64   Joint
  Ventures 65   Direct Foreign
  Investment 65   Countertrade 66
THREATS AND OPPORTUNITIES IN THE
GLOBAL MARKETPLACE 66
  Political Considerations 66   Cultural
  Differences 67   Economic
  Environment 67
THE IMPACT OF MULTINATIONAL COR-
PORATIONS 69
  The Multinational Advantage 70

Section 2
  Capitalizing on Trends in Business 71
  Market Expansion 71   Resource
  Acquisition 72   Competition 72
  Technological Change 72   Government
  Actions 72

Section 3
  Applying This Chapter's Topics 73
  Continue Your Education 73
  Study the Role of a Global Manager 73

  SUMMARY OF LEARNING GOALS 74
  PREPARING FOR TOMORROW'S
  WORKPLACE 76
  WORKING THE NET 76
  CREATIVE THINKING CASE 77
  VIDEO CASE 78
  E-COMMERCE CASE 79

>3   MAKING ETHICAL DECISIONS AND
      MANAGING A SOCIALLY RESPONSIBLE
      BUSINESS 80

Section 1
  Business in the 21st Century 82
  INDIVIDUAL BUSINESS ETHICS 82
  Utilitarianism 82   Individual Rights 83
  Justice—The Fairness Question 83
  Stages of Ethical Development 83
HOW ORGANIZATIONS INFLUENCE ETHI-
CAL CONDUCT 84
  Recognizing Unethical Business
  Actions 85   Resolving Ethical Problems
  in Business 86   Leading By Example
  87   Ethics Training 88   Establishing
  a Formal Code of Ethics 89

MANAGING TO BE SOCIALLY
RESPONSIBLE 89
  Understanding Social Responsibility 92
RESPONSIBILITIES TO
STAKEHOLDERS 94
  Responsibility to Employees 94
  Responsibility to Customers 95
  Responsibility to the General Public 96
  Responsibilities to Investors 97

Section 2
  Capitalizing on Trends in Business 98
  Trends in Corporate Philanthropy 98
  A New Social Contract Trend Between
  Employer and Employee 99   Trends in
  Global Ethics and Social Responsibility 99

Section 3
  Applying This Chapter's Topics 100
  Ethics Are Part of Everyday Life 100
  Work for a Firm That Cares About Its Social
  Responsibilities 101

  SUMMARY OF LEARNING GOALS 102
  PREPARING FOR TOMORROW'S
  WORKPLACE 103
  WORKING THE NET 103
  CREATIVE THINKING CASE 103
  VIDEO CASE 104
  E-COMMERCE CASE 105

>PART 2 STARTING AND GROWING A
         BUSINESS

>4   FORMS OF BUSINESS OWNERSHIP 106

Section 1
  Business in the 21st Century 108
  TYPES OF BUSINESS ORGANIZATION
  109
  SOLE PROPRIETORSHIPS 109
  Advantages of Sole Proprietorships 110
  Disadvantages of Sole Proprietorships 110
PARTNERSHIPS 111
  Advantages of Partnerships 112
  Disadvantages of Partnerships 112
CORPORATIONS 114
  The Incorporation Process 115   The
  Corporate Structure 116   Advantages
  of Corporations 117   Disadvantages
  of Corporations 118   Types of
  Corporations 118
SPECIALIZED FORMS OF BUSINESS ORGA-
NIZATION 120
  Cooperatives 120   Joint Ventures 121
FRANCHISING 121
  Advantages of Franchises 122
  Disadvantages of Franchises 123
  Franchise Growth 124   International
  Franchising 125

80

138

CORPORATE GROWTH THROUGH MERGERS AND ACQUISITIONS 125

Merger Motives 126 Types of Mergers 127

Section 2 Capitalizing on Trends in Business 128
Niche Markets 128
New Twists for Existing Franchises 128
The Big Get Bigger 129
Hands Across the Sea 129

Section 3 Applying This Chapter's Topics 130
Is Franchising in Your Future? 130
Mergers and You 132

SUMMARY OF LEARNING GOALS 132
PREPARING FOR TOMORROW'S WORKPLACE 134
WORKING THE NET 135
CREATIVE THINKING CASE 135
VIDEO CASE 136
E-COMMERCE CASE 137

>5 ENTREPRENEURSHIP: STARTING AND GROWING A BUSINESS 138

Section 1 Business in the 21st Century 140
ENTREPRENEURSHIP TODAY 141
Entrepreneur or Small Business Owner? 141 Types of Entrepreneurs 141
Why Become an Entrepreneur? 143
CHARACTERISTICS OF SUCCESSFUL ENTREPRENEURSHIPS 143
The Entrepreneurial Personality 144
Managerial Ability and Technological Knowledge 144
SMALL BUSINESS 145
What is a Small Business? 146
Advantages of Small Business 147
Disadvantages of Small Business 148
The Small Business Administration 149
STARTING YOUR OWN BUSINESS 150
Getting Started 150 Developing the Business Plan 151 Financing the Business 153 Buying a Small Business 154 Risks of Small Business Ownership 154

MANAGING A SMALL BUSINESS 155
Using Outside Consultants 156 Hiring and Retaining Employees 156
Operating Internationally 157

Section 2 Capitalizing on Trends in Business 157
Home Is Where the Office Is 158
Ownership Trends 158
The Internet Explosion 161

Section 3 Applying This Chapter's Topics 162
Taking the First Steps 162
Working at a Small Business 163

SUMMARY OF LEARNING GOALS 164
PREPARING FOR TOMORROW'S WORKPLACE 166
WORKING THE NET 167
CREATIVE THINKING CASE 167
VIDEO CASE 168
E-COMMERCE CASE 169

>PART 3 MANAGING FOR COMPETITIVE SUCCESS

>6 MANAGEMENT AND LEADERSHIP IN TODAY'S ORGANIZATION 170

Section 1 Business in the 21st Century 172
THE ROLE OF MANAGEMENT 172
PLANNING 172
ORGANIZING 176
LEADING 177
Leadership Styles 178 Employee Empowerment 179 Corporate Culture 180
CONTROLLING 181
MANAGERIAL ROLES 183
Managerial Decision-Making 183
MANAGERIAL SKILLS 185
Technical Skills 185
Human Relations Skills 187
Conceptual Skills 187
Global Management Skills 188

Section 2 Capitalizing on Trends in Business 188
Managers Empowering Employees 188
Managers and Information Technology 189
Managing in a Global Marketplace 189

Section 3 Applying This Chapter's Topics 189
Effective Time Management 190
Decision-Making Skills 190

SUMMARY OF LEARNING GOALS 191
PREPARING FOR TOMORROW'S WORKPLACE 193
WORKING THE NET 193
CREATIVE THINKING CASE 193

VIDEO CASE   194
E-COMMERCE CASE   195

>7   DESIGNING ORGANIZATIONAL STRUCTURES   196

Section 1
Business in the 21st Century   198
STRUCTURAL BUILDING BLOCKS   198
Division of Labor   198
Departmentalization   199   Managerial
Hierarchy   200   Span of Control   202
Centralization of Decision-Making   203
**MECHANISTIC VERSUS ORGANIC
STRUCTURES   205**
**COMMON ORGANIZATIONAL
STRUCTURES   206**
Line Organization   207   Line-and-Staff
Organization   207   Committee Structure
207   Matrix Structure   208
**REENGINEERING ORGANIZATION
STRUCTURE   210**
THE INFORMAL ORGANIZATION   212
Functions of the Informal Organization
212

Section 2
Capitalizing on Trends in Business   214
The Virtual Corporation   214
Structuring for Global Mergers   215

Section 3
Applying This Chapter's Topics   215
SUMMARY OF LEARNING GOALS   217
PREPARING FOR TOMORROW'S WORK-
PLACE   218
WORKING THE NET   219
CREATIVE THINKING CASE   219
VIDEO CASE   220
E-COMMERCE CASE   221

**>8   ACHIEVING WORLD-CLASS OPERATIONS
MANAGEMENT   222**

Section 1
Business in the 21st Century   224
**PRODUCTION AND OPERATIONS
MANAGEMENT—AN OVERVIEW   225**
PRODUCTION PLANNING   226
Production Process   227   Site Selection
229   Facility Layout   232   Resource
Planning   232   Supply Chain
Management   237

**PRODUCTION AND OPERATIONS
CONTROL   238**
Routing Production   238   Scheduling
238
**IMPROVING PRODUCTION AND
OPERATIONS   241**
Total Quality Management   241   The
Move toward Lean Manufacturing   241
Automation in Productions and Operations
Management   242   Technology and
Automation in Nonmanufacturing
Operations   244

Section 2
Capitalizing on Trends in Business   245
Modular Production   245
Agile Manufacturing   246
Trends in Facility Layout   246

Section 3
Applying This Chapter's Topics   246
SUMMARY OF LEARNING GOALS   247
PREPARING FOR TOMORROW'S WORK-
PLACE   250
WORKING THE NET   250
CREATIVE THINKING CASE   251
VIDEO CASE   251
E-COMMERCE CASE   253

**>PART 4   Managing and Leading Human
Resources**

>9   MANAGING HUMAN RESOURCES   254

Section 1
Business in the 21st Century   256
**DEVELOPING PEOPLE TO HELP REACH
ORGANIZATIONAL GOALS   256**
HUMAN RESOURCE PLANNING   257
Job Analysis and Design   258   Human
Resource Planning and Forecasting   259
EMPLOYEE RECRUITMENT   260
EMPLOYEE SELECTION   262
**EMPLOYEE TRAINING AND DEVELOP-
MENT   264**
On-the-Job Training   265   Off-the-Job
Training   265
**PERFORMANCE PLANNING AND
EVALUATION   266**
**EMPLOYEE COMPENSATION AND
BENEFITS   267**
Types of Compensation or Pay   268
**ORGANIZATIONAL CAREER
MANAGEMENT   269**
Job Changes within the Organization   269
Separations   270
**LAWS AFFECTING HUMAN RESOURCE
MANAGEMENT   271**
The Role of Government in Human
Resource Management   274   Making
Affirmative Action Work   274

196

Section 2   Capitalizing on Trends in Business   275

Social Change   275   Demographics 275   Advancing Technology   276 Global Competition   277

Section 3   Applying This Chapter's Topics   278

You Will Be Involved In Human Resources Decision Making   279

SUMMARY OF LEARNING GOALS   279
PREPARING FOR TOMORROW'S
WORKPLACE   281
WORKING THE NET   282
CREATIVE THINKING CASE   282
VIDEO CASE   283
E-COMMERCE CASE   285

>10   MOTIVATING EMPLOYEES AND CREATING SELF-MANAGED TEAMS   286

Section 1   Business in the 21st Century   288

THE EVOLUTION OF MOTIVATION
THEORY   288

Frederick Taylor's Scientific Management 288   The Hawthorne Studies   289 Maslow's Hierarchy of Needs   290 McGregor's Theories X and Y   291 Herzberg's Motivator-Hygiene Theory   292

CONTEMPORARY VIEWS ON
MOTIVATION   293

Expectancy Theory   293   Equity Theory 294   Goal-Setting Theory   295

FROM MOTIVATION THEORY TO
APPLICATION   296

Motivational Job Design   296   Work-Scheduling Options   297   Recognition, Empowerment, and Economic Incentives   297

USING TEAMS TO ENHANCE MOTIVA-TION AND PERFORMANCE   298

Understanding Group Behavior   298 Wok Groups versus Work Teams   299 Types of Teams   299   Building High-Performance Teams   300

Section 2   Capitalizing on Trends in Business   302

Education and Training   303   Employee Ownership   303   Work-Life Benefits 303

Section 3   Applying This Chapter's Topics   303

SUMMARY OF LEARNING GOALS   304
PREPARING FOR TOMORROW'S
WORKPLACE   307
WORKING THE NET   308
CREATIVE THINKING CASE   308
VIDEO CASE   309
E-COMMERCE CASE   311

>PART 5   MARKETING: DELIVERING VALUE TO THE CUSTOMER

>11   UNDERSTANDING THE CUSTOMER AND CREATING GOODS AND SERVICES THAT SATISFY   312

Section 1   Business in the 21st Century   314

THE MARKETING CONCEPT   314

Customer Value   315   Customer Satisfaction   315   Building Relationships   316

CREATING A MARKETING STRATEGY   317

Understanding the External Environment 318   Defining the Target Market   318 Creating a Competitive Advantage   319

DEVELOPING A MARKETING MIX   320

Product Strategy   321   Pricing Strategy 321   Distribution Strategy   321 Promotion Strategy   322   Not-for-Profit Marketing   323

BUYER BEHAVIOR   323

Influences on Consumer Decision-Making 324   Business-to-Business Purchase Decision-Making   325

MARKET SEGMENTATION   325

Demographic Segmentation   326 Geographic Segmentation   327 Psychographic Segmentation   328 Benefit Segmentation   328   Volume Segmentation   328

USING MARKETING RESEARCH TO SERVE EXISTING CUSTOMERS AND FIND NEW CUSTOMERS   329

Define the Marketing Problem   329 Choose a Method of Research   330 Collect the Data   330   Analyze the Data 331   Make Recommendations to Management   331

Section 2   Capitalizing on Trends in Business   332

Advanced Observation Research Methods 332   Decision Support Systems   332 Using Databases for Micromarketing   333

Section 3   Applying This Chapter's Topics   334

Participate in Marketing Research Surveys 334   Understand Cognitive Dissonance 334

SUMMARY OF LEARNING GOALS 335
PREPARING FOR TOMORROW'S
WORKPLACE 336
WORKING THE NET 336
CREATIVE THINKING CASE 337
VIDEO CASE 338
E-COMMERCE CASE 339

>12 DEVELOPING THE MARKETING MIX 340

Business in the 21st Century 342

Section 1

THE ROLE OF THE PRODUCT IN THE
MARKETING MIX 342
Types of Consumer Products 342 Types
of Business Products 343 Branding
344 Packaging 346 Developing New
Products 346 How New Products Are
Developed 346
PRODUCT LIFE CYCLE 348
PRICING PRODUCTS RIGHT 349
Pricing Strategies 350
THE ROLE OF DISTRIBUTION IN THE
MARKETING MIX 351
Marketing Intermediaries in the
Distribution Channel 351 Wholesalers
and Retailers 351 How Channels
Organize and Cover Markets 354 Using
Physical Distribution to Increase Efficiency
and Customer Satisfaction 355
CREATING AN EFFECTIVE PROMOTION
STRATEGY 356
The Promotional Mix 357 Advertising
357 Personal Selling 358 Sales
Promotion 358 Public Relations 359

Section 2

Capitalizing on Trends in Business 359
Mass Customization 359
Services and Physical Distributon 360
Integrated Marketing Communications
360

Section 3

Applying This Chapter's Topics 361
Custom Products and Services 361
Always Sell Yourself 361

SUMMARY OF LEARNING GOALS 362
PREPARING FOR TOMORROW'S
WORKPLACE 364
WORKING THE NET 364

CREATIVE THINKING CASE 365
VIDEO CASE 366
E-COMMERCE CASE 367

>PART 6 USING TECHNOLOGY AND MAN-
AGING FINANCIAL RESOURCES

>13 USING TECHNOLOGY TO MANAGE
INFORMATION 368

Business in the 21st Century 370

Section 1

COMPUTER NETWORKS 371
Local Area Networks 372 Wide Area
Networks 372 Intranets 373
BUSINESS INFORMATION SYSTEMS 373
Transaction Processing Systems 374
Management Support Systems 375
Office Automation Systems 377
MANAGING INFORMATION
TECHNOLOGY 377
Technology Planning 378 Protecting
Computers and Information 378

Section 2

Capitalizing on Trends in Business 383
Managing Knowledge Resources 383
End of the Personal Computer Era? 383
Searching for Information Technology
Talent 384

Section 3

Applying This Chapter's Topics 384
Preparation Pays Off 385
Keeping Secrets 385

SUMMARY OF LEARNING GOALS 386
PREPARING FOR TOMORROW'S
WORKPLACE 386
WORKING THE NET 387
CREATIVE THINKING CASE 387
VIDEO CASE 388
E-COMMERCE CASE 389

>14 USING FINANCIAL INFORMATION AND
ACCOUNTING 390

Business in the 21st Century 392

Section 1

THE PURPOSE OF ACCOUNTING 392
Who Uses Financial Reports? 393 The
Accounting Profession 394
BASIC ACCOUNTING PROCEDURES 395
The Accounting Equation 395 The
Accounting Cycle 396 Computers in
Accounting 396
THE BALANCE SHEET 397
Assets 398 Liabilities 400 Owners'
Equity 401
THE INCOME STATEMENT 401
Revenues 401 Expenses 401 Net
Profit or Loss 403

418

SUMMARY OF LEARNING GOALS   434
PREPARING FOR TOMORROW'S
WORKPLACE   435
WORKING THE NET   435
CREATIVE THINKING CASE   435
VIDEO CASE   436
E-COMMERCE CASE   437

THE STATEMENT OF CASH FLOWS   403
ANALYZING FINANCIAL STATEMENTS
404
Liquidity Ratios   405   Profitability
Ratios   407   Activity Ratios   408
Debt Ratios   408

Section 2
Capitalizing on Trends in Business   409
Accountants Expand Their Role   409
Valuing Knowledge Assets   410
Tightening the GAAP   410

Section 3
Applying This Chapter's Topics   410
SUMMARY OF LEARNING GOALS   412
PREPARING FOR TOMORROW'S
WORKPLACE   413
WORKING THE NET   415
CREATIVE THINKING CASE   415
VIDEO CASE   416
E-COMMERCE CASE 417

>15   UNDERSTANDING MONEY AND FINANCIAL
INSTITUTIONS   418
Section 1
Business in the 21st Century   420
MONEY   420
Characteristics of Money   420   Functions
of Money   421   The U.S. Money Supply
421
THE FEDERAL RESERVE SYSTEM   422
Carrying Out Monetary Policy   422
Setting Rules on Credit   423   Distributing
Currency   423   Making Check Clearing
Easier   423
THE U.S. FINANCIAL SYSTEM   424
Depository Financial Institutions   426
Nondepository Financial Institutions   428
INSURING BANK DEPOSITS   429
Role of the FDIC   430   Enforcement by
the FDIC   430

Section 2
Capitalizing on Trends in Business   430
Online Banking   431   Consolidation
431   The Integration of Banking,
Brokerage, and Insurance Services   431

Section 3
Applying This Chapter's Topics   432
Getting Connected   433   Finding
Financing   433

>16   FINANCIAL MANAGEMENT AND
SECURITIES MARKETS   438
Section 1
Business in the 21st Century   440
THE ROLE OF FINANCE AND THE
FINANCIAL MANAGER   440
The Financial Manager's Responsibilities
and Activities   441   The Goal of the
Financial Manager   442
HOW ORGANIZATIONS USE FUNDS   442
Short-Term Expenses   442   Long-Term
Expenditures   444
OBTAINING SHORT-TERM FINANCING
444
Unsecured Short-Term Loans   445
Secured Short-Term Loans   446
RAISING LONG-TERM FINANCING   446
Debt versus Equity Financing   447   Debt
Financing   448   Bond Ratings   449
Equity Financing   449
SECURITIES MARKETS   451
Types of Markets   452   The Role of
Investment Bankers and Stockbrokers   452
Other Popular Securities   452
SECURITIES EXCHANGES   454
U.S. Stock Exchanges   454   Global
Trading and Foreign Exchanges   455
The Over-the-Counter Market   455
Regulation of Securities Markets   456

Section 2
Capitalizing on Trends in Business   457
Risk Management   457
Market Competition Heats Up   458

Section 3
Applying This Chapter's Topics   459
SUMMARY OF LEARNING GOALS   460
PREPARING FOR TOMORROW'S
WORKPLACE   462
WORKING THE NET   463
CREATIVE THINKING CASE   463
VIDEO CASE   464
E-COMMERCE CASE   465

APPENDICES

>A   UNDERSTANDING THE LEGAL AND TAX
ENVIRONMENT   466
The Main Sources of Law   466   Business
Law   466   The Court System   467

Nonjudicial Methods of Settling Disputes
467   Contract Law   468   Warranties
470   Patents, Copyrights, and Trademarks
470   Tort Law   471   Product-Liability
Law   471   Bankruptcy Law   472   Laws
to Promote Fair Competition   472
Taxation of Business   475

>B   **MANAGING RISK AND INSURANCE   477**

Overview   477   Risk Management   477
    Types of Risk   477
    Strategies to Manage Risk   477
Insurance Concepts   478
    Insurable Risks   478
    Premium Costs   479
    Insurance Providers   479
Types of Insurance   481
    Property and Liability Insurance   481
    Special Types of Business Liability
    Insurance   482

ENRICHMENT CHAPTERS

>A   **USING THE INTERNET FOR BUSINESS SUCCESS**

Find it on the Student Companion CD-ROM.

>B   **MANAGING YOUR PERSONAL FINANCES**

Find it on the Student Companion CD-ROM.

GLOSSARY   483

END NOTES   493

SUBJECT INDEX   502

COMPANY INDEX   515

Lawrence J. Gitman

Lawrence J. Gitman is a professor of finance at San Diego State University. He received his Bachelor's Degree from Purdue University, his M.B.A. from the University of Dayton, and his Ph.D. from the University of Cincinnati. Professor Gitman is a prolific textbook author and has over 50 articles appearing in *Financial Management, Financial Review, Journal of Financial Planning, Journal of Risk and Insurance, Journal of Financial Research, Financial Practice and Education, Journal of Financial Education,* and other publications.

His singly authored major textbooks include *Principles of Managerial Finance: Brief,* Second Edition, *Principles of Managerial Finance,* Ninth Edition, and *Foundations of Managerial Finance,* Fourth Edition. In addition, he is co-author of *Introduction to Finance* with Jeff Madura. Other major textbooks include *Personal Financial Planning,* Ninth Edition, and *Fundamentals of Investing,* Eighth Edition, both co-authored with Michael D. Joehnk. Gitman and Joehnk also wrote *Investment Fundamentals: A Guide to Becoming a Knowledgeable Investor,* which was selected as one of 1988's ten best personal finance books by *Money* magazine.

An active member of numerous professional organizations, Professor Gitman is past president of the Academy of Financial Services, the San Diego Chapter of the Financial Executives Institute, the Midwest Finance Association, and the FMA National Honor Society. In addition he is a Certified Financial Planner (CFP) and a Certified Cash Manager (CCM). Gitman recently served as Vice-President, Financial Education for the Financial Management Association, Director of the San Diego MIT Enterprise Forum, and member of the CFP Board of Standards. He lives with his wife and two children in La Jolla, California, where he is an avid bicyclist.

Carl McDaniel

Carl McDaniel is a professor of marketing at the University of Texas—Arlington, where he is Chairman of the Marketing Department. He has been an instructor for more than 20 years and is the recipient of several awards for outstanding teaching. McDaniel has also been a District Sales Manager for Southwestern Bell Telephone Company. Currently, he serves as a board member of the North Texas Higher Education Authority, a one billion dollar financial institution.

In addition to this text, McDaniel also has co-authored a number of textbooks in marketing. Professor McDaniel's research has appeared in such publications as *Journal of Marketing Research, Journal of Marketing, Journal of Business Research, Journal of the Academy of Marketing Science,* and *California Management Review.*

He is a member of the American Marketing Association, Academy of Marketing Science, Society for Marketing Advances, Southwestern Marketing Association, and Western Marketing Association. Professor McDaniel is the past president of the Southwestern Marketing Association

Besides his academic experience, McDaniel has business experience as the co-owner of a marketing research firm. Recently, McDaniel served as senior consultant to the International Trade Centre (ITC), Geneva, Switzerland. The ITC's mission is to help developing nations increase their exports. McDaniel also teaches international business each year in France. He has a Bachelor's Degree from the University of Arkansas and his Master's Degree and Doctorate from Arizona State University.

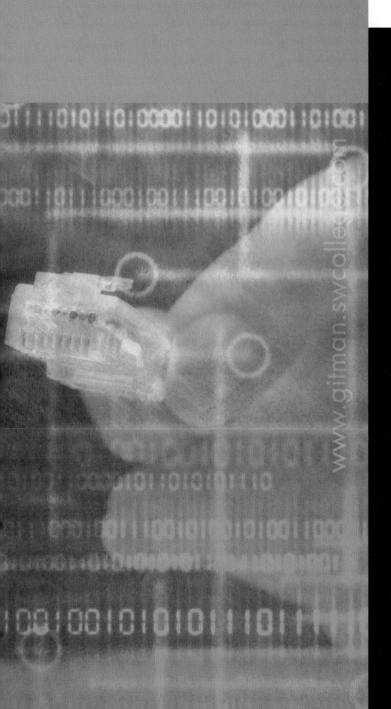

Special Feature

THE BEST OF THE FUTURE OF BUSINESS

Sampler

www.gitman.swcollege.com

Remember way back in the ancient history of commerce, when running a business was so much simpler? Say 2000 or so? So much has changed since then. Only those few short years ago managers could focus on producing a competitive product or service, keeping workers motivated, holding down costs, and keeping prices in line.

Today's managers must manage these same issues, and so much more. Our new interactive economy demands new skills, new perspective, and new resources. In this new century, the primary competitive tool of many organizations is knowledge. Organizations that obtain it, harness it, and apply it faster than competitors will reap extraordinary results. Technology is another tool organizations use to create a competitive advantage. Yesterday's companies competed locally, statewide, and sometimes nationally. In the blink of an eye, the Internet has enabled even the smallest entrepreneur to produce and sell in the global marketplace. Moreover, domestic markets that once had relatively little connection with the rest of world now are utilized and served by giant global corporations.

To succeed in our rapidly changing, increasingly interactive and interconnected business environment, a successful organization—now more than ever—requires fast and accurate knowledge. To help prepare students for their futures in business, *The Best of The Future of Business*, showcases the dramatic changes occurring in the business environment.

NEW ANGLES ON BUSINESS: UNIQUE CHAPTER STRUCTURE

The new shape, pace and spirit of the global economy require new ways of looking at business and careers. We've organized every chapter of **The Best of The Future of Business** with a unique chapter structure to support three essential themes:

BUSINESS IN THE 21ST CENTURY Students begin their study of each chapter with a glimpse into the strategies of popular business organizations. These lively vignettes draw students into the chapter and stimulate classroom discussion.

Each chapter delivers a comprehensive overview of current business principles and practices. Students will learn what is happening in today's businesses with examples from the largest global corporate giants, such as Ford and Airbus Industries, to the smallest Internet start-ups.

Business in the 21st Century

CAPITALIZING ON TRENDS IN BUSINESS

The second part of each chapter explores new business trends and how they are reshaping today's business and altering tomorrow's competitive environment. Technology and the global economy are covered extensively in every trends section. We expose students to the fundamental factors that are reshaping the business world in which they will soon begin professional careers. With this preview of the future, students gain a keen advantage when entering the workplace.

Capitalizing on Trends in Business

APPLYING THIS CHAPTER'S TOPICS

This unique feature, found only in **The Best of The Future of Business**, brings the chapter topics to life for students with relevant and interesting tips for making the most of a professional career or becoming a smart consumer. Students can utilize these suggestions throughout their careers; many are applicable immediately after reading the chapter in everyday life. In Chapter 4 (Forms of Business Ownership), students explore their readiness for starting a franchise or learn how to protect their jobs during a merger.

Applying This Chapter's Topics

THE INTERACTIVE PERSPECTIVE: MAJOR BUSINESS TOPICS UP CLOSE

In 16 chapters, *The Best of The Future of Business* explores important business issues and trends that are reshaping today's workplace. Students will be exposed to these and other important topics:

- **Customer value**
- **Knowledge management**
- **Relationship management**
- **Euro and the European Union**
- **New Internet economy**
- **Multinational corporations**
- **Entrepreneurs/intrapreneurs**
- **Database marketing**
- **Mass customization**
- **Integrated marketing communications**
- **Decision support systems (DSS)**

- **Global management skills**
- **Motivational job design**
- **Work cell design**
- **Online trading**
- **Online banking**
- **Risk management**
- **Agile manufacturing**
- **Intranets and extranets**
- **Electronic data interchange (EDI)**

TECHNOLOGY AND E-COMMERCE

Technology not only touches all areas of business; it often revolutionizes it. That's why each chapter addresses how businesses are applying technology to improve processes and maximize value to the customer.

Enrichment Chapter A, Using the Internet for Business Success, looks at the impact of the Internet on business operations. Found on the CD that accompanies this book, this chapter describes the growth of e-commerce in both consumer and business-to-business markets. This chapter also explores the process for launching an e-business and looks ahead to the future of the Internet in business.

Technology issues are integrated throughout the chapters, where appropriate, and featured in Applying Technology boxes. For example, the Applying Technology box in Chapter 5 (Entrepreneurship: Starting and Growing a Business) describes how travel-related companies have thrived in an online environment.

APPLYING TECHNOLOGY

RESERVATIONS ABOUND, YET SO DO PROFITS

While many dot-com companies were disappearing from sight, travel-related companies continued making inroads into the e-tail space. This sector accounts for about 30 percent of online consumer spending. These companies are a natural for online operations, because they don't have physical products that require warehouse and shipping. Most tickets and confirmations can be delivered electronically, keeping overhead to a minimum.

Dallas-based Hotel Reservations Network operates several discount reservations sites. Established in 1991 as a telephone-based reservations service, founder David Litman added the first Web site, **www.hoteldiscount.com**, in 1995. Moving online provided a cost-effective way for the company to grow quickly and reach a global customer base. "It didn't change what we do," says Litman. "It just put the company on steroids."

Since 1995 the company's average annual revenue growth has been 80 percent, compared to on estimated 20 percent to 30 percent if it hadn't migrated to the Web. As more customers discovered how easy it was to save 10 percent to 30 percent over the lowest published fares, demand grew. Hotels liked the service, too, which gave them an inexpensive distribution channel to fill unbooked rooms. The Web also allowed the company to track rates so it could guarantee customers the best prices and follow booking trends to decide what cities to add. The 1997 introduction of interactive

technology improved the company's efficiency even more. About two-thirds of customers now book online instead of by phone, saving staffing costs.

With its own system firmly in place, the company launched an affiliate program to be the exclusive hotel booking resource on other travel sites. Arrangements with such sites as Travelocity.com and Cheap Tickets now account for over half its business, and that figure is growing. The affiliates receive about 5 percent of hotel sales booked at their sites.

To broaden its product line even further, Hotel Reservations added condominium and vacation rentals to its main site. In mid-2001 the company went upscale with its second Web site, **www.allluxuryhotels.com**, for four- and five-star hotels. On the drawing boards were sites dedicated to boutique hotels and budget lodging.

Critical Thinking Questions:
1. What are the advantages to Hotel Reservations Network of adding Web-based reservations to its phone-based service? Disadvantages? Are hotel reservations and the Internet a good fit?
2. Would you book hotel reservations online through **www.hoteldiscount.com?** Why or why not? What features should Hotel Reservations Network offer at its sites to improve the reservations process?

GLOBAL BUSINESS ECONOMY

Chapter 2 (Competing in the Global Marketplace) offers a complete and exciting picture of competition in the global marketplace. We discuss why global trade is important to the United States, why nations trade, barriers to international trade, how companies enter the global marketplace, and a host of other international concepts and topics. The trends section found in each chapter frequently explains how globalization will affect specific business activities. For example, the trends section in Chapter 9 (Managing Human Resources) examines the unique problems faced by human resource managers as more and more companies "go global."

ENTREPRENEURSHIP AND SMALL BUSINESS MANAGEMENT

Because many students will either open their own businesses or go to work for small organizations, entrepreneurship and small business principles are presented throughout the text. Chapter 5 (Entrepreneurship: Starting and Growing a Business) delivers insightful discussions on issues related to starting and managing a small business including the advantages and disadvantages of small business ownership.

In addition, each chapter contains a feature called Focusing on Small Business that offers practical insights into the challenges and rewards of actually owning and managing a small business. In Chapter 11, for example, the Focusing on Small Business box explains how Michael Bracken's small landscape nursery took on Wal-Mart and Home Depot and survived. In Chapter 10 (Motivating Employees and Creating Self-Managed Teams), students see how a small technology start-up business motivates employees to perform their best.

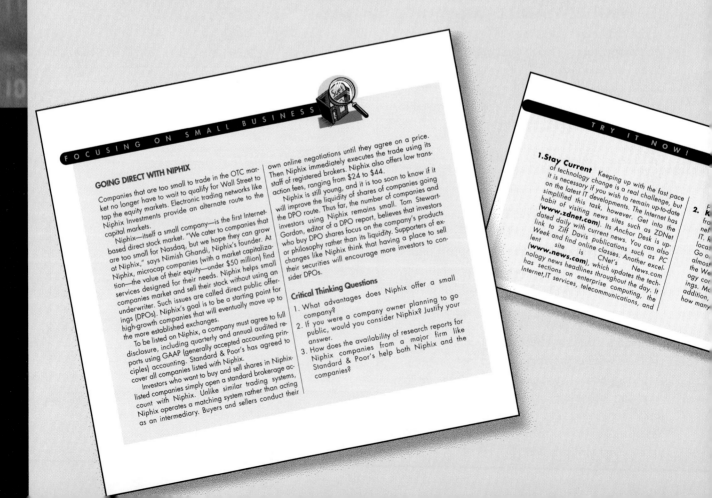

FOCUSING ON SMALL BUSINESS

GOING DIRECT WITH NIPHIX

Companies that are too small to trade in the OTC market no longer have to wait to qualify for Wall Street to tap the equity markets. Electronic trading networks like Niphix Investments provide an alternate route to the capital markets.

Niphix—itself a small company—is the first Internet-based direct stock market. "We cater to companies that are too small for Nasdaq, but we hope they can grow at Niphix," says Nimish Ghandi, Niphix's founder. At Niphix, microcap companies (with a market capitalization—the value of their equity—under $50 million) find services designed for their needs. Niphix helps small companies market and sell their stock without using an underwriter. Such issues are called direct public offerings (DPOs). Niphix's goal is to be a starting point for high-growth companies that will eventually move up to the more established exchanges.

To be listed on Niphix, a company must agree to full disclosure, including quarterly and annual audited reports using GAAP (generally accepted accounting principles) accounting. Standard & Poor's has agreed to cover all companies listed with Niphix.

Investors who want to buy and sell shares in Niphix-listed companies simply open a standard brokerage account with Niphix. Unlike similar trading systems, Niphix operates a matching system rather than acting as an intermediary. Buyers and sellers conduct their own online negotiations until they agree on a price. Then Niphix immediately executes the trade using its staff of registered brokers. Niphix also offers low transaction fees, ranging from $24 to $44.

Niphix is still young, and it is too soon to know if it will improve the liquidity of shares of companies going the DPO route. Thus far, the number of companies and investors using Niphix remains small. Tom Stewart-Gordon, editor of a DPO report, believes that investors who buy DPO shares focus on the company's products or philosophy rather than its liquidity. Supporters of exchanges like Niphix think that having a place to sell their securities will encourage more investors to consider DPOs.

Critical Thinking Questions

1. What advantages does Niphix offer a small company?

2. If you were a company owner planning to go public, would you consider Niphix? Justify your answer.

3. How does the availability of research reports for Niphix companies from a major firm like Standard & Poor's help both Niphix and the companies?

TRY IT NOW!

1. Stay Current Keeping up with the fast pace of technology change is a real challenge, but it is necessary if you wish to remain up-to-date on the latest IT developments. The Internet has simplified this task, however. Get into the habit of visiting news sites such as ZDNet (**www.zdnet.com**). Its Anchor Desk is updated daily with current news. You can also link to Ziff Davis publications such as PC Week and find online classes. Another excellent site is CNet's News.com (**www.news.com**), which updates the technology news headlines throughout the day. It has sections on enterprise computing, the Internet, IT services, telecommunications, and

ETHICS AND SOCIAL RESPONSIBILITY

A paramount theme of this text is that business must be conducted in an ethical and socially responsible manner. Chapter 3 (Making Ethical Decisions and Managing a Socially Responsible Business) is completely devoted to business ethics and social responsibility. We discuss techniques for setting personal ethical standards and the stages of ethical development. Also presented are ways managers influence organizational ethics, tools for creating employee ethical awareness, and the concept of social responsibility.

Each chapter drives this important theme home with a Making Ethical Choices box. Each box presents sticky ethical issues, taken from actual business situations, and poses provocative questions about right and wrong. For example, the Making Ethical Choices box in Chapter 13 (Using Technology to Manage Information) tests students' reactions to false and misleading information on the Internet.

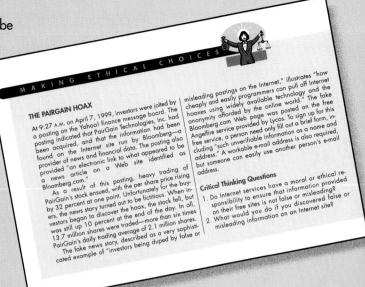

MAKING ETHICAL CHOICES

THE PAIRGAIN HOAX

At 9:27 A.M. on April 7, 1999, investors were jolted by a posting on the Yahoo! finance message board. The posting indicated that PairGain Technologies, Inc. had been acquired, and that the information had been found on the Internet site run by Bloomberg—a provider of news and financial data. The posting also provided "an electronic link to what appeared to be a news article on a Web site identified as Bloomberg.com."

As a result of this posting, heavy trading of PairGain's stock ensued, with the per share price rising by 32 percent at one point. Unfortunately for the buyers, the news story turned out to be fictitious. When investors began to discover the hoax, the stock fell, but was still up 10 percent at the end of the day. In all, 13.7 million shares were traded—more than six times PairGain's daily trading average of 2.1 million shares.

The fake news story, described as a very sophisticated example of "investors being duped by false or misleading postings on the Internet," illustrates "how cheaply and easily programmers can pull off Internet hoaxes using widely available technology and the anonymity afforded by the online world." The fake Bloomberg.com Web page was posted on the free Angelfire service provided by Lycos. To sign up for this free service, a person need only fill out a brief form, including "such unverifiable information as a name and address." A workable e-mail address is also required, but someone can easily use another person's e-mail address.

Critical Thinking Questions

1. Do Internet services have a moral or ethical responsibility to ensure that information provided on their free sites is not false or misleading?
2. What would you do if you discovered false or misleading information on an Internet site?

CAREERS IN BUSINESS

This edition features a comprehensive online career center at **http://gitman.swcollege.com** that provides the tools, information, and resources students need to explore career options in business. Not only will students explore the step-by-step process for finding a job, they will learn more about the following:

- Preparing a cyber resume.
- Researching the history, financial status, and mission of potential employers.
- Researching economic, demographic, and climatic information about cities in which they might work.
- Calculating the cost of living in various cities and obtaining details on crime rates.
- Ensuring success in a new job and winning the first promotion.

Hiring you can benefit age of technology person- think you want a job in employment ads in your he Wall Street Journal. e employment ads from aper and surf through stings. Many technol- also post job open- hat interest you. In job listings to see skills.

Students will find valuable career guidance in the Hot Links activities and in the last part of each chapter, Applying This Chapter's Topics. For example, in Chapter 3 (Competing in the Global Marketplace), students are given insights into the importance of developing global management skills. Try It Now! boxes also emphasize career development. For instance, the Try It Now! box in Chapter 13 (Using Technology to Manage Information), tells students how to stay tuned to the latest information technology developments to enhance employment opportunities.

TECHNOLOGY AND SKILLS FOR

Professors told us that one of their course goals is to strengthen research, communication, business writing, Web, and teamwork skills. To aid in skills development, **The Best of The Future of Business** integrates the following features in each chapter:

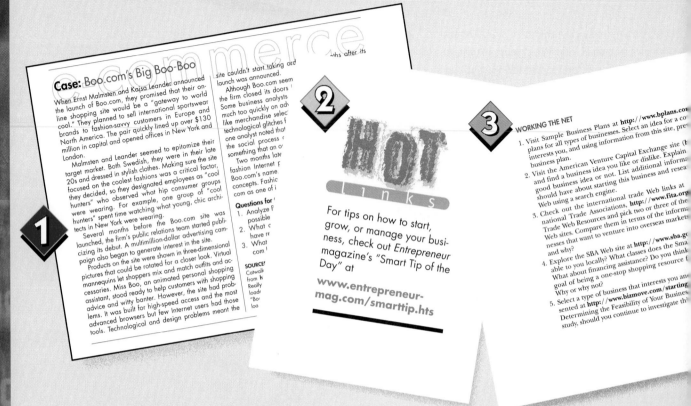

① E-Commerce cases.
Because leading-edge companies are quickly embracing e-commerce as an avenue for future growth and profitability, **The Best of The Future of Business** takes a peak inside 16 different organizations that use state-of-the-art information technology to launch online business ventures. In each e-commerce case, students are invited to explore business strategies of various companies, analyze business decisions and prepare open-response comments.

② Hot Link activities.
Hot Links take students to the web sites of well-known companies and show them how to find the web's most reliable and valuable business resources. These activities demonstrate actual e-commerce practices and policies, covering issues as diverse as online security, new distribution systems, mass customization and more.

③ Working the Net activities.
These guide students through a step-by-step analysis of actual e-business practices and give them opportunities to build online skills.

THE INTERACTIVE WORKPLACE

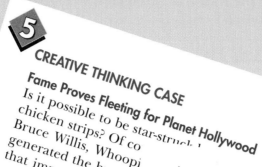

PREPARING FOR TOMORROW'S WORKPLACE

1. Divide the class into teams of five. Each group should select a form of a⁻ plicant testing and defend why their form of testing should be used screen applicants.
2. What kind of training and development program would be best for asser line workers? For first-line supervisors? For industrial sales representa For maintenance workers? For computer programmers?
3. Would an overseas job assignment be good for your career developr you think so, what country would you prefer to live and work in fe three years, and what type of job would you like to have in that co⁻
4. The fringe benefit package of many employers includes numer tarily provided items such as health insurance, life insurance, pe paid vacations, tuition reimbursement, employee price discou⁻ ucts of the firm, and paid sick leave. At your age, what are the most important benefits? Why? Twenty years from now, wha will be your three or four most important benefits? Why?

a bu⁻ r feasibility

CREATIVE THINKING CASE

Fame Proves Fleeting for Planet Hollywood

Is it possible to be star-struck chicken strips? Of co Bruce Willis, Whoopi generated the huge b that immediately form eateries made it the env And then all those pe chicken-strips appetizer, taste. They squinted into watched oversized video absent from the restauran ber the experience.

INFOTRAC®
COLLEGE EDITION
Exclusively from Gale Group and Thomson Learning

 Preparing for Tomorrow's Workplace. These activities, found at the end of each chapter, are designed to help students develop their writing, research, and teamwork skills.

 Critical Thinking Activities. Each boxed feature has two purposes—to amplify and reinforce chapter concepts while encouraging in-depth analysis. Critical thinking questions can be used to generate class discussion or prompt further student analysis. In addition, each chapter contains a Creative Thinking Case featuring interesting organizations such as the New England Aquarium, the Internet Monster Board, Girl Scouts of America, Ford's Acquisition of Volvo, and the American Automobile Association.

 INFOTRAC™ College Edition. With InfoTrac College Edition, students have full access to articles from hundreds of scholarly journals and popular periodicals such as Newsweek, Time, and USA Today. The Gitman Web site (**http://gitman.swcollege.com**) features a list of InfoTrac™ articles that will help students analyze the creative thinking cases within each chapter.

KEEPING PACE WITH BUSINESS: STUDENT-ORIENTED PEDAGOGY

The Best of The Future of Business is designed to engage students and arouse interest in all facets of business for today and tomorrow. Delivered in a precise, crisp writing style, each chapter includes various applications to strengthen students' understanding and involve them in actual business practices.

INTEGRATED LEARNING SYSTEM

To anchor key concepts and provide a framework for study, an integrated learning system links all major concepts with the chapter, end-of-chapter, and supplements package. Learning goals at the beginning of each chapter outline the goals for study. Major headings within the chapter are identified by icons and supported with concept checks and a chapter summary. In addition, the study guide, instructor's manual, PowerPoint™ slides, and test bank are all framed around the integrated learning system. Each piece of the integrated learning system reinforces the other components to help students learn quickly and to ease lecture preparation.

HUNDREDS OF ACTUAL BUSINESS APPLICATIONS

We focused this book on the needs, abilities, and experience of the typical student. We drew on our experiences inside and outside the classroom to create the most readable and enjoyable textbook in business administration. We believe that the actual business applications interspersed throughout the chapters set the standard for readability and lucid explanation of key concepts.

OPENING VIGNETTES THAT CONNECT

Many texts use short stories to open the chapters but fail to make connections to these stories elsewhere in the chapters. We take a different approach. We begin each chapter with a vignette about a prominent, student-friendly company that previews that chapter's content. We then provide several questions to prompt critical thinking about the chapter content. At the end of the chapter content, we provide an update on the company featured in the opening vignette and offer suggestions on how it may have to adapt to meet emerging trends.

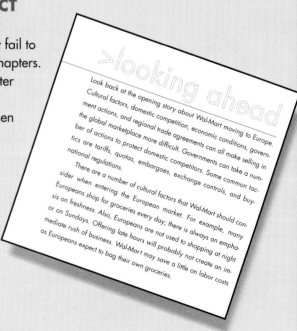

>looking ahead

Look back at the opening story about Wal-Mart moving to Europe. Cultural factors, domestic competition, economic conditions, government actions, and regional trade agreements can all make selling in the global marketplace more difficult. Governments can take a number of actions to protect domestic competitors. Some common tactics are tariffs, quotas, embargoes, exchange controls, and buy-national regulations.

There are a number of cultural factors that Wal-Mart should consider when entering the European market. For example, many Europeans shop for groceries every day; there is always an emphasis on freshness. Also, Europeans are not used to shopping at night or on Sundays. Offering late hours will probably not create an immediate rush of business. Wal-Mart may save a little on labor costs as Europeans expect to bag their own groceries.

THE BEST OF THE FUTURE OF BUSINESS STUDENT WEB SITE

(http://gitman.swcollege.com)

The Best of The Future of Business Web site provides rich content
to maximize student learning and build online skills.

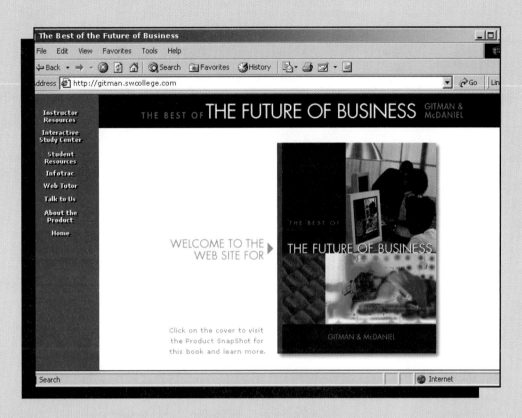

1 **Each text chapter is supported by two online quizzes** that test student understanding and offer clear, customized feedback for incorrect answers.

2 **The Web site includes Internet Exercises** that demonstrate how actual companies are applying key chapter concepts. These exercises are organized by chapter and include discussion questions and links to related Web sites.

3 **PowerPoint™ slides** overview the important concepts and principles within each chapter.

4 **Crossword puzzles** utilizing key terms from each chapters make learning business vocabulary more fun and interactive.

5 **The Web site also offers voluminous support resources** for students seeking career information and links to helpful sites.

6 **InfoTrac Resources** includes a bibliography of InfoTrac articles that relate to the critical thinking cases. These articles will help students analyze and develop responses to the critical thinking case questions. A second list of InfoTrac articles, organized by chapter, provides in-depth insight into chapter topics.

INTERACTIVE STUDENT SUPPLEMENTS

The Best of The Future of Business is supported by the following student resources to maximize success in the course and help students learn fundamental business terminology, key business concepts, and practice what they learn.

Web Tutor™ Advantage harnesses the power of the Internet to deliver innovative learning aids that actively engage students. WebTutor™ Advantage was designed to help students grasp complex concepts and to provide several forms of interactive learning reinforcements. This rich collection of content is available to students online.

In addition to a wide variety of skills activities, WebTutor™ Advantage includes new video lectures that enhance the online study of key concepts. Supplementing each PowerPoint™ slide is an audio summary that provides extra explanation of the more challenging key concepts. Narrated and scripted by a university business professor, these video lectures are available only in WebTutor™ Advantage for this textbook.

Student Companion CD-ROM

Free with every new textbook, the Student Companion CD-ROM contains two additional chapters, complete with skills development activities and cases. These chapters offer in-depth insight into using the Internet in business and managing personal finances:

- **Enrichment Chapter A, Using the Internet for Business Success,** explores the best strategies for using the Internet to enhance business functions.
- **Enrichment Chapter B, Managing Your Personal Finances,** introduces students to the skills needed to manage their personal finances.

Student Study Guide (ISBN: 0-324-18550-2).

Designed using the integrated learning system, the Student Study Guide tests student comprehension of concepts through the use of multiple-choice questions and matching exercises. A vocabulary builder reinforces business and non-business terms used within the text.

Zapitalism

Zapitalism, a business simulation game where students run a retail business on the imaginary island of Zapinalia, gets students excited about and involved in real business strategies. Zapitalism gives students the opportunity to make smart business decisions on investing in stocks and bonds, negotiating with unions, sabotaging competition, and advertising their products and services.

MarketingBuilder Express

An "express" version of JIAN's popular marketing builder software, this workbook and software provides everything students need to develop a marketing plan.

A NETWORK OF RESOURCES TO MEET
A VARIETY OF TEACHING OBJECTIVES

Business success is stimulated by access to and mastery of vital resources. The same is true for the classroom. Whether teaching an online course or simply enhancing your course with Web resources, *The Best of The Future of Business* offers a vast, complementary system of teaching and learning resources designed to aid the instructor and drive student interactivity.

Each component of the comprehensive supplements package has been carefully crafted by outstanding teachers to ensure your course is a rewarding learning experience for students. The supplements package includes time-tested teaching tools as well as new supplements designed for the electronic classroom.

Comprehensive Instructor's Manual with Transparency Masters and Video Guide (ISBN: 0-324-18551-0).

Instructor's Manual with
Transparency Masters

THE BEST OF
THE FUTURE OF BUSINESS

GITMAN & McDANIEL

Prepared by
James P. Hess

At the core of the integrated learning system for *The Best of The Future of Business* is the Instructor's Manual. Developed in response to numerous suggestions from instructors teaching this course, each chapter is designed to provide maximum guidance for delivering the content in an interesting and dynamic manner. Each chapter begins with learning goals that anchor the integrated learning system. A detailed lecture outline guides professors through key terminology and concepts. Lecture enhancers provide additional information and examples from actual businesses to illustrate key chapter concepts. Each chapter includes lecture support for teaching the e-commerce cases and guidance for integrating PowerPoint™ slides and other visuals that illustrate and reinforce the lecture. A comprehensive Video Guide includes the running time of each video segment, concepts illustrated in the video segments, teaching objectives for the case, and solutions for video case study questions. A complete set of transparency masters is available to create overhead acetates. The transparency masters include exhibits from the text and additional teaching notes designed to add fresh examples to your lectures.

PowerPoint™ Lecture System (IRCD ISBN: 0-324-18554-5).
Key chapter concepts and actual business examples are available in PowerPoint™ presentation software to improve lecture organization and reduce preparation time. The PowerPoint™ slides wereprepared by Carol Luce, Arizona State University.

Instructor's Resource CD (ISBN: 0-324-18554-5).
For maximum convenience, the Instructor's Manual, the PowerPoint™ slides, and the ExamView Testing System are all available on a CD.

Color Acetate Transparencies (ISBN: 0-324-18558-8).
Color acetate transparencies feature key concepts, exhibits from the text, and additional examples and exhibits not found in the text.

Test Bank (ISBN: 0-324-18557-X).
The comprehensive test bank is organized by learning goal to support the integrated learning system. Designed to provide multiple options for testing every concept in a chapter, the test bank contains true/false, multiple-choice, fill-in-the-blank, and short-answer questions. These test questions may be arranged and customized to support a variety of course objectives. The Test Bank is available in print and computerized test bank format (ExamView Testing Software: IRCD ISBN: 0-324-18554-5)

Comprehensive Video Library (ISBN: 0-324-18560-X; 0-324-185618).
Designed to enrich and support chapter concepts, each of the 16 videos presents real business issues faced by a variety of service and manufacturing organizations. The video cases challenge students to study business issues and develop solutions to business problems. The instructor's video guide outlines the key teaching objectives of each video case and suggests answers to the thinking questions.

This book could not have been written and published without the generous, expert assistance of many people. First, we wish to thank Marlene Bellamy, Writeline Associates, for her major and outstanding contributions to numerous aspects of this text. We wish to thank Jim Hess, Ivy Tech State College, for his comprehensive, creative, and timely work on the Instructor's Manual, PowerPoint slides, and e-lectures. We extend special thanks to Tom and Betty Pritchett, Kennesaw State University, for their conscientious development of the test bank. In addition, we appreciate the creative energy of Jonas Falik and Brenda Hersh, Queensborough Community College, who wrote the study guide.

A special word of appreciation goes to the editorial team at South-Western/Thomson Learning, including Mary Draper, Steve Hazelwood, Kelly Keeler, Christine Wittmer, Amy Wilson, and Casey Gilbertson.

We have benefited from the detailed and constructive reviews provided by many individuals. In particular, we wish to thank the following educators who have served as reviewers in this and prior editions:

Joseph H. Atallah
Devry Institute of Technology

Hal Babson
Columbus State Community College

Herm Baine
Broward Community College

Iris Berdrow
Bentley College

Susan C. Borkowski
La Salle University

Lorenzo Bowman
DeVry Institute of Technology/Georgia

Harvey Bronstein
Oakland Community College

Bonnie R. Chavez
Santa Barbara City College

Kevin Collins
Lehigh University

M. Bixby Cooper
Michigan State University

Jonas Falik
Queensborough Community College

Janice M. Feldbauer
Austin Community College—Northridge

Dennis Foster
Northern Arizona University

James Giles
Bergen Community College

Carnella Hardin
Glendale College

Frederic H. Hawkins
Westchester Business Institute

Henry J. Jackson
Delaware County Community College

Connie Johnson
Tampa College

Jerry Kinskey
Sinclair Community College

Jeffrey Klivans
University of Maine at Augusta

Raymond T. Lamanna
Berkeley College

Carol Luce
Arizona State University

Carl Meskimen
Sinclair Community College

Andrew Miller
Hudson Valley Community College

H. Lynn Moretz
Central Piedmont Community College

Joseph Newton
Bakersfield College

Teresa Palmer
Illinois State University

Lila Prigge
University of North Dakota

Robert F. Reck
Western Michigan University

Ann Squire
Blackhawk Technical College

Ron Weidenfeller
Grand Rapids Community College

Dedicated to the memory of my mother,
Dr. Edith Gitman, who instilled in me the
importance of education and hard work.

To my brother and his wife,
Maxwell and Dawn McDaniel.

acknowledgments

prologue

Understanding Trends in Business

The pace of change in the world seems faster and faster. Recessions, technology, global mergers, terrorist attacks, rapid changes in oil prices, and global alliances, such as the European Union, all impact today's business. The businesses that will still be competing at the end of this new century are the ones that best adapt to the ever-changing business environment. The one thing we know is that tomorrow's businesses will be quite different from today's.

To understand how fast our lives can change, consider the world of 1975. The Volkswagen Beetle was the hot imported car. Japanese imports were just starting to be sold in the United States. The personal computer was an idea yet to be born. Business communication was primarily by telephone or mail—Federal Express was in its infancy and "faxing" was unknown. There were no videocassette recorders, CDs, or video cameras for personal use, and cellular phone technology was not widely used.

These and other changes in the way we live and work affect business organizations. To survive in tomorrow's business world, businesspeople must do their best to continually answer the question "What will tomorrow hold?" Managers, workers, and tomorrow's graduates must have visions, goals, and ideas based on their best guess of what the future will be. How can they even guess? The smart ones look at today's trends and the issues that seem to be changing fastest, and try to imagine where they'll lead.

To help you look ahead and anticipate tomorrow's business environment, this prologue examines the following trends:

- Social factors that influence consumer choices
- Demographic trends
- Evolving economic systems
- Emerging technologies
- Global competition

Throughout the text special theme boxes will give you specific examples of these trends, and an eighth category will focus on interesting stories from other areas of business.

CAPITALIZING ON TRENDS IN BUSINESS

Business owners and managers use their skills and resources to create goods and services that will satisfy customers and prospective customers. Owners and managers have a wide latitude of control over day-to-day business decisions such as which supplies are purchased, which employees are hired, what products are sold, and where they are sold. However, certain environmental conditions that affect a business cannot be controlled. These conditions are constantly changing and include social change, demographics, economic conditions, technology, and global competition, as shown in Exhibit P-1. Successful owners and managers must continuously study these conditions and adapt their businesses, or they will lose their ability to compete.

Consider two examples of how companies have responded to changes in the business environment:

e x h i b i t P - 1 | The Environment of Business

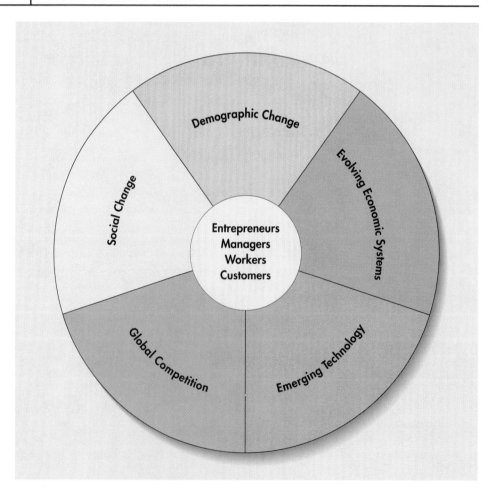

- The average age of the traditional buyer of some Cadillac models is approaching 70. An aging target market means big problems for the company. Cadillac's share of the roughly 1.2 million-unit luxury market is now 15 percent, down from 24 percent in the early 1990s. To offset this trend, Cadillac created the Catera. Its target market is entry-level luxury car buyers, such as buyers of the BMW 3 series or the Lexus ES300. The car has been modestly successful.

What else is Cadillac doing to respond to a changing business environment? Take a look at the company's plans and new car models at http://www.cadillac.com

- The social trend toward casualness has finally reached the office. Many firms now have a "dress-down" day on Fridays, when coats and ties aren't required. When Charles Schwab, the discount stockbroker, considered offering a "dress-down" day, it called Levi Strauss and Co., the blue jeans and casual wear manufacturer, for a little fashion advice. Recognizing the significance of this trend, Levi Strauss responded with more than advice. It provided brochures showing how dress could be casual without being sloppy, names of other companies that had successfully shed traditional attire, and studies that showed how the apparel shift had improved workers' productivity and morale. By capitalizing on a new social trend, Levi's Dockers now capture one-third of all department store pants sales.[1]

No one business is large or powerful enough to create major changes in the external environment. Thus, managers are basically adapters to rather than agents of change. For example, despite the huge size of General Motors, Ford, and DaimlerChrysler, these companies have only recently been able to stem the competitive push by the Japanese for an ever-growing share of the U.S. automobile market. Global competition is basically an uncontrollable element in the external environment. This section examines trends in the business environment that are reshaping today's business landscape.

SOCIAL TRENDS

Social change is perhaps the most difficult environmental factor for owners and managers to forecast, influence, or integrate into business plans. Social factors include our attitudes, values, and lifestyles. Social factors influence the products people buy, the prices paid for products, the effectiveness of specific promotions, and how, where, and when people expect to purchase products.

The Growth of Component Lifestyles

component lifestyle
A lifestyle made up of a complex set of interests and choices.

People in the United States today are piecing together component lifestyles. A lifestyle is a mode of living; it is the way people decide to live their lives. A **component lifestyle** is a lifestyle made up of a complex set of interests and choices. In other words, people are choosing products and services that meet diverse needs and interests rather than conforming to traditional stereotypes.

In the past, a person's profession—for instance, banker—defined that person's lifestyle. Today a person can be a banker, gourmet, fitness enthusiast, dedicated single parent, and conservationist—all at once. Each of these lifestyles is associated with different goods and services and represents a unique market.

The Changing Role of Families and Working Women

Component lifestyles have evolved because consumers can choose from a growing number of goods and services, and most have the money to exercise more options. Increased purchasing power is largely a result of the growth of dual-income families. Wives' incomes amounted to only 26.6 percent of their families' household incomes in 1970, but make up over 42 percent today. Now more than 72 percent of women with children under 18 are working in the paid labor force, compared with 47 percent in 1970. The increase is even sharper for women with children younger than three, from 34 percent to 62 percent.[2] The phenomenon of working women has had a greater effect on business than any other social change.

As women's earnings grow, so do their levels of expertise, experience, and authority. The word *handyman* may no longer be politically correct—or correct at all—as women become a more potent force in buying tools and hardware for both inside and outside the home. From simply using more "feminine" colors to designing tools especially for women do-it-yourselfers, companies are responding by creating products with women in mind. "Our research shows more females are the primary decision-makers and buyers of home items," says Lorrie Crum, a spokeswoman for Rubbermaid, Inc.[3]

Other hardware companies have assembled "kits" for customers tackling a specific home project for the first time. The Miracle Restoration Kit includes a Miracle Eraser pumice stone sander and rejuvenation oil for refinishing furniture. "The stores say that women are the people who refinish furniture, and we came up with a product that doesn't take any pressure at all and doesn't get clogged up like sandpaper," said Hank Greenfield, who makes the kit.[4]

concept check

- Why are social changes the most difficult environmental factor to predict?
- How do component lifestyles make it more difficult to predict a consumer's buying habits?
- What social change has had the greatest impact on business?

DEMOGRAPHIC TRENDS

demography
The study of people's vital statistics, such as their age, race and ethnicity, and location.

Demographic trends—another uncontrollable factor in the business environment—are also extremely important to managers. **Demography** is the study of people's vital statistics, such as their age, race and ethnicity, and location. Demographics are significant because the basis for any market is people. Demographics also determine the size and composition of the workforce. Let's begin by taking a closer look at key age groups.

Generation Y—Born to Shop

Generation Y
Americans born after 1978.

Today there are about 58 million Americans age 19 and under. These people—those born after 1978—make up **Generation Y.** And though Generation Y is much smaller than the baby boom, which lasted nearly 20 years and produced 78 million children, its members are plentiful enough to put their own footprints on society.

The marketing impact of Generation Y has been immense. Companies that sell toys, videos, software, and clothing to kids have boomed in recent years. Nine of the 10 best-selling videos of all time are animated films from Walt Disney Co. Club Med, the French vacation company, now earns half its U.S. revenues from family resorts. The members of Generation Y were born into a world vastly different from the one their parents entered. The changes in families, the workforce, technology, and demographics in recent decades will no doubt affect their attitudes, but in unpredictable ways. Among those changes:

Members of Generation Y love to shop. Born into a world of technology, they're big consumers of high-tech products like cellular phones.

Generation X
Americans born between 1965 and 1978.

baby boomers
Americans born between 1946 and 1964.

- Some 61 percent of U.S. children aged three to five are attending preschool, compared with 38 percent in 1970.
- Over 60 percent of households with children aged seven or younger have personal computers, according to IDC/LINK Resources Corp., a market research firm in New York.
- Approximately 15 percent of U.S. births in recent years were to foreign-born mothers, with origins so diverse that more than 100 different languages are spoken in the school systems of New York City, Chicago, Los Angeles, and Fairfax County, Virginia.[5]

Generation X—Savvy and Cynical

There are approximately 47 million people between the ages of 23 and 34. These people—those born between 1965 and 1978—have been labeled **Generation X.** They are the first generation of latchkey children—products of dual-career households or, in roughly half the cases, of divorced or separated parents. The members of Generation X began entering the workforce in the era of downsizing, so they are likelier than the previous generation to be unemployed, underemployed, and living at home with mom and dad. Still, 18 million are married and not living at home, and 8 million are full-time college students. As a generation that's been bombarded by multiple media since their cradle days, they're savvy and cynical consumers.

For decades, Ford marketed its light-duty pickups by emphasizing their roughness and toughness. Advertisements featured trucks climbing rugged mountains or four-wheeling through mud. But Ford quickly realized that this approach was not going to work with Generation Xers. Instead, Ford chose to lead with a new product. The company created a new version of its popular Ranger pickup, giving it flares on the fenders, jazzy graphics, and a youthful new name—Splash. The promotion campaign attempted to infuse the vehicle with personality by combining the truck with adventuresome sports.

Baby Boomers—America's Mass Market

People born between 1946 and 1964 are called **baby boomers.** Many baby boomers are now over 50, but they still cling to their youth. Most continue to live a very active life. This group cherishes convenience, which has resulted in a growing demand for home delivery of large appliances, furniture, groceries, and other items. In addition, the spreading culture of convenience explains the tremendous appeal of prepared take-out foods, VCRs, portable telephones, and the Internet.

Baby boomers' parents raised their children to think for and of themselves. Studies of child-rearing practices show that parents of the 1950s and 1960s consistently ranked "to think for themselves" as the number-one trait they wanted to nurture in their children. Postwar affluence also enabled parents to indulge their children as never before. They invested in their children's skills by sending them to college. They encouraged their children to succeed in a job market that rewarded competitive drive more than cooperative spirit and individual skills more than teamwork.

In turn, the sheer size of the generation encouraged businesses to play to the emerging individuality of baby boomers. Even before the oldest baby boomers started earning a living more than two decades ago, astute businesspeople anticipated the profits that could come from giving millions of young people what they wanted. Businesses offered individualistic baby boomers a growing array of customized products and services—houses, cars, furniture, appliances, clothes, vacations, jobs, leisure time, and even beliefs.

Firms like Ford Motor Company market their products to the growing number of Spanish-speaking immigrants, whose buying power boosts the U.S. economy.

Older Consumers—Not Just Grandparents

The oldest baby boomers have already crossed the 50-year threshold that many demographers use to define the "mature market." Yet today's mature consumers are wealthier, healthier, and better educated than those of earlier generations.[6] Although they make up only 26 percent of the population, 50-plus consumers buy half of all domestic cars, half of all silverware, and nearly half of all home remodeling. By 2020, over a third of the population will be age 50 or older.

Businesspeople who want to actively pursue the mature market must understand it. Aging consumers create some obvious opportunities. JC Penney's Easy Dressing clothes feature Velcro-fasteners for women with arthritis or other ailments who may have difficulty with zippers or buttons. Sales from the first Easy Dressing catalog were three times higher than expected. Chicago-based Cadaco offers a line of games with easy-to-read big print and larger game pieces. The series focuses on nostalgia by including Michigan rummy, hearts, poker, and bingo. Trivia buffs more familiar with Mitch Miller than Guns 'n' Roses can play Parker Brothers' "The Vintage Years" edition of Trivial Pursuit.

Americans on the Move

The average U.S. citizen moves every six years. This trend has implications for business. A large influx of new people into an area creates many new opportunities for all types of businesses. Conversely, significant out-migration from a city or town may force many of its businesses to move or close down because they can't find qualified employees. The cities with the greatest projected population growth from 1995 to 2005 are Houston, Washington D.C., Atlanta, San Diego, Phoenix, Orlando, and Dallas.

The United States experiences both immigration from other countries and migration within its borders. In the 1990s, the six states with the highest levels of immigration from abroad were California, New York, New Jersey, Illinois, Texas, and Massachusetts. The six states with the greatest population increases due to interstate migration were Florida, Georgia, North Carolina, Virginia, Washington, and Arizona. Areas with large numbers of immigrants face increased costs of public services, but the influx benefits the U.S. economy overall. Immigrants add approximately $10 billion to the economy each year with little negative impact on job opportunities for most other residents.[7]

Growing Ethnic Markets

The United States is undergoing a new demographic transition: it is becoming a society composed of people from multiple cultures. Over the next decades, the United States will shift further away from a society dominated by whites and rooted in Western culture toward a society characterized by three large racial and ethnic minorities: African Americans, U.S. Hispanics, and Asian Americans. All three minorities will grow in size and in share of the population, while the white majority declines as a percentage of the total. Native Americans and people with roots in Australia, the Middle East, the former Soviet Union, and other parts of the world will further enrich the fabric of U.S. society.

The labor force of the past was dominated by white men who are now retiring. They will be replaced by a multicultural labor force who began their careers in entry-level jobs in 2000. The proportion of workers who are non-Hispanic whites will decrease from 77 percent in 1997 to 74 percent in 2005. A diverse workforce is a healthy workforce. Diversity leads to new ideas, new ways of doing things, and greater income equality among ethnic groups.

Multiculturalism exists when all major ethnic groups in an area—such as a city, county, or census tract—are roughly equally represented. Because of the current demographic transition, the trend in the United States is toward greater multiculturalism, although the degree varies in different parts of the country.

Four of New York City's five boroughs are among the 10 most ethnically diverse counties in the country. People of various ancestries have long been attracted to San Francisco County, and not surprisingly, it is the most diverse county in the nation. The proportions of major ethnic groups are closer to being equal there than anywhere else. The least multicultural region is a broad swath stretching from northern New England through the Midwest and into Montana. These counties have few people other than whites. The counties with the very lowest level of diversity are found in the agricultural heartland—in Nebraska and Iowa.

Employees from different ethnic and racial backgrounds will continue to enrich the workplace with their diverse views and ideas.

multiculturalism
The condition when all major ethnic groups in an area, such as a city, county, or census tract, are about equally represented.

concept check

- How has the changing role of women affected business?
- Explain how Generation X, Generation Y, and baby boomers differ.
- How is multiculturalism changing business?

EVOLVING GLOBAL ECONOMIC SYSTEMS

In addition to social and demographic factors, managers must understand and adapt to the economic system or systems in which they operate. Economic systems found in the world today include capitalism, command economies, socialism, and mixed economies.

Capitalism

A remarkable trend in global economies today is the move toward capitalism. Sometimes, as in the case of the former East Germany, the transition to capitalism has been painful, but fairly quick. In other countries, such as Russia, the

Entrepreneurs like Fred Wagenhals thrive in a capitalist system. Wagenhals recognized Americans' growing interest in car racing and launched his own business selling toy NASCAR race cars.

capitalism

An economic system based on competition in the marketplace and private ownership of the factors of production (resources); also known as the *private enterprise system.*

command economy

An economic system characterized by government ownership of virtually all resources and economic decision making by central government planning; also known as *communism.*

movement has been characterized by false starts and backsliding. **Capitalism,** also known as the *private enterprise system,* is based on competition in the marketplace and private ownership of the factors of production (resources). In a competitive economic system, a large number of people and businesses buy and sell products freely in the marketplace. In pure capitalism all the factors of production are owned privately, and the government does not try to set prices or coordinate economic activity.

A capitalist system guarantees certain economic rights: the right to own property, the right to make a profit, the right to make free choices, and the right to compete. The right to own property is central to capitalism. The main incentive in this system is profit, which encourages entrepreneurship. Profit is also necessary for producing goods and services, building plants, paying dividends and taxes, and creating jobs. The freedom to choose whether to become an entrepreneur or to work for someone else means that people have the right to decide what they want to do on the basis of their own drive, interest, and training. The government does not create job quotas for each industry or give people tests to determine what they will do.

In a capitalist system, competition is good for both businesses and consumers. It leads to better and more diverse products, keeps prices stable, and increases the efficiency of producers. Producers try to produce their goods and services at the lowest possible cost and sell them at the highest possible price. But when profits are high, more firms enter the market to seek those profits. The resulting competition among firms tends to lower prices. Producers must then find new ways of operating more efficiently if they are to keep making a profit—and stay in business.

The Command Economy

The complete opposite to capitalism is a command economy. A **command economy,** or communism, is characterized by government ownership of virtually all resources and economic decision making by central government planning. The government decides what will be produced, where it will be produced, how much will be produced, where the raw materials and supplies will come from, and who will get the output.

Pure capitalism and the command economy are extremes; real-world economies fall somewhere between the two. The U.S. economy leans toward pure capitalism, but government policies are used to promote economic stability and growth. Also, through policies and laws, the government transfers money to the poor, the unemployed and the elderly. American capitalism has produced some very powerful organizations in the form of huge corporations, such as General Motors and Microsoft. Laws have been enacted to help smaller firms and entrepreneurs by requiring that the giants compete fairly against weaker competitors.

Before the Soviet Union collapsed in 1991, it had a command economy, but even so it relied to some extent on market-determined prices and allowed some private ownership. Recent reforms in Russia, China, and most of the eastern European nations have moved these economies toward more capitalistic, market-oriented systems. North Korea and Cuba are the best remaining examples of command economies.

Socialism

socialism

An economic system in which the basic industries are owned either by the government itself or by the private sector under strong government control.

Socialism is an economic system in which the basic industries are owned by the government or by the private sector under strong government control. A socialist state controls critical, large-scale industries such as transportation, communications, and utilities. Smaller businesses may be privately owned. To varying degrees the state also determines the goals of businesses, the prices and selection of goods, and the rights of workers. Socialist countries typically provide their citizens with a higher level of services, such as health care and unemployment benefits, than do most capitalist countries. As a result, taxes and unemployment may also be quite high in socialist countries.

Many countries, including Great Britain, Denmark, China, Israel, and Sweden, have socialist systems, but the systems vary from country to country. In Denmark, for example, most businesses are privately owned and operated, but two-thirds of the population is sustained by the state through government welfare programs.

Socialism is proving to be surprisingly resilient in western Europe. France, for example, inched toward a capitalistic form of government after the presidency of François Mitterrand ended in 1995. Yet several years later the country elected Lionel Jospin, who won the election based upon a pledge of more government control and intervention in the workplace. Tony Blair, Great Britain's prime minister, is a member of the Labour Party, which historically has stood for the preeminence of government, nationalized industry, extraordinary social regulation, and massive taxation to support it all.

Mixed Economic Systems

mixed economies

Economies that combine several economic systems; for example, an economy where the government owns certain industries but others are owned by the private sector.

Canada, Great Britain, and Sweden, among others, are also called **mixed economies;** that is, they use more than one economic system. Sometimes, the government is basically socialist and owns basic industries. In Canada, for example, the government owns the communications, transportation, and utilities industries, as well as some of the natural resource industries. It also supplies health care to its citizens. But most other activity is carried on by private enterprises, as in a capitalist system.

The United States, surprisingly, is also considered a mixed economy. The few factors of production owned by the government include some public lands, the Postal Service, and some water resources. But the government is extensively involved in the economic system through taxing, spending, and welfare activities. The economy is also mixed in the sense that the country tries to achieve many social goals—income redistribution and Social Security, for example—that may not be attempted in purely capitalist systems. Exhibit P-2 summarizes key factors of the world's economic systems.

concept check

- What is capitalism and why is it growing?
- Explain the concept of a planned economy.
- What is socialism and why is it still popular?
- Why are most economies mixed?

TECHNOLOGICAL TRENDS

technology

The application of science and engineering skills and knowledge to solve production and organizational problems.

The application of technology can stimulate growth under capitalism or any other economic system. **Technology** is the application of science and engineering skills and knowledge to solve production and organizational problems. New

exhibit P-2 | The Basic Economic Systems of the World

	Capitalism	Command Economy (Communism)	Socialism	Mixed Economy
Ownership of Business	Businesses are privately owned with minimal government ownership or interference	Government owns all or most enterprises	Basic industries such as railroads and utilities are owned by government. Very high taxation as government redistributes income from successful private businesses and entrepreneurs	Private ownership of land and businesses but government control of some enterprises. The private sector is typically large
Control of Markets	Complete freedom of trade. No or little government control	Complete government control of markets	Some markets are controlled and some are free. Significant central government planning. State enterprises are managed by bureaucrats. These enterprises are rarely profitable	Some markets such as nuclear energy and the post office are controlled or highly regulated
Worker Incentives	Strong incentive to work and innovate because profits are retained by owners	No incentive to work hard or produce quality products	Private-sector incentives the same as capitalism and public-sector incentives the same as a planned economy	Private-sector incentives the same as capitalism. Limited incentives in the public sector
Management of Enterprises	Each enterprise is managed by owners or professional managers with little government interference	Centralized management by the government bureaucracy. Little or no flexibility in decision making at the factory level	Significant government planning and regulation. Bureaucrats run government enterprises	Private-sector management similar to capitalism. Public sector similar to socialism
Forecast for 2020	Continued steady growth	No growth and perhaps disappearance	Stable with probable slight growth	Continued growth

productivity

The amount of goods and services one worker can produce.

Get the scoop on the latest technologies affecting our lives at

http://www.cnet.com

machines that improve productivity and reduce costs can be one of a firm's most valuable assets. **Productivity** is the amount of goods and services one worker can produce. Our ability, as a nation, to maintain and build wealth depends in large part on the speed and effectiveness with which we invent and adopt machines that lift productivity. For example, coal mining is typically thought of as unskilled, backbreaking labor. But visit Cyprus Amax Mineral Co.'s Twenty-mile Mine near Oak Creek, Colorado, and you will find workers with push-button controls who walk along massive machines that shear 30-inch slices from an 850-foot coal wall. Laptop computers help miners track equipment breakdowns and water quality.

Internet technology connects buyers and sellers of goods and services throughout the world. This man visiting the E-Bay Web site can make a purchase with just a click of his mouse.

American business is becoming better at using technology to create change. The development pipelines at many high-tech companies already showcase a whole new breed of miniaturized inventions with capabilities well beyond today's computer chips. During the next five years, these microelectromechanical systems (MEMS)— which combine sensors, motors, and digital smarts on a single sliver of silicon— are likely to replace more expensive components in computer hardware, automobile engines, factory assembly lines, and dozens of other processes and products. The operating software for these devices is now being written.

High-tech visionaries foresee far more radical developments in the next 15 to 20 years. Scientists are speaking of using nature's own creative machinery. In medicine, this means replacing the body's failing organs. In manufacturing, it means creating innovative, new devices that will save time and money. The coming wave of miniaturization and molecular electronics—sometimes called "nanotechnology"—is taking shape at the intersection of chemistry, physics, biology, and electrical engineering.[8] And if it works as many scientists predict, it will bring a wholesale industrial transformation that will be more dramatic than the growth of microelectronics in the late 20th century.

Perhaps the technology that is having the most impact on individuals and businesses is the Internet. In fact, we are said to be living in the "click here" economy.

concept check

- What is technology?
- What benefits can businesses experience through the application of technology?
- What technology is having the most impact on business today?

TRENDS IN GLOBAL COMPETITION

exports

Goods and services sold outside a firm's domestic market.

gross domestic product (GDP)

The total market value of all final goods and services produced within a nation's borders in a year.

Global competition is another element of the external business environment that is driving changes in the way business is conducted. Agreements among nations and laws of individual countries have generally been supportive of global competition and trade. If current trends continue, world **exports** (goods and services sold outside a firm's domestic market) will reach $11 trillion by 2005, or 28 percent of world gross domestic product. This is up from 24.3 percent in 1998; 20 years ago, world trade's share was only 9.3 percent.[9] **Gross domestic product (GDP)** is the total market value of all final goods and services produced within a nation's borders in a year. World gross domestic product is the sum of all countries' GDP.

Global competition is fiercer than ever. A firm must watch out for competitors around the world as well as across town. In addition, businesses must often seek out suppliers from around the world to create world-class products. For example, we

Which country has the largest GDP? The answer is at

http://www.zurich-base-line.com

usually think of Boeing airplanes as a uniquely American product. Yet firms from around the world play a role in producing the Boeing 777.

Global competition is being stimulated and bolstered by advances in technology and communications and the continuous search for improved productivity.

Technology and Communications

Advances in technology and communications have allowed more companies than ever before to participate in the world arena. Large U.S.-based multinational corporations have operations in many countries. For example, Gillette manufactures in 57 locations in 28 countries and markets in over 200 countries. When companies like Gillette have offices all over the world, they can pick up winning ideas for new products just about anywhere. For example, in June 1997, Häagen-Dazs began serving a new flavor called *dulce de leche* at its sole ice cream shop in Buenos Aires. Named after the caramelized milk that is one of the most popular flavors in Argentina, the locally developed line was an immediate hit. Within weeks, the supersweet, butterscotch-like confection was the store's best-seller.

See what new flavors Häagen-Dazs is offering around the world. Go to http://www.haagen-dazs.com

Just one year later, consumers from Boston to Los Angeles to Paris could find *dulce de leche* at the supermarket or in one of Häagen-Dazs's 700 retail stores. In U.S. stores that carry it, only vanilla sells better. In Miami, *dulce* sells twice as fast as any other flavor. In the United States, it does $1 million a month in revenue. And in Europe, it will soon move up from a seasonal flavor to year-round status.[10]

Boeing is one of many U.S. companies that benefit from global competition. While the Boeing 777 may be assembled in the U.S., the actual parts of this airplane come from both U.S. and international suppliers.

KEY TERMS

baby boomers 5
capitalism 8
command economy 8
component lifestyle 3
demography 4
exports 11
Generation X 5
Generation Y 4
gross domestic product (GDP) 11
mixed economies 9
multiculturalism 7
productivity 10
Socialism 9
technology 9

Other companies are hoping for similar outcomes. Levi Strauss, famous for exporting the all-American look of blue jeans to the world, is hoping to bring an offshore trend to U.S. consumers. For three years, a dark version of Levi's denim has been the hot seller in Japan. Now Levi's is launching an offshoot to U.S. customers; called "hard jeans," it will be darker and stiffer than typical denim. Levi's has told its U.S. managers that looking abroad for ideas is part of their job.[11]

Improvements in Productivity

Good planning and efficient use of resources have made American companies world-class competitors. American businesses are now the most productive in the world. During the 1990s American businesses downsized to become more efficient. Downsizing means terminating employees, or laying off workers, to reduce costs and become more efficient. The goal is to produce as many or more goods and services with fewer employees. Many companies including AT&T, Boeing, and General Motors laid off tens of thousands of workers to become more competitive.

The American Society for Quality is a professional organization that helps firms improve their quality. Find out more at

http://www.asq.org

Often downsizing has been coupled with a greater use of technology, thereby greatly increasing productivity. Today, for example, there are about 65 personal computers per 100 workers in the United States. In Japan there are 20 personal computers per 100 workers. Contrary to popular belief, American businesses are much more productive than the Japanese. American manufacturers are 20 percent more productive than Japanese manufacturers, and American service providers are 50 percent more productive than Japan's service sector.

concept check

• What factors are stimulating global competition?
• What is gross domestic product (GDP)?
• Describe the trend in world exports.

learning goals

>lg 1   How do businesses and not-for-profit organizations help create our standard of living?

>lg 2   What is economics, and how are the three sectors of the economy linked?

>lg 3   How do economic growth, full employment, and price stability indicate a nation's economic health?

>lg 4   What is inflation, how is it measured, and what causes it?

>lg 5   How does the government use monetary policy and fiscal policy to achieve its macroeconomic goals?

>lg 6   What are the basic microeconomic concepts of demand and supply, and how do they establish prices?

>lg 7   What are the four types of market structure?

>lg 8   Which trends are reshaping micro- and macroeconomic environments?

Understanding Economic Systems and Competition

chapter 1

The Smart car—today
Europe, tomorrow the world

It's as big as an oversized go-cart with a plastic exterior that never rusts or dents. It can be swapped for another color for about the price of an evening dress. Designed for city commuting, it can turn on a dime, goes easy on fuel, and barely pollutes.

Alexis Mannes, a Brussels car dealer, says, "This may be the car that will change the car business." That's just what Daimler-Benz AG has in mind for its joint project with Société Cease de Microelectronic et d'Horlogerie SA, (SMH), maker of Swatch watches. Nicknamed the "Smart" car, the ultra-light, ultrafuel-efficient two-seater is being marketed as the ideal European city car, selling for the equivalent of $8,500.

Daimler-Benz has no current plans to market the Smart car in the United States, but both Daimler and its new partner, Chrysler Corp., view the project as a laboratory. Both see the Smart car as an idea factory for the automotive technology and industrial cooperation of the future. "Daimler sees the Smart as a playground to test things," says Peter Soliman, a consultant with Booz-Allen Hamilton in Düsseldorf. "Even if it never makes any money, it has already taught the operation a lot about manufacturing, research and development, and distribution that they can carry over to their main business."

Some rival auto makers scoff at the idea of plastic doors, hoods, and trunks. But the lightweight materials are critical in increasing fuel efficiency, which is important in Europe where auto makers have agreed to reduce their fleets' carbon dioxide emissions by some 25 percent by the year 2008. The Smart car is one of Europe's most fuel-efficient autos, using just 4.8 liters of gasoline per 100 kilometers—or roughly 1 gallon per 59 miles—compared with 6.8 liters for Ford Motor Co.'s Ka and 6.6 liters for a Volkswagen Polo.

To make the car dramatically smaller than existing subcompacts, Micro Compact Car, the Daimler-SMH joint venture that makes the Smart, was forced to redesign the basic "three-box" concept of the traditional car, which has a hood, a cockpit, and a trunk. Designers put the engine in the back, as in the original VW Beetle. Then they shoved the rest of the car's mechanics below the passenger cabin, something that had previously been done only with minivans. As a result, the Smart factory in Hambach, France, is capable of building 900 cars a day with virtually no parts inventory of its own. Because only 25 percent of the Smart's value is added in final assembly, it takes just 4.5 hours to assemble one, compared with 20 hours for a VW Polo.

Critical Thinking Questions:

As you read this chapter, consider the following questions as they relate to the Smart car:

- What factors determine the price of the Smart?
- In what type of environment does Daimler-Benz compete?
- How can the changing economic environment affect the demand for the Smart?

Business in the 21st Century

Auto history is littered with cars of tomorrow that landed on the scrap heap, including the Edsel, the Tucker, and the DeLorean sports car. And for every Smart enthusiast there seems to be a Smart skeptic. "Too expensive," says Shuhei Toyoda, chief engineer for Toyota Motor Corp.'s new Yaris, another small city car. Ferdinand Piech, chairman of rival Volkswagen AG, suggests that the Smart car isn't even new: "We already have a city car," he scoffs, referring to the VW Polo. "And it has four seats."[1]

BUSINESS IN THE 21ST CENTURY

economic system

The combination of policies, laws, and choices made by a nation's government to establish the systems that determine what goods and services are produced and how they are allocated.

Whether the Smart car will be a success depends in part on the economic systems of the countries where it is marketed. A nation's **economic system** is the combination of policies, laws, and choices made by its government to establish the systems that determine what goods and services are produced and how they are allocated. Capitalism and a planned economy, which we discussed in the Prologue, are examples of economic systems. In a planned economy, government bureaucrats would determine whether to build a car like the Smart car. Historically, planned economies have done a much worse job of stimulating economic growth and creating a higher standard of living for their citizens than capitalist economies have. Even though the Smart car is not very expensive, most people in planned economies like Cuba and North Korea could not afford one.

This chapter will help you understand how economies provide jobs for workers and also create and deliver products to consumers and businesses. We'll begin with a look at how businesses and not-for-profit organizations create our standard of living. You will also learn how governments attempt to influence economic activity through policies such as lowering or raising taxes. Next, we discuss how supply and demand determine prices for goods and services. We conclude by examining trends in evolving economic systems and competition.

business

An organization that strives for a profit by providing goods and services desired by its customers.

THE NATURE OF BUSINESS

goods

Tangible items manufactured by businesses.

services

Intangible offerings of businesses that can't be held, touched, or stored.

standard of living

A country's output of goods and services that people can buy with the money they have.

A **business** is an organization that strives for a profit by providing goods and services desired by its customers. Businesses meet the needs of consumers by providing movies, medical care, autos, and countless other goods and services. **Goods** are tangible items manufactured by businesses, such as desks. **Services** are intangible offerings of businesses that can't be held, touched, or stored. Physicians, lawyers, restaurants, car washes, and airlines all provide services. Businesses also serve other organizations, such as hospitals, retailers, and governments, by providing machinery, goods for resale, computers, and thousands of other items.

Thus, businesses create the goods and services that are the basis of our standard of living. The **standard of living** of any country is measured by the output of goods and services people can buy with the money they have. The United States has one of the highest standards of living in the world. Several countries such as Switzerland and Germany have higher wages than the United States, but their standard of living isn't higher. The reason is that prices are so much higher in those countries that people are able to purchase less than people in the United States with the same amount of money. For example, a "Real Meal Deal" at McDonald's in Geneva, Switzerland, costs about $9 compared to less than $4 in the United States.

Businesses play a key role in determining our quality of life by providing jobs and goods and services to society. **Quality of life** refers to the general level of human happiness based on such things as life expectancy, educational standards, health, sanitation, and leisure time. Countries with the highest quality of life are Canada, the United States, Japan, the Netherlands, and Norway. In a list of 174 countries, Russia ranks 57th, China 108th, and India 135th.[2] Building a high quality of life is a combined effort of businesses, government, and not-for-profit organizations.

Creating a quality of life is not without risks. **Risk** is the potential to lose time and money or otherwise not be able to accomplish an organization's goals. The Boy Scouts of America, for example, face the risk of not recruiting enough new scouts each year, while Compaq Computer risks not reaching its revenue goals. **Revenue** is the money a company earns from providing services or selling goods to customers. **Costs** are expenses for rent, salaries, supplies, transportation, and many other items that a company incurs from creating and selling goods and services. Some of the costs incurred by a clothing manufacturer, for example, include expenses for cloth, pattern designers, cutting machines, workers, managers, building rental or purchase, advertising, and transportation. **Profit** is the money left over after all expenses are paid.

Not-for-Profit Organizations

Not all organizations strive to make a profit. A **not-for-profit organization** is an organization that exists to achieve some goal other than the usual business goal of profit. The United Way, Keep America Beautiful, the American Cancer Society, Greenpeace, and the Sierra Club are all not-for-profit organizations. Most hospitals, zoos, museums, and charities are also not-for-profit organizations. Government is our largest and most pervasive not-for-profit group. Not-for-profit organizations (not including government expenditures) now account for over 28 percent of the economic activity in the United States.

Successful not-for-profit organizations follow sound business principles. These groups have goals they hope to accomplish, but the goals are not focused on profits. For example, a not-for-profit organization's goal might be feeding the poor, stopping destruction of the environment, increasing attendance at the ballet, or preventing drunk driving. Reaching such goals takes good planning, management, and control. Not-for-profit organizations do not compete directly with each other as, for example, American and United Airlines do, but they do compete for people's scarce volunteer time and donations.

Factors of Production: The Building Blocks of Business

Factors of production are the resources used to create goods and services. By using the factors of production efficiently, a company can produce more output with the same resources. Four traditional factors of production are common to all productive activity: natural resources, labor, capital, and entrepreneurship. A fifth factor, knowledge, is gaining in importance.

Commodities that are useful inputs in their natural state are known as natural resources. They include farmland, forests, mineral and oil deposits, and water. Sometimes natural resources are simply called *land*, although, as you can see, the term means more than just land. Today, urban sprawl, pollution, and limited resources have raised questions about resource use. Conservationists,

---

quality of life
The general level of human happiness based on such things as life expectancy, educational standards, health, sanitation, and leisure time.

risk
The potential to lose time and money or otherwise not be able to accomplish an organization's goals.

revenue
The money a company earns from providing services or selling goods to customers.

costs
Expenses incurred in creating and selling goods and services.

profit
The money left over after all expenses are paid.

not-for-profit organization
An organization that exists to achieve some goal other than the usual business goal of profit.

factors of production
The resources used to create goods and services.

ecologists, and government bodies are proposing laws to require land-use planning and resource conservation.

The economic contributions of people working with their minds and muscles are called labor. This input includes the talents of everyone—from a restaurant cook to a nuclear physicist—who performs the many tasks of manufacturing and selling goods and services.

The tools, machinery, equipment, and buildings used to produce goods and services and get them to the consumer are known as **capital.** Sometimes the term *capital* is also used to mean the money that buys machinery, factories, and other production and distribution facilities. However, because money itself produces nothing, it is *not* one of the basic inputs. Instead, it is a means of acquiring the inputs. Therefore, in this context, capital does not include money.

Entrepreneurs are people who combine the inputs of natural resources, labor, and capital to produce goods or services with the intention of making a profit. These people make all the decisions that set the course for their firms; they create products and production processes. Because they are not guaranteed a profit in return for their time and effort, they must be risk takers. Of course, if their firms succeed, the rewards may be great.

Today, Americans between the ages of 14 and 34 are creating almost half of the new businesses in the country.[3] One study found that 87 percent of young people ages 16 to 25 want to own a business.[4] They are attracted by the opportunity to be their own boss and reap the financial rewards of a successful business. Many start their first business from their dorm rooms or while living at home, so their cost is almost zero.

Entrepreneurs include people like Bill Gates, the founder of Microsoft, who is now one of the richest people in the world. The list of entrepreneurs also includes countless thousands of individuals who have started small companies that, while remaining small, still contribute to America's economic well-being.

A number of outstanding managers and noted academics are beginning to emphasize a fifth factor of production—knowledge. **Knowledge** is the combined talents and skills of the workforce. As the world becomes ever more uncertain, the very nature of work, organizations, and management is changing. The new competitive environment places a premium on knowledge and learning. Lester Thurow, a leading world expert on economic issues, says that "the dominant competitive weapon of the 21st century will be the knowledge of the workforce."[5] The companies that will become and remain successful will be the ones that can learn fast, assimilate this learning, and develop new insights. General Electric and Coca-Cola are two firms often cited as learning-based organizations because they utilize their human resources so effectively.

capital

The inputs, such as tools, machinery, equipment, and buildings, used to produce goods and services and get them to the customer.

entrepreneurs

People who combine the inputs of natural resources, labor, and capital to produce goods or services with the intention of making a profit or accomplishing a not-for-profit goal.

knowledge

The combined talents and skills of the workforce.

Knowledge gives businesses a competitive edge. For insight into how companies are turning themselves into learning-based organizations, go to

http://www.brint.com

HOW BUSINESSES AND ECONOMIES WORK

>lg 2

economics

The study of how a society uses scarce resources to produce and distribute goods and services.

Economics is the study of how a society uses scarce resources to produce and distribute goods and services. The resources of a person, a firm, or a nation are limited. Hence, economics is the study of choices—what people, firms, or nations choose from among the available resources. Every economy is concerned with what types and amounts of goods and services should be produced, how they should be produced, and for whom. These decisions are made by the marketplace,

Daimler Chrysler considered the economic system of European nations in developing its compact, affordable, and highly fuel-efficient Smart car.

---

macroeconomics
The subarea of economics that focuses on the economy as a whole by looking at aggregate data for large groups of people, companies, or products.

microeconomics
The subarea of economics that focuses on individual parts of the economy such as households or firms.

the government, or both. In the United States the government and the free market system together guide the economy.

You probably know more about economics than you realize. Every day many news stories deal with economic matters: a union wins wage increases at General Motors; the Federal Reserve Board lowers interest rates; Wall Street has a record day; the president proposes a cut in income taxes; consumer spending rises as the economy grows; or retail prices are on the rise, to mention just a few examples.

Macroeconomics and Microeconomics

The state of the economy affects both people and businesses. How you spend your money (or save it) is a personal economic decision. Whether you continue in school and whether you work part-time are also economic decisions. Every business also operates within the economy. Based on their economic expectations, businesses decide what products to produce, how to price them, how many people to employ, how much to pay these employees, how much to expand the business, and so on.

Economics has two main subareas. **Macroeconomics** is the study of the economy as a whole. It looks at *aggregate* data, data for large groups of people, companies, or products considered as a whole. In contrast, **microeconomics** focuses on individual parts of the economy, such as households or firms.

Both *macroeconomics* and *microeconomics* offer a valuable outlook on the economy. For example, Ford might use both to decide whether to introduce a new line of cars, like the Smart car, from Europe. The company would consider such macroeconomic factors as the national level of personal income, the unemployment rate, interest rates, fuel costs, and the national level of sales of imported cars. From a microeconomic viewpoint, Ford would judge consumer demand for new cars versus the existing supply, competing models, labor and material costs and availability, and current prices and sales incentives.

Economics as a Circular Flow

circular flow
The movement of inputs and outputs among households, businesses, and governments; a way of showing how the sectors of the economy interact.

Another way to see how the sectors of the economy interact is to examine the **circular flow** of inputs and outputs among households, businesses, and governments as shown in Exhibit 1-1. Let's review the exchanges by following the purple circle around the inside of the diagram. Households provide inputs (natural resources, labor, capital, entrepreneurship) to businesses, which convert these inputs into outputs (goods and services) for consumers. In return, consumers receive income from rent, wages, interest, and ownership profits (green circle). Businesses receive income from consumer purchases of goods and services.

The other important exchange in Exhibit 1-1 takes place between governments (federal, state, and local) and both individuals and businesses. Governments supply many types of publicly provided goods and services (highways, schools, police, courts, health services, unemployment insurance, Social Security) that benefit individuals and businesses. Government purchases from businesses also contribute to business profits. The contractor who repairs a local stretch of state highway, for example, is paid by government for the work. As the diagram shows, government receives taxes from individuals and businesses to complete the flow.

e x h i b i t   1 - 1 | Economics as a Circular Flow

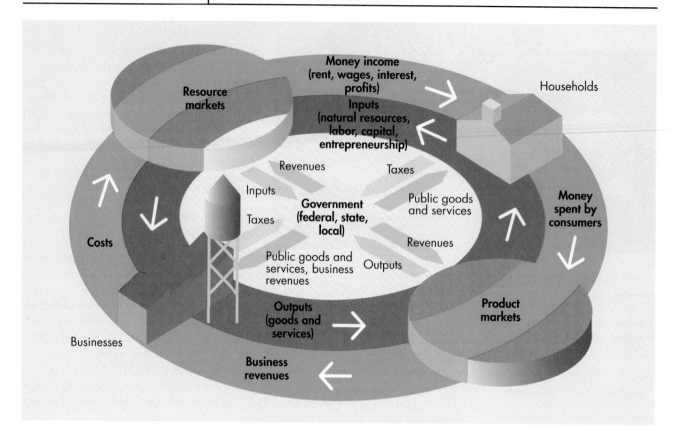

concept check

- What is economics?
- What is the difference between macro-economics and microeconomics?
- How do resources flow among the house-hold, business, and government sectors?

Changes in one flow affect the others. If government raises taxes, households have less to spend on goods and services. Lower consumer spending causes businesses to reduce production, and economic activity declines; unemployment may rise. In contrast, cutting taxes can stimulate economic activity. Keep the circular flow in mind as we continue our study of economics. The way economic sectors interact will become more evident as we explore macroeconomics and microeconomics.

MACROECONOMICS: THE BIG PICTURE

>lg 3

Have you ever looked at Headline News on the Internet or turned on the radio or television and heard something like, "Today the Labor Department reported that for the second straight month unemployment declined"? Statements like this are macroeconomic news. Understanding the national economy and how changes in government policies affect households and businesses is a good place to begin our study of economics.

Let's look first at macroeconomic goals and how they can be met. The United States and most other countries have three main macroeconomic goals: economic growth, full employment, and price stability. A nation's economic well-being depends on carefully defining these goals and choosing the best economic policies to reach them.

Striving for Economic Growth

Perhaps the most important way to judge a nation's economic health is to look at its production of goods and services. The more the nation produces, the higher its standard of living. An increase in a nation's output of goods and services is **economic growth.**

economic growth
An increase in a nation's output of goods and services.

Economic growth is usually a good thing, but it also has a bad side. Increased production yields more pollution. Growth may strain public facilities, such as roads, electricity, schools, and hospitals. Thus, the government tries to apply economic policies that will keep growth to a level that does not reduce the quality of life.

The most basic measure of economic growth is the *gross domestic product (GDP).* GDP is the total market value of all final goods and services produced within a nation's borders each year. It is reported quarterly and is used to compare trends in national output. When GDP rises, the economy is growing.

The *rate* of growth in real GDP (GDP adjusted for inflation) is also important. Recently, the U.S. economy has been growing at about 2 to 3 percent annually. This growth rate has meant a slow, steady increase in output of goods and services and low unemployment. When the growth rate slides toward zero, the economy will begin to stagnate and perhaps decline.

The U.S. Bureau of Economic Analysis tracks national and regional economic statistics, including the GDP. To find the latest GDP statistics, visit the BEA at

http://www.bea.doc.gov

business cycles
Upward and downward changes in the level of economic activity.

recession
A decline in GDP that lasts for at least two consecutive quarters.

The level of economic activity is constantly changing. These upward and downward changes are called **business cycles.** Business cycles vary in length, in how high or low the economy moves, and in how much the economy is affected. Changes in GDP trace the patterns as economic activity expands and contracts. An increase in business activity results in rising output, income, employment, and prices. Eventually, these all peak, and output, income, and employment decline. A decline in GDP that lasts for two consecutive quarters

The housing industry is a leading economic indicator. A rise in new home construction typically translates into a robust economy.

(each a three-month period) is called a **recession.** It is followed by a recovery period when economic activity once again increases. The most recent recession began in 2001.

Businesses must monitor and react to the changing phases of business cycles. When the economy is growing, companies often have a difficult time hiring good employees and finding scarce supplies and raw materials. When a recession hits, many firms find they have more capacity than the demand for their goods and services requires. During the recession of the early 1990s, many firms operated at 75 percent or less of their capacity. When plants use only part of their capacity, they operate inefficiently and have higher costs per unit produced. Let's say that Mars Corp. has a plant that can produce one million Milky Way candy bars a day, but because of a recession Mars can sell only half a million candy bars a day. Mars has a huge plant with large, expensive machines designed to produce a million candy bars a day. Producing Milky Ways at 50 percent capacity does not efficiently utilize Mars's investment in the plant and equipment.

Keeping People on the Job

full employment

The condition when all people who want to work and can work have jobs.

Another macroeconomic goal is **full employment,** or having jobs for all who want to and can work. Full employment doesn't actually mean 100 percent employment. Some people choose not to work for personal reasons (attending school, raising children) or are temporarily unemployed while they wait to start a new job. Thus, the government defines full employment as the situation when about 94 to 96 percent of those available to work actually have jobs. During the early 2000s, the economy operated at close to full employment until the recession of 2001.

unemployment rate

The percentage of the total labor force that is actively looking for work but is not actually working.

Measuring Unemployment To determine how close we are to full employment, the government measures the **unemployment rate.** This rate indicates the percentage of the total labor force that is not working but is *actively looking for work.* It excludes "discouraged workers," those not seeking jobs because they think no one will hire them. Each month the Department of Labor releases statistics on employment. These figures help us understand how well the economy is doing. In the past two decades, unemployment rose as high as 9.7 percent in 1982, which was a recession year. It then declined steadily through the remainder of the 1980s and most of the 1990s. In 2000, the rate fell to under 4 percent, which was the lowest rate in almost 30 years. However, it rose to around 5 percent in 2001.[6]

How are the job prospects in your area? Your region's unemployment statistics can give you an idea of how hard it will be to find a job. Find the most recent unemployment statistics from the Bureau of Labor Statistics at
http://www.bls.gov

Types of Unemployment Economists classify unemployment into four types: frictional, structural, cyclical, and seasonal. The categories are of small consolation to someone who is unemployed, but they help economists understand the problem of unemployment in our economy.

frictional unemployment

Short-term unemployment that is not related to the business cycle.

Frictional unemployment is short-term unemployment that is not related to the business cycle. It includes people who are unemployed while waiting to start a better job, those who are reentering the job market, and those entering for the first time such as new college graduates. This type of unemployment is always present and has little impact on the economy.

structural unemployment

Unemployment that is caused by a mismatch between available jobs and the skills of available workers in an industry or region; not related to the business cycle.

Structural unemployment is also unrelated to the business cycle but is involuntary. It is caused by a mismatch between available jobs and the skills of available workers in an industry or a region. For example, if the birthrate declines, fewer teachers will be needed. Or the available workers in an area may lack the skills that employers want. Retraining and skill-building programs are often required to reduce structural unemployment.

cyclical unemployment

Unemployment that occurs when a downturn in the business cycle reduces the demand for labor throughout the economy.

Cyclical unemployment, as the name implies, occurs when a downturn in the business cycle reduces the demand for labor throughout the economy. In a long recession, cyclical unemployment is widespread, and even people with good job skills can't find jobs. The government can partly counteract cyclical unemployment with programs that boost the economy.

In the past, cyclical unemployment affected mainly less skilled workers and those in heavy manufacturing. Typically, they would be rehired when economic growth increased. During the 1990s, however, competition forced many American companies to downsize so they could survive in the global marketplace. Motorola cut 15,000 jobs, or 10 percent of its workforce, to lower costs so that it could compete with Asian, European, and other U.S. semiconductor and telecommunications firms.[7]

seasonal unemployment
Unemployment that occurs during specific seasons in certain industries.

>lg 4

inflation
The situation in which the average of all prices of goods and services is rising.

purchasing power
The value of what money can buy.

demand-pull inflation
Inflation that occurs when the demand for goods and services is greater than the supply.

cost-push inflation
Inflation that occurs when increases in production costs push up the prices of final goods and services.

During busy summer months, theme parks like Disney World hire many young people and adults—a group of employees subject to seasonal unemployment.

The last type is **seasonal unemployment,** which occurs during specific seasons in certain industries. Employees subject to seasonal unemployment include retail workers hired for the Christmas buying season, lettuce pickers in California, and restaurant employees in Aspen during the summer.

Keeping Prices Steady

The third macroeconomic goal is to keep overall prices for goods and services fairly steady. The situation in which the average of all prices of goods and services is rising is called **inflation.** Inflation's higher prices reduce **purchasing power,** the value of what money can buy. If prices go up but income doesn't rise or rises at a slower rate, a given amount of income buys less. For example, if the price of a basket of groceries rises from $30 to $40 but your salary remains the same, you can buy only 75 percent as many groceries ($30 ÷ $40). Your purchasing power declines by 25 percent ($10 ÷ $40).

Inflation affects both personal and business decisions. When prices are rising, people tend to spend more—before their purchasing power declines further. Businesses that expect inflation often increase their supplies, and people often speed up planned purchases of cars and major appliances.

During the early 2000s and late 1990s, inflation in the United States was in the 2 to 4 percent range. This level is generally viewed as quite low. In the 1980s we had periods of inflation in the 12 to 13 percent range. Some nations have had triple-digit inflation or even higher in recent years. In the late 1990s, Bulgaria had an annual rate of inflation of 123 percent; Turkmenistan, 992 percent; and Angola, 4,145 percent!

Want to know where the consumer price index stands today? Go to
http://www.bls.gov/cpi/

Types of Inflation There are two types of inflation. **Demand-pull inflation** occurs when the demand for goods and services is greater than the supply. Would-be buyers have more money to spend than the amount needed to buy available goods and services. Their demand, which exceeds the supply, tends to pull prices up. This situation is sometimes described as "too much money chasing too few goods." The higher prices lead to greater supply, eventually creating a balance between demand and supply.

Cost-push inflation is triggered by increases in production costs, such as expenses for materials and wages. These increases push up the prices of final goods and services. Wage increases are a major cause of cost-push inflation, creating a "wage-price spiral." For example, assume the United Auto Workers union negotiates a three-year labor agreement that raises wages 3 percent per year and increases overtime pay. Car makers will then raise car prices to cover their higher labor costs. Also, the higher wages will give auto workers more money to buy goods and services, and this increased demand may pull up other prices. Workers in other industries will demand higher wages to keep up with the increased prices, and the cycle will push prices even higher.

consumer price index (CPI)

An index of the prices of a market basket of goods and services purchased by typical urban consumers.

How Inflation Is Measured The rate of inflation is most commonly measured by looking at changes in the **consumer price index (CPI),** an index of the prices of a "market basket" of goods and services purchased by typical urban consumers. It is published monthly by the Department of Labor. Major components of the CPI, which are weighted by importance, are food, clothing, transportation, housing, health, and recreation. Data are collected from about 23,000 retail and service businesses in 87 areas around the country.

The CPI sets prices in a base period at 100. The base period, which now is 1982–1984, is chosen for its price stability. Current prices are then expressed as a percentage of prices in the base period. A rise in the CPI means prices are increasing. For example, the CPI was 172.6 in July 2000, meaning that prices had increased 72.6 percent from the 1982–1984 base period.

Changes in wholesale prices are another important indicator of inflation. The **producer price index (PPI)** measures the prices paid by producers and wholesalers for such commodities as raw materials, partially finished goods, and finished products. The PPI is actually a family of indexes for many different product categories. For example, the PPI for finished goods was 134.7 in June 2000. Examples of other PPI indexes include containers, fuels and lubricants, and construction. Because the PPI measures prices paid by producers for raw materials, energy, and other commodities, it may foreshadow subsequent price changes for businesses and consumers.

HOT
links

How do the PPI and the CPI differ? Get the answers to this and other questions about the PPI by visiting the Bureau of Labor Statistics PPI site at

http://www.bls.gov/ppi/

producer price index (PPI)

An index of the prices paid by producers and wholesalers for various commodities such as raw materials, partially finished goods, and finished products.

concept check

• What is a business cycle? How do businesses adapt to periods of contraction and expansion?
• Why is full employment usually defined as a target percentage below 100 percent? How is unemployment measured?
• What is the difference between demand-pull and cost-push inflation?

The Impact of Inflation Inflation has several negative effects on people and businesses. For one thing, inflation penalizes people who live on fixed incomes. Let's say that a couple receives $1,000 a month retirement income beginning in 2002. If inflation is 10 percent in 2003, then the couple can buy only 90 percent of what they could purchase in 2002. Similarly, inflation hurts savers. As prices rise, the real value, or purchasing power, of a nest egg of savings deteriorates.

ACHIEVING MACROECONOMIC GOALS

>lg 5

To reach macroeconomic goals, countries must often choose among conflicting alternatives. Sometimes political needs override economic ones. For example, bringing inflation under control may call for a politically difficult period of high unemployment and low growth. Or, in an election year, politicians may resist raising taxes to curb inflation. Still, the government must try to guide the economy to a sound balance of growth, employment, and price stability. The two main tools it uses are monetary policy and fiscal policy.

Monetary Policy

monetary policy

A government's programs for controlling the amount of money circulating in the economy and interest rates.

Monetary policy refers to a government's programs for controlling the amount of money circulating in the economy and interest rates. Changes in the money supply affect both the level of economic activity and the rate of inflation. The **Federal Reserve System (the Fed),** the central banking system, prints money and controls how much of it will be in circulation. The money supply is also controlled by the Fed's regulation of certain bank activities.

Federal Reserve System (the Fed)

The central banking system of the United States.

When the Fed increases or decreases the amount of money in circulation, it affects interest rates (the cost of borrowing money and the reward for lending it). The Fed can change the interest rate on money it lends to banks to signal the banking system and financial markets that it has changed its monetary policy. Banks, in turn, may pass along this change to consumers and businesses that receive loans from the banks. If the cost of borrowing increases, the economy slows because interest rates affect consumer and business decisions to spend or invest. The housing industry, business, and investments react most to changes in interest rates.

Eight times a year, the Federal Reserve Board issues the Beige Book with up-to-the-minute information abut the state of the U.S. economy. Find it at the Federal Reserve's home page, http://www.federalreserve.gov/

As you can see, the Fed can use monetary policy to contract or expand the economy. With **contractionary policy,** the Fed restricts, or tightens, the money supply by selling government securities or raising interest rates. The result is slower economic growth and higher unemployment. Thus, contractionary policy reduces spending and, ultimately, lowers inflation. With **expansionary policy,** the Fed increases, or loosens, growth in the money supply. An expansionary policy stimulates the economy. Interest rates decline, so business and consumer spending go up. Unemployment rates drop as businesses expand. But increasing the money supply also has a negative side: more spending pushes prices up, increasing the inflation rate.

contractionary policy

The use of monetary policy by the Fed to tighten the money supply by selling government securities or raising interest rates.

expansionary policy

The use of monetary policy by the Fed to increase the growth of the money supply.

Fiscal Policy

fiscal policy

The government's use of taxation and spending to affect the economy.

The other economic tool used by the government is **fiscal policy,** its program of taxation and spending. By increasing its spending or by cutting taxes, the government can stimulate the economy. Look again at Exhibit 1-1. The more government buys from businesses, the greater business revenues and output are. Likewise, if consumers or businesses have to pay less in taxes, they will have more income to spend for goods and services. Tax policies in the United States therefore affect business decisions. High corporate taxes can make it harder for U.S. firms to compete with companies in countries with lower taxes. As a result, companies may choose to locate facilities overseas to reduce their tax burden.

Nobody likes to pay taxes, although we grudgingly accept that we have to. Although most U.S. citizens complain that they are overtaxed, we pay lower taxes per capita (per person) than citizens in many countries similar to ours, as Exhibit 1-2 shows.

Taxes are, of course, the major source of revenue for our government. Every year the president prepares a budget for the coming year based upon estimated revenues and expenditures. Congress receives the president's report and recommendations and then, typically, debates and analyzes the proposed budget for several months. The president's original proposal is always modified in numerous ways. Exhibit 1-3 shows sources of revenue and expenses for the U.S. budget.

While fiscal policy has a major impact on businesses and consumers, continual increases in government spending raise another important issue. When government takes more money from businesses and consumers (the private sector) and uses these funds for increased government spending (the public

e x h i b i t   1 - 2 | Tax Revenues, by Country (Per Capita and Percentage of GDP)

	Per Capita	Percentage of GDP
United States	$ 7,234	27.6%
Japan	10,434	27.8
Australia	5,589	29.9
United Kingdom	5,968	34.1
Canada	6,858	36.1
Germany	12,197	39.3
Norway	11,706	41.2
Italy	7,416	41.7
France	10,129	44.1
The Netherlands	9,983	45.9
Belgium	10,500	46.6
Sweden	11,481	51.0
Denmark	14,460	51.6

crowding out

The situation that occurs when government spending replaces spending by the private sector.

sector), a phenomenon known as **crowding out** occurs. Here are three examples of crowding out:

1. The government spends more on public libraries, and individuals buy fewer books at bookstores.
2. The government spends more on public education, and individuals spend less on private education.
3. The government spends more on public transportation, and individuals spend less on private transportation.

In other words, government spending is crowding out private spending.

e x h i b i t   1 - 3 | Revenues and Expenses for the Federal Budget

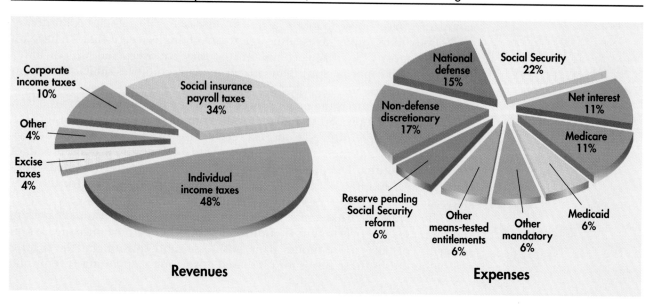

Revenues

Corporate income taxes 10%
Other 4%
Excise taxes 4%
Social insurance payroll taxes 34%
Individual income taxes 48%

Expenses

National defense 15%
Social Security 22%
Non-defense discretionary 17%
Net interest 11%
Medicare 11%
Reserve pending Social Security reform 6%
Other means-tested entitlements 6%
Other mandatory 6%
Medicaid 6%

federal budget deficit
The condition that occurs when the federal government spends more for programs than it collects in taxes.

If the government spends more for programs (social services, education, defense) than it collects in taxes, the result is a **federal budget deficit.** To balance the budget, the government can cut its spending, increase taxes, or do some combination of the two. When it cannot balance the budget, the government must make up any shortfalls by borrowing (just like any business or household).

In 1998, for the first time in a generation, there was a federal budget surplus (revenue exceeded spending) of about $70 billion. Whenever the government finds itself with a surplus, Congress begins an often heated debate about what to do with the money. Some members of Congress, for example, want to spend more on social programs or for defense. Others say that this money belongs to the people and should be returned in the form of tax cuts. Another alternative is to reduce the national debt.

See how the national deficit has changed since the nation began by visiting

http://www.budget.org/NationalDebt/Deficit

national debt
The accumulated total of all of the federal government's annual budget deficits.

Despite the recent federal budget surplus, the U.S. government has run budget deficits for many years. The accumulative total of these past deficits is the **national debt,** which now amounts to about $5 trillion or about $20,000 for every man, woman, and child in the United States. Interest on the debt is more than $360 billion a year. To cover the deficit, the U.S. government borrows money from people and businesses in the form of Treasury bills, Treasury notes, and Treasury bonds. These are federal IOUs that pay interest to the owners.

The national debt is an emotional issue debated not only in the halls of Congress, but by the public as well. Some believe that deficits contribute to economic growth, high employment, and price stability. Others have the following reservations about such a high national debt.

Want to know the current public debt per citizen? Go to

http://www.budget.org/NationalDebt/Debt

Not Everyone Holds the Debt One issue is who actually bears the burden of the national debt. If only the rich were bondholders, then they alone would receive the interest payments. Depending on how many bonds they held, they could end up receiving more in interest than they paid in taxes. In the meantime, poorer people, who held no bonds, would end up paying taxes that would be transferred to the rich as interest. Under these conditions, the debt would indeed be a burden to some.

The government is very conscious of this burden effect and has kept a watchful eye on who holds what bonds. For example, it has at times instructed commercial banks to reduce their total debt by divesting some of their bond holdings. That's also why the Treasury created **savings bonds.** Because these bonds are issued in relatively small denominations, they allow more people to buy and hold government debt.

savings bonds
Government bonds of relatively small denominations.

c o n c ə p t   c h ə c k

- What are the two kinds of monetary policy? How does the government use monetary policy to achieve its macroeconomic goals?
- What is fiscal policy? What fiscal policy tools can the government use to achieve its macroeconomic goals?
- What problems can a large national debt present?

Crowding Out Private Investment Another concern is the effect of the national debt on private investment. If, to sell its bonds, the government raises the interest rate on the bonds it offers, it forces private businesses, which must stay competitive as suppliers of bonds in the bond market, to raise the rates they offer on their corporate bonds (long-term debt obligations issued by a company). In other words, financing government spending by government debt makes it more costly for private industry to finance its own investment. As a result, government debt may end up crowding out private investment and slowing economic growth in the private sector.

MICROECONOMICS: ZEROING IN ON BUSINESSES AND CONSUMERS

Now let's shift our focus from the whole economy to *microeconomics*, the study of households, businesses, and industries. This field of economics is concerned with how prices and quantities of goods and services behave in a free market. It stands to reason that people, firms, and governments try to get the most from their limited resources. Consumers want to buy the best quality at the lowest price. Businesses want to keep costs down and revenues high to earn larger profits. Governments also want to use their revenues to provide the most effective public goods and services possible. These groups choose among alternatives by focusing on the prices of goods and services.

As consumers in a free market, we influence what is produced. If Mexican food is popular, the high demand attracts entrepreneurs who open more Mexican restaurants. They want to compete for our dollars by supplying Mexican food at a lower price, of better quality, or with different features such as Santa Fe Mexican food rather than Tex-Mex. This section explains how business and consumer choices influence the price and availability of goods and services.

The Nature of Demand

demand

The quantity of a good or service that people are willing to buy at various prices.

demand curve

A graph showing the quantity of a good or service that people are willing to buy at various prices.

Demand is the quantity of a good or service that people are willing to buy at various prices. The higher the price, the lower the quantity demanded, and vice versa. A graph of this relationship is called a **demand curve.**

Let's assume you own a store that sells jackets for snowboarders. From past experience you know how many jackets you can sell at different prices. The demand curve in Exhibit 1-4 depicts this information. The x-axis (horizontal axis) shows the quantity of jackets, and the y-axis (vertical axis) shows the related price of those jackets. For example, at a price of $60, customers will buy (demand) 500 snowboard jackets.

In the graph the demand curve slopes downward and to the right. This means that as the price falls, people will want to buy more jackets. Some people

e x h i b i t   1 - 4 | Demand Curve for Jackets for Snowboarders

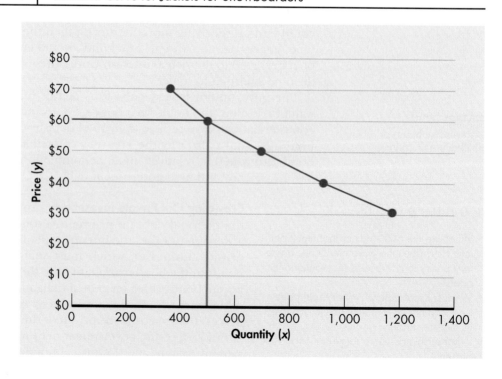

who were not going to buy a jacket will purchase one at the lower price. Also, some snowboarders who already have a jacket will buy a second one. The graph also shows that if you put a large number of jackets on the market, you will have to reduce the price to sell all of them.

The Nature of Supply

supply
The quantity of a good or service that businesses will make available at various prices.

supply curve
A graph showing the quantity of a good or service that a business will make available at various prices.

Demand alone is not enough to explain how the market sets prices. We must also look at **supply,** the quantity of a good or service that businesses will make available at various prices. The higher the price, the greater the amount a jacket manufacturer is willing to supply, and vice versa. A graph of the relationship between various prices and the quantities a manufacturer will supply is a **supply curve.**

We can again plot the quantity of jackets on the *x*-axis and the price on the *y*-axis. As Exhibit 1-5 shows, 900 jackets will be available at a price of $60. Note that the supply curve slopes upward and to the right, the opposite of the demand curve. If snowboarders are willing to pay higher prices, manufacturers of jackets will buy more inputs (Goretex, dye, machinery, labor) and produce more jackets. The quantity supplied will be higher at higher prices, because producers can earn higher profits.

How Demand and Supply Interact to Determine Prices

In a stable economy, the number of jackets that snowboarders demand depends on the jackets' price. Likewise, the number of jackets that suppliers provide depends on price. But at what price will consumer demand for jackets match the quantity suppliers will produce?

To answer this question, we need to look at what happens when demand and supply interact. By plotting both the demand curve and the supply curve on the same graph in Exhibit 1-6, we see that they cross at a certain quantity and price. At that point, labeled E, the quantity demanded equals the quantity supplied.

e x h i b i t   1 - 5 | Supply Curve for Jackets for Snowboarders

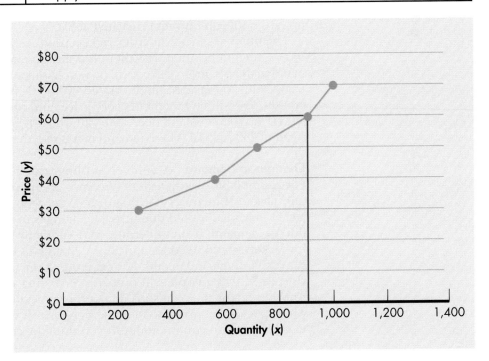

e x h i b i t   1 - 6 | Equilibrium Price and Quantity

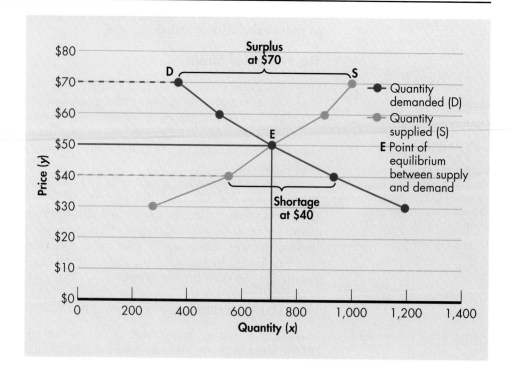

equilibrium

The point at which quantity demanded equals quantity supplied.

This is the point of **equilibrium.** The equilibrium price is $50; the equilibrium quantity is 700 jackets. At that point there is a balance between the amount consumers will buy and the amount the manufacturers will supply.

Market equilibrium is achieved through a series of quantity and price adjustments that occur automatically. If the price increases to $70, suppliers produce more jackets than consumers are willing to buy, and a surplus results. To sell more jackets, prices will have to fall. Thus, a surplus pushes prices downward until equilibrium is reached. When the price falls to $40, the quantity of jackets demanded rises above the available supply. The resulting shortage forces prices upward until equilibrium is reached at $50.

The number of snowboarder jackets produced and bought at $50 will tend to rest at equilibrium unless there is a shift in either demand or supply. If demand increases, more jackets will be purchased at every price, and the demand curve shifts to the right (as illustrated by line D_2 in Exhibit 1-7). If demand decreases, less will be bought at every price, and the demand curve shifts to the left (D_1). When demand decreased, snowboarders bought 500 jackets at $50 instead of 700 jackets. When demand increased, they purchased 800.

Changes in Demand   A number of things can increase or decrease demand. For example, if snowboarders' incomes go up, they may decide to buy a second jacket. If incomes fall, a snowboarder who was planning to purchase a jacket may wear an old one instead. Changes in fashion or tastes can also influence demand. If snowboarding were suddenly to go out of fashion, demand for jackets would decrease quickly. A change in the price of related products can also influence demand. For example, if the average price of a snowboard rises to $1,000, people will quit snowboarding and jacket demand will fall. Another factor that can shift demand is expectations about future prices. If you expect jacket prices to increase significantly in the future, you may decide to go ahead and get one today. If you think prices will fall, you will postpone

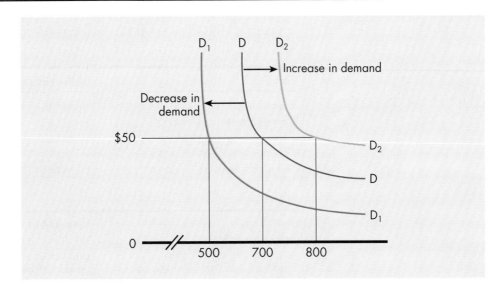

your purchase. Finally, changes in the number of buyers will affect demand. Snowboarding is a young person's sport. The number of teenagers will increase in the next few years. Therefore, the demand for snowboarding jackets should increase.

Changes in Supply   New technology typically lowers the cost of production. For example, North Face, a manufacturer of ski and snowboarder jackets, has just purchased laser-guided pattern-cutting equipment and computer-aided pattern-making equipment. Each jacket is now cheaper to produce, resulting in a higher profit per jacket. This becomes an incentive to supply more jackets at every price. If the price of resources such as labor or fabric goes up, North Face will earn a smaller profit on each jacket, and the amount supplied will decrease at every price. The reverse is also true. Changes in the prices of other goods can also affect supply. Let's say that snow skiing becomes a really hot sport. The number of skiers jumps dramatically and the price of ski jackets soars. North Face can use its machines and fabrics to produce either ski or snowboard jackets. If the company can make more profit from ski jackets, it will produce fewer snowboarding jackets at every price. Also, simply a change in the number of producers will shift the supply curve. If the number of manufacturers increases, more jackets will be placed on the market at every price and vice versa. Taxes can also affect supply. If the government decides, for some reason, to tax the manufacturer for every snowboard jacket produced, then profits will fall and fewer jackets will be offered at every price. Exhibit 1-8 summarizes the factors that can shift demand and supply curves.

c o n c ə p t   c h ə c k

- What is the relationship between prices and demand for a product?
- How is market equilibrium achieved?
- Draw a graph that shows an equilibrium point.

COMPETING IN A FREE MARKET

>lg 7

market structure

The number of suppliers in a market.

One of the characteristics of a free market system is that suppliers have the right to compete with one another. The number of suppliers in a market is called **market structure.** Economists identify four types of market structures: (1) perfect competition, (2) pure monopoly, (3) monopolistic competition, and (4) oligopoly.

| | Shift Demand | |
Factor	To the Right if:	To the Left if:
Buyers' incomes	increase	decrease
Buyers' preferences/tastes	increase	decrease
Prices of substitute products	increase	decrease
Expectations about future prices	will rise	will fall
Number of buyers	increases	decreases
	Shift Supply	
Technology	lowers costs	increases costs
Resource prices	fall	increase
Changes in prices of other products that can be produced with the same resources	profit of other product falls	profit of other product increases
Number of suppliers	increases	decreases
Taxes	lowered	increased

Perfect Competition

perfect (pure) competition
A market structure in which a large number of small firms sell similar products, buyers and sellers have good information, and businesses can be easily opened or closed.

Characteristics of **perfect (pure) competition** include:

- A large number of small firms are in the market.
- The firms sell similar products; that is, each firm's product is very much like the products sold by other firms in the market.
- Buyers and sellers in the market have good information about prices, sources of supply, and so on.
- It is easy to open a new business or close an existing one.

In a perfectly competitive market, firms sell their products at prices determined solely by forces beyond their control. Because the products are very similar and because each firm contributes only a small amount to the total quantity supplied by the industry, price is determined by supply and demand. A firm that raised its price even a little above the going rate would lose customers. In the wheat market, for example, the product is essentially the same from one wheat producer to the next. Thus, none of the producers has control over the price of wheat.

Perfect competition is an ideal. No industry shows all its characteristics, but the stock market and some agricultural markets, such as those for wheat and corn, come closest. Farmers, for example, can sell all of their crops through national commodity exchanges at the current market price.

Pure Monopoly

pure monopoly
A market structure in which a single firm accounts for all industry sales and in which there are barriers to entry.

barriers to entry
Factors, such as technological or legal conditions, that prevent new firms from competing equally with a monopoly.

At the other end of the spectrum is **pure monopoly,** the market structure in which a single firm accounts for all industry sales. The firm is the industry. This structure is characterized by **barriers to entry**—factors that prevent new firms from competing equally with the existing firm. Often the barriers are technological or legal conditions. Polaroid, for example, has held major patents on instant photography for years. When Kodak tried to market its own instant camera, Polaroid sued, claiming patent violations. Polaroid collected millions of dollars from Kodak. Another barrier may be one firm's control of a natural resource. DeBeers Consolidated Mines Ltd., for example, controls most of the world's supply of uncut diamonds.

Public utilities like gas and water are pure monopolies. Some monopolies are created by a government fiat that outlaws competition. The U.S. Postal Service is currently one such monopoly.

Monopolistic Competition

monopolistic competition

A market structure in which many firms offer products that are close substitutes and in which entry is relatively easy.

Three characteristics define the market structure known as **monopolistic competition:**

- Many firms are in the market.
- The firms offer products that are close substitutes but still differ from one another.
- It is relatively easy to enter the market.

Under monopolistic competition, firms take advantage of product differentiation. Industries where monopolistic competition occurs include clothing, food, and similar consumer products. Firms under monopolistic competition have more control over pricing than do firms under perfect competition because consumers do not view the products as exactly the same. Nevertheless, firms must demonstrate those product differences to justify their prices to customers.

MAKING ETHICAL CHOICES

GASOLINE PRICE GYRATIONS AND OPEC

In March 1999, gasoline prices skyrocketed in anticipation that the Organization of Petroleum Exporting Countries (OPEC) would decide, at a meeting on March 23, to restrict the world's supply of crude oil. OPEC was expected to approve cuts in petroleum production totaling 2.1 million barrels a day. The purpose was to strengthen the price of crude oil. Over the preceding 18 months, crude oil prices had fallen from $22 per barrel to around $11 per barrel. At one point, crude oil prices had sunk as low as $9 per barrel.

The average price of all grades of gasoline at U.S. service stations increased by more than 9 percent in the two-week period preceding OPEC's March 23 meeting. About half of the price increase was blamed on refiners who were quick to pass crude oil cost increases through to consumers. The other half was attributed to dwindling supplies of refined gasoline that resulted from the depletion of the huge refined gasoline inventories of the preceding autumn and winter. By summer 2000, crude oil prices were over $30 per barrel.

Historically, OPEC has been unable "to maintain supply discipline among its members for very long." Some industry observers expected petroleum prices to fall back rather quickly due to an oversupply of crude oil in the global market. Analysts pointed out that a major problem for OPEC was that other oil-producing countries were ready to increase their production if OPEC members restricted their output of crude oil.

Critical Thinking Questions

1. Should businesses raise prices in anticipation of cost increases? Or should they wait to raise prices until the cost increases actually occur?
2. In your opinion, is it ethical or unethical for a group of nations to restrict the supply of a commodity such as crude oil so as to force a price increase?

e x h i b i t   1 - 9 | Types of Market Structures

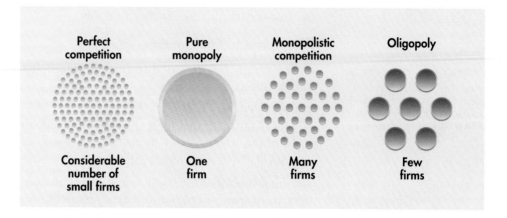

Consequently, companies use advertising to distinguish their products from others. Such distinctions may be significant or superficial. For example, Nike says "Just Do It," and Tylenol is advertised as being easier on the stomach than aspirin.

Oligopoly

oligopoly

A market structure in which a few firms produce most or all of the output and in which large capital requirements or other factors limit the number of firms.

An **oligopoly** has two characteristics:

- A few firms produce most or all of the output.
- Large capital requirements or other factors limit the number of firms.

Boeing and McDonnell Douglas (aircraft manufacturers) and USX (formerly U.S. Steel) are major firms in different oligopolistic industries.

With so few firms in an oligopoly, what one firm does has an impact on the other firms. Thus, the firms in an oligopoly watch one another closely for new technologies, product changes and innovations, promotional campaigns, pricing, production, and other developments. Sometimes they go so far as to coordinate their pricing and output decisions, which is illegal. Many antitrust cases—legal challenges arising out of laws designed to control anticompetitive behavior—occur in oligopolies. Exhibit 1-9 summarizes the primary types of market structures.

c o n c ə p t   c h ə c k

- What is meant by market structure?
- Describe the four types of market structure.

CAPITALIZING ON TRENDS IN BUSINESS

>lg 8

Trends in business occur at both the macroeconomic and the microeconomic level. We will begin by taking a look at some microeconomic trends.

Delivering Value and Quality

Companies today are facing accelerating change in many areas, including better educated and more demanding consumers, new technology, and the globalization of markets. As a result, competition is the toughest it has ever been. More and more, the key to building and sustaining a long-range advantage is a commitment to delivering superior customer value.

customer value

The customer's perception of the ratio of benefits (functionality, performance, durability, design, ease of use, and serviceability) to the sacrifice (of money, time, and effort) necessary to obtain those benefits.

Customer value is the customer's perception of the ratio of benefits to the sacrifice necessary to obtain those benefits. Customers receive benefits in the form of functionality, performance, durability, design, ease of use, and serviceability. To receive those benefits, they give up money, time, and effort.

Customer value is not simply a matter of high quality. A high-quality product that is available only at a high price will not be perceived as a value. Nor will bare-bones service or low-quality goods selling for a low price. Instead, customers value goods and services of the quality they expect that are sold at prices they are willing to pay. Value marketing can be used to sell a $150,000 Rolls-Royce as well as a $3 Tyson frozen chicken dinner.

Businesses provide customer value by:

- *Offering products that perform.* This is the bare minimum. Consumers have lost patience with shoddy merchandise.
- *Giving consumers more than they expect.* Soon after Toyota launched Lexus, the company had to order a recall. The weekend before the recall, dealers personally phoned all the Lexus owners in the United States and arranged to pick up their cars and provide replacement vehicles.
- *Avoiding unrealistic pricing.* Consumers couldn't understand why Kellogg's cereals commanded a premium over other brands, so Kellogg's market share fell 5 percent.
- *Giving the buyer facts.* Today's sophisticated consumer wants informative advertising and knowledgeable salespeople.

In today's business world, if a firm doesn't deliver customer value it doesn't survive. Firms that provide customer value end up with satisfied customers. Exhibit 1-10 lists some companies that are especially good at satisfying customers.

e x h i b i t   1 - 1 0 | Some Companies and Products That Deliver Satisfaction

Company or Division
Mercedes-Benz
H.J. Heinz (food processing)
Colgate-Palmolive (pet foods)
H.J. Heinz (pet foods)
Mars (food processing)
Maytag
Quaker Oats
Cadillac
Hershey Foods
Coca-Cola
Toyota
Volvo
Zenith Electronics
Buick
Cadbury Schweppes

Creating Long-Term Relationships

relationship management

The practice of building, maintaining, and enhancing interactions with customers and other parties in order to develop long-term satisfaction through mutually beneficial partnerships.

Customer satisfaction helps build long-term relationships between a company and its clients. Today, companies are focusing on **relationship management,** which involves building, maintaining, and enhancing interactions with customers and other parties so as to develop long-term satisfaction through mutually beneficial partnerships. In general, the longer a customer stays with a company, the more that customer is worth. Long-term customers buy more, take less of a company's time, are less sensitive to price, and bring in new customers. Best of all, they require no acquisition or start-up costs. Good long-standing customers are worth so much that in some industries, reducing customer defections by as little as five points—from, say, 15 percent to 10 percent per year—can double profits.

Travelodge practices relationship management by launching Travelodge Miles, a guest rewards program featuring swipe-card technology. The program thanks frequent Travelodge and Thriftlodge guests for their patronage with value-added rewards such as frequent-flyer miles, free hotel nights, free rental cars, and other travel perks. Guests earn one Travelodge Mile for each qualified lodging dollar spent at participating economy Travelodge and Thriftlodge properties. With 250 Miles, members can redeem them for Sleepy Bear dolls, T-shirts, or a road atlas or keep saving the Miles for other rewards at higher levels. The enhanced level is already paying off with an increase in the average stay of preferred guests—almost a full night longer per stay. The system makes it easy to track and gather data on the company's best customers and enabled the creation of a "Gold Level" for preferred customers. These Gold Level customers receive preferred rates and free local phone calls.

strategic alliance

A cooperative agreement between business firms; sometimes called a *strategic partnership.*

By building strong customer relationships, retailers can turn a one-time buyer into a loyal, long-term customer.

Relationship management also means creating long-term relationships with suppliers. Suppliers are making major adjustments in their thinking, management styles, and methods of responding to purchasers' standards and operational requirements. A satisfied customer is one of the best sources of new business because the customer already knows that the supplier can meet expectations and deliver on its promises. Thus, the supplier has created trust, and trust is the foundation of most successful relationships.

A **strategic alliance,** sometimes called a strategic partnership, is a cooperative agreement between business firms. The trend toward forming strategic alliances is accelerating rapidly, particularly among high-tech firms. These companies have realized that strategic partnerships are more than just important—they are critical. Xerox management, for example, has decided that to maintain its leadership position in the reprographics industry, the company must "include suppliers as part of the Xerox family." This strategy often means reducing the number of suppliers, treating those that remain as allies, sharing strategic information freely, and drawing on supplier expertise in developing new products that can meet the quality, cost, and delivery standards of the marketplace.

Another way to build long-term relationships is to provide products designed specifically for the individual customer and then make it very easy to reorder. Could a mass producer like Levi Strauss implement such a strategy? Absolutely, with the help of technology, as the Applying Technology box describes.

APPLYING TECHNOLOGY

LEVI'S ORIGINAL SPIN PROGRAM CREATES JEANS JUST FOR YOU

Finding a pair of jeans that fit as if they were made for you and you alone is one of life's perfect moments. It certainly beats the wasted hours spent in dressing rooms, yanking on and peeling off pair after pair of denim duds. Thanks to technology, the perfect jeans, just for you, can be a reality.

Levi's Original Spin Program allows you to create the perfect jeans for your lifestyle and your figure. Here is how it works: Go to a Levi's store that features the Original Spin Program. There you can choose from three basic jean models: relaxed, classic, or low cut. Plus, you can make your jeans as baggy or as fitted as you want and pick a color. Next, choose from five leg openings: flare, wide, boot cut, straight, or tapered. Finally, pick a fly: button or zipper.

When you've made your choices, the clerk will measure your waist, rear, and inseam and then hunt up a test pair for you to try on. If you like what you see, all that info goes into the computer and is zapped to the Levi's factory in Tennessee, where your personal pair will be stitched. The jeans cost about $55, plus $6 if you want them shipped to your home. (There's no charge if you go back to the store to pick them up.) All this takes about two weeks. Want more jeans but perhaps a different model or color? Call the Original Spin Store or go to the Web site at **http://www.levi.com/original_spin/**

Critical Thinking Questions

1. Do you think the Original Spin Program will help build long-term relationships?
2. How might other types of manufacturers or retailers create similar programs?
3. Would you use the Original Spin Program? Why or why not?

Creating a Competitive Workforce

Creating customer value and building long-term relationships require a world-class workforce. The goal of leading companies such as Coca-Cola and Intel is for all workers to add value to every job they do every day. Such firms place a strong emphasis on training and the use of technology to improve worker productivity.

For example, the state of California employs around 200,000 workers who, for the most part, stay and build their careers in state government. Taxpayer investment in training state workers can result in significant savings for the state. California is one of the first states to offer Internet courses for its employees. Now workers are getting high-quality training from their computers either at work or home.[8]

Entrepreneurial Spirit in Former Command Economies

A key trend in macroeconomics is the surprising entrepreneurial spirit among many citizens of former command economies.

Russia and China have inched away from planned economies. Today, China has a population of 1.3 billion and they all want more and better goods and services.[9] Already there are 21 million *ge-ti-hu* (entrepreneurs) in China.

One entrepreneur, Robert Kuok, helped bring Coca-Cola to China. Kuok grew up in Hong Kong, where he started a chain of hotels. When Coca-Cola decided to enter mainland China, the company realized that careful handling would be needed to sell the most American product in the world (Coca-Cola) to the Chinese. Every entrepreneur in Asia coveted the opportunity to license Coke in China, a deal that could in time be worth $8 billion.[10] Coke chose Robert Kuok. "I thought, 'My God, this is a gift from Heaven,'" Kuok recalls. Kuok is being modest. It was not a gift. Coke knew what it was doing. Soft drinks were not Kuok's business, but Coke didn't need expertise in soft drinks. It needed a smart guy with contacts. And that's Kuok, a 73-year-old hotel owner, commodities trader, investor, and cosmopolite. Keeping 12.5 percent of the bottling venture, Coke granted 87.5 percent to Kerry Group, Kuok's Hong Kong-based conglomerate.[11]

Another example of an entrepreneur is Russia's Konstantin Borovoi. Borovoi was a math professor until he made a small fortune selling his knowledge of computer software. When the floodgates opened for capitalism, he started the Russian

FOCUSING ON SMALL BUSINESS

MONEY OFFERS NEW HOPE TO STRUGGLING ENTREPRENEURS

Sekororo, South Africa, is a place of abundant sunshine and scarce opportunity. Nurse Leshabane had lived for years in a cycle of subsistence, surviving on odd jobs and the charity of family and friends. Then, in the spring of 1998, hope arrived at her door in the form of Ben Nkuna. He couldn't offer her a job because virtually none were to be had in this dusty village of tin shacks and grass huts in South Africa's Northern Province, one of the country's most impoverished regions. But if she could find three or four friends willing to go in with her, Nkuna would provide money to start a small business.

This wasn't an offer of charity: Leshabane and her friends would be expected to repay the money in regular quarterly installments at an interest rate of about 20 percent, slightly below South Africa's prime rate at the time. Many Africans avoid credit, but Leshabane accepted the offer—after some hesitation.

Today, Leshabane operates a tiny vending stand at a busy Sekororo crossroads, selling fruit and a kind of porridge called *pap* to passersby. For the first time in her life, she has a steady income, however small, to help support her extended family of 11. "I thought it was some kind of robbery," says Leshabane of

Nkuna and his associates. "But this has changed my life."

Neither robber nor loan shark, Nkuna represents the Small Enterprise Foundation, a nonprofit organization in the vanguard of those bringing "microcredit" to Africa. Known also as microfinance, the program provides small amounts of start-up capital to the poor as a way of helping them out of poverty. The notion has made some headway in Asia, where almost 13 million people living below the World Bank's official poverty line—defined as those subsisting on $1 a day or less—participate in microcredit programs.

Critical Thinking Questions

1. Do you think that programs like the Small Enterprise Foundation can help lift rural Africa out of poverty?
2. Do you think that a 20 percent interest rate is fair?
3. Won't Leshabane basically end up working for Nkuna because she will be unable to get out of debt?

Commodities and Raw Materials Exchange and ended up indirectly controlling about 12 percent of Russia's economy.[12] The Russian economy is divided into two parts—the very profitable part and the rest. The very profitable part is under the patronage of the state, which has created a host of privileges that favor tycoons such as Borovoi. "Without these privileges," says Olga Kryshtanovska, a specialist on Russian elites, "all the other enterprises experience all the difficulties that exist in this country. No one helps them. They are completely defenseless."[13]

The entrepreneurial spirit is not limited to the evolving old command economies. Struggling developing countries are also creating their own share of entrepreneurs. The Focusing on Small Business box tells one such story.

concept check

- How do businesses provide customer value?
- How does relationship management make a business more competitive?
- Explain the entrepreneurial movement in former command economies.

APPLYING THIS CHAPTER'S TOPICS

This chapter has been about micro- and macroeconomics. Economics is not something you should learn for an exam and then forget. Economics is an analytical science that will help you understand the world around you. It can help you be more imaginative and insightful in everyday life. You should now better understand why prices are going up or down, when interest rates will fall, and when and why the unemployment rate will fall. Understanding these basic economic concepts can help you decide whether to change jobs

TRY IT NOW!

1. **Understand Your Tax Commitment** Soon you will enter the permanent job market, if you are not there already. Typically, your earnings will rise over the next 35 years, but as your earnings increase, so will your taxes. The average American works five months out of every year just to cover taxes. Are taxes too high in our country? Since taxes will be a major part of your financial life for the next 35 to 45 years, you need to be informed. Visit a few organizations that advocate tax reform, such as Americans for Tax Reform (**http://www.atr.org/**) and Citizens for Tax Justice (**http://www.ctj.org/**).

2. **Learn a Foreign Language** Consider taking a job outside the United States for a while. If you decide to work overseas, having basic skills in a second language will go a long way toward ensuring that you have a rewarding and pleasant experience. Learning a second language can also bring a lot of self-satisfaction. Go to **http://www.learnalanguage. com.** and learn more about learning a foreign language.

(and how much money to ask for) and whether to buy a car now or wait until next year. When you hear that Ford Motor Co. has 115 days of inventory, understanding supply and demand will tell you that now may be the time to buy that new car.

>looking ahead
at Daimler-Benz AG

Consider the opening story about the Smart car. The two basic determinants of price for the Smart car are demand and supply: the number of people who want to purchase the car at various prices, and the number of cars Daimler-Benz is willing to produce at various price points. Daimler-Benz competes in a market with a few large competitors. What one auto manufacturer does will have an impact on the others. Therefore, Daimler-Benz competes in an oligopolistic market. How will changes in the economy such as a recession or inflation affect the Smart car? During a recession, demand for the Smart car might decline, but it could also increase if people look for a low-price alternative to a traditional car. With inflation prices of resources used to produce the Smart car will increase, so Daimler-Benz would probably raise the price of the car.

Similarly, economics will help you become a better informed citizen. Almost every political issue is, in some way, grounded in economic concepts. You should now know what it means to balance the budget and what problems occur with monopoly power. In short, economics can help you make more thoughtful and informed decisions.

Economics can also help you understand what is happening in other countries and can help you become aware of opportunities there. As more and more countries have moved away from command economies, American and foreign multinational firms are moving in to take advantage of ground floor opportunities. Consider accepting a foreign assignment. It's a wonderful way to experience other cultures and, at the same time, get ahead in your career. More and more large organizations are requiring that their middle and upper-level managers have foreign field experience. When you have an opportunity for a foreign assignment, don't let it slip by.

KEY TERMS

barriers to entry 32
business 16
business cycles 21
capital 18
circular flow 19
consumer price
 index (CPI) 24
contractionary
 policy 25
costs 17
cost-push inflation
 23
crowding out 26
customer value 35
cyclical
 unemployment 22
demand curve 28
demand 28

SUMMARY OF LEARNING GOALS

>lg 1 **How do businesses and not-for-profit organizations help create our standard of living?**

Businesses attempt to earn a profit by providing goods and services desired by their customers. Not-for-profit organizations, though not striving for a profit, still deliver many needed services for our society. Our standard of living is measured by the output of goods and services. Thus, businesses and not-for-profit organizations help create our standard of living. Our quality of life is not simply the amount of goods and services available for consumers but rather the society's general level of happiness.

Economists refer to the building blocks of a business as the factors of production. To produce anything, one must have natural resources, labor, capital, and entrepreneurship to assemble the resources and manage the business. The competitive environment of our new millennium is based upon knowledge and learning. The companies that will succeed in this new era will be those that learn fast, use knowledge effectively, and develop new insights.

>lg 2 **What is economics, and how are the three sectors of the economy linked?**

Economics is the study of how individuals, businesses, and governments use scarce resources to produce and distribute goods and services. The two major areas in economics are macroeconomics, the study of the economy as a whole, and microeconomics, the study of particular markets. The individual, business, and government sectors of the economy are linked by a series of two-way flows. The government provides public goods and services for the other two sectors and receives income in the form of taxes. Changes in one flow affect the other sectors.

>lg 3 **How do economic growth, full employment, and price stability indicate a nation's economic health?**

A nation's economy is growing when the level of business activity, as measured by gross domestic product, is rising. GDP is the total value of all goods and services produced in a year. The goal of full employment is to have a job for all who can and want to work. How well a nation is meeting its employment goals is measured by the unemployment rate. There are four types of unemployment: frictional, structural, cyclical, and seasonal. With price stability, the overall prices of goods and services are not moving very much either up or down.

>lg 4 **What is inflation, how is it measured, and what causes it?**

Inflation is the general upward movement of prices. When prices rise, purchasing power falls. The rate of inflation is measured by changes in the consumer price index (CPI) and the producer price index (PPI). There are two main causes of inflation. If the demand for goods and services exceeds the supply, prices will rise. This is called demand-pull inflation. With cost-push inflation, higher production costs, such as expenses for materials and wages, increase the final prices of goods and services.

>lg 5 **How does the government use monetary policy and fiscal policy to achieve its macroeconomic goals?**

Monetary policy refers to actions by the Federal Reserve System to control the money supply. When the Fed restricts the money supply, interest rates rise, the inflation rate drops, and economic growth slows. By expanding the money supply, the Fed stimulates economic growth.

The government also uses fiscal policy—changes in levels of taxation and spending—to control the economy. Reducing taxes or increasing spending stimulates the economy; raising taxes or decreasing spending does the opposite. When the government spends more than it receives in tax revenues, it must borrow to finance the deficit. Some economists favor deficit spending as a way to stimulate the economy; others worry about our high level of national debt.

>lg 6 **What are the basic microeconomic concepts of demand and supply, and how do they establish prices?**

Demand is the quantity of a good or service that people will buy at a given price. Supply is the quantity of a good or service that firms will make available at a given price. When the price increases, the quantity demanded falls but the quantity supplied rises. A price decrease leads to increased demand but a lower supply. At the point where the quantity demanded equals the quantity supplied, demand and supply are in balance. This equilibrium point is achieved by market adjustments of quantity and price.

>lg 7 **What are the four types of market structure?**

Market structure is the number of suppliers in a market. Perfect competition is characterized by a large number of buyers and sellers, very similar products, good market information for both buyers and sellers, and ease of entry and exit into the market. In a pure monopoly, there is a single seller in a market. In

demand-pull inflation 23
economic growth 21
economic system 16
economics 18
entrepreneurs 18
equilibrium 30
expansionary policy 25
factors of production 17
federal budget deficit 27
Federal Reserve System (the Fed) 25
fiscal policy 25
frictional unemployment 22
full employment 22
goods 16
inflation 23
knowledge 18
macroeconomics 19
market structure 31
microeconomics 19
monetary policy 24
monopolistic competition 33
national debt 27
not-for-profit organization 17
oligopoly 34
perfect (pure) competition 32
producer price index (PPI) 24
profit 17
purchasing power 23
pure monopoly 32
quality of life 17
recession 21
relationship management 36
revenue 17
risk 17
savings bonds 27
seasonal unemployment 23
services 16
standard of living 16
strategic alliance 36
structural unemployment 22
supply 29
supply curve 29
unemployment rate 22

monopolistic competition, many firms sell close substitutes in a market that is fairly easy to enter. In an oligopoly, a few firms produce most or all of the industry's output. An oligopoly is also difficult to enter and what one firm does will influence others.

>lg 8   **Which trends are reshaping the micro- and macroeconomic environments?**
One micro trend is that firms are placing more emphasis on delivering value and quality to the customer. Companies are also establishing long-term relationships with both customers and suppliers. To compete in today's environment, companies and industries must build a competitive workforce. At the macro level, budding entrepreneurial spirit in former command economies is sparking wealth among individual business owners and fueling the growth of capitalism.

PREPARING FOR TOMORROW'S WORKPLACE

1. Form small groups with three or four members each. Each group should then go to a small business that has opened in the past two years. Ask the owner to describe (1) the most important lesson learned since opening the business, (2) unexpected pitfalls the business encountered, and (3) the information that helped the most prior to opening the business.

2. Assume that the U.S. economy is sluggish and the government wants to stimulate it just before a national election. Write a paper explaining which type of policy—monetary or fiscal—the government is more likely to use and why.

3. Use the Internet or go to the library and determine the current trends in GDP growth, unemployment, and inflation. What do these trends tell you about the level of business activity and the business cycle? If you owned a personnel agency, how would this information affect your decision making?

4. Divide the class into four teams. One pair of teams will debate the pros and cons of airline deregulation. The other pair will debate electric utility deregulation. One team should take the pro and the other the con for each issue. If you have Internet access, use the Dow Jones news service or Lexis-Nexis to obtain current articles on the subjects.

5. As a manufacturer of in-line roller skates, you are questioning your pricing policies. You note that over the past five years, the CPI increased an average of 2 percent per year, but the price of a pair of skates increased an average of 8 percent per year for the first three years and 2 percent for the next two years. What does this information tell you about demand, supply, and other factors influencing the market for these skates?

6. Write a paper describing an occasion when you received outstanding customer value and an occasion when you received very poor customer value.

WORKING THE NET

1. Go to **http://www.ipo.org/**. Tell the class what is new at this site. Explain to the class how a business might use the information from the **ipo** site. Be sure to provide an example.

2. Go to an Internet search engine, such as Excite, Infoseek, Lycos, or AltaVista, and look up the "North Korean economy." North Korea is probably the best example of a command economy in the world. Write a report on the current economic conditions in North Korea.

3. Point your browser toward the Bureau of Economic Analysis Regional Accounts Data at **http://www.bea.doc.gov/bea/regional/data.htm.** Find the historical information for your state's gross domestic product (GDP). What trends do you see? Can you think of reasons for these trends? How does your state's GDP compare with the U.S. GDP overall? Federal GDP figures are available at **http://www.bea.doc.gov/bea/dn1.htm.**

4. Read more about how the consumer price index (CPI) is computed at **http://www.stats.bls.gov/cpi/cpifaq.htm.** Look at the relative importance of each category included in the CPI. How well do these weightings match your own expenditures on each of these categories? What are some of the drawbacks of computing the CPI this way? Do you think these categories give a realistic picture of how most Americans spend their money? Why or why not?

5. Ever think about what you'd do differently if you were president? Here's your chance to find out how your ideas would affect the federal budget. The National Budget Simulator at **http://garnet.berkeley.edu:3333/budget/budget. html** lets you see how government officials make tradeoffs in planning the federal budget. Experiment with your own budget ideas at the site. What are the effects of your decisions?

CREATIVE THINKING CASE

Should Network Solutions Have a "Dot-Com" Monopoly on the Internet?

It's often said that no one owns the Internet. But a little company in Herndon, Virginia, comes pretty close. Since 1994, Network Solutions, Inc. has held an exclusive federal contract to handle distribution of addresses for the World Wide Web, including its most widely recognized feature: the ".com" suffix. Currently appended to more than 2 million Web addresses, .com covers the preeminent domain for doing cyberbusiness. If Web addresses were California real estate, Network Solutions would own the coastline.

Like most monopolies, this one is lucrative. Registering Web addresses for $70 a pop, Network Solutions has metamorphosed from a minority contractor scrambling for government computer jobs into a publicly traded Internet player with revenues at $77 million.

But now that monopoly is under siege. Network Solutions's original contract with the government has expired, and competitors are demanding a piece of the action. To fight back, the company has hired top-dollar lobbyists.

When Network Solutions received its monopoly, there were only 7,500 Web addresses; now there are millions. Network Solutions argues that taking away its monopoly will create chaos in cyberspace. The federal government agrees that stability of the Internet is very important. Government officials also claim that maintaining a monopoly will stifle competition and strangle the growth of the global network.

The company does more than merely collect registrations. Each evening, Network Solutions adds the day's newly registered names to the Internet's master list of addresses. And at midnight Eastern Standard Time, the company releases this updated master list to engineers around the world who maintain the Internet's 13 "root servers." Without the updated list, these digital hubs wouldn't know where to direct traffic. Right now, Network Solutions is the sole guardian of the master list.

The critical nature of that task in today's economy was demonstrated on July 17, 1997, when a software bug rendered portions of Network Solutions's nightly master list invisible. The following day, roughly a third of all Internet sites were inaccessible. Since then, Network Solutions has upgraded its software and installed a number of safety features. The company's competitors argue that the breakdown shows precisely why Network Solutions needs competition. But the company and its defenders counter that such problems are more manageable with one experienced company.

Critical Thinking Questions

1. Should Network Solutions maintain its ".com" monopoly? Why or why not?
2. What might be a possible compromise solution?
3. What can Network Solutions do to try and maintain its monopoly?
4. Go to **http://www.netsol.com** and learn how to register a Web address. How do you determine if someone has already registered the name that you want? What is the current cost to register?

VIDEO CASE

Black Forest Motors: The Mercedes-Benz Strategy in Action

Mercedes-Benz (**http://www.mbusa.com**), a manufacturer headquartered in Germany, produces luxury and near-luxury automobiles for distribution in Germany, the United States, and elsewhere. To increase its sales and perceived customer value in the U.S. market, Mercedes-Benz decided to pursue a corporate strategy called the "Customer Value Triad." This strategy had three components: goods quality, service quality, and value-based pricing. While goods quality and value-based pricing are established by the manufacturer, dealerships are the key element in service quality.

Black Forest Motors is a Mercedes-Benz dealership located in Acme, Michigan, near Lake Michigan's Grand Traverse Bay. Black Forest Motors is a prime example of the Mercedes-Benz corporate strategy in action, particularly the service quality component of the Customer Value Triad. Black Forest prides itself on exceeding customers' expectations of product quality, price, and service. As a result, Black Forest's customer base, fondly referred to as its "family of owners," has continued to grow. Black Forest Motors describes itself as "a great place to purchase a car."

Some employees have been with Black Forest Motors since its founding. Black Forest views this as evidence that the dealership is also a great place to work. This translates directly into quality customer service and helps the dealership to be a great place to purchase a vehicle.

The sales, service, and parts departments powerfully demonstrate Black Forest's commitment to service quality, as well as to goods quality and value-based pricing. The sales department's sole purpose is to exceed customer expectations from test drive to delivery of the vehicle. This commitment begins with the test drive, which customers can schedule online through Black Forest's Web page. The sales staff is dedicated to providing the information that customers need to make an educated buying decision. Black Forest wants all of its customers to drive away in a Mercedes-Benz that they feel is the perfect choice.

The service department has a state-of-the-art facility, featuring the latest diagnostic and repair equipment used by highly trained, factory technicians. The department's operations are based on the premise that "you and your vehicle deserve only the best of care." Goods quality and service quality are also emphasized in the parts department. It is stocked with a large inventory of the same high-quality parts used in manufacturing Mercedes-Benz vehicles.

With its commitment to the Customer Value Triad of goods quality, service quality, and value-based pricing, Black Forest Motors asks only one thing of its clients: "If you were treated well, your expectations met, and the service was good, please tell others."

Critical Thinking Questions

1. Do you think the Mercedes-Benz Customer Value Triad is an effective way to formulate a corporate strategy?
2. How might a strategy based on the Customer Value Triad help Mercedes-Benz and its dealerships to compete effectively in the American marketplace?
3. Why are product and service quality important elements of operating a successful business? What is the impact on the price of the cars?
4. Does Mercedes-Benz operate in an oligopolistic marketplace?

Case: APX Powers Deregulation Through the Internet

"Electricity is the perfect e-commerce commodity," says Edward Cazalet, chairman of Automated Power Exchange (APX), **http://www.apx.com**, a Santa Clara, California firm that runs an online electricity trading marketplace. "You can't do deregulation without the Internet."

In 1998, California became the first state to deregulate how electricity is bought, sold, and delivered. Prior to deregulation, by law electricity prices in California were carefully monitored and controlled by a state commission that gave just a few utility firms the right to sell electricity in specific parts of the state. In effect, these utilities had a monopoly on selling power in their region. Deregulation, however, opened up the power market to competition. Although the state's existing utilities continue to own and maintain the power lines in the state, other companies can now use those lines to deliver electricity directly to consumers and businesses. There are, however, still some price caps placed on the prices charged to consumers.

APX is one of several Internet-based power exchanges. APX doesn't sell power to consumers; instead its Web marketplace functions as a central meeting place for companies that generate power and those that supply it to customers. Through the APX exchange, these trading partners can offer and bid on electricity supplies. Over $250 million in power deals have been made through the APX electronic commerce market. APX also operates online exchanges in Japan and Great Britain.

In addition to California, 25 other states have either passed or are considering energy deregulation. The road to deregulation has bumps, however. Although California legislators promised that electric bills would drop after deregulation, electricity prices in some parts of the state soared. There were also problems with power shortages. Some industry experts said the higher prices were simply a result of supply and demand operating in a free economy for the first time. They pointed out that computer use, spurred by the growth of the Internet, has increased, boosting the demand for electricity. The booming economy has also raised electrical demand. At the same time, few new power-generating plants are being built in the United States, reducing supply.

The U.S. Department of Energy Secretary says that the situation in California "could be an ominous sign." The Silicon Valley Manufacturing Group, a trade organization representing high technology firms, also warns that high energy prices and shortages could cripple the economy if they are allowed to spread.

Questions for Critical Thinking

1. Do you agree or disagree with Edward Cazalet's statement that the Internet has a central role in making electricity deregulation work? Why?
2. Explain how rising electricity prices could affect the economy. How could they affect the growth of electronic commerce?

SOURCES: Jarret Adams, "British Traders Swap Volts," *Redherring.com*, June 8, 2000; Mark Boslet, "Electrical Storm Hits the New Economy," *The Standard*, September 11, 2000, downloaded from **http://www.thestandard.com**; Peter Coy and Christopher Palmeri, "Gridlock on the Power Grid," *Business Week*, August 28, 2000, p. 48; Scott Harris, "New Power Generation," *The Standard*, September 11, 2000, downloaded from **http://www.thestandard.com**; "Nationwide Thirst for Power Worries Utilities, Officials," *The Dallas Morning News*, July 9, 2000, p. 29A.

learning goals

>lg 1 Why is global trade important to the United States?

>lg 2 How is global trade measured?

>lg 3 Why do nations trade?

>lg 4 What are the barriers to international trade?

>lg 5 How do governments and institutions foster world trade?

>lg 6 What are international economic communities?

>lg 7 How do companies enter the global marketplace?

>lg 8 What threats and opportunities exist in the global marketplace?

>lg 9 What are the advantages of multinational corporations?

>lg 10 What are the trends in the global marketplace?

Competing in the Global Marketplace

chapter 2

Wal-Mart Creates a Beachhead in Europe

Looking down the long, long aisle, past the garden tools and the baby diapers, to the other end of the Wal-Mart store in Dortmond, Germany, 68-year-old Liselotte Schnellboegl commented that the store was really too big, but she liked it anyway. Gesturing at her brimming shopping cart, Mrs. Schnellboegl explained, "Other stores don't have all this merchandise. Here, I can find all the items I'm looking for."

In keeping with German preferences, the store has more food than a comparable American Wal-Mart, including a huge sausage bin, a fresh-fish department, and a big tray of exotic fruits in the fruit department.

Wal-Mart Stores Inc. has arrived in Europe and the Liselotte Schnellboegls of the shopping set are happy, if tired. All the company needs now is more customers like her, in more European countries.

The world's biggest retailer has bought and converted retail chains in Germany and Britain over the past three years. But it is not the leading retailer in either country, and analysts say it needs to expand and gain significant market share in at least three big European countries for its high-volume, centralized distribution strategy to make sense. Furthermore, Wal-Mart's competitors in Europe are ready to fight. In France, two leading retail chains merged in part to fend off a Wal-Mart acquisition. In Germany, well-established discount chains are restructuring and reducing prices.

"Wal-Mart has made its intention quite clear: It wants to dominate European retailing like it dominates American retailing," said Richard Hyman, chairman of the British retail consultancy Verdict Research Ltd.

Europe is already used to near-American-sized discount stores in its suburbs and outlying areas. The days are long past when citizens shopped only at open-air markets and small specialty stores. In Britain, France, and Germany, the big discount supermarket is the rule rather than the exception. But high taxes and extensive regulations make retail operations on this side of the Atlantic a very different game than in rural and suburban America. Lack of space means that building new stores is virtually impossible; the only way to invade is to buy.

Thus, in Germany, Wal-Mart bought two troubled chains, Wertkauf and InterSpar, giving it a total of 95 stores. But these stores needed to be entirely renovated; so far, only 12, including the shiny-clean, white-floored one here, have been revived. "The general perspective is that Wal-Mart will have to acquire more stores in Germany to get the economies of scale it needs," said Michael Pohn, an analyst at Deutsche Genossenschaftsbank in Frankfurt. "The trouble is, there's nothing left to buy at the moment."

The rules are different, too. In Germany, this Wal-Mart is required by law, like all other German stores, to close at 8 P.M. on weekdays and 4 P.M. on Saturdays, and it is not open at all on Sundays. And costs are astronomical. Derek Rowe, an American brought over to supervise the $5 million renovation of the Dortmund store, estimated that construction costs here are five times what they are in the United States.[1]

As the Wal-Mart story illustrates, selling in the global marketplace isn't always easy. Competition, for example, can be very difficult on European supermarket chains' home turf.

Critical Thinking Questions:

As you read this chapter, consider the following questions as they relate to Wal-Mart:

- What are several other factors that can make success difficult in the global marketplace?

- What can governments do to protect domestic competitors?

- What cultural differences should Wal-Mart consider when entering the European market?

BUSINESS IN THE 21ST CENTURY

Today, global revolutions are under way in many areas of our lives: management, politics, communications, technology. The word *global* has assumed a new meaning, referring to a boundless mobility and competition in social, business, and intellectual arenas. No longer just an option, having a global vision has become a business imperative. Having a **global vision** means recognizing and reacting to international business opportunities, being aware of threats from foreign competitors in all markets, and effectively using international distribution networks to obtain raw materials and move finished products to the customer.

U.S. managers must develop a global vision if they are to recognize and react to international business opportunities, as well as remain competitive at home. Often a U.S. firm's toughest domestic competition comes from foreign companies. Moreover, a global vision enables a manager to understand that customer and distribution networks operate worldwide, blurring geographic and political barriers and making them increasingly irrelevant to business decisions. Sometimes, too, as Wal-Mart discovered, that global vision must be fine-tuned. The purpose of this chapter is to explain how global trade is conducted. We also discuss the barriers to international trade and the organizations that foster global trade. The chapter concludes with trends in the global marketplace.

global vision

The ability to recognize and react to international business opportunities, be aware of threats from foreign competition, and effectively use international distribution networks to obtain raw materials and move finished products to customers.

AMERICA GOES GLOBAL

>lg 1

Over the past two decades, world trade has climbed from $200 billion a year to more than $4 trillion. Countries and companies that were never considered major players in global markets are now contributing to this growth in world trade. Gillette, for example, derives two-thirds of its revenue from its international division. Although this has contributed tremendously to the company's growth, it has also opened the company to new problems. In 1998 Gillette was unable to meet its 20 percent annual profit growth goal because of recessions in Asia. At the same time, global financial turmoil also presents opportunities to buy small consumer products companies outside the United States at a very good price. Gillette has agreed to an extensive licensing and supply arrangement with Rocket Electric Co., one of South Korea's largest battery makers. For a payment of about $60 million, Gillette effectively doubled its share of the world's 10th-largest battery market, to about 22 percent. Although best known as a maker of razors, Gillette bought battery maker Duracell International, Inc. in late 1996 and is now a world leader in that industry as well.[2]

Although Cheetos and Ruffles haven't done very well in Japan, the potato chip has been quite successful. PepsiCo's (owner of Frito-Lay) overseas snack business brings in more than $3.25 billion annually. Recently, Frito-Lay spent $20 million on advertising in Europe in one month to convince European consumers to eat more tortilla chips.[3]

Global business is not a one-way street, where only U.S. companies sell their wares and services throughout the world. Foreign competition in

While pursuing its global vision, Wal-Mart has tailored its products to suit the preferences of European customers. For example, German customers expect large selections of fish, sausage, and exotic fruits.

the domestic market used to be relatively rare but now occurs in almost every industry. In fact, U.S. makers of electronic goods, cameras, automobiles, fine china, tractors, leather goods, and a host of other consumer and industrial products have struggled to maintain their domestic market shares against foreign competitors. Nevertheless, the global market has created vast, new business opportunities for many U.S. firms.

The Importance of Global Business to the United States

Many countries depend more on international commerce than the United States does. For example, France, Great Britain, and Germany all derive more than 19 percent of their gross domestic product (GDP) from world trade, compared to about 12 percent for the United States. Nevertheless, the impact of international business on the U.S. economy is still impressive:

- The United States exports about a fifth of its industrial production and a third of its farm products.
- One of every 16 jobs in the United States is directly or indirectly supported by exports.
- U.S. businesses export nearly $850 billion in goods to foreign countries every year, and almost a third of U.S. corporate profits is derived from international trade and foreign investment.
- Exports account for almost one-third of America's economic growth.
- Chemicals, office machinery, computers, automobiles, aircraft, and electrical and industrial machinery make up almost half of all nonagricultural exports.[4]

The U.S. International Trade Administration (ITA) helps U.S. firms do business in foreign markets. To get the inside scoop on what it takes to do business in hundreds of countries, visit the ITA's Trade Compliance Center at

http://www.mac.doc.gov/tcc

These statistics might seem to imply that practically every business in the United States is selling its wares throughout the world, but nothing could be further from the truth. About 85 percent of all U.S. exports of manufactured goods are shipped by 250 companies. Only the very large multinational companies have seriously attempted to compete worldwide. Fortunately, more small companies are now aggressively pursuing international markets.

concept check

- What is global vision, and why is it important?
- What impact does international trade have on the U.S. economy?

MEASURING TRADE BETWEEN NATIONS

>lg 2

International trade improves relationships with friends and allies, helps ease tensions among nations, and—economically speaking—bolsters economies, raises people's standard of living, provides jobs, and improves the quality of life. The value of international trade is over $4 trillion a year and growing. This section takes a look at some key measures of international trade: exports and imports, the balance of trade, the balance of payments, and exchange rates.

Exports and Imports

exports
Goods and services produced in one country and sold in other countries.

imports
Goods and services that are bought from other countries.

The developed nations (those with mature communication, financial, educational, and distribution systems) are the major players in international trade. They account for about 70 percent of the world's exports and imports. **Exports** are goods and services made in one country and sold to others. **Imports** are goods and services that are bought from other countries. The United States is both the largest exporter and the largest importer in the world. During a four-year period

The United States is the world leader in exports and imports, which are a key measure of international trade.

ending in 2000, U.S. exports accounted for almost one-third of U.S. economic growth and 2.6 million additional American jobs. Today, U.S. exports amount to approximately $998 billion annually. Exports support more than 12 million U.S. jobs.[5]

Each year the United States exports more food, animal feed, and beverages than the year before. A third of U.S. farm acreage is devoted to crops for export. The United States is also a major exporter of engineering products and other high-tech goods, such as computers and telecommunications equipment. For more than 40,000 U.S. companies (the majority of them small), international trade offers exciting and profitable opportunities. Among the largest U.S. exporters are Boeing Co., General Motors Corp., General Electric Co., Ford Motor Co., and IBM.

Despite our impressive list of resources and great variety of products, imports to the United States are also growing. Some of these imports are raw materials that we lack, such as manganese, cobalt, and bauxite, which are used to make airplane parts, exotic metals, and military hardware. More modern factories and lower labor costs in other countries make it cheaper to import industrial supplies (like steel) and production equipment than to produce them at home. Most of Americans' favorite hot beverages—coffee, tea, and cocoa—are imported. We also import Scotch whiskey, English bicycles, German and Japanese automobiles, Italian and Spanish shoes, Central American bananas, Philippine plywood, Hong Kong textiles, and French wines.

Balance of Trade

balance of trade

The difference between the value of a country's exports and the value of its imports during a certain time.

trade surplus

A favorable balance of trade that occurs when a country exports more than it imports.

trade deficit

An unfavorable balance of trade that occurs when a country imports more than it exports.

The difference between the value of a country's exports and the value of its imports during a certain time is the country's **balance of trade.** A country that exports more than it imports is said to have a *favorable* balance of trade, called a **trade surplus.** A country that imports more than it exports is said to have an *unfavorable* balance of trade, or a **trade deficit.** When imports exceed exports, more money flows out of the country than flows into it.

Check out the current U.S. balance of trade with various countries at

http://www.bea.doc.gov/bea/di1.htm

Although U.S. exports have been booming, we still import more than we export. We have had an unfavorable balance of trade throughout the 1990s and early 2000s. In 1999 the United States had a trade deficit of approximately $254 billion.[6] Part of the problem is that most U.S. companies still avoid the export market. Many medium-size and small producers think "going global" is more trouble than it's worth. And as we've seen, Americans are buying more foreign goods than ever before. As long as we continue to import more than we export, the United States will continue to have a trade deficit.

balance of payments

A summary of a country's international financial transactions showing the difference between the country's total payments to and its total receipts from other countries.

Balance of Payments

Another measure of international trade is called the **balance of payments,** which is a summary of a country's international financial transactions showing the difference between the country's total payments to and its total receipts from other countries. The balance of payments includes imports and exports (balance of trade), long-term investments in overseas plants and equipment, government loans to and from other countries, gifts and foreign aid, military expenditures made in other countries, and money transfers in and out of foreign banks.

From 1900 until 1970, the United States had a trade surplus, but in the other areas that make up the balance of payments, U.S. payments exceeded receipts, largely due to the large U.S. military presence abroad. Hence, almost every year since 1950, the United States has had an unfavorable balance of payments. And since 1970, both the balance of payments *and* the balance of trade have been unfavorable. What can a nation do to reduce an unfavorable balance of payments? It can foster exports, reduce its dependence on imports, decrease its military presence abroad, or reduce foreign investment.

In the late 1990s and early 2000s, Japan, Russia, and much of the rest of the developing world were in a recession. America's relatively strong economy drew in the exports of crisis-stricken countries at the same time that foreign demand for American products weakened. As a result, the U.S. balance of payments deficit soared, rising from $290 billion in 1999 to over $375 billion in 2000.[7]

The Changing Value of Currencies

The exchange rate is the price of one country's currency in terms of another country's currency. If a country's currency *appreciates,* less of that country's currency is needed to buy another country's currency. If a country's currency *depreciates,* more of that currency will be needed to buy another country's currency.

How do appreciation and depreciation affect the prices of a country's goods? If, say, the U.S. dollar depreciates relative to the Japanese yen, U.S. residents have to pay more dollars to buy Japanese goods. To illustrate, suppose the dollar price of a yen is $0.012 and that a Toyota is priced at 2 million yen. At this exchange rate, a U.S. resident pays $24,000 for a Toyota ($0.012 × 2 million yen = $24,000). If the dollar depreciates to $0.018 to one yen, then the U.S. resident will have to pay $36,000 for a Toyota.

As the dollar depreciates, the prices of Japanese goods rise for U.S. residents, so they buy fewer Japanese goods—thus, U.S. imports decline. At the same time, as the dollar depreciates relative to the yen, the yen appreciates relative to the dollar. This means prices of U.S. goods fall for the Japanese, so they buy more U.S. goods—and U.S. exports rise.

Currency markets operate under a system called **floating exchange rates.** Prices of currencies "float" up and down based upon the demand for and supply of each currency. Global currency traders create the supply of and demand for a particular currency based on that currency's investment, trade potential, and economic strength.

Get up-to-the-minute exchange rates at http://xe.net/currency

If a country decides that its currency is not properly valued in international currency markets, the government may step in and adjust the currency's value. In a **devaluation,** a nation lowers the value of its currency relative to other currencies. In August 1998, Russia devalued the ruble by 34 percent.[8] A month later, Colombia and Ecuador also devalued their currencies but by much less than Russia. Russia not only devalued its currency but also restructured government short-term debt to long term and imposed strict financial controls on Russian banks and companies. As a result, companies and banks could not meet their foreign debt obligations.

floating exchange rates

A system in which prices of currencies move up and down based upon the demand for and supply of the various currencies.

devaluation

A lowering of the value of a nation's currency relative to other currencies.

concept check

- Describe the position of the United States in world trade.
- Explain the difference between balance of trade and balance of payments.
- Explain the impact of a currency devaluation.

WHY NATIONS TRADE

>lg 3

One might argue that the best way to protect workers and the domestic economy is to stop trade with other nations. Then the whole circular flow of inputs and outputs would stay within our borders. But if we decided to do that, how would we get resources like cobalt and coffee beans? The United States simply can't produce some things, and it can't manufacture some products, such as steel and most clothing, at the low costs we're used to. The fact is that nations—like people—are good at producing different things: you may be better at balancing a ledger than repairing a car. In that case you benefit by "exporting" your bookkeeping services and "importing" the car repairs you need from a good mechanic. Economists refer to specialization like this as *advantage*.

Absolute Advantage

absolute advantage

The situation when a country can produce and sell a product at a lower cost than any other country or when it is the only country that can provide the product.

A country has an **absolute advantage** when it can produce and sell a product at a lower cost than any other country or when it is the only country that can provide a product. The United States, for example, has an absolute advantage in reusable spacecraft and other high-tech items.

Suppose that the United States has an absolute advantage in air traffic control systems for busy airports and that Brazil has an absolute advantage in coffee. The United States does not have the proper climate for growing coffee, and Brazil lacks the technology to develop air traffic control systems. Both countries would gain by exchanging air traffic control systems for coffee.

Comparative Advantage

principle of comparative advantage

The concept that each country should specialize in the products that it can produce most readily and cheaply and trade those products for those that other countries can produce more readily and cheaply.

Even if the United States had an absolute advantage in both coffee and air traffic control systems, it should still specialize and engage in trade. Why? The reason is the **principle of comparative advantage,** which says that each country should specialize in the products that it can produce most readily and cheaply and trade those products for goods that foreign countries can produce most readily and cheaply. This specialization ensures greater product availability and lower prices. Even small businesses have learned how to capitalize on comparative advantage as demonstrated in the Focusing on Small Business box.

free trade

The policy of permitting the people of a country to buy and sell where they please without restrictions.

For example, Mexico and China have a comparative advantage in producing clothing because of low labor costs. Japan has long held a comparative advantage in consumer electronics because of technological expertise. America has an advantage in computer software, airplanes, some agricultural products, heavy machinery, and jet engines.

protectionism

The policy of protecting home industries from outside competition by establishing artificial barriers such as tariffs and quotas.

Thus, comparative advantage acts as a stimulus to trade. When nations allow their citizens to trade whatever goods and services they choose without government regulation, free trade exists. **Free trade** is the policy of permitting the people of a country to buy and sell where they please without restrictions. The opposite of free trade is **protectionism,** in which a nation protects its home industries from outside competition by establishing artificial barriers such as tariffs and quotas. In the next section, we'll look at the various barriers, some natural and some created by governments, that restrict free trade.

concept check

- Explain the difference between absolute advantage and comparative advantage.
- Describe the principle of comparative advantage.
- Describe the policy of free trade and its relationship to comparative advantage.

BARRIERS TO TRADE

>lg 4

International trade is carried out by both businesses and governments—as long as no one puts up trade barriers. In general, trade barriers keep firms from sell-

SMALL AMERICAN BUSINESSES SCRAMBLE FOR SUCCESS IN CHINA

From an office overlooking Beijing's crowded streets, former Beverly Hills businessman Jian Lin plots what he hopes will become China's next cultural revolution: family entertainment American style. "We found a lot of young Chinese are doing well in business. They are starving for entertainment," Jian said.

Along with big corporations such as Microsoft and Motorola, small-business entrepreneurs from the United States are starting to launch their own businesses and joint ventures across China. The obstacles to success can be daunting. Language is a barrier for most Americans. They also must deal with bureaucratic corruption and an unfamiliar business culture based on *guanxi*, the contacts needed to cut through governmental red tape. "A lot of Americans come here with a lot of hope, a lot of money, but they are killed by doing business with the wrong people," said Jian.

To businesspeople like Jian and his Chinese partner, Liu Tie, China represents a vast, largely untapped market. The joint venture launched by Liu's Beijing Dazhong Trading Group and Jian's Innovation Capital Corp. includes a traveling carnival, complete with cotton candy, corn dogs, and midway games, that played through the summer in Chinese coastal cities. They are renovating space in Beijing's main railroad station to house a motion simulation theater and two bars, one with a theme of outer space and the other of New Orleans' Bourbon Street. The pair also won rights to turn a quiet park into a family-fun center with rides, arcades, and a cowboy-

themed restaurant. Eventually, Jian and Liu want to create an entertainment empire of similar ventures in cities across China.

A Chinese native who immigrated to the United States as a child, Jian speaks fluent Mandarin Chinese and knows China's culture. In Liu, chairman of a $5 million-a-year real estate and food services company, Jian gained a partner with money to invest and connections needed to secure permits and leases. Jian brings American connections to the deal. He bought equipment for the traveling carnival and hired an American carnival company to run it. He also negotiated the purchase of a $700,000, 45-seat motion simulation theater from Los Angeles-based Showscan Entertainment.

Younger Chinese businesspeople, such as Liu, 30, understand capitalism and are eager to reap its rewards, said Jian, who is 44. "The easiest way to do business in China is to find a young entrepreneur," he said. "They will take command of the problem. All that you have to do is assist them in the way a normal American does business. They love that."

Critical Thinking Questions

1. How is the principle of comparative advantage working here?
2. What type of American small businesses might do best in China?
3. In what areas does America have an absolute advantage over China?

---

ing to one another in foreign markets. The major obstacles to international trade are natural barriers, tariff barriers, and nontariff barriers.

Natural Barriers

Natural barriers to trade can be either physical or cultural. For instance, even though raising beef in the relative warmth of Argentina may cost less than raising beef in the bitter cold of Siberia, the cost of shipping the beef from South America to Siberia might drive the price too high. *Distance* is thus one of the natural barriers to international trade. Jet airplanes cut the time needed to ship goods long distances, but weight is a factor. Thus, air cargo is limited to products with a high value per pound. For example, it would not make sense to ship coal or gravel by air, although orchids, seafood, computers, and replacement parts for machinery are often moved this way. With advances in technology, liquefied natural gas, asphalt, and other hard-to-transport products can now be moved by ship or barge—something not feasible 15 or 20 years ago. Further improvements in technology should help lower other distance barriers as well.

Language is another natural trade barrier. People who can't communicate effectively may not be able to negotiate trade agreements or may ship the wrong goods.

Tariff Barriers

tariff

A tax imposed on imported goods.

A **tariff** is a tax imposed by a nation on imported goods. It may be a charge per unit, such as per barrel of oil or per new car; it may be a percentage of the value of the goods, such as 5 percent of a $500,000 shipment of shoes; or it may be a combination. No matter how it is assessed, any tariff makes imported goods more costly, so they are less able to compete with domestic products.

protective tariffs

Tariffs that are imposed in order to make imports less attractive to buyers than domestic products are.

Protective tariffs make imports less attractive to buyers than domestic products are. The United States, for instance, has protective tariffs on imported poultry, textiles, sugar, and some types of steel and clothing. On the other side of the world, Japan imposes a tariff on U.S. cigarettes that makes them cost 60 percent more than Japanese brands. U.S. tobacco firms believe they could get as much as a third of the Japanese market if there were no tariffs on cigarettes. With tariffs, they have under 2 percent of the market.

Arguments for and against Tariffs Congress has debated the issue of tariffs since 1789. The main argument against tariffs is that they discourage free trade, and free trade lets the principle of comparative advantage work most efficiently. The main argument for tariffs is that they protect domestic businesses and workers.

One of the oldest arguments in favor of protectionism is the *infant-industry argument.* By protecting new domestic industries from established foreign competitors, so this argument goes, a tariff can give a struggling industry time to become an effective competitor. A tariff protected the infant U.S. motorcycle industry against British firms. But eventually the Japanese drove most European and American producers from the market. Harley-Davidson is the only remaining large U.S. motorcycle maker.

A second argument for tariffs is the *job-protection argument.* Supporters—especially unions—say we should use tariffs to keep foreign labor from taking away U.S. jobs. U.S. jobs are lost, they say, when low-wage countries sell products at lower prices than those charged in the United States. The higher prices charged by the U.S. firms help pay the higher wages of U.S. workers. More than 200,000 U.S. manufacturing jobs have been lost since 1997 because of high U.S. wages.

Defense suppliers and the military often use the *preparedness argument* for tariffs. They say that industries and technology that are vital to our military should be protected during peace-

Tariffs on the imported goods arriving on this foreign ship at a port in Seattle, Washington, make the products more expensive than those of U.S. competitors.

time because these industries will be needed in the event of war. U.S. ship-builders, gunpowder manufacturers, and uniform manufacturers are helped by this sort of tariff.

An argument against tariffs is that they raise prices, thereby decreasing consumers' purchasing power. Over the long run tariffs may also be too protective, if they cause domestic companies to stop innovating and fall behind technologically. An example is the Italian car builder Fiat. Protective tariffs helped keep Fiat's Italian market share very high. As Europe's trade barriers fell, foreign competitors moved in with cars that Italian drivers preferred. Fiat is now desperately spending billions of dollars to revamp its factories and design new models.

Details about Japan's tariffs and regulations for foreign companies are available at http://www.ita.doc.gov/

Nontariff Barriers

Governments also use other tools besides tariffs to restrict trade. Among them are import quotas, embargoes, buy-national regulations, custom regulations, and exchange controls.

import quota
A limit on the quantity of a certain good that can be imported.

Import quotas   One type of nontariff barrier is the **import quota** or limits on the quantity of a certain good that can be imported. The goal of setting quotas is to limit imports to the optimum amount of a given product. America protects its shrinking textile industry with quotas.

The Trade and Development Act of 2000 was passed to help economically struggling sub-Saharan African nations and Caribbean countries by bypassing U.S. textile quotas. The bill grants these nations "quota-free access for clothing assembled for U.S. companies." Without quotas, big U.S. clothing manufacturers have a great incentive to move work to those nations. In effect, the bill moves textile assembly from low-cost Asian countries to those favored under the new law.[9]

embargo
A total ban on imports or exports of a product.

Embargoes   A complete ban against importing or exporting a product is an **embargo.** Often embargoes are set up for defense purposes. For instance, the United States does not allow various high-tech products, such as supercomputers and lasers, to be exported to countries that are not allies. Although this embargo costs U.S. firms billions of dollars each year in lost sales, it keeps enemies from using the latest technology in their military hardware.

Buy-national regulations   Government rules that give special privileges to domestic manufacturers are called buy-national regulations. One such regulation in the United States bans the use of foreign steel in constructing U.S. highways. Many state governments have buy-national rules for supplies and services.

Custom regulations   In a more subtle move, a country may make it hard for foreign products to enter its markets by establishing custom regulations that are different from generally accepted international standards, such as requiring bottles to be quart size rather than liter size. The French seem most adept at using this tactic. For example, to reduce imports of foreign VCRs, at one time France ruled that all VCRs had to enter through the customs station at Poitiers. This customs house is located in the middle of the country, was woefully understaffed, and was open only a few days each week. What's more, the few customs agents at Poitiers opened each package separately to inspect the merchandise. Within a few weeks, imports of VCRs in France came to a halt.

concept check

- Discuss the concept of natural trade barriers.
- Describe several tariff and nontariff barriers to trade.

Exchange controls **Exchange controls** are laws that require a company earning foreign exchange (foreign currency) from its exports to sell the foreign exchange to a control agency, usually a central bank. For example, assume that Rolex, a Swiss company, sells 300 watches to Zales Jewelers, a U.S. chain, for $120,000 (U.S.). If Switzerland had exchange controls, Rolex would have to sell its U.S. dollars to the Swiss central bank and would receive Swiss francs.

FOSTERING GLOBAL TRADE

>lg 5

exchange controls
Laws that require a company earning foreign exchange (foreign currency) from its exports to sell the foreign exchange to a control agency, such as a central bank.

dumping
The practice of charging a lower price for a product in foreign markets than in the firm's home market.

From our discussion so far, it might seem that governments act only to restrain global trade. On the contrary, governments and international financial organizations work hard to increase it as this section explains.

Antidumping Laws

U.S. firms don't always get to compete on an equal basis with foreign firms in international trade. To level the playing field, Congress has passed antidumping laws. **Dumping** is the practice of charging a lower price for a product (perhaps below cost) in foreign markets than in the firm's home market. The company might be trying to win foreign customers, or it might be seeking to get rid of surplus goods. Sometimes, too, to help create an export market, a government will subsidize certain industries so that they can sell their goods for less. In the past, Japanese steel was sold below cost in world markets, and the losses were covered by government subsidies.

When the variation in price can't be explained by differences in the cost of serving the two markets, dumping is suspected. Most industrialized countries have antidumping regulations. They are especially concerned about *predatory dumping,* the attempt to gain control of a foreign market by destroying competitors with impossibly low prices. Many businesspeople feel that Japan has engaged in predatory dumping of semiconductors in the U.S. market. Without import quotas, companies such as Intel wouldn't exist.

One of the most famous dumping cases in U.S. history involved Japanese color television sets during the 1960s and 1970s. In 1971 U.S. television makers filed a complaint, alleging that Japanese television makers were selling below cost and offering distributors rebates, while also restricting imports into Japan. The Treasury Department, which then enforced the antidumping laws, took no action for three years and then failed to collect duties even though it had determined that dumping was occurring. The U.S. television industry was effectively destroyed. Today, there are no U.S.-owned television makers. As a result of that experience, Congress transferred the authority to enforce antidumping laws from the Treasury Department to the Commerce Department.[10]

The Uruguay Round and the World Trade Organization

Uruguay Round
A 1994 agreement by 117 nations to lower trade barriers worldwide.

The **Uruguay Round** of trade negotiations is an agreement to dramatically lower trade barriers worldwide. Adopted in 1994, the agreement was signed by 117 nations in Marrakesh, Morocco. The most ambitious global trade agreement ever negotiated, the Uruguay Round reduced tariffs by one-third worldwide, a move that is expected to increase global income by $235 billion annually by 2005. Perhaps the most notable aspect of the agreement is its recognition of new global realities. For the first time, an agreement covers services, intellectual property rights, and trade-related investment measures such as exchange controls.

FOREIGN STEEL: FRIEND OR FOE OF AMERICAN STEEL?

As a result of the global competitive pressures that emerged during the 1980s, the American steel industry eliminated hundreds of thousands of jobs in an effort to cut costs and become more competitive and more profitable. As part of this downsizing, many U.S. steel producers closed some or all of their basic steelmaking operations but retained their more profitable rolling mills. Consequently, American steelmakers began importing more steel slabs—the output from the basic steelmaking operation. In fact, imports of steel slabs increased from 155,343 tons in 1980 to 6.8 million tons in 1998. Steel slabs are finished into various hot-rolled, cold-rolled, or galvanized products.

The American steel industry is still fighting for survival. Interestingly, the beleaguered industry has begun to attack the very imports that it has embraced in the past several years. Complaining that foreign steel producers are engaging in unfair trade practices, American steel producers have lobbied the U.S. Congress to provide legislative relief from foreign companies that are dumping steel into the American market.

The legal test for product dumping is based on two criteria. First, the product must be priced unfairly low—either below its production costs or below the selling price in the home country. Second, the imported product must harm the domestic industry.

Steel producers in Brazil, Japan, and Russia, among others, have been accused of dumping steel into the American market. Meanwhile, U.S. steel producers say they will not import steel that is priced below fair market value. However, "one steel trader scoffs at the notion that U.S. steelmakers would pay the fair-value price of steel they import if others are paying a price below fair value."

Critical Thinking Questions

1. Is it ethical for the steel industry to benefit from pricing policies and practices that it complains are unfair?
2. How might the ethical climate of a steel producer be affected by simultaneously complaining about and benefiting from dumping?
3. What role, if any, can government play in establishing an ethical position with regard to dumping?

The Uruguay Round made several major changes in world trading practices:

- *Entertainment, pharmaceuticals, integrated circuits, and software.* Under new rules, patents, copyrights, and trademarks are protected for 20 years. Computer programs are protected for 50 years and semiconductor chips for 10 years. Many developing nations will have a decade to phase in patent protection for drugs. However, France, which limits the number of U.S. movies and television shows that can be shown, refused to liberalize market access for the U.S. entertainment industry.

- *Financial, legal, and accounting services.* Services were brought under international trading rules for the first time, potentially creating a vast opportunity for these competitive U.S. industries. Now it is easier to admit managers and key personnel into a country.

- *Agriculture.* Europe will gradually reduce farm subsidies, opening new opportunities for such U.S. farm exports as wheat and corn. Japan and Korea will begin to import rice. But subsidies for U.S. growers of sugar, citrus fruit, and peanuts will be reduced.

- *Textiles and apparel.* Strict quotas limiting imports from developing countries are being phased out over 10 years, causing further job losses in the U.S. clothing industry. But retailers and consumers will be the big winners because quotas now add $15 billion a year to clothing prices.

- *A new trade organization.* The new **World Trade Organization (WTO)** replaces the old General Agreement on Tariffs and Trade (GATT), which was created in 1948. The GATT contained extensive loopholes that enabled countries to evade agreements to reduce trade barriers. Today, all WTO members must fully comply with all agreements under the Uruguay Round. The WTO also has an effective dispute settlement procedure with strict time limits to resolve disputes.

World Trade Organization (WTO)

An organization established by the Uruguay Round in 1994 to oversee international trade, reduce trade barriers, and resolve disputes among member nations.

The WTO has emerged as the world's most powerful institution for reducing trade barriers and opening markets. Approximately 135 nations now belong to the organization. The advantage of WTO membership is that member countries lower trade barriers among themselves. Countries that don't belong must negotiate trade agreements individually with all their trading partners. To date, China and Russia are the largest countries that have not qualified for WTO membership.

The World Trade Organization tracks the latest trade developments between countries and regions around the world. For the most recent global trading news, visit the WTO's site at

http://www.wto.org

The United States has had mixed results in bringing disputes before the WTO. To date, it has won slightly less than half of the cases it has presented to the WTO. America has also won about one-third of the cases brought by other countries against the United States. One of America's biggest losses came when a WTO panel ruled that the Japanese government's attempt to protect Fuji Film from competition by Kodak was not illegal. In late 2000, the United States targeted Europe, India, South Korea, Canada, and Argentina to file cases against. The disputes ranged from European aviation practices to Indian barriers affecting U.S. automakers.

The World Bank and International Monetary Fund

World Bank

An international bank that offers low-interest loans, as well as advice and information, to developing nations.

Two international financial organizations are instrumental in fostering global trade. The **World Bank** offers low-interest loans to developing nations. Originally, the purpose of the loans was to help these nations build infrastructure such as roads, power plants, schools, drainage projects, and hospitals. Now the World Bank offers loans to help developing nations relieve their debt burdens. To receive the loans, countries must pledge to lower trade barriers and aid private enterprise. In addition to making loans, the World Bank is a major source of advice and information for developing nations. The United States has granted the organization $60 million to create knowledge databases on nutrition, birth control, software engineering, creating quality products, and basic accounting systems.[11]

International Monetary Fund (IMF)

An international organization, founded in 1945, that promotes trade, makes short-term loans to member nations, and acts as a lender of last resort for troubled nations.

The **International Monetary Fund (IMF)** was founded in 1945, one year after the creation of the World Bank, to promote trade through financial cooperation and eliminate trade barriers in the process. The IMF makes short-term loans to member nations that are unable to meet their budgetary expenses. It operates as a lender of last resort for troubled nations. In exchange for these emergency loans, IMF lenders frequently extract significant commitments from the borrowing nations to address the problems that led to the crises. These steps may include curtailing imports or even devaluing the currency.

In the late 1990s, South Korea, Thailand, Malaysia, and Indonesia were hit by a severe recession. IMF intervention to rescue these economies did not seem to work as unemployment and interest rates soared. The crisis also hit Russia and several countries of Latin America including Brazil. Private money for economic development simply quit flowing into these economies. The basic problem was that capital (money) had flowed into these emerging economies with little attention paid to the creditworthiness of the borrowers. With easy money, borrowers took on more debt than they could repay. To make matters worse, banks and other financial institutions were so closely intertwined with governments that decisions were made for political reasons and not based on sound economics.

Such global financial problems do not have a simple solution. One option would be to pump a lot more funds into the IMF, giving it enough resources to bail out troubled countries and put them back on their feet. In effect, the IMF would be turned into a real lender of last resort for the world economy.

The danger of counting on the IMF, though, is the "moral hazard" problem. Investors would assume that the IMF would bail them out and would therefore be encouraged to take bigger and bigger risks in emerging markets, leading to the possibility of even deeper financial crises in the future.

Gain additional insight into the workings of the International Monetary Fund at

http://www.imf.org

concept check

- Describe the purpose and role of the WTO.
- What are the roles of the World Bank and the IMF in world trade?

INTERNATIONAL ECONOMIC COMMUNITIES

>lg 6

Nations that frequently trade with each other may decide to formalize their relationship. The governments meet and work out agreements for a common economic policy. The result is an economic community or, in other cases, a bilateral trade agreement (an agreement between two countries to lower trade barriers). For example, two nations may agree upon a **preferential tariff,** which gives advantages to one nation (or several nations) over others. For instance, when members of the British Commonwealth trade with Great Britain, they pay lower tariffs than do other nations. In other cases, nations may form free-trade associations. In a **free-trade zone,** few, if any, duties or rules restrict trade among the partners, but nations outside the zone must pay the tariffs set by the individual members. A *customs union* sets up a free-trade area and specifies a uniform tariff structure for members' trade with nonmember nations. In a *common market,* or economic union, members go beyond a customs union and try to bring all of their government trade rules into agreement.

preferential tariff

A tariff that is lower for some nations than for others.

free-trade zone

An area where the nations allow free, or almost free, trade among each other while imposing tariffs on goods of nations outside the zone.

North American Free Trade Agreement (NAFTA)

The **North American Free Trade Agreement (NAFTA)** created the world's largest free-trade zone. The agreement was ratified by the U.S. Congress in 1993. It includes Canada, the United States, and Mexico, with a combined population of 360 million and an economy of $6 trillion.

Canada, the largest U.S. trading partner, entered a free-trade agreement with the United States in 1988. Thus, most of the new long-run opportunities opened for U.S. business under NAFTA are in Mexico, America's third largest trading partner. Before NAFTA, tariffs on Mexican exports to the United States averaged just 4 percent, and most goods entered the United States duty-free, so

North American Free Trade Agreement (NAFTA)

A 1993 agreement creating a free-trade zone including Canada, Mexico, and the United States.

Want to learn the latest info about NAFTA? Go to http://www.NAFTA-customs.org

NAFTA's primary impact was to open the Mexican market to U.S. companies. When the treaty went into effect, tariffs on about half the items traded across the Rio Grande disappeared. Since NAFTA came into effect, U.S.-Mexican trade has increased by 250 percent, from $80 billion to $200 billion annually.[12] The pact removed a web of Mexican licensing requirements, quotas, and tariffs that limited transactions in U.S. goods and services. For instance, the pact allows U.S. and Canadian financial services companies to own subsidiaries in Mexico for the first time in 50 years.

The real test of NAFTA will be whether it can deliver rising prosperity on both sides of the Rio Grande. For Mexicans, NAFTA must provide rising wages, better benefits, and an expanding middle class with enough purchasing power to keep buying goods from the United States and Canada. That scenario is plausible in the long run, but not guaranteed. As for the United States, the full implementation of NAFTA will add about $30 billion to GDP annually. But for Americans, the trade agreement will need to prove that it can produce more well-paying jobs than it destroys. Although estimates of the employment effects of NAFTA vary widely, almost every study agrees that there will be gains. The Labor Department has certified—under a program that gives displaced workers retraining and unemployment relief—that 128,303 U.S. workers have lost their jobs so far because of increased competition from Mexico and Canada. That compares with 2.2 million jobs created each year since NAFTA took effect.[13]

Ultimately, some U.S. politicians would like to expand NAFTA to include other Latin American countries and perhaps even Great Britain. Chile was to be the first new entrant, but wrangling within the U.S. Congress has blocked NAFTA expansion so far. Concerns that NAFTA will eventually cost more American jobs than it creates have stalled congressional expansion of the agreement. As a result, countries south of the U.S. border have been forming their own trade agreements.

The largest new trade agreement is **Mercosur,** which includes Brazil, Argentina, Uruguay, and Paraguay. The elimination of most tariffs among the trading partners has resulted in trade revenues that currently exceed $16 billion annually.[14] The economic boom created by Mercosur will undoubtedly cause other nations to either seek trade agreements on their own or enter Mercosur. The European Union, discussed next, hopes to have a free-trade pact with Mercosur by 2005.

The European Union

In 1993, the member countries of the European Community (EC) ratified the **Maastricht Treaty,** which proposed to take the EC further toward economic, monetary, and political union. Officially called the Treaty on European Union, the document outlined plans for tightening bonds among the member states and creating a single market. The European Commission, which drafted the treaty, predicted that Maastricht will create over 2 million new jobs. Also, retail prices in the **European Union (EU),** as the EC is now called, are expected to fall by a minimum of 6 percent. Exhibit 2-1 shows the members of the EU.

Although much of the treaty deals with developing a unified European market, Maastricht is also intended to increase integration among the EU members in areas much closer to the heart of national sovereignty. The treaty called for economic and monetary coordination, including a common currency and an

Mercosur

A trade agreement among Argentina, Brazil, Paraguay, and Uruguay that eliminates most tariffs among the member nations.

Maastricht Treaty

A 1993 treaty concluded by the members of the European Community (now the European Union) that outlines plans for tightening bonds among the members and creating a single market; officially called the Treaty on European Union.

European Union (EU)

An organization of 15 European nations (as of 1999) that works to foster political and economic integration in Europe; formerly called the European Community.

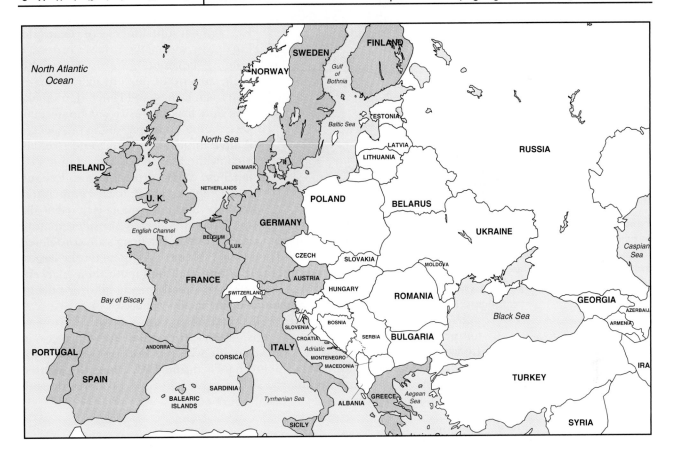

independent central bank. In addition, EU members will eventually share foreign security and defense policies as well as European citizenship—any EU citizen will be able to live, work, vote, and run for office in any member country. The treaty also coordinated health and safety regulations and standardized trade rules, duties, customs procedures, and taxes. A driver hauling cargo from Amsterdam to Lisbon can now clear four border crossings by showing a single piece of paper. Before the Maastricht Treaty, a driver had to carry two pounds of paper to cross the same borders. By setting uniform standards, the treaty's goal is to eliminate the need for manufacturers to produce a separate product for each country—one Braun electric razor for Italy, a slightly different one for Germany, and a third one for France, for example. Goods marked GEC (goods for EC) can be traded freely without being retested at each border.

Some economists have called the EU the "United States of Europe." It is an attractive market, with 320 million consumers and purchasing power almost equal to that of the United States. But the EU will probably never be a United States of Europe. For one thing, even in a united Europe, businesses will not be able to produce a single Europroduct for a generic Euroconsumer. With nine languages and different national customs, Europe will always be far more diverse than the United States. Thus, product differences will continue. It will be a long time, for instance, before the French begin drinking the same instant coffee that Britons enjoy. Even preferences for washing machines differ: British homemakers want front-loaders, and the French want top-loaders; Germans like lots of settings and high spin speeds, while Italians like lower speeds.

The eurodollar replaces the individual currencies of 12 European Union nations. The new common currency enables the countries to do business as a single trading bloc.

An entirely different type of problem facing global businesses is the possibility of a protectionist movement by the EU against outsiders. For example, European automakers have proposed holding Japanese imports at roughly their current 10 percent market share. The Irish, Danes, and Dutch don't make cars and have unrestricted home markets; they are unhappy at the prospect of limited imports of Toyotas and Hondas. Meanwhile France has a strict quota on Japanese cars to protect its own Renault and Peugeot. These local automarkers could be hurt if the quota is raised at all.

Interestingly, a number of big U.S. companies are already considered more "European" than many European companies. Coke and Kellogg's are considered classic European brand names. Ford and General Motors compete for the largest share of auto sales on the continent. IBM and Dell dominate their markets. General Electric, AT&T, and Westinghouse are already strong all over Europe and have invested heavily in new manufacturing facilities there.

Although many U.S. firms are well prepared to contend with European competition, the rivalry is perhaps more intense there than anywhere else in the world. In the long run, it is questionable whether Europe has room for eight mass-market automakers, including Ford and GM, when the United States sustains just three. Similarly, an integrated Europe probably doesn't need 12 national airlines.

The Euro

Twelve of the 15 members of the European Union have converted their currencies to the eurodollar, or "euro" for short, a new currency that circulates in all 12 nations. Due to internal policies, Great Britain, Denmark, and Sweden will not convert to the euro; the currencies that have become obsolete are listed in Exhibit 2-2. The conversion began in January 1999 and was completed in 2002 when the euro notes began circulating. With the conversion, the participating European nations are doing business as a single trading bloc, which is the largest economy in the world in terms of percentage of world GDP.

concept check

- Explain the pros and cons of NAFTA.
- What is the European Union? Will it ever be a United States of Europe?
- Discuss the concept of the euro.

PARTICIPATING IN THE GLOBAL MARKETPLACE

>lg 7

Companies decide to "go global" for a number of reasons. Perhaps the most urgent reason is to earn additional profits. If a firm has a unique product or technological advantage not available to other international competitors, this advantage should result in major business successes abroad. In other situations, management may have exclusive market information about foreign customers, marketplaces, or market situations not known to others. In this case, although exclusivity can provide an initial motivation for going global, managers must realize that competitors will eventually catch up. Finally, saturated domestic markets, excess capacity, and potential for cost savings can also be motivators to expand into international markets. A company can enter global trade in several ways, as this section describes.

Countries Converted to the Eurodollar/Currency Replaced

Austria/Schilling	Ireland/Pound
Belgium/Franc	Italy/Lira
Finland/Markka	Luxembourg/Franc
France/Franc	Netherlands/Guilder
Germany/Deutsche mark	Portugal/Escudo
Greece/Drachma	Spain/Peseta

Exporting

When a company decides to enter the global market, usually the least complicated and least risky alternative is **exporting,** or selling domestically produced products to buyers in another country. A company, for example, can sell directly to foreign importers or buyers. Exporting is not limited to huge corporations such as General Motors or Westinghouse. Indeed, small companies account for 96 percent of all U.S. exporters, but only 30 percent of the export volume.[15] The United States is the world's largest exporter. Many small businesses claim that they lack the money, time, or knowledge of foreign markets that exporting requires. The U.S. Small Business Administration (SBA) now offers the Export Working Capital Program, which helps small and medium-size firms obtain working capital (money) to complete export sales. The SBA also provides counseling and legal assistance for small businesses that wish to enter the global marketplace. Companies such as American Building Restoration Products of Franklin, Wisconsin, have benefited tremendously from becoming exporters. American Building is now selling its chemical products to building restoration companies in Mexico, Israel, Japan, and Korea. Exports account for more than 5 percent of the firm's total sales.[16]

The Internet is an excellent source of information for any firm that is considering entering the global marketplace by exporting. The Applying Technology box describes some of the new information sources found on the Web.

IBM's entry in global markets includes exporting, which helps the company to expand the global distribution of products like the OS/2 Warp operating system to businesses and consumers in Japan.

exporting
The practice of selling domestically produced goods to buyers in another country.

Licensing

Another effective way for a firm to move into the global arena with relatively little risk is to sell a license to manufacture its product to a firm in a foreign country. **Licensing** is the legal process whereby a firm (the *licensor*) agrees to let another firm (the *licensee*) use a manufacturing process, trademark, patent, trade secret, or other proprietary knowledge. The licensee, in turn, agrees to pay the licensor a royalty or fee agreed on by both parties.

licensing

The legal process whereby a firm agrees to allow another firm to use a manufacturing process, trademark, patent, trade secret, or other proprietary knowledge in exchange for the payment of a royalty.

U.S. companies have eagerly embraced the licensing concept. For instance, Philip Morris licensed Labatt Brewing Company to produce Miller High Life in Canada. The Spaulding Company receives more than $2 million annually from license agreements on its sporting goods. Fruit-of-the-Loom lends its name through licensing to 45 consumer items in Japan alone, for at least 1 percent of the licensee's gross sales.

The licensor must make sure it can exercise sufficient control over the licensee's activities to ensure proper quality, pricing, distribution, and so on. Licensing may also create a new competitor in the long run, if the licensee decides to void the license agreement. International law is often ineffective in stopping such actions. Two common ways that a licensor can maintain effective control over its licensees are by shipping one or more critical components from the United States and by locally registering patents and trademarks in its own name.

Franchising, covered in Chapter 5, is a form of licensing that has grown rapidly in recent years. Over 350 U.S. franchisors operate more than 32,000 outlets in foreign countries, bringing in sales of $6 billion. More than half of the international franchises are for fast-food restaurants and business services. McDonald's's international division is responsible for over 50 percent of the chain's sales and 60 percent of its profits.[17]

Contract Manufacturing

contract manufacturing
The practice in which a foreign firm manufactures private-label goods under a domestic firm's brand name.

In **contract manufacturing,** a foreign firm manufactures private-label goods under a domestic firm's brand. Marketing may be handled by either the domestic company or the foreign manufacturer. Levi Strauss, for instance, entered into an agreement with the French fashion house of Cacharel to produce a new Levi's line called "Something New" for distribution in Germany.

The advantage of contract manufacturing is that it lets a company "test the water" in a foreign country. By allowing the foreign firm to produce a certain volume of products to specification, and put the domestic firm's brand name on the goods, the domestic firm can broaden its global marketing base without investing in overseas plants and equipment. After establishing a solid base, the domestic firm may switch to a joint venture or direct investment, explained below.

Joint Ventures

joint venture
An agreement in which a domestic firm buys part of a foreign firm or joins with a foreign firm to create a new entity.

Joint ventures are somewhat similar to licensing agreements. In a **joint venture,** the domestic firm buys part of a foreign company or joins with a foreign company to create a new entity. A joint venture is a quick and relatively inexpensive way to enter the global market. It can also be very risky. Many joint ventures fail. Others fall victim to a takeover, in which one partner buys out the other.

E*Trade, one of the hottest U.S. Internet-based stockbrokers, recently entered into a joint venture with Softbank Corp. of Japan to offer online investing services in Asia. E*Trade also entered a second joint venture with the British company Electronic Share Information (ESI). The agreement provides E*Trade the opportunity to serve ESI's 170,000 customers and gives ESI access to E*Trade's software and brand name.[18]

In a successful joint venture, both parties gain valuable skills from the alliance. In the General Motors–Suzuki joint venture in Canada, for example, both parties have contributed and gained. The alliance, CAMI Automotive, was formed to manufacture low-end cars for the U.S. market. The plant, which is run by Suzuki management, produces the Geo Metro/Suzuki Swift—the smallest, most fuel-efficient GM car sold in North America—as well as the Geo Tracker/Suzuki Sidekick sport utility vehicle. Through CAMI, Suzuki has gained access to GM's dealer network and an expanded market for

Find out more about Suzuki's international joint ventures at
http://www.suzuki.co.jp/cpd/koho_e/kaigai.htm

parts and components. GM avoided the cost of developing low-end cars and obtained models it needed to revitalize the lower end of its product line and its average fuel economy rating. The CAMI factory may be one of the most productive plants in North America. There GM has learned how Japanese automakers use work teams, run flexible assembly lines, and manage quality control.

Direct Foreign Investment

direct foreign investment
Active ownership of a foreign company or of manufacturing or marketing facilities in a foreign country.

Active ownership of a foreign company or of overseas manufacturing or marketing facilities is **direct foreign investment.** Direct investors have either a controlling interest or a large minority interest in the firm. Thus, they stand to receive the greatest potential reward but also face the greatest potential risk. A firm may make a direct foreign investment by acquiring an interest in an existing company or by building new facilities. It might do so because it has trouble transferring some resources to a foreign operation or obtaining that resource locally. One important resource is personnel, especially managers. If the local labor market is tight, the firm may buy an entire foreign firm and retain all its employees instead of paying higher salaries than competitors. Sometimes firms make direct investments because they can find no suitable local partners. Also, direct investments avoid the communication problems and conflicts of interest that can arise with joint ventures. IBM, for instance, insists on total ownership of its foreign investments because it does not want to share control with local partners.

Kodak paid more than $1 billion to acquire and upgrade three government-owned film manufacturers in China. In return, the Chinese government granted Kodak a virtual monopoly to manufacture film in the country. In the past, the Chinese government would simply erect more trade barriers to keep companies like Kodak and Fuji out. In a more pragmatic move, the government decided to sell the debt-ridden, inefficient plants to outside investors and exit the film manufacturing business.[19]

How does Argent Trading help companies like Nestlé and Sherwin Williams conduct business internationally? Find out by reading some of the case studies at the Argent Trading home page,

http://www.argenttrading.com

countertrade

A form of international trade in which part or all of the payment for goods or services is in the form of other goods and services.

Countertrade

International trade does not always involve cash. Today, countertrade is a fast-growing way to conduct international business. In **countertrade,** part or all of the payment for goods or services is in the form of other goods or services. Countertrade is a form of barter (swapping goods for goods), an age-old practice whose origins have been traced back to cave dwellers. The U.S. Commerce Department says that roughly 30 percent of all international trade involves countertrade. Each year about 300,000 U.S. firms engage in some form of countertrade. American companies, including General Electric, Pepsi, General Motors, and Boeing, barter about $7.5 billion of goods and services every year.[20]

Argent Trading is the world's largest countertrade organization. Argent reviews a client's unsold products and issues trade credits in exchange. The credits can be used to obtain other products and services Argent has acquired—everything from hotel rooms and airline tickets to television advertising time, forklift trucks, carpeting, pulp, envelopes, steel castings, or satellite tracking systems.

concept check

- Discuss several ways that a company can enter international trade.
- Explain the concept of countertrade.

THREATS AND OPPORTUNITIES IN THE GLOBAL MARKETPLACE

>lg 8

To be successful in a foreign market, companies must fully understand the foreign environment in which they plan to operate. Politics, cultural differences, and the economic environment can represent both opportunities and pitfalls in the global marketplace.

Political Considerations

We have already discussed how tariffs, exchange controls, and other governmental actions threaten foreign producers. The political structure of a country may also jeopardize a foreign producer's success in international trade.

Intense nationalism, for example, can lead to difficulties. **Nationalism** is the sense of national consciousness that boosts the culture and interests of one country over those of all other countries. Strongly nationalistic countries, such as Iran and New Guinea, often discourage investment by foreign companies. In other, less radical forms of nationalism, the government may take actions to

nationalism

A sense of national consciousness that boosts the culture and interests of one country over those of all other countries.

hinder foreign operations. France, for example, requires that pop music stations play at least 40 percent of their songs in French. This law was enacted because the French love American rock and roll. Without airtime, American CDs sales suffer. Coca-Cola recently attempted to purchase Orangina, France's only domestically owned and distributed soft drink. The French government blocked the sale saying that it would be "anticompetitive."[21] The real reason was nationalism.

In a hostile climate, a government may *expropriate* a foreign company's assets, taking ownership and compensating the former owners. Even worse is *confiscation,* when the owner receives no compensation. This happened during rebellions in several African nations during the 1990s.

Cultural Differences

Central to any society is the common set of values shared by its citizens that determine what is socially acceptable. Culture underlies the family, educational system, religion, and social class system. The network of social organizations generates overlapping roles and status positions. These values and roles have a tremendous effect on people's preferences and thus on marketers' options. Inca Kola, a fruity, greenish yellow carbonated drink, is the largest selling soft drink in Peru. Despite being described as "liquid bubble gum," the drink has become a symbol of national pride and heritage. The drink was invented in Peru and contains only fruit indigenous to the country. A local consumer of about a six-pack a day says, "I drink Inca Kola because it makes me feel like a Peruvian." He tells his young daughter, "This is our drink, not something invented overseas. It is named for your ancestors, the great Inca warriors."

Language is another important aspect of culture. Marketers must take care in selecting product names and translating slogans and promotional messages so as not to convey the wrong meaning. For example, Mitsubishi Motors had to rename its Pajero model in Spanish-speaking countries because the term refers to a sexual activity. Toyota Motors' MR2 model dropped the number 2 in France because the combination sounds like a French swearword. The literal translation of Coca-Cola in Chinese characters means "bite the wax tadpole."

Each country has its own customs and traditions that determine business practices and influence negotiations with foreign customers. In many countries, personal relationships are more important than financial considerations. For instance, skipping social engagements in Mexico may lead to lost sales. Negotiations in Japan often include long evenings of dining, drinking, and entertaining; only after a close personal relationship has been formed do business negotiations begin. Exhibit 2-3 presents some cultural "dos and don'ts."

Economic Environment

The level of economic development varies considerably, ranging from countries where everyday survival is a struggle, such as the Sudan and Eritrea, to countries that are highly developed, such as Switzerland and Japan. In general, complex, sophisticated industries are found in developed countries, and more basic industries are found in less developed nations. Average family incomes are higher in the more developed countries than in the least developed markets. Larger incomes mean greater purchasing power and demand not only for consumer goods and services but also for the machinery and workers required to produce consumer goods. Exhibit 2-4 provides a glimpse of what families earn throughout the world.

Business opportunities are usually better in countries that have an economic infrastructure in place. **Infrastructure** is the basic institutions and public facilities

infrastructure
The basic institutions and public facilities upon which an economy's development depends.

e x h i b i t   2 - 3 | Cultural Dos and Don'ts

DO:

- **Read up** on the culture of the country where you will be doing business. Pointing or beckoning with the forefinger is considered rude in some Asian countries, for example; pointing your foot at another person is considered rude in Thailand.
- **Remember** that pleasure and personal relationships are often a determining factor when Latin Americans and Asians do business.
- **Treat business cards** seriously almost everywhere. In many cultures, a business card is as important as a résumé. Don't glance at the card and shove it in your pocket. Take the card in your right hand, carefully examine it, and memorize the person's name, title, and company and the company's address. You may be tested later.
- **Be aware** of dietary taboos. Pork is considered unclean, for example, by Muslims. Nor should you offer a Hindu a meal containing beef; the cow is considered a sacred animal in the Hindu religion.

DON'T:

- **Dress too casually.** Americans view casual as comfortable or even as part of the breakdown of phony corporate hierarchical rules. In many Asian and Latin American countries, though, casual equals sloppy.
- **Use your left hand** to eat, or to give or receive objects, unless you are certain it is acceptable. In many Asian, Middle Eastern, and African cultures, the left hand is used for personal hygiene and is considered unclean.

Some Examples of Cultural Differences That Can Affect Business Dealings

- The Japanese do not like to say no. If your Japanese business partner tells you that your proposition would "be very difficult," she means "no, we don't want to do it that way."
- In Asia, companies usually do not provide employee evaluations, or performance reviews, unless the employee is about to be fired.
- A powerful Chinese buyer will buy the highest-quality product. He doesn't care about marketing or advertising pitches.
- In many parts of Latin America, the business day begins about 11 A.M., and proceeds until about 3 P.M., when there is a two-to-three-hour break; the last part of the work day runs from about 6 to 9 P.M.
- Hype doesn't sell in many countries, such as Germany and China. A good product stands on its own merits. If you have to hype a product, people believe that something must be wrong with it.
- European and Asian résumés include only the facts: a complete professional history and a copy of every degree, certificate or award earned. Expressions of professional accomplishment on the job are frowned on.
- Cultural norms vary from culture to culture. You might have to turn your head to avoid being kissed on the lips by another man in Russia, for example, as a sign of affection or expression of celebration. But a Chinese businessperson, even one who is a close friend, would generally be uncomfortable with physical contact beyond a handshake.

SOURCE: Bill Bowen, "Culture Clash," *Fort Worth Star Telegram* (September 28, 1998), pp. 14–15.

concept check

- Explain how political factors can affect international trade.
- Describe several cultural factors that a company involved in international trade should consider.
- How can economic conditions affect trade opportunities?

upon which an economy's development depends. When we think about how our own economy works, we tend to take our infrastructure for granted. It includes the money and banking system that provides the major investment loans to our nation's businesses; the educational system that turns out the incredible varieties of skills and basic research that actually run our nation's production lines; the extensive transportation and communications systems—interstate highways, railroads, airports, canals, telephones, Internet sites, postal systems, television stations—that link almost every piece of our geography into one market; the energy system that powers our factories; and, of course, the market system itself, which brings our nation's goods and services into our homes and businesses.

e x h i b i t   2 - 4

What the World Earns
High consumption levels are concentrated in a small share of
households worldwide.

Percent distribution of households by annual consumption level.

■ **Less than $5,000**   ■ **$5,000 to $9,999**

□ **$10,000 to $19,999**   ▨ **$20,000 and above**

South Asia	75% 21% 4% 1%
Sub-Saharan Africa	75% 16% 7% 2%
East Asia/Pacific	73% 17% 7% 4%
Former socialist economies	21% 32% 30% 17%
Middle Eastern crescent	22% 32% 28% 18%
Latin America	24% 23% 26% 27%
Established market economies	3% 8% 24% 65%

0%   20%   40%   60%   80%   100%

Note: Consumption is in U.S. dollars on a purchase-power-parity basis. Percentages may add to more than 100 percent due to rounding.

SOURCE: World Bank and Global Business Opportunities.

THE IMPACT OF MULTINATIONAL CORPORATIONS

>lg 9

multinational corporations
Corporations that move resources, goods, services, and skills across national boundaries without regard to the country in which their headquarters are located.

Corporations that move resources, goods, services, and skills across national boundaries without regard to the country in which their headquarters are located are **multinational corporations.** Some are so rich and have so many employees that they resemble small countries. For example, the sales of both Exxon Mobil and General Motors are larger than the GDP of all but 22 nations in the world. Multinational companies are heavily engaged in international trade. The successful ones take political and cultural differences into account.

Today, dozens of America's top names—including General Electric, Gillette, Xerox, Dow Chemical, and Hewlett-Packard—sell more of their products outside the United States than they do at home. U.S. service companies—such as McDonald's, Service Master (cleaning services), and Federal Express—are close behind.

A multinational company may have several worldwide headquarters, depending on the location of its markets or technologies. Britain's APV, a maker of food-processing equipment, has a different headquarters for each of its worldwide businesses. Hewlett-Packard recently moved the headquarters of its personal computer business to Grenoble, France. Siemens A.G., Germany's electronics giant, is relocating its medical electronics division headquarters from Germany to Chicago. Honda is planning to move the worldwide headquarters for its power-products division to Atlanta, Georgia. The largest multinational corporations in the world are shown in Exhibit 2-5.

e x h i b i t   2 - 5 | The World's Largest Multinational Corporations

Rank	Company (Country)	Rank	Company (Country)
1	General Electric (U.S.)	11	NTT Docomo (Japan)
2	Microsoft (U.S.)	12	American International Group (6) (U.S.)
3	Exxon Mobil (U.S.)	13	Intel (U.S.)
4	Pfizer (U.S.)	14	Vadafone Group (Britain)
5	Citigroup (U.S.)	15	GlaxoSmithKline (Britain)
6	Wal-Mart Stores (U.S.)	16	Merck (U.S.)
7	AOL Time Warner (U.S.)	17	Verizon Communications (U.S.)
8	Royal Dutch/Shell (1) (Neth./Britain)	18	SBC Communications (U.S.)
9	BP (Britain)	19	CISCO Systems (U.S.)
10	Internationl Business Machines (U.S.)	20	Nokia (Finland)

SOURCE: "The Top 100 Companies," *Business Week* (July 9, 2001), p. 75.

The Multinational Advantage

Large multinationals have several advantages over other companies. For instance, multinationals can often overcome trade problems. Taiwan and South Korea have long had an embargo against Japanese cars for political reasons and to help domestic automakers. Yet Honda USA, a Japanese-owned company based in the United States, sends Accords to Taiwan and Korea. In another example, when the environmentally conscious Green movement challenged the biotechnology research conducted by BASF, a major German chemical and drug manufacturer, BASF moved its cancer and immune-system research to Cambridge, Massachusetts.

Another advantage for multinationals is their ability to sidestep regulatory problems. U.S. drugmaker SmithKline and Britain's Beecham decided to merge in part so that they could avoid licensing and regulatory hassles in their largest markets. The merged company can say it's an insider in both Europe

Procter & Gamble employees test different detergents formulated at P&G facilities worldwide, giving the company a technology advantage as a multinational corporation.

and the United States. "When we go to Brussels, we're a member state [of the European Union]," one executive explains. "And when we go to Washington, we're an American company."[22]

Multinationals can also shift production from one plant to another as market conditions change. When European demand for a certain solvent declined, Dow Chemical instructed its German plant to switch to manufacturing a chemical that had been imported from Louisiana and Texas. Computer models help Dow make decisions like these so it can run its plants more efficiently and keep costs down.

Multinationals can also tap new technology from around the world. Xerox has introduced some 80 different office copiers in the United States that were designed and built by Fuji Xerox, its joint venture with a Japanese company. Versions of the superconcentrated detergent that Procter & Gamble first formulated in Japan in response to a rival's product are now being sold under the Ariel brand name in Europe and being tested under the Cheer and Tide labels in the United States. Also, consider Otis Elevator's development of the Elevonic 411, an elevator that is programmed to send more cars to floors where demand is high. It was developed by six research centers in five countries. Otis' group in Farmington, Connecticut, handled the systems integration, a Japanese group designed the special motor drives that make the elevators ride smoothly, a French group perfected the door systems, a German group handled the electronics, and a Spanish group took care of the small-geared components. Otis says the international effort saved more than $10 million in design costs and cut the process from four years to two.

Finally, multinationals can often save a lot in labor costs, even in highly unionized countries. For example, when Xerox started moving copier-rebuilding work to Mexico to take advantage of the lower wages, its union in Rochester, New York, objected because it saw that members' jobs were at risk. Eventually, the union agreed to change work styles and to improve productivity to keep the jobs at home.

c o n c ə p t   c h ə c k

- What is a multinational corporation?
- What are the advantages of multi-nationals?

CAPITALIZING ON TRENDS IN BUSINESS

>lg 10

In this section we will examine several underlying trends that will continue to propel the dramatic growth in world trade. These trends are market expansion, resource acquisition, competition, technological change, and governmental actions.

Market Expansion

The need for businesses to expand their markets is perhaps the most fundamental reason for the growth in world trade. The limited size of domestic markets often motivates managers to seek markets beyond their national frontiers. The economies of large-scale manufacturing demand big markets. Domestic markets, particularly in smaller countries like Denmark and the Netherlands, simply can't generate enough demand. Nestlé was one of the first businesses to "go global" because its home country, Switzerland, is so small. Nestlé was shipping milk to 16 different countries as early as 1875. Today, hundreds of thousands of businesses are recognizing the potential rich rewards to be found in international markets.

Resource Acquisition

More and more companies are going to the global marketplace to acquire the resources they need to operate efficiently. These resources may be cheap or skilled labor, scarce raw materials, technology, or capital. Nike, for example, has opened manufacturing facilities in many Asian countries in order to use cheap labor. Honda opened a design studio in southern California to put that "California flair" into the design of some of its vehicles. Large multinational banks such as Bank of New York and Citigroup have offices in Geneva, Switzerland. Geneva is the private banking center of Europe and attracts capital from around the globe.

Competition

As multinational firms continue to enter new markets, their competitors will often do the same to maintain their competitive position. Starbucks, for example, recently entered Great Britain. Nestlé quickly developed Starbucks-type stores and moved into London shortly after Starbucks. Mazda has struggled for years in Japan because it lacked the resources of its larger domestic competitors—Toyota and Nissan. It entered the U.S. market in an effort to keep pace with its Japanese rivals by gaining market share and profitability. With the opening of Eastern Europe and China, thousands of businesses are racing to capture new customers. Each realizes that if it falls behind its competitors, it may have a difficult time catching up.

Technological Change

New technology, particularly the Internet, transportation systems, and information processing, fosters continued growth in international trade. Transportation improvements from computerized container ships to cargo jetliners have dramatically improved the efficiency of distribution throughout the world. Moreover, Federal Express and other shippers use advanced computerized tracking software to tell shippers where their packages are at any point in time. Shippers can use special software that enables them to enter FedEx's database and track the packages themselves, if they so desire. It's a far cry from the sailing ships of yesteryear when voyages took weeks or months, and there was no way to communicate with the ship once it left port.

The Internet opens up the world to any seller with a Web site. Markets no longer have geographic boundaries. E-mail enables a manager in London to receive reports from Dallas, Moscow, Capetown, and Tokyo in a matter of minutes rather than days. Thus, coordinating global business strategies is now a workable reality.

concept check

- What trends will foster continued growth in world trade?
- Describe some of the ways businesses can take advantage of these trends to "go global."

Government Actions

Governments around the globe, working with the WTO, have significantly lowered barriers to world trade. Sellers in the global marketplace have a more level playing field than ever before. Regional trade organizations, such as the European Union, NAFTA, and Mercosur, also have reduced trade barriers in large geographic areas. As these governmental actions continue to make it easier to "go global," world trade will continue to grow.

APPLYING THIS CHAPTER'S TOPICS

Continue Your Education

The handwriting is on the wall. Low-skilled jobs are rapidly disappearing in America. U.S. businesses know that to compete globally, they must find cheap labor for labor-intensive businesses. This means establishing plants in Mexico, Asia, or other places in the world where labor in inexpensive. It also means that unskilled or low-skilled American workers will find it increasingly difficult to secure a permanent job. By continuing your education, you won't fall into this very undesirable trap.

Study the Role of a Global Manager

As business becomes more global, chances are that you may become a global manager. Start learning right now what this means and if it's right for you. The life of a global manager can be hectic, as these examples illustrate:

> As president of DoubleClick International, a unit of the New York Internet advertising company, Barry Salzman spends about 75% of his time traveling. He takes a laptop and four battery packs so he can wade through the 200 e-mail messages he averages daily. Welcome to the world of global management. It's a punishing pace, but it's the only way Mr. Salzman knows how to manage his network of 13 offices worldwide.
>
> Global managers spend proportionately more of their energy combating the sense of isolation that tends to gnaw at employees in remote offices. Mr. Salzman conducts a conference call every Monday morning for international managers in Canada, Europe and Asia. Only those who are flying somewhere are excused. "We try to maintain voice contact," he says. "We lose that with computers and e-mail."
>
> Top overseas performers at Secure Computing, a San Jose, Calif., software developer, are treated to a dinner for two by Christine Hughes, senior vice president of marketing and business development. Ms. Hughes supervises a 24-person staff in North and South America and Asia. One of her missions on trips is to combat the tendency of foreign-based employees to think the organization is "U.S.-centric," she says. Because they take much longer flights than the typical corporate road warrior, global managers wind up turning airplanes into offices. When she is overseas, Ms. Hughes has her office ship her a package of paperwork overnight, so she can work on the flight home. Mr. Salzman considers flight time some of his most productive; he uses it to answer e-mail and review contracts.
>
> Indeed, a global manager's workday never really ends. Wherever they are, it's still business hours somewhere else. When she's working in Australia, Ms. Hughes usually ends her day in a hotel room, talking with someone at the home office. "I'm on the phone until two in the morning dealing with issues," she says. "You just have to accept that."[23]

Your position may not be as hectic as that of Salzman or Hughes, but you can easily see the differences between a person who is a global manager and one who is not. Is this the life for you? Would you enjoy living abroad? Can you adapt easily to other cultures?

Changing Money Abroad   If you travel, work, or study abroad, you are going to need to change U.S. dollars to foreign currency. Making mistakes when changing money can cost you 10 to 20 percent of your bankroll. Here are a few tips about changing money abroad.

1. Know the exchange rate between U.S. dollars and the currencies of the countries you plan to visit before you go. Go to **http://money.cnn.com/markets/currencies/** for the latest quotations. Keep up with the changing rates by reading *USA Today International* or the *International Herald Tribune* every day.

2. Avoid changing money at airports, train stations, and hotels. These places usually have the worst rates. Ask local people where they change money. Locals know where the best rates are.

3. Try to bargain with the clerk. Sometimes you can do better than the posted rate simply by asking.

4. Rather than making several small transactions, make one large exchange. This will often get you a better rate.

5. Don't change more than you will need. You'll pay another fee to change the foreign currency back to U.S. dollars.

6. Use a credit card. Typically, any major credit card will give you a better rate than a change booth or bank. Sometimes the spread is substantial, so minimize cash and use credit.

7. Traveler's checks usually have a worse exchange rate than cash. In other words, a $100 American Express traveler's check will give you less in exchange than a $100 bill. If your traveler's checks are lost or stolen, however, they will be replaced, so the peace of mind is usually worth the added expense.

One way to see if you might be cut out to be a global manager is to spend some time abroad. The ideal situation is to find a job overseas during the summer months. This experience will help you decide if you want to be a global manager. Also, it will look good on your résumé. One source of international job information is **http://www.internationaljobs.org/**.

If you can't find a job overseas, save your money and travel abroad. Seeing how others live and work will broaden your horizons and give you a more enlightened view of the world. Even international travel can help you decide what you want to do in the global marketplace.

SUMMARY OF LEARNING GOALS

>lg 1   **Why is global trade important to the United States?**
International trade improves relations with friends and allies, eases tensions among nations, helps bolster economies, raises people's standard of living, and improves the quality of life. The United States is still the largest importer and exporter in the world. We export a fifth of our industrial production and about a third of our farm crops. One out of every 16 jobs in the United States is supported by exports.

>lg 2   **How is global trade measured?**
Two concepts important to global trade are the balance of trade (the difference in value between a country's exports and its imports over some period) and the

>looking ahead

Look back at the opening story about Wal-Mart moving to Europe. Cultural factors, domestic competition, economic conditions, government actions, and regional trade agreements can all make selling in the global marketplace more difficult. Governments can take a number of actions to protect domestic competitors. Some common tactics are tariffs, quotas, embargoes, exchange controls, and buy-national regulations.

There are a number of cultural factors that Wal-Mart should consider when entering the European market. For example, many Europeans shop for groceries every day; there is always an emphasis on freshness. Also, Europeans are not used to shopping at night or on Sundays. Offering late hours will probably not create an immediate rush of business. Wal-Mart may save a little on labor costs as Europeans expect to bag their own groceries.

balance of payments (the difference between a country's total payments to other countries and its total receipts from other countries). The United States now has both a negative balance of trade and a negative balance of payments. Another import concept is the exchange rate, which is the price of one country's currency in terms of another country's currency. Currencies float up and down based upon the supply of and demand for each currency. Sometimes a government steps in and devalues its currency relative to the currencies of other countries.

>lg 3   Why do nations trade?
Nations trade because they gain by doing so. The principle of comparative advantage states that each country should specialize in the goods it can produce most readily and cheaply and trade them for those that other countries can produce most readily and cheaply. The result is more goods at lower prices than if each country produced by itself everything it needed. Free trade allows trade among nations without government restrictions.

>lg 4   What are the barriers to international trade?
The three major barriers to international trade are natural barriers, such as distance and language; tariff barriers, or taxes on imported goods; and nontariff barriers. The nontariff barriers to trade include import quotas, embargoes, buy-national regulations, customs regulations, and exchange controls. The main argument against tariffs is that they discourage free trade and keep the principle of comparative advantage from working efficiently. The main argument for using tariffs is that they help protect domestic companies, industries, and workers.

>lg 5   How do governments and institutions foster world trade?
The World Trade Organization created by the Uruguay Round has dramatically lowered trade barriers worldwide. For the first time a trade agreement covers services, intellectual property rights, and exchange controls. The World Bank makes loans to developing nations to help build infrastructures. The International Monetary Fund makes loans to member nations that cannot meet their budgetary expenses.

>lg 6   What are international economic communities?
International economic communities reduce trade barriers among themselves while often establishing common tariffs and other trade barriers toward non-member countries. The best-known economic communities are the European Union, NAFTA, and Mercosur.

>lg 7   How do companies enter the global marketplace?
There are a number of ways to enter the global market. The major ones are exporting, licensing, contract manufacturing, joint ventures, and direct investment.

KEY TERMS

absolute advantage 52

balance of payments 50

balance of trade 50

contract manufacturing 65

countertrade 66

devaluation 51

direct foreign investment 65

dumping 56

embargo 55

European Union (EU) 60

exchange controls 56

exporting 63

exports 49

floating exchange rates 51

free trade 52

free-trade zone 59

global vision 48

import quota 55

imports 49

infrastructure 67

International Monetary Fund (IMF) 58

joint venture 65

licensing 63

Maastricht Treaty 60

Mercosur 60

multinational corporations 69

nationalism 66

North American Free Trade Agreement (NAFTA) 59

preferential tariff 59

principle of comparative advantage 52

protectionism 52

protective tariffs 54

tariff 54

trade deficit 50

trade surplus 50

Uruguay Round 56

World Bank 58

World Trade Organization (WTO) 58

>lg 8   **What threats and opportunities exist in the global marketplace?**

Domestic firms entering the international arena need to consider the politics, economies, and culture of the countries where they plan to do business. For example, government trade policies can be loose or restrictive, countries can be nationalistic, and governments can change. In the area of culture, many products fail because companies don't understand the culture of the country where they are trying to sell their products. Some developing countries also lack an economic infrastructure, which often makes it very difficult to conduct business.

>lg 9   **What are the advantages of multinational corporations?**

Multinational corporations have several advantages. First, they can sidestep restrictive trade and licensing restrictions because they frequently have headquarters in more than one country. Multinationals can also move their operations from one country to the next depending on which location offers more favorable economic conditions. In addition, multinationals can tap into a vast source of technological expertise by drawing upon the knowledge of a global workforce.

>lg 10   **What are the trends in the global marketplace?**

Global business activity will continue to escalate due to several factors. Firms that desire a larger customer base or need additional resources will continue to seek opportunities outside their country's borders. When an organization moves into a new global market, competitors typically follow its lead and enter the same new market. In addition, technological improvements in communication and transportation will continue to fuel growth in global markets by making it easier to sell and distribute products internationally.

PREPARING FOR TOMORROW'S WORKPLACE

1. How can a country's customs create barriers to trade? Ask foreign students to describe such barriers in their country. American students should give examples of problems that foreign businesspeople might experience with American customs.

2. Should Great Britain be admitted to NAFTA? Why might Britain not wish to join?

3. Write a paper on how the euro may affect American business.

4. Divide the class into teams. Each team should choose a country and research its infrastructure to determine how it will help or hinder trade. Include a variety of countries, ranging from the most highly developed to the least developed.

5. What do you think is the best way for a small company to enter international trade? Why?

6. What impact have foreign multinationals had on the U.S. economy? Give some examples.

7. Write a paper on why countertrade will probably continue to grow.

8. Identify some U.S. multinational companies that have been successful in world markets. How do you think they have achieved their success?

WORKING THE NET

1. Go to the market access database maintained by the U.S. International Trade Department at **http://mac.doc.gov/TCC/DATA/index_reports.html.** Pick a country that interests you from the index and read either the Commercial Guide or the Report on Trade Practices for that country. Would this country

be a good market for a small U.S. clothing manufacturer interested in expanding internationally? Why or why not? What are the main barriers to trade the company might face?

2. Review the historical data about exchange rates between the U.S. dollar and the Japanese yen available at **http://ia.ita.doc.gov/exchange.** List any trends you spot. What years would have been best for a U.S. company to enter the Japanese marketplace? Given current exchange rate conditions, do you think Japanese companies are increasing or decreasing their exporting efforts in the United States?

3. Pretend that you are the president of a mid-sized U.S. software company who is trying to decide whether to export. Read several of the articles in the Software Export Guide at **http://www.swexport.com.** What opportunities might exporting hold for your firm? What barriers might you face?

4. Visit Export Today's Global Business Online site at **http://www.gbmag.com.** Read one of the articles from the current issue. Make a list of additional information you would need if you were the owner of a business affected by the events described in the article. Do a search on the search engine AltaVista, **http://www.altavista.com,** to uncover additional Internet sites related to the topic. Pick one site and write a review of the information and resources available on it. Rate the usefulness of the site and the information it offers.

CREATIVE THINKING CASE

Adaptive Eyecare Limited

Professor Joshua Silver is a physicist at Oxford University who spends much of his time exploring the mysteries of subatomic particles. But for the last 13 years he has quietly pursued a more earthly passion: to devise low-cost adjustable spectacles for the 1 billion people in the world who need glasses, but don't have them. He also hopes to turn some of these people into paying customers.

The lenses of Silver's glasses are made from pairs of transparent plastic membranes, filled with a colorless silicone fluid. Attached to the spectacle frame are two circular "focus adjusters," which contain the fluid. A user can adjust the power of the lenses by twirling the adjusters. This injects fluid through a tiny hole in the frame.

A fatter lens increases magnification, helping those who are nearsighted; a thinner lens reduces magnification, helping the farsighted. Once each eye has been properly focused, the adjusters are snapped off, sealing the holes, and the spectacles are ready for use.

A pair could cost as little as $10. There is no need for a vision test, a visit to an optician, or an expensive prescription. "There's a strong argument to get these specs out to the millions of people who need them," says Bjorn Thylefors, who heads the World Health Organization's campaign to prevent blindness and has seen Silver's glasses. He calls the lack of spectacles "a sizable health problem in the developing world, with economic and educational repercussions."

Silver's start-up, Adaptive Eyecare Ltd., hopes to sell the glasses, for a profit, in developing countries. It has assembled a management group, including two manufacturing optometrists and a business consultant.

I N F O T R A C® COLLEGE EDITION **Critical Thinking Questions**

1. Should Professor Silver "go global"?
2. If so, how should he enter the global marketplace?
3. What are several threats and opportunities Adaptive Eyecare may face?
4. Will the product be successful in the United States? In Ghana?

VIDEO CASE

Enforcement Technology, Inc.

Enforcement Technology, Inc., or ETEC (**http://www.autocite.com/**), located in Irvine, California, specializes in utilizing computer technology to address selected law enforcement challenges. ETEC's products are used primarily in parking and traffic enforcement and related purposes. AutoCITE and AutoPARK form the core of ETEC's business.

AutoCITE (Automated Citation Issuance System) is a portable citation system used by police and campus parking enforcement departments worldwide for issuing parking and traffic tickets. The AutoCITE device has a built-in printer, display, and user-friendly keyboard. It weighs less than three pounds and is designed to be held in one hand. AutoCITE is also programmed to schedule court appearances and "also uses the violator's birth date to reassign juveniles to a juvenile court appearance." With AutoCITE, a police officer can quickly check drivers' license information against law enforcement databases. "Using a pre-stored 'hotsheet,' the AutoCITE will alert the officer with 'wants or warrants' keyed to the driver's license number and/or name."

AutoPARK is an automated parking citation management system and ticket processing service. Used to handle millions of citations for clients, AutoPARK covers all aspects of processing parking citations and collecting parking fines. The system's features include handheld computer issuance of parking tickets, ticket book inventory management, Department of Motor Vehicle (DMV) registered owner address inquiries, generation and mailing of notices, court scheduling, collections, a residential/parking permit system, and interfaces with DMV reporting systems.

ETEC markets its AutoCITE and AutoPARK systems throughout the United States and the world. One method that ETEC uses to reach potential customers is by being an exhibitor at trade shows such as the International Parking Conference and Exposition. This conference is attended by representatives from small, medium, and large cities throughout North America, Latin America, Asia, and Europe, as well as from American colleges and universities, domestic and international airports, major hospital systems in North America, commercial parking operations in North and Central America, and large theme parks in the United States.

ETEC's pursuit of a global distribution strategy is not without its challenges, however. In particular, ETEC must adapt the AutoCITE and AutoPARK systems to the language and legal requirements of the various nations where it markets its products and services.

Critical Thinking Questions

1. Why would a company like ETEC wish to pursue global marketing of its products?
2. How can trade shows help a company implement its business strategy?
3. What trends have influenced and will continue to influence ETEC's global business strategy?

Case: REI Rides the Web to Japan

Seattle-based Recreation Equipment Inc. (REI) was started in 1938 by a group of 23 mountain climbers in the Pacific Northwest. Seeking quality climbing equipment at reasonable prices, they formed a buying cooperative. REI now has 1.5 million members who pay a one-time membership fee of $15 and receive an annual dividend from the company equal to about 10 percent of the purchases they make. Helping customers make informed purchases and providing a broad variety of choices have always been central focuses at REI.

Launched in 1996, REI's Web site, **http://www.REI. com,** was an immediate success. Developed and maintained in-house, the site offered 10,000 products and over 45,000 pages of original content, including product descriptions and tips, feature articles, and tutorials on outdoor activities in five languages. "Our value proposition for REI.com is to deliver any product, at any time, to any place, and to answer any question," said Matt Hyde, online vice president.

Although REI.com received orders from around the world, nearly half came from Japan. The number of Internet users in Japan is second only to the United States and analysts predict that Japanese consumers will buy $8 billion over the Internet by 2001. There was no REI store in Japan, yet REI has 86,000 Japanese members who order products via catalog. Based on these facts, REI decided to develop a fully-translated Japanese Internet site.

Creating the site was complex. REI hired native Japanese speakers to write and develop it. Cultural differences had to be addressed. For example, when a customer orders a product that is out-of-stock at REI.com, they see a "sorry" message next to a figure shrugging with his palms up. In Japan, this gesture is considered impolite, so the figure was replaced with a bowing figure.

The site debuted with just 1,000 products for sale, and prices were shown in dollars. REI management planned to ship orders from the United States initially, although they hoped to eventually be able to ship within Japan. This would allow for a greater number of products, pricing in Japanese yen, and faster delivery.

Questions for Critical Thinking

1. Do you agree with REI's decision to open a Web site specifically for Japanese consumers? What alternatives could REI use to reach this market?
2. Do you think that the "value proposition" for the Japanese site is different than for the REI.com site?
3. What are REI's main barriers to trade in Japan via the Internet?
4. Would you recommend that REI launch specialized sites for other countries? Explain.

SOURCES: Lawrence M. Fisher, "REI Climbs Online: A Clicks-and-Mortar Chronicle," *ECompany,* First Quarter, 2000, downloaded from **http://www.ecompany.com,** September 17, 2000; Ken Yamada, "REI Treks to Profits on Web," *RedHerring.com,* May 9, 2000; REI Company press releases, downloaded from **http://www.REI.com.**

learning goals

>lg 1   What philosophies and concepts shape personal ethical standards, and what are the stages of ethical development?

>lg 2   How can managers influence organizational ethics?

>lg 3   What are the techniques for creating employee ethical awareness?

>lg 4   What is social responsibility?

>lg 5   How do businesses meet their social responsibilities to various stakeholders?

>lg 6   What are the global and domestic trends in ethics and social responsibility?

Making Ethical Decisions and Managing a Socially Responsible Business

chapter 3

Searching for Solutions at the Miami International Airport

Smarte Carte luggage carts can be found in most major airports. But are they available at the Miami International Airport, the world's twelfth largest airport? Not until recently. Each year, tens of millions of passengers passed through Miami International toting everything from tractor tires to swing sets. Yet there were no luggage carts.

Letters from disgruntled travelers poured in to the airport offices, pleading for carts. "I can't carry six bags and do not intend on paying a porter each time I need to use the bathroom," writes Nomi Lyonns of Vancouver, British Columbia. Even airport officials professed shame. "Last year, I was in an airport in Foz do Iguacu" (on Brazil's border with Paraguay), says Hernando Vergara, a spokesman for the Miami airport. "It had carts. It's kind of embarrassing we don't have them."

From Smarte Carte, Inc. headquarters in White Bear Lake, Minnesota, Miami airport looks like the mother lode of luggage concessions. Smarte Carte's chief executive officer, Brad Stanius, has lusted after its business for at least 12 years. "It's a no-brainer," says Stanius, whose company has a virtual lock on the U.S. market, with carts in 159 U.S. airports and 21 abroad.

But managers at the Miami airport do business in ways that leave outsiders and investors dumbfounded, especially at the airport. "No one seems to get a deal in the airport unless they have a local contractor in partnership who has the right political connections," complains Allen Harper, a real estate executive and chairman of the transportation commission at the Greater Miami Chamber of Commerce. "It really ties things up."

Smarte Carte, however, has been nothing if not persistent. For years, airport directors balked at luggage carts, fretting that they would jam the narrow concourses. By 1990, however, airport officials began warming to the idea. The lack of carts had become the No. 1 complaint among passengers. Smarte Carte, at the airport's invitation, brought down a couple of demonstration carts.

Airport executives spent weeks rolling them down ramps and handing them off to passengers. "Wherever we went, people asked us, 'Where did you get the cart?'" says Rick Elder, the airport director at the time. In the mid-1990s, airport officials took off on a 10-day around-the-world trip to airports in Singapore, Hong Kong, San Francisco, Frankfurt, and New York to study cart concessions and other amenities—bathrooms, for instance. (Frankfurt, which has carts that can scale escalators, was their favorite.) They returned home energized. "The vision was to make Miami International Airport the best airport in the world," says John Van Wezel, who headed the cart effort.

Critical Thinking Questions:

As you read this chapter, consider the following questions as they relate to the Miami International Airport:

- Has the Miami Airport Authority acted in an ethical and responsible manner?
- Was it ethical for airport officials to go on an around-the-world trip to evaluate carts?
- Would it have been ethical for Smarte Carte to enter into a partnership with Albo?

About that same time, Lazaro Albo, a prominent political fund-raiser and a close friend of several county commissioners, had a vision of his own. He formed his own airport-cart company, called Miami Baggage Cart, Inc. He didn't have any carts, employees, or experience. But he did have one thing Smarte Carte lacked: connections. "Politics is my hobby," says Albo, a Cuban exile. "I have lived in Miami for 40 years. I have friends—lawyers, judges, county commissioners. I help my friends."

Albo says he got Smarte Carte's phone number off a cart at some other airport and arranged a meeting with the company in Minnesota. But the negotiations went nowhere. Smarte Carte, which charges passengers about $1.50 to use its carts, was willing to give Albo 20 percent of the proceeds to satisfy a county requirement that any airport service contract must include a "minority" partner with a 20 percent interest. (A long list of approved minorities includes women, African Americans, Hispanics, Asians, and Native Americans.) Albo wanted 50 percent of the profits and a consulting contract to help oversee operations. Finally, Smarte Carte paid lobbyists almost $200,000 and only then received the cart concession in 1999.[1]

BUSINESS IN THE 21ST CENTURY

ethics

A set of moral standards for judging whether something is right or wrong.

Every day, managers and business owners like Lazaro Albo make business decisions based on what they believe to be right and wrong. Through their actions, they demonstrate to their employees what is and is not acceptable behavior and shape the moral standard of the organization. **Ethics** is a set of moral standards for judging whether something is right or wrong. As you will see in this chapter, personal and professional ethics are important cornerstones of an organization and shape its ultimate contributions to society. First, let's consider how individual business ethics are formed.

INDIVIDUAL BUSINESS ETHICS

>lg 1

Individual business ethics are shaped by personal choices and the environments in which we live and work. In addition, the laws of our society are guideposts for choosing between right and wrong. This section describes personal philosophies and legal factors that influence the choices people make when confronting ethical dilemmas.

Utilitarianism

utilitarianism

A philosophy that focuses on the consequences of an action to determine whether it is right or wrong; holds that an action that affects the majority adversely is morally wrong.

One of the philosophies that may influence choices between right and wrong is **utilitarianism,** which focuses on the consequences of an action taken by a person or organization. The notion that "people should act so as to generate the greatest good for the greatest number" is derived from utilitarianism. When an action affects the majority adversely, it is morally wrong. One problem with this philosophy is that it is nearly impossible to accurately determine how a decision will affect a large number of people. Another problem is that utilitarianism always involves both winners and losers. If sales are slowing and a manager decides to fire 5 people rather than putting everyone on a 30-hour workweek, the 20 people who keep their full-time jobs are winners, but the other 5 are losers.

A final criticism of utilitarianism is that some "costs," although small relative to the potential good, are so negative that some segments of society find them unacceptable. Reportedly, the backs of up to 3,000 animals a year are deliberately broken so that scientists can conduct spinal cord research that could someday lead to a cure for spinal cord injuries. To a number of people, however, the "costs" are simply too horrible for this type of research to continue.

Individual Rights

In our society, individuals and groups have certain rights that exist under certain conditions regardless of any external circumstances.[2] These rights serve as guides when making individual ethical decisions. The term *human rights* implies that certain rights—to life, to freedom, to the pursuit of happiness—are conveyed at birth and cannot be arbitrarily taken away. Denying the rights of an individual or group is considered to be unethical and illegal in most, though not all, parts of the world. Certain rights are guaranteed by the government and its laws, and these are considered *legal rights*. The U.S. Constitution and its amendments, as well as state and federal statutes, define the rights of American citizens. Those rights can be disregarded only in extreme circumstances, such as during wartime. Legal rights include the freedom of religion, speech, and assembly; protection from improper arrest and searches and seizures; and proper access to counsel, confrontation of witnesses, and cross-examination in criminal prosecutions. Also held to be fundamental is the right to privacy in many matters. Legal rights are to be applied without regard to race, color, creed, gender, or ability.

Justice—the Question of Fairness

justice
What is considered fair according to the prevailing standards of society; in the twentieth century, an equitable distribution of the burdens and rewards that society has to offer.

Another factor influencing individual business ethics is **justice**, or what is fair according to prevailing standards of society.[3] We all expect life to be reasonably fair. You expect your exams to be fair, the grading to be fair, and your wages to be fair, based on the type of work being done.

In the 21st century, we take *justice* to mean an equitable distribution of the burdens and rewards that society has to offer. The distributive process varies from society to society. Those in a democratic society believe in the "equal pay for equal work" doctrine, in which individuals are rewarded based on the value the free market places on their services. Because the market places different values on different occupations, the rewards, such as wages, are not necessarily equal. Nevertheless, many regard the rewards as just. A politician who argued that a supermarket clerk should receive the same pay as a physician, for example, would not receive many votes from the American people. At the other extreme, communist theorists have argued that justice would be served by a society in which burdens and rewards were distributed to individuals according to their abilities and their needs, respectively.

Stages of Ethical Development

preconventional ethics
A stage in the ethical development of individuals in which people behave in a childlike manner and make ethical decisions in a calculating, self-centered, selfish way, based on the possibility of immediate punishment or reward.

We can view an individual's ethical development as having reached one of three levels: preconventional, conventional, or postconventional. The behavior of a person at the level of **preconventional ethics** is childlike in nature; it is calculating, self-centered, and even selfish, based on the possibility of immediate punishment or reward. Thus, a student may not cheat on a test because she is afraid of receiving a failing grade for the course. The student's behavior is based not on a sense of what's right or wrong, but instead on the threat of punishment.

conventional ethics

The second stage in the ethical development of individuals in which people move from an egocentric viewpoint to consider the expectations of an organization of society.

HOT
l i n k s

Find out which companies test their products on animals and which don't at

http://www.peta-online.org/mall/cc.html

Conventional ethics moves from an egocentric viewpoint toward the expectations of society. Loyalty and obedience to the organization (or society) become paramount. At the conventional ethics level, a businessperson might say, "I know that our advertising is somewhat misleading, but as long as it will increase sales we should continue the campaign." Right or wrong is not the issue; the only question is whether the campaign will benefit the organization.

postconventional ethics

The third stage in the ethical development of individuals in which people adhere to the ethical standards of a mature adult and are less concerned about how others view their behavior than about how they will judge themselves in the long run.

Postconventional ethics represents the ethical standards of the mature adult. At the postconventional level, businesspeople are concerned less about how others might see them and more about how they see and judge themselves over the long run. A person who has attained this ethical level might ask, "Even though this action is legal and will increase company profits, is it right in the long run? Might it do more harm than good in the end?" A manager at a soda bottler might refuse to offer disposable cans because he knows a certain percentage would end up as litter. An advertising agency manager might refuse a tobacco account because of the health hazards of smoking. A lab technician might refuse to recommend a new whitener for a detergent because it could harm the environment. All of these individuals are exhibiting postconventional morality.

Many people believe that the Internet is a vast anonymous place where they can say and do just about anything. When they think that they can't be caught, they sometimes revert to preconventional ethics. Yet e-mail servers owned by businesses and governmental agencies can quickly tell what is being sent and to whom. In the state of Washington, state auditors and ethics officials are trying to stem Internet ethics violations, as the Applying Technology box describes.

c o n c ə p t   c h ə c k

- Define ethics.
- What is utilitarianism?
- Discuss the stages of ethical development.

HOW ORGANIZATIONS INFLUENCE ETHICAL CONDUCT

>lg 2

People choose between right and wrong based on their personal code of ethics. They are also influenced by the ethical environment created by their employers. Consider the following newspaper headlines that announce legal claims against organizations that failed to manage their employees ethically:

- "Texaco's $176M Race Bias Settlement Gets Tentative OK." Then, adding to this financial hit: "Rights Groups Urge Boycott of Texaco" and "Stock Drops in Latest Fallout from Bias Case." Still more: "Texaco Agrees to Report to EEOC on Promotion of Racial Minorities."
- "Publix Super Markets Will Pay $81.5 Million to Settle Bias Suit." This figure includes plaintiffs' legal fees and "$2.5 million for monitoring the company's compliance."
- "Home Depot Pays $87.5 Million for Not Promoting More Women" and "Home Depot's Agreement to Settle Suit Could Cut 3rd-Quarter Earnings by 21%."[4]

As these headlines illustrate, poor business ethics can be very expensive for a company. Organizations can reduce the potential for these types of liability claims by educating their employees about ethical standards through various

HEY, YOU! BACK TO WORK

The Information Superhighway is a playground for some public employees. State auditors and ethics officials are doing their best to stem abuse, but it will take ongoing scrutiny to stop surfing for pleasure on taxpayers' dime.

The law prohibits use of public computers for private work or play. Yet, according to the state Auditor's Office, in the last two years, 14 investigations of whistle-blower complaints about computer misuse have been substantiated and three more are pending. Among the activities investigated: using the Internet to run sports betting pools, conducting private business or hobbies, and installing and playing recreational games during work time.

Taxpayers don't have to wait for the Auditor's Office or curious reporters to catch Web weasels in the act. Watchdogs can use technology to fight back. Using a free, online search tool called DejaNews, Dave Wickham of Cle Elum discovered the variety of ways state workers waste their time online. His web site **http://www.adsnet.net/wickhamd/indexs.htm** blows the whistle on cyber-slacking public employees throughout the country. By identifying the government domain name on e-mail messages posted to Internet bulletin boards, Wickham found:

- A Department of Health and Human Services worker running a fly-fishing business online;
- A Department of Ecology official giving advice on making homemade explosives;
- A Department of Revenue employee opining about the "Goddam United States";
- Another DSHS employee posting over a dozen messages about her favorite episodes of "The Simpsons."

We all may have an occasional hankering for Solitaire between meetings. But public employees continually abusing desktop computers and Internet access make it all too easy for government bashers eager to pounce on new examples of government and bureaucratic waste.

Critical Thinking Questions

1. Although what Washington state employees were doing was against the law, was their behavior unethical in each case?
2. At what level of ethical development are these workers?

informal and formal programs. The first step, however, in making a good ethical decision is to recognize unethical business activities when they occur.

Recognizing Unethical Business Actions

Researchers from Brigham Young University tell us that all unethical business activities will fall into one of the following categories:

1. *Taking things that don't belong to you.* The unauthorized use of someone else's property or taking property under false pretenses is taking something that does not belong to you. Even the smallest offense, such as using the postage meter at your office for mailing personal letters or exaggerating your travel expenses, belongs in this category of ethical violations.

2. *Saying things you know are not true.* Often, when trying for a promotion and advancement, fellow employees discredit their coworkers. Falsely assigning blame or inaccurately reporting conversations is lying. Although "This is the way the game is played around here" is a common justification, saying things that are untrue is an ethical violation.

3. *Giving or allowing false impressions.* The salesperson who permits a potential customer to believe that cardboard boxes will hold the customer's tomatoes

for long-distance shipping when the salesperson knows the boxes are not strong enough has given a false impression. A car dealer who fails to disclose that a car has been in an accident is misleading potential customers.

4. *Buying influence or engaging in a conflict of interest.* A conflict of interest occurs when the official responsibilities of an employee or government official are influenced by the potential for personal gain. Suppose a company awards a construction contract to a firm owned by the father of the state attorney general while the state attorney general's office is investigating that company. If this construction award has the potential to shape the outcome of the investigation, a conflict of interest has occurred.

5. *Hiding or divulging information.* Failing to disclose the results of medical studies that indicate your firm's new drug has significant side effects is the ethical violation of hiding information that the product could be harmful to purchasers. Taking your firm's product development or trade secrets to a new place of employment constitutes the ethical violation of divulging proprietary information.

6. *Taking unfair advantage.* Many current consumer protection laws were passed because so many businesses took unfair advantage of people who were not educated or were unable to discern the nuances of complex contracts. Credit disclosure requirements, truth-in-lending provisions, and new regulations on auto leasing all resulted because businesses misled consumers who could not easily follow the jargon of long, complex agreements.

7. *Committing improper personal behavior.* Although the ethical aspects of an employee's right to privacy are still debated, it has become increasingly clear that personal conduct outside the job can influence performance and company reputation. Thus, a company driver must abstain from substance abuse because of safety issues. Even the traditional company Christmas party and picnic have come under scrutiny due to the possibility that employees at and following these events might harm others through alcohol-related accidents.

8. *Abusing another person.* Suppose a manager sexually harasses an employee or subjects employees to humiliating corrections in the presence of customers. In some cases, laws protect employees. Many situations, however, are simply interpersonal abuse that constitutes an ethical violation.

9. *Permitting organizational abuse.* Many U.S. firms with operations overseas, such as Levi Strauss, The Gap, and Esprit, have faced issues of organizational abuse. The unfair treatment of workers in international operations appears in the form of child labor, demeaning wages, and excessive work hours. Although a business cannot change the culture of another country, it can perpetuate—or stop—abuse through its operations there.

10. *Violating rules.* Many organizations use rules and processes to maintain internal controls or respect the authority of managers. Although these rules may seem burdensome to employees trying to serve customers, a violation may be considered an unethical act.

11. *Condoning unethical actions.* What if you witnessed a fellow employee embezzling company funds by forging her signature on a check that was to be voided? Would you report the violation? A winking tolerance of others' unethical behavior is itself unethical.[5]

Resolving Ethical Problems in Business

In many situations, there are no right or wrong answers. Instead, organizations must provide a process to resolve the dilemma quickly and fairly. Two approaches for resolving ethical problems are the "three-questions test" and the newspaper test.

The Three-Questions Test   In evaluating an ethical problem, managers can use the three-questions test to determine the most ethical response: "Is it legal?" "Is it balanced?" and "How does it make me feel?" Companies such as Southwest Airlines, Texas Instruments, Marriott, and McDonald's rely on this test to guide employee decision making. If the answer to the first question is "no," then don't do it. Many ethical dilemmas, however, involve situations that aren't illegal. For example, the sale of tobacco is legal in the United States. But, given all the research that shows that tobacco use is dangerous to one's health, is it an ethical activity?

The second question, "Is it balanced?" requires you to put yourself in the position of other parties affected by your decision. For example, as an executive, you might not favor a buyout of your company because you will probably lose your job. Shareholders, however, may benefit substantially from the price to be paid for their shares in the buyout. At the same time, the employees of the business and their community may suffer economically if the purchaser decides to close the business or focus its efforts in a different product area. The best situation, of course, is when everybody wins or shares the burden equally.

The final question, "How does it make me feel?" asks you to examine your comfort with a particular decision. Many people find that after reaching a decision on an issue they still experience discomfort that may manifest itself in a loss of sleep or appetite. Those feelings of conscience can serve as a guide in resolving ethical dilemmas.

Read more about the ethical issues facing businesses at http://condor.depaul.edu/ethics/

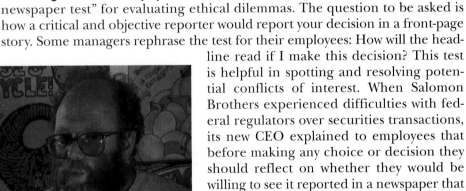

Employees of Ben & Jerry's are influenced by the ethical values of company founders Ben Cohen and Jerry Greenfield, who created an environment of equity in compensating employees.

Front Page of the Newspaper Test   Many managers use the "front page of the newspaper test" for evaluating ethical dilemmas. The question to be asked is how a critical and objective reporter would report your decision in a front-page story. Some managers rephrase the test for their employees: How will the headline read if I make this decision? This test is helpful in spotting and resolving potential conflicts of interest. When Salomon Brothers experienced difficulties with federal regulators over securities transactions, its new CEO explained to employees that before making any choice or decision they should reflect on whether they would be willing to see it reported in a newspaper that their family, friends, and communities would read.[6]

Leading by Example

Employees often follow the examples set by their managers. That is, leaders and managers establish patterns of behavior that determine what's acceptable and what's not within the organization. While Ben Cohen was president of Ben & Jerry's ice cream, he followed a policy that no one could earn a salary more than seven times the lowest-paid worker. He wanted all employees to feel that they were equal (remember the "balance

>lg 3

Ben & Jerry's recently announced that it would no longer use bleached paper for its ice cream cartons because the chemicals used in the bleaching process pollute the environment. For a closer look at why and how Ben & Jerry's made this decision, travel to

http://lib.benjerry.com/ pressrel/unbleached.html

Discover what Texas Instruments's "Ethics Quick Test" includes at

http://www.ti.com/corp/ docs/company/citizen/ ethics/quicktest.shtml

question"). At the time he resigned, company sales were $140 million and the lowest-paid worker earned $19,000 per year. Ben Cohen's salary was $133,000 based on the "seven times" rule. A typical top executive of a $140 million company might have earned ten times Cohen's salary. Ben Cohen's actions helped shape the ethical values of Ben & Jerry's.

Ethics Training

In addition to providing a system to resolve ethical dilemmas, organizations also provide formal training to develop an awareness of questionable business activities and practice appropriate responses. About 35 percent of all American companies have some type of ethics training programs.[7] The ones that are most effective, like those created by Levi Strauss, American Express, and Campbell Soup Company, begin with techniques for solving ethical dilemmas such as those discussed earlier. Next, employees are presented with a series of situations and asked to come up with the "best" ethical solution. One of these ethical dilemmas is shown in Exhibit 3-1.[8] Some companies have tried to add a bit of excitement and fun to their ethics training programs by presenting them in the form of games. Citigroup, for example, has created The Work Ethic, a board game in which participants strive to correctly answer legal, regulatory, policy-related, and judgment ethics questions.

e x h i b i t   3 - 1 | An Ethical Dilemma Used for Employee Training

Donations and Vendors

As CEO of a large Chicago hotel, you and your purchasing manager are in the midst of the annual review of several vendors' contracts. One of the suppliers is Sherman Distributors, a restaurant supply company that furnishes straws, salt, pepper, condiments, and related items for the restaurants and room service in your hotel. Your spouse, an associate dean at a local university's business school, has informed you that Sherman's CEO, who serves on the school's council of advisers, has mentioned Sherman's supply contract and a willingness to endow a scholarship fund. Your spouse's primary area of responsibility at the school is fund-raising.

Discussion Questions
1. What ethical issues does the situation raise?
2. Would it make a difference if Sherman's bid were the lowest?
3. Would renewing Sherman's contract create an appearance of impropriety?
4. What would you do to avoid negative perceptions?
5. Should the university be concerned about perceptions?

Establishing a Formal Code of Ethics

code of ethics

A set of guidelines prepared by a firm to provide its employees with the knowledge of what the firm expects in terms of their responsibilities and behavior toward fellow employees, customers, and suppliers.

Most large companies and thousands of smaller ones have created, printed, and distributed codes of ethics. In general, a **code of ethics** provides employees with the knowledge of what their firm expects in terms of their responsibilities and behavior toward fellow employees, customers, and suppliers. Some ethical codes offer a lengthy and detailed set of guidelines for employees. Others are not really codes at all but rather summary statements of goals, policies, and priorities. Some companies have their codes framed and hung on office walls or printed on cards to be carried at all times by executives. The code of ethics for Costco Wholesale, the chain of membership warehouse clubs, is shown in Exhibit 3-2.

Do codes of ethics make employees behave in a more ethical manner? Some people believe that they do. Others think that they are little more than public relations gimmicks. One research study found that corporate codes of ethics were not influential in determining a person's ethical decision-making behavior.[9]

Fortunately, most workers only rarely face an ethical dilemma. A survey of 1,002 American adults found that 75 percent had never been asked or told to do something that they thought was unethical on the job.[10] Of those who were asked to do something unethical, 4 out of 10 people did the unethical act. When asked what they would do if they found their boss doing something unethical, most (78 percent) said that they would try to talk to the boss or otherwise try to resolve the situation without losing their jobs. Nine percent said that they would "look the other way" and 5 percent claimed that they would quit. The rest weren't sure what they would do.

When faced with an ethical dilemma, entrepreneurs and large-business managers responded differently, however, as shown in the Focusing on Small Business box.

c o n c ǝ p t   c h ǝ c k

- Discuss two approaches to resolving ethical problems.
- What is the role of top management in organizational ethics?
- What is a code of ethics?

MANAGING TO BE SOCIALLY RESPONSIBLE

>lg 4

social responsibility

The concern of businesses for the welfare of society as a whole; consists of obligations beyond those required by law or contracts.

Acting in an ethical manner is one of the four components of the pyramid of corporate social responsibility. **Social responsibility** is the concern of businesses for the welfare of society as a whole. It consists of obligations beyond those required by law or union contract. This definition makes two important points. First, social responsibility is voluntary. Beneficial action required by law, such as cleaning up factories that are polluting air and water, is not voluntary. Second, the obligations of social responsibility are broad. They extend beyond investors in the company to include workers, suppliers, consumers, and communities.

Exhibit 3-3 portrays economic performance as the foundation for the other three responsibilities. At the same time that a business pursues profits (economic responsibility), however, it is expected to obey the law (legal responsibility); to do what is right, just, and fair (ethical responsibility); and to be a good corporate citizen (philanthropic responsibility). These four components are distinct but together constitute the whole. Still, if the company doesn't make a profit, then the other three responsibilities are moot.

Many companies are already working to make the world a better place to live. Consider these examples:

- Colby Care Nurses, Inc., a home health care service located in Los Angeles County, is offering much-needed health care to predominantly African American and Hispanic communities that are often not covered by other

exhibit 3 - 2 | Costco Wholesale's Code of Ethics

CODE OF ETHICS

By Jim Sinegal

OBEY THE LAW

The law is irrefutable! Absent a moral imperative to challenge a law, we must conduct our business in total compliance with the laws of every community where we do business.

• Comply with all statutes.

• Cooperate with authorities.

• Respect all public officials and their positions.

• Avoid all conflict of interest issues with public officials.

• Comply with all disclosure and reporting requirements.

• Comply with safety and security standards for all products sold.

• Exceed ecological standards required in every community where we do business.

• Comply with all applicable wage and hour laws.

• Comply with all applicable anti-trust laws.

• Protect "inside information" that has not been released to the general public.

TAKE CARE OF OUR MEMBERS

The member is our key to success. If we don't keep our members happy, little else that we do will make a difference.

• Provide top-quality products at the best prices in the market.

• Provide a safe shopping environment in our warehouses.

• Provide only products that meet applicable safety and health standards.

• Sell only products from manufacturers who comply with "truth in advertising/packaging" standards.

• Provide our members with a 100% satisfaction guaranteed warranty on every product and service we sell, including their membership fee.

• Assure our members that every product we sell is authentic in make and in representation of performance.

• Make our shopping environment a pleasant experience by making our members feel welcome as our guests.

• Provide products to our members that will be ecologically sensitive.

Our member is our reason for being. If they fail to show up, we cannot survive. Our members have extended a "trust" to Costco by virtue of paying a fee to shop with us. We can't let them down or they will simply go away. We must always operate in the following manner when dealing with our members:
   Rule #1– The member is always right.
   Rule #2 – In the event the member is ever wrong, refer to rule #1.

There are plenty of shopping alternatives for our members. We will succeed only if we do not violate the trust they have extended to us. We must be committed at every level of our company, with every ounce of energy and grain of creativity we have, to constantly strive to "bring goods to market at a lower price."

If we do these four things throughout our organization, we will realize our ultimate goal, which is to REWARD OUR SHAREHOLDERS.

TAKE CARE OF OUR EMPLOYEES

To claim "people are our most important asset" is true and an understatement. Each employee has been hired for a very important job. Jobs such as stocking the shelves, ringing members' orders, buying products and paying our bills are jobs we would all choose to perform because of their importance. The employees hired to perform these jobs are performing as management's "alter egos." Every employee, whether they are in a Costco warehouse or whether they work in the regional or corporate offices, is a Costco ambassador trained to give our members professional, courteous treatment.

Today we have warehouse managers who were once stockers and callers and vice presidents who were once in clerical positions for our company. We believe that Costco's future executive officers are currently working in our warehouses, depots, buying offices and accounting departments, as well as in our home offices.

To that end, we are committed to these principles:

• Provide a safe work environment.

• Pay a fair wage.

• Make every job challenging, but make it fun!

• Consider the loss of any employee as a failure on the part of the company and a loss to the organization.

• Teach our people how to do their jobs and how to improve personally and professionally.

• Promote from within the company to achieve the goal of a minimum of 80% of management positions being filled by current employees.

• Create an "open door" attitude at all levels of the company that is dedicated to "fairness and listening."

RESPECT OUR VENDORS

Our vendors are our partners in business, and for us to prosper as a company, they must prosper with us. It is important that our vendors understand that we will be tough negotiators but fair in our treatment of them.

• Treat all vendors and their representatives as you would expect to be treated if visiting their places of business.

• Pay all bills within the allocated time frame.

• Honor all commitments.

• Protect all vendor property assigned to Costco as though it were our own.

• Always be thoughtful and candid in negotiations.

• Provide a careful review process with at least two levels of authorization before terminating business with an existing vendor of more than two years.

• Do not accept gratuities of any kind from a vendor.

These guidelines are exactly that - guidelines, some common sense rules for the conduct of our business. Intended to simplify our jobs, not complicate our lives, these guidelines will not answer every question or solve every problem. At the core of our philosophy as a company must be the implicit understanding that not one of us is required to lie or cheat on behalf of Costco. In fact, dishonest conduct will not be tolerated. To do any less would be unfair to the overwhelming majority of our employees who support and respect Costco's commitment to ethical business conduct.

If you are ever in doubt as to what course of action to take on a business matter that is open to varying ethical interpretations, take the high road and do what is right.

If you want our help, we are always available for advice and counsel. That's our job, and we welcome your questions or comments.

Our continued success depends on you. We thank each of you for your contribution to our past success and for the high standards you have insisted upon in our company.

97HR1005

FOCUSING ON SMALL BUSINESS

ARE ENTREPRENEURS MORE ETHICAL?

In a recent survey of 165 entrepreneurs and 128 large-company business managers, the entrepreneurs proved more apt to regard certain business activities as unethical. Seventy-four percent of the entrepreneurs and 71 percent of the managers said a prescribed code of ethics would help them in making decisions.

The following table presents the actions described to the survey participants and shows the percentage of entrepreneurs and business managers who said each action was unethical.

Critical Thinking Questions

1. Does the survey prove that entrepreneurs are more ethical than business managers?
2. Why would it make a difference if one group were more ethical than the other?
3. Are you surprised at the results? Why or why not?

Business Activity	Percentage Considered Unethical	
	Entrepreneurs	Business Managers
Using company services for personal purposes	82%	72%
Using company supplies for personal purposes	93	86
Overstating an expense account by more than 10%	99	95
Overstating an expense account by less than 10%	93	87
Using company time for personal benefit	81	70
Taking longer than necessary to do a job	91	78

providers. The company prides itself on giving back to the community by employing its residents and providing role models for its young people.

- Wrigley, the Chicago chewing gum maker, is producing a $10 million commercial campaign aimed at getting African, Asian, and Hispanic Americans to use doctors for regular health maintenance instead of as a last resort.
- Ben & Jerry's, the premium ice cream maker, sent seven workers to live with Cree Indians in Canada to see how they've been displaced by a new hydro-electric power complex.
- Jantzen, the world's leading swimsuit manufacturer, makes direct grants through its clean water campaign to organizations that preserve and clean up beaches and waterways.
- Apple Computer donates almost $10 million in computer equipment and advice to U.S. schools annually.
- Ricoh, a Japanese office equipment maker, has developed a reverse copier that strips away the toner and allows the copy paper to be used again.[11]

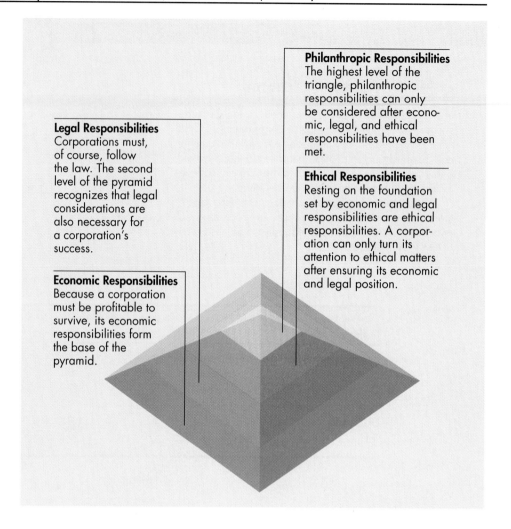

Philanthropic Responsibilities
The highest level of the triangle, philanthropic responsibilities can only be considered after economic, legal, and ethical responsibilities have been met.

Ethical Responsibilities
Resting on the foundation set by economic and legal responsibilities are ethical responsibilities. A corporation can only turn its attention to ethical matters after ensuring its economic and legal position.

Legal Responsibilities
Corporations must, of course, follow the law. The second level of the pyramid recognizes that legal considerations are also necessary for a corporation's success.

Economic Responsibilities
Because a corporation must be profitable to survive, its economic responsibilities form the base of the pyramid.

Understanding Social Responsibility

Peter Drucker, a management expert, said that we should look first at what an organization does *to* society and second at what it can do *for* society. This idea suggests that social responsibility has two basic dimensions: legality and responsibility.

Illegal and Irresponsible Behavior The idea of social responsibility is so widespread today that it is hard to conceive of a company continually acting in illegal and irresponsible ways. Nevertheless, such actions do sometimes occur. For example, Royal Caribbean Cruise Lines, the world's second-largest cruise line, had to pay a $9 million fine for dumping oily bilge waste into the ocean and then lying about it.[12] In another case, Louisiana-Pacific Corp. pleaded guilty to pollution violations and agreed to pay $37 million in penalties, including the biggest criminal fine in the 28-year history of the Clean Air Act. The Portland, Oregon–based timber company was fined $5.5 million under the act for higher-than-allowed emissions from a plant in Colorado that makes floorboards and siding. It was fined an additional $31 million for offenses such as doctoring reports, tampering with pollution-monitoring equipment, and lying to inspectors. U.S. District Judge Lewis Babcock in Denver also placed the company on probation for five years. Louisiana- Pacific will also donate $500,000 to environmental groups under the agreement.[13]

Federal, state, and local laws determine whether an activity is legal or not. The laws that regulate business are discussed in Appendix B.

Irresponsible but Legal Behavior   Sometimes companies act irresponsibly, yet their actions are legal. For example, in 1998 Congress was considering comprehensive tobacco legislation that would curb industry promotion and open the industry to liability lawsuits from the health hazards of smoking. A key aspect of the legislation focused on the 3,000 teenagers who become addicted to smoking each day. The bill included all manner of protections aimed at teenagers: no billboard advertising near schools, serious restrictions on advertising in publications with significant teen readership, and in-store restrictions on cigarette merchandising. The five major U.S. tobacco companies began a six-month, $60 million advertising campaign to kill the legislation. The campaign successfully shifted the focus from the ills of tobacco to the tax and spend policies of Washington. Once the legislation died, the campaign was dropped.[14] Other controversial advertising campaigns include Budweiser's ad featuring talking frogs and lizards and the cuddly Spuds McKenzie. Joe Camel, however, was perhaps the advertising symbol most disliked by activists.

Yoplait's national sponsorship of the Race for the Cure represents a legal and socially responsible activity. The nationwide series of 98 running and fitness walks that draw more than 700,000 participants benefit the Susan G. Komen Breast Cancer Foundation.

Legal and Responsible Behavior The vast majority of business activities fall into the category of behavior that is both legal and responsible. Most firms act legally, and most try to be socially responsible. Lucent Technologies (formerly Bell Labs) each year has 10,000 employees participate in "Global Days of Caring," assisting community projects worldwide. Richard McGinn, chairman of Lucent, says, "Global Days are a celebration of the generosity and spirit of Lucent people who live the value of social responsibility year around."[15] A recent Global Days of Caring found employees working on specific projects in 25 states and 20 countries. The projects included engaging in environmental cleanup, fixing up child care and senior citizens centers, and assisting organizations like Camp DaKaNi in Oklahoma City, home to the local Camp Fire Boys and Girls, which was significantly damaged during a tornado. Ongoing projects include painting maps on elementary school playgrounds to help teach geography and making "smart" teddy bears for children to ease the trauma of a hospital stay. Lucent gives employees paid time off for the projects and provides coordination and money. The company also engages in a number of other socially responsible activities including hiring and training the unemployed, giving equipment and grants to schools, and making grants to community agencies where Lucent employees volunteer.

MAKING ETHICAL CHOICES

COSTAS FOODS

Should business be socially responsible? Can business be socially responsible? Some executives, like Jack Welch, General Electric's CEO, believe that business can and should be socially responsible, but say that the marketplace alone is insufficient for achieving social responsibility. These executives are "calling faith in value-free, self-regulating markets a dangerous illusion and urging governments to protect people and the planet before it's too late." Other people, however, believe that business should be ethically neutral and focus on "profit as the primary measure of corporate success." They argue that the most socially responsible thing a business can do is to make as much profit as possible.

One business that operates on the basis of values and commitment to social responsibility is Costas Foods, an independently owned and operated grocer based in Valparaiso, Indiana. Not only does Costas Foods operate a values-driven business, but it emphasizes a particular set of values—Christian values.

When new employees watch a training video made by owner Bill Costas, they hear about the company's Christian values, not the ins and outs of the grocery

business. Costas talks "to employees about values, how to treat customers, God and the Bible (handed out along with the W-2 forms to every new hire)." But Costas is not holier-than-thou. He also talks of his early days in the grocery business; his struggles with alcohol, marital infidelity, and tax cheating; and how he conquered those challenges through religious faith. That faith became the foundation for Bill Costas, the grocer and businessman. He operates Costas Foods according to Christian values, and all new employees are told that.

Critical Thinking Questions

1. Is it ethical for a business not to be socially responsible? Explain your answer.
2. Should a particular doctrine or set of principles, such as the Christian tradition, be used as the basis of running an ethical business? Why or why not?
3. How might the ethical actions of a business that operates on the basis of religious principles differ, if at all, from those of one that does not?

concept check

- What are the four components of social responsibility?
- Give an example of legal but irresponsible behavior.

Many other companies are also trying to do more. For example, Bristol-Myers, Coca-Cola, General Motors, Exxon Mobil, Ford Motor, Citigroup, JP Morgan, and many others have agreed to help the National Black MBA Association persuade young African Americans to look for executive jobs. The group, which has about 2,000 members, has built a scholarship fund that hands out $450,000 a year.

RESPONSIBILITIES TO STAKEHOLDERS

>lg 5

stakeholders
Individuals or groups to whom a business has a responsibility; include employees, customers, the general public, and investors.

What makes a company admired or perceived as socially responsible? Such a company meets its obligations to its stakeholders. **Stakeholders** are the individuals or groups to whom a business has a responsibility. The stakeholders of a business are its employees, customers, the general public, and investors.

Responsibility to Employees

An organization's first responsibility is to provide a job to employees. Keeping people employed and letting them have time to enjoy the fruits of their labor is the finest thing business can do for society. Beyond this fundamental responsibility, employers must provide a clean, safe working environment that is free from all forms of discrimination. Companies should also strive to provide job security whenever possible.

Enlightened firms are also empowering employees to make decisions on their own and suggest solutions to company problems. Empowerment contributes to an employee's self-worth, which, in turn, increases productivity and reduces absenteeism. The Ritz Carlton hotel chain, for example, empowers *all* employees to solve *any* guest problem on the spot. Dana Corp., an automotive-components manufacturer based in Toledo, Ohio, has created a culture where empowerment has become a reality. The company has implemented a number of programs and practices that encourage and recognize individual contributions. These include a commitment to 40 hours of education for each employee every year; an internal promotion policy in which the people who help create the company's success share in the rewards; a suggestion system in which each employee is encouraged to submit two ideas per month and the company strives for 80 percent implementation of those ideas; an organizational structure that supports individual responsibility; a retirement program that encourages longevity; and a stock-purchase program that encourages eligible employees to own a share of the company.

Levi Strauss's unique corporate culture rewards and recognizes employee achievements. To learn about working for a company that values employee efforts, go to the Levi Strauss home page at
http://www.levistrauss.com

Many companies are doing an excellent job in meeting their responsibilities toward their employees. Each year *Fortune* conducts an extensive survey of the best places to work in America. The top 10 are shown in Exhibit 3-4. Some companies offer unusual benefits to their employees. CMP Media gives employees $30,000 for infertility treatments and adoption aid. FedEx allows free rides in the jump seats of company planes. Steelcase has a 1,200-acre camping and recreational area for employee use.

Responsibility to Customers

A central theme of this text is that to be successful in the new millennium a company must satisfy its customers. Satisfied customers lead to long-term relationships and a long-term stream of revenue and profits for the firm. Poor customer service or shoddy products will drive customers away. However, nothing drives customers away faster or breaks the bonds of a long-term relationship quicker than failure to treat a customer fairly or honestly.

consumer fraud

The practice of deceiving customers by such means as failing to honor warranties or other promises or selling goods or services that do not meet advertised claims.

IOMEGA Corp. learned this lesson the hard way. Recently, the company agreed to provide free customer support via the Internet or by telephone as part of a settlement of a **consumer-fraud** lawsuit. The lawsuit accused the disk drive maker of not honoring product warranties and failing to provide adequate technical support. Customers said they had trouble installing IOMEGA products despite packaging claims that installation was easy. When they tried to call IOMEGA, they learned the company charged up to $19.99 for the help. Even then, they had trouble getting help because technical-support lines were severely understaffed. Customers were often left waiting on hold for an hour or more.[16]

See how IOMEGA now supports customers online at
http://www.IOMEGA.com/support/

Allegations of consumer fraud have also been made in a case involving Computer Learning Centers. Based in Fairfax, Virginia, the company provides training in computer programming, network administration, and other computer skills at 25 centers across the country. The Illinois Attorney General's Office accused the company of making misrepresentations to students who enrolled at its Illinois campus. The company allegedly

e x h i b i t   3 - 4 | America's Best Places to Work

Company (Headquarters Location; Number of U.S. Sites)	Comments
1 Container Store (Dallas; 20)	Why is this small retailer of boxes No. 1? For starters, it pays well. Moreover, it doesn't act like a retailer: After 10 years employees get sabbaticals, and everyone's expected to know daily sales information.
2 Southwest Airlines (Dallas; 67)	Listen to a typical comment from the more than 100 received from enthusiastic employees: "Working here is truly an unbelievable experience. They treat you with respect, pay you well, and empower you. They use your ideas to solve problems. They encourage you to be yourself. I love going to work!"
3 Cisco Systems (San Jose; 126)	The computer network giant is growing fast—adding 5,000 new employees in a year—but still boasts stock options for everyone as well as on-the-spot bonuses of up to $2,000 for exceptional performance.
4 TDIndustries (Dallas; 200)	The employee-owned construction company indexed health-insurance premiums to income: The more you make, the more you pay. Workers get two weeks of paid personal time off after one year.
5 Synovus Financial (Columbus, GA; 343)	Benefits are lush at this credit card processor and bank holding company. Pay for all team members is supplemented by pension and bonuses of up to 21% of gross salary, plus stock options.
6 SAS Institute (Cary, NC; 51)	The world's largest privately held computer software company, SAS Institute offers superb on-site child care for $200 a month, an on-site clinic that offers primary medical care at zero cost to employees, and an award-winning cafeteria, where a pianist plays during lunch. It's no surprise that turnover, at 4% a year, is among the lowest in the software industry.
7 Edward Jones (St. Louis; 4,740)	Most brokers here qualify for twice-a-year, expenses-paid jaunts for two to places like Alaska or Pebble Beach. When it comes to flextime requests, managers are encouraged to "do what is right and human."
8 Charles Schwab (San Francisco; 375)	The anti-Wall Street brokerage certainly seems to work for its employees: Ten percent of them have more than $1 million in their ESOP accounts. Plus massages during busy periods.
9 Goldman Sachs (New York; 19)	When this bastion of Wall Street went public in 1999, after 130 years as a partnership, every employee received a stock award. Those working late into the night are ferried home by a free limo service.
10 MBNA (Wilmington, DE; 21)	If you get married while at this credit card company, you get an extra week of vacation. Stick around to have a family: six child-care centers and college scholarships of up to $32,000 for employees' kids.

SOURCE: Robert Levering and Milton Moskowitz, "The 100 Best Companies to Work For in America," *Fortune* (January 10, 2000), pp. 108–110.

made unrealistic promises of high earning potential and job placement to entice students to sign up for courses. Some students paid the school thousands of dollars. "When students enrolled, they often found overcrowded classrooms, unprepared instructors, few computers, books or other necessary materials," the attorney general said.[17]

Responsibility to the General Public

A business must also be responsible to the general public. A business provides a community with jobs, goods, and services. It also pays taxes that go to support schools, hospitals, and better roads. Most companies try to be good citizens in their communities. Corning, Inc., for example, located in Corning, New York, has made a point of acting responsibly toward its namesake. When the company constructed new headquarters in the early 1990s, it deliberately kept the building's height low enough to avoid overshadowing the town. The corporation also distributes leaflets warning of the dangers of smoking, bulimia, anorexia nervosa, and herpes to its employees, who include half of the town's 12,000 inhabitants.

Environmental Protection   Business is also responsible for protecting and improving the world's fragile environment. The world's forests are being destroyed fast. Every second, an area the size of a football field is laid bare. Plant and animal species are becoming extinct at the rate of 17 per hour. A continent-size hole is opening up in the earth's protective ozone shield. Each year we throw out 80 percent more refuse than we did in 1960; as a result, more than half of the nation's landfills are filled to capacity.

Want to see how the global environment is changing? Go to:

http://edcwww.cr.usgs.gov/earthshots/slow/tableofcontents

To slow the erosion of the world's resources, many companies are becoming more environmentally responsible. Toyota is now using "renewable" energy sources to power its facilities, making it the largest single user of clean power in the world. Toyota's first step in the United States was to turn to renewable sources such as solar, wind, geothermal, and water power for the electricity at its headquarters in Torrance and Irvine, California.

corporate philanthropy
The practice of charitable giving by corporations; includes contributing cash, donating equipment and products, and supporting the volunteer efforts of company employees.

Corporate Philanthropy   Companies also display their social responsibility through corporate philanthropy. **Corporate philanthropy** includes cash contributions, donations of equipment and products, and support for the volunteer efforts of company employees as at Lucent Technologies. Corporate philanthropy totals about $9 billion a year.[18] Coca-Cola has a multiyear $60 million strategic partnership with the Boys and Girls Clubs of America. It funds concerts, sports tournaments, and other activities for club members. Restaurant chain Denny's has become Save the Children's largest corporate supporter—contributing $2.5 million over three years from selling special meals, scarves, and neckties. Tanqueray has spent more than $2 million a year in major markets around the country to sponsor its Tanqueray AIDS Rides—bicycle races that get the attention of consumers between the ages of 25 and 40. The AIDS Rides have picked up a few hitchhikers, including Gatorade and Starbucks.

To preserve the environment, businesses must become more environmentally responsible. These digital images of Earth illustrate how a strip mining firm altered the same area over a 24-year period.

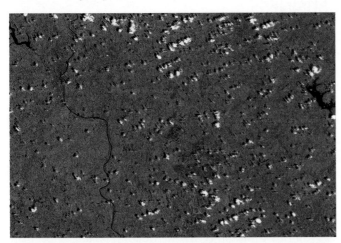

More and more companies are donating products and research findings rather than cash. IBM, for example, donates about $100 million a year to various organizations. About $70 million of IBM's donations are in noncash items. In a recent year, Merck, the giant pharmaceutical firm, donated $5 million in cash and $116 million in noncash items.[19] Such giving makes business sense because companies can value their donations at fair-market prices, rather than the cost to produce them. Better yet, a generous tax law allows corporations to write off the cost of producing the donation as well as the difference between the cost and retail value. In contrast, a business that donates $1 million in cash can write off only that amount.

Responsibilities to Investors

Companies' relationships with investors also entail social responsibility. Although a company's

98/**part one** Participating in the Global Business Environment

Capitalizing on Trends in Business

social investing

The practice of limiting invest-ments to securities of compa-nies that behave in accordance with the investor's beliefs about ethical and social responsibility.

economic responsibility to make a profit might seem to be its main obligation to its shareholders, many investors increasingly are putting more emphasis on other aspects of social responsibility.

Some investors are limiting their investments to securities that fit within their beliefs about ethical and social responsibility. This is called **social investing.** For example, a social investment fund might eliminate from consideration the securities of all companies that make tobacco products or liquor, manufacture weapons, or have a history of polluting. Not all social investment strategies are alike. Some ethical mutual funds will not invest in government securities because they help to fund the military; others freely buy government securities, with managers noting that federal funds also support the arts and pay for AIDS research. Today, about $100 billion is invested in social investment funds.

When investors are dissatisfied with corporate managers, they are less passive than in the past. They are pressuring corporations with tactics such as exposés on television and other media and calling government attention to perceived wrong-doings. Groups of owners are pressuring companies to increase prof-its, link executive pay to performance, and oust inefficient manage-ment. Consequently, executives and managers are giving more weight to the concerns of owner stakeholders in the decision-making process. For example, shareholders of pharmaceutical giant Pfizer forced the company to stop selling flavoring agents to tobacco com-panies. In the 1990s, a number of chief executives from major corpo-rations—General Motors, IBM, Apple, and Eastman Kodak, to name a few—were expelled by dissatisfied investors.[20]

concept check

- How do businesses carry out their social responsibilities to consumers?
- What is corporate philanthropy?
- Is a company's only responsibility to its in-vestors to make a profit? Why or why not?

CAPITALIZING ON TRENDS IN BUSINESS

>lg 6

Three important trends related to ethics and social responsibility for the new millennium are changes in corporate philanthropy, a new social contract be-tween employers and employees, and the growth of global ethics and social re-sponsibility. This section will examine each trend in turn.

Trends in Corporate Philanthropy

strategic giving

The practice of tying philan-thropy closely to the corporate mission or goals and targeting donations to regions where a company operates.

Corporate philanthropy has typically involved seeking out needy groups and then giving them money or company products. Today, the focus is shifting to **strategic giving,** which ties philanthropy more closely to the corporate mission or goals and targets donations to regions where a company operates.

Thomas Kimble is the chairman of the General Motors Foundation, which is GM's philanthropic organization. Kimble notes, "Prior to 1997 our giving was sim-ply for unselfish purposes. Now our thinking is that we need to balance unselfish giving with strategic donations to target groups." Most of the foundation's gifts now go to areas such as education, health and human services, and public policy that are related to GM's corporate goals such as lowering costs. Funding for research on a major health threat such as cancer makes both social and economical sense, GM believes. "Health care was the company's highest cost, so funding health, espe-cially cancer-related research, became a priority," explains Kimble.[21]

Similarly, IBM "focuses like a laser beam" on areas related to its mission as "an information technology solutions provider," says Stanley Litow, IBM's director of community relations.[22] As we noted earlier, product and research donations account for most of the more than $100 million IBM contributes to philanthropic causes each year. IBM launched its nation-wide Reinventing Education effort by singling out a number of school systems, including Philadelphia's public schools, to serve as test centers. The computer giant committed $2 million in research, products, and some 50 employees, including researchers and marketing and technology professionals, who worked over a 22-month period to find ways to boost literacy and improve teaching methods. As a result, IBM adapted the voice recognition technology used in its products to young children's high-pitched voices and pronunciations to come up with software that would enable a child working on a computer to recognize word and sentence patterns.

Corporate philanthropy has also become a target for special-interest groups. AT&T, General Electric, and Eastman Kodak have come under attack by abortion foes for their donations to Planned Parenthood. The conservative Capital Research Center has criticized Anheuser-Busch, Hewlett-Packard, and other manufacturers for supporting what the center claims are radical groups seeking to undermine the capitalist system. When Philip Morris gave money to conservative political causes, the gay activist group ACT-UP encouraged consumers to stop buying its products.

A New Social Contract Trend between Employer and Employee

Another trend in social responsibility is the effort by organizations to redefine their relationship with their employees. Many people have viewed social responsibility as a one-way street that focuses on the obligations of business to society, employees, and others. Now, companies are telling employees that they also have a responsibility when it comes to job security. The new contract goes like this: "There will never be job security. You will be employed by us as long as you add value to the organization, and *you* are continuously responsible for finding ways to add value. In return, you have the right to demand interesting and important work, the freedom and resources to perform it well, pay that reflects your contribution, and the experience and training needed to be employable here or elsewhere." Coca-Cola, for example, requires extensive employee re-training each year. The idea, according to a Coke executive, is to become a more valuable employee by adding 25 percent to your existing knowledge every year.

Hot Links

General Motors is often recognized as a top participant in philanthropic activities. Which charities and organizations does GM support, and how? Read GM's Annual Philanthropic Report online at

http://www.gm.com

Computer firms that link their product donations to schools with their corporate goals represent the corporate philanthropy trend of strategic giving.

Trends in Global Ethics and Social Responsibility

As U.S. businesses expand into global markets, their corporate codes of ethics and policies on social responsibility must travel with them. As a citizen of several countries, a multinational corporation has several responsibilities. These include respecting local practices and customs, ensuring that there is harmony between the organization's staff and the host population, providing management leadership, and developing a cadre of local managers who will be a credit to their community. When a multinational makes an investment in a foreign country, it should commit to a long-term relationship. That means involving all stakeholders in the host country in

Applying This Chapter's Topics

Human rights problems plague athletic shoemaker Nike. When Phil Knight, Nike's chief executive, visited Stanford University, students and faculty protested the company's practice of paying employees working at its contract plants in Asia wages too low to support an adequate living standard.

concept check

- Describe strategic giving.
- What role do employees have in improving their job security?
- How do multinational corporations demonstrate social responsibility in a foreign country?

decision making. Finally, a responsible multinational will implement ethical guidelines within the organization in the host country. By fulfilling these responsibilities, the company will foster respect for both local and international laws.

Multinational corporations often must balance conflicting interests of stakeholders when making decisions regarding social responsibilities, especially in the area of human rights. Questions involving child labor, forced labor, minimum wages, and workplace safety can be particularly difficult. Levi Strauss was strongly praised when it announced it was leaving China in 1993 because of the country's poor human rights record. China is also an inexpensive place to manufacture clothing, and the temptation to stay there was simply too great. In fact, Levi Strauss never stopped making clothes in China; its Hong Kong subsidiary continues to manufacture clothes on a contract basis. Levi recently announced that it would begin selling clothes in China. One might argue that Levi Strauss must remain competitive and profitable, or it will not be able to be a leader in the cause of social responsibility. When the announcement came, however, human rights activists quickly set up a picket at Levi's San Francisco headquarters.[23]

APPLYING THIS CHAPTER'S TOPICS

Are you at the preconventional, conventional, or postconventional stage of ethical development? If you determine that you are at the preconventional level, you should begin striving for a more mature ethical outlook. This may mean taking an ethics course, reading a book on ethics, or engaging in a lot of introspection about yourself and your values. A person with preconventional ethics will probably have a difficult time succeeding in today's business world.

Ethics Are Part of Everyday Life

Realize that ethics play a part in our lives every day. We all must answer questions such as these:

How do I balance the time and energy obligations of my work and my family? How much should I pay my employees? What should I do with the child of my husband's first marriage who is disrupting our new family? How am I spending my money? Should I "borrow" a copy of my friend's software? If I know my employee is having troubles at home, should I treat her differently? What should I do if I know a neighbor's child is getting into serious trouble? How do I react to a sexist or racist joke?

Too many people make decisions about everyday questions without considering the underlying moral and ethical framework of the problems. They are simply swept along by the need to get through the day. Our challenge to you is to always think about the ethical consequences of your actions. Make doing so a habit.

Waiting for dramatic events before consciously tackling ethical considerations is like playing a sport only on the weekend. Just as a weekend warrior often ends

1. **Support a Good Cause** You don't have to wait until graduation to start demonstrating your social responsibility. Go to HubHeaven right now at **http://www.heavens.org**. Heaven seeks to bring about positive social change through a unique mix of innovative initiatives and celebrity involvement. An innovative ANGELS program couples computer training with community service. Heavenly programs include the following:

- Heavenly Bodies. Features celebrities who serve as role models. They describe causes they care about and explain how to get involved in supporting the cause. Participating celebrities include models Tyra Banks, Frederique, and Lauren Wacht; actors Martin Sheen, Billy Baldwin, Malik Yoba, and Andrew Shue; musicians MC Hammer and Adam Yauch; dancer Reg E. Gaines; and political commentator Chris Cuomo.
- Good Company. Profiles and publicizes companies and organizations that effect change.
- Do Something. Provides leadership training, guidance, and grants to those who take action to improve their communities.

- Volunteer Now! Connects young adults with local volunteer opportunities in their areas of interest.
- Cloud Nine. Features issue-oriented articles and essays by leading writers, activists, and artists and encourages participation in dialogue and debate.
- ANGELS (America's Network of Givers, Educators, Linkers, and Servers). Administers a real-world computer training and community service program for inner-city high school students. ANGELS is a nationwide effort to lessen the divide between the information haves and have-nots.

2. **Know Your Ethical Values** To get a better idea of your own level of ethical development, take an ethics test. Go to **http://www. ethicsandbusiness.org/stylequiz.htm**. This test will give you better insight into yourself.

up with pulled muscles and poor performance, people who seldom consider the ethical implications of daily activities won't have the coordination to work through the more difficult times in their lives. Don't let this happen to you.

>looking ahead
at Miami International Airport

Given the hardship that the lack of luggage carts at the Miami International Airport imposed on passengers, many people would argue that the Miami Airport Authority had not acted in an ethical and responsible manner. Mr. Albo seemed to be selling his political connections. Although this is done routinely in the United States and most other countries, many people view this practice as unethical. Also, it is highly unlikely that airport officials needed to go on an around-the-world trip to evaluate luggage carts. Many would also consider this action unethical.

Work for a Firm That Cares about Its Social Responsibilities

When you enter the job market, make certain that you are going to work for a socially responsible organization. Ask a prospective employer "how the company gives back to society." If you plan to work for a large company, check out *Fortune*'s current list of America's most admired corporations. It appears around March 1.

If you plan to work for a multinational, examine *Fortune*'s most globally admired corporations, which appears in October. The list is broken down by industry and includes 10 to 15 companies in each industry. Working for an ethical, socially responsible organization will make you proud of the place where you work.

SUMMARY OF LEARNING GOALS

>lg 1   **What philosophies and concepts shape personal ethical standards, and what are the stages of ethical development?**
Ethics is a set of moral standards for judging whether something is right or wrong. A utilitarianism approach to setting personal ethical standards focuses on the consequences of an action taken by a person or organization. According to this approach, people should act so as to generate the greatest good for the greatest number. Every human is entitled to certain rights such as freedom and the pursuit of happiness. Another approach to ethical decision making is justice, or what is fair according to accepted standards.

There are three stages of ethical development. At the level of preconventional ethics, behavior is childlike in nature and self-centered. Conventional ethics moves from an egocentric point of view toward the expectations of society or an organization. Postconventional ethics represents the ethical standards of the mature adult.

>lg 2   **How can managers influence organizational ethics?**
The first step management should take is to recognize the categories of unethical business actions. Managers should educate employees to use the three-questions test or the front page of the newspaper test when faced with ethical dilemmas. Top management must shape the ethical culture of the organization. They should lead by example.

>lg 3   **What are the techniques for creating employee ethical awareness?**
The most common way companies raise employee ethical awareness is through ethics training. Typically, this involves analyzing and discussing ethical dilemmas. Companies also create and distribute codes of ethics to heighten ethical awareness.

>lg 4   **What is social responsibility?**
Social responsibility is the concern of businesses for the welfare of society as a whole. It consists of obligations beyond just making a profit. Social responsibility also goes beyond what is required by law or union contract. Companies may engage in illegal and irresponsible behavior, irresponsible but legal behavior, or legal and responsible behavior. The vast majority of organizations act legally and try to be socially responsible.

>lg 5   **How do businesses meet their social responsibilities to various stakeholders?**
Stakeholders are individuals or groups to whom business has a responsibility. Businesses are responsible to employees. They should provide a clean, safe working environment. Organizations can build employees' self-worth through empowerment programs. Businesses also have a responsibility to customers to provide good, safe products and services. Organizations are responsible to the general public to be good corporate citizens. Firms must help protect the environment and provide a good place to work. Companies also engage in corporate philanthropy, which includes contributing cash, donating goods and services, and supporting volunteer efforts of employees. Finally, companies are responsible to investors. They should earn a reasonable profit for the owners.

>lg 6   **What are the global and domestic trends in ethics and social responsibility?**
Today, corporate philanthropy is shifting away from simply giving to any needy group and is focusing instead on strategic giving, in which the philanthropy relates more closely to the corporate mission or goals and targets donations to areas where the firm operates. Corporate philanthropy is coming under increasing attacks from special-interest groups, however.

A second trend is toward a new social contract between employer and employee. Instead of the employer having the sole responsibility for maintaining jobs, now the employee must assume part of the burden and find ways to add value to the organization.

KEY TERMS

code of ethics 89
consumer fraud 95
conventional ethics 84
corporate philanthropy 97
ethics 82
justice 83
postconventional ethics 84
preconventional ethics 83
social investing 98
social responsibility 89
stakeholders 94
strategic giving 98
utilitarianism 82

As the world increasingly becomes a global community, multinational corporations are now expected to assume a global set of ethics and responsibility. Global companies must understand local customs. They should also involve local stakeholders in decision making. Multinationals must also make certain that their suppliers are not engaged in human rights violations.

PREPARING FOR TOMORROW'S WORKPLACE

1. Divide the class into two teams. Representatives from each team should debate whether ethics can be taught.
2. Write a paper that explains how utilitarianism may conflict with human rights.
3. You have been asked to give a speech on creating employee ethical awareness. Prepare an outline for your speech.
4. Divide the class into teams. Debate whether the only social responsibility of the employer to the employee is to provide a job. Include a discussion of the employee's responsibility to bring value to the firm.
5. Identify the potential ethical and social responsibility issues confronting the following organizations: Microsoft, Columbia Hospitals, Nike, American Cancer Society, and R.J. Reynolds. Make recommendations on how these issues should be handled.

WORKING THE NET

1. Visit the Web site of the People for the Ethical Treatment of Animals (PETA) at **http://furisdead.com.** Read about PETA's view of the fur industry. Do you agree or disagree with this view? Why? How do you think manufacturers who make fur clothing would justify their actions to someone from PETA? Would you work for a store that offered fur-trimmed clothing in addition to other items? Explain your answer.
2. Use a major search engine such as Yahoo (**http://www.yahoo.com**) or Lycos (**http://www.lycos.com**) to look for several examples of corporate codes of ethics. What common elements appear in the examples you found? Suggest how one of the codes could be improved.
3. At **http://www.goodmoney.com/wpubco.htm**, you will find a list of public companies that have been identified as being socially responsible. Pick one of the companies and find its Internet home page (Yahoo at **http://www.yahoo.com** is one way to find this). Read about the firm's operations and marketing efforts. Do you agree or disagree that this firm is socially responsible? Give specific examples from the company's Web site to support your answer.
4. Read about Bank of America's community development and environmental protection programs at **http://www.bankofamerica.com**. Why do you think Bank of America runs these programs? How do these programs benefit Bank of America's stockholders/investors? Customers? Employees? Use a search engine like Dogpile (**http://www.dogpile.com**) to find other examples of corporate philanthropy.

CREATIVE THINKING CASE

Limited Too Helps Girl Scouts Earn a Merit Badge in Shopping

Draped shoulder to waist, the kelly-green Girl Scout sash is the showcase of its wearer's badges and patches. The insignia denote achievement in fields such as first aid, plants and animals, folk art, or shopping. Yes, shopping. It's part of the

Fashion Adventure program, offered nationwide inside Limited Too stores, which merchandise clothing specifically for girls age 7 to 14. To earn the patch, the Girl Scouts must troop off to a Limited Too, where they learn about fabrics, markdowns, store security, and what merchandisers do. The girls get to browse among clothes racks, choose their favorite outfits, and model in front of others. They also get 15 percent off coupons from the store.

"It's nauseating," says Peggy Charren, consumer activist and founder of Action for Children's Television. The Fashion Adventure program, she says, is a "pure and simple sales pitch under the auspices of the Girl Scouts."

"We're trying to make sure that our program activities remain contemporary," says Marianne Ilaw, spokeswoman for the Girl Scouts of the U.S.A. Defending business-sponsored programs such as Fashion Adventure, she says, "It's a real life experience for girls who will be working. It's just a learning environment."

Officials at Limited Too stress that the five-year-old Fashion Adventure program is strictly a community service, to educate the girls about fashion and grooming. Michael Rayden, president and chief executive of Limited Too, says the program is part of any good corporation's "three legs of the stool: community, family, and business."

INFOTRAC® COLLEGE EDITION Critical Thinking Questions

1. Do you think it is ethical for the Girl Scouts to offer a Fashion Adventure merit badge tied in with Limited Too? Why or why not?

2. Is the Limited Too simply meeting its public social responsibility, as it claims?

3. Would you view the situation differently if the Fashion Adventure badge could be earned at any retailer of the girls' choosing? Why or why not?

VIDEO CASE

The Bank of Alma

Founded more than 100 years ago as a community-oriented banking institution, the Bank of Alma has 10 offices and 7 automatic teller machines (ATMs) located throughout Gratiot County in central Michigan. The bank is also the lead bank in Firstbank Corporation, a multibank holding company.

The bank's four-point mission statement guides its operation. First and foremost, it is committed to customer service. John McCormack, the president and chief executive officer, says this means the bank's main goal is making each customer's "experience with the Bank of Alma delightful in every way." Other goals in the corporate mission statement include meeting employee needs, supporting the communities that the bank serves, and enhancing shareholder value.

The bank offers a wide selection of checking services, savings account options, and loans designed to fit customers' current lifestyles and future needs. Other customer services include trust and investment management services, employee benefit plans, business accounts, ATM and check cards, safety deposit boxes, electronic payroll direct deposits, and electronic tax payments.

In addition to trying to satisfy customers with its broad range of products and services, the bank pushes decision making down to the lowest level. This helps the Bank of Alma to provide quick and effective service. For instance, the bank has a well-established reputation for providing loans that customers qualify for and can afford.

Another way the bank seeks to delight its customers is by vigorously enforcing its policies regarding confidentiality, honesty, and privacy. Bank employees view these policies, and the actions governed by them, as essential to developing trusting relationships with customers. Adhering to these ethical standards is important because customers entrust their financial assets and a variety of financial information to the bank.

An additional, though less obvious, means of delighting customers is through local outreach programs. The Bank of Alma provides significant financial support to the communities it serves, and also encourages employees to be involved meaningfully in the communities where they work.

Critical Thinking Questions

1. Is the Bank of Alma operated as an ethical business? Explain your answer.
2. Why is trust so crucial for the Bank of Alma? To what extent can (or should) trust be applied to other businesses?
3. To what extent do you apply standards such as confidentiality, honesty, privacy, and nondisclosure of information to your own interactions with other people?

Case: Geekcorps: From Dot.com to Dot.org

What would you do if you helped start a successful Internet company and made your first million before you turned 30? If you're Ethan Zuckerman, you found Geekcorps (**http://www.Geekcorps.org**), a nonprofit organization with the goal of spreading electronic commerce to developing nations.

Zuckerman, a 1993 graduate of Williams College, made his fortune as vice president of research and development at Tripod, an online personal publishing site. When Lycos bought Tripod in 1999, Zuckerman became an instant millionaire. With $100,000 of his own money, Zuckerman started Geekcorps in 2000. A kind of Peace Corps for techies, Geekcorps hopes to send techno-savvy volunteers to countries like Ghana, Nicaragua, and Bolivia, where Internet technology is limited. The volunteers, on sabbaticals from their current jobs, will spend three months in each country helping local firms and governments develop and implement electronic commerce initiatives.

Zuckerman says he has no lack of volunteers interested in joining Geekcorps. "My generation has made a lot of money at a very young age," says Zuckerman. "Rather than the Yuppie boom of the '80s and '90s where wealth led to excess, I believe we'll see people interested in building things intelligently."

Sending GeekCorp volunteers abroad, however, will take more capital than Zuckerman's initial investment. It will cost about $10,000 for each three-month volunteer stint. Zuckerman has already secured some contributions, including $250,000 from Tripod's founder Bo Peabody. Zuckerman hopes to convince more private and corporate donors to contribute. "If I

can give $100,000 just with my modest net worth, others in the industry can give a lot more," he says.

To raise the needed funds, Zuckerman says Geekcorps needs to get creative. He arranged a partnership with Dewar's, the whisky brand, that will feature Geekcorps in Dewar's ads. He hopes to convince emerging high technology firms to place a small percentage of their initial stock in Geekcorps' name. As these firms mature, Geekcorps would receive dividends from the stock. Zuckerman is considering other plans as well, such as starting a for-profit consulting arm of Geekcorps.

Questions for Critical Thinking

1. If you were Ethan Zuckerman, how would you explain to high technology firms why contributing to Geekcorps would be a strategic giving choice?
2. Do you think other consumer goods firms like Dewar's would see this as an opportunity to meet their social responsibilities to employees, customers, or investors? Explain.
3. Do you agree with Zuckerman's assessment that the generation building their wealth from electronic commerce will be more likely to take on social causes?

SOURCES: Eddy Goldberg, "Investing in Tommorrow: Dot-Com Multimillionaires Are Changing the Nature of Giving," *Success,* July/August 2000, downloaded from **http://www.successmagazine. com**; S. E. Slack, "Spreading the Geek Gospel," *Office.com,* August 23, 2000, downloaded from **http://www.office.com**; "Volunteerism: Good Will Geeks," *The Standard,* July 24, 2000, downloaded from **http://www.thestandard.com**; "Computer Advocate Works to Develop Geekcorps," *Chicago Tribune,* February 21, 2000, downloaded from **http://chicagotribune.com**.

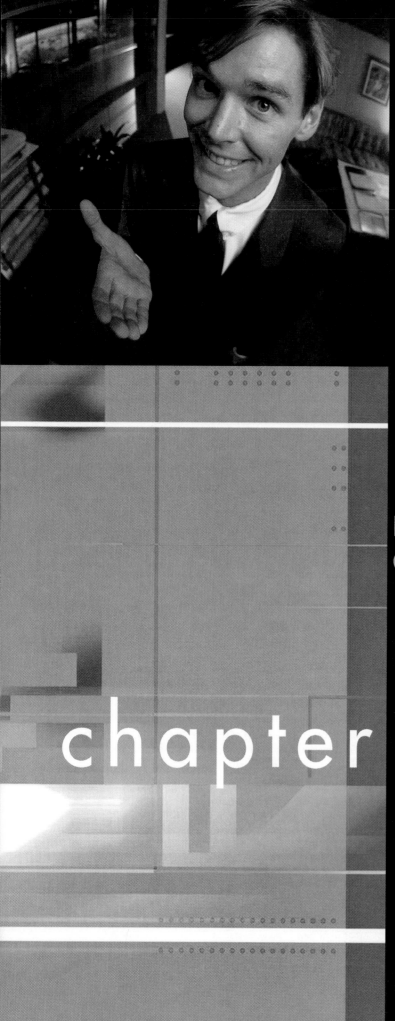

learning goals

>lg 1   What are the three main forms of business organization, and what factors should a company's owners consider when selecting a form?

>lg 2   What are the advantages and disadvantages of sole proprietorships?

>lg 3   Why would a new business venture choose to operate as a partnership, and what downside would the partners face?

>lg 4   How does the corporate structure provide advantages and disadvantages to a company, and what are the major types of corporations?

>lg 5   Does a company have any business organization options besides sole proprietorship, partnership, and corporation?

>lg 6   Why is franchising growing in importance?

>lg 7   Why would a company use mergers and acquisitions to grow?

>lg 8   What trends will affect business organization in the future?

Forms of Business Ownership

chapter 4

It's a Match with JobDirect, Inc.

Sometimes the best ideas are born out of desperation. Sharing a taxi in Boston in June 1995 and commiserating about their difficulties finding jobs, college juniors Sara Sutton and Rachel Bell wondered why there wasn't an Internet service geared toward entry-level jobs and internships. Taking Bell's father's advice—"When you go out into the real world, you don't have to work for a company. You can start one yourself."—the two women spent several months testing the feasibility of using Internet technology to match students with jobs. Although they had no business or technical experience, they believed that their idea had merit and took leaves of absence—Sutton from the University of California at Berkeley and Bell from Hobart & William Smith College—to start JobDirect (**http://www.jobdirect.com**).

After developing a business plan and raising about $60,000 from family and friends, they were ready to start the company. But what form should their business take? Should they be partners or form a corporation? Although partnerships are easy to set up, Sutton and Bell would be personally liable for all the company's financial obligations. And could a partnership attract enough money to grow the company? In June 1996, they formed an S corporation because of tax advantages and limited liability.

Sutton and Bell also realized they needed professional managers and technology experts. In the spring of 1996, they hired former Tufts University professor and small business consultant Robert Ford as president and chief operating officer and Microsoft alumnus Jesse Keller as vice president, development in charge of Web systems, along with sales and marketing staff.

As the scope of their venture grew, so did the need for additional funding. By getting their corporate house in order from the earliest stages, JobDirect gained credibility and flexibility to attract investors in a fast-moving Internet business environment. They also wanted a structure that allowed them to develop JobDirect as a national brand. In August 1996, JobDirect incorporated in Connecticut as a regular, or C, corporation, which was better suited to the company's long-term growth plan. Soon after, the company's new law firm—a specialist in small high-growth companies—advised JobDirect to reincorporate in Delaware to avoid Connecticut's restrictive securities laws.

To differentiate JobDirect from other Web database services, the management group decided to take their service directly to college campuses to create awareness of their free Internet service and build relationships. They also developed the

Critical Thinking Questions:
As you read this chapter, consider the following questions as they relate to JobDirect, Inc.:

- What factors should Sutton and Bell consider when selecting a form of business organization?
- What are some of the pros and cons they would encounter if they organized as a partnership?
- How does incorporating benefit their business?

technology to cross-reference the qualifications on posted résumés with current positions and notify the students directly about appropriate positions via e-mail. Students could also search the job database, and employers could perform targeted searches of student résumés.

In September 1996, Sutton and Bell took their show on the road—literally. They visited 43 colleges in a "JobDrive" recreational vehicle with 15 laptop computers so students could submit résumés directly into JobDirect's database. Word of JobDirect's novel approach spread as people learned about this efficient way for entry-level job seekers and potential employers to exchange information. By June 1997, JobDirect, Inc. had three JobDrive RVs traveling throughout the United States to over 300 campuses. Through 1998 the corporation raised $3.5 million from about 60 private stockholders and venture capital firms (institutional investors that finance young companies). Today about 500,000 students from over 2,000 campuses have résumés in JobDirect's databank.[1]

BUSINESS IN THE 21ST CENTURY

If you want to start a small business, you may want to consider owning a franchise. Through franchising, Mail Boxes Etc. allows entrepreneurs to own a small business without starting from scratch.

As business novices, Sara Sutton and Rachel Bell knew very little about choosing a form of business organization for their new venture. They were fortunate to have good advisers who helped them understand the pros and cons of partnerships, limited liability companies, and corporations. They also learned that a company may need to change its legal form as it grows.

If you, like Sara and Rachel, dream of owning your own business, you are not alone. About 900,000 new companies open their doors for business each year—and that includes only firms with employees. If one-person businesses were counted, the number would be even higher.

Regardless of size, every new business must choose a form of business organization that reflects its goals. In this chapter we will look at the different ways to organize a business. The three main types of business organization—sole proprietorships, partnerships, and corporations—all have advantages and disadvantages. Other business structures, such as cooperatives, joint ventures, and franchising, are appropriate for special situations. Next we will explore how corporations use mergers and acquisitions to grow. Finally, we'll look ahead at trends shaping business organization in the future.

TYPES OF BUSINESS ORGANIZATION

>lg 1

Congratulations! You've decided to start a company. You've got a great idea and some start-up funding. Before you go any further, however, you must set up your business entity. Which form of business organization best suits the needs of your particular business?

To choose wisely, you must ask several key questions: Do you want to own the business alone or with other participants? How much operating control do the owners want? Who will be liable for the firm's debts and taxes? Can the firm attract employees? What costs are associated with the chosen ownership structure? How easy will it be to find financing? How will the business be taxed? The answers determine the legal ownership structure you will select.

Most businesses fall into one of three major ownership categories: sole proprietorships, partnerships, or corporations. As Exhibit 4-1 illustrates, sole proprietorships are the most popular form of business ownership. They account for 73 percent of all businesses, compared to 20 percent for corporations and 7 percent for partnerships. Most sole proprietorships and partnerships remain small, however, so corporations generate about 90 percent of total business sales and 71 percent of the profits.

Each form of business ownership has advantages and disadvantages. As we'll discover in the following sections, the form that offers the most advantages in the early stages of a company's life may no longer meet its needs as it grows.

SOLE PROPRIETORSHIPS

>lg 2

Starting Hot Pots, a San Diego company that specializes in container gardens for small spaces, gave owner Gail Cecil the chance to combine her love of gardening

exhibit 4-1 | Comparison of Forms of Business Organization

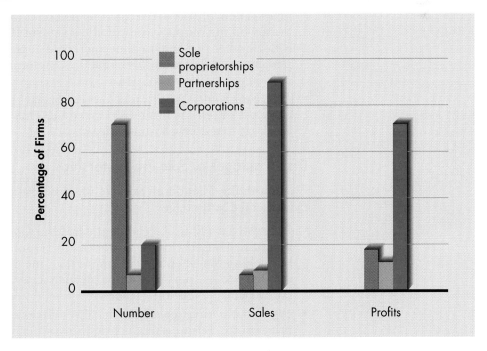

SOURCE: Internal Revenue Service, as reported in U.S. Bureau of the Census, *Statistical Abstract of the United States, 1999*, 119th ed. (Washington, DC.: Government Printing Office, 1999), p. 545.

with her desire to bring beauty into people's homes. All she needed to get started was her expertise in horticulture, a business license, and the money for business cards, plants, pots, and related materials. "I love being my own boss and the challenge of creating new designs for each location," she says. At the same time, Gail has no guaranteed paycheck, and the work can be lonely: "It's hard to stay motivated. Some days I really have to push myself to look for new clients."[2]

Gail Cecil formed Hot Pots as a **sole proprietorship,** a business that is established, owned, operated, and often financed by one person. Your neighborhood florist, shoe repair shop, construction company, and hair salon are usually sole proprietorships. Small service businesses, such as lawyers, accountants, consultants, landscapers, and real estate agents, often operate as sole proprietorships. In fact, almost half of all sole proprietorships offer services.

sole proprietorship
A business that is established, owned, operated, and often financed by one person.

Advantages of Sole Proprietorships

Sole proprietorships have several advantages that make them popular:

- *Easy and inexpensive to form.* As Gail Cecil discovered, sole proprietorships have few legal requirements, and forming one doesn't cost much. Once the owner obtains the start-up funds and necessary local licenses and permits, he or she can start the business.
- *Profits that all go to the owner.* The owner of a sole proprietorship gets all the profits the business earns. The more efficiently the firm operates, the higher the profits.
- *Direct control of the business.* Successful sole proprietors like Gail Cecil thrive on their independence. They like being their own boss and controlling all business decisions without having to consult anyone else. It's easy to respond quickly to changing business conditions.
- *Freedom from government regulations.* Although all businesses are subject to some government controls, sole proprietorships have more freedom than other forms of business.
- *No special taxation.* Proprietorships do not pay special franchise or corporate taxes. Their profits are treated as personal income of the owner and reported on the owner's individual tax return. Business income is combined with all other personal income and taxed at personal rates ranging from 15 percent to 39.6 percent (as of 2000). Combining business and personal income may provide a tax break.
- *Ease of dissolution.* With no co-owners or partners involved, the proprietor can close or sell the business at any time. Thus, sole proprietorships are an ideal way to test new business ideas.

Disadvantages of Sole Proprietorships

Along with the freedom to operate the business as they wish, sole proprietors face several disadvantages:

- *Unlimited liability.* In the eyes of the law, the sole proprietor and the firm are identical. Thus, the owner is personally responsible for all the debts of the business—even when they are more than the company is worth. The owner may have to sell personal property, such as a car, house, or investments, to satisfy claims against the business.
- *Difficulty in raising capital.* Financial resources are more limited for sole proprietorships. Business lenders view the owner's unlimited liability as a high risk. Business assets are not protected from claims of personal creditors. Owners must often use personal funds—borrowing on credit cards, taking

second mortgages on their homes, and selling investments—to finance the business. Inability to raise additional funding may curtail expansion plans.

- *Limited managerial expertise.* The success of a sole proprietorship depends entirely on the owner's skills and talents. The owner is fully responsible for all business decisions and must be a "jack-of-all-trades." Not all owners are equally skilled in all areas. An inventor who creates a new product may not be a good salesperson, production manager, or accountant.

- *Trouble finding qualified employees.* Sole proprietors have difficulty finding and keeping good employees. Small firms cannot offer the same fringe benefits and opportunities for advancement as larger companies.

- *Personal time commitment.* Running a sole proprietorship requires a huge time commitment and often dominates the owner's life. The owner must be willing to make sacrifices, often working 12 or more hours a day, six or seven days a week.

- *Unstable business life.* The life span of a sole proprietorship is uncertain. If the owner loses interest, retires, or dies, the business will cease to exist unless the owner finds a buyer.

- *Losses that all go to the owner.* The sole proprietor is responsible for all losses. However, tax law allows the proprietor to deduct these losses from other types of personal income.

The sole proprietorship may be a suitable choice for a one-person start-up operation that has no employees and little risk of liability exposure, like Hot Pots. For many sole proprietors, however, this is a temporary choice. As the business grows, the owner may not have the managerial and financial resources to operate alone. At this point she or he may decide to go into partnership with one or more co-owners.

concept check

- What is a sole proprietorship?
- Why do so many businesspeople choose this form of business organization?
- What are the drawbacks to being a sole proprietor?

PARTNERSHIPS

>lg 3

Brett Cosor had an idea for a company that provides big-screen multimedia installations for special events. However, he realized that his strengths were in the creative vision rather than the nuts-and-bolts details of the business. In 1988 he recruited his cousin Jeff Studley to handle the operational side of CPR MultiMedia Solutions, based in Gaithersburg, Maryland. The cousins' abilities were complementary. "Brett is a goal-oriented guy; I'm a task-oriented guy," explains Studley. Within 10 years, their partnership had grown into a business with two divisions, 47 employees, and revenues of $10 million.[3]

For those like Brett Cosor who don't want to "go it alone," the partnership offers another form of business ownership. A **partnership** is an association of two or more persons who agree to operate a business together for profit. Some professional service firms—for example, law firms, accounting firms, investment banks, stock brokerages, and real estate companies—are set up as partnerships.

Forming a partnership is simple. The parties agree, either orally or in writing, to share in the profits and losses of a joint enterprise. Written partnership agreements that spell out the terms and conditions of the partnership can prevent later conflicts between the partners. These agreements typically include the name and purpose of the partnership, contributions of each partner (financial, talent, equipment, etc.), management responsibilities and duties of each partner, compensation arrangements (salaries and shares of profits), provisions covering the addition of new partners and sale of partnership interests, and procedures for resolving conflicts, dissolving the business, and distributing assets.

partnership

An association of two or more persons who agree to operate a business together for profit.

general partnership

A partnership in which all partners share in the management and profits. Each partner can act on behalf of the firm and has unlimited liability for all its business obligations.

limited partnership

A partnership with one or more *general partners,* who have unlimited liability, and one or more *limited partners,* whose liability is limited to the amount of their investment.

general partners

Partners who have unlimited liability for all of the firm's business obligations and who control its operations.

limited partners

Partners whose liability for the firm's business obligations is limited to the amount of their investment. They help to finance the business, but do not participate in the firm's operations.

There are two basic types of partnerships: general and limited. In a **general partnership,** all partners share in the management and profits. They co-own assets, and each can act on behalf of the firm. Each partner has unlimited liability for all the business obligations of the firm. A **limited partnership** has two types of partners: one or more **general partners,** who have unlimited liability, and one or more **limited partners,** whose liability is limited to the amount of their investment. In return for limited liability, limited partners agree not to take part in the day-to-day management of the firm. They help to finance the business, but the general partners maintain operational control.

Advantages of Partnerships

Some advantages of partnerships come quickly to mind:

- *Ease of formation.* Like sole proprietorships, partnerships are easy to form. The partners agree to do business together and develop a partnership agreement. For most partnerships, applicable state laws are not complex.

- *Availability of capital.* Because two or more people contribute financial resources, partnerships can raise funds more easily for operating expenses and business expansion. The partners' combined financial strength also increases the firm's ability to raise funds from outside sources.

- *Diversity of skills and expertise.* Partners share the responsibility for managing and operating the business. Ideal partnerships bring together people with complementary backgrounds, rather than those with similar experience. Combining partner skills to set goals, manage the overall direction of the firm, and solve problems increases the likelihood of the partnership's success. Finding the right partner entails looking at your own strengths and weaknesses and examining what you're looking for in a partner. In Exhibit 4-2 you'll find some advice on choosing a partner.

- *Flexibility.* General partners take an active role in managing their firm and can respond quickly to changes in the business environment.

- *No special taxes.* Partnerships pay no income taxes. A partnership must file a partnership return with the Internal Revenue Service that reports the amount of profit and how it was divided among the partners. Each partner's profit or loss is then reported on the partner's personal income tax return, with profits taxed at personal tax rates.

- *Relative freedom from government control.* Except for state rules for licensing and permits, the government has little control over partnership activities.

Disadvantages of Partnerships

Despite their advantages, partnerships also have their downside:

- *Unlimited liability.* All general partners have unlimited liability for the debts of the business. In fact, any one partner can be held personally liable for all partnership debts and legal judgments (like malpractice)—regardless of who caused them. As with sole proprietorships, business failure can lead to a loss of the general partners' personal assets. To overcome this disadvantage, many states now allow the formation of limited liability partnerships (LLPs). The LLP limits each individual partner's liability to harm resulting from his or her own acts, but not for the acts of the other partners.

- *Potential for conflicts between partners.* Partners may have different ideas—personal or business—about such matters as how and when to expand the business, which employees to hire, and how to allocate responsibilities. As CPR MultiMedia's business grew, so did the strain of managing a larger company. Differences in their personalities and work styles caused major clashes and a communications breakdown between Cosor and Studley. "We stopped

e x h i b i t   4 - 2 | Picking the Right Partner

Picking a partner is an art, not a science. Be prepared to talk, talk, talk—about everything. On paper someone may have all the right business credentials. But does that person share the ideas you have for your company? And honesty, integrity, and ethics are equally, if not more, important. After all, you may be liable for what your partner does. Be willing to trust your intuition. "Trust those gut feelings—they're probably right," advises Irwin Gray, author of *The Perils of Partners*. First, ask yourself the following questions. Then ask a potential partner and see how well your answers match.

1. Why do you want a partner?
2. What characteristics and talents does each person bring to the partnership?
3. How will you divide partnership responsibilities? Consider every aspect of the business, from long-range planning to daily operations. Who will handle marketing, sales, accounting, customer service?
4. What is your long-term vision for the business (size, life span, financial commitment, etc.)?
5. What are your personal reasons for forming this company—for example, steady paycheck, independence, creating a company that stays small, building a large company?
6. Are all parties willing to put in the same amount of time, and if not, is there an alternative arrangement that is acceptable to everyone?
7. Do you have similar work ethics and values on how to run the company? Is the person honest?
8. What requirements should be included in the partnership agreement?

SOURCES: Julie Bawden Davis, "Buddy System," *Business Start Ups* (June 1998), downloaded from **http://www.entrepreneurmag.com;** Azriela Jaffe, "'Till Death Do Us Part' Is No Way to Start a Business," *Business Week Online* (October 23, 1998), downloaded from **http://www.businessweek.com/smallbiz;** Jerry Useem, "Partners on the Edge," *Inc.* (August 1998), pp. 54, 59.

pulling in the same direction in the same harness," says Studley. "All of a sudden there were two moons pushing tides in different directions, and that creates a lot of turbulence." To save the business, the cousins began working through their differences with the help of a psychologist who specialized in counseling troubled business partners.[4]

- *Sharing of profits.* Dividing the profits is relatively easy if all partners contribute about the same amount of time, expertise, and capital. But if one partner provides more money and the other puts in more time, it is more difficult to arrive at a fair profit-sharing formula.

- *Difficulty in leaving or ending a partnership.* Partnerships are easier to form than to leave. Suppose one partner wants to leave. How much is that partner's share worth? Is there a buyer who is acceptable to the other partners? If a partner owning more than 50 percent of the entity withdraws, dies, or becomes disabled, the partnership must reorganize or end. To avoid these problems, most partnership agreements include specific guidelines for transfer of partnership interests and buy-sell agreements so that surviving partners can buy a deceased partner's interest. Partners often buy special life insurance policies on each partner that fund this purchase.

You can see why business partnerships are often compared to marriages. As with marriage, choosing the right partner is critical. If you're considering forming a partnership, allow plenty of time to evaluate both your own and your potential partner's goals, personalities, business values, and work habits. You might even decide to go into partnership with your spouse. Learn more about this growing trend in the Focusing on Small Business box.

c o n c ə p t   c h ə c k

- How does a partnership differ from a sole proprietorship?
- Describe briefly the three types of partnerships and explain the difference between a general partner and a limited partner.
- What are the main advantages and disadvantages of partnerships, and how do they compare to sole proprietorships?

PERFECT PARTNERS

Looking for the perfect partner for your business? Sometimes the best person is close at hand—your spouse. It worked for Paula Mae Schwartz, who needed a partner to handle the growing demands of her public relations (PR) firm for high-tech companies. She convinced her husband Steve, a vice president at a software developer, to join her in 1990. It was a natural fit. He understood the services her target clients required and could also "talk the talk," while Paula Mae knew how to pull together PR campaigns. The business partnership worked as well as their personal one. Today, Schwartz Communications is one of the country's fastest growing high-tech PR agencies, with 150 employees, East and West Coast offices, and over 80 clients.

The Schwartzes represent two growing trends: married couples teaming up for business ventures and people leaving corporate life to start their own companies. Whether they organize as a partnership or become co-owners of a corporation, spouses have a head start. They know each other's strengths and weaknesses and can also structure the firm to allow for more family time, perhaps by working at home.

Going into business with a spouse has pitfalls as well, however. "You have to have a strong marriage going into it," advises Fran Rogers of Work/Family Directions, a national consulting firm (who also partners with her husband). One risk is too much togetherness. The Schwartzes avoided problems from the start by carefully structuring their business relationship and setting rules. They acknowledged their separate identities, allocating responsibilities based on individual strengths and weaknesses. Steve ran sales and marketing; Paula Mae, internal operations. Physical separation—offices at opposite ends of the company—helped, too. Mutual respect is also important. They learned to trust each other's judgment, to compromise, and to keep personal issues and egos out of the business—no easy task.

Critical Thinking Questions

1. What are the pros and cons of going into business with your spouse, as opposed to a non-family partner?
2. How did the Schwartzes' approach to their business venture contribute to its success?
3. Suggest some ground rules to help the Schwartzes separate their work and personal lives.

CORPORATIONS

When people think of corporations, they typically think of major, well-known corporations like IBM, Microsoft, General Electric, and Procter & Gamble. Corporations range in size from large multinational corporations like these, with sales in the billions of dollars and thousands of employees, to small firms with a few employees and revenues under $25,000.

A **corporation** is a legal entity with an existence and life separate from its owners. Because of this separation, the owners are not personally liable for the corporation's debts. A corporation is subject to the laws of the state in which it is formed. The state issues a charter that gives the corporation the right to operate as a business and specifies its business goals. A corporation can own property, enter into contracts, sue and be sued, and engage in business operations under the terms of its charter. Unlike sole proprietorships and partnerships, corporations are taxable entities.

Corporations play an important role in the U.S. economy. As we saw in Exhibit 4-1, corporations account for only 20 percent of all businesses but generate about 90 percent of all revenues and 71 percent of the profits. Just scan

corporation

A legal entity with an existence and life separate from its owners, who therefore are not personally liable for the entity's debts. A corporation is chartered by the state in which it is formed and can own property, enter into contracts, sue and be sued, and engage in business operations under the terms of its charter.

Exhibit 4-3, the 10 largest U.S. corporations, and you will see many familiar names that affect our lives every day. In 1999, the top 500 industrial and service corporations, as ranked by *Fortune,* accounted for over $6.3 trillion in sales and $410 billion in profits. Yet many individuals and small businesses also incorporate to benefit from the advantages of this form of business organization. Over 70 percent of all corporations have sales under $500,000.

The Incorporation Process

Setting up a corporation is more complex than starting a sole proprietorship or partnership. Most states base their laws for chartering corporations on the Model Business Corporation Act of the American Bar Association. Nevertheless, registration procedures, fees, taxes, and laws regulating corporations do vary from state to state.

A firm doesn't have to incorporate in the state where it is based. It may benefit by comparing the rules in several states before choosing a state of incorporation. Although it is a small state with few corporations actually based there, Delaware's pro-corporate policies have made it the state of incorporation for many companies, including about half of the Fortune 500.

Incorporating a company involves five main steps:

1. Selecting the company's name
2. Writing the *articles of incorporation* (see Exhibit 4-4) and filing them with the appropriate state office, usually the secretary of state
3. Paying required fees and taxes
4. Holding an organizational meeting
5. Adopting bylaws, electing directors, and passing the first operating resolutions

HoT links

Which Fortune 500 company had the biggest revenue increase? The highest profits? Highest return to investors? What is the largest entertainment company? Get all the details on the largest U.S. companies at

http://www.fortune.com

Note: you will have to then click on Fortune 500.

---

e x h i b i t   4 - 3 | The 10 Largest U.S. Corporations (ranked by 1999 sales)

1999 Rank	Company	Sales ($ millions)	Profits ($ millions)
1	General Motors, Detroit	$189,058	$ 6,002
2	Wal-Mart Stores, Bentonville, Ark.	166,809	5,377
3	Exxon Mobil, Irving, Texas	163,881	7,910
4	Ford Motor, Dearborn, Mich.	162,558	7,237
5	General Electric, Fairfield, Conn.	111,630	10,717
6	Intl. Business Machines, Armonk, N.Y.	87,548	7,712
7	Citigroup, New York	82,005	9,867
8	AT&T, New York	62,391	3,428
9	Philip Morris, New York	61,751	7,675
10	Boeing, Seattle	57,993	2,309

SOURCE: "The Fortune 500," *Fortune* (April 17, 2000), p. F-1.

The Company Corporation guides firms through the steps of incorporating and informs them of the corporate structure's many tax-deductible benefits.

The state issues the corporate charter based on the information in the articles of incorporation. Once the corporation has its charter, it holds an organizational meeting to adopt bylaws, elect directors, and pass initial operating resolutions. *Bylaws* provide the legal and managerial guidelines for operating the firm.

The Corporate Structure

As Exhibit 4-5 shows, corporations have their own organizational structure with three important components: stockholders, directors, and officers.

The owners of a corporation are its **stockholders,** or *shareholders,* who hold shares of stock that provide certain rights. They may receive a share of the corporation's profits in the form of dividends, and they can sell or transfer their ownership in the corporation (the shares of stock) at any time. Stockholders can attend annual meetings, elect the board of directors, and vote on matters that affect the corporation, as the charter and bylaws specify. They generally have one vote for each share of stock they own.

Stockholders elect a **board of directors** to govern the corporation. The directors handle overall management of the corporation. They set major corporate goals and policies, hire corporate officers, and oversee the firm's operations and finances. Small firms may have as few as 3 directors, whereas large corporations usually have 15 to 25. Large corporations typically include both corporate executives and *outside directors* (not employed by the organization) chosen for their professional and personal expertise. Because they are inde-

---

e x h i b i t   4 - 4 | Articles of Incorporation

stockholders

The owners of a corporation, who hold shares of stock that provide certain rights; also known as *shareholders.*

board of directors

A group of people elected by the stockholders to handle the overall management of a corporation, such as setting corporate goals and policies, hiring corporate officers, and overseeing the firm's operations and finances.

Articles of incorporation are prepared on a form authorized or supplied by the state of incorporation. Although they may vary slightly from state to state, all articles of incorporation include the following key items:

- Name of the corporation
- The company's goals
- Types of stock and number of shares of each type to issue
- Life of the corporation (usually "perpetual," meaning with no time limit)
- Minimum investment by the owners

- Methods for transferring shares of stock
- Address of the corporate office
- Names and addresses of the first board of directors
- Names and addresses of the incorporators
- Other public information the incorporators wish to include

e x h i b i t   4 - 5 | Organizational Structure of Corporations

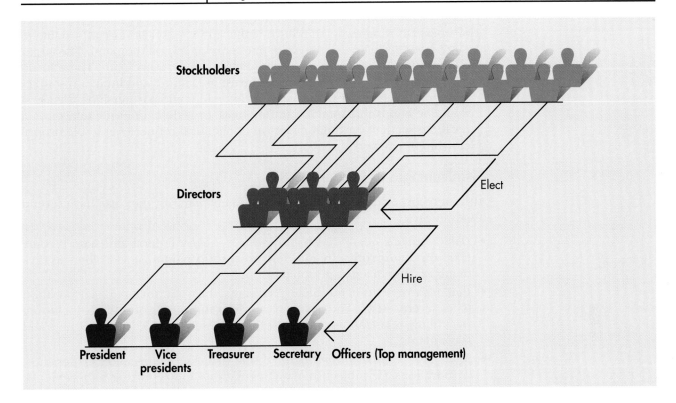

pendent of the firm, outside directors can bring a fresh view to the corporation's activities.

The *officers* of a corporation are its top management. Hired by the board, they include the president and chief executive officer (CEO), vice presidents, treasurer, and secretary and are responsible for achieving corporate goals and policies. Officers may also be board members and stockholders.

Advantages of Corporations

Certain features enable corporations to merge financial and human resources into enterprises with great potential for growth and profits:

- *Limited liability.* This is one of the key advantages of corporations. Because a corporation is a legal entity that exists apart from its owners, a stockholder's liability for the debts of the firm is limited to the amount of the stock owned. If the corporation goes bankrupt, creditors can look only to the assets of the corporation for payment.

- *Ease of transferring ownership.* Stockholders of public corporations can sell their shares to someone else at any time without affecting the status of the corporation.

- *Unlimited life.* The life of a corporation is unlimited. Although corporate charters specify a number of years of life, they also include rules for renewal. The corporation is separate from its owners, so unlike a sole proprietorship or partnership, death or withdrawal of an owner does not affect its existence.

- *Tax deductions.* Corporations also are allowed certain tax deductions, such as for operating expenses, that reduce their taxable income. Under the current

2000 tax code, corporate tax rates range from 15 to 35 percent, compared to 15 to 39.6 percent for individuals.

- *Ability to attract financing.* Corporations can raise money by selling new shares of stock. Dividing ownership into smaller units makes it more affordable to more investors, who can purchase one share or several thousand. The larger size and stability of corporations also help them get bank loans. These financial resources allow corporations to invest in facilities and human resources and grow much larger than sole proprietorships and partnerships. Clearly, it would be impossible to make automobiles, provide nationwide telecommunications services, or build major oil or chemical refineries as a sole proprietorship or partnership.

Disadvantages of Corporations

Although corporations offer businesses many benefits, they also have several disadvantages:

- *Double taxation of profits.* Corporations must pay federal and state income taxes on their profits. In addition, any profits paid to stockholders as dividends are also taxed as personal income.
- *Cost and complexity of formation.* As discussed earlier, forming a corporation takes several steps. The cost can run into thousands of dollars, including state filing, registration, and license fees, as well as the cost of attorneys and accountants.
- *More government restrictions.* Unlike sole proprietorships and partnerships, corporations are subject to many regulations and reporting requirements. For example, corporations must register in each state where they want to do business. Before selling stock to the public, they must register with the Securities and Exchange Commission (SEC). Unless it is closely held, the firm must publish financial reports on a regular basis. It must also file other special reports with the SEC and state and federal agencies. These reporting requirements impose substantial costs. Publishing information on corporate operations may also give an advantage to competitors.

Types of Corporations

Three types of corporate business organization provide limited liability. The "basic" corporate form of organization is the *conventional, or C, corporation.* Small businesses can also achieve limited liability through two other options: the S corporation and the limited liability company.

S Corporations

S corporation

A hybrid entity that is organized like a corporation, with stockholders, directors, and officers, but taxed like a partnership, with income and losses flowing through to the stockholders and taxed as their personal income.

limited liability company (LLC)

A hybrid organization that offers the same liability protection as a corporation but may be taxed as either a partnership or a corporation.

Confused about the differences between regular corporations, S corporations, and LLCs? Compare the three business structures at

http://www.4inc.com/compare.htm

S Corporations Double taxation of corporate profits is a major disadvantage for some small corporations. To avoid this problem, firms that meet certain size and ownership constraints can organize as S corporations. An **S corporation** is a hybrid entity that is organized like a corporation, with stockholders, directors, and officers, but taxed like a partnership. Income and losses flow through to the stockholders and are taxed as the personal income of the stockholders. S corporations can have only 75 qualifying shareholders and one class of stock. The owners of an S corporation are not personally liable for the debts of the corporation. About 2.2 million U.S. businesses enjoy the benefits of limited liability and special tax treatment that S corporations offer.

Limited Liability Companies   A newer type of business entity, the **limited liability company (LLC)** is also a hybrid organization. Although LLCs are not corporations, like S corporations they appeal to small businesses. LLCs are easy to set up and are not subject to many restrictions. LLCs provide the same liability protection as corporations but offer the option of being taxed as either a partnership or a corporation. First authorized by Wyoming in 1977, LLCs became popular after a 1988 tax ruling that treats them like partnerships for tax purposes. Today, all states allow the formation of LLCs.

Exhibit 4-6 summarizes the advantages and disadvantages of each form of business ownership.

concept check

- What is a corporation? Describe how corporations are formed and structured.
- Summarize the advantages and disadvantages of corporations. Which features contribute to the dominance of corporations in the business world?
- Why do S corporations and limited liability companies appeal to small businesses?

e x h i b i t   4 - 6 | Advantages and Disadvantages of Major Types of Business Organization

	Sole Proprietorship	Partnership	Corporation
Advantages			
	Owner receives all profits.	More expertise and managerial skill available	Limited liability protects owners from losing more than they invest.
	Low organizational costs	Relatively low organizational costs	Can achieve large size due to marketability of stock (ownership)
	Income taxed as personal income of proprietor.	Income taxed as personal income of partners.	Ownership is readily transferable.
	Independence	Fund-raising ability is enhanced by more owners.	Long life of firm (not affected by death of owners)
	Secrecy		Can attract employees with specialized skills
	Ease of dissolution		Greater access to financial resources allows growth.
			Receives certain tax advantages
Disadvantages			
	Owner receives all losses.	Owners have unlimited liability; may have to cover debts of other, less financially sound partners.	Double taxation because both corporate profits and dividends paid to owners are taxed
	Owner has unlimited liability; total wealth can be taken to satisfy business debts.	Dissolves or must reorganize when partner dies	More expensive and complex to form
	Limited fund-raising ability can inhibit growth.	Difficult to liquidate or terminate	Subject to more government regulation
	Proprietor may have limited skills and management expertise.	Potential for conflicts between partners	Financial reporting requirements make operations public.
	Few long-range opportunities and benefits for employees	Difficult to achieve large-scale operations	
	Lacks continuity when owner dies		

SPECIALIZED FORMS OF BUSINESS ORGANIZATION

>lg 5

In addition to the three main forms, several specialized types of business organization play a role in our economy. We'll look at cooperatives and joint ventures in this section and take a more detailed look at franchising in the following section.

Cooperatives

Have you eaten a Sunkist orange or spread Land O' Lakes butter on your toast? If so, you've used items produced by cooperatives. **Cooperatives** are typically formed by people with similar interests, such as customers or suppliers, to reduce costs and gain economic power. The member-owners pay annual fees and share in any profits. Cooperatives may be organized to provide just about any good or service, such as business services, child care, financial services, food, health care, marketing of agricultural and other products, and utilities and cable television. Today, over 100 million people are members of 48,000 U.S. cooperatives with revenues of over $120 billion. The top 100 cooperatives, led by the agriculture, grocery, and hardware/lumber industries, typically generate over $4 billion in revenues.[5]

cooperatives

Legal entities typically formed by people with similar interests, such as customers or suppliers, to reduce costs and gain economic power. A cooperative has limited liability, an unlimited life span, an elected board of directors, and an administrative staff; all profits are distributed to the member-owners in proportion to their contributions.

Did you know that cooperatives market about 30 percent of farmers' products in the United States? For more co-op statistics, head to the National Cooperative Business Association Web site, http://www.ncba.org/stats.cfm

A cooperative is a legal entity with several corporate features, such as limited liability, an unlimited life span, an elected board of directors, and an administrative staff. Cooperatives distribute all profits to the members in proportion to their contributions. Because they do not keep any profits, cooperatives do not pay taxes.

There are two types of cooperatives. *Seller cooperatives* are popular in agriculture. Individual producers join to compete more effectively with large producers. Member dues support market development, national advertising, and other business activities. In addition to Sunkist and Land O' Lakes, other familiar cooperatives are Calavo (avocados), Ocean Spray (cranberries and juices), and Blue Diamond (nuts). Farmland Industries, the largest cooperative in the United States, sells feed, fertilizer, petroleum, and grain. *Buyer cooperatives* combine members' purchasing power. Buying in volume results in lower prices. Food cooperatives are one example. College bookstores may operate as buyer cooperatives. At the end of the year, members get shares of the profits based on how much they bought.

Cooperatives help small-business owners like the proprietor of this True Value hardware store compete with larger corporations.

By forming cooperatives to obtain discounts, small companies can lower costs, increase their efficiency, and compete with larger corporations. Many independent hardware store owners belong to True Value, Doing It Best, or Ace cooperatives. Robin Bryant, owner of a Doing It Best hardware store in Burlington, North Carolina, paid $2,700 to join that cooperative. In return, she received training in store management, as well as support from the cooperative. "They always get the answers I need quickly," she says. "They work with owners like myself because they really want us to succeed."

For Bryant, the cooperative route was the only way to survive against chain discounters like Home Depot and Lowe's. Among the benefits are the lower prices and greater merchandise variety she gets by ordering from the cooperative's centralized purchasing system.[6]

Joint Ventures

In a *joint venture* (defined in Chapter 2), two or more companies form an alliance to pursue a specific project, usually for a specific time period. There are many reasons for joint ventures. The project may be too large for one party to handle on its own. By forming joint ventures, companies can gain access to new markets, products, or technology. Both large and small companies benefit from joint ventures. Software giant Microsoft Corp. teamed up with Citibank and other partners for its TransPoint joint venture to offer nationwide online billing and bill-paying services. Young technology companies often form joint ventures with more established players to get wider distribution for their products. The joint venture brings the larger company access to the latest technology.

FRANCHISING

Andrea Brinkman, a critical care nurse, was burned out after seven years working for large health care organizations. After researching various franchise concepts, she joined the more than 500,000 Americans who own franchises. In 1996 she decided to capitalize on the growing demand for used retail goods and opened Children's Orchard, a resale franchise specializing in children's clothing, toys, and equipment. In addition to being her own boss, running her own retail outlet gave Brinkman the opportunity to develop personal relationships with her customers.[7]

Franchises come in all sizes, from McDonald's, with 23,000 franchises in over 100 countries, to Children's Orchard with about 90 units in several states, to new concepts still on the drawing boards. Chances are you deal with one of the more than 2,100 franchise systems in the United States and Canada almost every day. When you have lunch at Taco Bell or Jamba Juice, make copies at Kinko's, change your oil at Jiffy Lube, buy candles at Wicks 'n' Sticks, or drop your film off at Moto Photo, in each case you are dealing with a franchised business. These and other familiar name brands have come to mean quality, consistency, and value to customers.

Franchising, one of the fastest growing segments of the economy, provides a way to own a business without starting it from scratch. **Franchising** is a form of business organization that involves a business arrangement between a **franchisor,** the company that supplies the product concept, and the **franchisee,** the individual or company that sells the goods or services in a certain geographic area. With a franchise, the business owner buys a package: a proven product, proven operating methods, and training in managing the business.

The **franchise agreement** is a contract allowing the franchisee to use the franchisor's business name and its trademark and logo. The agreement outlines the rules for running the franchise, the services provided by the franchisor, and the financial terms. The franchisee agrees to keep inventory at certain levels, buy a standard equipment package, keep up sales and service levels, follow the franchisor's operating rules, take part in the franchisor's promotions, and maintain a relationship with the franchisor. In return, the franchisor generally provides the use of a proven company name and symbols, building plans and help finding a site, guidance and training, management assistance, managerial and accounting procedures, employee training, wholesale prices on supplies, and financial assistance.

franchising

A form of business organization based on a business arrangement between a *franchisor,* which supplies the product concept, and the *franchisee,* who sells the goods or services of the franchisor in a certain geographic area.

franchisor

In a franchising arrangement, the company that supplies the product concept to the franchisee.

franchisee

In a franchising arrangement, the individual or company that sells the goods or services of the franchisor in a certain geographic area.

franchise agreement

A contract setting out the terms of a franchising arrangement, including the rules for running the franchise, the services provided by the franchisor, and the financial terms. Under the contract, the franchisee is allowed to use the franchisor's business name, trademark, and logo.

Advantages of Franchises

Like other forms of business organization, franchising offers some distinct advantages:

- *Increased ability for franchisor to expand.* Because franchisees finance their own units, franchisors can grow without making a major investment. Although franchisors give up a share of profits to their franchisees, they receive ongoing revenues in the form of royalty payments. In 1998 Diedrich Coffee, Inc., a 36-unit specialty coffee chain based in southern California, turned to franchising to expand nationally. It signed a franchise agreement with Tacala, Inc., the largest U.S. Taco Bell franchisee, to develop 44 coffee houses and 35 carts and kiosks in North Carolina. Over the next five years, Diedrich plans to add 1,500 coffee houses through regional franchising agreements in new geographic areas. "It would take us 10 years to build out what we can do in less than half that time using franchisees," said Tim Ryan, Diedrich's president. He added that franchisees are in a better position to adapt the company's concepts to local markets.[8]

- *Recognized name, product, and operating concept.* The franchisee gets a widely known and accepted business with a proven track record, as well as operating procedures, standard goods and services, and national advertising. Consumers know they can depend on products from such franchises as Pizza Hut, Hertz, and Holiday Inn. As a result, the franchisee's risk is reduced and the opportunity for success rises.

MAKING ETHICAL CHOICES

JOHN PARK'S UNUSUAL BUSINESS PRACTICES

John Park, one of the hottest Athlete's Foot franchisees in the nation, owns nine stores in some of Chicago's toughest neighborhoods. Park estimates that about 90 percent of his sales staff have criminal records. Occasionally, he hires people right out of prison.

Park has a rather unusual working arrangement with his sales staff. Park says, "From 9:30 to 6 is my time . . . whatever you do after that is your time." He does not ask many questions about his employees' outside activities, yet he is ready with bail money or short-term loans. Of course, such financial favors are eventually deducted from the employee's wages. None of the sales staff are allowed to work the cash register. A Korean American himself, Park hires only Korean American managers to handle the money.

By hiring people who have criminal records, "Park gets something that has proved indispensable (in the rough neighborhoods where his stores are located): salesmen who have genuine currency on these streets—and clout." Park has never been robbed, but two of his stores have been burglarized. After one of the burglaries, a salesclerk—who was also a gang member—was called to guard the store through the night. The clerk subsequently talked to another local gang member, and Park's stores have not been burglarized since. Having salespeople who are in touch with the street can also prove beneficial in moving the store's merchandise. "Stock changes from neighborhood to neighborhood, sometimes depending on gang allegiances."

Critical Thinking Questions

1. In your judgment, are Park's business practices ethical or unethical?
2. Suppose that you represent the franchisor, Athlete's Foot. Would you be concerned about Park's business practices?

- *Management training and assistance.* The franchisor provides a structured training program that gives the new franchisee a crash course in how to start and operate the business. Ongoing training programs for managers and employees are another plus. In addition, franchisees have a peer group to provide support and share ideas.
- *Financial assistance.* Being linked to a nationally known company can help a franchisee obtain funds from a lender. Also, the franchisor typically gives the franchisee advice on financial management, referrals to lenders, and help in preparing loan applications. Many franchisors also offer payment plans, short-term credit for buying supplies from the franchise company, and loans to buy real estate and equipment.

Disadvantages of Franchises

Franchising also has disadvantages, of course:

- *Loss of control.* The franchisor has to give up some control over operations and has less control over its franchisees than over company employees.
- *Costs of franchising.* Franchising can be a costly form of business. A recent Gallup survey reports that the average franchise start-up cost is about $143,000. These costs vary, depending on the type of business, and may include expensive facilities and equipment. The franchisee also pays ongoing fees or royalties (usually a percentage of sales). Fees for national and local advertising and management advice may add to the franchisee's cost. Franchise fees are higher for better known franchises, but even newer companies may charge $10,000 to $25,000 or more. Industry averages range from a low of $12,000 for real estate franchises to $36,000 in the lodging industry. Lodging franchises require the highest average total initial investment—$1.8 million, excluding real estate.[9] Exhibit 4-7 compares the total start-up costs and ongoing royalty fees for several types of franchise units.

e x h i b i t 4 - 7 | Cost Comparison of Selected Franchises

Name	Description	Total Start-up Costs, Including Franchise Fee	Royalty
Jiffy Lube Int'l	Fast oil change	$174,000–$194,000	Up to 5%
McDonald's	Fast-food restaurant	$433,800–$14 million	12.5%+
Sylvan Learning Centers	Children's tutoring services	$134,600–$215,300	8–9%
Chem-Dry	Carpet, drapery, upholstery cleaning	$29,900–$55,600	$192 per month
Jani-King	Commercial cleaning services	$15,100–$68,800	10%
Candy Bouquet	Designer gifts and confections	$11,000–$63,000	6–8%
Super 8 Motels	Economy motels	$271,400–$2.3 million	5%
Hilton Inns, Inc.	Hotels and resorts	$30–$45 million	5%
Re/Max International	Real estate services	$25,500–$200,000	Varies
Liberty Tax Service	Income tax preparation	$34,800–$40,000	Varies

- *Restricted operating freedom.* The franchisee agrees to conform to the franchisor's operating rules and facilities design, as well as inventory and supplies standards. Some franchises require franchisees to purchase only from the franchisor or approved suppliers. The franchisor may restrict the franchisee's territory or site, which can limit growth. Failure to conform to franchisor policies can mean loss of the franchise.

Franchise Growth

Many of today's major names in franchising, such as McDonald's and Kentucky Fried Chicken, started in the 1950s. Franchising grew rapidly in the 1960s and 1970s as more types of businesses—clothing, business services, convenience stores, and many others—used franchising to distribute their goods and services. The popularity of franchising continued as more business own-

Have a sweet tooth? Indulge yourself by finding out the requirements for owning a Rocky Mountain Chocolate Factory franchise at

http://www.rmcf.com

ers turned to franchising as a way to expand operations quickly and in new geographic areas, with limited capital investment. For example, between 1980 and 1999 the number of franchise units counted by *Entrepreneur* magazine's Franchise 500 nearly doubled.

Today, there are more than 2,100 franchise systems in the United States and Canada. The more than 500,000 business units in the United States employ over 8 million people and generate revenues of $800 billion. Franchises account for an estimated 50 percent of U.S. retail sales.[10] Fast food is the industry with the largest number of franchises, as Exhibit 4-8 shows.

e x h i b i t   4 - 8 | Franchise Population by Industry

Industry	Percentage of Total Units
Fast food	18%
Retail	11
Service businesses	9
Restaurants	9
Automotive	8
Maintenance	7
Building and construction	7
Business services	5
Retail food	5
Lodging	5
Other*	16

*3 percent or less: Baked goods, personnel services, sports and recreation, real estate, education, printing, child-related, travel.
SOURCE: *Profile of Franchising,* vol. III (Washington, DC: IFA Educational Foundation, 2000), p. 27, Chart 1.1.

International Franchising

Like other areas of business, franchising is part of the global marketplace. Most franchise systems either operate units internationally already or plan to expand overseas as the demand for all types of goods and services grows. "Our research has shown us that this is an ideal time to move into the Korean market," says Doug Dwyer, president of Worldwide Refinishing Systems, a bath and kitchen remodeling franchise. "Because the average living standard now is fairly high in Korea, people not only desire but also can afford a better living environment that refinishing and restoring can provide."[11] Currently, among the most popular types of international franchises are restaurants, hotels, business services, educational products, car rentals, and nonfood retail stores.

Franchisors in foreign countries face many of the same problems as other firms doing business abroad. In addition to tracking the market and currency changes, franchisors must be aware of the local culture, language differences, and political risks.

Franchisors in foreign countries also face the challenge of aligning their business operations with the goals of their franchisees, who may be located half a globe away. Technology improves communication with the franchisee and unites worldwide suppliers and customers, as described in the Applying Technology box.

concept check

- Describe franchising and the main parties to the transaction.
- Summarize the major advantages and disadvantages of franchising.
- Why has franchising proved so popular?

CORPORATE GROWTH THROUGH MERGERS AND ACQUISITIONS

>lg 7

As the 20th century came to a close, corporations continued to merge at record levels. In 1999 alone, the worldwide total was $3.4 trillion, including over 10,800 acquisition announcements totaling $1.7 trillion for U.S. companies. Exhibit 4-9 lists some of the largest mergers in recent years.

e x h i b i t   4 - 9 | Selected Recent Mergers

Year*	Acquirer	Target	Industry	Value** ($ Billions)
2000	America Online	Time Warner	Media/Internet	$183.0
1999	Vodafone AirTouch	Mannesmann	Telecommunications	124.8
1999	Pfizer	Warner-Lambert	Pharmaceuticals	87.4
1998	Exxon	Mobil	Oil and gas	86.4
1998	Travelers Group	Citicorp	Financial services	72.6
1999	AT&T	MediaOne	Telecommunications/Cable	56.0
1999	Vodafone Group	AirTouch Communications	Telecommunications	60.3
1998	Daimler-Benz	Chrysler	Motor vehicles	40.5
1999	Qwest	U.S. West	Telecommunications	38.5
1999	Viacom	CBS	Media	35.9

*Announced.
**Based on stock value on announcement date; excludes debt of target assumed by acquirer. Actual price at completion may differ.
SOURCE: "1999's Megamergers," *The Wall Street Journal* (January 3, 2000), p. R8; "Top Ten Deals of 1998," *Fortune* (January 11, 1999), p. 71; and various news sources.

FOR MENUS, CLICK HERE

Imagine trying to coordinate operations for Tricon Restaurants International's 10,000 Kentucky Fried Chicken (KFC), Pizza Hut, and Taco Bell franchises around the world. "When you're in 83 countries, it's nearly impossible to get consistency and discipline in building a global brand," comments Elana Gold, Tricon's KFC brand manager. "We needed to get everyone on the same page." Frustrated by the inadequacies and expense of paper-filled marketing binders, Tricon turned to an electronic business solution for global marketing management. In collaboration with Chicago software developer DNA Visual Solutions, Tricon created Brand Toolkit, a multimedia CD-ROM application with marketing resources. The CD-ROM provides Tricon franchisees with clearly organized information in an easy-to-use, cost-effective format.

With the click of a mouse, franchisees access detailed information about brand history, advertising, promotions, menu management, pricing, and operations. Guidelines on the best marketing practices and samples of effective ads teach franchisees how to develop ads to meet corporate standards. After working through a tutorial on menu guidelines, the franchisee can download actual menu models.

The CD-ROM format allows Tricon to design graphically rich interactive content such as video, three-dimensional (3-D) images, photographs, and animation that would take too long to send via the Internet. Adding an Internet connection to the next version of Brand Toolkit will allow franchisees to receive current news and updates to the CD-ROM and eventually do online transactions. In addition, the CD will take franchisees on a virtual reality tour through a 3-D restaurant model and show them the effect of layout and decorating modifications.

Since implementing the Brand Toolkit, relationships between Tricon and its franchisees have improved. As Howard Weinzimmer, DNA vice president, explains, "What does a franchise really have to sell? Product, methodology, and brand. Our technology helps them deliver that to all of their constituents."

Critical Thinking Questions

1. Summarize Brand Toolkit's benefits to both Tricon and its franchisees.
2. Describe several other ways Tricon could use different forms of technology to improve communications and franchise operations.

---

merger

The combination of two or more firms to form a new company, which often takes on a new corporate identity.

acquisition

The purchase of a corporation by another corporation or by an investor group; the identity of the acquired company may be lost.

A **merger** occurs when two or more firms combine to form one new company, which often takes on a new corporate identity. In an **acquisition,** a corporation or an investor group buys a corporation, and the identity of the acquired company may be lost. (A company can also acquire divisions or subsidiaries of another firm.) In Pfizer's 1999 $87 billion acquisition of Warner-Lambert, Pfizer was the *acquirer* and Warner-Lambert the *target*. Normally, an acquiring company finds a target company and, after analyzing the target carefully, negotiates with its management or stockholders.

Merger Motives

Although the headlines tend to focus on mega-mergers, the current "merger mania" affects small companies as well. The motives for undertaking mergers and acquisitions are similar regardless of size. Often the goal is strategic: improving the overall performance of the merged firms through cost savings, elimination of overlapping operations, improved purchasing power, increased market share, or reduced competition. Growth, widening of product lines, and the ability to quickly acquire technology or management skill are other mo-

In announcing their merger, Exxon CEO Lee Raymond and Mobil CEO Lucio Noto stated that the merged firms will improve their profitability with annual cost savings of almost $3 billion.

tives. Acquiring a company is often faster, less risky, and less costly than developing products internally or expanding internationally.

One of 1998's largest mergers, for example, involved giant oil companies: Exxon acquired Mobil. In the oil industry, size counts; larger companies have historically earned higher returns. With crude oil prices at record lows, these major oil companies had already cut costs as much as possible and saw the merger route as the only way to improve profitability. Exxon and Mobil merged the two companies' technological expertise with Exxon's lower exploration and production costs and Mobil's larger reserves outside the United States. Although the new corporation has more operating units, it eliminated duplication in nonoperational areas such as headquarters facilities, executive team, and marketing organization. The result was annual cost savings of $2.8 billion.[12]

Another motive for acquisitions is financial restructuring—cutting costs, selling off units, laying off employees, refinancing the company—to increase the value of the company to its stockholders. Financially motivated mergers are based not on the potential to achieve economies of scale, but rather on the acquirer's belief that the target has hidden value that can be unlocked through restructuring. Most financially motivated mergers involve larger companies.

Types of Mergers

The three main types of mergers are horizontal, vertical, and conglomerate. In a **horizontal merger,** companies at the same stage in the same industry merge to reduce costs, expand product offerings, or reduce competition. Many of the large mergers in the late 1990s were horizontal mergers to achieve economies of scale. For example, in 1999, Qwest acquired former regional Bell operating company U.S. West. Qwest's goal was to create a larger company to dominate the newly deregulated telecommunications industry.

In a **vertical merger,** a company buys a firm in its same industry that is involved in an earlier or later stage of the production or sales process. Buying a supplier of raw materials, a distribution company, or a customer gives the acquiring firm more control. America Online (AOL), Inc. acquires companies that address different Internet-related markets and capabilities. In 1999 AOL completed its $4.2 billion acquisition of Netscape Communications Corp. AOL had focused on the consumer market, while Netscape had a strong presence in the corporate market. AOL gained Netscape's software technology, including powerful Web browser software and the behind-the-scenes software to run Web sites and conduct electronic commerce.[13]

A **conglomerate merger** brings together companies in unrelated businesses to reduce risk. Combining with a company whose products have a different seasonal pattern or that respond differently to the business cycle can result in a more stable sales pattern. GE Capital Corp., the financial unit of General Electric Co., targets acquisitions that balance each other: risky companies

horizontal merger
A merger of companies at the same stage in the same industry; done to reduce costs, expand product offerings, or reduce competition.

vertical merger
A merger of companies at different stages in the same industry; done to gain control over supplies of resources or to gain access to different markets.

conglomerate merger
A merger of companies in unrelated businesses; done to reduce risk.

To learn more about the latest information technology industry mergers, explore the Broadview Associates site at http://www.broadview.com

concept check

- Differentiate between a merger and an acquisition.
- What are the most common motives for corporate mergers and acquisitions?
- Describe the different types of corporate mergers.

whose performance fluctuates with changing financial markets and companies that perform consistently regardless of market conditions. GE Capital has 28 separate business lines in five major product groups: specialty insurance; consumer services such as credit card operations and auto and home financing; equipment leasing, ranging from aircraft to satellites to portable toilets; commercial financing; and financing for smaller businesses. Recently, it entered the rapidly growing information technology services market as well.[14]

A specialized financially motivated type of merger, the **leveraged buyout (LBO),** became popular in the 1980s but is less common today. LBOs are corporate takeovers financed by large amounts of borrowed money—as much as 90 percent of the purchase price. LBOs can be started by outside investors or the corporation's management. Believing that the company is worth more than the value of all the stock, they buy the stock and take the company private. The purchasers expect to generate cash flow by improving operating efficiency or by selling off some units for cash that can be used to pay the debt. Although some LBOs did improve efficiency, many did not live up to investor expectations or generate enough cash to pay the debt.

CAPITALIZING ON TRENDS IN BUSINESS

>lg 8

As we learned in the Prologue, an awareness of trends in the business environment is a critical component of business success. Many of the social, demographic, and technology trends described affect how businesses organize. When studying options for organizing a business or choosing a career path, consider the following trends in franchising and mergers and acquisitions.

Niche Markets

More franchises are catering to niche markets. For example, former Denver dentist Scott Menough now operates two Colorado Wild Birds Unlimited, Inc. franchises. Started by Jim Carpenter in 1981, this franchise system now has more than 280 units around the United States. Used goods are another growing segment of the retail market. GrowBiz offers franchisees resale outlets in five concepts: Once Upon a Child, Play It Again Sports, Music Go Round (instruments), Plato's Closet, and ReTool. Within 10 years the company opened 1,200 outlets. At its 700 Play It Again Sports stores, used items sell so quickly that the units now carry new items as well, amounting to about 60 percent of inventory.[15]

To boost its share of the $18 billion coffee market, Starbucks is expanding beyond coffee cafes by operating kiosks in airports, providing coffee service to businesses, and selling its coffee in supermarkets.

New Twists for Existing Franchises

As more franchise systems crowd into growing industry categories, established franchises must find ways to differentiate themselves:

- *Multiple franchise concepts.* Like GrowBiz, other franchisors offer more than one type of outlet. Precision Tune Auto Care's 650 franchisees like the option of choosing from Precision Auto Care, Precision Lube Express, or Precision Auto Wash stores. Many operate all three. Precision is also taking its successful multiple-option concept overseas to countries where people drive older cars.[16]

- *New types of outlets and expanded product offerings.* Pioneering postal service franchisor Mail Boxes Etc. added MBE Business Express, 24-hour self-service business centers in hotel lobbies. Coffee franchises like Diedrich's operate coffee carts in office complexes. Food franchises now offer broader menus. Smoothie franchise Jamba Juice added soup and snacks, and bagel franchises serve soups, salads, and gourmet sandwich creations.

- *Cross-branding.* Operating two or more franchises in one location generates more customer traffic and maximizes space, personnel, and management utilization. Jim Hobold of Cincinnati runs a Burger King and Frullati Cafe and Bakery (healthy fast food) franchises. "Every day mothers come into Burger King for chicken tender meals or burgers and fries for their kids, then come to Frullati for fruit smoothies and salads or sandwiches for themselves," he says. "With both operations in one place, we only need one general manager."[17]

The Big Get Bigger

As noted earlier, consolidation to achieve economies of scale is driving strategic mergers in industries such as automobiles, defense, oil, telecommunications, utilities, and financial services. These and other industries overexpanded due to an abundance of investment capital, globalization, better information technology, deregulation, and privatization. The result was fierce price competition and a search for other ways to improve financial performance.[18] Consolidation is affecting companies of all sizes, from small businesses to industry leaders like Mobil and Citicorp, which surprised many when they became targets.

In addition to the oil and telecommunications mergers described earlier, consolidation is changing the competitive environment in other industries as well. In the supermarket industry, announced mergers as of year-end 1998 increased the market share of the top 10 supermarket chains to almost 50 percent, compared to 30 percent in 1993. And between 1986 and 1998, the number of grocery wholesalers plummeted from 366 to 97 firms. Bank consolidations represented over 25 percent of 1998's total deal value.[19]

Hands across the Sea

Because size is also an advantage when competing in the global marketplace, cross-border mergers are also on the rise. In particular, U.S. and European companies want new markets around the world. German automaker Daimler-Benz's 1998 acquisition of Chrysler, the number three U.S. automaker, created the world's third largest auto manufacturer based on revenues. Other trans-Atlantic acquisitions in recent years include the 2000 acquisition of Bestfoods by British-Dutch consumer firm Unilever for $20 billion and the $56 billion 1999 merger between Britain's Vodafone Group and its joint venture partner AirTouch Communications to create the world's largest cellular phone company.

European companies are also seeking partners closer to home. In 1999 Hoechst AG (Germany) and France's Rhone-Poulenc SA merged to form the world's largest life sciences company. Both U.S. and European companies are buying Latin American companies, especially in the telecommunications, utility, and financial services industries.

Cross-border mergers present special challenges for the combined entity. It must contend with differences in language and social and workplace cultures in addition to the usual complexities of merging two companies. Regulatory considerations also increase.

c o n c ə p t   c h ə c k

- What are the important trends in franchising?
- How will the performance of the stock market affect future merger activity?
- What are the important trends in mergers and acquisitions?

APPLYING THIS CHAPTER'S TOPICS

Clearly, you need to understand the benefits of different forms of business organization if you start your own company. If you decide to work for someone else, this information will help you match a business entity with your goals. Suppose you are considering two job offers for computer programming positions: a two-year-old consulting firm with 10 employees owned by a sole proprietor or a publicly traded software developer with sales of $500 million. In addition to comparing the specific job responsibilities, consider the following:

- Which company offers the better training? Do you prefer the on-the-job training you'll get at the small company, or do you want formal training programs as well?
- Which position offers the chance to work on a variety of assignments?
- What are the opportunities for advancement? Employee benefits?
- What happens if the owner of the young firm gets sick or decides to sell the company?
- Which company offers a better work environment for you?

Answering these and similar questions will help you decide which job meets your particular needs.

Is Franchising in Your Future?

If the franchise route to business ownership interests you, begin educating yourself about the franchise process and investigate various types of franchise opportunities. You should research a franchise company thoroughly before making a financial commitment, because there are considerable differences among the more than 2,100 franchise systems. Once you've narrowed your choices to several specific franchises, ask for the *Uniform Franchise Offering Circular (UFOC)* for that franchisor and read it thoroughly. The Federal Trade Commission (FTC) requires franchisors to prepare this document. The UFOC provides a wealth of information about the franchisor, including its history, operating style and management, past or pending litigation against the franchisor, the franchisee's financial obligations, and any restrictions on the sale of units. Interviewing current and past franchisees is another essential step.

Would-be franchisees should check recent issues of small-business magazines such as *Inc., Entrepreneur,* and *Entrepreneur's Be Your Own Boss* for industry trends, ideas on promising franchise opportunities, and advice on how to choose and run a franchise. The International Franchise Association Web site at **www.franchise.org** has links to *Franchise World* magazine and other useful sites. (For other franchise-related sites, see the Try It Now box and the Working the Net questions.)

Is franchising for you? Assertiveness, desire to be your own boss, willingness to make a substantial time commitment, passion about the franchise concept, optimism, patience, and integrity rank high on franchisors' lists. Prior business experience is also a definite plus, and some franchisors prefer or require experience in their field. The information in Exhibit 4-10 can help you make a realistic self-assessment and increase your chances of success.

1. **Learn the Laws** Before starting your own company, you should know the legal requirements in your area. Call the appropriate city or county departments, such as licensing, health, and zoning, to find out what licenses and permits you need and any other requirements you must meet. Do the requirements vary depending on the type of company? Are there restrictions on starting a home-based business? Then contact your secretary of state or other agency that handles corporations to get information on how to incorporate.

2. **Study Franchise Opportunities** Franchising offers an alternative to starting a business on your own. Do you have what it takes to be successful? Start by making a list of your interests and skills, and do a self-assessment using some of the suggestions in the last section of this chapter. Next you need to narrow the field of thousands of different franchise systems. At Franchise Handbook: On-line **http://www. franchise1.com**, you'll find articles with checklists to help you thoroughly research a franchise and its industry, as well as a directory of franchise opportunities. Armed with this information, you can develop a questionnaire to evaluate a prospective franchise.

e x h i b i t   4 - 1 0 | Are You a Perfect Franchisee?

What traits do franchisors look for in a prospective franchisee? Specific preferences vary depending on the type of franchise company. For example, most lodging franchisors want prior experience in hotel management. The following questions are based on characteristics franchisors cited in a *Nation's Business* magazine survey:

- How long have you wanted to own a business?
- Are you willing to work hard and put in long hours?
- Do you have the required financial resources for your chosen franchise?
- Does the idea of running *all* aspects of a small business, from dealing with customers to bookkeeping and maintenance, appeal to you?
- Are you excited about the specific franchise concept?
- Do you have prior business experience? In what fields?
- Can you balance your entrepreneurial tendencies with the need to follow the franchisor's operating procedures?
- Are you competitive and a high achiever?
- Do your expectations and personal goals match the franchisor's?

SOURCE: Adapted from Thomas Love, "The Perfect Franchisee," *Nation's Business* (April 1, 1998), downloaded from **http://business.elibrary.com**.

Mergers and You

The high level of merger and acquisition activity changes the business environment for employees, business owners, and customers. You may work for an acquiring or a target company. What does this mean careerwise?

It's important in any job to take opportunities to develop a portfolio of transferable skills. This increases your chances of finding another job, either at the new company or at a new firm. Announcement of a merger increases the stress level for all employees. You will have to live with uncertainty for many months while the companies work out the details of integrating two operations. You may lose your job when overlapping departments are combined. According to outplacement firm Challenger, Gray & Christmas, in 1998 mergers were responsible for almost 74,000 lost jobs, or about 11 percent of all job cuts.[20] Even if you keep your job, the corporate culture may change, whether the acquirer is a U.S. company or one based overseas. The best approach is keep the quality and quantity of your work at the highest levels and be flexible.

If you own a small company, you may become a target. Or your customers may disappear as they are acquired by other companies. Should the large number of mergers discourage you from starting your own company? Not at all! Even though size is an advantage in many industries, the worldwide economy still needs small, entrepreneurial firms. Despite consolidation trends, large corporations still prefer to outsource many projects to companies with specialized expertise in such areas as design and technology. Also, many niche markets exist where being small provides benefits such as personal service and quick, creative solutions to customer problems.

Mergers also affect vendors, competing firms, and customers. If you own or work for a supplier in an industry with lots of merger activity, increase your efforts to acquire new customers, perhaps in different sectors. Maintain and nurture customer contacts. Those employees often move to other companies where they can recommend your firm. As a customer, you may find that your local bank branch or supermarket disappears after a merger. If competition decreases as a result of a merger, you may face fewer choices and higher prices.

at JobDirect, Inc.

Choosing the corporate structure early in its life paid off for JobDirect, Inc. Despite competition from other electronic job posting Web sites, in just a few years JobDirect has differentiated itself through its marketing expertise and unique interactive matching service that runs matches every 24 hours. Over 250 college career offices use its proprietary Resume Exchange software. Its clients range from major firms like PaineWebber, Sears, Oracle, Xerox, and Macy's, IBM, Chase Manhattan, Charles Schwab, and DoubleClick, to not-for-profits like the Peace Corps and Teach for America and smaller companies. In a nationwide survey, college students ranked JobDirect first among Web job search services. Corporate and online partnerships with companies like Barnes and Noble College Bookstores and Yahoo! help JobDirect reach more students.

The ultimate tribute to Sara and Rachel's vision came in July 2000, when Korn/Ferry International, a leading executive recruitment firm, acquired JobDirect to enter the rapidly growing college recruitment market and develop an early career management relationship with entry-level professionals. "The prestige of the Korn/Ferry brand along with their blue chip client relationships uniquely position us for success in serving and developing the online recruitment market for entry-level graduates," said Kevin Gage, CEO of JobDirect.com.[21]

SUMMARY OF LEARNING GOALS

>lg 1 **What are the three main forms of business organization, and what factors should a company's owners consider when selecting a form?**
A sole proprietorship is a business owned and operated by an individual. A partnership is an association of two or more people who operate a business

as co-owners. A corporation is a legal entity with an existence separate from its owners. When choosing a form of organization for a business, evaluate the owner's liability for the firm's debts, the ease and cost of forming the business, the ability to raise funds, the taxes, the degree of operating control the operator can retain, and the ability to attract employees.

>lg 2   What are the advantages and disadvantages of sole proprietorships?

The advantages of sole proprietorships include ease and low cost of formation, the owner's rights to all profits, the owner's control of the business, relative freedom from government regulation, absence of special taxes, and the ease of dissolution. Disadvantages include unlimited liability of the owner for debts, difficulty in raising capital, limited managerial expertise, large personal time commitment, unstable business life, difficulty in attracting qualified employees, and the owner's personal absorption of all losses.

>lg 3   Why would a new business venture choose to operate as a partnership, and what downside would the partners face?

Partnerships can be formed as either general partnerships or limited partnerships. In a general partnership, the partners co-own the assets and share in the profits. Each partner is individually liable for all debts and contracts of the partnership. The operations of a limited partnership are controlled by one or more general partners, who have unlimited liability. Limited partners are financial partners whose liability is limited to their investment; they do not participate in the firm's operations. The advantages of partnerships include ease of formation, availability of capital, diversity of managerial expertise, flexibility to respond to changing business conditions, and relative freedom from government control. Disadvantages include unlimited liability for general partners, potential for conflict between partners, limited life, sharing of profits, and difficulty in leaving a partnership.

>lg 4   How does the corporate structure provide advantages and disadvantages to a company, and what are the major types of corporations?

A corporation is a legal entity chartered by a state. Its organizational structure includes stockholders, who own the corporation; the board of directors, who are elected by the stockholders and govern the firm; and officers who carry out the goals and policies set by the board. Stockholders can sell or transfer their shares at any time and are entitled to receive profits in the form of dividends.

Advantages of corporations include limited liability, ease of transferring ownership, stable business life, and ability to attract financing. Disadvantages are double taxation of profits, the cost and complexity of formation, and government restrictions.

>lg 5   Does a company have any business organization options besides sole proprietorship, partnership, and corporation?

Businesses can also organize as limited liability companies, cooperatives, joint ventures, and franchises. A limited liability company (LLC) provides limited liability for its owners but is taxed like a partnership. These two features make LLCs an attractive form of business organization for many small firms.

Cooperatives are collectively owned by individuals or businesses with similar interests that combine to achieve more economic power. Cooperatives distribute all profits to their members. Two types of cooperatives are buyer and seller cooperatives.

A joint venture is an alliance of two or more companies formed to undertake a special project. Joint ventures can be set up in various ways, such as through partnerships or special-purpose corporations. By sharing management expertise, technology, products, and financial and operational resources, companies can reduce the risk of new enterprises.

>lg 6   Why is franchising growing in importance?

Franchising is one of the fastest growing forms of business ownership. It involves an agreement between a franchisor, the supplier of goods or services, and a

KEY TERMS

acquisition 126
board of directors
   116
conglomerate
   merger 127
cooperatives 120
corporation 114
franchise
   agreement 121
franchisee 121
franchising 121
franchisor 121
general partners
   112
general partnership
   112
horizontal merger
   127
leveraged buyout
   (LBO) 128
limited liability
   company (LLC)
   119
limited partners
   112
limited partnership
   112
merger 126
partnership 111
S corporation 118
sole proprietorship
   110
stockholders 116
vertical merger
   127

franchisee, the individual or company that buys the right to sell the franchisor's products in a specific area. With a franchise, the business owner does not have to start from scratch but buys a business concept with a proven product and operating methods. The franchisor provides management training and assistance; use of a recognized brand name, product, and operating concept; and financial assistance. Franchises can be costly to start, however, and restrict operating freedom because the franchisee must conform to the franchisor's standard procedures.

>lg 7 **Why would a company use mergers and acquisitions to grow?**
In a merger, two companies combine to form one company; in an acquisition, one company or investor group buys another. Companies merge for strategic reasons, such as growth, diversification of product lines, increased market share, and economies of scale. The other main motive for merging is financial restructuring—cutting costs, selling off units, laying off employees, refinancing the company—to increase the value of the company to its stockholders.

There are three types of mergers. In a horizontal merger, companies at the same stage in the same industry combine to have more economic power, to diversify, or to win greater market share. A vertical merger involves the acquisition of a firm that serves an earlier or later stage of the production or sales cycle, such as a supplier or sales outlet. In a conglomerate merger, unrelated businesses come together to reduce risk through diversification.

>lg 8 **What trends will affect business organization in the future?**
Americans continue to open new businesses, from sole proprietorships to multi-unit franchise operations, at record rates. The service sector is growing fastest to meet the increased demand for convenience from working women and two-income families. Good franchise opportunities include those providing services for children and senior citizens, as well as resale shops and other specialty markets. To remain competitive, established franchisors are offering multiple concepts, new types of outlets, and expanded products. Key merger trends include increasing numbers of mergers between companies that wish to consolidate to achieve economies of scale and cross-border mergers.

PREPARING FOR TOMORROW'S WORKPLACE

1. Susan Atkinson is thinking about opening a business to sell her homemade barbeque sauces over the Internet. Although she has enough money saved to start the business on her own, she is worried about her lack of knowledge of accounting and finance. A friend mentions that he knows someone with 10 years of business management experience who wants to get involved with a start-up company. As Susan's business consultant, prepare a memo for Susan that recommends a form of business organization, including the issues she should consider, advantages, disadvantages, and risks involved, and reasons for your choice.

2. At the end of a late night study session, you wonder why someone doesn't provide an on-campus coffee delivery service and decide this is a great business for you. There's just one catch: you're broke, so you'll need a partner. Summarize the management and technical skills and financial resources you need for your company; then make a list of the qualities and resources you bring to the team and what you want in a partner. Select a potential partner from your class to interview using the advice in Exhibit 4-2 as a starting point. Evaluate the proposed partnership.

3. You and a partner co-own Glow Auto, a successful car-detailing business. Because sales at the first location have tapered off, you want to open additional outlets in a large city about 20 miles away. Because of the cost of expanding, you

decide to sell Glow Auto franchises. The idea takes off, and soon you have 25 units throughout the region. Your success results in an invitation to speak at the local Rotary Club. Prepare a brief presentation that describes how you evaluated the benefits and risks of becoming a franchisor, the problems you encountered, and how you've established good working relationships with your franchisees.

4. Choose one of the selected recent mergers of 1998 from Exhibit 4-9. Research the background of the merger using a variety of sources, including the acquirer's corporate Web site and news articles from business periodicals like *Business Week, Fortune,* and *The Wall Street Journal.* Report on the motives behind the merger, the problems facing the new entity, and the company's progress toward achieving its objectives.

WORKING THE NET

1. Research how to form a corporation and an LLC in your state using a search engine to find relevant sites. Here are two to get you started: **http://www.corporate.com** and **http://www.incorporate-usa.com.** What steps are necessary to set up a corporation in your state? How do the fees compare to other states? If you were incorporating a business, what state would you choose and why?

2. Select three franchises that interest you. Research them at sites such as the Franchise Handbook: On-Line (**http://www.franchise1.com/directory**), *Entrepreneur* magazine's Franchise Zone (**http://www.entrepreneur.com/Franchise_Zone**), and Be the Boss Virtual Franchise Expo (**http://www.vifexpo.com**). Prepare a chart comparing them, including history, number and location of units, financial requirements (initial franchise fee, other start-up costs, royalty and advertising fees), and any other information that would help you evaluate the franchise.

3. Check out the latest merger trends at Industry Week (**http://www.industryweek.com**). Find examples of a horizontal merger and a merger that failed.

CREATIVE THINKING CASE

Should Jason Take the Subway?

Jason Braden's dream of starting and running a business in his hometown became reality when he inherited $35,000 from his grandfather. Jason, who wanted a low-risk venture that provided a decent income, decided that his town needed a sandwich store near two large office parks. Jason had worked during college at a Subway sandwich store and knew that designing the store, rent, and equipment and supply costs would quickly eat up his $35,000, leaving little for advertising or promotion. Jason also didn't know much about finding suppliers, setting up an accounting system, and hiring employees.

Jason contacted his former boss José Gonzalez, who owned five Subway franchises. Mr. Gonzalez was very positive about his experiences, telling Jason that Subway was one of the lowest cost food franchises to start and pointing to his late-model sports car and house in an affluent neighborhood as proof of the income potential.

Jason requested information about becoming a franchisee from Subway's corporate offices. He learned that his total initial investment could range from $60,000 to $103,000, depending on store size and location. The company could help with financing for most of the costs and provide training to help him set up an efficient operation. The only cash down payment was the $10,000 franchise fee. After the store opened, out of weekly gross sales Jason would pay 8 percent royalties and 3.5 percent to Subway's fund for national advertising.

Jason had two other options. His parents would lend him $20,000 to open his own independent sandwich store or to buy a different type of franchise. His girlfriend said she'd contribute about $30,000, so they could pool their funds and go into business as partners. After all, they got along really well and this would give them a chance to spend more time together.

INFOTRAC® COLLEGE EDITION

Critical Thinking Questions

1. Should Jason purchase a Subway sandwich franchise? Defend your answer.
2. How could Jason minimize the potential risks of opening an independent sandwich shop? Would you recommend this course of action? Why?
3. What potential problems might Jason encounter if he goes into partnership with his girlfriend? How could they reduce these problems?
4. If you were Jason, which course of action would you take? Why?

VIDEO CASE

Second Chance Body Armor

Second Chance Body Armor (**http://www.sruniforms.com/second.html**) makes protective clothing—body armor that is worn underneath a person's street clothes.

Second Chance Body Armor produces comfortable, concealable, everyday body armor. It is made with lightweight materials that stop the penetration of a bullet or a knife, thereby protecting the wearer against serious or fatal injury. The armor is designed to be comfortable so that people will wear it on a daily basis.

Richard Davis, president of Second Chance Body Armor, invented the concept of concealable body armor in 1971. Though he had a good product, he found that the market was not aware of it. To promote market awareness, Davis developed advertisements in which he shot himself at point-blank range while wearing the body armor. He survived, sustaining only superficial abrasions.

Since those early days, Second Chance Body Armor has expanded its line of personal protection products. Second Chance's business strategy is quite simple: focus on customer needs for comfortable, custom-fit body armor. Carrying out this strategy requires strong customer service, the use of new technology, and the creation and maintenance of brand identity.

Second Chance now produces several different types of concealable body armor. The SUPERfeatherlite Body Armor, advertised as its "good" armor, is made with DuPont Kevlar 129. The SUPERfeatherlite SC229 is billed as the "better" model. It is made with Akzo-Nobel TWARON T-2000 Microfilament fibers and Butterfly Lite fabrication technology. Second Chance's "best" body armor, the Monarch, combines three fourth-generation ballistics technologies "to produce revolutionary improvement in wearability and performance." The Monarch model incorporates ARAFLEX IV ballistics fibers; Butterfly Lite stitch patterns to protect against multihits, multiangle hits, and blunt trauma; and Gore-Tex ComfortCOOL ballistic pad covers for moisture protection and breathability. Second Chance also produces the Monarch +P+, which combines antiballistic properties and antipuncture properties into a single body armor model. Promoted as Second Chance's "bonus" model, this product provides protection from both gunshots and penetration by knives and other sharp instruments. No matter which type of body armor a Second Chance customer purchases, it is designed for comfort and custom fit to the customer using five different body measurements.

The Second Chance brand has become so widely accepted in law enforcement circles that it has become a generic name just as Kleenex has for facial tissue. There is only one Second Chance brand, but people commonly refer to any body armor as "providing them with their second chance." By following the business strategy of focusing on customer needs for comfortable, custom-fit body armor, Second Chance has developed into the worldwide leader in body armor.

Critical Thinking Questions

1. What advantages and disadvantages of the sole proprietorship might Davis have experienced? Would another form of business ownership have been better?
2. Suppose that you wish to go into business for yourself in the future. What insights does the Second Chance Body Armor experience provide for you?

Case: AOL and Time Warner Try to Reinvent the Internet

America Online (AOL) and Time Warner had a great deal in common when they announced plans to merge into one mega-corporation in a $183 billion deal. Time Warner controlled a large media enterprise that included magazine publishing, film production, cable television broadcasting, and music recording. AOL commanded the largest and fastest growing slice of Internet access and content service for millions of subscribers around the world.

In announcing the deal, AOL CEO Steve Case and Time Warner Chairman Gerald Levin said that the merger would allow them to reinvent how entertainment, communications, and information are delivered to consumers. "What we are creating is really the first Internet-powered media communications company of the 21st Century," said Levin. Plans included introducing an interactive service, delivered via cable, that would let consumers surf the Internet and send emails through their home television screens using a wireless keyboard.

Before the merger could be completed, it required government approval both in the United States and in Europe. In hearings, critics of the deal said that they worried the combined entity would dominate Internet access. Not only did AOL already have millions of subscribers, but Time Warner also owned approximately 20 percent of high-speed cable connections that could bring the Internet to millions of other homes. Critics feared that the merged company would block other Internet service providers from using Time Warner's ca-

ble lines. Another concern was that the huge corporation would overly control Internet content if AOL favored using Time Warner content over that created by other firms.

Case and Levin dismissed these criticisms by saying they operate in different markets and are fully committed to keeping high-speed cable lines open to other entertainment and online companies. "To my view, I don't think there are any regulatory issues," says Levin. "This is not a conventional horizontal merger. There are no business overlaps."

Questions for Critical Thinking

1. Do you agree with Levin that this isn't a horizontal merger? Explain.
2. Evaluate how the merger may affect the stakeholders of both companies.
3. Using the Internet, research the status of this merger. What challenges have the two companies faced? Make suggestions for overcoming these challenges.

SOURCES: Marilyn Geewax, "Regulatory Scrutiny Increases for AOL-Time Warner Deal," *The Atlanta Journal and Constitution* (September 2, 2000), p. E3; Alec Klein, "AOL, Time Warner Officials to Testify; Merger Critics Seeking Voice in Hill Hearings," *The Washington Post* (September 2, 2000), p. E01; Richard Siklos, Catherine Yang, "Welcome to the 21st Century," *Business Week* (January 24, 2000), downloaded from **http://www.businessweek.com**; "Behind Case, the Visionary, Lies a Monopolist," *Independent* (September 6, 2000), p. 15; "Courtship of 2 Companies Spanned 3 Months," *Minneapolis Star Tribune* (January 11, 2000), p. 5D.

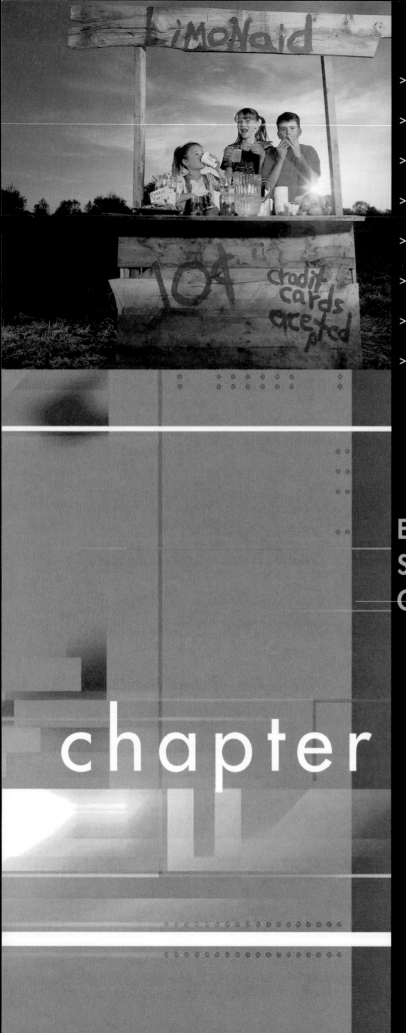

learning goals

>lg 1 Why do people become entrepreneurs, and what are the different types of entrepreneurs?

>lg 2 Which characteristics do successful entrepreneurs share?

>lg 3 How do small businesses contribute to the U.S. economy?

>lg 4 What are the advantages and disadvantages facing owners of small businesses?

>lg 5 How does the Small Business Administration help small businesses?

>lg 6 What are the first steps to take if you are starting your own firm?

>lg 7 Why does managing a small business present special challenges for the owner?

>lg 8 What trends are shaping the small business environment?

Entrepreneurship: Starting and Growing a Business

chapter 5

The Juice Guys Squeeze Their Way to Success

From a small boat in Nantucket Harbor to a $60 million company named one of *Inc.* magazine's fastest growing firms—that kind of success is every potential entrepreneur's dreams. "If I were on the outside looking in, I would say, 'These guys were an overnight success,'" says Tom Scott, co-president of Nantucket Nectars (**http://www.juiceguys.com**). "Being on the inside, it's been a long, long time. We almost went out of business a thousand times." As Scott and his partner and co-president Tom First acknowledge, "Nantucket Nectars is one big collection of mistakes." But they learned through experience, relying on their creativity and instincts.

Scott didn't set out to develop a multimillion dollar juice company. During the summer of 1988, he started Allserve from a small boat in Nantucket Harbor. "It was like a floating 7-Eleven," Scott recalls. He made the rounds of the yachts in the harbor, selling newspapers and snacks, taking trash, and doing laundry. Despite the 18-hour days, seven days a week, Scott loved being his own boss and vowed to find a way to make enough money to live on Nantucket.

Classmate Tom First became Scott's partner in Allserve the summer following graduation. During the winter, however, business was nonexistent. With lots of time on their hands, the Toms and their friends would gather for dinner. One night First re-created a fresh peach juice he'd tasted in Spain. It was an instant hit, so the two Toms named it Nantucket Nectar, bottled it in recycled wine bottles, and sold it the next summer from the boat and a small store.

Though the peach juice was a success, Allserve was too seasonal and too small to support both partners. Pooling their $17,000 savings, they hired a bottler to produce 1,400 cases of Nantucket Nectars. The initial production run sold out so quickly that they began investigating mass production. By 1993, Nantucket Nectars reached $400,000 in sales.

To expand, Scott and First needed to raise more money. One of the investors they contacted was Michael Egan, then chairman of Alamo Rent a Car and a former Allserve customer. Egan liked Scott, First, and their company so much that he provided $500,000 in first-round financing. "It was very hard to dissuade them from their mistakes," he says. "But I've never been involved with two such fast learners in my life."

As demand increased, the "juice guys" encountered their first major problem: distributing their juice to enough markets. In 1994 they lost $2 million by handling their own distribution. In 1995, after Egan contributed an additional $1.5 million, they hired outside distributors and made a profit of $850,000 on $15 million in sales.

Critical Thinking Questions

As you read this chapter, consider the following questions as they relate to Nantucket Nectars, Inc.:

- What type of entrepreneur is Scott? What were his motives in starting Nantucket Nectars?

- What personal characteristics contributed to Scott and First's success?

- What advantages and disadvantages did Scott and First face as small business owners, and how did they overcome them?

By 1997, Nantucket Nectars was a $50 million company and one of *Inc.* magazine's 20 fastest growing private companies. In November of that year, Scott and First sold a large ownership stake to Ocean Spray Cranberries, Inc., retaining about half the company. They are still active in management, and although their corporate offices are now in Cambridge, Massachusetts, the company maintains its original entrepreneurial feeling. "Employees don't walk into the job with a procedures manual," says First. "We figure it out ourselves. Trial and error. That's entrepreneurial. That's fun."[1]

BUSINESS IN THE 21ST CENTURY

The entrepreneurial spirit is capturing the interest of people from all backgrounds and age groups. Teenagers are starting fashion clothing and high-tech companies. Recent college graduates like Tom Scott and Tom First shun the "jacket and tie" corporate world to make it on their own. Downsized employees and midcareer executives form another large group of small business owners. Retirees who worked for others all their lives may form the company they always wanted to own.

Although the number of new businesses started in the United States each year has declined slightly in the past three years, they continue to be formed at high rates. In the first 9 months of 2000, an average of 2,600 businesses were launched each week across the country.[2] Small companies are the lifeblood of the U.S. economy. In fact, 99 percent of all U.S. companies have fewer than 500 employees, yet they employ 60 percent of the nation's workforce. Small businesses provide 40 percent of the nation's goods and services.[3] Some firms start small but grow into multimillion dollar corporations.

Companies started by entrepreneurs and small business owners make significant contributions to the global economy. They are hotbeds of innovation, taking leadership roles in technological change and the development of new goods and services. They account for 51 percent of the gross domestic product and 47 percent of all retail sales. Small businesses also create most of the new jobs in the United States. Since the 1970s, approximately two-thirds of the total net gain in new jobs has been created by small businesses.[4] In addition, they provide women, minorities, and immigrants with opportunities for economic and social advancement.

You may be one of the millions of Americans who's considering joining the ranks of business owners. As you read this chapter, you'll get the information and tools you need to help you decide whether owning your own company is the right career path for you. You'll discover why entrepreneurship continues to be one of the hottest areas of business activity, as well as the characteristics you need to become a successful entrepreneur. Then we'll look at the importance of small businesses in the economy, their ad-

In launching Nantucket Nectars, entrepreneurs Tom Scott and Tom First join the growing number of college graduates who choose to start their own businesses rather than working for someone else.

vantages and disadvantages, and the role of the Small Business Administration. Next, the chapter offers guidelines for starting and managing a small business. Finally, it explores the trends that will shape entrepreneurship and small business ownership in the 21st century.

ENTREPRENEURSHIP TODAY

>lg 1

Although he's only 25, Jared Schutz already has five companies to his credit. At 16, he started a company to trade government scrap metal. While in college he used those earnings to open a technical consulting firm, American Information Systems, Inc. (AIS), with two partners. Soon after he founded Stardot Consulting to create Web sites for politicians, he helped a friend start Internet athletic equipment dealer Sportscape.com. His latest venture is Proflowers.com, an Internet flower retailer that's growing 25 percent a month. A high-energy person described by his partners as "a classic idea man," Schutz also has top marketing and strategy skills and knows how to use Internet technology to his advantage.[5]

The United States is blessed with a wealth of entrepreneurs like Schutz. According to research by the Small Business Administration, 16 million Americans—about 13 percent of all nonagricultural workers—are involved in either full- or part-time entrepreneurial activities. And their ranks continue to swell as up-and-coming entrepreneurs aspire to become the next Bill Gates or Marc Andreessen (co-founder of Netscape).

Why has entrepreneurship remained a strong part of the foundation of the U.S. business system for so many years? Today's global economy rewards innovative, flexible companies that respond quickly to changes in the business environment. These companies are started by **entrepreneurs,** people with vision, drive, and creativity who are willing to take the risk of starting and managing a business to make a profit.

entrepreneurs
People with vision, drive, and creativity who are willing to take the risk of starting and managing a new business to make a profit or of greatly changing the scope and direction of an existing firm.

Entrepreneur or Small Business Owner?

The term *entrepreneur* is often used in a broad sense to include most small business owners. But there is a difference between entrepreneurship and small business management. Entrepreneurship involves taking a risk, either to create a new business or to greatly change the scope and direction of an existing firm. Entrepreneurs typically are innovators who start companies to pursue their ideas for a new product or service. They are visionaries who spot trends.

While entrepreneurs may be small business owners, not all small business owners are entrepreneurs. They are managers or people with technical expertise who started a business or bought an existing business and made a conscious decision to stay small. For example, the proprietor of your local independent bookstore is a small business owner. Jeff Bezos, founder of Amazon.com, also sells books. But Bezos is an entrepreneur: he developed a new model—a Web-based book retailer—that revolutionized the world of book selling. The two groups share some of the same characteristics, and we'll see that some of the reasons for becoming an entrepreneur or a small business owner are very similar. However, entrepreneurs are less likely to accept the status quo and generally take a longer-term view than the small business owner.

Types of Entrepreneurs

Entrepreneurs fall into several categories: classic entrepreneurs, multipreneurs, and intrapreneurs.

Classic Entrepreneurs   *Classic entrepreneurs* are risk takers who start their own companies based on innovative ideas. Some classic entrepreneurs are *micropreneurs* who start small and plan to stay small. They often start businesses just for personal satisfaction and the lifestyle. Michael McVey got the entrepreneurial urge after the 1994 baseball players' strike when he lost his job selling hot dogs at Colorado Rockies baseball games. McVey developed Treebats, roughly cut decorative baseball bats carved from recycled Colorado Christmas trees, to combine his love of baseball with an opportunity to recycle the wood. His company, Colorado Rules, sells Treebats to baseball teams, to tourists as souvenirs, and to corporations that want to give the Colorado-inspired bats as gifts instead of coffee mugs or T-shirts.[6]

In contrast, *growth-oriented entrepreneurs* want their businesses to grow into major corporations. Most high-tech companies are formed by growth-oriented entrepreneurs. Jeff Bezos' recognized that with Internet technology he could compete with large chains of traditional book retailers. Bezos' goal was to build his company into a high-growth enterprise—and he even chose a name that reflected this strategy: Amazon.com. Now he's moved beyond books to sell CDs, toys, and other products in an effort to make his company a one-stop shopping site.[7]

Multipreneurs   Then there are *multipreneurs,* entrepreneurs who start a series of companies. Jim Clark is the quintessential multipreneur, starting three high-tech companies with market values of more than $1 billion each. A former Stanford professor, Clark founded Silicon Graphics, Inc., which makes powerful high-end graphics computers, in 1982. His next venture, Internet pioneer Netscape, was formed in 1994 and went public in 1995. While Clark was still Netscape's chairman, he shifted his attention to his newest company, Healtheon, which he founded in 1996 and took public in early 1999. Healtheon provides online medical data for physicians, insurers, and hospitals. A visionary who's better at creating companies, putting together a management team, and advising the company than at day-to-day management, Clark began looking for his next start-up before Netscape went public.[8]

How can Jim Clark help you? Get answers to your medical questions at the consumer solutions area or learn more about the company at the Healtheon Web site whose site appears when entering

http://www.healtheon.com

intrapreneurs

Entrepreneurs who apply their creativity, vision, and risk taking within a large corporation, rather than starting a company of their own.

Intrapreneurs   Some entrepreneurs don't own their own companies but apply their creativity, vision, and risk taking within a large corporation. Called **intrapreneurs,** these employees enjoy the freedom to nurture their ideas and develop new products, while their employers provide regular salaries and financial backing. Intrapreneurs have a high degree of autonomy to run their own mini-companies within the larger enterprise. They share many of the same personality traits as classic entrepreneurs but take less personal risk. According to Gifford Pinchot, who coined the term *intrapreneur* in 1985, corporations have lost billions of dollars by rejecting ideas from employees who then leave to start their own companies. Corporations that create supportive environments for intrapreneurship retain their most innovative employees—as well as ownership of the products they develop.[9] Xerox Technology Ventures (XTV) funds promising research projects that don't quite fit the overall corporate objectives until the projects are ready for outside financing. This gives them the chance to develop into profitable businesses, rather than be shunted aside.[10]

Why Become an Entrepreneur?

As the examples in this chapter show, entrepreneurs are found in all industries and have different motives for starting companies. The most common reason cited by CEOs of the *Inc.* 500, the magazine's annual list of fastest growing private companies, is the desire to control their own destiny. Related to this is a desire for job security now that large corporations regularly downsize staff and streamline operations. Other reasons, as Exhibit 5-1 shows, include making money and building a new company. Two other important basic motives mentioned in other surveys are feeling personal satisfaction with your work and creating the lifestyle that you prefer.

Do entrepreneurs feel that going into business for themselves is worth it? The answer is a resounding yes. In one survey, over 80 percent said they would do it over again. And as we've seen, many thrive on creating multiple companies around their ideas. "The first time, you go and take a risk and push it, and you succeed, then the next time, you take more risk; you push further," says Kamran Elahan, who's started seven successful technology companies. "It becomes an addiction. Each time you want to push it further, further, further."[11]

concept check

- What is an entrepreneur? Describe several types of entrepreneurs.
- What differentiates an entrepreneur from a small business owner?
- What are some major factors that motivate entrepreneurs to start businesses?

CHARACTERISTICS OF SUCCESSFUL ENTREPRENEURS

>lg 2

Do you have what it takes to become an entrepreneur? Being an entrepreneur requires special drive, perseverance, passion, and a spirit of adventure in addition to managerial and technical ability. Having a great concept is not enough. An entrepreneur must also be able to develop and manage the company that implements the idea. In addition, entrepreneurs *are* the company; they cannot leave problems at the office at the end of the day. Most entrepreneurs tend to work longer hours and take fewer vacations once they have their own company. They also share other common characteristics, as described in the next section.

e x h i b i t 5 - 1 | Reasons Entrepreneurs Start Companies

Reason	Percentage Citing
To be my own boss or control my own life	41%
To make money	16
To create something new	12
To prove I could do it	9
Because I was not rewarded at my old job	6
Because I was laid off from my old job	5
Other	11

SOURCE: "Inc. 500 Almanac," *Inc.* 500 (October 22, 1996), p. 24.

The Entrepreneurial Personality

Many of the studies of the entrepreneurial personality have found similar traits.[12] In general, entrepreneurs are:

- *Ambitious.* Entrepreneurs have a high need for achievement and are competitive.
- *Independent.* They are self-starters who prefer to lead rather than follow. They are also individualists. "I've done between 400 and 500 acquisitions in my career, so I know a lot about entrepreneurs. Entrepreneurs don't march left, right, left, right. They march left, left, right, right, left, hop, skip," comments Paul M. Verrochi, chairman and CEO of Provant, a Boston company that provides business training services.[13]
- *Self-confident.* They understand the challenges of starting a business but are decisive and have faith in their abilities to resolve problems. Entrepreneurs trust their hunches and act on them.
- *Risk taking.* Though they are not averse to risk, most successful entrepreneurs prefer situations with a moderate degree of risk, where they have a chance to control the outcome, to highly risky ventures that depend on luck.
- *Visionary.* "Entrepreneurs believe they can create the future," says Marc Andreessen, Netscape co-founder.[14] Their ability to spot trends and act on them sets entrepreneurs apart from small business owners and managers.
- *Creative.* To compete with larger firms, entrepreneurs need to have creative product designs, marketing strategies, and solutions to managerial problems.
- *Energetic.* Starting a business takes long hours. Some entrepreneurs start companies while still employed full-time. Each week, Elle Hamm, founder of the Beverly Hills–based Rudwear Collection, worked 40 hours at a hotel job and another 40 hours developing her line of funky clothing and accessories.[15]
- *Passionate.* Entrepreneurs love their work. "If you're not passionate about what you're doing, you can't be an entrepreneur," says Judy Estrin, founder of three successful high-tech companies. "It just takes too many compromises and too much effort."[16]
- *Committed.* They make personal sacrifices to achieve their goals. Because they are so committed to their companies, entrepreneurs are persistent in seeking solutions to problems. Tom Scott and Tom First, for example, believed in their product and refused to lower their quality standards, even if it meant financial hardship.

The Edward Lowe Foundation's mission is to "champion the entrepreneurial spirit." Find out how it accomplishes that goal by exploring its site at

http://www.lowe.org

The Hagberg Consulting Group, a leadership development consulting firm, studied over 2,000 executives for 12 years. In addition to the characteristics already mentioned, the study found that in comparison to the average executive, entrepreneurs are much more opinionated, emotionally aloof, impatient, focused, and aggressive. They also tend to get upset when things don't go their way.[17]

Managerial Ability and Technical Knowledge

A person with all the characteristics of an entrepreneur might still lack the business skills to run a successful business. As we'll discuss later in this chapter, entrepreneurs believe they can learn many of these technical skills.

concept check

- Describe the personality traits and other skills characteristic of successful entrepreneurs.
- What does it mean to say that an entrepreneur should work on the business, not in it?

Entrepreneurs need managerial ability to organize a company, develop operating strategies, obtain financing, and manage day-to-day activities. Good interpersonal and communication skills are also essential in dealing with employees, customers, and other businesspeople, such as bankers, accountants, and attorneys. They also need the technical knowledge to carry out their ideas. For instance, an entrepreneur may have a great idea for a new computer game and be a self-confident, hardworking, motivated person with good interpersonal skills. But without a detailed knowledge of computers, that entrepreneur would find it nearly impossible to produce a computer game that would sell.

Michael Gerber, author of *The E-Myth Revisited,* agrees that entrepreneurs need both managerial ability and technical skills to succeed. "Everybody who goes into business is actually three people in one: the Entrepreneur, the Manager, and the Technician," Gerber says. He explains that the technician can do the work but cannot run and grow the business; those are the jobs of the other two. Owners need to get their roles straight: work *on* the business, not *in* it.[18]

Working on the business often requires entrepreneurs to take Jim Clark's approach: focus on what they do best and hire others to do the rest. As Lillian Vernon, founder of the successful mail-order business that bears her name, explains, "My biggest mistake was trying to do it all. As the business grew, I had a hard time relinquishing responsibility. I finally realized the only healthy way to grow a business is with a qualified, dedicated management team."[19]

SMALL BUSINESS

>lg 3

Although large corporations dominated the business scene for many decades, in recent years small businesses have once again come to the forefront of the U.S. economy. Ninety-eight percent of the businesses in the United States have less than 100 employees and nearly three-quarters of all U.S. businesses are owned by self-employed people who have no other employees.[20] By some estimates, U.S. small businesses in the aggregate would rank third among the world's economic powers based on the total value of goods and services they provide.[21]

Let's look at some of the main reasons behind the increase in small business formation:

- *Independence and a better lifestyle.* Large corporations no longer represent job security or offer as many fast-track career opportunities. Midcareer employees leave the corporate world in search of new opportunities. Many new college and business school graduates shun the corporate world altogether and start their own companies or look for work in small firms.

- *Personal satisfaction from work.* Many small business owners cite this as one of the primary reasons for starting their companies. They love what they do.

- *Best route to success.* Small businesses offer their owners the potential for profit. Also, business ownership provides greater advancement opportunities for women and minorities, as we discuss later in this chapter.

- *Rapidly changing technology.* Advances in computer and telecommunications technology, as well as the sharp decrease in the cost of this technology, have given individuals and small companies the power to compete in industries that were formerly closed to them. The arrival of the Internet and World Wide Web is responsible for the formation of many small businesses, as we'll discuss in the trends section later in this chapter.

- *Outsourcing.* As a result of downsizing, corporations often contract with outside firms for services they used to provide in-house. This "outsourcing" creates opportunities for smaller companies, many of which offer specialized goods and services.

- *Major corporate restructurings and downsizings.* These force many employees to look for other jobs or careers.

What Is a Small Business?

How many small businesses are there in the United States? Estimates range from over 5 million to almost 20 million, depending on how government agencies and other groups define a business and the size limits they use. The database of the federal Small Business Administration, which uses the number of business enterprises, lists about 5.4 million firms with fewer than 500 employees as of 1995. The Bureau of Labor Statistics estimates that another 10.5 million individuals are self-employed.[22]

So what makes a business "small"? As we've seen, there are different interpretations, and the range is extremely broad. Generally, though, a **small business** has the following characteristics:

- Independently managed
- Owned by an individual or a small group of investors
- Based locally (although the market it serves may be widespread)
- Not a dominant company (thus it has little influence in its industry)

Exhibit 5-2 shows some of the characteristics of the typical American small business.

Small businesses in the United States can be found in almost every industry group, as shown in Exhibit 5-3. Small businesses include the following:

- *Services.* Service firms are the most popular category of small businesses because they are easy and low cost to start. They are often small; very few service-oriented companies are national in scope. They include repair services, restaurants, specialized software companies, accountants, travel agencies, management consultants, and temporary help agencies.
- *Wholesale and retail trade.* Retailers sell goods or services directly to the end user. Wholesalers link manufacturers and retailers or industrial buyers; they assemble, store, and distribute products ranging from heavy machinery to produce. About 85 percent of all wholesale firms have fewer than 20 employees. Most retailers also qualify as small businesses, whether they operate one store or a small chain.

small business

A business that is independently owned, is owned by an individual or a small group of investors, is based locally, and is not a dominant company in its industry.

---

e x h i b i t 5 - 2 | The Typical American Small Business

Median number of employees	3
Median annual revenues	$150,000–$500,000
Average annual earnings of owner	$40,000
Average hours per week owner works	50
Percentage with Internet access	78%
Percentage that maintain a Web site	40%

SOURCES: "Dun & Bradstreet 19th Annual Survey Finds Significant Rise in U.S. Businesses Offering Healthcare Benefits, But Growing Concern Over Costs," Dun & Bradstreet Company press release, May 27, 2000; and "Small Business: An Economic Powerhouse," National Federation of Independent Businesses (1998), downloaded from **www.nfibonline.com**.

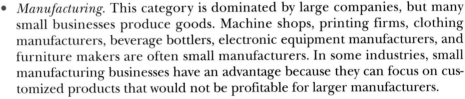

e x h i b i t   5 - 3 | Types of Small Business, by Industry

Industry	Percentage of All Small Businesses
Services	39.2%
Retail trade	20.4
Construction	11.8
Finance, insurance, real estate	8.0
Wholesale trade	7.4
Manufacturing	6.0
Transportation, public utilities	3.9
Agriculture, mining, other	3.3

SOURCE: Office of Advocacy, U.S. Small Business Administration, as reported in *Statistical Abstract of the United States*, 118th ed. (Washington, DC: Government Printing Office, 1998), p. 548.

- *Manufacturing.* This category is dominated by large companies, but many small businesses produce goods. Machine shops, printing firms, clothing manufacturers, beverage bottlers, electronic equipment manufacturers, and furniture makers are often small manufacturers. In some industries, small manufacturing businesses have an advantage because they can focus on customized products that would not be profitable for larger manufacturers.
- *Construction.* Firms employing under 20 people account for about 90 percent of the nation's construction companies. They include independent builders of industrial and residential properties and thousands of contractors in such trades as plumbing, electrical, roofing, and painting.
- *Agriculture.* Small businesses dominate agriculture-related industry, including forestry and fisheries. The Small Business Administration estimates that 99 percent of all agricultural firms have fewer than 100 employees.

>lg 4

Thousands of small manufacturers like this metal platemaker flourish because of their flexibility, efficiency, and ability to serve specialized markets.

Advantages of Small Business

Small businesses have advantages directly related to their size:

- *Greater flexibility.* Because most small businesses are owner-operated, they can react more quickly to changing market forces. They can develop product ideas and market opportunities without going through a lengthy approval process.
- *More efficient operation.* Small businesses are less complex than large organizations. They have fewer employees doing things that are not directly related to producing or selling the company's product (such as accounting and legal work). Thus, they can keep their total costs down.
- *Greater ability to serve specialized markets.* Small businesses excel in serving specialized markets. Large firms tend to focus on goods and services with an established demand and the potential for high sales.

MAKING ETHICAL CHOICES

BEING AN INFORMATION BROKER

Are you interested in going into business for yourself? Do you have access to the Internet? If you answered yes to both questions, you might be interested in becoming the proprietor of an information brokerage service.

Information brokers "specialize in hunting down confidential financial data" for lawyers working on behalf of their clients and individuals or firms seeking to collect payments on bills, among others. Some firms in this fast-growing industry use only legitimate public records to conduct their searches. Other information brokers use unscrupulous methods. Indeed, Julie Williams, acting Comptroller of the Currency for the United States, says that dishonest information brokering is both "growing and alarming."

According to federal and state authorities, "the most widely used [information brokering] practice involves impersonating an account holder to obtain balances." The Internet has enabled information brokers to easily gather information on individuals. In turn, this information makes it easier for the broker to impersonate an account holder when calling a financial institution. Other tactics used by unscrupulous information brokers

include mailing phony rebate checks to targets in order to obtain their bank account numbers from returned checks and using bogus offers of preapproved credit to trick people into revealing bank information and Social Security numbers.

An investigation of Summer Associates Information Services in Stamford, Connecticut, shows how easy it is for someone to start an information brokerage business. Summer was a small operation located in a three-room suite in a converted factory in Stamford. The entire business operated with just a few people, a telephone, and a computer modem.

Critical Thinking Questions

1. How does the information brokerage industry reflect trends in business?
2. What should an information broker do to ensure that the business is operated ethically?
3. Suppose that you wish to become an entrepreneur. What insights, if any, does the information brokerage industry provide?

Many products would not exist were it not for small firms' ability to provide them cost-effectively. Narrative Television Network (NTN), for example, is a Tulsa firm that provides narrated movies and television shows for the visually impaired and blind. Founders Jim Stovall, totally blind since age 29, and Kathy Harper, a legally blind legal researcher, wanted careers that they could manage despite their disability. Stovall came up with the idea of providing narration to supplement the soundtracks on movies and television shows (similar to the closed captioning service for the hearing impaired).[23]

- *More personal service.* Another advantage of small businesses is their ability to give the personal touch. In businesses like gourmet restaurants, health clubs, fashion boutiques, and travel agencies, customers place a high value on personal attention. Through this direct relationship with customers, the owner-manager also gets feedback on how well the firm is meeting customer needs.

Disadvantages of Small Business

Small businesses also face several disadvantages:

- *Limited managerial skill.* Small business owners may not have the wide variety of skills they need to respond quickly to change. As noted earlier, they often lack knowledge in areas like finance, marketing, taxation, and business law. They may have experience in one area of business but not in the specific type of business they choose to start. Others have the technical skills but not the management ability. Nantucket Nectars' founders, Scott and First, were business novices with no experience in managing a company or producing, distributing, or marketing juice. They learned on the job—and quickly. Other entrepreneurs hire consultants to help them solve problems. Later this chapter discusses how these problems can be overcome when starting and managing a small business.

- *Fund-raising difficulty.* Another big problem for small businesses is obtaining adequate financing. Small firms must compete with larger, more established firms for the same pool of investment funds. Getting loans can be difficult because new businesses are obviously more risky than established ones. And the interest rates charged by banks and private investors are usually higher for small firms than for large ones. Sources of financing are examined in greater detail later in the chapter.

- *Burdensome government regulations.* The addition of new federal, state, and local regulations creates more compliance and reporting requirements for small businesses. Expanded federal, state, and local environmental regulations on water pollution and toxic wastes are especially burdensome. Local laws regulate noise pollution and traffic related to home-based businesses. With limited staff and financial resources, small firms may have to hire outside consultants to help prepare the many types of reports the government requires.

- *Extreme personal commitment of the owner.* Starting and managing a small business requires a major commitment by the owner. According to Dun & Bradstreet's 17th Annual Small Business Survey, more than half of all entrepreneurs work more than 51 hours a week, and 26 percent work over 60 hours a week. Long hours, the need for owners to do much of the work themselves, and the stress of being personally responsible for the success of the business are big disadvantages.

The Small Business Administration

Many small business owners turn to the **Small Business Administration (SBA)** for assistance. The SBA's mission is to help people start and manage small businesses, help them win federal contracts, and speak on behalf of small business. Through its national network of local offices, the SBA advises and helps small businesses in the areas of finance and management. Its toll-free number—1-800-U-ASK-SBA (1-800-827-5722)—provides general information, and its Web site at **www.sba.gov** offers details on all its programs.[24]

Financial Assistance Programs   The SBA offers financial assistance to qualified small businesses that cannot obtain financing on reasonable terms through normal lending channels. This assistance takes the form of guarantees on loans made by private lenders. (The SBA no longer provides direct loans.) These loans can be used for most business purposes, including purchasing real estate, equipment, and materials. Between 1993 and 2000, the SBA helped more than 375,000 businesses get more than $80 billion in loans, including $30 billion in loans to women- and minority-owned businesses.[25]

More than 300 SBA-licensed **Small Business Investment Companies (SBICs)** provide long-term financing for small businesses. These privately owned and managed investment companies hope to earn a substantial return on their investments as the small

>lg 5

Small Business Administration (SBA)
A government agency that helps people start and manage small businesses, helps small business owners win federal contracts, and speaks on behalf of small business.

Small Business Investment Company (SBIC)
Privately owned and managed investment companies that are licensed by the Small Business Administration and provide long-term financing for small businesses.

What does it take to qualify for one of the many SBA loan programs? Find out at http://www.sba.gov/financing

businesses grow. In 1999, SBICs invested a record $3.7 billion in about 66,541 small businesses. The not-for-profit Angel Capital Electronic Network (ACE-Net, **http://ace-net.sr.unh.edu**) offers an Internet-based matching service for small businesses seeking funding of up to $5 million from individual investors.[26]

Management Assistance Programs   The SBA also provides a wide variety of management advice. Its Business Development Library has publications on most business topics. Its "Starting Out" series offers more than 30 brochures on how to start a business in different fields (from ice cream stores to fish farms).

The Office of Business Development and local Small Business Development Centers offer advice, training, and educational programs. Business development officers counsel small business owners. The SBA also offers free management consulting through the Service Corps of Retired Executives (SCORE). Executives in this program use their business background to help small business owners. The more than 11,000 SCORE volunteers and approximately 1,000 Small Business Development Centers provide management and technical assistance to about 300,000 small businesses each year. The Internet is helping SCORE expand its outreach into new markets by offering email counseling through its Web site (**http://ww.score.org**).

The SBA is committed to helping minority-owned businesses through its Office of Minority Enterprise Development. It has special programs and support services for socially and economically disadvantaged persons, including women, Native Americans, and Hispanics. The SBA also makes a special effort to help veterans go into business for themselves.

concept check

- What is a small business? Why are small businesses becoming so popular?
- Discuss the major advantages and disadvantages of small business ownership.
- What is the Small Business Administration? Describe the financial and management assistance program offered by the SBA.

STARTING YOUR OWN BUSINESS

>lg 6

You may have decided that you'd like to go into business for yourself. If so, what's the best way to go about it? You can (1) start from scratch, (2) buy an existing business, or (3) buy a franchise. The first two options are covered in this section. Franchising was covered in Chapter 4.

Getting Started

The first step in starting your own business is a self-assessment to determine whether you have the personal traits you need to succeed and, if so, what type of business would be best for you. The Your Career feature that follows this chapter includes a questionnaire and other information to help you make these decisions. Finding the idea and choosing a form of business organization come next.

Finding the Idea   Entrepreneurs get ideas for their businesses from many sources. It is not surprising that 60 percent of *Inc.* 500 executives got the idea for their company while working in the same industry. Starting a firm in a field where you have experience improves your chances of success. Other sources of inspiration are hobbies and personal interests; suggestions from customers, family, and friends; and college courses or other education.

Ideas are all around you. Do you have a problem that you need to solve or a product that doesn't work as well as you'd like? Maybe one of your coworkers has a complaint. Raising questions about the way things are done is a great way to generate ideas. Many successful businesses get started because someone notices problems and needs and then finds a way to fill them. In 1996 Bill Gross founded Idealab, a company that develops Internet-related companies based on his ideas, on that premise. "Just about every idea I've ever pursued has been something that I . . . passionately feel I would want in my life," Gross says.[27]

What Pennsylvania interior designer Julie Margaret wanted was convenience. Tired of struggling with heavy mattresses and box springs when she arranged model homes, she wondered if there was a way to make beds look real without incurring the expense and hassle of real mattresses. The answer was Mimics, cardboard box "mattresses" reinforced with ribs so they won't collapse if someone sits on them. Margaret began selling the lightweight, reusable substitute cardboard beds in 1996. Mimics, which are easy to ship and cost only $30 to $50 depending on size, quickly became popular with contractors, department stores, bedding manufacturers, and photography studios.[28] Later in this chapter we'll offer more suggestions for ways to generate business ideas.

For tips on how to start, grow, or manage your business, check out *Entrepreneur*'s "Tip of the Day" at

http://www.entrepreneur.com

Choosing a Form of Business Organization   Another key decision for a person starting a new business is whether it will be a sole proprietorship, partnership, corporation, or limited liability company. As discussed in Chapter 4, each type of business organization has advantages and disadvantages. The choice depends on the type of business, number of employees, capital requirements, tax considerations, and level of risk involved.

Developing the Business Plan

Once you have the basic concept for a product, you must develop a plan to create the business. The planning process is one of the most important steps in starting a business and helps minimize the risks involved. A good business plan can be a critical determinant of whether a firm succeeds or fails. Debbie Gallagher, head of the Center for Entrepreneurship at New York's Nassau Community College, points out that two-thirds of all businesses fail in the first five years. "Why are these businesses failing? They haven't educated themselves as to what it takes to run a business," she says.[29]

business plan

A formal written statement that describes in detail the idea for a new business and how it will be carried out; includes a general description of the company, the qualifications of the owner(s), a description of the product or service, an analysis of the market, and a financial plan.

One of the best ways to get that education is by preparing a formal, written **business plan** that describes in detail the idea for the new business and how it will be carried out. A well-prepared, comprehensive business plan helps business owners take an objective and critical look at their business venture and set goals that will help them manage the business and monitor its growth and performance.

Key features of a business plan are a general description of the company, the qualifications of the owner(s), a description of the product or service, an analysis of the market (demand, customers, competition), and a financial plan. It should focus on the uniqueness of the business and explain why customers will be attracted to it. Exhibit 5-4 is a brief outline of what a business plan should include.

Writing a good business plan may take many months. Many businesspeople, in their eagerness to begin doing business, neglect planning. They immediately get caught up in day-to-day operations and have little time for planning. But taking the time to develop a good business plan pays off. Writing the plan forces you to analyze your concept carefully and make decisions about marketing, production, staffing, and financing. A venture that seems sound at the idea stage may not look so good after closer analysis. The business plan also serves as the first operating plan for the business.

e x h i b i t   5 - 4 | Outline for a Business Plan

Title page: Provides names, addresses, and phone numbers of the venture and its owners and management personnel; date prepared; copy number; and contact person.

Table of contents: Provides page numbers of the key sections of the business plan.

Executive summary: Provides a one- to three-page overview of the total business plan. Written after the other sections are completed, it highlights their significant points and, ideally, creates enough excitement to motivate the reader to continue reading.

Vision and mission statement: Concisely describes the intended strategy and business philosophy for making the vision happen.

Company overview: Explains the type of company, such as manufacturing, retail, or service; provides background information on the company if it already exists; describes the proposed form of organization—sole proprietorship, partnership, or corporation. This section should be organized as follows: company name and location, company objectives, nature and primary product or service of the business, current status (start-up, buyout, or expansion) and history (if applicable), and legal form of organization.

Product and/or service plan: Describes the product and/or service and points out any unique features; explains why people will buy the product or service. This section should offer the following descriptions: product and/or service; features of the product or service providing a competitive advantage; available legal protection—patents, copyrights, trademarks—and dangers of technical or style obsolescence.

Marketing plan: Shows who the firm's customers will be and what type of competition it will face; outlines the marketing strategy and specifies the firm's competitive edge. This section should offer the following descriptions: analysis of target market and profile of target customer; methods of identifying and attracting customers; selling approach, type of sales force, and distribution channels; types of sales promotions and advertising; and credit and pricing policies.

Management plan: Identifies the key players—active investors, management team, and directors—citing the experience and competence they possess. This section should offer the following descriptions: management team, outside investors, and/or directors and their qualifications, outside resource people and their qualifications, and plans for recruiting and training employees.

Operating plan: Explains the type of manufacturing or operating system to be used; describes the facilities, labor, raw materials, and product processing requirements. This section should offer the following descriptions: operating or manufacturing methods, operating facilities (location, space, and equipment), quality-control methods, procedures to control inventory and operations, sources of supply, and purchasing procedures.

Financial plan: Specifies financial needs and contemplated sources of financing; presents projections of revenues, costs, and profits. This section should offer the following descriptions: historical financial statements for the last three to five years or as available; pro forma financial statements for three to five years, including income statements, balance sheets, cash flow statements, and cash budgets (monthly for first year and quarterly for second year); break-even analysis of profits and cash flows; and planned sources of financing.

Appendix of supporting documents: Provides materials supplementary to the plan. This section should offer the following descriptions: management team biographies, any other important data that support the information in the business plan, and the firm's ethics code.

SOURCE: From *Small Business Management*, 11th edition, by Justin G. Longenecker and Carlos W. Moore. © 2000. Reprinted with permission of South-Western College Publishing, a division of Thomson Learning. Fax 800 730-2215.

The most common use of business plans is to persuade lenders and investors to finance the venture. The detailed information in the business plan helps them decide whether to invest. Even though the business plan may have taken months to write, it must capture the potential investor's interest in only a few minutes. For that reason, the basic business plan should be written with a particular reader in mind; it should be tailored to the type of investor you plan to approach and his or her investment goals.

The business plan should not be set aside once financing is obtained and the company is operational. Entrepreneurs who think the business plan is only for raising money make a huge mistake. Owners should review the plan on a regular basis—monthly, quarterly, or annually, depending on how fast their particular industry changes. "A business plan is a dynamic plan," says Jerry Kleinman, co-founder of Optimal Resolutions, Inc., a Manhasset (New York) family business consulting group. "It needs to be constantly updated as both internal and external conditions change. . . . As you meet your projections, you then want to set higher goals." Reviewing your plan will help you identify strengths and weaknesses in marketing strategies and management and also help you analyze possible opportunities for expansion in light of current trends and your original mission.[30]

Many business students get firsthand experience writing business plans by participating in their school's business plan competitions. As the Focus on Small Business box explains, many contest winners launch successful companies.

Financing the Business

Once the business plan is complete, the next step is to get the financing to set up the business. The amount required depends on the type of business and the

FOCUSING ON SMALL BUSINESS

FROM CLASSROOM TO COMPANY

What do 1-800 Contacts, Direct Hit Technologies, and Ampersand Art Supply have in common? These companies were all winners of major business plan competitions. 1-800 Contacts, for example, won the 1995 Brigham Young University tournament. The mail-order contact lens replacement company sold almost $4 million in lenses the following year.

About 35 business schools sponsor the contests, where students (usually in MBA programs) present plans for a new business. Students compete first at intramural contests at their own schools. Winners of those contests go on to intercollegiate contests at the University of Texas, Austin; San Diego State University (SDSU); the University of Oregon; or the University of Nebraska.

By creating a business from the ground up, students use every aspect of their business education. "Going through a competition teaches students how to present a plan and exposes them to the type of questions investors will be asking," says Alex de Noble, SDSU professor of management and entrepreneurship and director of its tournament. The contest also provides valuable networking opportunities and exposes would-be entrepreneurs to businesspeople who can advise them as they refine their plans.

Elaine Salazar, CEO and president of Ampersand Art Supply, which manufactures and sells art supplies at over 400 U.S. and overseas outlets, won the Texas and California competitions. "I didn't just get an education on putting together a good business plan at the University of Texas," she says. "I had access to people and resources that helped me launch my business." One of the judges liked the company so much that he invested $300,000.

Winning does not guarantee success, however. University of Texas student Eric Hills, whose computer software start-up won second place at the San Diego contest, was unable to raise financing for Partnerware Technologies. "Some folks automatically assumed the company . . . was more of an academic exercise than a real business," he says. Hayes Batson, another software developer who placed second at the University of Chicago, fared better: "Coming in second helped provide us with the credibility we needed to raise $1 million."

Critical Thinking Questions

1. You and a friend decide to enter your school's business plan competition with an idea for a new interactive computer game based on the stock market. How would you prepare a business plan to convince judges that your idea is a winner?
2. As a judge at a business plan competition, what characteristics would you look for in a winning business plan, and why?

debt

A form of business financing consisting of borrowed funds that must be repaid with interest over a stated time period.

equity

A form of business financing consisting of funds raised through the sale of stock in a business.

angel investors

Individual investors or groups of experienced investors who provide funding for start-up businesses.

venture capital

Financing obtained from investment firms that specialize in financing small, high-growth companies and receive an ownership interest and a voice in management in return for their money.

Looking for your own angel? Visit the SBA's Angel Capital Electronic Network (ACE-Net) at

http://ace-net.sr.unh.edu/pub

entrepreneur's planned investment. Businesses started by lifestyle entrepreneurs require less financing than growth-oriented businesses. The National Federation of Independent Businesses estimates that about half of all small business owners started their companies with less than $20,000, and 37 percent of the 1998 Inc. 500 were started with $10,000 or less.[31] Of course, manufacturing and high-tech companies generally require a larger initial investment.

The two forms of business financing are **debt,** borrowed funds that must be repaid with interest over a stated time period, and **equity,** funds raised through the sale of stock in the business. Those who provide equity funds get a share of the profits. Lenders usually limit debt financing to no more than a quarter to a third of the firm's total needs. Thus, equity financing usually amounts to about 65 to 75 percent of total start-up financing.

Two sources of equity financing for young companies are angel investors and venture capital firms. **Angel investors** are individual investors or groups of experienced investors who provide funding for start-up businesses. Angels often get involved with companies at a very early stage. **Venture capital** is financing obtained from investment firms that specialize in financing small, high-growth companies and receive an ownership interest and a voice in management in return for their money. They typically invest at a later stage than angel investors. We'll discuss venture capital in greater detail in Chapter 16.

Who provides the start-up funding, whether debt or equity, for small companies? Almost 80 percent of all business owners contribute personal savings to their new companies. Exhibit 5-5 shows how the founders of the *Inc.* 500 companies financed their start-ups.

Buying a Small Business

Another route to small business ownership is buying an existing business. Although this approach is less risky, it still requires careful and thorough analysis. Several important questions must be answered: Why is the owner selling? Does he or she want to retire or move on to another challenge, or are there some problems with the business? Is the business operating at a profit? If not, can the problems be corrected? What are the owner's plans after selling the company? Depending on the type of business, customers may be more loyal to the owner than to the product or service. They could leave the firm if the current owner decides to open a similar business. To protect against this situation, a "noncompete clause" can be included in the contract of sale.

Many of the same steps for starting a business from scratch apply to buying an existing company. A business plan that thoroughly analyzes all aspects of the business should be prepared. Get answers to all your questions, and determine, via the business plan, that the business is a good one. Then you must negotiate the purchase price and other terms and get financing. This can be a difficult process, and it may require the use of a consultant.

Risks of Small Business Ownership

Running your own business may not be as easy as it sounds. Despite the many advantages of being your own boss, the risks are great as well. Many businesses fail each year. The SBA estimates that about a quarter of all new businesses fail after two years, half after three years, and almost two out of every three by the end of the sixth year.[32]

| Sources of Start-up Funding

Source	Percentage Using
Owner's personal savings	79%
Family members	16
Partners	14
Personal charge cards	10
Friends	7
Bank loans	7
Angel investors	5
Mortgaged property	4
Venture capital	3
Other	8

SOURCE: "The Inc. 500 Almanac," *Inc. 500* (October 21, 1997), p. 28.

Businesses close down for many reasons. Here are the most common causes:

- Economic factors—business downturns and high interest rates
- Financial causes—inadequate capital, low cash balances, and high expenses
- Lack of experience—inadequate business knowledge, management experience, and technical expertise

Many of the causes of business failure are interrelated. For example, low sales and high expenses are often directly related to poor management.

Inadequate planning is often at the core of business problems. As described earlier, a thorough feasibility analysis, from market assessment to financial plan, is critical to business success. And even with the best plans, business conditions change and unexpected situations arise. An entrepreneur may start a company based on a terrific new product only to find that a large firm with more marketing and distribution clout introduces a similar item.

The stress of managing a business can take its toll. The business can consume your whole life. Owners may find themselves in over their heads and unable to cope with the pressures of business operations, from the long hours to being the main decision-maker.

Even successful businesses may have to deal with many of these difficulties. For example, growing too quickly can cause as many problems as sluggish sales. Growth can strain a company's finances. Additional capital is required to fund the expanded operations, from hiring additional staff to purchasing more equipment. Successful business owners must respond quickly as the business changes and develop plans to manage growth.

c o n c e p t   c h e c k

- How can potential business owners find new business ideas?
- Why is it important to develop a business plan? What should such a plan include?
- What financing options do small business owners have?
- Summarize the risks of business ownership.

MANAGING A SMALL BUSINESS

>lg 7   Whether you start a business from scratch or buy an existing one, you must be able to keep it going. The main job of the small business owner is to carry out the business plan through all areas of the business—from personnel to

production and maintenance. The small business owner must be ready to solve problems as they arise and move quickly when market conditions change. Hiring, training, and managing employees is another crucial responsibility. Clearly, managing a small business is quite a challenge.

Over time, the owner's role will change. As the company grows, others will make many of the day-to-day decisions while the owner focuses on managing employees and making plans for the firm's long-term success. The owner must always watch performance, evaluate company policies in light of changing conditions, and develop new policies as required. She or he must nurture a continual flow of ideas to keep the business growing. The type of employees needed may also change as the firm grows. A larger firm may need more managerial talent and technical expertise.

Using Outside Consultants

One way to ease the burden of managing a business is to hire outside consultants. Nearly all small businesses need a good certified public accountant (CPA) who can help with financial record keeping, tax planning, and decision making. An accountant who works closely with the owner to help the business grow is a valuable asset. An attorney who knows about small business law can provide legal advice and draw up essential documents. Consultants in other areas, such as marketing, employee benefits, and insurance, can be hired as needed. Outside directors with business experience are another way for small companies to get advice. Resources like these free the small business owner to concentrate on planning and day-to-day operations.

Want to know more about Employease? Read about its services at its Web site,

http://www.employease.com

Some aspects of the business can be *outsourced,* or contracted out to specialists in that area. Seventy-four percent of small businesses outsource at least one business function.[33] For example, Employease is an Internet-based human resources system that manages benefits information for small and mid-size companies. At a secure Web site, a company's employees can review, change, or update benefits information. The company's personnel managers can analyze its benefits data to see how employees are using the benefits. The service costs less than buying the sophisticated software, which would be too expensive for most small firms.[34]

Hiring and Retaining Employees

Small companies may have to be creative to find new employees and to convince applicants to join their firm. Jonathan Hirshon knew that Horizon Communications, a public relations (PR) firm in Silicon Valley, couldn't afford to compete with established high-tech PR firms for experienced staffers. Instead, he hires career changers with no PR background and trains them. "I can train people about technology, but I can't train them to be smart," he says. Hirshon's strategy is working: revenues jumped from $300,000 in 1996 to an anticipated $1 million in 1998. Horizon also benefits from the fresh perspective these employees bring.[35]

Attracting good employees can be hard for a small firm, which may not be able to match the salaries, benefits, and advancement potential offered by larger firms. Compounding the problem is the general labor shortage. With unemployment rates below 5 percent, small companies are finding it even harder to compete for qualified workers.

Once they hire employees, small business owners must promote employee satisfaction to retain them. Comfortable working conditions, flexible hours,

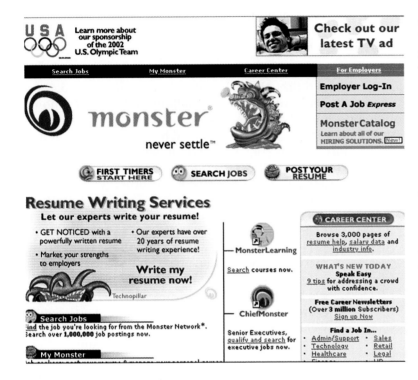

Small firms can use the Internet as a recruiting source by listing positions at job boards such as Monster, which reaches millions of job seekers.

employee benefit programs, opportunities to help make decisions, and a share in profits and ownership are some of the ways to do this.

Later chapters of the book present detailed discussions of management, production, human resources, marketing, accounting, computers, and finance, all of which are useful to small business owners.

Operating Internationally

More and more small businesses are discovering the benefits of looking beyond the United States for markets. As we learned in Chapter 2, the global marketplace represents a huge opportunity for U.S. businesses, both large and small. About 40 percent of the *Inc.* 500 companies do business overseas, and more companies are joining their ranks each year. According to the Department of Commerce (DOC), 60 percent of American firms that export have fewer than 100 employees. Small businesses decide to export because of foreign competition in the United States, new markets in growing economies, economic conditions (such as recession) in the United States, and the need for increased sales and higher profits.

Many small businesses hire international trade specialists to get started selling overseas. They have the time, knowledge, and resources that most small businesses lack. Export trading companies buy goods at a discount from small businesses and resell them abroad. *Export management companies (EMCs)* act on a company's behalf. For fees of 5 to 15 percent of gross sales and multi-year contracts, they handle all aspects of exporting, including finding customers, billing, shipping, and helping the company comply with foreign regulations.

concept check

- How does the small business owner's role change over time?
- Discuss strategies small business owners can use to acquire the expertise they need to help them run the business, either from outside sources or employees.
- Why should a small business consider exporting?

Want a quick course on how to expand into global markets? Check out the SBA's Office of International Trade at

http://www.sba.gov/oit

CAPITALIZING ON TRENDS IN BUSINESS

>lg 8   Social and demographic trends, combined with the challenges of operating in the fast-paced technology-dominated business climate of the 1990s, have changed the face of entrepreneurship and small business ownership. About

two-thirds of all new business owners launch their ventures from home. New ownership trends are emerging as well as more young people choose entrepreneurship over traditional career paths. The number of women and minority business owners continues to grow. Finally, the Internet is creating numerous opportunities for new types of small businesses.

Home Is Where the Office Is

For an increasing number of business owners, their daily commute is a walk down the hall to their home office. Home-based businesses make up 52 percent of all businesses and contribute about $314 billion to the U.S. economy each year. Although most home-based businesses are small, with average revenues of $40,000 a year, more than 55,000 home-based businesses report annual sales of $1 million or more. Technology has made it easier to start a home-based business by connecting home offices to customers through the Internet. Most home-based business owners wouldn't have it any other way; less than 5 percent eventually move out of their homes to a more traditional office. Exhibit 5-6 shows the reasons home-based business owners give for starting their business.[36]

Considering starting a business at home? You'll find tips and advice at the American Association of Home-Based Businesses Web site,

http://www.aahbb.org

No longer does running a business from home carry a stigma. In fact, many home-based entrepreneurs who could afford outside offices choose to stay home. "The home office used to be a stage in growth for many businesses," comments Sandy Weinberg, professor of entrepreneurship at Muhlenberg College in Allentown, Pennsylvania. "Now there's less of a need for many to ever move out of the home." Two trends that contribute to the rising popularity of working at home are the availability of low-cost technology—from voice mail to powerful computers and the Internet—and the large number of former corporate executives who consult or start businesses from home.[37]

Ownership Trends

At one time, most entrepreneurs were career changers starting second or third careers and corporate executives deciding to go out on their own. Today, many

| e x h i b i t   5 - 6 | Reasons for Starting a Home-Based Business |

Reason	Percentage Citing
For second income	44%
To be my own boss	21
For primary income	18
Family responsibilities	12
Health, unemployed, new ideas, or other	15

SOURCE: Joanne H. Prait, "Homebased Business: The Hidden Economy," SBA Office of Advocacy (March 2000), downloaded from **http://www.sba.gov**.

young people are choosing entrepreneurship as their first career. For women and minorities, entrepreneurship and small business ownership are a route to economic independence and personal and professional fulfillment. These groups are starting small businesses at rates far above the general population.

Entrepreneurs are getting younger all the time. About 30 percent of new entrepreneurs are age 30 or younger. An even higher number—over 60 percent of Americans ages 14 to 29—want to start their own business. A Wells Fargo Bank–National Federation of Independent Business (NFIB) study showed that Generation X-ers are among the most entrepreneurial of all age groups. "Instead of marching to the beat of corporate drums, many Gen X-ers are opting to build or buy their own drum, allowing them to pound out their own beat," explains study author William J. Dennis of the NFIB Education Foundation. As Exhibit 5-7 shows, almost half of the people starting their own businesses, either from scratch or buying a business, were under 35. Another key factor is the Internet, which makes it easier for technology-literate people in their teens and 20s to get into business.

Women start businesses at a rate twice the national average, making them one of the most dynamic small business segments. The SBA Office of Advocacy estimates that about 9.1 million American women own businesses that generate $3.6 trillion in revenue and employ almost 27.5 million workers.[38]

What motivates women to start their own firms? A study sponsored by three major women's business organizations found that the two leading reasons are the inspiration of an entrepreneurial idea and frustration with the previous work environment. More women business owners than men report dissatisfaction with their corporate jobs, mentioning inflexibility, the "glass ceiling" (lack of promotional opportunities), contributions not valued, unpleasant environment, and lack of challenge as specific reasons for going the entrepreneurial route.

Women-owned businesses make a significant contribution to today's business environment. They favor such workplace innovations as flexible scheduling, employee autonomy, and a family-like work environment and are more likely to commit to socially responsible business practices. Phyllis Adams found success in a nontraditional field for women—highway and heavy construction. After 16 years in her father's general contracting business, she started

e x h i b i t   5 - 7 | People Starting a Business, by Age

Age	Percentage of Total
Under 26	12.5%
26–35	34.1
36–45	30.1
46–55	16.9
56–65	4.9
Over 65	1.5

SOURCE: Wells Fargo/NFIB series on Business Starts and Stops, cited in "Generation X Leads the Way in Small Business Starts," NFIB Press Release, March 26, 1998, downloaded from **http://www.nfib.org.**

Women entrepreneurs like Heather Howitt, founder of Oregon Chai Tea Company, are launching their own firms at twice the rate of the national average.

For an overview of SBA services for women and links to its Online Women's Business Center and other program sites, visit the SBA Office of Women's Business Ownership site at

http://www.sba.gov/womeninbusiness/

Phylway Construction in Thibodaux, Louisiana, in 1992 with just $10,000 and an old truck. Her dedication to getting the work done during the cleanup after the devastation of Hurricane Andrew gave her company a good reputation right from the start. By 1998, sales were over $10 million and growing. Adams attributes her success to her positive attitude and team-building management style. "As a company, we've worked on building open communication and trust," she says.[39]

Firms owned by minorities—nonwhite people—are another fast-growing business sector. There are now 3.25 million minority-owned businesses in the United States, a 168 percent increase since 1990. These firms generate $495 billion in annual revenues, an astounding 343 percent increase since 1990. Minority businesses now employ over 4 million workers. Businesses owned by Hispanics are the fastest-growing minority business segment, with 1.4 million businesses. Asians own 1.1 million businesses and African Americans own 880,000.[40]

Like women business owners, today's minority entrepreneurs have more education and prior business experience than their predecessors and are branching out into new industries. "Traditionally, minorities owned businesses in retail, but we've seen a diversification into high tech, construction, and the service industries," says George Herrera, president of the U.S. Hispanic Chamber of Commerce. Contributing to this trend is the increase in government high-tech contracting and the globalization of U.S. business.[41]

The passage of NAFTA has opened doors for Hispanic entrepreneurs in particular. Their bilingual and bicultural skills help them form stronger trade relationships with Mexico. Javier Pacheco's firm, Mercantile Transport, Inc., has grown over 20 percent a year. Based near Los Angeles with offices in El Paso, San Diego, and Tijuana, the firm carries textiles, computer components, and other products between *maquiladora* plants in Mexico and the United States. Pacheco attributes part of his success to his understanding of Mexican business culture, which makes it easier to work effectively with Mexican customs officials.[42]

African Americans are less likely than other minorities to own their own enterprises. Although self-employment has been a route to advancement for other minority groups in the United States, the rate of self-employment for blacks is one-third that of whites. African American–owned businesses also tend to have lower revenues than other businesses, averaging $70,000 a year. A major obstacle for African American business owners is poor access to financing. Though other minority businesses also have problems obtaining financing, loan rejection rates for African American business owners were twice that of white-owned businesses, even after taking into account that African American–owned businesses tended to be younger, smaller, and owned by less experienced managers. This lack of financing discourages African Americans from becoming business owners. To remedy this situation, the SBA has pledged to double the number of loan guarantees for African Americans.[43]

The Internet Explosion

As noted earlier, advances in technology make it easier than ever to start a company and develop a loyal customer following. The Internet has opened new opportunities for small businesses, and research shows that small businesses are taking advantage of its benefits. Seventy percent of small business owners have Internet access, up from just 47 percent in 1998. Small businesses use the Internet for email, to purchase goods and services, to conduct business research, and, of course, to sell their products and communicate with customers. Thirty-eight percent of small business owners reported they have a Web

What services does the Minority Business Development Agency provide for small business owners? Click over to

http://www.mbda.gov/

to find out.

APPLYING TECHNOLOGY

RESERVATIONS ABOUND, YET SO DO PROFITS

While many dot-com companies were disappearing from sight, travel-related companies continued making inroads into the e-tail space. This sector accounts for about 30 percent of online consumer spending. These companies are a natural for online operations, because they don't have physical products that require warehouse and shipping. Most tickets and confirmations can be delivered electronically, keeping overhead to a minimum.

Dallas-based Hotel Reservations Network operates several discount reservations sites. Established in 1991 as a telephone-based reservations service, founder David Litman added the first Web site, **www.hoteldiscount. com,** in 1995. Moving online provided a cost-effective way for the company to grow quickly and reach a global customer base. "It didn't change what we do," says Litman. "It just put the company on steroids."

Since 1995 the company's average annual revenue growth has been 80 percent, compared to an estimated 20 percent to 30 percent if it hadn't migrated to the Web. As more customers discovered how easy it was to save 10 percent to 30 percent over the lowest published fares, demand grew. Hotels liked the service, too, which gave them an inexpensive distribution channel to fill unbooked rooms. The Web also allowed the company to track rates so it could guarantee customers the best prices and follow booking trends to decide what cities to add. The 1997 introduction of interactive

technology improved the company's efficiency even more. About two-thirds of customers now book online instead of by phone, saving staffing costs

With its own system firmly in place, the company launched an affiliate program to be the exclusive hotel booking resource on other travel sites. Arrangements with such sites as Travelocity.com and Cheap Tickets now account for over half its business, and that figure is growing. The affiliates receive about 5 percent of hotel sales booked at their sites.

To broaden its product line even further, Hotel Reservations added condominium and vacation rentals to its main site. In mid-2001 the company went upscale with its second Web site, **www.allluxuryhotels.com,** for four- and five-star hotels. On the drawing boards were sites dedicated to boutique hotels and budget lodging.

Critical Thinking Questions:

1. What are the advantages to Hotel Reservations Network of adding Web-based reservations to its phone-based service? Disadvantages? Are hotel reservations and the Internet a good fit?
2. Would you book hotel reservations online through **www.hoteldiscount.com?** Why or why not? What features should Hotel Reservations Network offer at its sites to improve the reservations process?

Applying This Chapter's Topics

What's topping the pop music charts? Find out at CDNow's site,

http://www.cdnow.com

site and 38 percent of those sites transact business directly over the Internet. About 8 percent of small business revenues currently come through electronic commerce–enabled Web sites.[44] CDNow took on the major music chains with its virtual music store. Instead of spending money on warehouses and distribution systems to place CDs on racks in stores around the country, the company focused on creating an informative and entertaining site. Visitors can search a huge inventory of all types of music, read interviews with their favorite artists, download sound clips, and, of course, order CDs and music in all categories.

Companies like InfoSpace simplify the process of setting up Web stores. Its Hypermart (**http://www.hypermart.com**) gives free space to small businesses that allow Hypermart to run ads on their Web pages. Its clients range from high-tech companies to home-based entrepreneurs selling handcrafts, and over 90,000 companies have taken advantage of the service in two years.[45]

Hotel Reservations Network, profiled in the Applying Technology box, tapped the full power of the Web to add vacation rentals and expand its discount reservations services.

concept check

- What significant trends are occurring in small business management?
- How is the Internet affecting small business?

APPLYING THIS CHAPTER'S TOPICS

After reading Chapters 4 and 5, you may be ready to go into business. Perhaps you believe you have just the "better mousetrap" the world needs. Maybe you want to be your own boss or seek financial rewards. Job security or quality of life issues may be your primary motives.

Whatever your reasons, you'll have to do a lot of groundwork before taking the plunge. Do you know what you want from life and how the business fits into your overall goals? Do you have what it takes to start a business, from personal characteristics like energy and persistence to money to fund the venture? You'll also have to research the feasibility of your product idea and develop a business plan. No question about it, becoming an entrepreneur or small business owner is hard work.

Taking the First Steps

Maybe you know that you want to run your own business but don't know what type of business to start. In addition to the advice provided earlier in the chapter, here are some ways to gather possible ideas:

- Brainstorm with family and friends without setting any limits, and then investigate the best ideas, no matter how impossible they may seem at first.
- Look at products that don't meet your needs and find ways to change them.
- Focus on your interests and hobbies. Attorneys Tim and Nina Zagat turned a love of dining out into a publishing company that sells restaurant guides.

- Use your skills in new ways. Are you computer-savvy? You could start a business providing in-home consulting to novices who don't know how to set up or use their computers.
- Be observant—look for anything that catches your interest wherever you are, in your hometown or when you travel. What's special about it? Is there a niche market you can fill?
- Pay attention to the latest fads and trends.
- Surf the Web, especially the "What's New" or "What's Hot" sections of search engines.[46]

Working at a Small Business

Working for a small company can be a wonderful experience. Many people enjoy the less structured atmosphere and greater flexibility that often characterize the small business workplace. Several years' experience at a small company can be a good stepping-stone to owning your own company. You'll get a better understanding of the realities of running a small business before striking out on your own. Other potential benefits include:

- *More diverse job responsibilities.* Small companies may not have formal job descriptions, giving you a chance to learn a wider variety of skills to use later. At a large company your job may be strictly defined.

TRY IT NOW!

1. **Explore the Possibilities** Starting a business at home is one of the easiest ways to become self-employed. Using the businesses listed in the Home Office Association of America (HOAA) Web site (http://www.hoaa.com) for ideas, choose a possible business opportunity that interests you. Then explore both the HOAA site and the American Association of Home-Based Businesses Web site (http://www.aahbb.org) to learn more about how to set up your business.

2. **Learn from an Entrepreneur** What does it really take to become an entrepreneur? Find out by interviewing a local entrepreneur or researching an entrepreneur you've read about in this chapter or in the business press. Get answers to the following questions, as well as any others you'd like to ask:

- How did you develop your vision for the company?
- What are the most important entrepreneurial characteristics that helped you succeed?
- Where did you learn the business skills you needed to run and grow the company?
- How did you research the feasibility of your idea? Prepare your business plan?
- What were the biggest challenges you had to overcome?
- Where did you obtain financing for the company?
- What are the most important lessons you learned by starting this company?
- What advice do you have for would-be entrepreneurs?

- *Less bureaucracy.* Small companies typically have fewer formal rules and procedures. This creates a more relaxed working atmosphere.
- *Your ideas more likely to count.* You'll have greater access to top management and be able to discuss your ideas.
- *Greater sense of your contribution to business.* You can see how your work contributes to the firm's success.

However, you should also be aware of the disadvantages of being a small business employee:

- *Lower compensation packages.* Although the gap between large and small businesses is narrowing, salaries are likely to be lower at small businesses. In addition, there may be few, if any, employee benefits such as health insurance and retirement plans.
- *Less job security.* Small businesses may be more affected by changing economic and competitive conditions. A change in ownership can put jobs at risk as well.
- *Greater potential for personality clashes.* When two employees don't get along, their hostility really stands out. Such conflicts can affect the rest of the staff. Also, if you have a problem with your boss, you don't have anyone to go to if the boss owns the company.
- *Fewer opportunities for career advancement.* After a few years, you may outgrow a small firm. There may be no chances for promotion. And with fewer people within the firm with whom to network, you'll have to join outside organizations for these connections.

Evaluating these factors will help you decide whether working at a small business is the right opportunity for you.

>looking ahead
at Nantucket Nectars, Inc.

Nantucket Nectars now has about 120 employees and five different lines of all-natural fruit juices, juice cocktails, iced teas, and lemonades. Despite its growth, Tom Scott and Tom First have kept the unique touches that made the company special, from homey labels and company trivia under the bottlecaps to the casual dress code. And the sentimental duo still owns their first business, Nantucket Allserve.

Although they are enjoying their financial success, they are far from complacent. "We're both paranoid people," Scott says. "Neither of us goes home and says, 'All right, now we're where we want to be.'" With competitors nipping at their heels, they are experimenting with new packaging, increased nutritional content for their Super Nectar line, and other products such as the Protein Smooth nutritional drink and an all-natural lemonade. Their long-range plan is to eventually become the country's largest juice producer. What could stand in their way? "Only ourselves—if we're not willing to improve ourselves and to strengthen our product over the next few years," says First.[47]

SUMMARY OF LEARNING GOALS

>lg 1 Why do people become entrepreneurs, and what are the different types of entrepreneurs?

Entrepreneurship involves taking the risk of starting and managing a business to make a profit. Entrepreneurs are innovators who start firms either to have a certain lifestyle or to develop a company that will grow into a major corporation. People become entrepreneurs for four main reasons: the opportunity for profit, independence, personal satisfaction, and lifestyle. Classic entrepreneurs may be micropreneurs, who plan to keep their businesses small, or growth-oriented entrepreneurs. Multipreneurs start multiple companies, while intrapreneurs work within large corporations.

>lg 2   **Which characteristics do successful entrepreneurs share?**
Successful entrepreneurs are ambitious, independent, self-confident, creative, energetic, passionate, and committed. They have a high need for achievement and a willingness to take moderate risks. They have good interpersonal and communication skills. Managerial skills and technical knowledge are also important for entrepreneurial success.

>lg 3   **How do small businesses contribute to the U.S. economy?**
A small business is independently owned and operated, has a local base of operations, and is not dominant in its field. The Small Business Administration further defines small business by size, according to the industry. Small businesses play an important role in the economy. About 98 percent of U.S. businesses have fewer than 100 employees. Small businesses are found in every field, but they dominate the construction, wholesale, and retail categories. Most new private-sector jobs created in the United States over the past decade were in small firms. Small businesses also create about twice as many new goods and services as larger firms.

>lg 4   **What are the advantages and disadvantages facing owners of small businesses?**
Small businesses have flexibility to respond to changing market conditions. Because of their streamlined staffing and structure, they can be efficiently operated. Small firms can serve specialized markets more profitably than large firms and provide a higher level of personal service. Disadvantages include limited managerial skill, difficulty in raising the capital needed for start-up and expansion, the burden of complying with increasing levels of government regulation, and the major personal commitment required on the part of the owner.

>lg 5   **How does the Small Business Administration help small businesses?**
The Small Business Administration is the main federal agency serving small businesses. It provides guarantees of private lender loans for small businesses. The SBA also offers a wide range of management assistance services, including courses, publications, and consulting. It has special programs for veterans, minorities, and women.

>lg 6   **What are the first steps to take if you are starting your own firm?**
After finding an idea that satisfies a market need, the small business owner should choose a form of business organization. The process of developing a formal business plan helps the business owner to analyze the feasibility of his or her idea. This written plan describes in detail the idea for the business and how it will be implemented. The plan also helps the owner obtain both debt and equity financing for the new business.

>lg 7   **Why does managing a small business present special challenges for the owner?**
At first, small business owners are involved in all aspects of the firm's operations. Wise use of outside consultants can free up the owner's time to focus on planning and strategy in addition to day-to-day operations. Other key management responsibilities are finding and retaining good employees and monitoring market conditions.

>lg 8   **What trends are shaping the small business environment?**
Women are starting businesses at a faster rate than any other group. Currently, they own about 30 percent of all businesses. Women often choose self-employment for lifestyle reasons and to overcome limited opportunities in large firms. Minority-owned businesses are another high-growth category. Minorities view business ownership as a way to overcome racial discrimination and economic hardship. Both women and minorities have made strides in overcoming

KEY TERMS

angel investors
    154
business plan 151
debt 154
entrepreneur 141
equity 154
intrapreneur 142
small business 146
Small Business
    Administration
    (SBA) 149
Small Business
    Investment
    Company (SBIC)
    149
venture capital
    154

barriers to entrepreneurship, such as discrimination, lack of formal business education, and limited business experience. Special training programs and financial assistance have helped increase business ownership among women and minorities. The Internet is also fueling small business growth by making it easier to open Web-based businesses.

PREPARING FOR TOMORROW'S WORKPLACE

1. After working in marketing with a major food company for 12 years, you are becoming impatient with corporate "red tape" (regulations and routines). You have an idea for a new snack product for nutrition-conscious consumers and are thinking of starting your own company. What are the entrepreneurial characteristics you will need? What other factors should you consider before quitting your job? Divide the class into two groups: one takes the role of the entrepreneurial employee, and the other takes the role of his or her current boss. Each should develop notes for a script. The employee will focus on why this is a good idea, reasons he/she will succeed, and so on, while the employer will play devil's advocate to convince him/her that staying on at the large company is a better idea.

2. Interview a small business owner in your community. Ask the owner why she/he chose this business, what she/he likes and dislikes most about running it, and the biggest challenges, advantages, and disadvantages. What would she/he do differently if starting over again today? Summarize your interview and prepare a brief report to present to your class.

3. Your class decides to participate in a local business plan competition. Divide the class into small groups and choose one of the following ideas:

   • A new computer game based on the stock market
   • A company with an innovative design for a skateboard
   • Travel services for college and high school students

   Prepare a detailed outline for the business plan, including the objectives for the business and the types of information you would need to develop product, marketing, and financing strategies. Each group will then present their outline for the class to critique.

4. A small catering business in your city is for sale for $150,000. The company specializes in business luncheons and smaller social events. The owner has been running the business for four years from her home but is expecting her first child and wants to sell. You will need outside investors to help you purchase the business. Develop questions to ask the owner about the business and its prospects and a list of documents you'd want to see. What other types of information would you need before making a decision to buy this company? Summarize your findings in a memo to a potential investor that explains the appeal of the business for you and how you plan to investigate the feasibility of the purchase.

5. Research the various types of assistance available to women and minority business owners. Call or visit the nearest SBA office to find out what services and resources it offers. Contact trade associations such as the U.S. Hispanic Chamber of Commerce, the Center for Women's Business Research (CWBR), and the Department of Commerce Minority Business Development Agency (MBDA). Call these groups or use the Web to develop a list of their resources and how a small business owner could use them.

WORKING THE NET

1. Visit Sample Business Plans at **http://www.bplans.com**/to review sample plans for all types of businesses. Select an idea for a company in a field that interests you, and using information from this site, prepare an outline for its business plan.

2. Visit the American Venture Capital Exchange site (**http://www.avce.com**) and find a business idea you like or dislike. Explain why you think this is a good business idea or not. List additional information the entrepreneur should have about starting this business and research the industry on the Web using a search engine.

3. Check out the international trade Web links at the Federation of International Trade Associations, **http://www.fita.org.** Click on International Trade Web Resources and pick two or three of the suggested global business Web sites. Compare them in terms of the information offered to small businesses that want to venture into overseas markets. Which is the most useful, and why?

4. Explore the SBA Web site at **http://www.sba.gov.** What resources are available to you locally? What classes does the Small Business Classroom offer? What about financing assistance? Do you think the site lives up to the SBA's goal of being a one-stop shopping resource for the small business owner? Why or why not?

5. Select a type of business that interests you and go through the checklist presented at **http://www.bizmove.com/starting/m1b.htm,** Starting a Business: Determining the Feasibility of Your Business Idea. Based on your feasibility study, should you continue to investigate this opportunity?

CREATIVE THINKING CASE

They Keep Going and Going . . .

For some entrepreneurs, once is not enough. They start multiple companies and become "multipreneurs." Even if their first attempts fail, they learn from their mistakes—and do whatever is necessary to avoid making those same mistakes in the future. Some investors like entrepreneurs who are willing to learn from their failures and plunge back in. "We prefer to back smart people who have stubbed their toes to backing smart people who have experienced nothing but smooth sailing," says Michael Moritz, a partner at venture capital firm Sequoia Capital.

Take, for example, Jerry Kaplan. In 1987, he founded Go Corporation, a pen-based computer company whose "Penpoint" computer won praise. Even though Kaplan had a great management team, Go's visionary, next-generation technology was ahead of its time and never gained market acceptance. Kaplan later wrote a best-selling book about his Go experiences, *Startup: A Silicon Valley Adventure.*

By 1995, Kaplan was ready to take the plunge again. With partner Alan Fisher, he started Onsale.com, an interactive online auction house. Kaplan's idea was to combine two popular trends—the Internet and the popularity of auctions—in an online format selling computers, consumer electronics, sports equipment, and other products. In many ways, Onsale.com was the opposite of Go: low technical risk, low capital risk, and quick time to market. Fisher and Kaplan funded the venture themselves with $500,000 in start-up capital, and took the firm public in 1997.

Initially, Onsale.com seemed destined for success. Over 1 million users registered at the site, and sales rose to over $200 million. By 1999, however,

Onsale.com was having problems. The company's stock price dropped when the firm posted several consecutive quarters of huge losses. In July 1999, Onsale.com and online computer merchant Egghead.com announced a merger valued at $400 million. Although the merger was supposed to help bring the two struggling companies back to profitability, results haven't met expectations. Today, Kaplan remains as co-chairman of the merged firm's board and says he doesn't expect to see a profit until the year 2002.

INFOTRAC®
COLLEGE EDITION

Critical Thinking Questions

1. Do you agree with Michael Moritz's preference for funding companies run by people who have experienced failure? Why?
2. How could Kaplan's experiences at Go have helped him to build Onsale.com into a successful company?

VIDEO CASE

Yahoo!, Inc.

Yahoo!, Inc. (**http://www.yahoo.com**) started out as an idea, grew into a hobby, and then became a rapidly expanding business. In 1994, David Filo and Jerry Yang were electrical engineering doctoral students at Stanford University. They started categorizing the sites they visited regularly on the Internet. Soon, the pair decided to transform their personal guide into an Internet search engine. They sold advertising space on the new service in order to make money.

Since then, Yahoo! has vigorously pursued a strategy of innovation, responding rapidly to user feedback, creating new services, and monitoring the Web for new content. Yahoo!'s services now include direct marketing, online shopping, Internet auctions, travel reservations, and communication tools such as email, chat, and personal calendars. The site also helps small businesses create a Web presence. Yahoo! Small Business offers resources for starting a business including planning tools, franchise opportunities, and marketing tips. Yahoo! Store lets merchants conduct commercial transactions online.

Yahoo! is one of the few Internet pioneers that has succeeded in making a profit online. The site gets 49 million visitors a day and has over 5,200 advertisers. Sales in 1999 were $588.6 million, a 189 percent increase over 1998. Still, not all analysts are convinced Yahoo!'s growth is sustainable. Recently, its stock prices dipped and its advertising revenues declined.

Critical Thinking Questions

1. Do you think David Filo and Jerry Yang have entrepreneurial personalities? Explain your answer.
2. What type of entrepreneurial business do you think Yahoo! is? Do you think it will continue to grow at the same rate over the next five years? Explain.
3. What insights can other potential entrepreneurs derive from Yahoo!'s example?

Case: HomePortfolio.com

Tom Ashbrook was a successful newspaper reporter when an old pal from college, Rolly Rouse, mentioned that he had a great idea for a new business: a CD-ROM that would help people design and furnish their homes. Rouse explained that Americans spend $300 billion a year on home design, construction, and furnishings.

Rouse had at least some knowledge of architecture and computer software, but neither Rouse nor Ashbrook had ever started a business before. Still, Ashbrook was convinced enough by the potential of Rouse's idea that he quit his job and invested $10,000 of his family's savings into the fledgling firm.

The two set up shop in a spare bedroom in Rouse's house. Soon the pair's initial idea changed. Instead of a CD-ROM, they would start a Web site where home manufacturers and retailers could display their wares, and homeowners could research available options. Although launching a Web site would be more costly than developing a CD-ROM, it would allow them to earn revenues by selling marketing space on the Web site to manufacturers. The entrepreneurs hired several employees to help them design and build their electronic commerce site, HomePortfolio.com (**http://www.HomePortfolio.com**).

To market the idea to manufacturers, and to build the site, Rouse and Ashbrook needed more money. They approached friends and family but couldn't raise enough cash to finance their idea. Their other option was to try to find angel investors or to convince a venture capital firm that their idea had merit. Rouse estimated that they would need a start-up fund of $5 million and an additional $5 million in operating funds once the site was up and running. They were able to raise $500,000 from independent investors, far short of the amount they needed.

Meanwhile, the company was burning through $75,000 a month in start-up and development costs. Their lead Internet developer announced he was quitting because he felt uncomfortable with the direction the firm was heading. Rouse and Ashbrook found themselves using their personal credit cards to keep the company afloat. Finally, Ashbrook's wife gave him an ultimatum: if the company didn't start making money within three months, she wanted him to quit.

Questions for Critical Thinking

1. Evaluate the advantages and disadvantages of deciding to start a Web site instead of developing a CD-ROM product. Do you think Rouse and Ashbrook made the right choice? Why?

2. If you were advising Rouse and Ashbrook, would you recommend they seek angel investors or go after venture capital? Why? How does the fact that they decided to become an electronic commerce business influence your advice?

3. Does an Internet entrepreneur need different characteristics than an entrepreneur starting a more traditional business? Explain your answer.

SOURCES: Tom Ashbrook, *The Leap,* Houghton Mifflin Company, New York, 2000; Carolyn Z. Lawrence, "Taking the Leap," *Office.com,* July 6, 2000, downloaded from **http://www.office.com**; Steven Syre and Charles Stein, "A Report from the Trenches," *The Boston Globe,* June 6, 2000, p. C1.

learning goals

>lg 1 What is the role of management?

>lg 2 What are the four types of planning?

>lg 3 What are the primary responsibilities of managers in organizing activities?

>lg 4 How do leadership styles influence a corporate culture?

>lg 5 How do organizations control activities?

>lg 6 What roles do managers take on in different organizational settings?

>lg 7 What set of managerial skills is necessary for managerial success?

>lg 8 What trends will affect management in the future?

Management and Leadership in Today's Organization

chapter 6

Using Toyota Techniques to Build Toys

It took a savvy group of investors to see the potential of Alexander Doll Co. (http://www.alexanderdoll.com), a small low-tech company located in the middle of Harlem. After 70 plus years, the company that handcrafts Madame Alexander collectible dolls found itself hoping to salvage its profitability by adopting the manufacturing and management methods used by one of the world's largest automakers. Headed for bankruptcy in 1995, Alexander Doll Co. was purchased by an investment group organized by TBM Consulting of North Carolina. The TBM partners specialize in teaching Toyota's lean management and manufacturing methods to American companies. TBM's investment group seeks out under-performing firms and changes the way their manufacturing process is managed, while retaining the company's original location and workforce.

The makeover at Alexander Doll Co. started with a change in leadership. New CEO Herbert Brown had lots of expertise in manufacturing, developed at companies such as Black & Decker, and he convinced employees to work with him in developing a new approach to making dolls. Empowering employees to share in decision making is one of the many lessons gleaned from the Toyota approach.

Managers and employees alike had to refocus on planning accurately for future production. Doll fabric is purchased in very small quantities that can't be reordered, and 75 percent of the styles change every year. Therefore, accurate forecasting of materials and production scheduling is crucial. In addition to reemphasizing accurate planning, the company needed to reorganize the entire production process. In contrast to the batch manufacturing method previously used at the company, Brown introduced employees to Toyota-style work teams. By working as teams, rather than producing parts individually, employees are able to fill orders much more quickly and have reduced work in progress by an astounding 96 percent. The company uses standard quality control methods to provide feedback for the continuous improvement of the production process.

And how did the Alexander Doll Co. respond to the Toyota techniques? The company is showing signs of financial good health and earned a profit for 2000, testimony to the ability of sound management techniques to cross the boundaries of culture, industry, and firm.[1]

Critical Thinking Questions:
As you read this chapter, consider the following questions as they relate to Alexander Doll Co.

- What is the role of management?
- Why did good planning at Alexander Doll make a difference?
- Was reorganization into work teams a key to success for Alexander Doll?

BUSINESS IN THE 21ST CENTURY

Using current management techniques appropriate to the production process is essential to the success of the Alexander Doll Co. Today's companies rely on managers to guide the daily process using human, technological, financial, and other resources to create competitive advantage. For many beginning business students, being in "management" is an attractive, but somewhat vague, future goal. This vagueness is due in part to an incomplete understanding of what managers do and how they contribute to organizational success or failure. This chapter introduces the basic functions of management and the skills required by managers to drive an organization toward its goals. We will also discuss how leadership styles influence a corporate culture and highlight the trends that are shaping the future role of managers.

THE ROLE OF MANAGEMENT

>lg 1

management
The process of guiding the development, maintenance, and allocation of resources to attain organizational goals.

planning
The process of deciding what needs to be done to achieve organizational objectives; identifying when and how it will be done; and determining by whom it should be done.

Management is the process of guiding the development, maintenance, and allocation of resources to attain organizational goals. Managers are the people in the organization responsible for developing and carrying out this management process. Management is dynamic by nature and evolves to meet needs and constraints in the organization's internal and external environments. In a global marketplace where the rate of change is rapidly increasing, flexibility and adaptability are crucial to the managerial process. This process is based in four key functional areas of the organization: planning, organization, leadership, and control. Although these activities are discussed separately in the chapter, they actually form a tightly integrated cycle of thoughts and actions. From this perspective, the managerial process can be described as (1) anticipating potential problems or opportunities and designing plans to deal with them, (2) coordinating and allocating the resources needed to implement plans, (3) guiding personnel through the implementation process, and (4) reviewing results and making any necessary changes. This last stage provides information to be used in ongoing planning efforts, and thus the cycle starts over again.

As shown in Exhibit 6-1, managerial work can be divided into four activities: planning, organizing, leading, and controlling. The four functions are highly interdependent, with managers often performing more than one of them at a time and each of them many times over the course of a normal workday. As you will learn in the following sections, all of the functions require sound decision-making and communication skills.

concept check

• Define the term *management*.
• What are the four key functions of managers?

PLANNING

>lg 2

Planning begins by anticipating potential problems or opportunities the organization may encounter. Managers then design strategies to solve current problems, prevent future problems, or take advantage of opportunities. These strategies serve as the foundation for goals, objectives, policies, and procedures. Put simply, planning is deciding what needs to be done to achieve organizational objectives, identifying when and how it will be done, and determining by whom it should be done. Effective planning requires extensive information

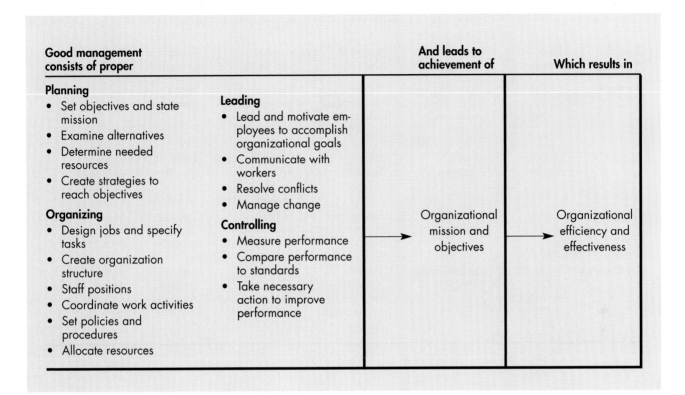

Good management consists of proper		And leads to achievement of	Which results in
Planning • Set objectives and state mission • Examine alternatives • Determine needed resources • Create strategies to reach objectives **Organizing** • Design jobs and specify tasks • Create organization structure • Staff positions • Coordinate work activities • Set policies and procedures • Allocate resources	**Leading** • Lead and motivate employees to accomplish organizational goals • Communicate with workers • Resolve conflicts • Manage change **Controlling** • Measure performance • Compare performance to standards • Take necessary action to improve performance	Organizational mission and objectives	Organizational efficiency and effectiveness

about the external business environment in which the firm competes, as well as its internal environment.

There are four basic types of planning: strategic, tactical, operational, and contingency. Most of us use these different types of planning in our own lives. Some plans are very broad and long term (more strategic in nature), such as planning to attend graduate school after earning a bachelor's degree. Some plans are much more specific and short term (more operational in nature), such as planning to spend a few hours in the library this weekend. Your short term plans support your long term plans. If you study now, you have a better chance of achieving some future goal, such as getting a job interview or attending graduate school. Like you, organizations tailor their plans to meet the requirements of future situations or events. A summary of the four types of planning appears in Exhibit 6-2.

Strategic planning involves creating long-range (one to five years), broad goals for the organization and determining what resources will be needed to accomplish those goals. An evaluation of external environmental factors such as economic, technological, and social issues is critical to successful strategic planning. Strategic plans, such as the organization's long-term **mission,** are formulated by top-level managers and put into action at lower levels in the organization. For example, Carly Fiorina, the forty-something new CEO of stodgy Hewlett-Packard, found a stagnating organization splintered into 83 autonomous businesses with no overall strategy. She immediately created a new strategic plan consolidating HP's 83 businesses into only 12. Her vision is to create a "winning e-company with a shining soul." She asked employees to commit their hearts, minds, and souls to the new mission.[2]

strategic planning

The process of creating long-range (one to five years), broad goals for the organization and determining what resources will be needed to accomplish those goals.

mission

An organization's purpose and reason for existing; its long-term goals.

e x h i b i t   6 - 2 | Types of Planning

Type of Planning	Time Frame	Level of Management	Extent of Coverage	Purpose and Goal	Breadth of Content	Accuracy/ Predictability
Strategic	1–5 years	Top management (CEO, vice presidents, directors, division heads)	External environment and entire organization	Establish mission and long-term goals	Broad and general	High degree of uncertainty
Tactical	Less than 1 year	Middle management	Strategic business units	Establish mid-range goals for implementation	More specific	Moderate degree of certainty
Operational	Current	Supervisory management	Geographic and functional divisions	Implement and activate specific objectives	Specific and concrete	Reasonable degree of certainty
Contingency	When an event occurs or a situation demands	Top and middle management	External environment and entire organization	Meet unforeseen challenges and opportunities	Both broad and detailed	Reasonable degree of certainty once event or situation occurs

mission statement

A formal document that states an organization's purpose and reason for existing and describes its basic philosophy.

tactical planning

The process of beginning to implement a strategic plan by addressing issues of coordination and allocating resources to different parts of the organization; has a shorter time frame (less than one year) and more specific objectives than strategic planning.

operational planning

The process of creating specific standards, methods, policies, and procedures that are used in specific functional areas of the organization; helps guide and control the implementation of tactical plans.

How does Ben & Jerry's mission statement translate into company action? Visit Ben & Jerry's home page at http://www.benjerry.com to learn more.

How have Mickey Drexler's plans for Gap, Inc. panned out? Read about the company's latest performance history under "company information" at http://www.gap.com

An organization's mission is formalized in its **mission statement,** a document that states the purpose of the organization and its reason for existing. For example, Ben & Jerry's mission statement addresses three fundamental issues and states the basic philosophy of the company (see Exhibit 6-3).

In all organizations, plans and goals at the tactical and operational levels should clearly support the organization's mission statement.

Tactical planning begins the implementation of strategic plans. Tactical plans have a shorter (less than one year) time frame than strategic plans and more specific objectives designed to support the broader strategic goals. Tactical plans begin to address issues of coordinating and allocating resources to different parts of the organization.

Operational planning creates specific standards, methods, policies, and procedures that are used in specific functional areas of the organization. Operational objectives are current, narrow, and resource focused. They are designed to help guide and control the implementation of tactical plans.

All of these types of planning are apparent in the history of Gap, Inc. Mickey Drexler is the driving force behind the company's strategic vision, namely, to become a global brand on the level of Coca-Cola, Gillette, and Disney.[3] On a strategic planning level, Drexler hopes to make Gap clothing a universal wardrobe staple by saturating the market with retail

e x h i b i t   6 - 3 | Ben & Jerry's Mission Statement

"Ben & Jerry's is dedicated to the creation and demonstration of a new corporate concept of linked prosperity. Our mission consists of three interrelated parts:

Product

To make, distribute and sell the finest quality all natural ice cream and related products in a wide variety of innovative flavors made from Vermont dairy products.

Economic

To operate the Company on a sound financial basis of profitable growth, increasing value for our shareholders, and creating opportunities and financial rewards for our employees.

Social

To operate the Company in a way that actively recognizes the central role that business plays in the structure of society by initiating ways to improve the quality of life of a broad community—local, national, and international. Underlying the mission of Ben & Jerry's is the determination to seek new and creative ways of addressing all three parts, while holding a deep respect for individuals inside and outside the Company and for the communities of which they are a part."

SOURCE: Ben & Jerry's, Inc.

stores and supplying the world with fundamental clothing such as pocket-Ts, khakis, and denim. At the tactical level, Drexler's planning focuses on different ways the company can grow the Gap brand. Creation of GapKids and Old Navy were both tactical plans designed to extend the Gap brand and increase market coverage. Even at the operational level, Drexler has a say in the planning process. After noticing that some stores were looking increasingly shabby, Drexler introduced a plan for completely remodeling every store every seven years. Such attention to detail at every level of planning has paid off for Drexler and his company. As of 2000, Gap's average return to investors was 59 percent.

contingency plans

Plans that identify alternative courses of action for very unusual or crisis situations; typically stipulate the chain of command, standard operating procedures, and communication channels the organization will use during an emergency.

The key to effective planning is anticipating future situations and events. Yet even the best-prepared organization must sometimes cope with unforeseen circumstances such as a natural disaster, an act of terrorism, or a radical new technology. Therefore, many companies have developed **contingency plans** that identify alternative courses of action for very unusual or crisis situations. The contingency plan typically stipulates the chain of command, standard operating procedures, and communication channels the organization will use during an emergency. Failure to have adequate contingency plans for emergencies can have serious consequences for an organization, as Potomac Electric Power Co. (Pepco) discovered on a cold night in January 1999.[4]

To learn more about how firms develop contingency plans for all sorts of crises, visit *Contingency Planning & Management* magazine's Web site at

http://www.
contingencyplanning.com

The ice storm that struck the Washington, DC area that night was, according to Pepco officials, the most devastating ever to hit the region. An estimated 400,000 residents and businesses were left powerless, some for as long as five days. A review of Pepco's response to the situation identified the following weaknesses in the company's planning: (1) despite forecasts of freezing rain, Pepco had only its standard number of line crews on duty; (2) customer service agents

concept check

- What is the purpose of planning, and what is needed to do it effectively?
- Identify the unique characteristics of each type of planning.

had little or no information about what was happening in the field during the crisis; (3) due to inadequate tracking mechanisms, Pepco could not always tell whether power had been restored to individual houses; and (4) repair staff had been reduced by one-third over the previous three years to trim costs. In the weeks following the power outage, Pepco executives spent long hours analyzing what went wrong and devising a new contingency plan to enable them to cope more effectively during the next emergency.

ORGANIZING

>lg 3

organizing

The process of coordinating and allocating a firm's resources in order to carry out its plans.

A second key function of managers is **organizing,** which is the process of coordinating and allocating a firm's resources in order to carry out its plans. Organizing includes developing a structure for the people, positions, departments, and activities within the firm. Managers can arrange the structural elements of the firm to maximize the flow of information and the efficiency of work processes. They accomplish this by doing the following:

- Dividing up tasks *(division of labor)*
- Grouping jobs and employees *(departmentalization)*
- Assigning authority and responsibilities *(delegation)*

These and other elements of organizational structure are discussed in detail in Chapter 7. In this chapter, however, you should understand the three levels of a managerial hierarchy. This hierarchy is often depicted as a pyramid as in Exhibit 6-4. The fewest managers are found at the highest level of the pyramid.

e x h i b i t 6 - 4 | The Managerial Pyramid

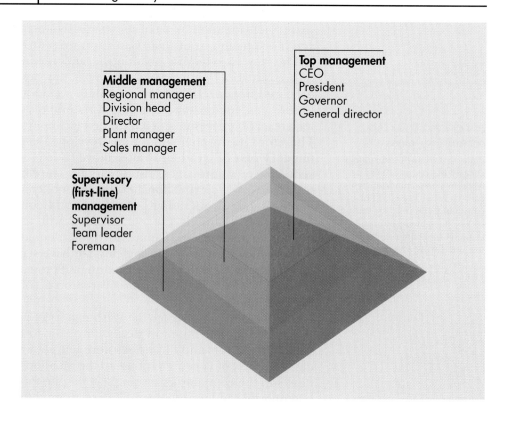

Top management
CEO
President
Governor
General director

Middle management
Regional manager
Division head
Director
Plant manager
Sales manager

Supervisory (first-line) management
Supervisor
Team leader
Foreman

top management

The highest level of managers; includes CEOs, presidents, and vice-presidents, who develop strategic plans and address long-range issues.

middle management

Managers who design and carry out tactical plans in specific areas of the company.

supervisory management

Managers who design and carry out operation plans for the ongoing daily activities of the firm.

 c o n c ə p t   c h ə c k

- Explain the managerial function of organizing.
- What is the managerial pyramid?

Called **top management,** they are the small group of people at the head of the organization (such as the CEO, presidents, and vice presidents). Top-level managers develop *strategic plans* and address long-range issues such as which industries to compete in, how to capture market share, and what to do with profits. These managers design and approve the firm's basic policies and represent the firm to other organizations. They also define the company's values and ethics and thus set the tone for employee standards of behavior. For example, at Booz Allen & Hamilton, Inc., a New York consulting company, employees are expected to model their behavior on that of the senior partners. Martha Gross Clark, vice president and chief financial officer (CFO) of the company, explains that employees are much more likely to take their cues from how top managers behave than to follow written rules.[5]

The second and third tiers of the hierarchy are called **middle management** and **supervisory management,** respectively. Middle managers (such as division heads, departmental managers, and regional sales managers) are responsible for beginning the implementation of strategic plans. They design and carry out *tactical plans* in specific areas of the company. They begin the process of allocating resources to meet organizational goals, and they oversee supervisory managers throughout the firm. Supervisors, the most numerous of the managers, are at the bottom of the managerial pyramid. These managers design and carry out *operational plans* for the ongoing daily activities of the firm. They spend a great deal of their time guiding and motivating the employees who actually produce the goods and services.

LEADING

>lg 4

leadership

The process of guiding and motivating others toward the achievement of organizational goals.

power

The ability to influence others to behave in a particular way.

legitimate power

Power that is derived from an individual's position in an organization.

reward power

Power that is derived from an individual's control over rewards.

coercive power

Power that is derived from an individual's ability to threaten negative outcomes.

expert power

Power that is derived from an individual's extensive knowledge in one or more areas.

referent power

Power that is derived from an individual's personal charisma and the respect and/or admiration the individual inspires.

Leadership, the third key management function, is the process of guiding and motivating others toward the achievement of organizational goals. Managers are responsible for directing employees on a daily basis as the employees carry out the plans and work within the structure created by management. Organizations need strong effective leadership at all levels in order to meet goals and remain competitive.

To be effective leaders, managers must be able to influence others' behavior. This ability to influence others to behave in a particular way is called **power.** Researchers have identified five primary sources, or bases, of power:

- **Legitimate power,** which is derived from an individual's position in an organization
- **Reward power,** which is derived from an individual's control over rewards
- **Coercive power,** which is derived from an individual's ability to threaten negative outcomes
- **Expert power,** which is derived from an individual's extensive knowledge in one or more areas
- **Referent power,** which is derived from an individual's personal charisma and the respect and/or admiration the individual inspires

Many leaders use a combination of all of these sources of power to influence individuals toward goal achievement. Bill Gates, for example, gets his legitimate power from his position as CEO of Microsoft. He is able to offer incentives such as stock options to reward high-performing employees and to threaten low performers with undesirable

Want to learn more about Bill Gates's management style? Go to **http://www.microsoft. com/BillGates** to read his official biography, speeches, and other information. For a different view, visit

http://www.zpub.com/ un/bill

consequences. His technical expertise in computer software, technological innovation, and financial management allows him to greatly influence the decisions made at Microsoft, and many people find his strong focus and ability to convey his vision compelling enough to warrant great respect and admiration.

Leadership Styles

Individuals in leadership positions tend to be relatively consistent in the way they attempt to influence the behavior of others, meaning that each individual has a tendency to react to people and situations in a particular way. This pattern of behavior is referred to as **leadership style.** As Exhibit 6-5 shows, leadership styles can be placed on a continuum that encompasses three distinct styles: autocratic, participative, and free rein.

Autocratic leaders are directive leaders, allowing for very little input from subordinates. These leaders prefer to make decisions and solve problems on their own and expect subordinates to implement solutions according to very specific and detailed instructions. In this leadership style, information typically flows in one direction, from manager to subordinate. The military, by necessity, is generally autocratic. When autocratic leaders treat employees with fairness and respect, they may be considered knowledgeable and decisive. But often autocrats are perceived as narrow-minded and heavy-handed in their unwillingness to share power, information, and decision making in the organization. The trend in organizations today is away from the directive, controlling style of the autocratic leader.

A recent merger took place that initially had Wall Street investors jumping for joy. HFS, one of the world's biggest franchisers of real estate brokerages, and

Microsoft CEO Bill Gates uses all five bases of power—legitimate, reward, coercive, expert, and referent—in leading his employees to achieve organizational goals.

leadership style

The relatively consistent way that individuals in leadership positions attempt to influence the behavior of others.

e x h i b i t   6 - 5 | Leadership Styles of Managers

Amount of authority held by the leader

Autocratic Style	Participative Style (democratic, consensual, consultative)	Free-Rein (Laissez-Faire) Style
• Manager makes most decisions and acts in authoritative manner. • Manager is usually unconcerned about subordinates' attitudes toward decisions. • Emphasis is on getting task accomplished. • Approach is used mostly by military officers and some production line supervisors.	• Manager shares decision making with group members and encourages teamwork. • Manager encourages discussion of issues and alternatives. • Manager is concerned about subordinates' ideas and attitudes. • Manager coaches subordinates and helps coordinate efforts. • Approach is found in many successful organizations.	• Manager turns over virtually all authority and control to group. • Members of group are presented with task and given freedom to accomplish it. • Approach works well with highly motivated, experienced, educated personnel. • Approach is found in high-tech firms, labs, and colleges.

Amount of authority held by group members

Many successful organizations use participative leadership styles that involve group members in discussing issues and making decisions.

autocratic leaders

Directive leaders who prefer to make decisions and solve problems on their own with little input from subordinates.

participative leadership

A leadership style in which the leader shares decision making with group members and encourages discussion of issues and alternatives; includes democratic, consensual, and consultative styles.

democratic leaders

Leaders who solicit input from all members of the group and then allow the members to make the final decision through a vote.

consensual leaders

Leaders who encourage discussion about issues and then require that all parties involved agree to the final decision.

CUC International, a billion dollar seller of club memberships, appeared at first to be a match made in heaven. But the partnership was a disaster, due at least in part to two very different leadership styles.[6] Henry Silverman, CEO of HFS, was an autocratic leader. He wanted to be in total control, to make every decision, and to know what was going on in every corner of his company. In contrast, Walter Forbes, CEO of CUC International, viewed himself as a visionary leader who left the operational details of running the company to others. Forbes's leadership style was so hands-off that he appeared to be unaware of massive accounting irregularities discovered in his organization after the merger. The distinctly different leadership styles of these two men resulted in a culture clash and a battle for power that ended up costing shareholders billions of dollars in lost earnings. In hindsight, perhaps both parties could have benefited from a more participative approach to management. There are three types of participative leadership: democratic, consensual, and consultative.

Democratic leaders solicit input from all members of the group and then allow the group members to make the final decision through a voting process. This approach works well with highly trained professionals. The president of a physicians' clinic might use the democratic approach. **Consensual leaders** encourage discussion about issues and then require that all parties involved agree to the final decision. This is the general style used by labor mediators. **Consultative leaders** confer with subordinates before making a decision, but retain the final decision-making authority. This technique has been used to dramatically increase the productivity of assembly-line workers.

The third leadership style, at the opposite end of the continuum from the autocratic style, is **free-rein** or **laissez-faire** (French for "leave it alone") **leadership.** Managers who use this style turn over all authority and control to subordinates. Employees are assigned a task and then given free rein to figure out the best way to accomplish it. The manager doesn't get involved unless asked. Under this approach, subordinates have unlimited freedom as long as they do not violate existing company policies. This approach is also sometimes used with highly trained professionals as in a research laboratory. Although one might at first assume that subordinates would prefer the free-rein style, this approach can have several drawbacks. If free-rein leadership is accompanied by unclear expectations and lack of feedback from the manager, the experience can be frustrating for an employee. Employees may perceive the manager as being uninvolved and indifferent to what is happening or as unwilling or unable to provide the necessary structure, information, and expertise.

Employee Empowerment

Participative and free-rein leaders use a technique called empowerment to share decision-making authority with subordinates. **Empowerment** means giving employees increased autonomy and discretion to make their own decisions, as well as control over the resources needed to implement those decisions. When decision-making power is shared at all levels of the organization, employees feel a greater sense of ownership in, and responsibility for, organizational outcomes.

consultative leaders
Leaders who confer with subordinates before making a decision, but who retain the final decision-making authority.

free-rein (laissez-faire) leadership
A leadership style in which the leader turns over all authority and control to subordinates.

empowerment
The process of giving employees increased autonomy and discretion to make decisions, as well as control over the resources needed to implement those decisions.

corporate culture
The set of attitudes, values, and standards that distinguishes one organization from another.

What management leadership traits do business executives believe are necessary to succeed in today's competitive business world? Read the results of a survey in *Entrepreneur* magazine at **http://www.entrepreneurmag.com** by doing a search for "leadership survey."

Jack Welch, ex-CEO of General Electric Corp. and a consummate manager, says that "Giving people self-confidence is by far the most important thing that I can do. Because then they will act."[7]

There is no one best leadership style. Each of the three styles described here works best in a particular type of business environment or situation. The most effective style for a given situation depends on elements such as the characteristics of the subordinates, the complexity of the task, the source of the leader's power, and the stability of the environment.

Corporate Culture

The leadership style of managers in an organization is usually indicative of the underlying philosophy, or values, of the organization. The set of *attitudes, values,* and *standards of behavior* that distinguishes one organization from another is called **corporate culture.** A corporate culture evolves over time and is based on the accumulated history of the organization, including the vision of the founders. It is also influenced by the dominant leadership style within the organization. Evidence of a company's culture is seen in its heroes (e.g., Andy Grove of Intel), myths (stories about the company that are passed from employee to employee), symbols (e.g., the Nike swoosh), and ceremonies. Procter & Gamble's corporate culture is so strong that it is sometimes referred to as a cult, and employees are said to be "Procterized," rather than socialized.[8]

Although culture is intangible and its rules are often unspoken, it can have a strong impact on a company's success. Therefore, managers must try to influence the corporate culture so that it will contribute to the success of the company. The 1998 merger of America's Chrysler Corp. with Germany's Daimler-Benz AG presented just such a challenge. Andreas Renschler, head of executive management development at DaimlerChrysler AG, was put in charge of "one of the world's biggest efforts to bridge corporate cultural differences."[9] Among the issues to be addressed in this corporate marriage are differences in language, customs, labor-management relations, worker autonomy, and compensation. What does Renschler see as the key to successfully combining the two corporate cultures? He plans to wed them by developing trust through team building and promoting managers who show a willingness to embrace change. Consider how a corporate culture may influence the success of a new technology business such as the one described in the Focusing on Small Business box.

In merging their companies, Chrysler's CEO Robert Eaton (front left) and Daimler-Benz's CEO Jurgen Schrempp (front right) are combining the firms' two different cultures by building trust through team building and rewarding managers who can adapt to change.

concept check
- How do leaders influence other people's behavior?
- How can managers empower employees?
- What is corporate culture?

HOW THE INTERNET CHANGED A LIFELONG GOAL

Gary Culliss spent years preparing to be a patent attorney. He earned his law degree from Harvard in 1997. But Culliss never practiced law for even one day. Instead, he took a leap of faith and started an Internet company. Now he is one of hundreds of young entrepreneurs with innovative ideas who have cashed in on the phenomenal growth of the World Wide Web. The hardest thing he's had to do so far? Tell his mom he's not going to be a lawyer.

Culliss's idea began to take shape as he worked on patent research during his law school years. He wanted a more efficient way to search the Web, so he wouldn't have to wade through thousands of irrelevant information sites before finding what he needed. Frustrated with the lack of existing alternatives, Culliss developed his own software program and named it Direct Hit. Called a "popularity engine," Culliss's software ranks Internet search results by using information such as length of viewing time to calculate how popular each Web site has been with people who ran similar searches. In early 1998 Culliss entered his idea in the prestigious Entrepreneurship Competition at the Massachusetts Institute of Technology and won $50,000.

"Within three months of his graduation, Culliss had founded a company dedicated to making Internet searching easier, raised $1.4 million in venture capital and landed contracts with America Online Inc., Apple Computer Inc., and Wired Digital, Inc. Without stopping for fancy planning and the usual business school stuff, Direct Hit raised another $2 million in the fall, hired 30 people, signed up more high-profile customers, released a string of new search features and . . . moved into 9,000 square foot digs near Boston." To make all of this happen in such a short time, Culliss needed help, and he found it in a man named Mike Cassidy, a man with some striking similarities to Culliss himself. Cassidy had also attended Harvard, and while there had won the same MIT contest. At age 22 Cassidy formed a technology company called Stylus Innovation, Inc., which he sold in 1996 for $13 million. In 1998 Cassidy went looking for a new challenge and found Culliss's Direct Hit. Culliss and Cassidy met, and after spending four hours together, Culliss offered Cassidy the CEO position in his new company. Cassidy accepted. Knowing how quickly business happens in the cyberworld, Cassidy immediately arranged an appointment with a large venture capital firm. By late afternoon of the day they presented their idea, Culliss and Cassidy had a check in hand, and Direct Hit became a reality.

Critical Thinking Questions

1. How did Culliss combine an entrepreneurial spirit with planning skills to make Direct Hit a success?
2. What type of management style should Mike Cassidy use to be most popular with Direct Hit employees?
3. Do you think that there will be a lot of employee empowerment at Direct Hit?

CONTROLLING

>lg 5

controlling

The process of assessing the organization's progress toward accomplishing its goals; includes monitoring the implementation of a plan and correcting deviations from the plan.

The fourth key function that managers perform is controlling. **Controlling** is the process of assessing the organization's progress toward accomplishing its goals. It includes monitoring the implementation of a plan and correcting deviations from that plan. As Exhibit 6-6 on p. 184 shows, controlling can be visualized as a cyclical process made up of five stages:

1. Setting performance standards (goals)
2. Measuring performance
3. Comparing actual performance to established performance standards
4. Taking corrective action (if necessary)
5. Using information gained from the process to set future performance standards

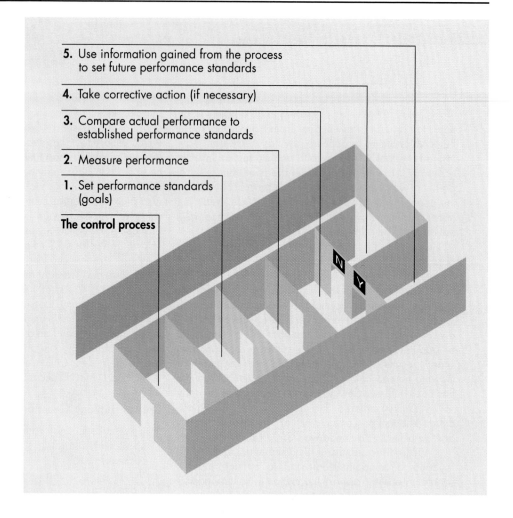

5. Use information gained from the process to set future performance standards

4. Take corrective action (if necessary)

3. Compare actual performance to established performance standards

2. Measure performance

1. Set performance standards (goals)

The control process

Performance standards are the levels of performance the company wants to attain. These goals are based on its strategic, tactical, and operational plans. The most effective performance standards state a measurable behavioral objective that can be achieved in a specified time frame. For example, the performance objective for the sales division of a company could be stated as "$100,000 in gross sales for the month of January." Each individual employee in that division would also have a specified performance goal. Actual firm, division, or individual performance can be measured against desired performance standards to see if a gap exists between the desired level of performance and the actual level of performance. If a performance gap does exist, the reason for it must be determined and corrective action taken.

Feedback is essential to the process of control. Most companies have a reporting system that identifies areas where performance standards are not being met. A feedback system helps managers detect problems before they get out of hand. If a problem exists, the managers take corrective action. Toyota uses a simple but effective control system on its automobile assembly lines. Each worker serves as the customer for the process just before his or hers. Each worker is empowered to act as a quality control inspector. If a part is defective or not installed properly, the next worker won't accept it. Any worker can alert the supervisor to a problem by tugging on a rope that turns on a warning light (i.e., feedback). If the problem isn't corrected, the worker can stop the entire assembly line.

M A K I N G   E T H I C A L   C H O I C E S

MANAGERIAL CHALLENGES IN A GARMENT FACTORY

For a number of years, the Mehserjian family ran a garment factory in Los Angeles, where they did contract sewing of T-shirts and other budget-priced clothing for a variety of clients. In 1997, their best year, they generated $2.9 million in sales from 120 sewing machines and made a profit of $400,000. The following year their business began a nose-dive. Their profits dwindled as some of their biggest customers shifted their contract sewing to factories in Mexico where labor costs were substantially lower.

Departing customers repeatedly said that they would continue to place orders with the Mehserjians if the family had a factory in Mexico. The Mehserjians reacted with a two-point strategy. First, they began sewing higher-priced garments in the Los Angeles factory. Second, they opened a factory on the outskirts of Guadalajara, Mexico, to sew lower-priced garments.

About half of the 100 sewing machines in the Mehserjians' Mexican factory are sitting idle. Finding enough workers to keep the Mexican facility running—even at half capacity—is a daily struggle. Improving productivity is a constant challenge as well. An even greater challenge, though, is trying to change the workers' attitudes. The Mehserjians pay above the prevailing market rate for the locale. Yet they still have difficulty getting employees to show up to work on a regular basis. To solve the attendance problem, the Mehserjians offered employees a 10 percent bonus for coming to work as scheduled for the entire week. In spite of this, absenteeism is still rampant.

Critical Thinking Questions

1. Can a business remain ethical while responding to the competitive pressures of the marketplace?
2. Do incentives for coming to work constitute bribery?
3. How far should companies go to ensure that employees conform to minimal work standards?

---

c o n c ə p t   c h ə c k

- Describe the control process.
- Why is the control process important to the success of the organization?

Why is controlling such an important part of a manager's job? First, it helps managers to determine the success of the other three functions: planning, organizing, and leading. Second, control systems direct employee behavior toward achieving organizational goals. Third, control systems provide a means of coordinating employee activities and integrating resources throughout the organization.

MANAGERIAL ROLES

>lg 6

informational roles

A manager's activities as an information gatherer, an information disseminator, or a spokesperson for the company.

interpersonal roles

A manager's activities as a figurehead, company leader, or liaison.

decisional roles

A manager's activities as an entrepreneur, resource allocator, conflict resolver, or negotiator.

In carrying out the responsibilities of planning, organizing, leading, and controlling, managers take on many different roles. A role is a set of behavioral expectations, or a set of activities that a person is expected to perform. Managers' roles fall into three basic categories: **informational roles, interpersonal roles,** and **decisional roles.** These roles are summarized in Exhibit 6-7. In an *informational role,* the manager may act as an information gatherer, an information distributor, or a spokesperson for the company. A manager's *interpersonal roles* are based on various interactions with other people. Depending on the situation, a manager may need to act as a figurehead, a company leader, or a liaison. When acting in a *decisional role,* a manager may have to think like an entrepreneur, make decisions about resource allocation, help resolve conflicts, or negotiate compromises.

Managerial Decision-Making

In every function performed, role taken on, and set of skills applied, a manager is a decision maker. Decision-making means choosing among alternatives.

exhibit 6 - 7 | The Many Roles That Managers Play in an Organization

Role	Description	Example
Informational Roles		
Monitor	Seeks out and gathers information relevant to the organization.	Finding out about legal restrictions on new product technology.
Disseminator	Provides information where it is needed in the organization.	Providing current production figures to workers on the assembly line.
Spokesperson	Transmits information to people outside the organization.	Representing the company at a shareholders' meeting.
Interpersonal Roles		
Figurehead	Represents the company in a symbolic way.	Cutting the ribbon at ceremony for the opening of a new building.
Leader	Guides and motivates employees to achieve organizational goals.	Helping subordinates to set monthly performance goals.
Liaison	Acts as a go-between among individuals inside and outside the organization.	Representing the retail sales division of the company at a regional sales meeting.
Decisional Roles		
Entrepreneur	Searches out new opportunities and initiates change.	Implementing a new production process using new technology.
Disturbance handler	Handles unexpected events and crises.	Handling a crisis situation such as a fire.
Resource allocator	Designates the use of financial, human, and other organizational resources.	Approving the funds necessary to purchase computer equipment and hire personnel.
Negotiator	Represents the company at negotiating processes.	Participating in salary negotiations with union representatives.

Managers made nonprogrammed decisions in preparing their automated production facilities like the microchip manufacturing system shown here for the unique situation presented by the year 2000.

Decision making occurs in response to the identification of a problem or an opportunity. The decisions managers make fall into two basic categories: programmed and nonprogrammed. Programmed decisions are made in response to routine situations that occur frequently in a variety of settings throughout an organization. For example, the need to hire new personnel is a common situation for most organizations. Therefore, standard procedures for recruitment and selection are developed and followed in most companies.

Infrequent, unforeseen, or very unusual problems and opportunities require **nonprogrammed decisions** by managers. Because these situations are unique and complex, the manager rarely has a precedent to follow. Preparing manufacturing companies for the year 2000 is an example of nonprogrammed decision making. The problem was that manufacturing equipment failed to operate properly when the computers that control their operations, which were designed to handle only two-digit years, failed to recognize the new millennium.[10] Although most of the attention was focused on mainframe computers, factories were actually the biggest Y2K challenge for managers. Because factory automation systems tend to be made by numerous manufacturers and assembled piecemeal using specialized software, there is no one blueprint for finding all

nonprogrammed decisions
Responses to infrequent, unforeseen, or very unusual problems and opportunities where the manager does not have a precedent to follow in decision making.

the electrical components and fixing all of the software. The final decision on how to adjust each manufacturing system must be made after carefully gathering information and weighing alternative courses of action.

Addressing the Y2K problem required a systematic approach to decision making as illustrated in Exihibit 6-8. Managers typically follow five steps in the decision-making process:

1. Recognize or identify a problem or opportunity. Although it is more common to focus on problems because of their obvious negative effects, managers who do not take advantage of new opportunities may lose competitive advantage to other firms.
2. Gather information so as to identify alternative solutions or actions.
3. Choose one or more alternatives after evaluating the strengths and weaknesses of each possibility.
4. Put the chosen alternative into action.
5. Gather information to obtain feedback on the effectiveness of the chosen plan. Some very practical questions to ask during the decision-making process are shown in Exhibit 6-9.

concept check

- What are the three types of managerial roles?
- Give examples of things managers might do when acting in each of the different types of roles.
- List the five steps in the decision-making process.

MANAGERIAL SKILLS

>lg 7

In order to be successful in planning, organizing, leading, and controlling, managers must use a wide variety of skills. A *skill* is the ability to do something proficiently. Managerial skills fall into three basic categories: conceptual, human relations, and technical skills. The degree to which each type of skill is used depends upon the level of the manager's position as seen in Exhibit 6-10. Additionally, in an increasingly global marketplace, it pays for managers to develop a special set of skills to deal with global management issues.

technical skills
A manager's specialized areas of knowledge and expertise, as well as the ability to apply that knowledge.

Technical Skills

Specialized areas of knowledge and expertise and the ability to apply that knowledge make up a manager's **technical skills.** Preparing a financial statement,

e x h i b i t   6 - 8 | The Decision-Making Process

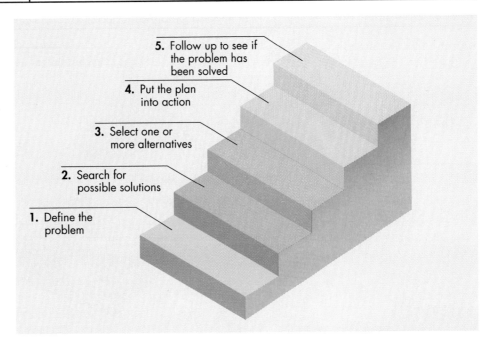

5. Follow up to see if the problem has been solved
4. Put the plan into action
3. Select one or more alternatives
2. Search for possible solutions
1. Define the problem

e x h i b i t   6 - 9 | Questions to Ask Yourself to Help Make Better Decisions

1. *What's my decision problem?* What, broadly, do I have to decide? What specific decisions do I have to make as a part of the broad decision?

2. *What are my fundamental objectives?* Have I asked "Why?" enough times to get to my bedrock wants and needs?

3. *What are my alternatives?* Can I think of more good ones?

4. *What are the consequences of each alternative in terms of the achievement of each of my objectives?* Can any alternatives be safely eliminated?

5. *What are the trade-offs among my more important objectives?* Where do conflicting objectives concern me the most?

6. *Do any uncertainties pose serious problems?* If so, which ones? How do they impact consequences?

7. *How much risk am I willing to take?* How good and how bad are the possible consequences? What are ways of reducing my risk?

8. *Have I thought ahead, planning out into the future?* Can I reduce my uncertainties by gathering information? What are the potential gains and costs in time, money, and effort?

9. *Is the decision obvious or pretty clear at this point?* What reservations do I have about deciding now? In what ways could the decision be improved by a modest amount of added time and effort?

10. *What should I be working on?* If the decision isn't obvious, what do the critical issues appear to be? What facts and opinions would make my job easier?

programming a computer, designing an office building, and analyzing market research are all examples of technical skills. These types of skills are especially important for supervisory managers because they work closely with employees who are producing the goods and/or services of the firm. Supervisory managers need to be knowledgeable about the specific production and operation tools, techniques, and methods relevant to their specific area of the organization, as demonstrated in the Applying Technology box.

e x h i b i t   6 - 1 0 | The Importance of Managerial Skills at Different Management Levels

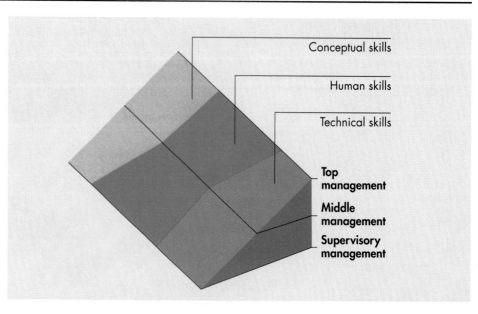

ADVANCED INFORMATION TECHNOLOGY IS A KEY TO DELL'S SUCCESS

Successful managers use new information technology to enhance corporate fitness. One of the best measures of corporate fitness is return on investment capital (ROIC). The two components that combine to create a high ROIC are the ability to charge a price much higher than actual cost (operating margin) and the ability to generate sales from a small base of invested capital (asset utilization). Dell Computers provides an excellent example of how both these elements can be significantly increased by effectively managing information technology. Dell's entrepreneurial approach to computer sales combines cutting-edge knowledge of Internet technology with sophisticated enterprise software that streamlines order processing and delivery, resulting in something known as mass customization.

Dell's reliance on advanced information technology systems allows it to build millions of personal computers a year to exact customer specifications and provide investors with a very comfortable ROIC. How does the company do it? Dell uses information technology in a number of ways to increase both operating margin and asset utilization. It uses sophisticated logistics software to reduce the cost of customization; yet it is able to charge a premium for the unique configurations customers want, thus increasing the operating margin. Asset utilization is improved by shortening the supply chain and tying up far less capital in inventory. Dell's managers use information technology aggressively to create value for their customers at a lower cost than the competition.

Critical Thinking Questions

1. Are technology skills important at all levels of management at Dell?
2. What other managerial skills are important at Dell?
3. Are technology skills important at other computer manufacturers like IBM and Gateway?

Human Relations Skills

human relations skills
A manager's interpersonal skills that are used to accomplish goals through the use of human resources.

Human relations skills are the interpersonal skills managers use to accomplish goals through the use of human resources. This set of skills includes the ability to understand human behavior, to communicate effectively with others, and to motivate individuals to accomplish their objectives. Giving positive feedback to employees, being sensitive to their individual needs, and showing a willingness to empower subordinates are all examples of good human relations skills.

Karl Eberle, general manager at Harley-Davidson's newest assembly plant, uses strong human relations skills to build cohesive self-directed work teams that run the production process.[11] Working closely with line workers and union representatives, Eberle empowers employees to make decisions about how to build a better bike and improve the work environment. This commitment to building relationships with Harley employees is in part responsible for the recent revitalization of the company and is a key to its continued success.

Conceptual Skills

conceptual skills
A manager's ability to view the organization as a whole, understand how the various parts are interdependent, and assess how the organization relates to its external environment.

Conceptual skills include the ability to view the organization as a whole, understand how the various parts

Most successful managers work hard at continually updating their managerial skills. One organization that offers many ongoing training and education programs is the American Management Association. Visit its site at

http://www.amanet.org

are interdependent, and assess how the organization relates to its external environment. These skills allow managers to evaluate situations and develop alternative courses of action. Good conceptual skills are especially necessary for managers at the top of the management pyramid where strategic planning takes place.

Global Management Skills

global management skills
A manager's ability to operate in diverse cultural environments.

The increasing *globalization* of the world market, as discussed in Chapter 2, has created a need for managers who have **global management skills,** that is, the ability to operate in diverse cultural environments. With more and more companies choosing to do business in multiple locations around the world, employees are often required to learn the geography, language, and social customs of other cultures. It is expensive to train employees for foreign assignments and pay their relocation costs; therefore, choosing the right person for the job is especially important. Individuals who are open-minded, flexible, willing to try new things, and comfortable in a multicultural setting are good candidates for international management positions.

c o n c ə p t c h ə c k

- Define the basic managerial skills.
- How important is each of these skill sets at the different levels of the management pyramid?
- What new challenges do managers face due to increasing globalization?

CAPITALIZING ON TRENDS IN BUSINESS

>lg 8

Three important trends in management today are: increasing employee empowerment, the growing use of information technology, and the increasing need for global management skills. Each will be examined in turn.

Managers Empowering Employees

The employee empowerment trend allows employers to tap the knowledge and talent of all employees and gives workers a greater sense of ownership in their work and commitment to their employers.

Most of the firms discussed in this chapter, including Ben & Jerry's, General Electric, and Harley-Davidson, are including more employees in the decision-making process than ever before. This increased level of employee involvement comes from the realization that people at all levels in the organization possess unique knowledge, skills, and abilities that can be of great value to the company. With empowerment, managers share information and responsibility with employees at all levels in the organization. Along with the authority to make decisions, empowerment also gives employees the control over resources needed to implement those decisions. Empowering employees enhances their commitment to the organization by giving them a feeling of ownership in the firm and an increased sense of competency.

In order for empowerment to work, managers have to facilitate employee decision making by providing access to necessary information, clear expectations for results, behavioral boundaries, and the resources employees need to carry out their decisions. This concept is illustrated by Steve Miller, group managing director of the Royal Dutch/Shell Group of Companies. Royal Dutch/Shell is one of the largest companies in the world with a strong sense of tradition and a very structured way of doing things. When Miller set out to

change the way things were done at his company, he knew he would have to involve the people on the front lines, the "grassroots" positions of the company. He calls his form of empowerment *grassroots leadership*. Grassroots leadership means finding a way to empower the frontline people, "to challenge them, to provide them with the resources they need, and then to hold them accountable."[12]

Managers and Information Technology

The second trend having a major impact on managers is the proliferation of information technology. An increasing number of organizations are selling technology, and an increasing number are looking for cutting-edge technology to make and market the products and services they sell. A brief look at PeopleSoft, a rapidly growing provider of automated human resource functions, provides some insight into the crucial role information technology can play in today's organizations.[13] Plenty of new technology is being used at PeopleSoft, but it is "people-oriented" technology, and it starts with a backpack. Every new employee is issued a backpack filled with a laptop, pager, cell phone, and digital assistant. Steve Zarate, chief information officer at PeopleSoft, calls it "information-to-go." Every employee has access to PeopleSoft's "massive information infrastructure that spans continents and time zones." PeopleSoft uses information systems to create an "infomacracy," an organization where members have access to the information they need to make and implement decisions. By using the latest technology to empower people and keep members of the organization connected, PeopleSoft has grown to be a $10 billion company.

Managing in a Global Marketplace

Geographic boundaries no longer constrain businesses the way they once did. To fully realize their potential, many companies must look to international markets to expand the sales of their products and services. This presents significant new challenges to managers. Global management can mean flying thousands of miles a week to keep up with business units spread across the world. Although new information technology makes communication easier than ever before, sometimes it cannot substitute for face-to-face contact. Ensuring that employees in far-flung locations still feel part of a cohesive organizational team can be difficult. Global managers often have to adapt to a new culture, learn a new language, manage a diverse workforce, and operate in a foreign economic system. For many managers, accepting an international position also means helping their spouses and children adapt to the new environment. And in some companies, managers must try to translate an entire company philosophy into another language and culture.

Find out more about how DoubleClick manages its worldwide operations by visiting the company's home page at
http://www.doubleclick.com

concept check

- What steps must managers take if employee empowerment is to work?
- How can information technology aid in decision-making?
- What special problems do global managers face?

APPLYING THIS CHAPTER'S TOPICS

Many of the skills managers use to accomplish organizational goals can be applied outside the organizational setting. You could be using these skills in your life right now to accomplish your personal goals. This section provides some examples.

Effective Time Management

Successful managers use their time wisely. Adopting the following time management techniques will help you become a more successful student now and will help prepare you for the demands of your future workplace:

- *Plan ahead.* This is first and most obvious. Set both long-term and short-term goals. Review your list often and revise it when your situation changes.
- *Establish priorities.* Decide what is most important and what is most urgent. Sometimes they are not the same thing. Keep in mind the 80–20 rule: 20 percent of one's effort delivers 80 percent of the results.
- *Delegate.* Ask yourself if the task can be accomplished as effectively by someone else. Empower other people, and you may be surprised by the quality of the outcome.
- *Learn to say no.* Be stingy with your time. Be realistic about how long tasks will take. Don't feel guilty when you don't have the time, ability, or inclination to take on an additional task.
- *Batch.* Group activities together so they take up less of your day. For example, set aside a certain time to return phone calls, answer email, and do any necessary written correspondence.
- *Stay on task.* Learn how to handle diversions. For example, let your answering machine take messages until you finish a particular task. Create a routine that helps you stay focused.
- *Set deadlines.* Don't let projects drag on. Reward yourself each time you cross a certain number of items off your "to do" list.

Decision-Making Skills

One of the best ways to prepare for any career, including a career in business, is to improve your ability to make good decisions. But what is a "good" decision? Is it one that is made quickly, but with incomplete information? Or is it one that is made more slowly, but with more facts and figures to support it? Is a good decision always objective? Or should it be based on a gut feeling? And, if you practice making decisions, do you actually get better at making them? Some recognized decision makers offer these guidelines:[14]

- *Have confidence in your judgment, and always go by the evidence,* says Ed Koch, former mayor of New York City.
- *Think about the long-term consequences of your decision,* says Pamela Lopker, CEO of QAD, Inc. and America's richest self-made woman.
- *Listen to your inner wisdom,* says W. Brian Arthur, Citigroup Professor at the Santa Fe Institute.
- *Be flexible,* says Chung-Jen Tan, senior manager at IBM's Watson Research Center.
- *Listen to your intuition,* says Deborah Triant, CEO of Check Point Software Technologies, Inc.
- *Ask yourself how you want things to turn out and how things could go wrong,* says Roger Rainbow, vice president at Shell International Ltd.
- *Think in terms of opportunities instead of problems,* says Howard Raiffa, Professor Emeritus at Harvard Business School.
- *Sometimes the "wrong" decision is the right thing to do,* says Chris Newell, executive director at the Lotus Institute.

Save Time and Money Successful managers use both their time and their money well. As a student, you may feel that you never have enough of either of these resources. You can save yourself some time and money by taking advantage of some of the bargains on the following Web sites:[15]

- Student Advantage (**http://www.studentadvantage.com**). One way to cut costs on everything from transportation to food to clothing is to use a student discount card. The Student Advantage Card is one such discount card, accepted at over 20,000 businesses nationwide.
- FastWeb.com (**http://www.fastweb.com**) and Sallie Mae (**http://www.salliemae.com/planning/scholarships.html**). Save valuable time and find out about "free" money available through academic scholarships and grants. These sites offer free online searches for scholarships and grants.

- VarsityBooks.com (**http://www.varsitybooks.com**), **Follett College Stores** (http://www.efollett.com), and BigWords.com (**http://www.BIGWORDS.com**). Students can spend hundreds of dollars per semester on textbooks and other course materials. Save up to 40 percent on textbooks by buying online.
- Travelocity (**http://www.travelocity.com**), Expedia Travel (**http://www.expedia.com**), United College Plus (**http://www.collegeplus.com**). Save time and money by using sites that make your travel arrangements for you, and do it at a discount price.
- Apple Computer (**http://www.apple.com/education/hed/students**) and Dell Faculty, students and staff (**http://www.dell.com/us/en/fss/default.htm**). Take advantage of special deals (discounts and rebates) on personal computers, and then use your new computer to find even more good deals on the Internet!

>looking ahead
at Alexander Doll Co.

Can the Alexander Doll Co. stay in Harlem and continue to increase its competitive position? Making collectible dolls is a labor-intensive process, so most of the company's competitors manufacture overseas to take advantage of cheaper labor. Alexander Doll has chosen to reduce costs by focusing on new production methods. In the coming years, the company will need to emphasize its commitment to mass customization in order to increase its customer base and remain profitable.

SUMMARY OF LEARNING GOALS

>lg 1 What is the role of management?
Management is the process of guiding the development, maintenance, and allocation of resources to attain organizational goals. Managers are the people in the organization responsible for developing and carrying out this management process. The four primary functions of managers are planning, organizing, leading, and controlling.

>lg 2 What are the four types of planning?
Planning is deciding what needs to be done, identifying when and how it will be done, and determining by whom it should be done. Managers use four different types of planning: strategic, tactical, operational, and contingency planning. Strategic planning involves creating long-range (one to five years), broad goals and determining the necessary resources to accomplish those goals. Tactical planning has a shorter time frame (less than one year) and more specific objectives that support the broader strategic goals. Operational planning creates specific standards, methods, policies, and procedures that are used in specific functional areas

KEY TERMS

autocratic leaders
178
coercive power
177
conceptual skills
187
consensual leaders
179
consultative leaders
179
contingency plans
175
controlling 181
corporate culture
180
decisional roles
183
democratic leaders
179
empowerment 179
expert power 177
free-rein (laissez-
faire) leadership
179
global management
skills 188
human relations
skills 187
informational roles
183
interpersonal roles
183
leadership 177
leadership style
178
legitimate power
177
management 172
middle
management 177
mission 173
mission statement
174
nonprogrammed
decisions 184
operational
planning 174
organizing 176
participative
leadership 179
planning 172
power 177
referent power
177
reward power 177
strategic planning
173
supervisory
management 177
tactical planning
174
technical skills 185
top management
177

of the organization. Contingency plans identify alternative courses of action for very unusual or crisis situations.

>lg 3   **What are the primary responsibilities of managers in organizing activities?**
Organizing involves coordinating and allocating a firm's resources in order to carry out its plans. It includes developing a structure for the people, positions, departments, and activities within the firm. This is accomplished by dividing up tasks (division of labor), grouping jobs and employees (departmentalization), and assigning authority and responsibilities (delegation).

>lg 4   **How do leadership styles influence a corporate culture?**
Leading is the process of guiding and motivating others toward the achievement of organizational goals. Managers have unique leadership styles that range from autocratic to free rein. The set of *attitudes, values,* and *standards of behavior* that distinguishes one organization from another is called corporate culture. A corporate culture evolves over time and is based on the accumulated history of the organization, including the vision of the founders. The dominant leadership style within the organization is a powerful determinant of corporate culture.

>lg 5   **How do organizations control activities?**
Controlling is the process of assessing the organization's progress toward accomplishing its goals. The control process is as follows: (1) set performance standards (goals), (2) measure performance, (3) compare actual performance to established performance standards, (4) take corrective action (if necessary), and (5) use information gained from the process to set future performance standards.

>lg 6   **What roles do managers take on in different organizational settings?**
In an *informational role,* the manager may act as an information gatherer, an information distributor, or a spokesperson for the company. A manager's *interpersonal roles* are based on various interactions with other people. Depending on the situation, a manager may need to act as a figurehead, a company leader, or a liaison. When acting in a *decisional role,* a manager may have to think like an entrepreneur, make decisions about resource allocation, help resolve conflicts, or negotiate compromises.

>lg 7   **What set of managerial skills is necessary for managerial success?**
Managerial skills fall into three basic categories: technical, human relations, and conceptual skills. Specialized areas of knowledge and expertise and the ability to apply that knowledge make up a manager's technical skills. Human relations skills include the ability to understand human behavior, to communicate effectively with others, and to motivate individuals to accomplish their objectives. Conceptual skills include the ability to view the organization as a whole, understand how the various parts are interdependent, and assess how the organization relates to its external environment.

>lg 8   **What trends will affect management in the future?**
Three important trends in management today are increasing employee empowerment, the increasing use of information technology, and the growing need for global management skills. Empowerment means giving employees increased autonomy and discretion to make their own decisions, as well as control of the resources needed to implement those decisions. When decision-making power is shared at all levels in the organization, employees feel a greater sense of ownership in, and responsibility for, organizational outcomes. Using the latest information technology, managers can make quicker, better-informed decisions. It also keeps organization members connected. As more companies "go global," the need for global management skills is growing. Global managers often have to adapt to a new culture, learn a new language, manage a diverse workforce, and operate in a foreign economic system.

PREPARING FOR TOMORROW'S WORKPLACE

1. Do not-for-profit organizations like the Red Cross and Boy Scouts of America need managers? Why or why not?
2. You have been asked to speak to the Rotary Club on sources of managerial power. Prepare an outline of your speech.
3. Talk to the dean or department head at your school. Ask for examples of strategic planning, tactical planning, and contingency planning at your university or college that can be shared with the class. Make your presentation.
4. Write a short paper on how you are using the four management functions to accomplish your goal of graduating.
5. Using a McDonald's restaurant manager as an example, give an example of a decision for each of the managerial functions: planning, organizing, leading, and controlling.

WORKING THE NET

1. Find information about how to develop a business plan by doing a search on the Dogpile mega-search engine (**http://www.dogpile.com**). Make a list of the resources available and suggest which ones would be most useful for (a) top executives of a large corporation, (b) a small business owner, and (c) a middle manager in a large corporation preparing an operational plan for her or his department. See if you can also find a site that has examples of completed business plans.
2. Go to the Management General Web site at **http://www.mgeneral.com.** Click on "Leaders.Now" and pick one of the short essays about management and leadership. Do you agree or disagree? Try to find real-world examples that support your argument by searching the archives of business magazines such as *Forbes* (**http://www.forbes.com**), *Fortune* (**http://www.fortune.com**), or *Business Week* (**http://www.businessweek.com**).
3. How do entrepreneurs develop corporate culture in their organizations? Do a search on the term "corporate culture" at the site of either *Inc.* magazine (**http://www.inc.com**) or *Entrepreneur* magazine (**http://www. entrepreneurmag.com**) to find answers to this question. Prepare a short presentation for your class explaining your findings.

CREATIVE THINKING CASE

Anatomy of Dragonflies and Empowerment

Once a week, Duncan Highsmith closets himself for two hours in a small room adjacent to his office and tries to wrap his brain around the world. Seated at a large wooden table, the president and CEO of Highsmith, Inc. sifts through stacks of articles on subjects ranging from juvenile crime to semiotics to the anatomy of dragonflies. In this eclectic mix he is searching for nascent trends, provocative contradictions, and, most important, *connections* that could eventually reshape his business.

Highsmith's pursuit—called Life, the Universe, and Everything—springs from his conviction that you can't take a narrow approach to the future. "We tend to behave as though the future will be like the present, only bigger and faster," says Highsmith, whose $55 million business is the country's leading mail order supplier of equipment such as book displays, audio-video tools, and educational software for schools and libraries.

Life, the Universe, and Everything is significant for the information it gathers, but Highsmith also intends it as a teaching tool that will ultimately prod everyone in the company to see and understand the kinds of big-picture connections CEOs generally make in isolation. Toward that end, he's beginning to broaden participation in the project, asking other staff members to pass along scraps of intriguing information and using his research as the basis for presentations at executive meetings.

Highsmith's overarching goal is for all employees in the company to shed their tactical blinders and begin thinking strategically—about customers, about the industry, and about forces for which the words *big picture* seem inadequate. "Life, the Universe, and Everything is in many ways in its infancy," says Highsmith. "The concrete benefits still have more to do with my role than with the rest of the organization. But thinking about what's next is becoming part of the routine work of the organization."

INFOTRAC COLLEGE EDITION

Critical Thinking Questions

1. How would you describe Duncan Highsmith's leadership style?
2. Is Life, the Universe, and Everything a tool for employee empowerment? Why or why not?
3. Is Life, the Universe, and Everything more beneficial for strategic planning or tactical planning, or is it equally beneficial for both?

VIDEO CASE

The Department Store Division of Dayton Hudson

Hudson's, Dayton's, and Marshall Field's are the components of the Department Store Division of Dayton Hudson Corp. (**http://www.target.com, http://www.marshallfields.com, http://www.mervyns.com**) Currently, Dayton Hudson's Department Store Division operates 19 Dayton's, 20 Hudson's, and 24 Marshall Field's stores—a total of 63 stores—in eight states. Every Hudson's, Dayton's, and Marshall Field's store seeks to be "the best store in town"—a mission they embarked on in 1996.

The stores refer to their customers as guests. The typical guest is female, married, and in her mid-40s. Approximately 40 percent of the guests have children living at home. Nearly 60 percent of the guests have earned at least an undergraduate degree, and about two-thirds hold white-collar jobs. The median household income of guests is about $58,000 annually.

Fashion leadership is the core of the division's business. The stores try to provide their guests with the widest possible assortment of the latest fashions and home products using national and private brands and by constantly monitoring product assortment.

The division recognizes that a wide assortment of trendy merchandise and guest friendly physical facilities are only part of the formula for making Hudson's, Dayton's, and Marshall Field's "the best store in town." The stores' employees are also a crucial element in this formula. Accordingly, the stores are investing significant sums in training their "team members to deliver consistently superior service."

The division's efforts have been well received by the company's customers. As a result, the Department Store division has enjoyed two consecutive years of strong earnings growth.

Critical Thinking Questions

1. How, if at all, are planning, organizing, leading, and controlling being used in Dayton Hudson Corp.'s Department Store Division?

2. Explain why conceptual, human relations, and technical skills are important to the development and successful execution of strategies to fulfill "the best store in town" mission.

Case: Fun and Games at Bigstep.com

"We really want to infuse a spirit of fun and fulfillment at Bigstep.com," says company co-founder and CEO Andrew Beebe. "Every month, I hand out a $10 bill to every employee to go buy toys for his or her desk—yo-yo's, Phantom Menace action figures, Bart Simpson dolls, whatever they want as long as they use the $10 to promote fun around the office."

Beebe and his co-founders launched Bigstep.com (**http://www.bigstep.com**) in 1998 with a clear objective: to become the premier online service center for small businesses to build their own Web sites and perform e-commerce transactions. Within a year, the company had 50,000 customers and 50 employees. "Most of us here are in a similar age-band—between 25 and 35," says Beebe, who is 27. "The culture of our company is very rooted in what some would call a Gen-X mentality. People here are very honest about what they think."

That honesty came in handy when Beebe decided it was time to come up with a formal mission statement. "We set out to nail the issue collectively," says Beebe. "All 50 of us went off-site for an entire day to begin formalizing our vision and values." During their meeting, the group visualized what they wanted Bigstep's impact and position to be over the next five years.

Later, an eight-member cross-company team drafted a core mission and value statement that was then presented and approved at a company-wide staff meeting. In part, it reads: "By tearing down the barriers of time, money and technology, we will ignite the power of small businesses and enable them to reap the benefits of the Internet." Core values include respecting customers and employees, empowering customers, pursuing quality, and creating an atmosphere where employees can learn and be challenged. "I think this document is going to prove invaluable as we continue to grow," says Beebe.

Bigstep's growth has been rapid. The firm now has 110 employees and over 100,000 customers. The company has landed $61.5 million in venture capital and forged partnerships with America Online, Compaq Computers, and S.C.O.R.E. With rapid growth, however, comes more challenges. Technical problems have crashed Bigstep's site at least twice, preventing customers from reaching their business Web sites. Recently, Beebe named Lucy Reid as the new Chief Executive Officer. Reid has over 20 years of executive experience, most recently as executive vice president of Wells Fargo Bank. Beebe will now become chairman of Bigstep's board of directors.

Questions for Critical Thinking

1. Describe Beebe's leadership style. How do you think this affected Bigstep's mission statement and core company values?
2. Why do you think Beebe has hired a new CEO with over 20 years of business experience? Discuss how this move might affect corporate culture.
3. Do you think an e-commerce firm needs a different type of leadership than a traditional firm? Why?

SOURCES: Andrew Beebe, "Diary of a Start Up," *Fast Company* (October 1999), downloaded from **http://www.fastcompany.com**; Jennifer Couzin, "Building MomandPop.com," *The Standard* (May 1, 2000), downloaded from **http://www.thestandard.com**; Patricia Fusco, "AOL Takes Big Step with Small Biz Service," *Internet News* (August 16, 2000), downloaded from **http://www.internetnews.com**; "Bigstep.com Names Former Wells Fargo Executive Vice President Lucy Reid as CEO," Bigstep.com company press release (September 12, 2000), downloaded from **http://www.bigstep.com**.

learning goals

>lg 1   What are the five structural building blocks that managers use to design organizations?

>lg 2   What are the five types of departmentalization?

>lg 3   How can the degree of centralization/ decentralization be altered to make an organization more successful?

>lg 4   How do mechanistic and organic organizations differ?

>lg 5   What is the difference between line positions and staff positions?

>lg 6   What is the goal of reengineering?

>lg 7   How does the informal organization affect the performance of the company?

>lg 8   What trends are influencing the way businesses organize?

Designing Organizational Structures

chapter 7

Procter & Gamble Reorganizes to Sell $70 Billion in 2005

The people who bring you Crest toothpaste, Pringles potato chips, and Hugo Boss cologne are really shaking things up. In an attempt to increase sales worldwide and bring new products to market more quickly, Procter & Gamble (**http://www.pg.com**) is reorganizing its corporate structure.[1] The consensus of consumers, chain-store customers, and industry insiders is that P&G needs to be simpler and to move faster.

To achieve these goals, the company has undertaken "Organization 2005!" To achieve its 2005 sales goal of $70 billion and reinvigorate its corporate culture, P&G is revamping its entire corporate management structure. The old P&G bureaucracy was based on geography, with four executive vice presidents overseeing the North American, Asian, Latin American, European, Middle Eastern, and African operations. Under this system, senior regional managers had wide latitude in setting prices and handling products. The old structure is being replaced by seven product-based global business units organized by category, such as baby care, food and beverage, and laundry and cleaning. These global business units will develop and sell products on a worldwide basis. P&G hopes that this shift from geographic departmentalization to a product-based structure will lead to faster product innovation and increase flexibility and response time.

As part of the restructuring process, P&G is streamlining its corporate staff and creating a global business services organization. Services that are currently spread throughout the organization, such as finance, accounting, and information technology, are being consolidated. According to top management, this will provide P&G with greater economies of scale and will improve both the quality and speed of those service areas. Additionally, P&G plans to introduce a new compensation system that will encourage employee innovation, flexibility, and customer service.

In 1998, P&G named Durk Jager to implement the new structure. Jager earned the nickname "Crazy Man Durk" for his earlier aggressive turnaround of P&G's failing Japanese operation. His aggressiveness, however, proved his undoing at rigidly structured P&G. He simply tried to do too much too fast.[2] A. G. Lafley, a man known for his people skills, was made CEO in the summer of 2000. Some observers say that the change was a mistake. Despite Jager's aggressive style, he may have been the best hope for changing P&G's entrenched bureaucracy.

Critical Thinking Questions:

As you read this chapter, consider the following questions as they relate to Procter & Gamble:

- What are the structural building blocks that Procter & Gamble can use in its reorganization?

- How does decentralization enter into the reorganization?

- How can the informal organization affect the reorganization?

BUSINESS IN THE 21ˢᵀ CENTURY

In today's dynamic business environment, organizational structures need to be designed so that the organization can quickly respond to new competitive threats and changing customer needs. In the future, companies such as Procter & Gamble will achieve long-term success only if they have the ability to manage change and organize their resources effectively. In this chapter, we'll present the five structural building blocks of organizations and look at how each can be used to build unique organizational structures. We'll explore how communication, authority, and job specialization are combined to create both formal and informal organizational structures. Finally, we'll consider how reengineering and new business trends are changing the way businesses organize.

STRUCTURAL BUILDING BLOCKS

>lg 1

As you learned in Chapter 6, the key functions that managers perform include planning, organizing, leading, and controlling. This chapter focuses specifically on the organizing function. Organizing involves coordinating and allocating a firm's resources so that the firm can carry out its plans and achieve its goals. This organizing, or structuring, process is accomplished by

- determining work activities and dividing up tasks *(division of labor)*,
- grouping jobs and employees *(departmentalization)*, and
- assigning authority and responsibilities *(delegation)*.

formal organization

The order and design of relationships within a firm; consists of two or more people working together with a common objective and clarity of purpose.

The result of the organizing process is a formal organizational structure. A **formal organization** is the order and design of relationships within the firm. It consists of two or more people working together with a common objective and clarity of purpose. Formal organizations also have well-defined lines of authority, channels for information flow, and means of control. Human, material, financial, and information resources are deliberately connected to form the business organization. Some connections are long lasting, such as the links among people in the finance or marketing department. Others can be changed at almost any time, as when a committee is formed to study a problem.

Five structural building blocks are used in designing an efficient and effective organizational structure. They are division of labor, departmentalization, managerial hierarchy, span of control, and centralization of decision making.

Division of Labor

division of labor

The process of dividing work into separate jobs and assigning tasks to workers.

specialization

The degree to which tasks are subdivided into smaller jobs.

The process of dividing work into separate jobs and assigning tasks to workers is called **division of labor.** In a fast-food restaurant, for example, some employees take or fill orders, others prepare food, a few clean and maintain equipment, and at least one supervises all the others. In an auto assembly plant, some workers install rearview mirrors, while others mount bumpers on bumper brackets. The degree to which the tasks are subdivided into smaller jobs is called **specialization.** Employees who work at highly specialized jobs, such as assembly-line workers, perform a limited number and variety of tasks. Employees who become specialists at one task, or a small number of tasks, develop greater skill in doing that particular job. This can lead to greater efficiency and consistency in production and other work activities. However, a high degree of specialization can also result in employees who are disinterested or bored due to the lack of variety and challenge.

Currently, most managers recognize that there is a trade-off between the economic benefits and the human costs associated with specialization. At Harley-Davidson's Kansas City assembly plant, managers and workers together have created an environment that maximizes the benefits and minimizes the drawbacks of highly specialized motorcycle assembly jobs.[3] To streamline the production process and at the same time keep employees involved and motivated, line workers are *required* to share their opinions and to make decisions about how to build better bikes. There is no denying the benefits of specialization in designing an efficient production system. But Harley has discovered that those benefits are best realized in an atmosphere that allows employees to experience challenge, empowerment, and ownership.

Departmentalization

The second building block used to create a strong organizational structure is called **departmentalization.** After the work is divided into jobs, jobs are then grouped together so that similar or associated tasks and activities can be coordinated. This grouping of people, tasks, and resources into organizational units facilitates the planning, leading, and control processes.

An **organization chart** is a visual representation of the structured relationships among tasks and the people given the authority to do those tasks. In the organization chart in Exhibit 7-1, each figure represents a job, and each job includes several tasks. The sales manager, for instance, must hire salespeople, establish sales territories, motivate and train the salespeople, and control sales operations. The chart also indicates the general type of work done in each position.

>lg 2

departmentalization
The process of grouping jobs together so that similar or associated tasks and activities can be coordinated.

organization chart
A visual representation of the structured relationships among tasks and the people given the authority to do those tasks.

e x h i b i t   7 - 1 | Organization Chart for a Typical Appliance Manufacturer

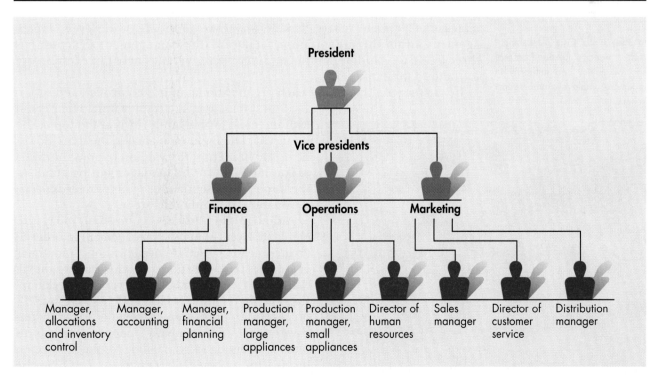

functional departmentalization

Departmentalization that is based on the primary functions performed within an organizational unit.

product departmentalization

Departmentalization that is based on the goods or services produced or sold by the organizational unit.

process departmentalization

Departmentalization that is based on the production process used by the organizational unit.

customer departmentalization

Departmentalization that is based on the primary type of customer served by the organizational unit.

geographic departmentalization

Departmentalization that is based on the geographic segmentation of the organizational units.

As Exhibit 7-2 shows, five basic types of departmentalization are commonly used in organizations:

- **Functional departmentalization,** which is based on the primary functions performed within an organizational unit (marketing, finance, production, sales, and so on).
- **Product departmentalization,** which is based on the goods or services produced or sold by the organizational unit (such as outpatient/emergency services, pediatrics, cardiology, and orthopedics).
- **Process departmentalization,** which is based on the production process used by the organizational unit (such as lumber cutting and treatment, furniture finishing, shipping).
- **Customer departmentalization,** which is based on the primary type of customer served by the organizational unit (such as wholesale or retail purchasers).
- **Geographic departmentalization,** which is based on the geographic segmentation of organizational units (such as U.S. and Canadian marketing, European marketing, South American marketing).

People are assigned to a particular organizational unit because they perform similar or related tasks, or because they are jointly responsible for a product, client, or market. Decisions about how to departmentalize affect the way management assigns authority, distributes resources, rewards performance, and sets up lines of communication. Many large organizations use several types of departmentalization. For example, a global company may be departmentalized first geographically (North American, European, and Asian units), then by product line (foods/beverages and health care), and finally by functional area (marketing, operations, finance, and so on). As Procter & Gamble illustrates, the type(s) of departmentalization an organization uses can directly affect organizational performance.

Managerial Hierarchy

The third building block used to create effective organizational structure is the **managerial hierarchy** (also called the *management pyramid*), or the levels of management within the organization. Generally, the management structure has three levels: top, middle, and supervisory management. These three levels were introduced in Chapter 6.

In a managerial hierarchy, each organizational unit is controlled and supervised by a manager in a higher unit. The person with the most formal authority is at the top of the hierarchy. The higher a manager, the more power he or she has. Thus, the amount of power *decreases* as you move down the management pyramid. At the same time, the number of employees *increases* as you move down the hierarchy.

Although the trend in organizations today is to eliminate layers of middle management in order to create a leaner, "flatter" organization, sometimes companies find that adding another layer to the hierarchy can actually simplify the reporting relationships in the company. Home Depot, the world's biggest home improvement retailer, recently discovered this.[4] The company's phenomenal growth rate was straining the capabilities of the six division heads who reported directly to the CEO. So the company hired four new group presidents, adding

At the Santa Cruz Amusement Park, a manager (second from left) has the power and authority to supervise employees who report to her.

e x h i b i t   7 - 2 | Five Ways to Organize

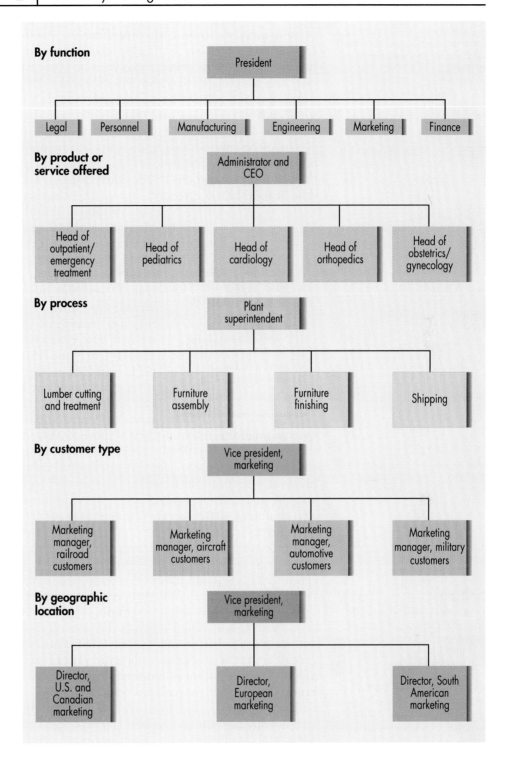

By function
- President
  - Legal
  - Personnel
  - Manufacturing
  - Engineering
  - Marketing
  - Finance

By product or service offered
- Administrator and CEO
  - Head of outpatient/emergency treatment
  - Head of pediatrics
  - Head of cardiology
  - Head of orthopedics
  - Head of obstetrics/gynecology

By process
- Plant superintendent
  - Lumber cutting and treatment
  - Furniture assembly
  - Furniture finishing
  - Shipping

By customer type
- Vice president, marketing
  - Marketing manager, railroad customers
  - Marketing manager, aircraft customers
  - Marketing manager, automotive customers
  - Marketing manager, military customers

By geographic location
- Vice president, marketing
  - Director, U.S. and Canadian marketing
  - Director, European marketing
  - Director, South American marketing

managerial hierarchy

The levels of management within an organization; typically, includes top, middle, and supervisory management.

a layer of management between the CEO and the division heads. As often happens when a structure is changed, there was some initial negative reaction to the decision. Eventually, most of the resistance was overcome as managers realized the new positions were needed to deal with business areas outside the company's traditional core competencies (for example, a direct marketing expert and a retail sales expert). Adding the new positions actually freed the division heads to concentrate on the duties central to their particular area of the business.

chain of command

The line of authority that extends from one level of an organization's hierarchy to the next, from top to bottom, and makes clear who reports to whom.

An organization with a well-defined hierarchy has a clear **chain of command,** which is the line of authority that extends from one level of the organization to the next, from top to bottom, and makes clear who reports to whom. The chain of command is shown in the organization chart and can be traced from the CEO all the way down to the employees producing goods and services. Under the *unity of command* principle, everyone reports to and gets instructions from only one boss. Unity of command guarantees that everyone will have a direct supervisor and will not be taking orders from a number of different supervisors. Unity of command and chain of command give everyone in the organization clear directions and help coordinate people doing different jobs.

The increasing number of mergers among organizations has given rise to an interesting trend. The unity of command principle used to be clearly evident in most top management hierarchies, but now a number of firms are choosing dual leadership at the very top of the organization.[5] At Ford Motor Co.,

How is Ford Motor Co.'s CEO partnership working? Get the latest performance statistics by clicking on "Investor Information" at
http://www.ford.com

William Ford, Jr. and Jacques Nasser have settled into adjacent offices and parallel responsibilities. At Citigroup, co-CEOs Sandy Weill and John Reed could not work out their differences, resulting in Reed's retirement in early 2000. Rampant globalization and the blistering rate of technological change have made it increasingly difficult for just one top manager to guide an organization toward success. Huge businesses created by megamergers such as Citigroup, DaimlerChrysler, Bell Atlantic/GTE, and Exxon Mobil must find creative ways to merge management hierarchies as well as corporate cultures. For many top managers, this new model of leadership means abandoning a competitive, stand-alone mentality for a more collaborative approach. The power-sharing concept can be very beneficial when top managers push the shared decision making all the way down the ranks of the organization. Problems arise, however, when co-executives cannot agree on common goals and objectives and the appropriate strategies for attaining those objectives. Co-leaders may also confuse and alienate their managerial subordinates if lines of communication and authority are not clear. And just like parents, co-commanders have to stand together on their decisions, being careful not to show favoritism to any one individual or group within the organization.

authority

Legitimate power, granted by the organization and acknowledged by employees, that allows an individual to request action and expect compliance.

delegation of authority

The assignment of some degree of authority and responsibility to persons lower in the chain of command.

Individuals who are part of the chain of command have authority over other persons in the organization. **Authority** is legitimate power, granted by the organization and acknowledged by employees, that allows an individual to request action and expect compliance. Exercising authority means making decisions and seeing that they are carried out. Most managers *delegate,* or assign, some degree of authority and responsibility to others below them in the chain of command. The **delegation of authority** makes the employees accountable to their supervisor. *Accountability* means responsibility for outcomes. Typically, authority and responsibility move downward through the organization as managers assign activities to, and share decision making with, their subordinates. Accountability moves upward in the organization as managers in each successively higher level are held accountable for the actions of their subordinates.

Span of Control

The fourth structural building block is the managerial span of control. Each firm must decide how many managers are needed at each level of the management hierarchy to effectively supervise the work performed within organiza-

span of control
The number of employees a manager directly supervises; also called *span of management.*

tional units. A manager's **span of control** (sometimes called *span of management*) is the number of employees the manager directly supervises. It can be as narrow as 2 or 3 employees or as wide as 50 or more. In general, the larger the span of control, the more efficient the organization. As Exhibit 7-3 shows, however, both narrow and wide spans of control have benefits and drawbacks.

If hundreds of employees perform the same job, one supervisor may be able to manage a very large number of employees. Such might be the case at a clothing plant, where hundreds of sewing machine operators work from identical patterns. But if employees perform complex and dissimilar tasks, a manager can effectively supervise only a much smaller number. For instance, a supervisor in the research and development area of a pharmaceutical company might oversee just a few research chemists due to the highly complex nature of their jobs.

The optimal span of control is determined by the following five factors:

- *Nature of the task.* The more complex the task, the narrower the span of control.
- *Location of the workers.* The more locations, the narrower the span of control.
- *Ability of the manager to delegate responsibility.* The greater the ability to delegate, the wider the span of control.
- *Amount of interaction and feedback between the workers and the manager.* The more feedback and interaction required, the narrower the span of control.
- *Level of skill and motivation of the workers.* The higher the skill level and motivation, the wider the span of control.

Centralization of Decision-Making

centralization
The degree to which formal authority is concentrated in one area or level of an organization.

>lg 3

The final component in building an effective organizational structure is deciding at what level in the organization decisions should be made. **Centralization** is the degree to which formal authority is concentrated in one

---

e x h i b i t   7 - 3 | Narrow and Wide Spans of Control

	Advantages	Disadvantages
Narrow span of control	• High degree of control. • Fewer subordinates may mean manager is more familiar with each individual. • Close supervision can provide immediate feedback.	• More levels of management, therefore more expensive. • Slower decision making due to vertical layers. • Isolation of top management. • Discourages employee autonomy.
Wide span of control	• Fewer levels of management means increased efficiency and reduced costs. • Increased subordinate autonomy leads to quicker decision making. • Greater organizational flexibility. • Higher levels of job satisfaction due to employee empowerment.	• Less control. • Possible lack of familiarity due to large number of subordinates. • Managers spread so thin that they can't provide necessary leadership or support. • Lack of coordination or synchronization.

Jack Welch, former Chairman of the Board for General Electric, encouraged boundaryless behavior so all employees, despite their positions or rank, felt free to share new ideas. Shown in this photo are Jack Welch, on the left, and new Chairman Jeffrey Immelt.

decentralization
The process of pushing decision-making authority down the organizational hierarchy.

concept check

- What are the five building blocks of organizational structure?
- List the five types of departmentalization.
- What factors determine the optimal span of control?
- What are the primary characteristics of a decentralized organization?

area or level of the organization. In a highly centralized structure, top management makes most of the key decisions in the organization, with very little input from lower-level employees. Centralization lets top managers develop a broad view of operations and exercise tight financial controls. It can also help to reduce costs by eliminating redundancy in the organization. But centralization may also mean that lower-level personnel don't get a chance to develop their decision-making and leadership skills and that the organization is less able to respond quickly to customer demands.

Decentralization is the process of pushing decision-making authority down the organizational hierarchy, giving lower-level personnel more responsibility and power to make and implement decisions. Benefits of decentralization can include quicker decision making, increased levels of innovation and creativity, greater organizational flexibility, faster development of lower-level managers, and increased levels of job satisfaction and employee commitment. But decentralization can also be risky. If lower-level personnel don't have the necessary skills and training to perform effectively, they may make costly mistakes. Additionally, decentralization may increase the likelihood of inefficient lines of communication, incongruent or competing objectives, and duplication of effort.

Several factors must be considered when deciding how much decision-making authority to delegate throughout the organization. These factors include the size of the organization, the speed of change in its environment, managers' willingness to give up authority, employees' willingness to accept more authority, and the organization's geographic dispersion. Decentralization is usually desirable when the following conditions are met:

- The organization is very large, like Exxon Mobil, Ford, or General Electric.
- The firm is in a dynamic environment where quick, local decisions must be made, as in many high-tech industries.
- Managers are willing to share power with their subordinates.
- Employees are willing and able to take more responsibility.
- The company is spread out geographically, such as JC Penney, or Procter & Gamble.

As organizations grow and change, they continually reevaluate the organizational structure to determine whether it is helping the company to achieve its goals. Firms can alter the degree of centralization/decentralization in the organizational structure as the needs of the company change. For example, Motorola has recently *centralized* functions and activities in an effort to increase operational efficiency and recapture market share. Motorola is restructuring both its cell phone division and its semiconductor business in a major effort to regain competitiveness in these markets.[6] The reorganization involves consolidating previously autonomous communications divisions. Motorola hopes this increased centralization will enable the divisions to share resources more efficiently and respond more quickly to customers.

HOT
links

Have Motorola's plans to centralize the functions and operations of its divisions been successful? Find out by clicking on "About Motorola" at

http://www.mot.com

MECHANISTIC VERSUS ORGANIC STRUCTURES

>lg 4

mechanistic organization

An organizational structure that is characterized by a relatively high degree of job specialization, rigid departmentalization, many layers of management, narrow spans of control, centralized decision making, and a long chain of command.

organic organization

An organizational structure that is characterized by a relatively low degree of job specialization, loose departmentalization, few levels of management, wide spans of control, decentralized decision making, and a short chain of command.

Using different combinations of the building blocks described above, organizations can build a wide variety of organizational structures. Nevertheless, structural design generally follows one of the two basic models described in Exhibit 7-4: mechanistic or organic. A **mechanistic organization** is characterized by a relatively high degree of job specialization, rigid departmentalization, many layers of management (particularly middle management), narrow spans of control, centralized decision making, and a long chain of command. This combination of elements results in what is called a *tall organizational structure*. Military organizations typically have tall structures. In contrast, an **organic organization** is characterized by a relatively low degree of job specialization, loose departmentalization, few levels of management, wide spans of control, decentralized decision making, and a short chain of command. This combination of elements results in what is called a *flat organizational structure*. Colleges and universities tend to have flat organizational structures, with only two or three levels of administration between the faculty and the president. Exhibit 7-5 shows examples of flat and tall organizational structures.

Although few organizations are purely mechanistic or purely organic, most organizations tend more toward one type or the other. The decision to create a more mechanistic or a more organic structural design is based on factors such as the firm's overall strategy, the size of the organization, the types of technologies used in the organization, and the stability of its external environment.

c o n c ə p t   c h ə c k

• Compare and contrast mechanistic and organic organizations.
• What factors determine whether an organization should be mechanistic or organic?

e x h i b i t   7 - 4 | Mechanistic versus Organic Structure

Structural Characteristic	Mechanistic	Organic
Job specialization	High	Low
Departmentalization	Rigid	Loose
Management hierarchy (levels of management)	Tall (many levels)	Flat (few levels)
Span of control	Narrow	Wide
Decision-making authority	Centralized	Decentralized
Chain of command	Long	Short

e x h i b i t   7 - 5 | Tall versus Flat Organizational Structures

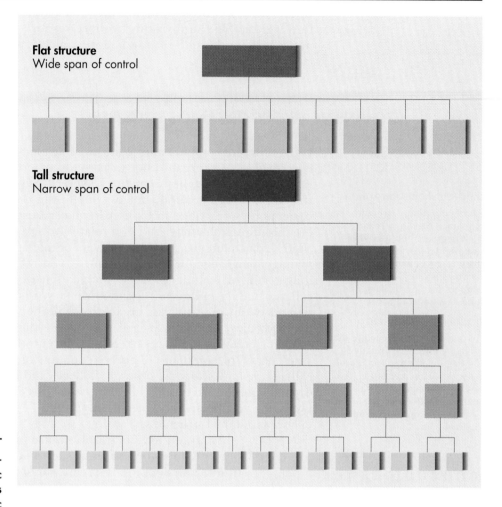

Flat structure
Wide span of control

Tall structure
Narrow span of control

Apple Computer's chief executive Steve Jobs uses an organic structure to develop new products like the iMac computer. Organic structures allow firms like Apple to succeed in rapidly changing environments.

collect
all
five

>lg 5

COMMON ORGANIZATIONAL STRUCTURES

There is no single best way to design an organization. Within the basic mechanistic and organic models and the hybrids that contain elements of both, an almost infinite variety of organizational structures can be developed. Many organizations use a combination of elements from different structural types to meet their unique organizational needs. Some of the most common structural designs are discussed in this section.

line organization

An organizational structure with direct, clear lines of authority and communication flowing from the top managers downward.

line-and-staff organization

An organizational structure that includes both line and staff positions.

line positions

All positions in the organization directly concerned with producing goods and services and which are directly connected from top to bottom.

staff positions

Positions in an organization held by individuals who provide the administrative and support services that line employees need to achieve the firm's goals.

committee structure

An organizational structure in which authority and responsibility are held by a group rather than an individual.

Line Organization

The **line organization** is designed with direct, clear lines of authority and communication flowing from the top managers downward. Managers have direct control over all activities, including administrative duties. An organization chart for this type of structure would show that all positions in the firm are directly connected via an imaginary line extending from the highest position in the organization to the lowest (where production of goods and services takes place). This structure with its simple design, clear chain of command, and broad managerial control is often well suited to small, entrepreneurial firms.

Line-and-Staff Organization

As an organization grows and becomes more complex, the line organization can be enhanced by adding staff positions to the design. Staff positions provide specialized advisory and support services to line managers in the **line-and-staff organization,** shown in Exhibit 7-6. In daily operations, those individuals in **line positions** are directly involved in the processes used to create goods and services. Those individuals in **staff positions** provide the administrative and support services that line employees need to achieve the firm's goals. Line positions in organizations are typically in areas such as production, marketing, and finance. Staff positions are found in areas such as legal counseling, managerial consulting, public relations, and human resource management.

Committee Structure

In **committee structure,** authority and responsibility are held by a group rather than an individual. Committees are typically part of a larger line-and-staff organization. Often the committee's role is only advisory, but in some situations the committee has the power to make and implement decisions. Committees can make the coordination of tasks in the organization much easier. At Toyota, for

e x h i b i t   7 - 6 | Line-and-Staff Organization

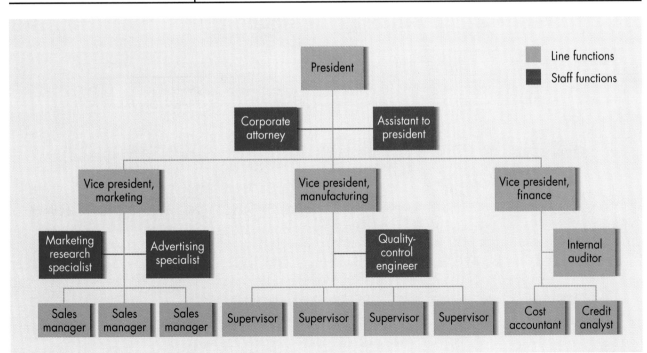

example, product and manufacturing engineers work together in committees. Using this process, factory machinery is developed concurrently with new car prototypes so it is able to accommodate them. Committees bring diverse viewpoints to a problem and expand the range of possible solutions, but there are some drawbacks. Committees can be slow to reach a decision and are sometimes dominated by a single individual. It is also more difficult to hold any one individual accountable for a decision made by a group.

Committee meetings can sometimes go on for long periods of time with little seemingly being accomplished. This is why many workers quickly develop an aversion to serving on committees. Stan Richards, president of the Richards Group, a Dallas-based advertising agency, developed a few simple tricks to creating short, effective committee meetings.[7] These are explained in the Focusing on Small Business box.

Matrix Structure

matrix structure (project management)

An organizational structure that combines functional and product departmentalization by bringing together people from different functional areas of the organization to work on a special project.

The **matrix structure** (also called the **project management** approach) is sometimes used in conjunction with the traditional line-and-staff structure in an organization. Essentially, this structure combines two different forms of departmentalization, functional and product, that have complementary strengths and weaknesses. The matrix structure brings together people from different functional areas of the organization (such as manufacturing, finance, and marketing) to work on a special project. Each employee has two direct supervisors: the line manager from her or his specific functional area and the project manager. Exhibit 7-7 shows a matrix organization with four special project groups (A, B, C, D), each with its own project manager. Because of the dual chain of command, the matrix structure presents some unique challenges for both managers and subordinates.

e x h i b i t 7 - 7 | Matrix Organization

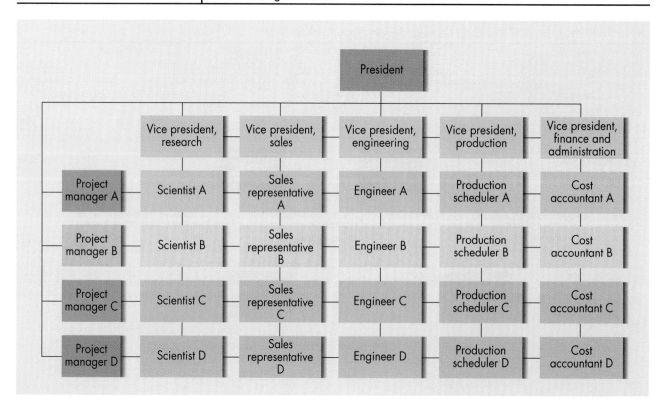

CREATING A STAIRWAY TO COMMITTEE HEAVEN

In 1987, when the Richards Group got big enough to take over a second floor in the building where it was then based, founder Stan Richards got worried that something special would get lost. "Everything changes when you move to multiple floors," he says. "People become tribal. Communication becomes more formal—and less effective." So Richards began convening regular committee meetings in the stairwell that connected the two floors. The idea: to gather everyone to hear news straight from the founder. Today those meetings seem downright quaint. The small agency has grown rapidly but the stairwell meetings continue.

Stairwell meetings are part of a strategy to maintain the spirit of small-company communication inside a fast-growing outfit. "Agencies can be hotbeds of paranoia," says Richards. "The best way to combat that tendency is simply not to keep secrets from each other."

Richards notes, "Being together is the key—all of us hearing something at exactly the same time. The event that brings us together varies. Another key point: Meeting in the staircase lets us be a little theatrical. Once, when we were courting an airline client, we even dropped oxygen masks from the fourth floor.

"If I call a committee meeting, we announce it over the loudspeaker, and people gather in the stairwell," says Richards. "I usually stand on the second level, so that everyone can hear me. We try to keep it short: I announce the news and offer a brief explanation. Then I might answer a question or two."

Critical Thinking Questions

1. How effective would stairwell meetings be in a large organization?
2. What are the advantages of a stairwell meeting?
3. What are other ways a large organization can retain the spirit of a small company?

Advantages of the matrix structure include:

- *Teamwork.* By pooling the skills and abilities of various specialists, the company can increase creativity and innovation and tackle more complex tasks.
- *Efficient use of resources.* Project managers use only the specialized staff they need to get the job done, instead of building large groups of underused personnel.
- *Flexibility.* The project structure is flexible and can adapt quickly to changes in the environment; the group can be disbanded quickly when it is no longer needed.
- *Ability to balance conflicting objectives.* The customer wants a quality product and predictable costs. The organization wants high profits and the development of technical capability for the future. These competing goals serve as a focal point for directing activities and overcoming conflict. The marketing representative can represent the customer, the finance representative can advocate high profits, and the engineers can push for technical capabilities.
- *Higher performance.* Employees working on special project teams may experience increased feelings of ownership, commitment, and motivation.
- *Opportunities for personal and professional development.* The project structure gives individuals the opportunity to develop and strengthen technical and interpersonal skills.

Disadvantages of the matrix structure include:

- *Power struggles.* Functional and product managers may have differing goals and management styles.
- *Confusion among team members.* Reporting relationships and job responsibilities may be unclear.
- *Lack of cohesiveness.* Team members from different functional areas may have difficulty communicating effectively and working together as a team.

How do you keep project teams on track in a matrix structure? Chris Higgins, BankAmerica's "Mr. Project," has some basic rules for getting things done.[8] Higgins joined the bank five years ago as a vice president in charge of project management in the payment services division. His span of control has increased from a team of 8 to 140 project managers, with a current combined budget of $100 million. Higgins gives this advice for keeping projects on track in a matrix organization:

1. Spend less time doing and more time planning. Higgins believes teams are often quick at acting, but slow to think things through. Planning is particularly important when the team is made up of members from different functional areas.

2. Don't rely on electronic communication. Face-to-face communication can prevent confusion, clarify expectations, and build relationships—all of which can be lost when only email is used to transmit information. Take time to communicate with team members.

3. Look for the commonality among projects. Although project teams often have unique challenges, not every challenge requires a unique plan of operation.

4. Project work isn't just about problem solving and timetables—it also requires encouraging employees to maintain momentum and keep up morale. Celebrate the achievement of interim goals, and make the project challenging as well as fun!

concept check

- How do line and staff positions differ?
- Why does the matrix structure have a dual chain of command?
- What are advantages of a matrix structure? Disadvantages?

REENGINEERING ORGANIZATIONAL STRUCTURE

>lg 6

reengineering

The complete redesign of business structures and processes in order to improve operations.

An excellent source of links and information about the ins and outs of the reengineering process is the Reengineering Resource Center at

http://www.reengineering. com

Periodically, all businesses must reevaluate the way they do business. This includes assessing the effectiveness of the organizational structure. To meet the formidable challenges of the future, companies are increasingly turning to **reengineering**—the complete redesign of business structures and processes in order to improve operations. An even simpler definition of reengineering is "starting over." In effect, top management asks, "If we were a new company, how would we run this place?" The purpose of reengineering is to identify and abandon the outdated rules and fundamental assumptions that guide current business operations. Every company has many formal and informal rules based on assumptions about technology, people, and organizational goals that no longer hold. Thus, the goal of reengineering is to redesign business processes to achieve improvements in cost control, product quality, customer service, and speed. The reengineering process

REENGINEERING THE IOC

In early 1999, the International Olympic Committee (IOC) received a wake-up call for reform when the Salt Lake City organizing committee "disclosed that it gave more than $1 million in cash and gifts to two dozen IOC members before it won the 2002 Winter Games." A report prepared by a panel appointed by the United States Olympic Committee (USOC) "offered a stinging rebuke of the IOC's structure and procedures and condemned it for failing to respond to warning signs about abuse as long ago as 1991." In the scandal's aftermath, 30 members—more than one-fourth of the IOC—were removed from the committee.

In addition to expelling the offending members, the IOC adopted some structural reforms in response to the scandal. The committee changed its process for selecting Olympics host cities and reduced the role of members. The IOC also agreed to create an ethics commission and a panel to recommend structural changes in the organization.

While praising the committee for taking quick action, corporate sponsors said the reforms had only be-

gun and that they would monitor future IOC actions. A Visa International spokesperson said, "We expect the IOC to review other opportunities to rebuild public trust and support." An executive from another Olympics sponsor was more critical. He observed that "[Juan Antonio] Samaranch [the IOC's president] could have taken his mandate and put it behind some very specific reforms. . . Instead they set up study groups."

The corporate world—and at least some of the IOC membership—recognizes that the scandal could reduce the number of corporate sponsors or lower the fees that sponsors are willing to pay. Some observers fear, however, that not all IOC members are serious about reform.

Critical Thinking Questions

1. Why might someone take a bribe or accept a substantial gift for voting in favor of a specific bidding city?
2. How might the IOC use reengineering to make structural changes to its organization?

should result in a more efficient and effective organizational structure that is better suited to the current (and future) competitive climate of the industry.

The many challenges of reengineering are well exemplified by the massive makeover currently in progress at VF Corp., a $5.5 billion-a-year apparel manufacturer headquartered in Greensboro, North Carolina. The project has been underway for four years and has already cost more than $70 million just for new software. Will the results be worth the cost? VF's reengineering goals included increasing annual revenue to $7 billion by the year 2001 by focusing on meeting the customer's needs, centralizing corporate functions, reducing costs, and pumping up marketing efforts. This requires structural change and new information technology. And if all goes well, VF's reengineering effort will have prepared the company to meet the competition head-on in the 21st century.

Is VF's reengineering effort paying off? Find out by clicking on "investor relations" at http://www.vfc.com

concept check

- What is meant by reengineering?
- What is the purpose of reengineering?

THE INFORMAL ORGANIZATION

>lg 7

informal organization
The network of connections and channels of communication based on the informal relationships of individuals inside an organization.

Informal relationships between coworkers promote friendships among employees and keep employees informed about what's happening in their firm.

Thus far in the chapter we have focused on the elements of formal organizational structures, many of which can be seen in the boxes and lines of the organization chart. Yet many important relationships within an organization do not show up on an organization chart. Nevertheless, these relationships can affect the decisions and performance of employees at all levels of the organization. The network of connections and channels of communication based on the informal relationships of individuals inside the organization is known as the **informal organization.** Informal relationships can be between people at the same hierarchical level or between people at different levels and in different departments. Some connections are work related, such as those formed among people who carpool or ride the same train to work. Others are based on nonwork commonalties such as belonging to the same church or health club or having children who attend the same school. The informal channels of communication of the informal organization are often referred to as the grapevine, the rumor mill, or the intelligence network.

Functions of the Informal Organization

The informal organization has several functions: First, it provides a source of friendships and social contact for organization members. Second, the interpersonal relationships and informal groups help employees feel better informed and connected with what is going on in their firm, thus giving them some sense of control over their work environment. Third, the informal organization can provide status and recognition that the formal organization cannot or will not provide employees. Fourth, the network of relationships can aid the socialization of new employees by informally passing along rules, responsibilities, basic objectives, and job expectations. Finally, the organizational grapevine helps employees to be more aware of what is happening in their workplace by transmitting information quickly and conveying it to places that the formal system does not reach.

Although the informal organization can help the formal organization to achieve its goals, it can also create problems if not managed well. Group *norms* (commonly accepted standards of behavior) may conflict with the company's standards and cause problems. For instance, during a merger or acquisition, informal groups may strongly resist change (especially structural change), spread incorrect information through the grapevine, and foster fear and low morale among employees. With this in mind, managers need to learn to use the existing informal organization as a tool that can potentially benefit the formal organization. An excellent way of putting the informal organization to work for the good of the company is to bring informal leaders into the decision-making process. For another approach to the informal organization, see the Applying Technology box.

concept check

- What is the informal organization?
- How can informal channels of communication be used to improve operational efficiency?

IT IS A SMALL WORLD AFTER ALL!

Ever been to Disneyland's "small, small world"? The reality may be closer than you think. Two Cornell University researchers have come up with a recipe for turning any large network of components into a "small world." This is an intriguing concept for managers looking for more effective ways to structure their organizations. The small-world model could be used to improve the operational efficiency of very large corporations like General Motors and Procter & Gamble. The key to the small-world model is shortcuts: well-connected individuals or components that can cut across traditional organizational boundaries. These shortcuts could significantly speed up the flow of information through a company. Using mathematical modeling, the researchers discovered that it takes only a very few random connections, or shortcuts, to reduce a large world to a small one. Of primary importance is linking well-connected people from each level, as in the accompanying illustration.

The small-world model is based on Stanley Milgram's "six degrees of separation" concept. In the 1960s Milgram, a social psychologist at Harvard, theorized that we were all much more closely connected by our web of social interactions than any of us realized. Milgram conducted an experiment that showed it took on average only five intermediaries to connect a person in the Midwest with a complete stranger in Massachusetts—hence the phrase "six degrees of separation." The Cornell researchers used experimental mathematics, a discipline that combines mathematical analysis with computer simulations, to explore different models of social interaction. To test the random network model, the two researchers applied it to three different fully mapped networks (including the nation's western electric power grid) and found that it is indeed a small, small world.

Critical Thinking Questions

1. What are shortcuts in the small-world model? What purpose do they serve?
2. How could an organization use the small-world model internally to improve efficiency?
3. How could an organization use the small-world model in its external environment?

MISSING LINK
The key to an efficient organization is the creation of shortcuts between different levels.

1. In what researchers call a "locally ordered system," communication occurs only between people on the same level.

2. Random shortcuts can be introduced into such a network—that is, people meet members of other levels at the water cooler and pass along information.

3. Only a few such shortcuts are needed to create a "a small world" in which information flows freely throughout the group. Productivity rises as a result.

CAPITALIZING ON TRENDS IN BUSINESS

To achieve long-term objectives, organizations constantly evaluate and alter their organizational structures. The increased use of information technology and globalization are creating new options for organizing a business.

The Virtual Corporation

One of the biggest challenges for companies today is adapting to the technological changes that are affecting all industries. Organizations are struggling to find new organizational structures that will help them transform information technology into a competitive advantage. One alternative that is becoming increasingly prevalent is the **virtual corporation,** which is a network of independent companies (suppliers, customers, even competitors) linked by information technology to share skills, costs, and access to one another's markets. This network structure allows companies to come together quickly to exploit rapidly changing opportunities. The key attributes of a virtual corporation are:

virtual corporation

A network of independent companies linked by information technology to share skills, costs, and access to one another's markets; allows the companies to come together quickly to exploit rapidly changing opportunities.

- *Technology.* Information technology helps geographically distant companies form alliances and work together.

For an inside look at a virtual corporation, point your browser to GeneraLife's corporate home page at
http://www.generalife.com

- *Opportunism.* Alliances are less permanent, less formal, and more opportunistic than in traditional partnerships.
- *Excellence.* Each partner brings its core competencies to the alliance, so it is possible to create an organization with higher quality in every functional area and increase competitive advantage.
- *Trust.* The network structure makes companies more reliant on each other and forces them to strengthen relationships with partners.
- *No borders.* This structure expands the traditional boundaries of an organization.

In the concept's purest form, each company that links up with others to create a virtual corporation is stripped to its essence. Ideally, the virtual corporation has neither central office nor organization chart, no hierarchy, and no vertical integration. It contributes to an alliance only its core competencies, or key capabilities. It mixes and matches what it does best with the core competencies of other companies and entrepreneurs. For example, a manufacturer would only manufacture, while relying on a product design firm to decide what to make and a marketing company to sell the end result.

How does Cisco handle continual change without chaos? Read about the company's strategies at
http://www.cisco.com

Although firms that are purely virtual organizations are still relatively scarce, many companies are embracing several of the characteristics of the virtual structure. One of the best examples is Cisco Systems, Inc., the global leader of networking for the Internet.[9] Cisco produces the tools needed to build the powerful networks that link businesses to their customers and suppliers—access products, Web scaling products, security products, and many more. Perhaps because of the nature of its products, Cisco has been at the forefront of developing a new approach to organizational structure and management, incorporating information technology in every conceivable way. Along with an innovative organizational design, Cisco has built a unique corporate culture, relentlessly pursued alliances to acquire and retain intellectual capital, focused obsessively on customer needs, and developed some of the most progressive human resource policies in the industry. Cisco CEO John Chambers believes strongly that organizations should be built on change, not stability; organized as networks, not hierarchies; based on interdependencies, not self-sufficiency; and, above all, based on technological advantage. According to Chambers, Cisco has found "the sweet spot" where technology and the future meet to transform not just business, but all of life.

Structuring for Global Mergers

Recent mergers creating megafirms (such as DaimlerChrysler and Exxon Mobil) raise some important questions regarding corporate structure. How can managers hope to organize the global pieces of these huge, complex new firms into a cohesive, successful whole? Should decision making be centralized or decentralized? Should the firm be organized around geographic markets or product lines? And how can managers consolidate distinctly different corporate cultures? These issues and many more must be resolved if mergers of global companies are to succeed. The merger of Pharmacia AB of Sweden and Michigan-based Upjohn Co. provides some insight into these structural dilemmas. Forging one company from two, while also boosting profits, presented some unique challenges to Fred Hassan, CEO of newly merged Pharmacia & Upjohn.[10]

The merger of Upjohn Co. and Pharmacia AB required restructuring the operations of both firms. Has the strategy worked? Uncover the details at

http://www.upjohn.com

When Hassan took over, sales and earnings were declining, turf wars were raging between regional offices, and the company's best talent was being hired away by its competitors. Hassan began his restructuring by reducing the number of senior executives from 19 to 8 so that they could make decisions as a team and collaborate more closely across different functional areas. Hassan lobbied to move the company's headquarters to a more strategic location that would be closer to other pharmaceutical firms and enable outside talent to be recruited more easily. Additionally, as is the case with many mergers, Hassan consolidated overlapping marketing, research, and administrative functions at the company's three regional offices. By restructuring the company, Hassan hopes his firm is now better positioned to compete with the other giants in the global pharmaceutical industry.

APPLYING THIS CHAPTER'S TOPICS

How is organizational structure relevant to you? A common thread linking all of the companies profiled in this chapter is you, the consumer. Companies structure their organizations to facilitate achieving their overall organizational

TRY IT NOW!

Build a Web Site   How computer literate are you? Have you ever built your own Web page? Could you build one for someone else? Find out what it takes to be a freelance Web builder! Visit **http://builder.cnet.com** to get information about building Web sites for fun and profit. You can set your own hours, name your own price, and choose your own projects. This site gives you a wide variety of information about Web-based businesses. Not sure whether you have the right skills, or uncertain what skills you should develop to work in this field? Don't know the difference between a content creator and a technical developer? Answers to those questions and many more can be found at this site. Companies are adapting their organizations to compete in cyberspace. Learn the skills you need to be a part of these new organizations.

goals. In order to be profitable, companies must have a competitive advantage, and competition is based on meeting customer expectations. The company that best satisfies customer wants and demands is the company that will lead the competition.

When companies make changes to their organizational structures, they are attempting to increase in some way their ability to satisfy the customer. For example, several of the companies profiled in this chapter were consolidating or centralizing parts of their operation. Why? Those companies hope to become more efficient and reduce costs, which should translate into better customer service and more reasonable prices. Some companies are decentralizing operations, giving departments or divisions more autonomy to respond quickly to changes in the market or to be more flexible in their response to customer demands. Many companies are embracing new information technology because it brings them closer to their customers faster than was previously possible. Internet commerce is benefiting consumers in a number of ways. When you buy books at **http://www.amazon.com** or use **http://www.ebay.com** to sell a used bicycle, you are sending the message that the virtual company is a structure you will patronize and support. Increasing globalization and use of information technology will continue to alter the competitive landscape, and the big winner should be the consumer, in terms of increased choice, increased access, and reduced price!

>looking ahead

at Procter & Gamble

The structural building blocks for any organization are: division of labor, departmentalization, and delegation. Durk Jager was not known as a great delegator. Decentralization can push decision making down into an organization. It can make an organization more responsive to local cultures and change. Under Jager, there was more decentralization resulting in improved earnings for some divisions because of their responsiveness to local market conditions. Durk Jager's alienation of the informal organization was a major factor in his termination.[11]

KEY TERMS

authority 202
centralization 203
chain of command
  202
committee structure
  207
customer
  departmental-
  ization 200
decentralization
  204
delegation of
  authority 202
departmentalization
  199
division of labor
  198
formal organization
  198
functional
  departmental-
  ization 200
geographic
  departmental-
  ization 200
informal
  organization 212
line-and-staff
  organization 207
line organization
  207
line positions 207
managerial
  hierarchy 201
matrix structure
  (project
  management)
  208
mechanistic
  organization 205
organic
  organization 205
organization chart
  199
process
  departmental-
  ization 200
product
  departmental-
  ization 200
reengineering 210
span of control
  203
specialization 198
staff positions 207
virtual corporation
  214

SUMMARY OF LEARNING GOALS

>lg 1 **What are the five structural building blocks that managers use to design organizations?**
The five structural building blocks that are used in designing an efficient and effective organizational structure are (1) division of labor, which is the process of dividing work into separate jobs and assigning tasks to workers; (2) departmentalization; (3) the managerial hierarchy (or the *management pyramid*), which is the levels of management within the organization (generally consists of top, middle, and supervisory management); (4) the managerial span of control (sometimes called *span of management*), which is the number of employees the manager directly supervises; and (5) the amount of centralization or decentralization in the organization, which entails deciding at what level in the organization decisions should be made. Centralization is the degree to which formal authority is concentrated in one area or level of the organization.

>lg 2 **What are the five types of departmentalization?**
Five basic types of departmentalization (see Exhibit 7-2) are commonly used in organizations:

- *Functional.* Based on the primary functions performed within an organizational unit.
- *Product.* Based on the goods or services produced or sold by the organizational unit.
- *Process.* Based on the production process used by the organizational unit.
- *Customer.* Based on the primary type of customer served by the organizational unit.
- *Geographic.* Based on the geographic segmentation of organizational units.

>lg 3 **How can the degree of centralization/decentralization be altered to make an organization more successful?**
In a highly centralized structure, top management makes most of the key decisions in the organization with very little input from lower-level employees. Centralization lets top managers develop a broad view of operations and exercise tight financial controls. In a highly decentralized organization, decision-making authority is pushed down the organizational hierarchy, giving lower-level personnel more responsibility and power to make and implement decisions. Decentralization can result in faster decision-making and increased innovation and responsiveness to customer preferences.

>lg 4 **How do mechanistic and organic organizations differ?**
A mechanistic organization is characterized by a relatively high degree of work specialization, rigid departmentalization, many layers of management (particularly middle management), narrow spans of control, centralized decision-making, and a long chain of command. This combination of elements results in a *tall organizational structure*. In contrast, an organic organization is characterized by a relatively low degree of work specialization, loose departmentalization, few levels of management, wide spans of control, decentralized decision-making, and a short chain of command. This combination of elements results in a *flat organizational structure*.

>lg 5 **What is the difference between line positions and staff positions?**
In daily operations, those individuals in *line positions* are directly involved in the processes used to create goods and services. Those individuals in *staff positions* provide the administrative and support services that line employees need to achieve the firm's goals. Line positions in organizations are typically in areas such as production, marketing, and finance. Staff positions are found in areas such as legal counseling, managerial consulting, public relations, and human resource management.

>lg 6 **What is the goal of reengineering?**
Reengineering is a complete redesign of business structures and processes in order to improve operations. The goal of reengineering is to redesign business processes to achieve improvements in cost control, product quality, customer service, and speed.

>lg 7 **How does the informal organization affect the performance of a company?**
The informal organization is the network of connections and channels of communication based on the informal relationships of individuals inside the organization. Informal relationships can be between people at the same hierarchical level or between people at different levels and in different departments; the relationships can be based on connections made inside or outside the workplace. Informal organizations give employees more control over their work environment by delivering a continuous stream of company information throughout the organization, thereby helping employees stay informed.

>lg 8 **What trends are influencing the way businesses organize?**
The virtual corporation is a network of independent companies (suppliers, customers, even competitors) linked by information technology to share skills, costs, and access to one another's markets. This network structure allows companies to come together quickly to exploit rapidly changing opportunities. The key attributes of a virtual corporation are technology, opportunism, excellence, trust, and no borders.

Large global mergers, like DaimlerChrysler created from the merger of America's Chrysler Corp. and Germany's Daimler-Benz, raise important issues in organizational structure. The ultimate question is how does management take two huge global organizations and create a single, successful, cohesive organization? Should it be centralized or decentralized? Should it be organized along product or geographic lines? These are some of the questions management must answer.

PREPARING FOR TOMORROW'S WORKPLACE

1. Divide the class into groups of five. Each group should be assigned a different type of organization: manufacturer, product retailer, service retailer, nonprofit organization, and governmental agency. Each group should interview managers at their assigned organization and report to the class on the structure of the organization. Be sure to ask the managers if they are satisfied with the current organizational structure and how it might be improved.

2. Would you like to work in a virtual organization? Why or why not?

3. Write a paper on why organizing is an important process. Give an example of how being disorganized can cause severe problems.

4. As the person in charge of homecoming, would you centralize or decentralize your operation? Explain why.

5. Why do you think that reengineering has become popular? Give an example of a company that has gone through reengineering.

6. Draw an organization chart of the firm you work for, your college, or a campus student organization. Show the lines of authority and formal communication. Describe the informal relationships that you think are important for the success of the organization.

7. Describe how the group norms in an informal organization with which you are familiar have influenced the company or organization. How can managers make informal organizations work for the good of the company?

WORKING THE NET

1. Find at least three examples of organization charts on the Internet by searching on AltaVista (**http://www.altavista.com**) for the term "company organizational charts." Analyze each company's organizational structure. Are the companies organized by function, product/service, process, customer type, or geographic location?

2. At either the *Fortune* magazine (**http://www.fortune.com**) or the *Forbes* (**http://www.forbes.com**) Web site, search the archives for stories about companies that have reengineered. Find an example of a reengineering effort that succeeded and one that failed and discuss why.

3. Visit the *Inc.* magazine Web site (**http://www.inc.com**) and use the search engine to find articles about virtual corporations. Using a search engine, find the Web site of at least one virtual corporation and look for information about how the company uses span of control, informal organization, and other concepts from this chapter.

CREATIVE THINKING CASE

Organizing the Monster

Tyrannosaurus rex, pterodactyl, and brontosaurus—dinosaurs all. But what's a trumpasaurus? In fact, he's no dinosaur at all, but a friendly monster—a 10-foot-high, bright green-and-purple mascot, affectionately dubbed "Trump"—who greets as you step off the fifth-floor elevator at the new 75,000-square-foot headquarters of Monster.com, a job search Web site. Founded in April 1994 by Jeffrey Taylor, Monster.com became part of the interactive division of TMP Worldwide in 1995. Today the company, based in Maynard, Massachusetts, and Indianapolis, Indiana, boasts that it is the most successful career center on the Internet. Serving both job seekers and recruiters, the site receives more than 29 million visits per month, contains more than 1 million job postings from 90,000 companies, and posts nearly 14 million résumés.

The Monster.com Web site makes it easy for job hunters and recruiters to find each other. That business model is reflected in the design principle behind the company's new headquarters—and especially in the 22 team areas built into the space. The goal: to make sure that people can connect with one another whenever and wherever they need to—without having to wait for an empty room.

Teams are encouraged to name their rooms—the Creative Group meets in "Brain Forest"; the Alliance Team convenes in "Raise the Roof"—and each group has a small budget for decorating its rooms. "There's something that happens when you get together in your own comfortable space," says Danielle McCabe, the creative director of Monster.com. "Ideas start to happen."

The largest, most-often-used meeting spot is the Monster Den—a cavernous area that features a kitchen, pool and Ping-Pong tables, oversize armchairs, and a mural decorated with monsters. Every Monday morning, Monster.com employees gather in the Den for a meeting whose purpose is to ensure that everyone in the company is on the same (Web) page.

I N F O T R A C® Critical Thinking Questions
COLLEGE EDITION

1. How would you describe the organizational structure at Monster.com?

2. Do you think that the informal organization might be very important at Monster.com?

3. Would you be happy working in this type of organizational structure? Why or why not?

VIDEO CASE

JIAN: A Virtual Organization

On its Web page (**http://www.jian.com**), JIAN, located in Mountain View, California, comments on the company's unusual name. "While a black belt is a master of the martial arts, a 'jian' is a *master of every art*—the ultimate human with extraordinary acumen, power and resourcefulness." JIAN describes itself as a contemporary software company that applies modern techniques to the art of building businesses. JIAN provides "expert knowledge and effective, time-saving tools that work with familiar Windows and Macintosh word processing and spreadsheet software."

JIAN, founded in July 1986 by Burke Franklin, was originally named Tools For Sales and focused on the development of sales promotion materials. Franklin also applied his experience to helping clients with their business plans. In 1988, Franklin took the best materials from each of these projects and developed BizPlan*Builder,* which became the flagship product for JIAN.

JIAN experienced rapid early growth. Franklin's challenge was to design an organization that would enable the company to continue to grow. Because it would be expensive and take him away from his software development and marketing expertise, Franklin rejected the common business approach of purchasing the equipment and hiring the people necessary to produce and distribute JIAN's products. Instead, Franklin decided to design JIAN as a virtual organization. He outsourced the production and distribution of JIAN's software to BINDCO and the human resources functions to EXECUSTAFF. BINDCO produces the software, packaging, manuals, and labels for JIAN's products, then assembles the products, and distributes them through JIAN's distribution channels. BINDCO also manages JIAN's inventory, takes its orders, and collects customer payments. EXECUSTAFF provides complete human resources services from hiring to firing and everything in between, including payroll, benefits administration, and workers' compensation claims. This virtual organization allows JIAN to concentrate on its core activities of designing business software and to increase its productivity and flexibility.

Critical Thinking Questions

1. What differentiates a virtual organization from other organizational structures?
2. What are the advantages and disadvantages of a virtual organization?
3. Would you like to work for a virtual organization? Why or why not?

Case: Oracle Changes Course

Oracle is one of the world's largest software firms, second only to Microsoft in size. Selling $10 billion of database software a year, Oracle has over 45,000 employees and operates in 70 countries. Now, founder Larry Ellison wants to turn Oracle into an Internet firm. He's had Oracle's software engineers build a line of "e-business" software products that allow businesses to manage all of their computers and databases through the Internet. "We have a chance to pass Microsoft and become the No. 1 software company," says Ellison. "If I said that two years ago, I would have been sedated and locked up. But now we're the Internet and they're not."

Ellison says his strategy hinges on being able to streamline Oracle's bloated organizational structure. Each of the countries where Oracle operates has its own management team, and its own way of tracking sales, accounting, revenues, and profits. Getting information about how the company or its individual divisions are doing is almost impossible. "I can't go to my PC and get an exact head count of how many people work at Oracle," says Ellison, "and I'm the CEO, for crying out loud." Ellison also believes that the company's sales force is inefficient. Several different salespeople, each selling a different company product, often call on the same customers.

Ellison shares leadership of the firm with company president Ray Lane and chief financial officer Jeff Henley. Each has run their own area—technology, sales, and finances respectively—relatively independently. Ellison has told Lane and Henley that he now plans to be actively involved with all facets of the company. He recently told a group of senior executives that they "report to me now and not Ray, and make no mistake about it."

In order to sell Oracle's Internet-based business systems to customers, Ellison believes that he has to first demonstrate that it can work. He's announced that all of the company's worldwide computers will now be run through a central system networked over the Internet.

Ellison says he wants to create an organizational structure for the Internet age. "When you're an e-business, everything is mediated by computers," he says. "All the individuality is bled out of the system and replaced by standards. People don't run their own show anymore."

Questions for Critical Thinking

1. What steps has Ellison taken to centralize Oracle's organizational structure? What else could he do? How can the Internet help implement Ellison's plan?
2. Do you think Ellison's plan to centralize decision making will work? Explain. What are other alternatives?
3. Do you agree with Ellison's statement about e-business removing individual decision making? Why?

SOURCES: Steve Hamm, "Oracle: Why It's Cool Again," *BusinessWeek Online* (May 8, 2000), downloaded from **http://www.businessweek.com**; G. Christian Hill, "Dog Eats Dog Food. And Damn if It Ain't Tasty," *Ecompany* (November 2000), downloaded from **http://www.ecompany.com**; Brent Schlender, "Oracle at Web Speed," *Fortune* (May 1999), downloaded from **http://www.ecompany.com**; Heather Wright, "Oracle Over the Pain of Switching to E-Business," *Infotech Weekly* (August 14, 2000), downloaded from **http://oracle.kjip.com**; "Oracle's Inside Story," *CNET* (July 13, 2000), downloaded from **http://news.cnet.com**.

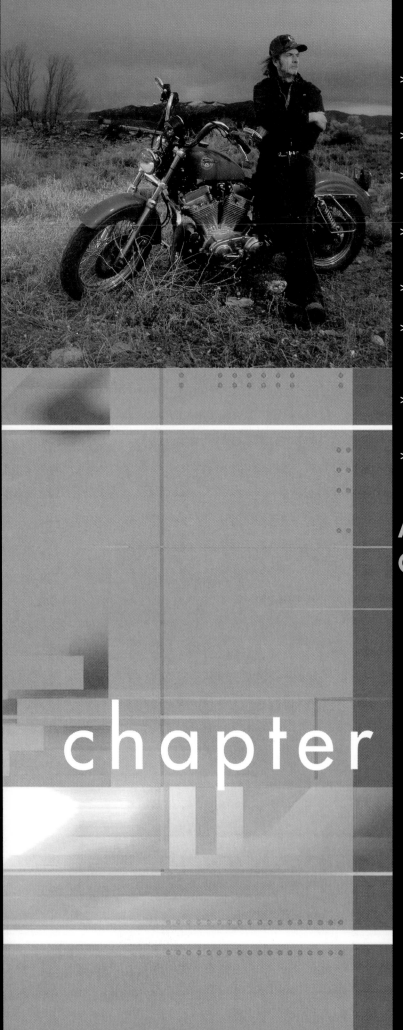

learning goals

>lg 1   Why is production and operations management important in both manufacturing and service firms?

>lg 2   What types of production processes are used by manufacturers and service firms?

>lg 3   How do organizations decide where to put their production facilities? What choices must be made in designing the facility?

>lg 4   Why are resource planning tasks like inventory management and supplier relations critical to production?

>lg 5   How do operations managers schedule and control production?

>lg 6   How can quality management and lean manufacturing techniques help firms improve production and operations management?

>lg 7   What roles do technology and automation play in manufacturing and service industry operations management?

>lg 8   What key trends are affecting the way companies manage production and operations?

Achieving World-Class Operations Management

chapter 8

Harley-Davidson Revs up Production

Harley-Davidsons (**http://www.harley-davidson. com**) aren't just motorcycles. They're an American legend, known for their unique style, sound, and power ever since the first one was assembled in a backyard workshop in 1903. "People want more than two wheels and a motor," explains Harley-Davidson CEO Jeffrey Bleustein. "Harleys represent something very basic—a desire for freedom, adventure, and individualism."

Back in the 1980s, Harleys also represented everything that was wrong with American manufacturing. The company's main factory in York, Pennsylvania, was outdated and inefficient, keeping prices high. Quality was so poor that owners sometimes joked they needed two Harleys—one to ride and one for parts. Fed-up consumers started buying motorcycles made by Japanese and German manufacturers. Harley-Davidson's future looked grim.

To turn things around, the company designed new models and borrowed state-of-the-art quality and production techniques from Japanese manufacturers. It cut the number of parts stored in inventory at the company's factories, keeping costs—and prices—under control. As quality improved and prices stabilized, Harley-Davidson's sales began to climb.

By the mid-1990s, however, Harley's existing factories were having trouble keeping up with demand. Customers often had to wait a year or longer to get a new Harley. The choice was clear: either the firm must rev up its production capability, or it would risk losing customers to foreign competitors once again.

First order of business? A new $86 million factory in Kansas City. The 330,000-square-foot plant, opened in 1998, puts Harley-Davidson at the forefront of modern manufacturing and management practice.

In a special lightproof room, lasers automatically pierce holes in fenders for taillights and other attachments. Robots then polish the finished fenders, along with gas and oil tanks, while other robots paint the various components needed to build a Harley. The components are loaded onto three dozen specially designed carts that swivel 360 degrees and can be lowered or raised to suit different workers or tasks. The carts move among workstations where employees assemble motorcycle frames. By the end of the line, 70 employees have assembled 650 parts at 20 different workstations.

No motorcycle leaves the plant without a final stop at Station 20. A team of test drivers revs up and rides each motorcycle, checking operating quality and listening for the classic

Critical Thinking Questions

As you read this chapter, consider the following questions as they relate to Harley-Davidson:

- How has a focus on manufacturing supported Harley-Davidson's growth?
- What factors outside the company have led to this focus?
- What future production changes will Harley need to make in order to continue to grow?

Harley sound. Any bikes that don't meet rigid standards are sent back to the factory for adjustments and fine-tuning.

Employees are integral to the success of Harley's new factory. They are grouped in work teams, and every employee is cross-trained to perform a variety of production tasks. Each work team must constantly look for ways to build a better Harley. The result has been many employee-generated ideas for better equipment, factory layout, and production processes.

Looking back, CEO Bleustein believes production and operations have been vital to Harley-Davidson's continued growth. "In the last 10 years, we were very much internally focused," he says. "We had to fix our manufacturing and bring it to a new level. With that in place, our focus can be more external, bringing new and exciting products to the marketplace."[1]

BUSINESS IN THE 21ST CENTURY

Finding the most efficient and effective methods of producing the goods or services it sells to customers is an ongoing focus of nearly every type of business organization. Today more than ever, changing consumer expectations, technological advances, and increased competition are all forcing business organizations to rethink where, when, and how they will produce products or services.

Like Harley-Davidson in the chapter's opening story, manufacturers are discovering that it is no longer enough to simply push products through the factory and onto the market. Consumers are demanding higher quality at reasonable prices. They also expect products to be delivered in a timely manner. Firms that can't meet these expectations often face strong competition from businesses that can. To compete, many manufacturers are reinventing how they make their products by automating their factories, developing new production processes, and tightening their relationships with suppliers.

Service organizations are also facing challenges. Their customers are demanding better service, shorter waits, and more individualized attention. Just like manufacturers, service organizations are using new methods to deliver what customers need and want. Banks, for example, are using technology such

Assembly-line employees at Harley-Davidson's new Kansas City plant suggested production process improvements that contributed to their firm's continued growth.

as ATMs and the Internet to make their services more accessible to customers. Many colleges now offer weekend courses for working students. Tax services are filing tax returns via computer.

In this chapter, we will examine how manufacturers and service firms manage and control the creation of products and services. Following a brief overview, we'll discuss production planning, including the choices firms must make concerning the type of production process they will use, the location where production will occur, and the management of resources needed in production. Next, we'll explain routing and scheduling, two critical tasks for controlling production and operations efficiency. Many businesses are improving productivity by employing new methods like quality control and automation. We'll discuss these methods before summarizing some of the trends affecting production and operations management.

PRODUCTION AND OPERATIONS MANAGEMENT—AN OVERVIEW

production >lg 1

The creation of products and services by turning inputs, such as natural resources, raw materials, human resources, and capital, into outputs, products and services.

operations management

Management of the production process.

Production, the creation of products and services, is an essential function in every firm. Production turns inputs, such as natural resources, raw materials, human resources, and capital, into outputs, products and services. This process is shown in Exhibit 8-1. Managing this conversion process is the role of **operations management.**

In the 1980s, many U.S. industries, such as automotive, steel, and electronics, lost customers to foreign competitors because their production systems could not provide the quality customers demanded. As a result, most American companies, both large and small, now consider a focus on quality to be a central component of effective operations management.

The goal of customer satisfaction, closely linked to quality, is also an important part of effective production and operations. In the past, the manufacturing

---

e x h i b i t   8 - 1 | Production Process for Products and Services

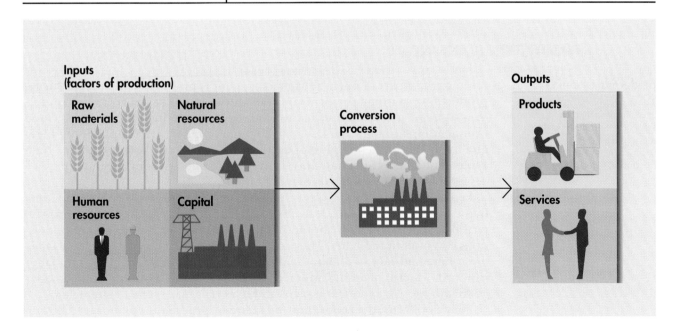

function in most companies was inwardly focused. Manufacturing had little contact with customers and didn't always understand their needs and desires. Today, however, stronger links between marketing and manufacturing have encouraged production managers to be more outwardly focused and to consider decisions in light of their effect on customer satisfaction. Service companies have also found that making operating decisions with customer satisfaction in mind can be a competitive advantage.

Operations managers, the personnel charged with managing and supervising the conversion process, play a vital role in today's firm. They control about three-fourths of a firm's assets, including inventories, wages, and benefits. They work closely with other major functions of the firm, such as marketing, finance, accounting, and human resources, to help ensure that the firm continually provides customer satisfaction. They face the challenge of combining people and other resources to produce high-quality goods, on time and at a reasonable cost. Working with marketing, they help to decide which products to make or which services to offer. They become involved with the development and design of goods and determine what production processes will be most effective.

Production and operations management involves three main types of decisions that are made at three different stages:

1. *Production planning.* The first decisions facing operations managers come at the *planning stage.* At this stage, decisions are made regarding where, when, and how production will occur. Resources are obtained and site locations determined.
2. *Production control.* At this stage, the decision-making process focuses on scheduling, controlling quality and costs, and the actual day-to-day operations of running a factory or service facility.
3. *Improving production and operations.* In the final stage, operations management focuses on developing more efficient methods of producing the firm's goods.

concept check

- Define production and explain how operations management is related to it.
- What are the three main types of decisions operations managers must make?

It is important to remember that these three types of decisions are ongoing and often occur simultaneously. In the following sections, we will take a closer look at the decisions and considerations firms face in each of these stages of production and operations management.

PRODUCTION PLANNING

production planning

The aspect of operations management in which the firm considers the competitive environment and its own strategic goals in an effort to find the best production methods.

An important part of operations management is **production planning.** During production planning, the firm considers the competitive environment and its own strategic goals in an effort to find the best production methods. Good production planning balances goals that may conflict such as providing high-quality service while keeping operating costs down, or keeping profits high while maintaining adequate inventories of finished products. Sometimes accomplishing all of these goals is quite difficult.

Production planning involves three phases. Long-term planning has a time frame of three to five years. It focuses on which goods to produce, how many to produce, and where they should be produced. Medium-term planning decisions cover about two years. They concern the layout of factory or service facilities, where and how to obtain the resources needed for production, and labor issues. Short-term planning, with a one-year time frame, converts these broader goals into specific production plans and materials management strategies.

Four important decisions must be made in production planning. They involve the type of production process that will be used, site selection, facility layout, and resource planning.

Production Process

>lg 2

production process
The way a good is made.

mass production
The ability to manufacture many identical goods at once.

In production planning, the first decision to be made is which type of **production process**—the way a good is made—best fits with the company's goals and customer demands. Another important consideration is the type of good or service being produced, as different goods may require different production processes. In general, there are three types of production: mass production, mass customization, and customization.

Mass Production   **Mass production,** the ability to manufacture many identical goods at once, was a product of the Industrial Revolution. Henry Ford's Model-T automobile is a good example of mass production. Each car turned out by Ford's factory was identical, right down to its color. If you wanted a car in any color except black, you were out of luck. Canned goods, over-the-counter drugs, and household appliances are examples of goods that are still mass-produced. The emphasis in mass production is on keeping manufacturing costs low by producing highly uniform products.

Increasingly, however, manufacturers are finding that mass production is becoming more complex. Many products are more complicated to produce. Automobile manufacturers, for example, are incorporating more sophisticated electronics into their car designs. As a result, the number of assembly stations in an auto assembly plant has increased. In many industries, customers are also demanding a wider array of choices and even customization. These trends have led to changes in the processes used to produce many goods.

A quality control employee inspects the uniformity of Trix yogurt, a product that is mass-produced to keep manufacturing costs low.

mass customization
A manufacturing process in which goods are mass-produced up to a point and then custom tailored to the needs or desires of individual customers.

customization
The production of goods or services one at a time according to the specific needs or wants of individual customers.

job shop
A manufacturing firm that produces goods in response to customer orders.

Mass Customization and Customization   In **mass customization,** a relatively new concept in manufacturing, goods are produced using mass production techniques, but only up to a point. At that point, the product or service is custom tailored to the needs or desires of individual customers. Golf club maker Taylor Made Golf devotes part of its production plant to mass customization. Customers needing longer club shafts, customized grips, or other options order through pro shops and golf instructors. Workers at Taylor Made's plant add the parts to the clubs based on the customer's requirements.[2]

Customization is the opposite of mass production. In customization, the firm produces goods one at a time according to the specific needs or wants of individual customers. Unlike mass customization, each product or service produced is unique. For example, a print shop may handle a variety of projects, including newsletters, brochures, stationery, and reports. Each print job varies in quantity, type of printing process, binding, color of ink, and type of paper. A manufacturing firm that produces goods in response to customer orders is called a **job shop.**

Some types of service businesses also deliver customized services. Doctors, for instance, usually must consider the individual illnesses and circumstances of each patient before developing a customized treatment plan. Real estate

Can customized Taylor Made clubs improve your golf game? Find out more about how Taylor Made Golf uses mass customization at
http://www.taylormadegolf.com

agents also develop a customized service plan for each customer based on the type of house the person is selling or wants to buy. The differences between mass production, mass customization, and customization are summarized in Exhibit 8-2.

In addition to production type, operations managers also classify production processes in two ways: (1) by how inputs are converted into outputs and (2) by the timing of the process.

Converting Inputs to Outputs   Production involves converting inputs (raw materials, parts, human resources) into outputs (products or services). In a manufacturing company, the inputs, the production process, and the final outputs are usually obvious. Harley-Davidson, for instance, converts steel, rubber, paint, and other inputs into motorcycles. The production process in a service company involves a less obvious conversion. For example, HCA–The Health Care Company converts the knowledge and skills of its medical personnel, along with equipment and supplies from a variety of sources, into health care services for patients. Examples of the inputs and outputs used by other types of businesses are shown in Exhibit 8-3.

There are two basic processes for converting inputs into outputs. In **process manufacturing,** the basic input (raw materials, parts) is *broken down* into one or more outputs (products). For instance, bauxite (the input) is processed to extract aluminum (the output). The **assembly process** is just the opposite. The basic inputs, like parts, raw materials, or human resources, are either *combined* to create the output or *transformed* into the output. An airplane, for example, is created by assembling thousands of parts. Iron and other materials are combined and transformed by heat into steel. In services, customers may play a role in the transformation process. For example, a tax preparation service combines the knowledge of the tax preparer with the customer's information about personal finances in order to complete tax returns.

Production Timing   A second consideration in choosing a production process is timing. A **continuous process** uses long production runs that may last days, weeks, or months without equipment shutdowns. It is best for high-volume, low-variety products with standardized parts, such as nails, glass, and paper.

---

process manufacturing
A production process in which the basic input is *broken down* into one or more outputs (products).

assembly process
A production process in which the basic inputs are either *combined* to create the output or *transformed* into the output.

continuous process
A production process that uses long production runs lasting days, weeks, or months without equipment shutdowns; generally used for high-volume, low-variety products with standardized parts.

---

e x h i b i t   8 - 2 | Classification of Production Types

Mass Production	Mass Customization	Customization
Highly uniform products or services. Many products made sequentially.	Uniform and standardized production to a point, then unique features added to each product.	Each product or service produced according to individual customer requirements.
Examples: Breakfast cereals, soft drinks, and computer keyboards.	Examples: Dell computers, tract homes, and Taylor Made Golf clubs.	Examples: Custom homes, legal services, and haircuts.

| Converting Inputs to Outputs

Type of Organization	Input	Output
Airline	Pilots, crew, flight attendants, reservations system, ticketing agents, customers, airplanes, fuel, maintenance crews, ground facilities	Movement of customers and freight
Grocery store	Merchandise, building, clerks, supervisors, store fixtures, shopping carts, customers	Groceries for customer sales
High school	Faculty, curriculum, buildings, classrooms, library, auditorium, gymnasium, students, staff, supplies	Graduates, public service
Manufacturer	Machinery, raw materials, plant, workers, managers	Finished products for consumers and other firms
Restaurant	Food, cooking equipment, serving personnel, chefs, dishwashers, host, patrons, furniture, fixtures	Meals for customers

intermittent process

A production process that uses short production runs to make batches of different products; generally used for low-volume, high-variety products.

Some services also use a continuous process. Your local electric company is one example. Per-unit costs are low and production is easy to schedule.

In an **intermittent process,** short production runs are used to make batches of different products. Machines are shut down to change them to make different products at different times. This process is best for low-volume, high-variety products such as those produced by mass customization or customization. Job shops are examples of firms using an intermittent process.

Although some service companies use continuous processes, most service firms rely on intermittent processes. For instance, a restaurant preparing gourmet meals, a physician performing physical examinations or surgical operations, and an advertising agency developing ad campaigns for business clients all customize their services to suit each customer. They use the intermittent process. Note that their "production runs" may be very short—one grilled salmon or one eye exam at a time.

Site Selection

>lg 3

One big decision that must be made early in production and operations planning is where to put the facility, be it a factory or a service office. Site selection affects operating costs, the price of the product or service, and the company's ability to compete. For instance, the costs of shipping raw materials and finished goods can be as much as 25 percent of a manufacturer's total cost. Locating a factory where these and other costs are as low as possible can make a major contribution to a firm's success. Mistakes made at this stage can be expensive. It is hard and costly to move a factory or service facility once production begins. Firms must weigh a number of factors to ensure that the right decision is made.

Ohio? France? Sri Lanka? Get a clear picture of what these and other business locations offer at the Economic Development Directory

http://www.ecodevdirectory. com

Availability of Production Inputs

As we discussed earlier, organizations need certain resources in order to produce products and services for sale. Access to these resources, or inputs, is a huge consideration in site selection. For example, the availability and cost of labor are very important to both manufacturing and service businesses. Payroll costs can vary widely from one location to another because of differences in the cost of living, the number of jobs available, and the skills and productivity of the local workforce. The unionization of the local labor force is another point to consider in many industries. Low labor costs were one reason Honeywell, a U.S. manufacturer, chose Ireland as the site for a new factory. Ireland has a skilled workforce, but high unemployment rates in the country have kept the cost of labor down. Honeywell and other companies pay employees significantly less in salary and fringe benefits in Ireland than they do in the United States.[3]

Learn more about Honeywell's worldwide operations at

http://www.honeywell.com

Executives must also assess the availability of raw materials, parts, and equipment for each production site under consideration. It can be costly to ship these resources long distances so companies that use heavy or bulky raw materials may choose to be located near suppliers. Mining companies want to be near ore deposits, oil refiners near oil fields, paper mills near forests, and food processors near farms.

Marketing Factors

Businesses must also evaluate how the location of their facility will affect their ability to serve their customers. For some firms, it may not be necessary to be located near customers. Instead, the firm will need to assess the difficulty and costs involved with distributing its goods to customers from the location chosen.

Other firms may find that locating near customers can provide marketing advantages. When a factory or service center is close to customers, the firm can often offer better service at a lower cost. Other firms may gain a competitive advantage by locating their facilities so that customers can easily buy their products or services. The location of competitors may also be a factor. Businesses with more than one facility may also need to consider how far to spread their locations in order to maximize market coverage.

Local Incentives

Incentives offered by countries, states, or cities may also influence site selection. Tax breaks are a common incentive. The locality may reduce the amount of taxes the firm will pay on income, real estate, utilities, or payroll. Tax incentives offered by state and city governments were a deciding factor in Mitsubishi's selection of Illinois as the site for its factory. For 13 years, Mitsubishi has enjoyed a 50 percent exemption from real estate taxes and receives a 50 percent rebate on its utility taxes.[4]

Other government incentives can also convince businesses to choose one location over another. Local governments sometimes offer exemption from certain regulations or financial assistance in order to attract or keep production

Detroit, Michigan, is a world-class manufacturing city where a high percentage of the local workforce is employed by General Motors and other firms in the automotive industry.

facilities in their area. When financial services firm Fidelity Mutual was looking for a site for its administrative and customer service operations, the company chose Cincinnati, Ohio. Cincinnati officials gave the firm a tax break equal to about 5 percent of the firm's construction costs. The city also constructed a free highway to the new site and built a center at Northern Kentucky University. There, 200 students answer customer telephone inquiries for less pay than Fidelity's former telephone center employees.[5]

Manufacturing Environment   Another factor to consider is the manufacturing environment in a potential location. Some localities have a strong existing manufacturing base. When a large number of manufacturers, perhaps in a certain industry, are already located in an area, that area is likely to offer greater availability of resources, such as manufacturing workers, better accessibility to suppliers and transportation, and other factors that can increase a plant's operating efficiency.

Every year, *Industry Week* evaluates the manufacturing climate of 315 U.S. cities. Each city is rated based on the productivity of its manufacturing sector, the percentage of the local workforce employed by manufacturing firms, the contribution of manufacturing to the area's overall economy, and several other factors. Though not necessarily the largest manufacturing cities in the United States, the top-ranked cities are considered "world-class" manufacturing cities by *Industry Week*. As Exhibit 8-4 shows, San Jose, California, and Houston, Texas, topped the most recent *Industry Week* survey.

What characteristics make a city a world-class manufacturing site? Read the *Industry Week* articles at

http://www.industryweek. com/iwinprint/communities

International Location Considerations   In recent years, manufacturers in many industries have opened new production facilities outside the United States. There are often sound financial reasons for considering a foreign location. Labor costs are considerably lower in countries like Singapore, Ireland, and

e x h i b i t   8 - 4 | Top 10 World-Class U.S. Manufacturing Cities

1. San Jose, California
2. Houston, Texas
3. Portland, Oregon
4. Dallas, Texas
5. Boston, Massachusetts
6. Chicago, Illinois
7. Austin, Texas
8. Los Angeles, California
9. Phoenix-Mesa, Arizona
10. Atlanta, Georgia

SOURCE: "The Atlas of U.S. Manufacturing," *Industry Week Special Report* (April 3, 2000), downloaded from *Industry Week* Web site, **http://www.industryweek.com**.

Mexico. Foreign countries may also have fewer regulations governing how factories operate. Or with a foreign location, production may be closer to new markets. That's exactly why Cabot Corp.'s Microelectronics Materials Division decided to open a plant in Japan. The company, which makes industrial slurries that are used to form computer chips, recognized a growing demand for its product in Asia. Opening a plant in Japan gave the company the ability to take advantage of this market growth.[6]

Facility Layout

After the site location decision has been made, the next focus in production planning is the facility's layout. Here, the goal is to determine the most efficient and effective design for the particular production process. A manufacturer might opt for a U-shaped production line, for example, rather than a long, straight one, to allow products and workers to move more quickly from one area to another.

Service organizations must also consider layout, but they are more concerned with how it affects customer behavior. It may be more convenient for a hospital to place its freight elevators in the center of the building, but doing so may block the flow of patients, visitors, and medical personnel between floors and departments.

There are three main types of facility layouts: process, product, and fixed-position layouts. All three layouts are illustrated in Exhibit 8-5.

process layout

A facility arrangement in which work flows according to the production process. All workers performing similar tasks are grouped together, and products pass from one workstation to another.

Process Layout   The **process layout** arranges work flow around the production process. All workers performing similar tasks are grouped together. Products pass from one workstation to another (but not necessarily to every workstation). For example, all grinding would be done in one area, all assembling in another, and all inspection in yet another. The process layout is best for firms that produce small numbers of a wide variety of products, typically using general-purpose machines that can be changed rapidly to new operations for different product designs. For example, a manufacturer of custom machinery would use a process layout.

product (assembly-line) layout

A facility arrangement in which workstations or departments are arranged in a line with products moving along the line.

Product Layout   The **product (or assembly-line) layout** is used for a continuous or repetitive production process. When large quantities of a product must be processed on an ongoing basis, the workstations or departments are arranged in a line with products moving along the line. Automobile and appliance manufacturers, as well as food-processing plants, usually use a product layout. Service companies may also use a product layout for routine processing operations. For example, overnight film processors use assembly-line techniques.

fixed-position layout

A facility arrangement in which the product stays in one place and workers and machinery move to it as needed.

Fixed-Position Layout   Some products cannot be put on an assembly line or moved about in a plant. A **fixed-position layout** lets the product stay in one place while workers and machinery move to it as needed. Products that are impossible to move—ships, airplanes, and construction projects—are typically produced using a fixed-position layout. Limited space at the project site often means that parts of the product must be assembled at other sites, transported to the fixed site, and then assembled. The fixed-position layout is also common for on-site services like housecleaning services, pest control, and landscaping.

Resource Planning

>lg 4

As part of the production planning process, firms must ensure that the resources needed for production, such as raw materials, parts, and equipment, will be available at strategic moments in the production process. This can be a

e x h i b i t   8 - 5 | Facility Layouts

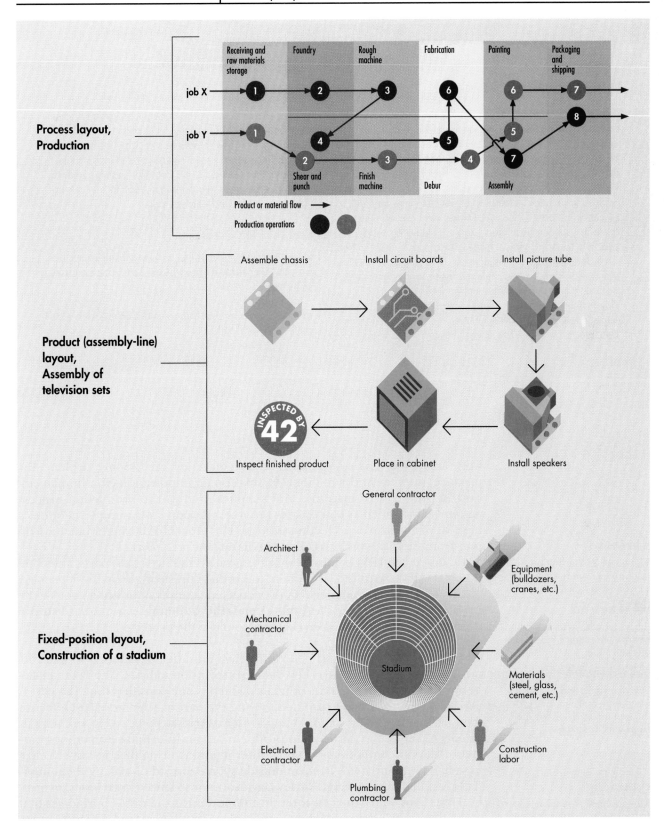

Process layout, Production

Receiving and raw materials storage | Foundry | Rough machine | Fabrication | Painting | Packaging and shipping

job X → 1 → 2 → 3 → 6 → 6 → 7

job Y → 1 → 4 → 5 → 5 → 8

2 → 3 → 4 → 7

Shear and punch | Finish machine | Debur | Assembly

Product or material flow →
Production operations ● ●

Product (assembly-line) layout, Assembly of television sets

Assemble chassis → Install circuit boards → Install picture tube

Inspect finished product ← Place in cabinet ← Install speakers

INSPECTED BY 42

Fixed-position layout, Construction of a stadium

General contractor

Architect

Mechanical contractor

Electrical contractor

Plumbing contractor

Stadium

Equipment (bulldozers, cranes, etc.)

Materials (steel, glass, cement, etc.)

Construction labor

SOURCE: From *Production and Operations Management, 8th edition*, by Gaither/Frazier. © 1999. Reprinted with permission of South-Western College Publishing, a division of Thomson Learning. Fax 800-730-2215

MAKING ETHICAL CHOICES

TWISTING SUPPLIERS' ARMS

In recent years, General Motors (GM)—like some other companies—has been using aggressive tactics to wring concessions out of its suppliers in order to cut the costs of the parts going into the vehicles that it manufactures. Purchased materials represent 50 to 60 percent of a new automobile's cost. Consequently, cost concessions from suppliers can result in enormous savings for GM.

Since the early 1990s, GM has used tactics such as "tearing up contracts and running multiple rounds of bidding to grind down prices." Harold Kutner, vice-president and group executive in charge of GM's worldwide purchasing, defends these tactics. He does not apologize for GM's unrelenting efforts to cut costs. According to Kutner, if a supplier can provide units less expensively a year from now, then the supplier ought to be able to meet the lower cost now. "We're trying to drive tomorrow's savings into today's programs. Some suppliers can't do that, so they write a check to give us those savings." A few suppliers say that "this amounts to demanding a rebate in return for new contracts." Kutner says that GM does not require these payments. Yet he concedes that "we open the door to any scheming by suppliers to find cost savings."

Critical Thinking Questions

1. Is it ethical for a business to use "strong-arm" tactics to pressure its suppliers for concessions? Why or why not?
2. How might Kutner's attitude affect the propensity of GM's suppliers and employees to behave ethically or unethically?

---

purchasing

The process of buying production inputs from various sources; also called *procurement*.

bill of material

A list of the items and the number of each required to make a given product.

make-or-buy decision

The determination by a firm of whether to make its own production materials or buy them from outside sources.

outsourcing

The purchase of items from an outside source rather than making them internally.

huge challenge. The components used to build just one Boeing airplane, for instance, number in the millions. Cost is also an important factor. In many industries, the cost of materials and supplies used in the production process amounts to as much as half of sales revenues. Resource planning is therefore a big part of any firm's production strategy. The process of buying production inputs from various sources is called **purchasing,** or *procurement*.

Resource planning begins by specifying which raw materials, parts, and components will be required, and when, to produce finished goods. To determine the amount of each item needed, the expected quantity of finished goods to be produced must be forecast. A **bill of material** is then drawn up that lists the items and the number of each required to make the product.

Insourcing and Outsourcing Next, the firm must decide whether to make its own production materials or buy them from outside sources. This is the **make-or-buy decision.** The quantity of items needed is one consideration. If a part is used in only one of many products, buying the part may be more cost-effective than making it. Buying standard items, such as screws, bolts, rivets, and nails, is usually cheaper and easier than producing them internally. Sometimes purchasing larger components from another manufacturing firm is cost-effective as well. Purchasing items from an outside source instead of making them internally is called **outsourcing.** Harley-Davidson, for example, purchases its tires, brake systems, and other motorcycle components from other businesses that make them to Harley's specifications. If a product has special design features that need to be kept secret to protect a competitive advantage, however, a firm may decide to produce all parts internally.

In deciding whether to make or buy, a firm must also consider whether outside sources can provide high-quality supplies in a reliable manner. Having to shut down production because vital parts weren't delivered on time can be a costly disaster. For example, General Motors relies on hundreds of suppliers for parts. When workers in two of the plants that supplied parts went on strike, GM was forced to shut down virtually all of its North American production.[7] Just as bad are inferior parts or materials, which can damage a firm's reputation for producing high-quality goods. Therefore, firms that buy some or all of their production materials from outside sources need to pay close attention to building strong relationships with quality suppliers.

Inventory Management   A firm's **inventory** is the supply of goods it holds for use in production or for sale to customers. Deciding how much inventory to keep on hand is one of the biggest challenges facing operations managers. On the one hand, with large inventories, the firm can meet most production and customer demands. Buying in large quantities can also allow a company to take advantage of quantity discounts. On the other hand, large inventories can tie up the firm's money, are expensive to store, and can become obsolete.

Inventory management involves deciding how much of each type of inventory to keep on hand and the ordering, receiving, storing, and tracking of it. The goal of inventory management is to keep down the costs of ordering and holding inventories while maintaining enough on hand for production and sales. Good inventory management enhances product quality, makes operations more efficient, and increases profits. Poor inventory management can result in dissatisfied customers, financial difficulties, and even bankruptcy.

One way to determine the best inventory levels is to look at three costs: the cost of holding inventory, the cost of reordering frequently, and the cost of not keeping enough inventory on hand. Managers must measure all three costs and try to minimize them.

To control inventory levels, managers often track the use of certain inventory items. Most companies keep a **perpetual inventory,** a continuously updated list of inventory levels, orders, sales, and receipts, for all major items. Today, companies often use computers to track inventory levels, calculate order quantities, and issue purchase orders at the right times.

Computerized Resource Planning   Many manufacturing companies have adopted computerized systems to control the flow of resources and inventory. **Materials requirement planning (MRP)** is one such system. MRP uses a master schedule to ensure that the materials, labor, and equipment needed for production are at the right places in the right amounts at the right times. The schedule is based on forecasts of demand for the company's products. It says exactly what will be manufactured during the next few weeks or months and when the work will take place. Sophisticated computer programs coordinate all the elements of MRP. The computer comes up with materials requirements by comparing production needs to the materials the company already has on hand. Orders are placed so items will be on hand when they are needed for production. MRP helps ensure a smooth flow of finished products.

Manufacturing resource planning II (MRPII) was developed in the late 1980s to expand on MRP. It uses a complex computerized system to integrate data from many departments, including finance, marketing, accounting, engineering, and manufacturing. MRPII can generate a production plan for the firm, as well as management reports, forecasts, and financial statements. The system lets managers make more accurate forecasts and assess the impact of production plans on profitability. If one department's plans change, the effects of these changes on other departments are transmitted throughout the company.

---

inventory

The supply of goods that a firm holds for use in production or for sale to customers.

inventory management

The determination of how much of each type of inventory a firm will keep on hand and the ordering, receiving, storing, and tracking of inventory.

perpetual inventory

A continuously updated list of inventory levels, orders, sales, and receipts.

materials requirement planning (MRP)

A computerized system of controlling the flow of resources and inventory. A master schedule is used to ensure that the materials, labor, and equipment needed for production are at the right places in the right amounts at the right times.

manufacturing resource planning II (MRPII)

A complex computerized system that integrates data from many departments to control the flow of resources and inventory.

enterprise resource planning (ERP)

A computerized resource planning system that includes information about the firm's suppliers and customers as well as data generated internally.

Whereas MRP and MRPII systems are focused internally, **enterprise resource planning (ERP)** systems go a step further and incorporate information about the firm's suppliers and customers into the flow of data. ERP unites all of a firm's major departments into a single software program. For instance, production can call up sales information and know immediately how many units must be produced to meet customer orders. By providing information about the availability of resources, including both human resources and materials needed for production, the system allows for better cost control and eliminates production delays. The system automatically notes any changes, such as the closure of a plant for maintenance and repairs on a certain date or a supplier's inability to meet a delivery date, so that all functions can adjust accordingly. ERP is being used to improve operations not only in large corporations, such as Boeing, Lockheed Martin, and General Motors, but in small businesses as well, as the Focusing on Small Business box describes.

FOCUSING ON SMALL BUSINESS

PUTTING ANTHRO'S PRODUCTION TOGETHER WITH ERP

Anthro Corp. (http://www.anthro.com) executives are clear about their strategic goal. They want to be the McDonald's of the furniture industry. To get there, they know they must find a way to make producing custom office furniture as simple as turning out burgers.

In its plant in Tualatin, Oregon, Anthro's 65 employees make furniture to hold electronic gear like personal computers, medical instruments, and video equipment. Once customers place their orders over the phone, the manufacturing workers assemble prefabricated parts to each customer's specifications. Anthro promises to ship the finished furniture within 24 hours.

Anthro's problems began when sales took off. Suddenly, the company was struggling to keep up with the 30,000 different production orders that streamed in each year. Managing inventory also became more difficult. The plant sometimes ran out of critical items like castors just when workers needed them.

The solution? Anthro purchased an enterprise resource planning (ERP) system from software maker SAP. The $500,000 system runs on 30 PCs and links together everyone from senior executives to production workers. When a customer places an order, it is immediately entered into the ERP system, which automatically calculates the costs of producing the order.

At the same time, the system releases a production order to the factory floor that alerts workers to the details of the customer's order. The system also checks on-hand inventory. If a part needed for assembly isn't available, the system either sends a purchase order to Anthro's suppliers or tells assembly workers what needs to be done.

It took Anthro six months to implement the system, but company president Shoaib Tareen says he expects benefits like faster production times to continue for many years. "You have to have a long-term focus, because the advantage is, once you get it going, you can grow with it."

Critical Thinking Questions

1. How might the benefits from ERP affect Anthro's other functions such as marketing, human resources, or financial management?
2. Why do you think Anthro decided to install an ERP system instead of an MRP or MRPII system?
3. Do you agree with Anthro's president that the $500,000 investment in ERP was worthwhile? What other changes in production planning could the company have made to improve operating efficiency?

Supply Chain Management

In the past, the relationship between purchasers and suppliers was often competitive and antagonistic. Businesses used many suppliers and switched among them frequently. During contract negotiations, each side would try to get better terms at the expense of the other. Communication between purchasers and suppliers was often limited to purchase orders and billing statements.

Today, however, many firms are moving toward a new concept in supplier relationships. The emphasis is increasingly on developing a strong **supply chain.** The supply chain can be thought of as the entire sequence of securing inputs, producing goods, and delivering goods to customers. If any of the links in this process are weak, chances are customers—the end point of the supply chain—will end up dissatisfied.

supply chain
The entire sequence of securing inputs, producing goods, and delivering goods to customers.

Strategies for Supply Chain Management Ensuring a strong supply chain requires that firms implement supply chain management strategies. **Supply chain management** focuses on smoothing transitions along the supply chain, with the ultimate goal of satisfying customers with quality products and services. A critical element of effective supply chain management is to develop tighter bonds with suppliers. In many cases, this means reducing the number of suppliers used and asking those suppliers to offer more services or better prices in return for an ongoing relationship. Instead of being viewed as "outsiders" in the production process, many suppliers are now playing an important role in supporting the operations of their customers. They are expected to meet higher quality standards, offer suggestions that can help reduce production costs, and even contribute to the design of new products.

supply chain management
The process of smoothing transitions along the supply chain so that the firm can satisfy its customers with quality products and services; focuses on developing tighter bonds with suppliers.

One company that is seeking to forge stronger bonds with its suppliers is AMD. AMD manufactures integrated circuits that are used to build computers and communications equipment. The company has manufacturing facilities in the United States, Asia, and Europe and regards its suppliers as partners in the production process. Before a company can sell to AMD, it must pass a rigorous evaluation by AMD managers and executives. Each supplier must show that it is willing to match AMD's dedication to quality, reliability, service, and flexibility in meeting demand. Suppliers who meet AMD's requirements are rewarded with a long-term relationship with the company.[8]

HOT links

Get a bird's eye view of AMD's manufacturing by viewing the quick-time video at
http://www.amd.com/video/manufac-qt.html

Improving Supplier Communications Underlying supply chain management is the development of strong communications with suppliers. Technology is providing new ways to do this. Some manufacturing firms are using the Internet to keep key suppliers informed about their requirements. Intel, for example, has set up a special Web site for its suppliers and potential suppliers. Would-be suppliers can visit the site to get information about doing business with Intel; once they are approved, they can access a secure area to make bids on Intel's current and future resource needs. The Internet also streamlines purchasing

HOT links

Want to do business with Intel? Check out the company's supplier site at
http://supplier.intel.com

c o n c ə p t ˌ c h ə c k

- What are the four main types of decisions that must be made in production planning, and what does each entail?
- Describe the various types of production processes and explain for what type of firm each is best suited.
- What factors does a firm consider when making a site selection decision?
- Describe the various types of facility layouts and explain for what type of production each is best suited.
- How is technology being used in resource planning?

by providing firms with quick access to a huge database of information about the products and services of hundreds of potential suppliers. The number of businesses using the Internet to buy materials, supplies, and services is skyrocketing. According to industry analysts, business-to-business purchases over the Internet will grow from $20 billion in 2000 to over $13 trillion in 2004, an increase of 650 percent.[9]

Another communications tool is **electronic data interchange (EDI),** in which two trading partners exchange information electronically. EDI can be conducted via a linked computer system or over the Internet. The advantages of exchanging information with suppliers electronically include speed, accuracy, and lowered communication costs.

PRODUCTION AND OPERATIONS CONTROL

>lg 5

electronic data interchange (EDI)
The electronic exchange of information between two trading partners.

Every company needs to have systems in place to see that production and operations are carried out as planned and to correct errors when they are not. The coordination of materials, equipment, and human resources to achieve production and operating efficiencies is called production control. Two of its key aspects are routing and scheduling.

Routing Production

Routing is the first step in controlling production. It sets out a work flow, that is, the sequence of machines and operations through which a product or service progresses from start to finish. Routing depends on the type of goods being produced and the facility layout. Good routing procedures increase productivity and cut unnecessary costs.

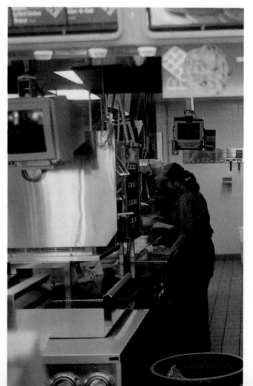

Redesigned food preparation routes and a computer system that links kitchen workers with order takers is helping McDonald's to serve customized food quickly.

McDonald's is experimenting with new food preparation routes in many of its restaurants. The changes are part of McDonald's "Made For You" program, a strategic decision to offer customers more choices in how their orders are prepared. First, the restaurant chain redesigned its kitchens to improve the way orders are prepared and routed through the kitchen. New high-tech food preparation equipment that automates much of the order preparation process was added. Finally, a centralized computer system improved the flow of communications between the customer counter and the kitchen. When a customer orders a Big Mac, the order taker enters it into a specially designed cash register that simultaneously sends the information to a video screen in the kitchen. Before the customer has even finished paying, kitchen workers have almost a third of the order completed. Within a few moments, the order, including customizations such as extra ketchup or tomatoes, is on its way out to the customer.[10]

Scheduling

Closely related to routing is **scheduling.** Scheduling involves specifying and controlling the time required for each step in the production process. The operations manager prepares timetables showing the most efficient sequence of production and then tries to ensure that the necessary materials and labor are in the right place at the right time.

routing

The aspect of production control that involves setting out the work flow—the sequence of machines and operations through which the product or service progresses from start to finish.

scheduling

The aspect of production control that involves specifying and controlling the time required for each step in the production process.

Gantt charts

Bar graphs plotted on a time line that show the relationship between scheduled and actual production.

Scheduling is important to both manufacturing and service firms. The production manager in a factory schedules material deliveries, work shifts, and production processes. Trucking companies schedule drivers, clerks, truck maintenance, and repair with customer transportation needs. Scheduling at a college entails deciding when to offer which courses in which classrooms with which instructors. A museum must schedule its special exhibits, ship the works to be displayed, market its services, and conduct educational programs and tours.

Scheduling can range from simple to complex. Giving numbers to customers waiting in a bakery and making interview appointments with job applicants are examples of simple scheduling. Organizations that must produce large quantities of products or services, or service a diverse customer base, face more complex scheduling problems.

Three common scheduling tools used for complex situations are Gantt charts, the critical path method, and PERT.

Gantt Charts   Named after their originator, Henry Gantt, **Gantt charts** are bar graphs plotted on a time line that show the relationship between scheduled and actual production. Exhibit 8-6 is an example. On the left, the chart lists the activities required to complete the job or project. Both the scheduled time and the actual time required for each activity are shown, so the manager can easily judge progress.

Gantt charts are most helpful when only a few tasks are involved, when task times are relatively long (days or weeks rather than hours), and when job routes are short and simple. One of the biggest shortcomings of Gantt charts is that they are static. They also fail to show how tasks are related. These problems can be solved, however, by using two other scheduling techniques, the critical path method and PERT.

e x h i b i t   8 - 6 | A Typical Gantt Chart

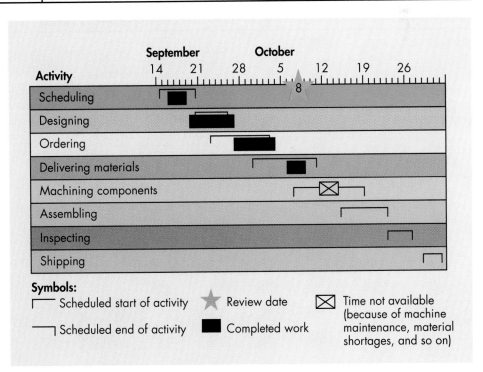

The Critical Path Method and PERT   To control large projects, operations managers need to closely monitor resources, costs, quality, and budgets. They also must be able to see the "big picture"—the interrelationships of the many different tasks necessary to complete the project. Finally, they must be able to revise scheduling and divert resources quickly if any tasks fall behind schedule. The critical path method (CPM) and the program evaluation and review technique (PERT) are related project management tools that were developed in the 1950s to help managers accomplish this.

In the **critical path method (CPM)**, the manager identifies all of the activities required to complete the project, the relationships between these activities, and the order in which they need to be completed. Then, the manager develops a diagram that uses arrows to show how the tasks are dependent on each other. The longest path through these linked activities is called the **critical path.** If the tasks on the critical path are not completed on time, the entire project will fall behind schedule.

To better understand how CPM works, look at Exhibit 8-7, which shows a CPM diagram for constructing a house. All of the tasks required to finish the house and an estimated time for each have been identified. The arrows indicate the links between the various steps and their required sequence. As you can see, most of the jobs to be done can't be started until the house's foundation and frame are completed. It will take five days to finish the foundation and another seven days to erect the house frame. The activities linked by red arrows form the critical path for this project. It tells us that the fastest possible time the house can be built is 38 days, the total time needed for all of the critical path tasks. The noncritical path jobs, those connected with black arrows, can be delayed a bit or done early. Short delays in installing appliances or roofing won't delay construction of the house because these activities don't lie on the critical path.

Like CPM, **program evaluation and review technique (PERT)** helps managers identify critical tasks and assess how delays in certain activities will affect operations or production. In both methods, managers use diagrams to see how

critical path method (CPM)

A scheduling tool that enables a manager to determine the critical path of activities for a project—the activities that will cause the entire project to fall behind schedule if they are not completed on time.

critical path

In a critical path method network, the longest path through the linked activities.

program evaluation and review technique (PERT)

A scheduling tool that is similar to the CPM method but assigns three time estimates for each activity (optimistic, most probable, and pessimistic); allows managers to anticipate delays and potential problems and schedule accordingly.

e x h i b i t   8 - 7 | A CPM Network for Building a House

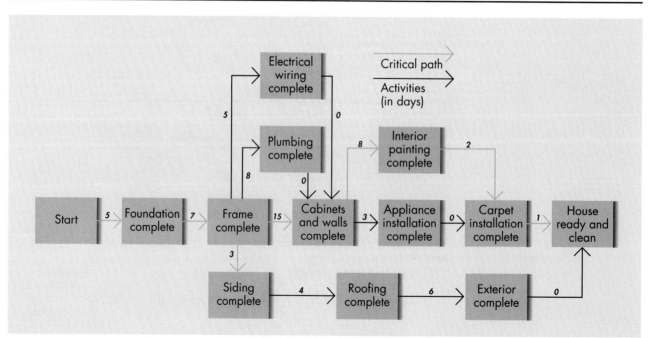

operations and production will flow. PERT differs from CPM in one important respect, however. CPM assumes that the amount of time needed to finish a task is known with certainty; therefore, the CPM diagram shows only one number for the time needed to complete each activity. In contrast, PERT assigns three time estimates for each activity: an optimistic time for completion, the most probable time, and a pessimistic time. These estimates allow managers to anticipate delays and potential problems and schedule accordingly.

c o n c ə p t   c h ə c k

- What is production control, and what are its key aspects?
- Identify and describe three commonly used scheduling tools.

IMPROVING PRODUCTION AND OPERATIONS

>lg 6

Competing in today's business world is difficult. The process of producing and delivering goods and services is becoming increasingly complex. Customers are demanding higher levels of quality and satisfaction. The lower production costs enjoyed by many foreign competitors can be difficult to compete against. In light of these challenges, businesses are continually looking for new ways to keep quality high, costs low, and production processes flowing smoothly. Among the methods that many companies have successfully implemented are total quality management, lean manufacturing, and automation.

Total Quality Management

Successful businesses recognize that quality and productivity must go hand in hand. Defective products waste materials and time, increasing costs. Worse, poor quality causes customer dissatisfaction, which usually means lost sales.

quality control

The process of creating standards for quality and then measuring finished products and services against them.

To a consumer, quality is how well a good serves its purpose. From the company's point of view, quality is the degree to which a good conforms to a set of predetermined standards. **Quality control** involves creating those quality standards and measuring finished products and services against them. Once quality control was simply a matter of inspecting products before they went out the door. Today, it's a company-wide commitment that involves every facet of operations.

One of the first to say that quality control should be a company-wide goal was an American, Dr. W. Edwards Deming. His ideas were adopted by the Japanese in the 1950s but largely ignored in the United States until the 1970s. Deming suggested that merely inspecting products after they are produced is not enough to ensure quality. He believed that quality control must start with top management, who must foster a culture dedicated to producing quality. Teamwork between managers and workers helps to identify ways to improve the production process, leading to better quality.

total quality management (TQM)

The use of quality principles in all aspects of a company's production and operations.

Total quality management (TQM) refers to the use of quality principles in all aspects of a company's production and operations. It emphasizes that all employees involved with bringing a product or service to customers—marketing, purchasing, accounting, shipping, manufacturing—contribute to its quality. TQM focuses on improving operations to achieve greater efficiency and, in turn, higher quality. Nearly every decision involved in production and operations management can affect a firm's ability to produce high-quality products and services.

The Move toward Lean Manufacturing

lean manufacturing

Streamlining production by eliminating steps in the production process that do not add benefits that customers are willing to pay for.

Manufacturers are discovering that they can better respond to rapidly changing customer demands, while keeping inventory and production costs down, by adopting lean manufacturing techniques. **Lean manufacturing** can be defined as streamlining production by eliminating steps in the production process that do not add benefits that customers are willing to pay for. In other words, non-value-added production processes are cut so that the company can concentrate its production and operations resources on items essential to satisfying customers. Toyota was a pioneer in developing these techniques, but today manufacturers in many industries have also adopted the lean manufacturing philosophy.

Another Japanese concept, **just-in-time (JIT)**, goes hand in hand with lean manufacturing. JIT is based on the belief that materials should arrive exactly when they are needed for production, rather than being stored on site. Relying closely on computerized systems such as MRP, MRPII, and ERP, manufacturers determine what parts will be needed and when, and then order them from suppliers so they arrive "just in time." Under the JIT system, inventory and products are "pulled" through the production process in response to customer demand. JIT requires close teamwork between vendors and production and purchasing personnel because any delay in deliveries of supplies could bring JIT production to a halt. If employed properly, however, a JIT system can greatly reduce inventory holding costs and can also smooth production highs and lows.

just-in-time (JIT)
A system in which materials arrive exactly when they are needed for production, rather than being stored on site.

Automation in Productions and Operations Management

Technology is helping many firms improve their operating efficiency and ability to compete. Computer systems, in particular, are enabling manufacturers to automate factories in ways never before possible.

>lg 7

Consider how technology and automation have helped Winnebago. Plagued with production problems, the recreational-vehicle maker decided to use technology to streamline production and improve product quality. Since 1995, the company has spent approximately $5 million annually to automate its factory. Now a single worker is able to oversee the routing of panels needed to produce customized models with the touch of a button. A $400,000 computer tells the plant's production machines how to cut materials to fit the desired floor plan and accessories. Using computerized equipment, one worker can now do tasks that previously required several workers.[11]

Travel through Winnebago's production processes company info section at http://www.winnebagoind.com

Among the technologies helping to automate manufacturing are computer-aided design and manufacturing, robotics, flexible manufacturing systems, and computer-integrated manufacturing.

computer-aided design (CAD)
The use of computers to design and test new products and modify existing ones.

computer-aided manufacturing (CAM)
The use of computers to develop and control the production process.

CAD/CAM systems
Linked computer systems that combine the advantages of computer-aided design and computer-aided manufacturing. The system helps design the product, control the flow of resources, and operate the production process.

Computer-Aided Design and Manufacturing Systems Computers have transformed the design and manufacturing processes in many industries. In **computer-aided design (CAD)**, computers are used to design and test new products and modify existing ones. Engineers use these systems to draw products and look at them from different angles. They can analyze the products, make changes, and test prototypes before making even one item. **Computer-aided manufacturing (CAM)** uses computers to develop and control the production process. The systems analyze the steps required to make the product. They then automatically send instructions to the machines that do the work. **CAD/CAM systems** combine the advantages of CAD and CAM by integrating design, testing, and manufacturing control into one linked computer system. The system helps design the product, control the flow of resources needed to produce the product, and operate the production process.

robotics

The technology involved in designing, constructing, and operating (computer-controlled machines that can perform tasks independently).

flexible manufacturing system (FMS)

A system that combines automated workstations with computer-controlled transportation devices—automatic guided vehicles (AGVs)—that move materials between workstations and into and out of the system.

computer-integrated manufacturing (CIM)

The combination of computerized manufacturing processes (like robots and flexible manufacturing systems) with other computerized systems that control design, inventory, production, and purchasing.

Automakers like General Motors have relied on CAD/CAM technology for some time. Using CAD/CAM systems, automotive designers are able to see a three-dimensional version of the car they are designing and make subtle adjustments to the design that can make a car model stand out in consumers' minds. The systems also detail and track all of the materials, parts, and processes necessary to move each car from the design stage to the showroom.[12]

Robotics *Robots* are computer-controlled machines that can perform tasks independently. **Robotics** is the technology involved in designing, constructing, and operating robots. The first robot, or "steel-collar worker," was used by General Motors in 1961.

Robots can be mobile or fixed in one place. Fixed robots have an arm that moves and does what the computer instructs. Some robots are quite simple, with limited movement for a few tasks such as cutting sheet metal and spot welding. Others are complex, with hands or grippers that can be programmed to perform a series of movements. Some robots are even equipped with sensing devices for sight and touch.

Robots usually operate with little or no human intervention. Replacing human effort with robots is most effective for tasks requiring accuracy, speed, or strength. Although manufacturers, such as Harley-Davidson as described at the beginning of this chapter, are most likely to use robots, some service firms are also finding them useful. Loyola University Medical Center in Maywood, Illinois, uses a $500,000 robot to sort and process hundreds of blood samples daily, freeing medical personnel from a tedious, and sometimes hazardous, repetitive task. The hospital estimates it saves about $200,000 a year in lab operating costs.[13]

Flexible Manufacturing Systems A relatively new way to automate a factory is to blend computers, robots, machine tools, and materials- and parts-handling machinery into a **flexible manufacturing system (FMS).** These systems combine automated workstations with computer-controlled transportation devices. Automatic guided vehicles (AGVs) move materials between workstations and into and out of the system.

Flexible manufacturing systems are expensive. Once in place, however, a system requires little labor to operate and provides consistent product quality. The system can be changed easily and inexpensively. FMS equipment can be programmed to perform one job and then quickly be reprogrammed to perform another. These systems work well when small batches of a variety of products are required or when each product is made to individual customer specifications.

With computer-aided design, engineers can design, analyze, modify, and test prototypes before products are manufactured.

Computer-Integrated Manufacturing **Computer-integrated manufacturing (CIM)** combines computerized manufacturing processes (like robots and FMS) with other computerized systems that control design, inventory, production, and purchasing. With CIM, when a part is redesigned in the CAD system, the changes are quickly transmitted both to the machines producing the part and to all other departments that need to know about and plan for the change.

Technology and Automation in Nonmanufacturing Operations

Manufacturers are not the only businesses benefiting from technology. Nonmanufacturing firms are also using automation to improve customer service and productivity. Banks now offer services to customers through automated teller machines (ATMs), via automated telephone systems, and even over the Internet. Retail stores of all kinds use point-of-sale (POS) terminals that track inventories, identify items that need to be reordered, and tell which products are selling well. Wal-Mart, the leader in retailing automation, has its own satellite system connecting POS terminals directly to its distribution centers and headquarters. As the Applying Technology box discusses, the restaurant industry is also streamlining operations with automation technology.

APPLYING TECHNOLOGY

AUTOMATION SPEEDS UP FAST FOOD

Tired of long lines at fast-food restaurants? Chains like McDonald's, Arby's, and Burger King are hoping technology can put the "fast" back into fast food by automating many of the processes used in taking and preparing food orders.

You may have already noticed changes on drive-thru menu boards. McDonald's and Hardee's restaurants have rotating menu boards that automatically change according to the time of day. Pull up at breakfast and the board will show only breakfast items. Visit at lunchtime and you'll see lunch items. By limiting the choices displayed on the menu board, the restaurant makes it easier and quicker for customers to order. McDonald's and Burger King have also put special LCD screens at the drive-thru that show what you've ordered so you can instantly see if your order isn't right. Next innovation for the drive-thru? Face-to-face video technology that will let you see the face of the cashier (and let the cashier see you) as you're ordering.

Inside, fast-food restaurants are also changing. Most chains have high-tech point-of-sale (POS) computer systems. When you order at the counter, the clerk enters the information at the register, and it is automatically transmitted to the kitchen. These systems also let managers keep track of customer sales and operating efficiency. Soon, some fast-food chains will be adding self-service terminals so that you can punch in and pay for your order without waiting in line.

In the kitchen, technology is speeding up food preparation. FAST, Inc. (http://www.fastinc.com), a computer automation company, has developed the SMART Commercial Kitchen system, which links computer technology with the cooking controls of all the kitchen's appliances. The system automatically tells appliances such as ovens, fryers, and holding cabinets when to turn on, how long and at what temperature to cook, and when to turn off. Arby's has connected its SMART system to its POS system. When customer orders reach a certain level, the SMART system tells workers in the kitchen to put more beef in the ovens and then instantly sets the right cooking times.

Perhaps the most intriguing technologies on the horizon are automated handwashing systems. Spurred by recent incidents of food contamination, many chains are looking into equipping workers with electronic handwashing badges. The badges will beep at selected intervals to remind employees to wash their hands or change their gloves. They'll also keep track of whether the employee does as told—and report any handwashing deadbeats to the restaurant manager!

Critical Thinking Questions

1. How is automation likely to change customers' opinions of fast-food restaurants? Why?
2. Discuss the effect of automation and technology on the employees of fast-food restaurants.
3. Do you think some of the technology being used in fast-food restaurants would work for the cafeteria in your school? How about for an expensive steakhouse? Defend your answers.

CAPITALIZING ON TRENDS IN BUSINESS

>lg 8

The past decade has seen the U.S. economy grow at an unprecedented rate. Stock prices and corporate profits in many industries have soared, and unemployment and inflation have plummeted. Changes in production and operations management have made a huge contribution to this success and are likely to continue to propel productivity and economic growth in the new millennium.

Manufacturing continues to play a huge role in the U.S. economy. The 380,000 manufacturing firms in this country contributed $1.43 trillion to the national Gross Domestic Product (GDP) in 1998. While the economy grew as a whole by 29 percent between 1992 and 1999, manufacturing output grew 42 percent. Although the number of people employed by manufacturing firms declined in the 1980s, in the 1990s the number stabilized at about 18.5 million. The United States continues to have the most productive manufacturing workers in the world.[14] In order to maintain this level of productivity in the face of growing global competition, more complex products, and more demanding consumers, manufacturers are having to rethink how, when, and where they produce the goods they sell. New production techniques and manufacturing technologies are vital to keep production costs as low as possible and productivity high.

Nonmanufacturing firms also face operating challenges. Like manufacturers, they must keep up with the constant pace of change and carefully manage how they use and deploy resources. As the service sector grows, so do customer expectations about the speed and quality of service. This puts increased pressure on nonmanufacturing firms to be ever vigilant in their search for new ways of streamlining service production and operations. In this section, we will look at some of the trends likely to alter how companies manage and control the production of goods and services in the future.

Modular Production

The executives at Palm Computing knew they had a good idea: a small electronic personal organizer called the Pilot. They also knew that their competitive advantage would depend on getting the Pilot on the market as quickly as possible, a schedule that would be impossible to meet without help. The Pilot's designers wrote detailed specifications for how the product should be produced; then the company invited 3,500 other firms to create different parts of the product. Working together, Palm and its suppliers soon had the Pilot on the market. It became one of history's hottest products, selling more than 1 million units in its first 18 months.

Palm Computing's success highlights a growing trend in the business world, *modular production*. Modular production involves breaking a complex product, service, or process into smaller pieces that can be created independently and then combined quickly to make a whole. Modular production not only cuts the cost of developing and designing innovative products, but it also gives businesses a tool for meeting rapidly changing conditions. Modular production also makes it easier to implement mass customization or pure customization strategies. With access to a variety of components that can be assembled in different ways, endless combinations of product features are possible.

Agile Manufacturing

Another concept businesses are using to stay flexible and move fast is *agile manufacturing*. Investing millions of dollars in production processes, resources, and equipment that can be used only to produce one particular product doesn't always make economic sense. When customer demands shift or new technological innovations occur, the firm must be able to adapt. In agile manufacturing, firms strive to develop a production system comprised of flexible tools and processes that can be quickly changed to produce new or different products. Toyota uses agile manufacturing methods at its Kentucky plant. The factory builds both Camry and Avalon cars and the Siena minivans on the same assembly line. All three vehicles basically rely on the same underlying body platform. As the vehicles move through the plant, different components and parts are added depending on whether workers are producing a car or a minivan.[15]

Trends in Facility Layout

Work cell design, also sometimes called module design or cellular manufacturing, is an innovation that some manufacturers are finding can help improve quality and production efficiency. Work cells are small, self-contained production units that include several machines and workers arranged in a compact, sequential order. Each work cell performs all or most of the tasks necessary to complete either a product or a major production sequence. There are usually between 5 and 10 workers in a cell, and they are trained to be able to do any of the steps in the production process. The goal is to create a team environment where team members are involved in production from beginning to end.

Work cell design can have dramatic results. Berne Apparel, a maker of cotton coveralls and jackets, has been using the concept for more than a year. Workers in each group now work together to complete entire garments, rather than just parts of a garment. Because they can communicate with each other better and fill different production roles to get the job done, production time has been cut and quality improved. The company also has less employee turnover.[16]

concept check

- Explain modular production.
- How can agile manufacturing help a company obtain a competitive advantage?
- Explain how work cell design can help a company improve quality and efficiency.

APPLYING THIS CHAPTER'S TOPICS

As we've seen throughout this chapter, every organization produces something. Cereal manufacturers turn grains into breakfast foods. Law firms turn the skills and knowledge of attorneys into legal services. Retailers provide a convenient way for consumers to purchase a variety of goods. Colleges and universities convert students into educated individuals. Therefore, no matter what type of organization you end up working for in the future, you will be involved, to one degree or another, with your employer's production and operations processes.

In some jobs, such as plant manager and quality control manager, you will have a direct role in the production process. But employees of manufacturing firms are not the only ones involved with production. Software developers, bank tellers, medical personnel, magazine writers, and a host of other jobs are also actively involved in turning inputs into outputs. If you manage people in these types of jobs, you'll need insight into the tools used to plan, schedule, and control production processes. Understanding production processes, resource management, and techniques for increasing productivity is vital to be-

Track a Project with a Gantt Chart Your teacher has just announced a huge assignment, due in three weeks. Where do you start? How can you best organize your time? A Gantt chart can help you plan and schedule more effectively. First, break the assignment down into smaller tasks. Say, for instance, that you have a 10-page research paper due in three weeks. Your list of tasks would include picking a topic, researching information at the library and on the Internet, organizing your notes, developing an outline, and writing and proofreading the paper. Next, estimate how much time each task will take.

Try to be realistic. There's no sense saying it will only take you a day to write the paper when you know you have spent a week or more writing similar papers in the past. At the top of a piece of paper, list all of the days until the assignment is due. Along the side of the paper, list all of the tasks you've identified in the order they need to be done. Starting with the first task, block out the number of days you estimate each task will take. If you run out of days, you'll know you need to adjust how you've scheduled your time. If you know that you will not be able to work on some days, note them on the chart as well. Hang the chart where you can see it. Your Gantt chart will give you a visual tool for tracking your progress. Instead of worrying about the entire project all at once, you'll be able to see exactly what you should be doing on a particular day. The end result should be a terrific paper turned in on time!

coming a more valuable employee, who sees how his or her job fits into "the big picture" of the firm's operating goals.

Other professionals also need to understand production and operations management in order to help the firm reach its goals. Want to be a sales representative? An awareness of how, when, and where goods or services are made will help you better serve customer needs. Or, perhaps you plan to work in new product development. The best idea for a new product will fail if production cannot produce it in a timely, cost-effective manner. Human resource managers need to know the type of work operations personnel do in order to do a good job of recruiting and retaining employees. Financial personnel, such as accountants, also need to understand what goes on in production and operations. That knowledge helps them in budgeting, pricing products, and managing financial resources.

If you plan to start your own business, you'll also face many production and operations decisions. You can use the information from this chapter to help you find suppliers, design an operating facility (no matter how small), and put customer-satisfying processes in place. This information can also help you make decisions about whether to manufacture goods yourself or rely on outside contractors to handle production.

SUMMARY OF LEARNING GOALS

>lg 1 **Why is production and operations management important in both manufacturing and service firms?**
In the 1980s, many U.S. manufacturers lost customers to foreign competitors because their production and operations management systems did not support the high-quality, reasonably priced products consumers demanded. Service organizations also rely on effective operations management in order to satisfy consumers.

>looking ahead
at Harley-Davidson

Operations managers, the personnel charged with managing and supervising the conversion of inputs into outputs, work closely with other functions in organizations to help ensure quality, customer satisfaction, and financial success.

Harley-Davidson's Kansas City plant has helped rev up the company's sales and profits. The new plant is so efficient that when daily production was recently increased from 161 bikes a day to 180, the factory only needed to hire 11 new workers. The factory's quality is high, too. The number of parts or sections rejected because of poor quality is only 5 percent at the Kansas City plant, compared with 20 percent at Harley's other finishing plants. Thanks in part to the greater efficiency of the new plant, the company was able to manufacture 204,000 motorcycles in 2000, up from just 177,000 the previous year. "That means we will have accomplished our goal of producing 200,000 units per year by 2003 a full three years ahead of our original schedule," says CEO Bleustein. The company also exceeded its target for 2001 (233,000 units) by almost 10,000 units and has set a 2002 goal of 256,000 units.

Harley-Davidson continues to increase production while slashing costs by making an enormous investment in new technology. New computer systems in its factories automate how production and operations information is managed and used throughout the company.

The company has also launched a new computer system that has improved its relationships with suppliers. Since 1995, the company has cut the number of its suppliers from 1,000 to just over 400. The new system allows the company to order parts, components, and materials electronically and involves suppliers more closely in the design and development of new products.

Although some analysts criticize Harley-Davidson's slow and deliberate pace of incorporating technology and other changes into production, others are convinced that's the secret to the motorcycle manufacturer's growing profits and success. "This is a company that gets better every quarter," says one analyst. "There's nothing wrong with being an intelligent tortoise as opposed to a hare."[17]

>lg 2 What types of production processes are used by manufacturers and service firms?

Products are made using one of three types of production processes. In mass production, many identical goods are produced at once, keeping production costs low. Mass production, therefore, relies heavily on standardization, mechanization, and specialization. When mass customization is used, goods are produced using mass production techniques up to a point, after which the product or service is custom tailored to individual customers by adding special features. In general, mass customization is more expensive than mass production, but consumers are often willing to pay more for mass-customized products. When a firm's production process is built around customization, the firm makes many products one at a time according to the very specific needs or wants of individual customers.

>lg 3 How do organizations decide where to put their production facilities? What choices must be made in designing the facility?

Site selection affects operating costs, the price of the product or service, and the company's ability to compete. In choosing a production site, firms must weigh the availability of resources—raw materials, human resources, and even capital—needed for production, as well as the ability to serve customers and take advantage of marketing opportunities. Other factors include the availability of local incentives and the manufacturing environment. Once a site is selected, the firm must choose an appropriate design for the facility. The three main production facility designs are process, product, and fixed-position layouts.

>lg 4 Why are resource planning tasks like inventory management and supplier relations critical to production?

Production converts input resources, such as raw materials and labor, into outputs, finished products and services. Firms must ensure that the resources

KEY TERMS

assembly process 228
bill of material 234
CAD/CAM systems 242
computer-aided design (CAD) 242
computer-aided manufacturing (CAM) 242
computer-integrated manufacturing (CIM) 243
continuous process 228
critical path 240
critical path method (CPM) 240
customization 227
electronic data interchange (EDI) 238
enterprise resource planning (ERP) 236
fixed-position layout 232
flexible manufacturing system (FMS) 243
Gantt charts 239
intermittent process 229
inventory 235
inventory management 235
job shop 227
just-in-time (JIT) 242
lean manufacturing 241
make-or-buy decision 234
manufacturing resource planning II (MRPII) 235
mass customization 227
mass production 227
materials requirement planning (MRP) 235
operations management 225
outsourcing 234
perpetual inventory 235
process layout 232
process manufacturing 228

needed for production will be available at strategic moments in the production process. If they are not, productivity, customer satisfaction, and quality may suffer. Carefully managing inventory can help cut production costs while maintaining enough supply for production and sales. Through good relationships with suppliers, firms can get better prices, reliable resources, and support services that can improve production efficiency.

>lg 5   How do operations managers schedule and control production?

Routing is the first step in scheduling and controlling production. Routing analyzes the steps needed in production and sets out a work flow, the sequence of machines and operations through which a product or service progresses from start to finish. Good routing increases productivity and can eliminate unnecessary cost. Scheduling involves specifying and controlling the time and resources required for each step in the production process. It can range from simple to complex. Operations managers use three methods to schedule production: Gantt charts, the critical path method, and PERT.

>lg 6   How can quality management and lean manufacturing techniques help firms improve production and operations management?

Quality and productivity go hand in hand. Defective products waste materials and time, increasing costs. Poor quality also leads to dissatisfied customers. By implementing quality-control methods, firms often reduce these problems and streamline production. Lean manufacturing also helps streamline production by eliminating unnecessary steps in the production process. When activities that don't add value for customers are eliminated, manufacturers can respond to changing market conditions with greater flexibility and ease.

>lg 7   What roles do technology and automation play in manufacturing and service industry operations management?

Many firms are improving their operational efficiency by using technology to automate parts of production. Computer-aided design and manufacturing systems, for example, help design new products, control the flow of resources needed for production, and even operate much of the production process. By using robotics, human time and effort can be minimized. Robots are especially useful for tasks that require accuracy, speed, and strength. Factories are being automated by blending computers, robots, and machinery into flexible manufacturing systems that require less labor to operate. Service firms are automating operations too. Banks, law firms, and utility companies have used technology to cut labor costs and control quality.

>lg 8   What key trends are affecting the way companies manage production and operations?

Faced with growing global competition, increased product complexity, and more demanding consumers, manufacturers are rethinking how, when, and where they produce the goods they sell. Agile manufacturing is a concept that helps manufacturers stay fast and flexible. Firms strive to develop production systems composed of tools and processes that can be quickly changed to produce new or different products. Cellular manufacturing creates small, self-contained production units that include several machines and workers. Each work cell performs all or most of the tasks necessary to complete a product or production sequence. Because of these trends and the increased use of technology in production, firms are recognizing that smarter, better motivated workers are an asset. Both manufacturing and nonmanufacturing firms are therefore putting new emphasis on empowering employees—giving them greater say in deciding how their jobs should be done and a larger role in company decision making.

product (or
   assembly-line)
   layout 232
production 225
production
   planning 226
production process
   227
program evaluation
   and review
   technique (PERT)
   240
purchasing 234
quality control 241
robotics 243
routing 238
scheduling 238
supply chain 237
supply chain
   management 237
total quality
   management
   (TQM) 241

PREPARING FOR TOMORROW'S WORKPLACE

1. Reliance Systems, headquartered in Oklahoma City, is a manufacturer of computer keyboards. The company plans to build a new factory and hopes to find a location with access to low-cost but skilled workers, national and international transportation, and favorable government incentives. The company has zeroed in on three possible states for the site: Connecticut, Kentucky, and Louisiana. Divide the class into three groups. Assign one state to each of the three groups. The state groups should start at **http://www. ecodevdirectory.com** to find URLs for their statewide agency, and use that information to develop a case for that state. Each group will make a brief presentation on behalf of their state.

2. Tom Lawrence and Sally Zickle are co-owners of L-Z Marketing, an advertising agency. Last week, they landed a major aerospace manufacturer as a client. The company wants the agency to create its annual report. Tom, who develops the art for the agency, needs about a week to develop the preliminary report design, another two weeks to set the type, and three weeks to get the report printed. Sally writes the material for the report and doesn't need as much time: two days to meet with the client to review the company's financial information and about three weeks to write the report copy. Of course, Tom can't set type until Sally has finished writing the report. Sally will also need three days to proofread the report before it goes to the printer. Develop either a Gantt chart or a critical path diagram for Tom and Sally to use in scheduling the project. Explain why you chose the method you did. How long will it take Tom and Sally to finish the project if there are no unforeseen delays?

3. Look for ways that technology and automation are used at your school, in the local supermarket, and at your doctor's office. As a class, discuss how automation affects the service you receive from each of these organizations. Does one organization use any types of automation that might be effectively used by one of the others? Explain.

4. Pick a small business in your community. Make a list of the resources critical to the firm's production and operations. What would happen if the business suddenly couldn't acquire any of these resources? Divide the class into small groups and discuss strategies that small businesses can use to manage their supply chain.

WORKING THE NET

1. Go to **http://purchasing.miningco.com/msub-corp.htm.** Pick two or three of the companies listed and visit their supplier information Web sites. Compare the requirements the companies set for their suppliers. How do the requirements differ? How are they similar?

2. Manufacturers face many federal, state, and local regulations. Visit the National Association of Manufacturers at **http://www.nam.org.** Pick two or three of the legislative or regulatory issues discussed there and use a search engine like Yahoo! (**http://www.yahoo.com**) to find more information.

3. Using a search engine like Google (**http://www.google.com**) or Info Seek (**http://www.infoseek.com**), search for information about technologies like robotics, CAD/CAM systems, or ERP. Find at least three suppliers for one of these technologies. Visit their Web sites and discuss how their clients are using their products to automate production.

CREATIVE THINKING CASE

New Patterns for Jody B Fashions

Jody Branson is the owner of Jody B Fashions, a small manufacturer of women's dresses. Jody designs the dresses herself and personally orders fabrics, trims, and other materials needed for production from a number of different suppliers. Jody has a work crew of 40. Production begins when the fabric is cut using Jody's patterns. After cutting, the pieces for each dress style are placed into bundles, which are then moved through the factory from worker to worker. Each worker opens each bundle and does one assembly task, such as sewing on collars, hemming the dresses, or adding decorative items like appliqués and lace. Then the worker puts the bundle back together and passes it on to the next person in the production process. Finished dresses are pressed and packaged for shipment.

Things were running smoothly until recently when Jody sold her first big order to Kmart. Unlike the small boutique stores Jody usually sells to, Kmart wants to buy hundreds of dresses in different style and fabric combinations all at one time. If Kmart is pleased with this first order, chances are good it will give Jody a steady stream of future business. In the past, some of Jody's suppliers haven't sent their fabrics on time, so she has always ordered extra material to avoid shortages. She tried to do the same to prepare for the Kmart order, but her inventory room has become a disorganized nightmare. Jody had to shut down production twice this week because the workers who do the cutting couldn't find the fabric she had specified.

Jody knows she is beginning to fall behind on the Kmart order. She needs to cut the amount of time her workers take to finish each dress, but she doesn't want to sacrifice quality. Luckily, Jody has set aside some emergency capital that she can use to help solve this problem. She sees only three options:

- Hire additional workers for her production crew and hope to speed up production.
- Automate some of her production systems.
- Call Kmart's buyer and ask for an extension on the order delivery deadline.

INFOTRAC® COLLEGE EDITION Critical Thinking Questions

1. Evaluate Jody's production processes. Could she change them in any way to increase production?
2. Discuss the effectiveness of Jody's supply chain. Make recommendations for improvement.
3. Draw a diagram of how work flows through Jody's factory. Could Jody improve production by using a different layout? Draw a diagram of how this might look.
4. What do you think Jody should do? Are there any other options she could consider? Discuss whether each option is a short-term or long-term solution.

VIDEO CASE

The Vermont Teddy Bear Company

The Vermont Teddy Bear Co. (**http://www.vermontteddybear.com**) in Shelburne, Vermont, produces handcrafted teddy bears of such quality that each bear is guaranteed for life. Vermont Teddy Bears are targeted toward customers seeking quality, personalized gifts.

A Vermont Teddy Bear can easily be personalized for a specific occasion because the company produces a wide variety of teddy bears. There are numerous birthday teddy bears, get-well bears, new baby bears, "I love you" bears, summer bears, sports and hobby bears, holiday bears, graduation bears, bears for kids, occupation bears, and all-occasion bears. The occupation bears include a businessman and businesswoman, a doctor, a nurse, a teacher, and a police officer. The sports and hobby bears include a soccer bear, a golfer bear, a martial arts bear, a cheerleader bear, and a fitness bear.

A Vermont Teddy Bear can also be personalized with a creative card message of 35 words or less that accompanies the gift. To help customers who are at a loss for a personalized message, the company offers a variety of suggestions that can be used as is or adapted.

Another personalized service is the Bear-Gram delivery service, which is the company's core business. By calling 1-800-829-BEAR, a customer is assisted by a Bear Counselor sales agent to design a perfect gift for a special holiday, to commemorate a life event such as a birthday, an anniversary, or the birth of a new baby, or to wish someone well during a stay in the hospital. The added value to the Bear-Gram delivery service includes a Vermont Teddy Bear customized to fit the occasion, optional embroidery, a personalized greeting card, a colorful gift box equipped with an AirHole and B'Air Bag to ensure a safe journey, all delivered with a candy treat.

The Vermont Teddy Bear Co. strives to make the best teddy bears in the world by "combining unparalleled design innovation, unmatched product quality, and a passion for service."

Employees, who are viewed as internal customers, function in "a results-oriented environment that encourages fairness, collaboration, mutual respect, and pride" in the company. The company also engages vendors in a partnership focusing on innovative product development and unsurpassed customer service.

Critical Thinking Questions

1. What characteristics of the Vermont Teddy Bear Co.'s manufacturing operations point to the use of mass customization?
2. How does mass customization benefit the Vermont Teddy Bear Co.?
3. Why is quality control important for the Vermont Teddy Bear Co.?

Case: AviationX Prepares for Take-Off

The average commercial airplane is an engineering marvel, with more than 3 million parts. Unfortunately, keeping those 3 million parts in working order is a gigantic operational task. Airlines spend $32 billion each year just on the parts they need to keep their airplanes flying safely and on-time. Major U.S. carriers often issue 3,000 purchase orders a day and buy parts from more than 13,000 suppliers around the world. Because airlines often can't wait when a part is needed to repair a plane, they keep up to 300,000 spare parts in inventory at all times. One major carrier estimates its parts inventory is worth $1.5 billion.

Airlines have to be extremely careful about the parts they buy. One bad screw can lead to catastrophe if it causes a plane crash. Airlines also operate on a very thin profit margin. In order to attract customers, they have to keep ticket prices low and that means operating costs need to be cut or controlled whenever possible.

AviationX (**http://www.aviationx.com**), a small startup in Arlington, Virginia, thinks the Internet can help. AviationX is planning to set up an e-commerce marketplace where airlines and suppliers can connect and do business. Instead of having to research the prices and availability of parts by phone, fax, or electronic data interchange, airlines will be able to sign on to AviationX's Web site and instantly find and order what is needed. AviationX says that the streamlined ordering process, combined with the ability to automatically compare the prices of different suppliers online, will save airlines at least 10 percent on every transaction, for an industry-wide savings of $300 million a year. To make money, AviationX will charge buyers a monthly fee and ask suppliers to pay a small commission on each sale.

AviationX isn't the only company planning to bring e-commerce to the airline industry. Several other small firms are launching their own online trading sites. Major parts manufacturers like Boeing and Airbus have also started their own e-commerce sites. Boeing's site handled $400 million in orders its first year.

In spite of these new sites, only about 3 percent of airline procurement is currently done through the Internet. Airlines aren't yet convinced of e-commerce's benefits. "We're entering an industry which, by nature, is rather prone to not making a change," admits Henrik Schroder, AviationX's CEO.

Questions for Critical Thinking

1. Evaluate the advantages and disadvantages for airlines if they buy parts through AviationX's e-commerce system. If you were in charge of purchasing for a major airline, would you sign up with AviationX? Why or why not?

2. Evaluate the advantages and disadvantages for suppliers and manufacturers if they sell parts through AviationX's e-commerce system. If you were a small manufacturer, would you sign up with AviationX? Why or why not?

3. What are the main challenges you see AviationX facing? Make suggestions for how the biggest challenges should be addressed.

SOURCES: Gregory Dalton, "Taxiing to the Net," *The Industry Standard* (February 28, 2000), downloaded from **http://www.thestandard.com**; Mickey Alam Khan, "iMarketing: AviationX Flies with Aerospace BTB Market," *dmnews.com* (March 7, 2000), downloaded from **http://www.dmnews.com**; Mark Roberti, "AviationX Charts Flight Plan," *InformationWeek Online* (March 27, 2000), downloaded from **http://www.informationweek.com**; "A New Kind of Hub: How B2B E-Marketplaces Will Revolutionize the Aviation Industry," AviationX company white paper, no date, downloaded from **http://www.aviationx.com**.

learning goals

>lg 1   What is the human resource management process?

>lg 2   How are human resource needs determined?

>lg 3   How do human resource managers find good people to fill the jobs?

>lg 4   What is the employee selection process?

>lg 5   What types of training and development do organizations offer their employees?

>lg 6   What is a performance appraisal?

>lg 7   How are employees compensated?

>lg 8   What is organizational career management?

>lg 9   What are the key laws and federal agencies affecting human resource management?

>lg 10 What trends are affecting human resource management?

Managing Human Resources

chapter 9

An Employee Problem at Don Pablo's

James Taylor is an assistant restaurant manager at Don Pablo's **(http://www.avado.com),** a Mexican restaurant chain of more than 130 units, many of which are located in larger cities of the East. In addition to being a shift manager several days a week, he is responsible for hiring and training employees and scheduling their weekly shift assignments. Most of the wait staff work part-time and attend the local university. After the restaurant closes at 11:00 P.M., James stays to check liquor and food inventories, count cash and credit card receipts, and clean. One recent morning, he came early to the restaurant to prepare work schedules for the next two weeks, check employee time sheets, prepare payroll information for electronic transfer to corporate headquarters, and decide how to address a performance problem with Sharon Young, a waitress who has worked at the restaurant for nearly a year.

Sharon had been 30 minutes late for work the previous night, the fifth time in the last four weeks she had been late. Her attendance record for the last three months revealed six absences; each time she called only a few minutes before the start of her work shift to say she could not come to work. Punctuality and attendance had obviously become a problem. As a part-time employee, Sharon was not eligible for any paid sick leave or health insurance coverage. At the same time, James was aware that Sharon was an excellent waitress; her service and customer relations skills are the best among the current wait staff, and several repeat customers ask for her table.

As James contemplated his approach and options in dealing with Sharon, he quickly reviewed job and performance requirements for wait staff employees. They had to have good communication skills, a strong service (or helpfulness) orientation, reasonably detailed knowledge of menu items, be neat and clean in physical appearance, and possess sufficient strength to carry large trays of food. Most importantly, however, they had to be dependable, or work when scheduled and report to work a few minutes before the start of the work shift. Sharon was obviously becoming less dependable. Training, counseling, a disciplinary warning, or termination were feasible options for dealing with her situation. Discharging her, however, won't improve her performance or correct her behavior.

Critical Thinking Questions

As you read this chapter, consider the following questions as they relate to Don Pablo's Mexican restaurant:

- Is James faced with a typical human resource problem?
- What areas does human resource management cover?
- How should James proceed in solving this employee problem?

BUSINESS IN THE 21ˢᵀ CENTURY

Human resource managers at FedEx train employees to use computer technology that improves communication among employees and increases worker efficiency and productivity.

Human resource management in contemporary organizations is instrumental in driving an organization toward its objectives. Today, human resource professionals face numerous challenges in recruiting, selecting, and retaining employees:

- Organizations are competing with each other for a shrinking pool of applicants.
- Workers seek to balance work and home/life activities.
- Technology is reshaping the way business is done.
- Laws govern many aspects of the employee-employer relationship.

Each day, human resource experts and front line supervisors deal with these challenges while sharing responsibility for attracting and retaining skilled, motivated employees. Whether faced with a large or small human resource problem, managers like James at Don Pablo's need to understand the process for finding and retaining excellent employees.

In this chapter, you will learn about the role of human resource management in building and maintaining an exceptional workforce. We will explore human resource planning, recruiting and selection, training, and motivating employees toward reaching organizational objectives. The chapter will also cover employee job changes within an organization and the laws guiding human resource decisions. Finally, we will look at important trends influencing human resource management.

DEVELOPING PEOPLE TO HELP REACH ORGANIZATIONAL GOALS

>lg 1

human resource management
The process of hiring, developing, motivating, and evaluating employees to achieve organizational goals.

Human resource management is the process of hiring, developing, motivating, and evaluating employees to achieve organizational goals. Organizational strategies and objectives form the basis for making all human resource management decisions. All companies strive to hire and develop well-trained, motivated employees. The human resources management process includes these steps, illustrated in Exhibit 9-1:

- Job analysis and design
- Human resource planning and forecasting
- Employee recruitment
- Employee selection
- Training and development
- Performance planning and evaluation

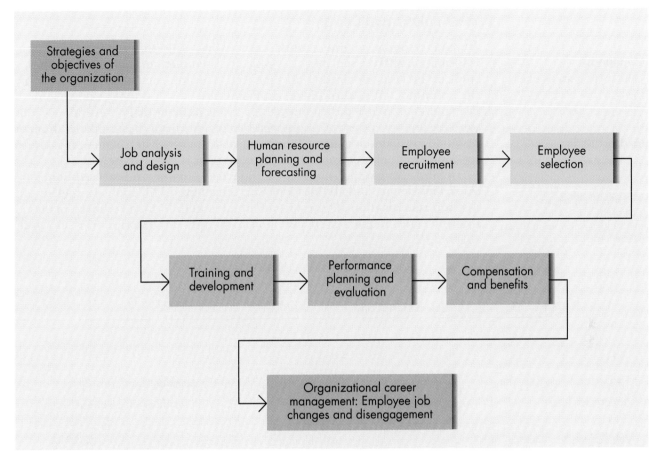

concept check

- Define human resource management.
- Describe the human resource management process.

- Compensation and benefits
- Organizational career management: employee job changes and disengagement.

In the following sections, you will learn more about each of these important functions.

HUMAN RESOURCE PLANNING

>lg 2

Firms need to have the right number of people, with the right training, in the right jobs, to do the organization's work when it needs to be done. Human resource specialists are the ones who must determine future human resource needs. Then they assess the skills of the firm's existing employees to see if new people must be hired or existing ones retrained.

Creating a strategy for meeting future human resource needs is called **human resource (HR) planning.** Two important aspects of HR planning are job analysis and forecasting the firm's people needs. The HR planning process begins with a review of corporate strategy and policy. By understanding the mission of the organization, planners can understand its human resource needs. When Compaq Computer bought Digital Equipment Corp. (DEC), the acquisition resulted in several thousand DEC employees losing their jobs, while hundreds of

human resource (HR) planning

Creating a strategy for meeting future human resource needs.

Compaq employees were transferred to DEC's former headquarters in Boston. Many transferred employees assumed managerial positions.

Job Analysis and Design

job analysis

A study of the tasks required to do a particular job well.

Human resource planners must know what skills different jobs require. Information about a specific job is typically assembled through a **job analysis,** a study of the tasks required to do a job well. This information is used to specify the essential skills, knowledge, and abilities. For instance, when General Dynamics was awarded the contract for a new military plane, several new jobs were created for industrial engineers. Job analysts from the company's human resource department gathered information from other department heads and supervisors to help recruiters hire the right people for the new jobs.

job description

The tasks and responsibilities of a job.

job specification

A list of the skills, knowledge, and abilities a person must have to fill a job.

The tasks and responsibilities of a job are listed in a **job description.** The skills, knowledge, and abilities a person must have to fill a job are spelled out in a **job specification.** These two documents help human resource planners find the right people for specific jobs. A sample job description is shown in Exhibit 9-2.

e x h i b i t   9 - 2 | Job Description

Position: College Recruiter

Reports to: Vice President of Human Resources

Location: Corporate Offices

Classification: Salaried/Exempt

Job Summary: Member of HR corporate team. Interacts with managers and department heads to determine hiring needs for college graduates. Visits 20 to 30 college and university campuses each year to conduct preliminary interviews of graduating students in all academic disciplines. Following initial interviews, works with corporate staffing specialists to determine persons who will be interviewed a second time. Makes recommendations to hiring managers concerning best qualified applicants.

Job Duties and Responsibilities:

Estimated time spent
and importance

15%   Working with managers and department heads, determines college recruiting needs.

10%   Determines colleges and universities with degree programs appropriate to hiring needs to be visited.

15%   Performs college relations activities with numerous colleges and universities.

25%   Visits campuses to conduct interviews of graduating seniors.

15%   Develops applicant files and performs initial applicant evaluations.

10%   Assists staffing specialists and line managers in determining who to schedule for second interviews.

5%   Prepares annual college recruiting report containing information and data about campuses, number interviewed, number hired, and related information.

5%   Participates in tracking college graduates who are hired to aid in determining campuses that provide the most outstanding employees.

Job Specification (Qualifications):

Bachelor's degree in human resource management or a related field. Minimum of two years of work experience with the firm in HR or department that annually hires college graduates. Ability to perform in a team environment, especially with line managers and department heads. Very effective oral and written communication skills. Reasonably proficient in Excel, Word, and Windows computer environment and familiar with People Soft.

Human Resource Planning and Forecasting

Forecasting an organization's human resource needs, known as an HR *demand forecast,* is an essential aspect of HR planning. This process involves two forecasts: (1) determining the number of people needed by some future time (in one year, for example), and (2) estimating the number of people currently employed by the organization who will be available to fill various jobs at some future time. This is an *internal* supply forecast.

Does TeamStaff, a PEO, live up to its motto "Simply a better way to employ people"? Find out at

http://www.teamstaff.com

By comparing human resource demand and supply forecasts, a future personnel surplus or shortage can be determined and appropriate action taken. For example, United Airlines hired approximately 2,000 additional flight attendants when it developed the Star Alliance, an air transport network consisting of United, Lufthansa, SAS, Thai, Varig, and Air Canada. On the other hand, One Plus Financial terminated hundreds of employees when it withdrew from the mortgage banking industry. Exhibit 9-3 summarizes the process of forecasting an organization's needs.

e x h i b i t   9 - 3 | Human Resource Planning Process

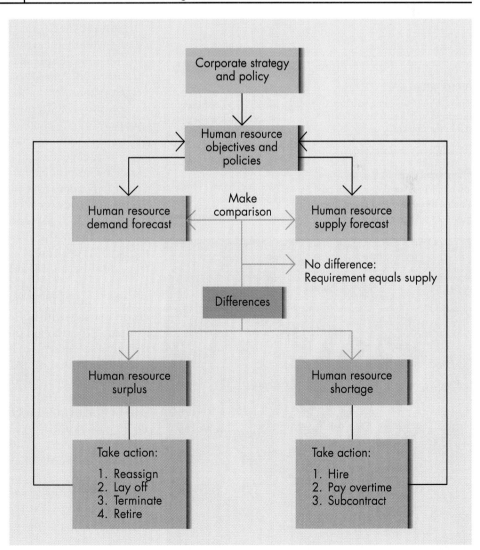

contingent workers

Persons who prefer temporary employment, either part-time or full-time.

In recent years many firms with employee shortages are hiring **contingent workers,** or persons who prefer temporary employment, either part-time or full-time. College students and retired persons comprise a big portion of America's contingent workforce. Other people who want to work but don't want to be permanent employees join a professional employer organization (PEO). A PEO performs staffing, training, and compensation functions by contracting with a business to provide employees for a specified period of time. A firm with a shortage of accountants can rent or lease an accountant from the PEO for the expected duration of the shortage.

concept check

- Describe the job analysis and design process.
- What is the process for human resource forecasting?

EMPLOYEE RECRUITMENT

>lg 3

When a firm creates a new position or an existing one becomes vacant, it starts looking for people with qualifications that meet the requirements of the job. Two sources of job applicants are the internal and external labor markets. The internal labor market consists of employees currently employed by the firm; the external labor market is the pool of potential applicants outside the firm.

recruitment

The attempt to find and attract qualified applicants in the external labor market.

Search the database of CareerBuilder.com (**http://www.careerbuilder.com**) for a job in a new city. It combines the listings of *The New York Times, Washington Post, Boston Globe, Chicago Tribune, Los Angeles Times,* and *San Jose Mercury News.*

Most companies including UPS, Southwest Airlines, and Wal-Mart follow a policy of promotion from within and try to fill positions with their existing employees. The internal search for job applicants usually means that a person must change his or her job. People are typically either promoted or transferred. A firm's *skills inventory* can help find the right person for a job opening. A skills inventory is a computerized employee database containing information on each employee's previous work experience, educational background, performance records, career objectives, and job location preferences. General Electric has used a skills inventory for many years as a means of determining promotions and transfers.

If qualified job candidates cannot be found inside the firm, the external labor market must be tapped. **Recruitment** is the attempt to find and attract qualified applicants in the external labor market. The type of position determines which recruitment method will be used and which segment of the labor market will be searched. Boeing will not recruit an experienced engineer the same way it would recruit a secretary or clerk typist.

Nontechnical, unskilled, and other nonsupervisory workers are recruited through newspaper, radio, and sometimes even television help wanted ads in local media. Starbucks placed ads in the *Beijing Youth Daily* to attract workers for its Beijing coffee shops.[1] Entry-level accountants, engineers, and systems analysts are commonly hired through college campus recruitment efforts. Each year Texas Instruments sends recruiters to dozens of colleges across the United States that have engineering degree programs. To recruit inexperi-

Many organizations find qualified job applicants for professional positions through recruitment programs at college campuses.

enced technicians, National SemiConductor visits junior and community college campuses with electronic and related technical programs that are within 50 to 100 miles of its facilities.

A firm that needs executives and other experienced professional, technical, and managerial employees may employ the services of an executive search firm such as Korn/Ferry. The hiring firm pays the search firm a fee equivalent to one to four months of the employee's first-year salary. Many search firms specialize in a particular occupation, industry, or geographic location.

job fair

An event, typically one day, held at a convention center to bring together thousands of job seekers and hundreds of firms searching for employees.

Many firms participate in local job fairs. A **job fair** is typically a one-day event held at a convention center to bring together thousands of job seekers and hundreds of firms searching for employees.

Some firms now use the Internet exclusively to attract new employees. A firm can post job announcements at its Web site, and applicants send their résumés via the Internet. Beacon Application Services Corp., a systems integration company, recruits only over the Internet. According to Dan Maude, president of the firm, "A year's worth of Web recruiting for us costs less than one agency fee. . . . it's also faster."[2] The Applying Technology box describes how Career Central uses the Internet to match job applicants with job openings.

APPLYING TECHNOLOGY

INTERNET HIRING AND E-RECRUITING: THE "TIDAL WAVE" OF THE FUTURE

Internet hiring is a tidal wave that keeps on growing. There are several approaches being used in e-recruiting. These include:

- **Job Boards.** You can search for candidates by region, industry, or demographics. Problems: Candidate quality is questionable.
- **Professional Portals.** Companies can add content other than job listings in their information. Benefits include direct marketing of jobs and the ability of employers to promote their brands to candidates.
- **Database Models.** These allow for fast "matches" and potentially broader selection pools. Companies pay per candidate. Problems: Data might not be fresh.

The Fortune 500's best practices to optimize internet use in corporate recruiting include:

- 73% link their careers section directly to their home page.
- 56% adhere to the "one click to apply" practice.
- 55% publish information on employee benefits.
- 44% publish information on corporate culture.
- 42% have a separate college recruiting section.
- 42% allow job seekers to search a database of open job positions.

A second study found that the most effective online sites share many of these characteristics:

- They allow candidates to navigate the site easily and use links to career pages and job openings.
- They describe career opportunities and individual jobs in greater detail than do typical help-wanted ads.
- Their information about the company, including profiles of archetypal employees, gives candidates a sense of what it would be like to work there.
- They let candidates paste resumes to an application page, e-mail then to a recruiter, or create online applications that allow information to be entered with a few clicks.

Critical Thinking Questions

1. What are the benefits of an electronic job search for an applicant?
2. What are the benefits to the employer?
3. How can an electronic job search improve the match between the applicant's skills and the job's requirements?
4. Would you consider applying for a job online? Why or why not?

Source: "Is Online Recruiting Becoming a Tidal Wave?" *HR Focus*, April 2001.

c o n c ə p t c h ə c k

- What is a skills inventory, and what are the two labor markets?
- Describe different ways that employees are recruited.
- How is technology helping firms find the right recruits?

Other firms including Coca-Cola, UBS PaineWebber, and NationsBank utilize artificial intelligence software to scan and track résumés.[3] Webhire, Inc. and HotJobs.com scan résumés for key words to identify qualified job candidates. Each system can scan and search thousands of résumés in minutes. With such systems, the words you use to describe your education, background, and work experience become very important.

EMPLOYEE SELECTION

>lg 4

selection

The process of determining which persons in the applicant pool possess the qualifications necessary to be successful on the job.

After a firm has attracted enough job applicants, employment specialists begin the selection process. **Selection** is the process of determining which persons in the applicant pool possesses the qualifications necessary to be successful on the job. The steps in the employee selection process are shown in Exhibit 9-4 and described below:

1. *Initial screening.* During the initial screening, an applicant usually completes an application form and has a brief interview of 30 minutes or less. The application form includes questions about education, work experience, and previous job duties. A personal résumé may be substituted for the application form. The interview is normally structured and consists of a short list of specific questions. For example: Are you familiar with any accounting software packages? Did you supervise anyone in your last job? Did you use a company car when making sales calls?

2. *Employment testing.* Following the initial screening, an applicant may be asked to take one or more employment tests, such as the Minnesota Clerical Test or the Wonderlic Personnel Test, a mental ability test. Some tests are designed to measure special job skills, others measure aptitudes, and some are intended to capture characteristics of one's personality. The Myers-Briggs

e x h i b i t   9 - 4 | Steps of the Employee Selection Process

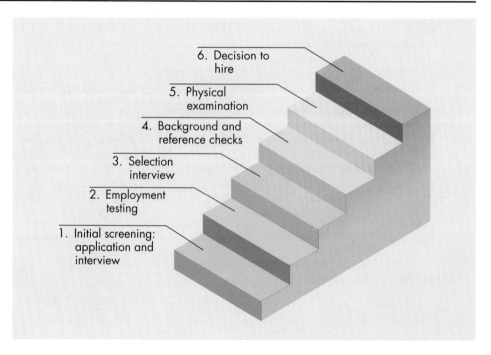

Type Indicator is a personality and motivational test widely used on college campuses as an aid in providing job and career counseling. Companies are increasingly using general attitude tests in job screening. John Pate, vice president of BT: Employee Screening Services, says, "You like to know what people are thinking. You don't want to hire their problems."[4]

selection interview

An in-depth discussion of an applicant's work experience, skills and abilities, education, and career interests.

3. *Selection interview.* The tool most widely used in making hiring decisions by Intel, Merck, and other firms is the **selection interview,** an in-depth discussion of an applicant's work experience, skills and abilities, education, and career interests. For managerial and professional positions, an applicant may be interviewed by several persons, including the line manager for the position to be filled. This interview is designed to determine an applicant's communication ability and motivation. It is also a means for gathering additional factual information from the applicant such as college major, years of part-time work experience, computer equipment used, and reason for leaving the last job. The applicant may be asked to explain how to solve a particular management problem or how she or he provided leadership to a group in a previous work situation when an important problem had to be solved quickly. United Airlines asks prospective flight attendants how they handled a conflict with a customer or coworker in a previous job.

Get advice for brushing up your interview skills at the Job Hunting Advice page of *The Wall Street Journal*'s Career site,

http://www.careerjournal.com

Carolyn Murray, a recruiter for W. L. Gore and Associates, makers of Gore-Tex, says she pays little attention to a candidate's carefully scripted responses to her admittedly easy questions. Instead, she listens for a casual remark that reveals the reality behind an otherwise thought-out reply. Using a baseball analogy, Carolyn gives examples of how three job candidates struck out in Exhibit 9-5.[5]

4. *Background and reference check.* If applicants pass the selection interview, most firms examine their background and check their references. In recent years an increasing number of employers such as American Airlines, Disney, and Microsoft are carefully researching applicants' backgrounds, particularly

---

e x h i b i t   9 - 5 | Striking Out with Gore-Tex

The Pitch (Question to Applicant)	The Swing (Applicant's Response)	The Miss (Interviewer's Reaction to Response)
"Give me an example of a time when you had a conflict with a team member."	"Our leader asked me to handle all of the FedExing for our team. I did it, but I thought that FedExing was a waste of my time."	"At Gore, we work from a team concept. Her answer shows that she won't exactly jump when one of her teammates needs help."
"Tell me how you solved a problem that was impeding your project."	"One of the engineers on my team wasn't pulling his weight, and we were closing in on a deadline. So I took on some of his work."	"The candidate may have resolved the issue for this particular deadline, but he did nothing to prevent the problem from happening again."
"What's the one thing that you would change about your current position?"	"My job as a salesman has become mundane. Now I want the responsibility of managing people."	"He's not maximizing his current position. Selling is never mundane if you go about it in the right way."

their legal history, reasons for leaving previous jobs, and even creditworthiness. Retail firms such as Men's Warehouse, JCPenney, RadioShack, and TD Industries, where employees have extensive contact with customers, tend to be very careful about checking applicant backgrounds. Some checking can be easily done using the Internet. In fact, many retired law enforcement officers have started their own firms that specialize in these investigations.

5. *Physical exams.* Companies frequently require job candidates to have a medical checkup to ensure they are physically able to perform a job. Drug testing is becoming a routine part of physical exams. Companies such as American Airlines, Burlington Northern Santa Fe Railway, and the U.S. Postal Service use drug testing for reasons of workplace safety, productivity, and employee health. A comprehensive study by the Postal Service found that employees who tested positive for drugs were 50 percent more likely to be fired, injured, disciplined, or absent than those who tested negative. Drug users also had lower performance ratings.[6]

6. *Decision to hire.* If an applicant progresses satisfactorily through all the selection steps, a decision to hire the individual is made. The decision to hire is nearly always made by the manager of the new employee.

concept check

- What are the steps in the employee selection process?
- Describe some ways that applicants are tested.

EMPLOYEE TRAINING AND DEVELOPMENT

>lg 5

training and development

Activities that provide learning situations in which an employee acquires additional knowledge or skills to increase job performance.

To ensure that both new and experienced employees have the knowledge and skills to perform their jobs successfully, organizations invest in training and development activities. **Training and development** involves learning situations in which the employee acquires additional knowledge or skills to increase job performance. Training objectives specify performance improvements, reductions in errors, job knowledge to be gained, and/or other positive organizational results. The design of training programs at General Electric, for example, includes determining instructional methods, number of trainees per class, printed materials (cases, notebooks, manuals, and the like) to be used, location of training, use of audiovisual equipment and software, and many other matters. The process of creating and implementing training and development activities is shown in Exhibit 9-6.

exhibit 9 - 6 | Employee Training and Development Process

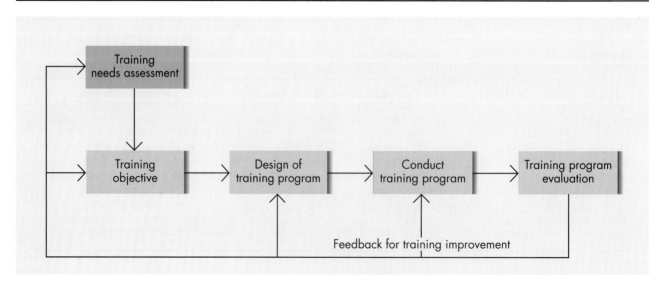

Training for new employees is instrumental in getting them up to speed and familiar with their job responsibilities. A study at MCI WorldCom found that in the first three months a new hire can accomplish only 60 percent as much as an experienced worker. And even a 5 percent drop in overall employee efficiency can cut MCI WorldCom's annual revenue by "several hundred million dollars."[7] The first type of training that new employees experience is **employee orientation,** which entails getting the new employee ready to perform on the job. Formal orientation (a half-day classroom program) provides information about company policies, salary and benefits, and parking. Although this information is very helpful, the more important orientation is about job assignments, work rules, equipment, and performance expectations provided by the new employee's supervisor and coworkers. This second briefing tends to be more informal and may last for several days or even weeks.

On-the-Job Training

Continuous training for both new and experienced employees is important to keep job skills fresh. Job-specific training, designed to enhance a new employee's ability to perform a job, includes **on-the-job training,** during which the employee learns the job by doing it with guidance from a supervisor or experienced coworker.

On-the-job training takes place at the job site or workstation and tends to be directly related to the job. This training involves specific job instructions, coaching (guidance given to new employees by experienced ones), special project assignments, or job rotation. **Job rotation** is the reassignment of workers to several different jobs over time. At Sears, management trainees work sequentially in two or three merchandise departments, customer service, credit, and human resources during their first year on the job.

An **apprenticeship** usually combines specific on-the-job instruction with classroom training. It may last as long as four years and can be found in the skilled trades of carpentry, plumbing, and electrical work.

With **mentoring,** another form of on-the-job training, a senior manager or other experienced employee provides job- and career-related information to a protégé. Mentoring is becoming increasingly popular with many firms, including Federal Express, Texaco, Merrill Lynch, and Bank of America, which uses "quad squads" composed of a mentor and three new hires (a male, female, and a minority group member). At Coca-Cola Roberto Goizueta mentored Douglas Ivester to become CEO of the company. When Goizueta died suddenly in 1997, Ivester's transition to CEO went very smoothly. The company clearly benefited from this mentoring relationship.

The primary benefits of on-the-job training are that it provides instant feedback about performance and is inexpensive. Trainees produce while learning, and no expensive classroom or learning tools are needed.

Off-the-Job Training

Even with the advantages of on-the-job training, many firms recognize that it is often necessary to train employees away from the workplace. With off-the-job training, employees learn the job away from the job. There are numerous popular methods of off-the-job training. Frequently, it takes place in a classroom where cases, role-play exercises, films, videos, lectures, and computer demonstrations are utilized to develop workplace skills.

Another form of off-the-job training takes place in a facility called a vestibule or a training simulator. In **vestibule training,** used by Honda and Kroger, trainees learn about products, manufacturing processes, and selling in a scaled-down version of an assembly line or retail outlet. When mistakes

---

employee orientation

Training that prepares a new employee to perform on the job; includes information about job assignments, work rules, equipment, and performance expectations, as well as about company policies, salary and benefits, and parking.

on-the-job training

Training in which the employee learns the job by doing it with guidance from a supervisor or experienced coworker.

job rotation

Reassignment of workers to several different jobs over time so that they can learn the basics of each job.

apprenticeship

A form of on-the-job training that combines specific job instruction with classroom instruction.

mentoring

A form of on-the-job training in which a senior manager or other experienced employee provides job- and career-related information to a protégé.

vestibule training

A form of off-the-job training in which trainees learn in a scaled-down version or simulated work environment.

By using vestibule training, airlines can teach pilots flight maneuvers and the controls of new aircraft in a safe and controlled off-the-job training environment.

c o n c ə p t c h ə c k

- Describe several types of on-the-job training.
- Explain vestibule training and programmed instruction.

are made, no customers are lost or products damaged. A training simulator, such as American Airlines' flight simulator for pilot training, is much like a vestibule facility. Pilots can practice hazardous flight maneuvers or learn the controls of a new aircraft in a safe, controlled environment with no passengers.

In a very rapidly developing trend that will undoubtedly accelerate in the 21st century, many companies including Compaq and Microsoft are using computer-assisted, electronically delivered training and development courses and programs. Many of these courses have their origins in **programmed instruction,** a self-paced, highly structured training method that presents trainees with concepts and problems using a modular format. Each module consists of a set of concepts, math rules, or task procedures with test questions at the end of the module. When the trainee or student masters all material presented in a module, he or she advances to the next module, which is somewhat more difficult. Some courses taught on your campus probably use programmed instructional materials.

Finally, trade associations, colleges and universities, and professional organizations offer professional and executive education courses at training centers or professional organization meetings.

Usually, off-the-job training is more expensive than on-the-job training, and its impact is less direct or the transfer of learning to the job is less immediate. Nevertheless, despite these shortcomings, some training can only be done away from the job.

PERFORMANCE PLANNING AND EVALUATION

>lg 6

programmed instruction

A form of computer-assisted off-the-job training.

performance appraisal

A comparison of actual performance with expected performance to assess an employee's contributions to the organization.

Along with employee orientation and training, new employees learn about performance expectations through performance planning and evaluation. Managers provide employees with expectations about the job. These are communicated as job objectives, schedules, deadlines, and product and/or service quality requirements. As an employee performs job tasks, the supervisor periodically evaluates the employee's efforts. A **performance appraisal** is a comparison of actual performance with expected performance to assess an employee's contributions to the organization and to make decisions about training, compensation, promotion, and other job changes. The performance planning and appraisal process is shown in Exhibit 9-7 and described below.

1. The manager establishes performance standards.
2. The employee works to meet the standards and expectations.
3. The employee's supervisor evaluates the employee's work in terms of quality and quantity of output and various characteristics such as job knowledge, initiative, relationships with others, and attendance and punctuality.
4. Following the performance evaluation, reward (pay raise) and job change (promotion) decisions can be made.
5. Rewards are positive feedback and provide reinforcement, or encouragement, for the employee to work harder in the future.

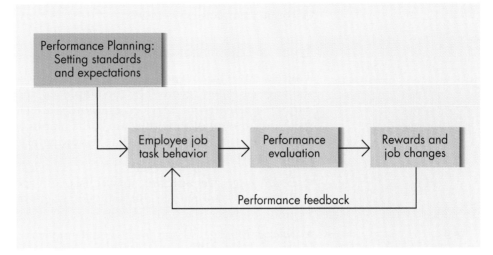

concəpt chəck

- What are the steps in the performance planning and appraisal process?
- What purposes do performance appraisals serve?

Performance appraisals serve a number of purposes, but they are most often used to make decisions about pay raises, training needs, and advancement opportunities.

EMPLOYEE COMPENSATION AND BENEFITS

>lg 7

External influences affect employee pay and benefits. With a high demand for skilled workers and high turnover rates, firms in the information technology industry offer high wages and many benefits to attract and retain workers like this Netscape employee.

Compensation, which includes both pay and benefits, is closely connected to performance appraisal. Employees who perform better tend to get bigger pay raises.[8] Several factors affect an employee's pay.

1. *Pay structure and internal influences.* Wages, salaries, and benefits usually reflect the importance of the job. The jobs that management considers more important are compensated at a higher rate; president, chief engineer, and chief financial officer are high-paying jobs. Likewise, different jobs of equal importance to the firm are compensated at the same rate. For instance, if a drill-press operator and a lathe operator are considered of equal importance, they may both be paid $21 per hour.

2. *Pay level and external influences.* In deciding how much to pay workers, the firm must also be concerned with the salaries paid by competitors. If competitors are paying much higher wages, a firm may lose its best employees. Larger firms conduct salary surveys to see what other firms are paying. Wage and salary surveys conducted by the Chamber of Commerce or the U.S. Department of Labor can also be useful.

An employer can decide to pay at, above, or below the going rate. Most firms try to offer competitive wages and salaries within a geographic area or an industry. If a company pays below-market wages, it may not be able to hire skilled people. The level, or competitiveness, of a firm's compensation is determined by the firm's financial condition (or profitability), efficiency, and employee productivity, as well as the going rates paid by competitors. Miller Brewing Co. is considered a high-paying firm ($22–$25 per hour for production employees); McDonald's is a lower paying company ($6–$8 per hour for counter employees).

Types of Compensation or Pay

There are two basic types of compensation: direct and indirect. Direct pay is the wage or salary received by the employee; indirect pay consists of various employee benefits and services. Employees are usually paid directly on the basis of the amount of time they work, the amount they produce, or some combination of time and output. The following are the most common types of compensation:

- *Hourly wages.* Technicians, machinists, and assembly-line workers at Miller Brewing Co. are paid by the hour with wages ranging from $22.50 to $26.50 per hour.

- *Salaries.* Managerial and professional employees are paid an annual salary either on a biweekly or a monthly basis. The annual salary of our U.S. president is $400,000.

- *Piecework and commission.* Some employees are paid according to how much they produce or sell. A car salesperson might be paid $500 for each car sold or a 3 percent commission on the car's sale price. Thus, a salesperson who sold four cars in one week at $500 per car would earn $2,000 in pay for that week. Alternatively, a 3 percent commission on four cars sold with total sales revenue of $70,000 would yield $2,100 in pay.

  Increasingly, business firms are paying employees using a base wage or salary and an incentive. The incentive feature is designed to increase individual employee, work group, and/or organizational performance. Incentive pay plans are commonly referred to as variable or contingent pay arrangements.

- *Accelerated commission schedule.* A salesperson could be paid a commission rate of 3 percent on the first $50,000 of sales per month, 4 percent on the next $30,000, and 5 percent on any sales beyond $80,000. For a salesperson who made $90,000 of sales in one month, the monthly pay would be as follows:

$$
\begin{array}{rcl}
3\% \times \$50,000 &=& \$1,500 \\
4\% \times \$30,000 &=& \$1,200 \\
5\% \times \underline{\$10,000} &=& \underline{\$500} \\
\$90,000 && \$3,200
\end{array}
$$

- *Bonus.* A bonus is a payment for reaching a specific goal; it may be paid on a monthly, quarterly, or annual basis. A bank with several offices or branches might set monthly goals for opening new accounts, making loans, and customer service. Each employee of a branch that meets all goals would be paid a monthly bonus of $100. Although the bonuses are paid to the employees individually, the employees must function as an effective, high-performing group to reach the monthly goals.

- *Profit sharing.* A firm that offers profit sharing pays employees a portion of the profits over a preset level. For example, profits beyond 10 percent of gross sales might be shared at a 50 percent rate with employees. The company retains the remaining profits. All employees may receive the same profit shares, or the shares may vary according to base pay.

- *Fringe benefits.* **Fringe benefits** are indirect compensation and include pensions, health insurance, vacations, and many others. Some fringe benefits are

fringe benefits

Indirect compensation such as pensions, health insurance, and vacations.

required by law: unemployment compensation, worker's compensation, and Social Security, which are all paid in part by employers. *Unemployment compensation* provides former employees with money for a certain period while they are unemployed. To be eligible, the employee must have worked a minimum number of weeks, be without a job, and be willing to accept a suitable position offered by the state Unemployment Compensation Commission. Some state laws permit payments to strikers. *Workers' compensation* pays employees for lost work time caused by work-related injuries and may also cover rehabilitation after a serious injury. *Social Security* is mainly a government pension plan, but it also provides disability and survivor benefits and benefits for people undergoing kidney dialysis and transplants. Medicare (health care for the elderly) and Medicaid (health care for the poor) are also part of Social Security.

Many employers also offer fringe benefits not required by law. Among these are paid time off (vacations, holidays, sick days, even pay for jury duty), insurance (health and hospitalization, disability, life, dental, vision, and accidental death and dismemberment), pensions and retirement savings accounts, and stock purchase options.

Some firms with numerous fringe benefits allow employees to mix and match benefit items or select items based on individual needs. This is a flexible or cafeteria-style benefit plan. A younger employee with a family may desire to purchase medical, disability, and life insurance, whereas an older employee may want to put more benefit dollars into a retirement savings plan. All employees are allocated the same number of benefit dollars but can spend these dollars on different items and in different amounts.

concept check

- How does a firm establish a pay scale for its employees?
- What is the difference between direct and indirect pay?

ORGANIZATIONAL CAREER MANAGEMENT

>lg 8

An important aspect of the human resource management process is organizational career management, or facilitating employee job changes, including promotions, transfers, demotions, layoffs, terminations, and retirements.

Job Changes within the Organization

promotion

An upward move in an organization to a position with more authority, responsibility, and pay.

A **promotion** is an upward move in an organization to a position with more authority, responsibility, and pay. Promotion decisions are usually based on merit (ability and performance) and seniority (length of service). Union employees usually prefer a strict seniority system for employee advancement. Managers and technical employees strongly prefer promotions based on merit.

transfer

A horizontal move in an organization to a position with about the same salary and at about the same organizational level.

A **transfer** is a horizontal move in an organization to a position with about the same salary and at about the same organizational level. An employee may seek a transfer for personal growth, for a more interesting job, for convenience (better work hours, work location, or training opportunity), or for a job that offers more potential for advancement. Employers may transfer workers from positions where they are no longer needed to ones where they are needed. Or the goal may be to find a better fit for the employee within the firm. Sometimes transfers are made to give employees a different perspective or to reenergize them. Consider Randy Lagman, a staff support technician for Internet operations at Lands' End, a billion-dollar clothing catalog company based in Dodgeville, Wisconsin. Randy was transferred from a self-described "Web-geek" position to a job with the title "technical adventurer outfitter."

Randy's transfer had a big impact on his work style. For most people, bringing work home means reading reports in front of the TV or analyzing spreadsheets in an office carved out of a spare bedroom. For Lagman, it means wearing a raincoat, sitting under a lawn sprinkler, and testing a weatherproof laptop. "I'm getting a reputation as the neighborhood crackpot," he jokes. His work has also had an impact on his understanding of risk and stress. Lots of information technology people believe that they work in high-stakes, high-pressure environments. But Lagman's role as technical adventurer outfitter brings him into contact with people who know the *real* meaning of risk.[9]

demotion

The downgrading or reassignment of an employee to a position with less responsibility.

When a person is downgraded or reassigned to a position with less responsibility, it is called a **demotion.** This usually occurs when an employee isn't performing satisfactorily. In most companies, a person is given several warnings before a demotion takes place.

Separations

separation

The departure of an employee from the organization; can be a layoff, termination, resignation, or retirement.

A **separation** occurs when an employee leaves the company. Layoffs, terminations, resignations, and retirements are all types of separations. Sometimes separations occur because companies are trying to remain competitive in the global marketplace. When oil prices dropped significantly early in 1997, many energy firms laid off or terminated workers. UPR, Inc., an oil exploration and drilling company, initially terminated 400 employees and later offered early retirement packages to other employees to encourage them to retire.

layoff

A temporary separation of an employee from the organization; arranged by the employer, usually because business is slow.

A **layoff** is a temporary separation arranged by the employer, usually because business is slow. Layoffs can be planned, such as seasonal reductions of employees, or unplanned, as when sales unexpectedly decline. Generally, employees with the least seniority are laid off first.

There are several alternatives to a layoff. With a *voluntary reduction in pay,* all employees agree to take less pay so that everyone can keep working. Other firms arrange to have all or most of their employees take vacation time during slow periods. Major league baseball teams, the Houston Astros, for example, encourage their full-time year-round employees to take vacations during the off-season from November through April. Other employees agree to take *voluntary time off,* or work fewer hours, which again has the effect of reducing the employer's payroll and avoiding the need for a layoff. Control Data Corp. avoids layoffs with what it calls a *rings of defense* approach. Temporary employees are hired with the specific understanding that they may be laid off at any time. When layoffs are needed, the temporary workers are the first "ring of defense." Permanent Control Data employees know they probably will never be laid off.

termination

A permanent separation of an employee from the organization, arranged by the employer.

A **termination** is a permanent separation arranged by the employer. Reasons for terminations include failure to perform as expected, violation of work rules, dishonesty, theft, sexual harassment, excessive absenteeism, or insubordination (disobedience).

Most companies follow a series of steps before terminating an employee. First, the employee is given an oral warning. The second step is a written statement that the employee's actions are not acceptable. If the employee fails to improve, he or she is suspended from work for a time. If the employee persists in wrongdoing after suspension, his or her employment is terminated.

resignation

A permanent separation of an employee from the organization, done voluntarily by the employee.

Resignation is a permanent form of separation that is undertaken voluntarily by the employee, whereas layoff and termination are involuntary. An employee may resign for almost any reason: to seek a new career, move to a different part of the country, accept an employment offer with a significant pay raise, or join a fast-growing firm with numerous advancement opportunities.

For companies in high-growth industries, keeping employees from resigning and moving to "greener pastures" is a number-one priority. This is particularly true in smaller entrepreneurial firms where losing a key employee can be disastrous. A good example of a company that emphasizes employee retention is Trilogy Software, discussed in the Focusing on Small Business box.

AT TRILOGY SOFTWARE, RESIGNATION IS A DIRTY WORD

At age 28, Danielle Rios has it all—a BS degree in computer science from Stanford, a great track record as a software developer for IBM, and the energy and savvy to market herself. With all that going for her, Rios could be a free-agent winner in the new economy, adding value by juggling different projects with different firms. Or she could have her pick of well-established corporate launch pads for her career.

But for the last three years, Rios has worked with Trilogy Software, Inc., a small, rapidly growing software firm based in Austin, Texas. Trilogy is on the cutting edge of sales-and-marketing software, and Rios is part of a team that shows potential customers how the software can work for them.

Joe Liemandt founded Trilogy in 1989, after dropping out of Stanford only a few months before graduation. To finance the start-up, Liemandt charged up 22 credit cards. Four years ago, Trilogy had 100 employees. Today it has almost 1,000 and plans to add another 1,000 soon. But to call Trilogy workers "employees" misses the point. They're all shareholders. They're all managers. They're all partners. That's how Liemandt, Trilogy's CEO, has chosen to run his company—and that's what makes it successful.

Liemandt knows that Trilogy depends on talented people. He also knows that people can go anywhere. Which means that his biggest competitive headache isn't companies like SAP AG, Baan Co., and PeopleSoft, Inc.—businesses he has to face down in the marketplace. His biggest worry is holding on to people like Rios. "There's nothing more important than recruiting and growing people," he says. "That's my number-one job."

It's a seller's market for talent. People with the right combination of savvy and ambition can afford to shop for the right boss, the right colleagues, the right environment. In the old economy, it was a buyer's market: Companies had their pick of the crop, and the question they asked was "Why hire?" Now the question is "Why join up?"

Critical Thinking Questions

1. Do you think that Trilogy overemphasizes the importance of employees?
2. What are some things that Trilogy can do to keep those workers in high demand?
3. Would you want to work for Trilogy?

---

retirement
The separation of an employee from the organization at the end of his or her career.

concept check

- What is organizational career management?
- Define promotion, transfer, termination, and retirement.

Retirement usually ends one's career. Common retirement ages are 55, 62, 65, and 70, but no one can be required to retire, according to the Age Discrimination in Employment Act. The law does, however, allow mandatory retirement in a few occupations, such as firefighter, police officer, and commercial airline pilot.

Workers in companies with too many employees may be offered early-retirement incentives. This option offers retirement benefits to younger employees or adds extra retirement benefits or both. Employees can thus retire more comfortably without working longer. Xerox, General Motors, IBM, Hewlett-Packard, and Phillips Petroleum, among others, have used early-retirement plans to reduce their workforces.

LAWS AFFECTING HUMAN RESOURCE MANAGEMENT

>lg 9

Federal laws help ensure that job applicants and employees are treated fairly and not discriminated against. Hiring, training, and job placement must be unbiased. Promotion and compensation decisions must be based on

AN UNFAIR DISMISSAL?

Alex Lambros, Jr., a stockbroker, has had just one customer complaint in 25 years in the business. Recruited in 1989 to work for Merrill Lynch & Co., Lambros soon became a top producer. He developed an "$88 million book of brokerage business" and was recognized by the company as one of the elite performers in the brokerage industry.

Several years later, when he was the acting branch manager of a Merrill Lynch office in Cape Coral, Florida, Lambros was fired for destroying company property. His apparent offense was that he tore open a payroll envelope addressed to the office's branch manager.

Lambros filed a complaint of wrongful termination and defamation with the New York Stock Exchange—one of several oversight authorities for the brokerage industry. Lambros contended that he was terminated because he "had repeatedly questioned the propriety of actions by superiors." He further contended that Merrill Lynch's managers were tempted by his "lush client base." High-performing brokers get a larger share of the commissions paid by clients. By redistributing Lambros's client base to brokers with lower commissions or by having managers take over the accounts, the company could retain a greater percentage of the commissions, and the managers would benefit. In addition, a brokerage firm benefits if client accounts are actively traded—"something that top producers with trusted relationships with their clients don't always do." Were Lambros's claims true? Merrill Lynch contends that his claims "were baloney from the start."

Critical Thinking Questions

1. In your opinion, was Lambros's dismissal fair and just?
2. How would you evaluate the action of a brokerage firm's managers who obtain new clients by firing a broker and taking his accounts?

performance. These laws help all Americans who have talent, training, and the desire to get ahead.

New legislation and the continual interpretation and reinterpretation of existing laws will continue to make the jobs of human resource managers challenging and complicated. In 1999, for example, the National Academy of Sciences reported a link between muscle and skeletal injuries and certain workplace activities, such as lifting. In response, OSHA, a federal agency discussed below, issued new standards for the handling and lifting of objects by employees. Of course, human resource managers must now integrate these standards into their organizations. The key laws that currently affect human resource management are shown in Exhibit 9-8.

Several laws govern wages, pensions, and unemployment compensation. For instance, the Fair Labor Standards Act sets the minimum wage, which is periodically raised by Congress. Many minimum-wage jobs are found in service businesses, such as restaurants and car washes. The Pension Reform Act protects the retirement income of employees and retirees. Federal tax laws also affect compensation, including employee profit-sharing and stock purchase plans.

Employers must also be aware of changes to laws concerning employee safety, health, and privacy. The Occupational Safety and Health Act requires employers to provide a workplace free of health and safety hazards. For instance, manufacturers must require employees working on loading docks to wear steel-toed shoes so their feet won't be injured if materials are dropped. Drug and AIDS testing are also governed by federal laws.

e x h i b i t 9 - 8	Laws Impacting Human Resource Management

Law	Purpose	Agency of Enforcement
Social Security Act (1935)	Provides for retirement income and old age health care	Social Security Administration
Fair Labor Standards Act (1938)	Sets minimum wage, restricts child labor, sets overtime pay	Wage and Hour Division, Department of Labor
Equal Pay Act (1963)	Eliminates pay differentials based on gender	Equal Employment Opportunity Commission
Civil Rights Act (1964), Title VII	Prohibits employment discrimination based on race, color, religion, gender, or national origin	Equal Employment Opportunity Commission
Age Discrimination in Employment Act (1967)	Prohibits age discrimination against those over 40 years of age	Equal Employment Opportunity Commission
Occupational Safety and Health Act (1970)	Protects worker health and safety, provides for hazard-free workplace	Occupational Safety and Health Administration
Vietnam Veterans Readjustment Act (1974)	Requires affirmative employment of Vietnam War veterans	Veterans Employment Service, Department of Labor
Employee Retirement Income Security Act (1974)—also called Pension Reform Act	Establishes minimum requirements for private pension plans	Internal Revenue Service, Department of Labor, and Pension Benefit Guaranty Corporation
Pregnancy Discrimination Act (1978)	Treats pregnancy as a disability, prevents employment discrimination based on pregnancy	Equal Employment Opportunity Commission
Immigration Reform and Control Act (1986)	Verifies employment eligibility, prevents employment of illegal aliens	Employment Verification Systems, Immigration and Naturalization Service
Americans with Disabilities Act (1990)	Prohibits employment discrimination based on mental or physical disabilities	Department of Justice, Equal Employment Opportunity Commission, others
Family and Medical Leave Act (1993)	Requires employers to provide unpaid leave for childbirth, adoption, or illness	Department of Labor

Another employee law that continues to strongly affect the work of human resource managers is the Americans with Disabilities Act. To be considered disabled, a person must have a physical or mental impairment that greatly limits one or more major life activities. More than 54 million Americans fall into this category.[10] Employers may not discriminate against disabled persons. They must make "reasonable accommodations" so that qualified disabled employees can perform the job, unless doing so would cause "undue hardship" for the business. Altering work schedules, modifying equipment so a wheelchair-bound person can use it, and making buildings accessible by ramps and elevators are considered reasonable. Two companies often praised for their efforts to hire the disabled are McDonald's and DuPont.

The Family and Medical Leave Act went into effect in 1993. The law applies to employers with 50 or more employees. It requires these employers to provide unpaid leave of up to 12 weeks during any 12-month period to workers

Human resource managers must ensure that their firms accommodate the needs of disabled employees like wheelchair-bound workers who need ramps to facilitate their mobility.

who have been employed for at least a year and work a minimum of 25 hours a week. The reasons for the leave include the birth or adoption of a child; the serious illness of a child, spouse, or parent; or a serious illness that prevents the worker from doing the job. Upon return, the employee must be given her or his old job back. The worker cannot collect unemployment compensation while on leave. A company can deny leave to a salaried employee in the highest-paid 10 percent of its workforce, if letting the worker take leave would create a "serious injury" for the firm.

The Role of Government Agencies in Human Resource Management

Several federal agencies oversee employment, safety, compensation, and related areas. The Occupational Safety and Health Administration (OSHA) sets workplace safety and health standards, provides safety training, and inspects places of work (assembly plants, construction sites, and warehouse facilities, for example) to determine employer compliance with safety regulations.

The Wage and Hour Division of the Department of Labor enforces the federal minimum-wage law and overtime provisions of the Fair Labor Standards Act. Employers covered by this law must pay certain employees a premium rate of pay (or time and one-half) for all hours worked beyond 40 in one week.

How does the Equal Employment Opportunity Commission promote equal opportunity in employment? Visit **http://www.eeoc.gov** to learn what the agency does.

The Equal Employment Opportunity Commission, created by the 1964 Civil Rights Act, investigates and resolves charges of discrimination. It also files lawsuits on its own against employers. Violators can be forced to promote, pay back wages to, or provide additional training for employees against whom they discriminated. Sears, Motorola, and AT&T have had to make large back-pay awards and to offer special training to minority employees after the courts found they had been discriminated against.

The Office of Federal Contract Compliance Programs (OFCCP) oversees firms with U.S. government contracts to make sure that applicants and employees get fair treatment. A big part of its job is to review federal contractors' affirmative action programs. Employers set up **affirmative action programs** to expand job opportunities for women and minorities. In the case of a major violation, the OFCCP can recommend cancellation of the firm's government contract.

affirmative action programs

Programs established by organizations to expand job opportunities for women and minorities.

Making Affirmative Action Work

Many firms have appointed an affirmative action officer to help ensure that they comply with antidiscrimination laws. At firms such as Coca-Cola, Snap-on Tools, Hilton Hotels, and Burlington Northern Santa Fe Railway, the affirmative action officer makes sure that job applicants and employees get fair treatment. He or she often reports directly to the company president rather than to the vice president of human resources.

Affirmative action officers watch for signs of *adverse impact,* or unfair treatment of certain classes of employees. **Protected classes** are the specific groups (women, African Americans, Native Americans, and others) who have legal protection against employment discrimination.

One example of adverse impact is a job qualification that tends to weed out more female applicants than male applicants. Suppose that an airline automatically rules out anyone under five feet seven inches tall who wants to

protected classes

The specific groups who have legal protection against employment discrimination; include women, African Americans, Native Americans, and others.

be a pilot. Many more female applicants than male applicants would be rejected because women tend to be shorter than men. But height has nothing to do with a pilot's ability, so this height requirement would be discriminatory.

The overall affirmative action record of the past decade has been mixed. The employment of women in professional occupations continues to grow, but minority representation among professionals has not significantly increased, even though professional jobs have been among the fastest growing areas. Technical jobs have the most equitable utilization rates of minorities.

concept check

- What are the key federal laws affecting employment?
- List and describe the functions of the two federal agencies that enforce employment discrimination laws.
- What is affirmative action?

CAPITALIZING ON TRENDS IN BUSINESS

>lg 10   Social change, evolving demographics, advancing technology, and global competition are driving the trends in human resource management in the 21st century.

Social Change

The most dramatic social change that is occurring is the increasing number of women joining the labor force—a trend that began in the 20th century and continues today. Today, women comprise about 45 percent of the American labor force. The entry of women into the workforce has created some new human resource management issues including dual-career couples, child and elder care, and workplace sexual harassment. American Airlines, for example, recently offered a new employee benefit called Life Balance Work/Life Services to assist employees in coping with some nonwork lifestyle issues. According to Allison Payne, the airline's vice president of human resources, Life Balance functions like a personal assistant who can help with child care arrangements, car repair services, mortgage rate information, parenting, and many other personal and family issues.[11]

For the latest news in the human resources field, visit the Web site of the Society for Human Resource Management at

http://www.shrm.org

Another social change is the new attitude toward changing jobs. Only a few years ago, recent college graduates could expect to change jobs and employers three to five times during their 25 to 40 years of professional experience. Now, a 22- to 25-year-old college graduate can expect six to ten of these changes and one or two significant occupational changes, such as from engineer to accountant. This increased frequency of job changes may mean that employees and employers are less loyal to one another.

Demographics

diversity
Employee differences in age, race and ethnicity, gender, educational background, and work experience.

Changes in demographics have resulted in a more diverse workforce, as shown in Exhibit 9-9. **Diversity** refers to employee differences in age, race and ethnicity, gender, educational background, and work experiences. Managing a diverse work group is more difficult than managing a homogeneous group, such as all white males, for example, because each group brings its own ideas, habits, culture, and communication skills to the work environment. Progressive human

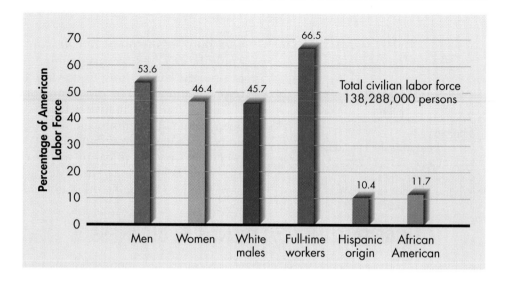

resource practices of diversity management focus on mentoring women and minority persons and removing the *glass ceiling*, or the invisible barrier in many firms that prevents women, minorities, and others from advancing to high-level management and executive positions. Nothing has prevented Darla Moore from advancing in her professional fields of banking and investments. She is CEO of Rainwater, Inc., and in 1998 she became the first woman ever to have a college of business named for her—the Moore School of Business at the University of South Carolina.[12]

Advancing Technology

Advances in information technology have greatly improved the efficiency of handling many transaction-based aspects (payroll and expense reimbursement) of employee services. Technology enables instant communication of human resource data from far-flung branches to the home office. Ease of communication has also led many companies to outsource some or all of their human resource functions. **Outsourcing** is the assignment of various functions, like human resources, accounting, or legal work, to outside organizations. The National Geographic Society outsourced all of its employee benefits programs to Workforce Solutions. Administaff is a large company that handles compensation and benefits processing, training, and even performance appraisal for many large corporate clients. Without computer databases and networks, such outsourcing would be impossible.

Technology has also made telecommuting a reality for almost 29 million workers. **Telecommuting** is now commonplace. In this arrangement, employees work at home and are linked to the office by phone, fax, and computer.[13] At Cisco Systems, a computer-networking giant based in San Jose, California, telecommuters have improved their productivity by up to 25 percent, while the company has saved about $1 million on overhead and retained key employees who might otherwise have left. What's more, those who have traded suits for sweats say they love setting their own schedules, skipping rush hour, spending more time with their kids, and working at least part-time in comfortable surroundings. "It's surprising the number of engineers who will respond to a question at 11:00 on a Saturday night," says John Hotchkiss, Cisco's human resource manager. "We can solve a problem that would not have been solved until Monday morning."[14]

outsourcing
The assignment of various functions, such as human resources, accounting, or legal work, to outside organizations.

telecommuting
An arrangement in which employees work at home and are linked to the office by phone, fax, and computer.

Telecommuting has also grown because of a strong economy in which employers must do what they can to attract the best and brightest workers. Telecommuting also offers environmental and political benefits as companies respond to Clean Air Act provisions aimed at reducing traffic. It also enables businesses to cut real estate costs by creating "hoteling" arrangements in which, say, 10 people share a single cubicle on an as-needed basis. Exhibit 9-10 lists some of the companies most friendly to telecommuting.

Global Competition

As more firms "go global," they are sending an increasing number of employees overseas. Procter & Gamble, IBM, Caterpillar, Microsoft, Federal Express, and many others have tens of thousands of employees abroad. Such companies face somewhat different human resource management issues than do firms that operate only within the United States. For example, criteria for selecting employees include not only technical skills and knowledge of the business, but also the ability to adapt to a local culture and to learn a foreign language.

Once an individual is selected for an overseas assignment, language training and cultural orientation become important. Salary and benefits, relocation expenses, and special allowances (housing, transportation, and education) can increase human resource costs by as much as three times normal annual costs. After an overseas assignment of one year or more, the firm must repatriate the employee, or bring the individual back home. Job placement and career progression frequently become issues during repatriation because the firm has changed and the employee's old job may no longer exist. After spending a year in Brussels, Belgium, Mike Rocca, a financial executive with Honeywell, experienced "reentry shock" when he returned to his corporate office in Minneapolis and saw how new software had changed accounting.

concept check

- How is the entry of more women into the workforce affecting human resource management?
- What is diversity, and how does it affect human resource management?
- What benefits does telecommuting offer?
- What issues does "going global" present for human resource management?

exhibit 9-10 | Telecommuting-Friendly Employers

Company	Percentage of Workforce that Telecommutes	Special Features
Aetna	2%	Telecommuter is assigned an office "buddy."
Arthur Andersen	20	Conducts safety inspections of home offices.
AT&T	55	Manager and employee work out details.
Boeing	1	Rules differ for each business unit.
Cisco Systems	66	24-hour technical support, ergonomic furniture required.
Georgia Power	5	May soon allow some to work at company sites near home.
Hewlett-Packard	8	Recommends ergonomically correct office.
IBM	20	Teleworkers use shared space in the office.
Merrill Lynch	5	Employees can test telecommuting in two-week simulation.
The Leisure Co./America West	16	Arranges monthly potluck team dinners to keep everyone in touch.

SOURCE: Reprinted *Business Week* from October 12, 1998, by special permission, copyright © 1998 by The McGraw-Hill Companies, Inc.

APPLYING THIS CHAPTER'S TOPICS

It's never too early to start thinking about your career in business. No, you don't have to decide today, but it's important to decide fairly soon how you will spend your life's work. A very practical reason for doing so is that it will save you a lot of time and money. We have seen too many juniors, seniors, or even graduate students who aren't really sure what they want to do upon graduation.

Interested in a career in human resources? At **http://www.ipma-hr.org/public/research_index.cfm** you'll find valuable tips to point you in the right direction.

The longer you wait to choose a profession, the more credit hours you may have to take in your new field and the longer it will be before you start earning real money.

A second reason to choose a career field early is that you can get a part-time or summer job and "test-drive" the profession. If it's not for you, you will find out very quickly.

Your school placement office can give you plenty of information about various careers in business. We also describe many career opportunities at the end of each part of this text. Another source of career information is the Internet. Go to any search engine,

TRY IT NOW!

Make Telecommuting Work for You Maybe a part-time job might require too much driving time. Perhaps there are simply no jobs in the immediate area that suit you. Try telecommuting right now. Is telecommuting for you? Nearly 75 percent of teleworkers responding to an AT&T survey said they were more satisfied with their personal and family lives than before they started working at home.[15] But telecommuting is not for every person or every job, and you'll need plenty of self-discipline to make it work for you. Ask yourself if you can perform your duties without close supervision. Also, think about whether you would miss your coworkers.

If you decide to give telecommuting a try, consider these suggestions to maintain your productivity:

• *Set ground rules with your family.* Spouses and small children have to understand that even though you're in the house, you are busy earning

a living. It's fine to throw in a few loads of laundry or answer the door when the plumber comes. It's another thing to take the kids to the mall or let them play games on your office PC.

• *Clearly demarcate your work space by using a separate room with a door you can shut.* Let your family know that, emergencies excepted, the space is off-limits during working hours.

• *If you have small children, you may want to arrange for child care during your working hours.*

• *Stay in touch with your coworkers and professional colleagues.* Go into the office from time to time for meetings to stay connected.

Above all, you can make telecommuting work for you by being productive. Doing your job well whether on-site or telecommuting will help assure you of a bright future.

such as Excite or Lycos, and enter "careers in business," or narrow your search to a specific area such as management or marketing.

Career planning will not end when you find your first professional job. It is a life-long process that ends only with retirement. Your career planning will include conducting a periodic self-assessment of your strengths and weaknesses, gathering information about other jobs both within the firm and externally, learning about other industries, and setting career goals for yourself.[16] You must always think about your future in business.

You Will Be Involved in Human Resources Decision Making

During your professional career in business, you will likely have the opportunity to become a manager. As a manager, you will have to make many human resource decisions, including hiring, firing, promoting, giving a pay raise, sending an employee to a training program, disciplining a worker, approving a college tuition reimbursement request, and reassigning an employee to a different job. In short, you will be involved in virtually every human resource decision or activity affecting the employees you manage.

Always treat people as you wish to be treated when making human resource decisions. Be fair, be honest, offer your experience and advice, and communicate frequently with your employees. If you follow this simple advice, you will be richly rewarded in your own career.

>looking ahead
at Don Pablo's

James was faced with a typical human resource problem with Sharon, the tardy waitperson. As presented in this chapter, James should utilize his human resource management skills and redirect Sharon toward improved performance. One approach is to offer additional training on company policies and the importance of good customer service. He might remind her that if she is late or doesn't come to work on a particular day, then her work must be shared by other waitpersons, which may lead to poor customer service. Finally, James may have to make the difficult decision to demote or fire Sharon if her performance does not meet desired levels.

Don Pablo's is expanding the number of its units and is part of a larger organization called Avado Brands. In addition to Don Pablo's, the company owns Canyon Cafe restaurants (southwestern theme) and Hops (a microbrewery with an American-style menu). The firm plans to open dozens of new restaurants over the next five years, which will create many new human resource challenges and opportunities.

SUMMARY OF LEARNING GOALS

>lg 1   What is the human resource management process?

The human resource management process consists of a sequence of activities that begins with job analysis and HR planning; progresses to employee recruitment and selection; then focuses on employee training, performance appraisal, and compensation; and ends when the employee leaves the organization. Human resource decisions and activities along this series of events increase the value and contributions the employee makes to the firm. Over several years for a given employee, training, performance appraisal, and changes in compensation form a repeated set of activities that facilitate career development and increase a person's contributions to the firm.

>lg 2   How are human resource needs determined?

Creating a strategy for meeting human resource needs is called human resource planning, which begins with job analysis. Job analysis is a process for studying a job to determine its tasks and duties for setting pay, determining

KEY TERMS

affirmative action
   programs 274
apprenticeship
   265
contingent workers
   260
demotion 270
diversity 275
employee
   orientation 265
fringe benefits 268
human resource
   (HR) planning
   257
human resource
   management 256
job analysis 258
job description
   258
job fair 261
job rotation 265
job specification
   258
layoff 270
mentoring 265
on-the-job training
   265
outsourcing 276
performance
   appraisal 266
programmed
   instruction 266
promotion 269
protected classes
   274
recruitment 260
resignation 270
retirement 271
selection 262
selection interview
   263
separation 270
telecommuting 276
termination 270
training and
   development 264
transfer 269
vestibule training
   265

employee job performance, specifying hiring requirements, and designing training programs. Information from the job analysis is used to prepare a job description, which lists the tasks and responsibilities of the job. A job specification describes the skills, knowledge, and abilities a person needs to fill the job described in the job description. By examining the human resource demand forecast and the *internal* supply forecast, human resource professionals can determine if the company faces a personnel surplus or shortage.

>lg 3   **How do human resource managers find good people to fill the jobs?**
When a job vacancy occurs, most firms begin by trying to fill the job from within. If a suitable *internal* candidate is not available, the firm begins an external search. Firms use local media to recruit nontechnical, unskilled, and nonsupervisory workers. To locate highly trained recruits, employers use college recruiters, executive search firms, job fairs, and company Web sites to promote job openings.

>lg 4   **What is the employee selection process?**
Typically, an applicant submits an application, or résumé, and then receives a short, structured interview. If an applicant makes it past the initial screening, he or she may be asked to take an aptitude, personality, or skills test. The next step is the selection interview which is an in-depth discussion of the applicant's work experience, skills and abilities, education, and career interests. An applicant seeking a professional or managerial position will typically be interviewed by several people. After the selection interview, successful applicants may be asked to undergo a physical exam before being offered a job.

>lg 5   **What types of training and development do organizations offer their employees?**
Training and development programs are designed to increase employees' knowledge, skills, and abilities in order to foster job performance improvements. Formal training (usually classroom in nature and off-the-job) takes place shortly after being hired. Development programs prepare employees to assume positions of increasing authority and responsibility. Job rotation, executive education programs, mentoring, and special project assignments are examples of employee development programs.

>lg 6   **What is a performance appraisal?**
A performance appraisal compares an employee's actual performance with the expected performance. Performance appraisals serve several purposes but are typically used to determine an employee's compensation, training needs, and advancement opportunities.

>lg 7   **How are employees compensated?**
Direct pay is the hourly wage or monthly salary paid to an employee. In addition to the base wage or salary, direct pay may include bonuses and profit shares. Indirect pay consists of various benefits and services. Some benefits are required by law: unemployment compensation, workers' compensation, and Social Security. Others are voluntarily made available by employers to employees. These include paid vacations and holidays, pensions, health and other insurance products, employee wellness programs, and college tuition reimbursement.

>lg 8   **What is organizational career management?**
Organizational career management is the facilitation of employee job changes, including promotions, transfers, layoffs, and retirements. A promotion is an upward move with more authority, responsibility, and pay. A transfer is a horizontal move in the organization. When a person is downgraded to a position with less responsibility, it is a demotion. A layoff is a temporary separation arranged by the employer, usually when business is slow. A termination is a permanent separation arranged by the employer. A resignation is a voluntary separation by the employee. Retirement is a permanent separation that ends one's career.

>lg 9 **What are the key laws and federal agencies affecting human resource management?**

A number of federal laws (listed in Exhibit 9-8) affect human resource management. Federal law prohibits discrimination based on age, race, gender, color, national origin, religion, or disability. The Americans with Disabilities Act bans discrimination against disabled workers and requires employers to change the work environment to accommodate the disabled. The Family and Medical Leave Act requires employers, with certain exceptions, to provide employees up to 12 weeks of unpaid leave a year. The leave can be for the birth or adoption of a child or due to serious illness of a family member.

Federal agencies that deal with human resource administration are the Equal Employment Opportunity Commission (EEOC), the Occupational Safety and Health Administration (OSHA), the Office of Federal Contract Compliance Programs (OFCCP), and the Wage and Hour Division of the Department of Labor. The EEOC and OFCCP are primary agencies for enforcement of employment discrimination laws; OSHA enforces safety regulation; and the Wage and Hour Division enforces the minimum wage and related laws. Many companies employ affirmative action and safety officers to ensure compliance with antidiscrimination and workplace safety laws.

>lg 10 **What trends are affecting human resource management?**

Women now comprise 45 percent of the workforce in America. As a result, we are seeing growing numbers of dual-career couples. In turn, companies are now facing issues like sexual harassment and nonwork lifestyle issues such as child care and elder care. Workers also now change jobs three to five times during their career. This lessens the loyalty between employer and employee. As the American workforce becomes increasingly more diverse, companies are offering diversity training and mentoring of minorities.

Technology continues to improve the efficiency of human resource management. It also enables firms to outsource many functions done internally in the past. Telecommuting is becoming increasingly popular among employers and employees.

As more firms enter the international market, they are sending an increasing number of employees overseas. In addition to normal job requirements, selected workers must have the ability to adapt to a local culture and perhaps to learn a foreign language.

PREPARING FOR TOMORROW'S WORKPLACE

1. Divide the class into teams of five. Each group should select a form of applicant testing and defend why their form of testing should be used to screen applicants.

2. What kind of training and development program would be best for assembly-line workers? For first-line supervisors? For industrial sales representatives? For maintenance workers? For computer programmers?

3. Would an overseas job assignment be good for your career development? If you think so, what country would you prefer to live and work in for two or three years, and what type of job would you like to have in that country?

4. The fringe benefit package of many employers includes numerous voluntarily provided items such as health insurance, life insurance, pension plan, paid vacations, tuition reimbursement, employee price discounts on products of the firm, and paid sick leave. At your age, what are the three or four most important benefits? Why? Twenty years from now, what do you think will be your three or four most important benefits? Why?

5. Select two teams of five. One team will take the position that employees are simply a business expense to be managed. The second team will argue that employees are an asset to be developed to enable the firm to gain a competitive advantage. The remainder of the class will judge which team provided the stronger argument.

6. How important is training likely to be in the future? What changes that are facing organizations will increase the importance of training?

7. Is reducing the number of employee resignations always a good thing? Why or why not?

8. You are applying for a job as a manager. Write down five critical questions that you would ask your prospective employer. Share these with the class.

WORKING THE NET

1. Go to Monster.com at **http://content.monster.com/resume/** to learn how to prepare an electronic résumé that will get results. Develop a list of rules for creating effective electronic résumés, and revise your own résumé into electronic format.

2. Working as a contingent employee can help you explore your career options. Visit the Manpower Web site at **http://www.manpower.com,** and search for several types of jobs that interest you. What are the advantages of being a temporary worker? What other services does Manpower offer job seekers?

3. As a corporate recruiter, you must know how to screen prospective employees. The Integrity Center Web site at **http://www.integctr.com** offers a brief tutorial on pre-employment screening, a glossary of key words and phrases, and related information. Prepare a short report that tells your assistant how to go about this process.

4. You've been asked to give a speech about the current status of affirmative action and equal employment to your company's managers. Starting with the Web site of the American Association for Affirmative Action (**http://www.affirmativeaction.org**) and its links to related sites, research the topic and prepare an outline for your talk. Include current legislation and recent court cases.

5. Web-based training is becoming popular at many companies as a way to bring a wider variety of courses to more people at lower costs. The Web-Based Training Information Center site at **http://www.filename.com/wbt** provides a good introduction. Learn about the basics of online training at its Primer page. Then link to the Resources section, complete a survey, and explore other areas that interest you.

CREATIVE THINKING CASE

"Do-It-Yourself" Human Resource Management at Spectrum Signal Processing

Some companies are now managing all or part of their human resource functions with employee teams. Martin McConnell decided that this was the way to go at Spectrum Signal Processing, Inc. McConnell is vice president of finance for Spectrum, a hardware and software designer with 155 employees in Burnaby, British Columbia. He says his company has no human resource department at all. Instead, it uses rotating human resource committees.

In a 1996 employee-satisfaction survey, Spectrum's managers discovered that its employees were not all that satisfied with the way the company was dealing with human resource issues. So Spectrum created a cross-functional employee team to focus on those issues. McConnell initially thought the committee would be only short term; it would deal with the immediate problems and then disband. "But it gained so much interest and momentum, it became part of our culture," he says.

Now the committee regularly discusses and addresses most of the company's typical human resource functions: performance appraisals and the employee handbook, as well as company training, recognition, mentoring, and orientation programs. (Payroll and benefits administration are handled by the accounting department.)

The committee consists of 12 elected members from various job functions. Member-involvement dates are staggered, so the committee is constantly getting new members and perspectives. McConnell and CEO Barry Jinks also serve on the team, albeit in an advisory role. According to group chair Carol Schulz, the bosses' presence doesn't present a hindrance. "They have the same say as anybody else," says Schulz. "Plus it gives employees the feeling that they really do care."

McConnell admits that at first he worried that the committee might establish some overly expensive policies. "But it's not us versus them," he says. "Whatever decision they made would be modified for what works for the environment. Or maybe we'd implement it in stages."

INFOTRAC
COLLEGE EDITION

Critical Thinking Questions

1. What are the advantages and possible disadvantages of a do-it-yourself human resource department?

2. Would this concept work at a large company like Ford Motor Co., or is it best suited for smaller organizations?

3. One problem that has surfaced at Spectrum is that serving on the committee takes a lot of time and distracts committee members from their jobs. McConnell is thinking about using a co-op student from a local university to do detail and legwork. Do you think that this is a good idea? Why or why not?

VIDEO CASE

Valassis Communications:
Matching People to the Company's Culture

Valassis Communications, Inc.(**http://www.valassis.com:**), headquartered in Livonia, Michigan, has been a leader in marketing services for over a quarter of a century. Valassis maintains that it has set the standard in its industry "for quality, reliability, service and expertise." A publicly held company with annual sales exceeding $740 million, Valassis has more than 1,300 employees across the United States and Canada.

The company's flagship product is the Free-Standing Insert (FSI), which is "distributed through newspapers to over 57 million households nearly every Sunday." The FSI is a booklet containing coupons, refunds, and other values from America's largest packaged goods companies. Other Valassis products include solo inserts that promote a single company's products or services; delivery of manufacturers' product samples and promotional messages through Sunday newspapers; direct placement of newspaper ads for clients; and oversight of clients' games and sweepstakes promotions.

Valassis Communications has a unique corporate culture that it calls "Change to Grow." The Change to Grow philosophy and culture are based on eight fundamental principles:

- Change is good.
- Don't point fingers—solve problems.
- Go—with speed.
- Create positive energy.
- Set the high bar high—don't fear failure.
- Be empowered, and be accountable.
- Communicate clearly and openly.
- Stick to fundamentals.

Executives at Valassis Communications believe the company's competitive advantage in the marketplace is based on its very capable and highly motivated employees. Accordingly, Valassis strives to match the abilities and motivation of the people it hires with the company's Change to Grow culture. With over 14,000 applicants for approximately 100 job openings annually, Valassis puts prospective employees through a rigorous screening and interview process to determine which individuals are most likely to embody and adhere to the eight fundamental principles of the "Change to Grow" culture.

Those who are fortunate enough to be hired by Valassis embark on unique career paths. The company does not "believe in rigid, standardized training methods or career paths, because . . . each employee has their own strengths, talents, and ultimate career goals."

Valassis also prefers to promote from within the company. Consequently, it invests heavily in employee training. Valassis University, a company-run educational program, "offers professional and personal development courses, as well as courses that cover specific areas and functions of the company. . . . Employees can work toward a variety of Valassis 'degrees' including a Bachelor and Master of Leadership." Valassis also supports continuing education for employees through an educational assistance reimbursement program.

When it comes to people, the bottom line for Valassis is to hire the right people through its recruitment and selection process and then to develop those people with appropriate training.

Critical Thinking Questions

1. What are the advantages of Valassis Communications' approach of hiring people with abilities and motivation that match the company's Change to Grow culture?
2. How does the Valassis approach to training and development help reinforce the company's culture?
3. Would you like to work for a company like Valassis Communications, given its Change to Grow culture? Why or why not?

Case: Value America Says Goodbye

Jennifer and Shawn Messmer were thrilled when Value America, a fast-growing Internet retailer, offered Jennifer a job as director of communications. Not only would Jennifer have a new job, but Value America also offered Shawn, a schoolteacher, a position in the company's merchandising department. It seemed like the perfect opportunity, so in September the couple packed up and moved to Value America's headquarters in Charlottesville, Virginia.

The three-year-old company sold everything from cheesecake to computers on its Web site. When a customer ordered a product, the order was sent directly to the product manufacturer who then shipped it to the customer. Founder Craig Winn had lined up top-notch investors in the firm, including Federal Express Chairman Fred Smith. Jennifer and Shawn weren't the only new employees. Sales were growing at 348 percent a year; to meet demand, the company had expanded its payroll by 78 percent in the past year alone.

On December 29, just four months after the Messmers had joined the company, all employees were summoned to a meeting at a local hotel. No one was quite sure why they were there. Maybe, some thought, the firm's executives were going to thank them for the long hours they'd just put in trying to process the rush of orders right before Christmas. Others, however, noticed an ominous sign. Instead of the soda, pizza, and snacks that were usually served at company meetings, only pitchers of water stood on the tables in the meeting room.

The company's new CEO, Glenda Dorchak, stood up in front of the room. Although sales were up, she said, the company was losing money at an alarming rate. The board of directors had decided that drastic measures were called for so, in addition to dropping 25 product categories from the Web site, 47 percent of Value America's staff—some 300 people—would be fired immediately. They were to return to their offices where their supervisors would let them know who would be laid off. Jennifer and Shawn Messmer both lost their jobs.

Questions for Critical Thinking

1. Suggest human resource strategies Value America could have used to avoid overstaffing.
2. In addition to financial considerations, what are some other human resource issues fast-growing Internet firms need to address when expanding their workforce?
3. Evaluate the effectiveness of Value America's method of terminating nearly half of its workforce. What effect do you think this had on remaining employees?

SOURCES: Keith Perine, "When Heads Roll," *The Standard* (May 8, 2000), downloaded from **http://www.thestandard.com**; Keith Perine, "Value America Files for Bankruptcy," *The Standard* (August 11, 2000), downloaded from **http://www.thestandard.com**.

learning goals

>lg 1   What are the basic principles of Frederick Taylor's concept of scientific management?

>lg 2   What did Elton Mayo's Hawthorne studies reveal about worker motivation?

>lg 3   What is Maslow's hierarchy of needs, and how do these needs relate to employee motivation?

>lg 4   How are McGregor's Theories X and Y used to explain worker motivation?

>lg 5   What are the basic components of Herzberg's motivator-hygiene theory?

>lg 6   What three contemporary theories on employee motivation offer insights into improving employee performance?

>lg 7   How can managers redesign existing jobs to increase employee motivation and performance?

>lg 8   What different types of teams are being used in organizations today?

>lg 9   What initiatives are organizations using today to motivate and retain employees?

Motivating Employees and Creating Self-Managed Teams

chapter 10

Motivating Employees at SAS Institute, Inc.

What would a company need to do to motivate you to work hard and stay committed? How would you feel about a 35-hour full-time workweek? What about two on-site day-care facilities so you'll know your children are safe and well cared for? And perhaps some fitness and recreational facilities to help you stay in shape and deal with job stress? Maybe a 36,000-square-foot gym, some pool and Ping-Pong tables, two basketball courts, a dance studio, and a yoga room? And to make workouts more convenient, your dirty gym clothes would be laundered for you each day. To help you stay healthy and happy, you might want full health insurance coverage (at no cost to you) and, of course, an on-site health clinic to make visiting the doctor more convenient. Are you motivated yet? Well, let's add on-site massages, elder-care referrals, casual dress every day of the week, and unlimited sick days. Not possible you say? Well, let me introduce you to SAS Institute, Inc. (**http://www.sas.com**), a software giant you've probably never heard of.[1]

On a secluded 200-acre campus in North Carolina is a company that believes in spoiling its employees. SAS Institute, the world's largest privately held software company,[2] has created a work environment that fosters intense loyalty. "I like happy people," explains co-founder, CEO, and majority owner James H. Goodnight, when discussing company perks such as bonuses, profit sharing, extra paid vacation time, private offices, fully stocked break rooms, discounted memberships to the local country club, and a pianist in the subsidized lunchroom. But the numbers tell the real story.

In a hypercompetitive industry where employee turnover is often around 20 percent, the annual turnover rate at SAS has hovered around 4 percent for years. High-performance employees at SAS seldom defect to the competition, and the company has hundreds of applications for any job openings. Revenue has increased by double-digit percentages each year for the past 24 years and went over $1 billion in 2000. The company is valued at about $5 billion, and Goodnight's personal net worth is an estimated $3.5 billion. Stanford University business professor Jeffrey Pfeffer has studied SAS and figures the company saves approximately $50 million a year from its low turnover rate. What may look like excessive employee coddling to outsiders makes good business sense to Goodnight. For instance, the free company clinic costs $1 million a year to operate, but that is about $500,000 less than the company would have to pay if employees were treated elsewhere.

The salaries at SAS are only average for the industry, and the company doesn't offer stock options like many of its high-tech competitors. Goodnight also refuses to pay sales commissions to SAS salespeople, claiming commissions encourage high-pressure sales tactics. Yet the company, recently named one of the "100 best companies to work for in America" by *Fortune* magazine,[3] is thriving. By providing a wide array of incentives that motivate SAS employees to achieve high levels of productivity and foster intense company loyalty, SAS seems to have found the magic formula.

Critical Thinking Questions

As you read this chapter, consider these questions as they relate to SAS Institute:

- Why don't most companies offer perks like those at SAS Institute?
- How do SAS Institute's generous benefits contribute to its low employee turnover rate?
- What else can SAS do to motivate its workers?

BUSINESS IN THE 21ˢᵀ CENTURY

People can be a firm's most important resource. They can also be the most challenging resource to manage well. Employees who are motivated and work hard to achieve personal and organizational goals can become a crucial competitive advantage for a firm. The key then is understanding the process of motivation, *what* motivates individuals, and *how* an organization like SAS can create a workplace that allows people to perform to the best of their abilities. Motivation is basically a need-satisfying process. A need is the lack of something, the gap between what is and what one desires. An unsatisfied need pushes (motivates) the individual to pursue behavior that will result in the need being met.

Successful managers help employees to achieve organizational goals and guide workers through the motivation process using the leadership skills discussed in Chapter 6. To succeed, managers must understand human relations, how employees interact with one another, and how managers interact with employees to improve effectiveness. Human relations skills include the ability to motivate, lead, communicate, build morale, and teach others. This chapter presents the traditional theories on human motivation and the modern application of these theories. We also explore the use of teams in creating and maintaining a motivated workforce.

THE EVOLUTION OF MOTIVATION THEORY

How can managers and organizations promote enthusiastic job performance, high productivity, and job satisfaction? Many studies of human behavior in organizations have contributed to our current understanding of these issues. A look at the evolution of management theory and research shows how managers have arrived at the practices used today to manage human behavior in the workplace. A sampling of the most influential of these theorists and research studies are discussed in this section.

Frederick Taylor's Scientific Management

>lg 1

scientific management

A system of management developed by Frederick W. Taylor and based on four principles: developing a scientific approach for each element of a job, scientifically selecting and training workers, encouraging cooperation between workers and managers, and dividing work and responsibility between management and workers according to who can better perform a particular task.

One of the most influential figures of the *classical era* of management, which lasted from about 1900 to the mid-1930s, was Frederick W. Taylor, a mechanical engineer sometimes called the "father of **scientific management.**" Taylor's approach to improved performance was based on economic incentives and the premise that there is "one best way" to perform any job. As a manager at the Midvale and Bethlehem Steel companies in Philadelphia in the early 1900s, Taylor was frustrated at the inefficiency of the laborers working in the mills.

Convinced that productivity could be improved, Taylor studied the individual jobs in the mill and redesigned the equipment and the methods used by workers. Taylor timed each job with a stopwatch and broke down every task into separate movements. He then prepared an instruction sheet telling exactly how each job should be done, how much time it should take, and what motions and tools should be used. Taylor's ideas led to dramatic increases in productivity in the steel mills and resulted in the development of four basic principles of scientific management:

Employers of factory workers in the early 1900s applied scientific methods to improve productivity. During this classical era of management, employers believed employee performance was motivated only by economic incentives.

1. Develop a scientific approach for each element of a person's job.
2. Scientifically select, train, teach, and develop workers.
3. Encourage cooperation between workers and managers so that each job can be accomplished in a standard, scientifically determined way.
4. Divide work and responsibility between management and workers according to who is better suited to each task.

Taylor published his ideas in *The Principles of Scientific Management*. His pioneering work vastly increased production efficiency and contributed to the specialization of labor and the assembly-line method of production. Taylor's approach is still being used nearly a century later in companies such as United Parcel Service (UPS), where industrial engineers maximize efficiency by carefully studying every step of the delivery process looking for the quickest possible way to deliver packages to customers. Though Taylor's work was a giant step forward in the evolution of management, it had a fundamental flaw in that it assumed that all people are primarily motivated by economic means. Taylor's successors in the study of management found that motivation is much more complex than he envisioned.

Want to find out more about organizational efficiency at United Parcel Service? Visit
http://www.ups.com

The Hawthorne Studies

>lg 2

The classical era of management was followed by the *human relations era,* which began in the 1930s and focused primarily on how human behavior and relations affect organizational performance. The new era was ushered in by the Hawthorne studies, which changed the way many managers thought about motivation, job productivity, and employee satisfaction. The studies began when engineers at the Hawthorne Western Electric plant decided to examine the effects of varying levels of light on worker productivity—an experiment that might have interested Frederick Taylor. The engineers expected brighter light to lead to increased productivity, but the results showed that varying the level of light in either direction (brighter or dimmer) led to increased output from the experimental group. In 1927, the Hawthorne engineers asked Harvard professor Elton Mayo and a team of researchers to join them in their investigation.

From 1927 to 1932, Mayo and his colleagues conducted experiments on job redesign, length of workday and workweek, length of break times, and incentive plans. The results of the studies indicated that increases in performance were tied to a complex set of employee attitudes. Mayo claimed that both experimental and control groups from the plant had developed a sense of group pride because they had been selected to participate in the studies. The pride that came from this special attention motivated the workers to increase their productivity. Supervisors who allowed the employees to have some

Hawthorne effect

The phenomenon that employees perform better when they feel singled out for attention or feel that management is concerned about their welfare.

control over their situation appeared to further increase the workers' motivation. These findings gave rise to what is now known as the **Hawthorne effect,** which suggests that employees will perform better when they feel singled out for special attention or feel that management is concerned about employee welfare. The studies also provided evidence that informal work groups (the social relationships of employees) and the resulting group pressure have positive effects on group productivity. The results of the Hawthorne studies enhanced our understanding of what motivates individuals in the workplace. They indicate that in addition to the personal economic needs emphasized in the classical era, social needs play an important role in influencing work-related attitudes and behaviors.

Maslow's Hierarchy of Needs

>lg 3

Another well-known theorist from the behavioral era of management history, psychologist Abraham Maslow, proposed a theory of motivation based on universal human needs. Maslow believed that each individual has a hierarchy of needs, consisting of physiological, safety, social, esteem, and self-actualization needs, as shown in Exhibit 10-1.

e x h i b i t   1 0 - 1 | Maslow's Hierarchy of Needs

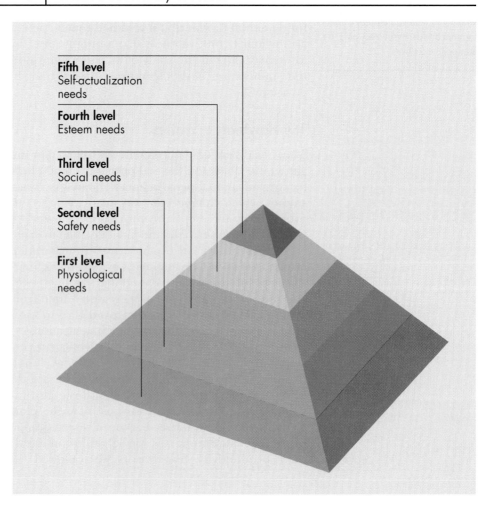

Fifth level
Self-actualization needs

Fourth level
Esteem needs

Third level
Social needs

Second level
Safety needs

First level
Physiological needs

Maslow's theory of motivation contends that people act to satisfy their unmet needs. When you're hungry, for instance, you look for and eat food, thus satisfying a basic physiological need. Once a need is satisfied, its importance to the individual diminishes, and a higher-level need is more likely to motivate the person.

Maslow's hierarchy of needs

A theory of motivation developed by Abraham Maslow; holds that humans have five levels of needs and act to satisfy their unmet needs. At the base of the hierarchy are fundamental physiological needs, followed in order by safety, social, esteem, and self-actualization needs.

According to **Maslow's hierarchy of needs,** the most basic human needs are physiological needs, that is, the needs for food, shelter, and clothing. In large part, it is the physiological needs that motivate a person to find a job. People need to earn money to provide food, shelter, and clothing for themselves and their families. Once people have met these basic needs, they reach the second level in Maslow's hierarchy, which is safety needs. People need to feel secure, to be protected from physical harm, and to avoid the unexpected. In work terms, they need job security and protection from work hazards. Companies such as Southwest Airlines, Harley-Davidson, and FedEx help meet employees' safety needs with their official "no layoffs" policies.[4]

Find out more about three companies that made *Fortune* magazine's "100 best companies to work for" by visiting

http://www.southwest.com, http://www.harleydavidson.com, and http://www.fedex.com

Physiological needs and safety are physical needs. Once these are satisfied, individuals focus on needs that involve relationships with other people. At Maslow's third level are social needs, or needs for belonging (acceptance by others) and for giving and receiving friendship and love. Informal social groups on and off the job help people satisfy these needs. At the fourth level in Maslow's hierarchy are esteem needs, which are needs for the respect of others and for a sense of accomplishment and achievement.

Finally, at the highest level in Maslow's hierarchy are self-actualization needs, or needs for fulfillment, for living up to one's potential, and for using one's abilities to the utmost. The Army recruiting slogan "Be all that you can be" describes the human need for self-actualization.

Managers who accept Maslow's ideas attempt to improve employee motivation by modifying organizational and managerial practices to increase the likelihood that employees will meet all levels of needs. Maslow's theory has also helped managers understand that it is hard to motivate people by appealing to already satisfied needs. For instance, overtime pay may not motivate employees who earn a high wage and value their leisure time.

McGregor's Theories X and Y

>lg 4

Theory X

A management style, formulated by Douglas McGregor, that is based on a pessimistic view of human nature and assumes that the average person dislikes work, will avoid it if possible, prefers to be directed, avoids responsibility, and wants security above all.

Douglas McGregor, one of Maslow's students, influenced the study of motivation with his formulation of two contrasting sets of assumptions about human nature—Theory X and Theory Y.

The **Theory X** management style is based on a pessimistic view of human nature and assumes the following:

- The average person dislikes work and will avoid it if possible.
- Because people don't like to work, they must be controlled, directed, or threatened with punishment to get them to make an effort.
- The average person prefers to be directed, avoids responsibility, is relatively unambitious, and wants security above all else.

This view of people suggests that managers must constantly prod workers to perform and must closely control their on-the-job behavior. Theory X managers tell people what to do, are very directive, like to be in control, and show little confidence in employees. They often foster dependent, passive, and resentful subordinates.

In contrast, a **Theory Y** management style is based on a more optimistic view of human nature and assumes the following:

Theory Y

A management style, formulated by Douglas McGregor, that is based on a relatively optimistic view of human nature; assumes that the average person wants to work, accepts responsibility, is willing to help solve problems, and can be self-directed and self-controlled.

- Work is as natural as play or rest. People want to and can be self-directed and self-controlled and will try to achieve organizational goals they believe in.
- Workers can be motivated using positive incentives and will try hard to accomplish organizational goals if they believe they will be rewarded for doing so.
- Under proper conditions, the average person not only accepts responsibility but seeks it out. Most workers have a relatively high degree of imagination and creativity and are willing to help solve problems.

Managers who operate on Theory Y assumptions recognize individual differences and encourage workers to learn and develop their skills. A secretary might be given the responsibility for generating a monthly report. The reward for doing so might be recognition at a meeting, a special training class to enhance computer skills, or a pay increase. In short, the Theory Y approach builds on the idea that worker and organizational interests are congruent. Marilyn Nelson, CEO of Carlson Co., is determined to create a corporate culture based on Theory Y assumptions.[5] Carlson Co. is one of the largest privately held companies in the world, with holdings that include Radisson Hotels, TGI Friday's franchises, and Carlson Wagonlit Travel. CEO Nelson is determined to replace the patriarchal micro-management style of her father (and predecessor) with leadership that empowers all levels of employees. Nelson's motto is "I want to lead with love, not fear," and she is changing the company culture by introducing expanded benefits, profit sharing, flextime schedules, and on-site day care.

motivating factors

Intrinsic job elements that lead to worker satisfaction.

hygiene factors

Extrinsic elements of the work environment that do not serve as a source of employee satisfaction or motivation.

>lg 5

Herzberg's Motivator-Hygiene Theory

Another important contribution to our understanding of individual motivation came from Frederick Herzberg's studies, which addressed the question, "What do people really want from their work experience?" In the late 1950s Herzberg surveyed numerous employees to find out what particular work elements made them feel exceptionally good or bad about their jobs. The results indicated that certain job factors are consistently related to employee job satisfaction while others can create job dissatisfaction. According to Herzberg, **motivating factors** (also called *job satisfiers*) are primarily intrinsic job elements that lead to satisfaction. **Hygiene factors** (also called *job dissatisfiers*) are extrinsic elements of the work environment. A summary of motivating and hygiene factors appears in Exhibit 10-2.

One of the most interesting results of Herzberg's studies was the implication that the opposite of satisfaction is not dissatisfaction. Herzberg believed that proper management of hygiene factors could prevent employee dissatisfaction, but that these factors could not serve as a source of satisfaction or motivation.

According to Herzberg's motivation theory, the job factors that motivate these Pacific Bell employees who install fiber optic cable are the work itself, achievement, recognition, responsibility, advancement, and growth.

Motivating Factors	Hygiene Factors
Achievement	Company policy
Recognition	Supervision
Work itself	Working conditions
Responsibility	Interpersonal relationships at work
Advancement	Salary and benefits
Growth	Job security

concept check

- What are the four principles of scientific management?
- What did Elton Mayo's studies reveal about employee productivity?
- How can a manager use an understanding of Maslow's hierarchy to motivate employees?
- How do the Theory X and Theory Y management styles differ?
- What is the difference between job satisfiers and job dissatisfiers?

expectancy theory

A theory of motivation that holds that the probability of an individual acting in a particular way depends on the strength of that individual's belief that the act will have a particular outcome and on whether the individual values that outcome.

Good working conditions, for instance, will keep employees at a job but won't make them work harder. But poor working conditions, which are job dissatisfiers, may make employees quit. According to Herzberg, a manager who wants to increase employee satisfaction needs to focus on the motivating factors, or satisfiers. A job with many satisfiers will usually motivate workers, provide job satisfaction, and prompt effective performance. But a lack of job satisfiers doesn't always lead to dissatisfaction and poor performance; instead, a lack of job satisfiers may merely lead to workers doing an adequate job, rather than their best.

CONTEMPORARY VIEWS ON MOTIVATION

The early management scholars laid a foundation that enabled managers to better understand their workers and how best to motivate them. Since then, new theories have given us an even better understanding of worker motivation. Three of these theories are explained in this section: the expectancy theory, the equity theory, and the goal-setting theory.

Expectancy Theory

One of the best-supported and most widely accepted theories of motivation is expectancy theory, which focuses on the link between motivation and behavior. According to **expectancy theory,** the probability of an individual acting in a particular way depends on the strength of that individual's belief that the act will have a particular outcome and on whether the individual values that outcome. The degree to which an employee is motivated depends on three important relationships, shown in Exhibit 10-3:

1. The link between *effort and performance,* or the strength of the individual's expectation that a certain amount of effort will lead to a certain level of performance.
2. The link between *performance and outcome,* or the strength of the expectation that a certain level of performance will lead to a particular outcome.
3. The link between *outcomes and individual needs,* or the degree to which the individual expects the anticipated outcome to satisfy personal needs. Some outcomes have more valence, or value, to individuals than others do.

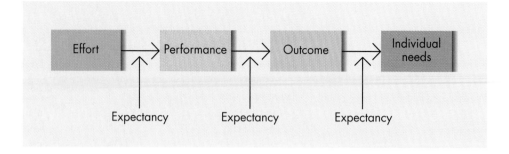

Based on the expectancy theory, managers should do the following to motivate employees:[6]

- Determine the rewards valued by each employee.
- Determine the desired performance level and then communicate it clearly to employees.
- Make the performance level attainable.
- Link rewards to performance.
- Determine what factors might counteract the effectiveness of an award.
- Make sure the reward is adequate for the level of performance.

For an example of expectancy theory at work, see the discussion of Trilogy Software in the Focusing on Small Business box on the next page.

Equity Theory

equity theory

A theory of motivation that holds that worker satisfaction is influenced by employees' perceptions about how fairly they are treated compared with their coworkers.

Another contemporary explanation of motivation, **equity theory** is based on individuals' perceptions about how fairly they are treated compared with their coworkers. Equity means justice or fairness, and in the workplace it refers to employees' perceived fairness of the way they are treated and the rewards they earn. Employees evaluate their own *outcomes* (e.g., salary, benefits) in relation to their *inputs* (e.g., number of hours worked, education, and training) and then compare the outcomes-to-inputs ratio to one of the following: (1) the employee's own past experience in a different position in the current organization, (2) the employee's own past experience in a different organization, (3) another employee's experience inside the current organization, or (4) another employee's experience outside the organization.

According to equity theory, if employees perceive that an inequity exists, they will make one of the following choices:

- *Change their work habits* (exert less effort on the job).
- *Change their job benefits and income* (ask for a raise, steal from the employer).
- *Distort their perception of themselves* ("I always thought I was smart, but now I realize I'm a lot smarter than my coworkers").
- *Distort their perceptions of others* ("Joe's position is really much less flexible than mine").
- *Look at the situation from a different perspective* ("I don't make as much as the other department heads, but I make a lot more than most graphic artists").
- *Leave the situation* (quit the job).

Managers can use equity theory to improve worker satisfaction. Knowing that every employee seeks equitable and fair treatment, managers can make an

FOCUSING ON SMALL BUSINESS

TRILOGY REWARDS RISK TAKERS

Does expectancy theory really explain employee motivation? A visit to Trilogy Software, Inc. in Austin, Texas, might convince you that it does. Joe Liemandt, the 33-year-old founder and CEO of Trilogy, is an entrepreneur with a vision, as well as a knack for motivating high-performing employees. In Liemandt's words, "at a software company, people are everything," so Trilogy focuses on recruiting the best people it can find, getting those recruits "up to speed" as quickly as possible, and then turning them loose so they can make immediate contributions. But once it has wooed them, how does Trilogy get its people to stay? That's where the expectancy model comes in.

According to expectancy theory, employees will be motivated when three important factors are addressed. First, Liemandt makes sure Trilogy recruits feel confident that exerting a given level of effort will result in a certain level of performance. Liemandt hires the most talented graduates he can find and thrusts responsibility on them immediately, giving them the power to make decisions and the resources to implement their decisions. Liemandt calls this the "just-do-it-now" spirit.

Expectancy theory is based not only on the link between effort and performance, but also on the link between *performance and outcomes*. Here again Liemandt has succeeded in creating a workplace conducive to high levels of motivation. On arriving at the company, all Trilogy recruits take part in a six- to eight-week "boot camp" called Industrial Trilogy University.

Liemandt's goal is to develop creative people who work well in teams, adapt swiftly to changes in customer demands, and are willing to take risks. New employees are immediately shown the clear link between performance and rewards. At the end of "boot camp," Liemandt takes 300 new employees on an all-expenses-paid trip to Las Vegas as a reward for their hard work.

The last component of expectancy theory is the *valence* of employee outcomes or rewards. Employees must meet very high performance goals, but if they do, the rewards include high salaries, bonuses, stock options, and participation in a unique corporate culture. Trilogy employees wear what they want, set their own hours, and socialize at the weekly company-sponsored happy hour. For some employees, the best reward of all is the chance to work with people like themselves—people who are creative, talented, and ambitious. In the words of one new recruit, "Trilogy hires people who are smart, talented, interesting, and cool. Those are exactly the sort of people I want to be around."

Critical Thinking Questions

1. Do you think expectancy theory works best in high-tech companies like Trilogy?
2. How does Liemandt's taking new employees to Las Vegas fit into expectancy theory?
3. Do you think that you would be highly motivated if you worked for Trilogy?

---

goal-setting theory
A theory of motivation based on the premise that an individual's intention to work toward a goal is a primary source of motivation.

Are you bright, talented, and ambitious? Are you willing to take a risk? Find out how to become a Trilogian by visiting

http://www.trilogy.com

effort to understand an employee's perceptions of fairness and take steps to reduce concerns about inequity.

Goal-Setting Theory

Goal-setting theory is based on the premise that an individual's intention to work toward a goal is a primary source of motivation. Once set, the goal clarifies for the employee what needs to be accomplished and how much effort will be required for completion. The theory has three main components: (1) specific goals lead to a higher level of performance than do more generalized goals ("do your best"); (2) more difficult goals lead to better performance than do easy goals (provided the individual accepts the goal); and (3) feedback on progress toward the goal enhances performance. Feedback is particularly important because it helps the individual identify the gap between the *real* (the actual performance) and the *ideal* (the desired outcome defined by the goal).

Bruce Tulgan, founder of Rainmaker Thinking, a consulting firm, emphasizes the relationship between goal achievement and feedback in his book *FAST Feedback.*[7] According to Tulgan, feedback that allows employees to meet their goals is FAST—frequent, accurate, specific, and timely. Because businesses operate in a dynamic environment, FAST feedback is necessary to ensure that employees stay in tune with what is working and what needs to be changed.[8] Managers can help employees meet goals by creating a feedback system based on day-to-day interactions and a variety of communication channels, such as routine meetings, memos, social events, e-mail, and voice mail.

Given the trend toward employee empowerment in the workplace, more and more employees are participating in the goal-setting process. Are employees who set their own work goals more motivated to achieve them? Research on the benefits of shared goal setting versus assigned goals has produced mixed results. Still, it is clear that when employees are encouraged to participate in the goal-setting process, they are more likely to accept a goal as desirable, especially if the goal is difficult.

concept check

- Discuss the three relationships central to expectancy theory.
- Explain the comparison process that is a part of equity theory.
- How does goal-setting theory contribute to our understanding of motivation?

FROM MOTIVATION THEORY TO APPLICATION

>lg 7

The material presented thus far in this chapter demonstrates the wide variety of theorists and research studies that have contributed to our current understanding of employee motivation. Now we turn our attention to more practical matters, to ways that these concepts can be applied in the workplace to meet organizational goals and improve individual performance.

Motivational Job Design

How might managers redesign or modify existing jobs to increase employee motivation and performance? The following three options have been used extensively in the workplace.

The horizontal expansion of a job, increasing the number and variety of tasks that a person performs is called **job enlargement.** Increasing task diversity can enhance job satisfaction, particularly when the job is mundane and repetitive in nature. A potential drawback to job enlargement is that employees may perceive that they are being asked to work harder and do more with no change in their level of responsibility or compensation. This can cause resentment and lead to dissatisfaction.

Job enrichment is the vertical expansion of an employee's job. Whereas job enlargement addresses the breadth or scope of a job, enrichment attempts to increase job depth by providing the employee with more autonomy, responsibility, and decision-making authority. In an enriched job, the employee can use a variety of talents and skills and has more control over the planning, execution, and evaluation of the required tasks. In general, job enrichment has been found to increase job satisfaction and reduce absenteeism and turnover.

Also called *cross-training,* **job rotation** is the shifting of workers from one job to another. This may be done to broaden an employee's skill base or because an employee has ceased to be interested in or challenged by a particular job. The organization may benefit from job rotation because it increases flexibility in scheduling and production, since employees can be shifted to cover for absent workers or changes in production or operations. It is also a valuable tool for training lower-level managers in a variety of functional areas. Drawbacks of job rotation include an increase in training costs and decreased productivity while employees are getting "up to speed" in new task areas.

job enlargement

The horizontal expansion of a job by increasing the number and variety of tasks that a person performs.

job enrichment

The vertical expansion of a job by increasing the employee's autonomy, responsibility, and decision-making authority.

job rotation

The shifting of workers from one job to another; also called *cross-training.*

Work-Scheduling Options

As companies try to meet the needs of a diverse workforce and retain quality employees, while remaining competitive and financially prosperous, managers are challenged to find new ways to keep workers motivated and satisfied. Increasingly popular are alternatives to the traditional work schedule, such as the compressed workweek, flextime, job sharing, and telecommuting.

One option for employees who want to maximize their leisure hours, indulge in three-day weekends, and avoid commuting during morning and evening rush hours is the compressed workweek. Employees work the traditional 40 hours, but fit those hours into a shorter workweek. Most common is the 4-40 schedule, where employees work four 10-hour days a week. By the mid-1990s, 25 percent of large U.S. companies offered a compressed workweek to some of their employees, double the percentage in the late 1980s.[9] Organizations that offer this option claim benefits ranging from increased motivation and productivity to reduced absenteeism and turnover.

Another scheduling option, called flextime, allows employees to decide what their work hours will be. Employees are generally expected to work a certain number of hours per week, but have some discretion as to when they arrive at work and when they leave for the day. The flexible work hours schedule offers many of the benefits of the compressed workweek, including increased morale and productivity and reduced absenteeism.

job sharing

A scheduling option that allows two individuals to split the tasks, responsibilities, and work hours of one 40-hour-per-week job.

Job sharing is a scheduling option that allows two individuals to split the tasks, responsibilities, and work hours of one 40-hour-per-week job. Though used less frequently than flextime and the compressed workweek, this option can also provide employees with job flexibility. The primary benefit to the company is that it gets "two for the price of one"—the company can draw on two sets of skills and abilities to accomplish one set of job objectives.

Recognition, Empowerment, and Economic Incentives

All employees have unique needs that they seek to fulfill through their jobs. Organizations must devise a wide array of incentives to ensure that a broad spectrum of employee needs can be addressed in the work environment, thus increasing the likelihood of motivated employees. A sampling of these motivational tools is discussed here.

Formal recognition of superior effort by individuals or groups in the workplace is one way to enhance employee motivation. Recognition serves as positive feedback and reinforcement, letting employees know what they have done well and that their contribution is valued by the organization. Some companies use formal awards ceremonies to acknowledge and celebrate their employees' accomplishments. Others take advantage of informal interaction to congratulate employees on a job well done and offer encouragement for the future.

Employee empowerment, sometimes called employee involvement or participative management, involves delegating decision-making authority to employees at all levels of the organization. Employees are given greater responsibility for planning, implementing, and evaluating the results of decisions. Empowerment is based on the premise that human resources, especially at lower levels in the firm, are an underutilized asset.

variable pay

A system of paying employees in which a portion of an employee's pay is directly linked to an individual or organizational performance measure.

Any discussion of motivation has to include the use of monetary incentives to enhance performance. Currently, companies are using a variety of variable-pay programs such as piece-rate plans, profit sharing, gain sharing, and bonuses to encourage employees to be more productive. Unlike the standard salary or hourly wage, **variable pay** means that a portion of an employee's pay is directly linked to an individual or organizational performance measure. In *piece-rate pay plans,* for example, employees are paid a given amount for each unit they produce, directly linking the amount they earn to their productivity. *Profit-sharing plans* are based on

concept check

- Explain the difference between job enlargement and job enrichment.
- What are the four work-scheduling options that can enhance employee performance?
- Are all employees motivated by the same economic incentives? Explain.

overall company profitability. Using an established formula, management distributes some portion of company profits to all employees. *Gain-sharing plans* are incentive programs based on group productivity. Employees share in the financial gains attributed to the increased productivity of their group. This encourages employees to increase productivity within their specific work area regardless of the overall profit picture for the organization as a whole. A *bonus* is simply a one-time lump-sum monetary reward.

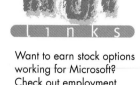

USING TEAMS TO ENHANCE MOTIVATION AND PERFORMANCE

>lg 8

One of the most apparent trends in business today is the use of teams to accomplish organizational goals. Using a team-based structure can increase individual and group motivation and performance. This section gives a brief overview of group behavior, defines work teams as specific types of groups, and provides suggestions for creating high-performing teams.

Understanding Group Behavior

Teams are a specific type of organizational group. Every organization contains *groups,* social units of two or more people who share the same goals and cooperate to achieve those goals. Understanding some fundamental concepts related to group behavior and group processes provides a good foundation for understanding concepts about work teams. Groups can be formal or informal in nature. Formal groups are designated and sanctioned by the organization; their behavior is directed toward accomplishing organizational goals. Informal groups are based on social relationships and are not determined or sanctioned by the organization.

Formal organizational groups must operate within the larger organizational system. To some degree, elements of the larger system, such as organizational strategy, policies and procedures, available resources, and corporate culture, determine the behavior of smaller groups within the organization. Other factors that affect the behavior of organizational groups are individual member characteristics (e.g., ability, training, personality), the roles and norms of group members, and the size and cohesiveness of the group. Norms are the implicit behavioral guidelines of the group, or the standards for acceptable and nonacceptable behavior. These standards are conveyed through socialization, a process by which new group members learn:

- The basic goals of the group.
- The preferred means for reaching those goals.
- The behavior patterns expected for effective performance within the group.
- The basic rules and attitudes that help maintain the group's identity and integrity.

Work socialization occurs both formally in training programs and informally by watching and talking with other group members. Group performance is related to how rapidly new members are socialized.

Group cohesiveness refers to the degree to which group members want to stay in the group and tend to resist outside influences (such as a change in

group cohesiveness
The degree to which group members want to stay in the group and tend to resist outside influences.

company policies). When group performance norms are high, group cohesiveness will have a positive impact on productivity. Cohesiveness tends to increase when the size of the group is small, individual and group goals are congruent, the group has high status in the organization, rewards are group-based rather than individual-based, and the group competes with other groups within the organization. Work group cohesiveness can benefit the organization in several ways including increased productivity, enhanced worker self-image because of group success, increased company loyalty, reduced employee turnover, and reduced absenteeism. On the other hand, cohesiveness can also lead to restricted output, resistance to change, and conflict with other work groups in the organization.

The opportunity to turn the decision-making process over to a group with diverse skills and abilities is one of the arguments for using work groups (and teams) in organizational settings. For group decision making to be most effective, however, both managers and group members must acknowledge its strengths and weaknesses (see Exhibit 10-4).

Work Groups versus Work Teams

We have already noted that teams are a special type of organizational group, but we also need to differentiate between work groups and work teams. **Work groups** share resources and coordinate efforts to help members better perform their individual duties and responsibilities. The performance of the group can be evaluated by adding up the contributions of the individual group members. **Work teams** require not only coordination but also *collaboration*, the pooling of knowledge, skills, abilities, and resources in a collective effort to attain a common goal. A work team creates *synergy*, causing the performance of the team as a whole to be greater than the sum of team members' individual contributions. Simply assigning employees to groups and labeling them a team does not guarantee a positive outcome. Managers and team members must be committed to creating, developing, and maintaining high-performance work teams. Factors that contribute to their success are discussed later in this section.

Types of Teams

The evolution of the team concept in organizations can be seen in three basic types of work teams: problem solving, self-managed, and cross-functional. Japanese companies used problem-solving teams, known as quality circles, as

work groups

Groups of employees who share resources and coordinate efforts so as to help members better perform their individual duties and responsibilities. The performance of the group can be evaluated by adding up the contributions of the individual group members.

work teams

Groups of employees who not only coordinate their efforts, but also collaborate by pooling their knowledge, skills, abilities, and resources in a collective effort to attain a common goal; causing the performance of the team to be greater than the sum of the members' individual efforts.

e x h i b i t   1 0 - 4 | Strengths and Weaknesses of Group Decision Making

Strengths	Weaknesses
• Groups bring more information and knowledge to the decision process.	• Groups typically take a longer time to reach a solution than an individual takes.
• Groups offer a diversity of perspectives and, therefore, generate a greater number of alternatives.	• Group members may pressure others to conform, reducing the likelihood of disagreement.
• Group decision making results in a higher-quality decision than individual decision making.	• The process may be dominated by one or a small number of participants.
• Participation of group members increases the likelihood that a decision will be accepted.	• Groups lack accountability, because it is difficult to assign responsibility for outcomes to any one individual.

Members of formal work groups share the same organizational goals and work together to achieve those goals. Group members are guided by norms that dictate acceptable behavior needed to accomplish effective group performance.

problem-solving teams

Teams of employees from the same department or area of expertise and from the same level of the organizational hierarchy who meet regularly to share information and discuss ways to improve processes and procedures in specific functional areas.

self-managed work teams

Highly autonomous teams of employees who manage themselves without any formal supervision and take responsibility for setting goals, planning and scheduling work activities, selecting team members, and evaluating team performance.

cross-functional teams

Teams of employees who are from about the same level in the organizational hierarchy but from different functional areas; for example, task forces, organizational committees, and project teams.

early as the 1950s to improve quality and efficiency in manufacturing processes. **Problem-solving teams** are typically made up of employees from the same department or area of expertise and from the same level of the organizational hierarchy. They meet on a regular basis to share information and discuss ways to improve processes and procedures in specific functional areas. Problem-solving teams generate ideas and alternatives and may recommend a specific course of action, but they typically do not make final decisions, allocate resources, or implement change.

Many organizations that experienced success using problem-solving teams were willing to expand the team concept to allow team members greater responsibility in making decisions, implementing solutions, and monitoring outcomes. These highly autonomous groups are called **self-managed work teams.** They manage themselves without any formal supervision, taking responsibility for setting goals, planning and scheduling work activities, selecting team members, and evaluating team performance. PepsiCo, Hewlett-Packard, and Xerox are just a few of the well-known, highly successful companies using self-managed work teams.

The most recent adaptation of the team concept is called a **cross-functional team.** These teams are made up of employees from about the same hierarchical level, but different functional areas of the organization. Many task forces, organizational committees, and project teams are cross-functional. Often the team members work together only until they solve a given problem or complete a specific project. Cross-functional teams allow people with various levels and areas of expertise to pool their resources, develop new ideas, solve problems, and coordinate complex projects. Both problem-solving teams and self-managed teams may also be cross-functional teams. The Applying Technology box describes yet another type of team that is becoming more common—the virtual team.

Visit Harley-Davidson's 2000 annual report at http://www.harleydavidson.com to learn how the circle organizational design promotes interdependent work teams.

Building High-Performance Teams

What are the factors that contribute to highly motivated and productive teams? Based on a study of teams in organizations, researchers have identified some basic building blocks of high-performance teams: (1) the skills of team members, (2) the accountability of the team, and (3) the commitment of the team members.[10] Exhibit 10-5 identifies some specific aspects of those building blocks that contribute to high performance.

The following are some guidelines for enhancing team performance:[11]

• Team work assignments should focus on specific, concrete issues.

MAKING ETHICAL CHOICES

ARE TEAMWORK AND EMPOWERMENT FOR EVERYONE?

Eaton Corp.'s plant in South Bend, Indiana, makes heavy-duty transmission gears. The manufacturing process requires employees to perform some very hot, heavy, noisy, dirty jobs. Large forge presses stamp hot steel into various shapes for transmission gear blanks. Long-handled tongs are used to lift white-hot parts and work them across the dies in the forge presses. The presses are so noisy that workers must communicate with hand signals.

Job success at Eaton's South Bend plant depends on teamwork. Each of the 106 employees is on at least three teams as well as a functional team. Work teams are self-directing; the employees are their own bosses. Employees are empowered to solve problems on their own, and they are expected to enforce the work rules themselves. Although there are no bosses, everyone watches everyone else, and "it can feel like having a hundred bosses."

Effective empowerment and teamwork at the South Bend plant rest on four pillars: trust, respect, communication, and involvement. Eaton's culture of empowerment, though resilient, is also delicate: a single breach of trust, respect, communication, or involvement can cause distrust to enter and the culture to atrophy.

Eaton's employees are expected to assume a great deal of responsibility in performing their jobs. As Alexander Cutler, Eaton's president and CEO, observes, however, "[T]he admission ticket for this kind of responsibility is accountability—and not everyone necessarily wants accountability." Indeed, some people try to work around the system, finding subtle ways to resist policies that they dislike. For instance, one worker refuses to note any problems when he does the daily locker check as part of the plant's general cleanliness campaign. His reasoning is that he is empowered and he is making the decision to ignore any problems.

The bottom line for Eaton is twofold: many workers thrive in a culture of teamwork and empowerment, but some discover that this culture is not for them.

Critical Thinking Questions

1. Does Eaton—or any business that relies on a culture of empowerment and teamwork—have an ethical responsibility to ensure that employees fit in with the culture and are motivated by it? Explain your answer.
2. Do employees of businesses like Eaton's South Bend plant have an ethical responsibility to do everything possible to function effectively as empowered team members? Explain your answer.

e x h i b i t 1 0 - 5 | Building Blocks of High-Performance Teams

Skills	Accountability	Commitment
• Problem solving	• Small number of members	• Specific goals
• Technical/functional	• Mutual accountability	• Common approach
• Interpersonal	• Individual accountability	• Meaningful purpose

concept check

- What is the difference between a work team and a work group?
- Identify and describe three types of work teams.
- What are some ways to build a high-performance team?

- Work should be broken down and delegated to individuals or subgroups (teams are not the same as group meetings).
- Team membership should be based on skills and abilities rather than formal authority or organizational position.
- Team members should do roughly the same amount of work to maintain equity within the group.
- Traditional hierarchical patterns of communication and interaction must be broken down.
- Teams must work to create an atmosphere of openness, commitment, and trust.

APPLYING TECHNOLOGY

VIRTUAL TEAMS

Increasing globalization and advances in information technology are changing the competitive landscape and forcing organizations to reevaluate organizational structures and work processes. Downsizing is common, and many organizations have become increasingly decentralized and geographically dispersed. The problem? Given these trends, it has become more and more challenging for organizations to retain the advantages of team-based organizational structures. The answer? Virtual teams.

Virtual teams are made up of employees in different geographic or organizational locations who come together as a team via a combination of telecommunications and information technologies. Virtual teams work together to accomplish a common goal, but rarely (if ever) meet in a face-to-face setting. Membership is often dynamic, changing to accommodate project or task requirements. The emergence of virtual teams can be attributed to five factors:

1. The increase in flat (horizontal) organizational structures.
2. Increased interorganizational cooperation (e.g., strategic alliances).
3. Changing employee expectations regarding the use of technology (i.e., increased technological sophistication).
4. The ongoing shift from production to service/ knowledge work environments.
5. The increasing globalization of business activities.

Virtual teams can exist because of relatively recent advances in computer and telecommunications technology. The infrastructure of virtual teamwork is made up of three basic types of technology: desktop videoconferencing systems (DVCS), collaborative software systems, and Internet/Intranet systems. These technologies allow virtual team members to interact and facilitate the accomplishment of complex work assignments.

Virtual teams provide an exciting opportunity to change the way in which work gets done, but they also present unique management challenges:

- The lack of traditional social interaction that facilitates trust and commitment.
- Increased team diversity (e.g., geographic location, language, culture, functional area, company outsiders).
- The need for team members to be technologically savvy.
- Increased difficulty coordinating resources and tasks (the teams are virtual, but the work is real).
- Increased difficulty monitoring individual and team performance.

In the workplace today, the use of virtual teams is an innovative way for companies to create competitive advantage. In the future such teams may become a necessity, perhaps even a dominant organizational form.

Critical Thinking Questions

1. What is meant by "virtual teams"?
2. Describe the technology that has enabled virtual teams to become a reality.
3. Would you like to be a member of a virtual team?

CAPITALIZING ON TRENDS IN BUSINESS

 >lg 9

According to a recent *Industry Week* article on the "100 best managed companies," people are the only real source of competitive advantage, and the only way companies can stay competitive is by "unleashing the full creative power of people at all levels of the organization."[12] This chapter has focused on understanding what motivates people and how employee motivation and satisfaction affect productivity and organizational performance. Organizations can improve performance by investing in people. In reviewing the ways companies are currently choosing to invest in their human resources, we can spot three obvious trends: (1) education and training, (2) employee ownership, and (3) work-life benefits. Every company in *Fortune* magazine's 2000 list of the "100 best companies to work for" has employee programs in at least one of those areas, and many offer programs in all three categories.[13]

Firms that train workers in new technologies such as videoconferencing increase employee motivation and satisfaction. Employers benefit from their investment in training and education with a more loyal, productive, and skilled workforce.

Education and Training

Companies that provide educational and training opportunities for their employees reap the benefits of a more motivated, as well as a more skilled, workforce. Employees who are properly trained in new technologies are more productive and less resistant to job change. Education and training provide additional benefits by increasing employees' feelings of competence and self-worth. When companies spend money to upgrade employee knowledge and skills, they convey the message "we value you and are committed to your growth and development as an employee." One of Allied Signal's goals is to better prepare its employees to take on new job assignments within the organization.[14] In 1991 only 20 percent of job openings at Allied were filled internally. The company's training and educational program, called a learning initiative, began in 1992, and today approximately 70 percent of job openings at Allied are filled with internal candidates.

Employee Ownership

Companies are always looking for new ways to increase employee commitment and thus decrease absenteeism and turnover. Jim Porter, vice president at Honeywell, Inc., claims that competitive advantage boils down to employees who are committed to making the company successful, and that commitment is driven by a sense of ownership in the organization.[15] In Porter's words, "owners behave very differently from hired hands." Like an increasing number of companies today, Honeywell creates a sense of economic ownership by giving employees stock options in the company. Employee stock ownership increases employees' feelings of responsibility for the performance of the organization.

Work-Life Benefits

In another growing trend in the workplace, companies are helping their employees to manage the numerous and sometimes competing demands in their lives. Organizations are taking a more active role in helping employees achieve a balance between their work responsibilities and their personal obligations. The desired result is employees who are less stressed, better able to focus on their jobs, and, therefore, more productive. Ford Motor Co. is a leader in providing work-life benefits for employees. The company offers telecommuting, part-time positions, job sharing, subsidized child care, elder-care referral, and on-site fitness centers.

concept check

- What benefits can an organization derive from offering training and educational opportunities for its employees?
- How can employee stock ownership programs benefit both the employees and the organization?
- How can work-life benefits help both an organization and its employees?

APPLYING THIS CHAPTER'S TOPICS

We've come a long way from the days of *scientific management*. Organizations now offer a wide variety of incentives to attract and retain high-quality employees. A knowledgeable, creative, committed, and highly skilled workforce provides a company with a source of sustainable competitive advantage in an increasingly competitive business environment. What does that mean to you? It means that companies are working harder than ever to meet employee needs. It means that when you graduate from college or university you may choose a prospective employer on the basis of its day-care facilities and fitness programs as well as its salaries. It means that you need to think about what motivates you. Would you forgo a big salary to work for a smaller company that gives you lots of freedom to be creative and make your own decisions? Would you trade extensive health coverage for a share of ownership in the company? Most organizations try to offer a broad spectrum of incentives to meet a variety of needs, but each company makes trade-offs, and so will you in choosing an employer. Do a little research on a company you are interested in working for (paying particular attention to its corporate culture); then use the exercise in the Try It Now section to help you determine how well your values fit with the company's values.

SUMMARY OF LEARNING GOALS

>lg 1   **What are the basic principles of Frederick Taylor's concept of scientific management?**

Scientific management is based on the belief that employees are motivated by economic incentives and that there is "one best way" to perform any job. The four basic principles of scientific management developed by Taylor are as follows:

1. Develop a scientific approach for each element of a person's job.
2. Scientifically select, train, teach, and develop workers.
3. Encourage cooperation between workers and managers so that each job can be accomplished in a standard, scientifically determined way.
4. Divide work and responsibility between management and workers according to who is better suited to each task.

>lg 2   **What did Elton Mayo's Hawthorne studies reveal about worker motivation?**

From 1927 to 1932, Mayo and his colleagues conducted experiments at the Hawthorne Western Electric plant on job redesign, length of workday and workweek, length of break times, and incentive plans. The results of the studies indicated that increases in performance were tied to a complex set of employee attitudes. Mayo claimed that both the experimental and the control groups at the plant had developed a sense of group pride because they had been selected to participate in the studies. The pride that came from this special attention motivated the workers to increase their productivity. Supervisors who allowed the employees to have some control over their situation appeared to further increase the workers' motivation. These findings gave rise to what is now known as the Hawthorne effect, which suggests that employees will perform better when they feel singled out for special attention or feel that management is concerned about employee welfare.

>lg 3   **What is Maslow's hierarchy of needs, and how do these needs relate to motivation?**

Maslow believed that each individual has a hierarchy of needs, consisting of physiological, safety, social, esteem, and self-actualization needs. The most basic needs are physiological such as air, food, clothing, and shelter. After these

The accompanying table lists 17 personal characteristics and 13 institutional values you might encounter at a company.[16] Select and rank order the 10 personal characteristics that best describe you; do the same for the 10 institutional values that would be most evident in your ideal workplace. Test your fit at a firm by seeing whether the characteristics of the company's environment match your top 10 personal characteristics.

The Choice Menu

Rank Order (1–17)	You Are	Rank Order (1–13)	Your Ideal Company Offers
_____	1. Flexible	_____	1. Stability
_____	2. Innovative	_____	2. High expectations of performance
_____	3. Willing to experiment	_____	3. Opportunities for professional growth
_____	4. Risk taking	_____	4. High pay for good performance
_____	5. Careful	_____	5. Job security
_____	6. Autonomy seeking	_____	6. A clear guiding philosophy
_____	7. Comfortable with rules	_____	7. A low level of conflict
_____	8. Analytical	_____	8. Respect for the individual's rights
_____	9. Team oriented	_____	9. Informality
_____	10. Easygoing	_____	10. Fairness
_____	11. Supportive	_____	11. Long hours
_____	12. Aggressive	_____	12. Relative freedom from rules
_____	13. Decisive	_____	13. The opportunity to be distinctive, or different from others
_____	14. Achievement oriented		
_____	15. Comfortable with individual responsibility		
_____	16. Competitive		
_____	17. Interested in making friends at work		

are satisfied, we have safety needs. People need to feel secure and to be protected from harm. At the third level are social needs, or needs for belonging (acceptance by others) and for giving and receiving friendship and love. At the fourth level in Maslow's hierarchy are esteem needs, which are needs for the respect of others and for a sense of accomplishment and achievement. Finally, at the highest level are self-actualization needs—the needs for fulfillment, for living up to one's potential, and for using one's abilities to the utmost.

>lg 4 **How are McGregor's Theories X and Y used to explain worker motivation?**
Douglas McGregor influenced the study of motivation with his formulation of two contrasting sets of assumptions about human nature—designated Theory

There is no doubt that most employees would say SAS Institute, Inc. is a great place to work. SAS's revenue growth and its very low employee turnover reflect its happy, motivated workers. The future, indeed, looks very bright. Nevertheless, SAS will have to continuously adapt its employee benefits to match employees' changing needs. One area SAS must monitor is employee salaries, which are only average for the industry. Perhaps some workers would rather have a fatter paycheck than a pianist in the lunchroom. A second challenge is the incredible wealth that managers and top executives of software and other high-tech companies are accumulating when their companies go public (issue common stock). SAS is still privately owned and simply can't match the wealth-generating opportunities of a public company. If SAS goes public, will it retain its intense employee loyalty and high job satisfaction ratings?

X and Theory Y. Theory X says people don't like to work and will avoid it if they can. Theory Y says work is as natural as play or rest. People want to be self-directed and will try to accomplish goals that they believe in. McGregor personally believed that Theory Y assumptions describe most employees and that managers seeking to motivate subordinates should develop management practices based on those assumptions.

>lg 5   **What are the basic components of Herzberg's motivator-hygiene theory?**
Frederick Herzberg's studies indicated that certain job factors are consistently related to employee job satisfaction while others can create job dissatisfaction. According to Herzberg, motivating factors (also called satisfiers) are primarily intrinsic job elements that lead to satisfaction, such as achievement, recognition, the (nature of) work itself, responsibility, advancement, and growth. What Herzberg termed hygiene factors (also called dissatisfiers) are extrinsic elements of the work environment such as company policy, relationships with supervisors, working conditions, relationships with peers and subordinates, salary and benefits, and job security. These are factors that can result in job dissatisfaction if not well-managed.

>lg 6   **What three contemporary theories on employee motivation offer insights into improving employee performance?**
According to expectancy theory, the probability of an individual acting in a particular way depends on the strength of that individual's belief that the act will have a particular outcome and on whether the individual values that outcome. The degree to which an employee is motivated depends on three important relationships: the link between *effort and performance,* the link between *performance and outcome,* and the link between *outcomes and personal needs.*

Equity theory is based on individuals' perceptions about how fairly they are treated compared with their coworkers. Equity means justice or fairness, and in the workplace it refers to employees' perceived fairness of the way they are treated and the rewards they earn. Employees evaluate their own *outcomes* (e.g., salary, benefits) in relation to *inputs* (e.g., number of hours worked, education and training) and then compare the outcomes-to-inputs ratio to their own past experiences or the experiences of another person whose situation is similar.

Goal-setting theory states that employees are highly motivated to perform when specific goals are established and feedback on progress is offered.

>lg 7   **How can managers redesign existing jobs to increase employee motivation and performance?**
The horizontal expansion of a job by increasing the number and variety of tasks that a person performs is called job enlargement. Increasing task diversity can enhance job satisfaction, particularly when the job is mundane and repetitive in nature. Job enrichment is the vertical expansion of an employee's job

KEY TERMS

cross-functional
  teams 300
equity theory 294
expectancy theory
  293
goal-setting theory
  295
group cohesiveness
  298
Hawthorne effect
  290
hygiene factors
  292
job enlargement
  296
job enrichment
  296
job rotation 296
job sharing 297
Maslow's hierarchy
  of needs 291
motivating factors
  292
problem-solving
  teams 300
scientific
  management 288
self-managed work
  teams 300
Theory X 291
Theory Y 292
variable pay 299
work groups 299
work teams 299

to provide the employee with more autonomy, responsibility, and decision-making authority. In general, job enrichment has been found to increase employee job satisfaction and reduce absenteeism and turnover. Job rotation, also called cross-training, is the shifting of workers from one job to another. This may be done to broaden an employee's skill base or when an employee ceases to be interested in or challenged by the job.

>lg 8 **What different types of teams are being used in organizations today?**
Work groups share resources and coordinate efforts to help members better perform their individual duties and responsibilities. The performance of the group can be evaluated by adding up the contributions of the individual group members. Work teams require not only coordination but also *collaboration*, the pooling of knowledge, skills, abilities, and resources in a collective effort to attain a common goal. The work team creates *synergy*, causing the performance of the team as a whole to be greater than the sum of team members' individual contributions.

Four types of work teams are used: problem solving, self-managed, cross-functional, and virtual teams. *Problem-solving teams* are typically made up of employees from the same department or area of expertise and from the same level of the organizational hierarchy; they meet on a regular basis to share information and discuss ways to improve processes and procedures in specific functional areas. *Self-managed work teams* are highly autonomous groups that manage themselves without any formal supervision. They take responsibility for setting goals, planning and scheduling work activities, selecting team members, and evaluating team performance. *Cross-functional teams* are made up of employees from about the same hierarchical level, but different functional areas of the organization. These teams allow people with various areas of expertise to pool their resources, develop new ideas, solve problems, and coordinate complex projects. In a *virtual team,* employees in different geographic or organizational locations come together as a team via a combination of telecommunications and information technologies. Virtual teams work together to accomplish a common goal, but rarely (if ever) meet face-to-face. Membership is often dynamic, changing to accommodate project or task requirements.

>lg 9 **What initiatives are organizations using today to motivate and retain employees?**
Today, firms are using three key tactics to motivate and retain workers. First, companies are investing more in employee education and training, which make workers more productive and less resistant to job change. Second, managers are offering employees a chance for ownership in the company. This can strongly increase employee commitment. Finally, enlightened employers are providing work-life benefits to help employees achieve a better balance between work and personal responsibilities. Examples include telecommuting, job sharing, subsidized child care, and on-site fitness centers.

PREPARING FOR TOMORROW'S WORKPLACE

1. Do you think the concept of scientific management is applicable today? Why or why not?

2. How are job satisfaction and employee morale linked to job performance? Do you work harder when you are satisfied with your job? Explain your answer.

3. Review the assumptions of Theories X and Y. Under which set of assumptions would you prefer to work? Is your current or former supervisor a Theory X manager or a Theory Y manager? Explain by describing the person's behavior.

4. Think about several of your friends who seem to be highly self-motivated. Talk with each of them and ask them what factors contribute the most to their motivation. Make a list of their responses and compare them to the factors that motivate you.

5. Is money a job satisfier or a job maintenance factor for you? Explain.

6. Both individual motivation and group participation are needed to accomplish certain goals. Describe a situation you're familiar with in which cooperation achieved a goal that individual action could not. Describe one in which group action slowed progress and individual action would have been better.

7. Explain the differences between equity theory and expectancy theory.

8. Using expectancy theory, analyze how you have made and will make personal choices, such as a major area of study, a career to pursue, or job interviews to seek.

9. If a famous executive or sports figure were to give a passionate motivational speech, trying to persuade people to work harder, what do you think the impact would be? Why?

WORKING THE NET

1. Looking for 1,001 ways to motivate or reward your employees? Bob Nelson can help. Visit his Nelson Motivation site at **http://www.nelson-motivation.com/** to get some ideas you can put to use to help you do a better job, either as a manager or as an employee.

2. More companies are offering their employees stock ownership plans. To learn the differences between an employee stock ownership plan (ESOP) and stock options, visit the National Center for Employee Ownership (NCEO) at **http://www.nceo.org** and the Foundation for Enterprise Development (FED) at **http://www.fed.org.** Which stock plan would you rather have? Why?

3. Open-book management is one of the better known ways to create a participatory work environment. Over 2,000 companies have adopted this practice, which involves sharing financial information with nonmanagement employees and training them to understand financial information. Does it really motivate employees and improve productivity? The NCEO's Articles page, **http://www.nceo.org/culture/culture_articles.html,** offers insights that will help you answer this question.

4. How do you keep your employees satisfied? The Business Research Lab has a series of articles on this topic at **busreslab.com/tips/tipses.htm.** Compile a list of the best ideas—the ones that would motivate *you.*

5. Knowing how to build and manage effective teams is a necessary skill in today's workplace. Team Building News, **http://www.teambuildingnews.com,** is a newsletter featuring ways America's top corporations use innovative team building to improve team performance. For a good summary of major issues facing teams, review the Team Building handout at the site for the Poynter Institute School for Journalists, **http://www.poynter.org/research/lm/lm_team.htm.**

CREATIVE THINKING CASE

A Clash of Cultures as Ford Meets Volvo

In Gothenburg, Sweden, Volvo car workers are nervous about what life will be like under their new owner, Ford Motor Co. After all, they might lose their badminton courts. At Volvo's flagship factory here, employees have the use of a company gym, Olympic-size swimming pool, badminton and tennis courts, an outdoor track, and tanning beds. There's also a hot-water pool, where workers go for physical therapy sessions after a hard day on the assembly line.

Some 1,800 Volvo workers, or roughly 9 percent of the total workforce at the company's headquarters, use the facilities. Unions and workers worry that Ford, which bought Volvo, may consider it all a bit too lavish. Although workers have to pay $1.50 a day to get in, Volvo pays as much as five million kronor ($605,500) a year to support the center. "Everybody at Volvo is wondering what Ford's takeover really means to our future," says Claes Andersson, vice president of the plant workers' union. "Will our Volvo traditions continue?"

For Ford, the Volvo purchase raises a big question of benefit equality. Ford workers in the United States are considerably less pampered than Swedish workers. Ford plants usually have free-of-charge fitness centers for employees, as well as weight-reduction programs, but U.S. workers have to do without the tanning beds and other goodies normally found only at the most exclusive health clubs.

Ford has been vague about its plans. "I respect the Swedish heritage," said Jacques Nasser, Ford's CEO. But he added that "nothing is safe in this world; there are no guarantees."

It's not just the health club that workers worry about, but a host of issues ranging from job security to quality of life. For example, Nasser said he wanted to make Volvo a "volume car" in the United States, which could mean a three-shift, round-the-clock production schedule, just like in the United States. Volvo employees currently work two shifts.

Nasser's comments disturbed 40-year-old Jari Saarelainen, a Volvo night-shift worker. He now works fewer than 30 hours a week, but gets paid about the same as day-shift workers, who work as many as 40 hours a week, because of a government-mandated allocation for late-shift employees. The setup allows him to spend lots of time with his wife and four children. "It's a human way of work," he says.

Saarelainen realizes he has it good, but argues that his relatively undemanding workload also helps the company because productivity and morale are higher than they would be under a more conventional employer. "We hope that Ford can grasp that this system is better for the company and the workers," he says. Indeed, the absentee rate at Volvo is roughly 4 percent a day, down from well over 10 percent in the late 1980s. "We like to think that the gym contributed to that," says Mats Edenborg, spokesman for Volvo Group.

Critical Thinking Questions

1. Do you think that Volvo has carried employee benefits and perks too far?

2. Swedish income taxes are far higher than in the United States. High salaries are taxed away, so many companies try to do a few things extra for their employees. Is this a sufficient reason for Ford to maintain Volvo's benefits for its workers?

3. A Ford worker in the United States can earn over $100,000 a year with overtime. A typical Volvo worker earns about $30,275 (U.S.) per year. Should Ford cut the perks and raise wages at Volvo? The government would take slightly over 50 percent.

4. Should Nasser simply leave benefits and perks at both places as they are? What if Ford workers start to complain or Volvo workers start demanding higher salaries?

VIDEO CASE

Motivational Initiatives at Valassis Communications

Valassis Communications, Inc. (**http://www.valassis.com**) has set the standard in the marketing services industry "for quality, reliability, service and expertise."

The company's products include the free-standing insert (FSI) in Sunday newspapers, which contains coupons, refunds, and other values from America's largest packaged goods companies; solo inserts that promote a single company's products or services; delivery of manufacturers' product samples and promotional messages through Sunday newspapers; direct placement of newspaper ads for customers; and oversight of customers' games and sweepstakes promotions.

Executives at Valassis Communications believe the company's success results from having highly motivated employees. The company has many programs that are intended to foster employee motivation. Three of the more notable programs involve employee recognition, perks, and employee communications.

Valassis has a variety of employee recognition programs that are designed to ensure that employees at all levels of the company understand the importance of their contributions. One program recognizes outstanding employees in four categories: Idea of the Year, Change to Grow (which reflects the company's corporate philosophy and culture), Team Player, and Employee of the Year. Employees nominate candidates for each category, and an election is held to select the winner. Other employee recognition programs include sales awards for the top performing account managers, various divisional recognition programs for outstanding performance, length of service awards, and perfect attendance awards.

In addition to a comprehensive benefits plan, Valassis provides employees with a variety of perks that address work/family issues. These benefits include flextime scheduling, job sharing, child care and dependent care reimbursement programs, and an adoption expense program. Health-related perks include an employee assistance plan and on-site fitness centers. At its corporate headquarters, Valassis also provides such amenities as an on-site hair salon/manicurist, an on-site automatic teller machine (ATM), dry cleaning pickup and delivery service, and an on-site cafeteria with indoor and outdoor dining.

Valassis also provides timely information to employees and seeks suggestions and feedback from employees. Among the primary communication vehicles are a monthly newsletter, a quarterly video magazine, public posting of all company press releases and outside articles written about the company, and a program in which employees have a brown bag lunch with the company's leaders. Other communication initiatives include a suggestion program to encourage employees to provide ideas; a semiannual survey that allows employees to provide feedback on any aspect of the company and its operations; and an annual daylong review where "employees receive a detailed update on company performance, learn about the corporate goals and initiatives for the upcoming year, and meet with their areas to set departmental and individual initiatives."

One result of these motivational initiatives is that Valassis Communications has acquired a reputation of being a great place to work. In 1997, *Fortune* magazine placed Valassis 67th in its list of the "100 best companies to work for." In 1998, Valassis placed 37th in the *Fortune* rankings.

Critical Thinking Questions

1. How could the motivational programs at Valassis be explained in the context of Maslow's needs hierarchy? Herzberg's motivator-hygiene theory?

2. How have Valassis's motivational programs contributed to the company being selected as one of the "100 best companies to work for"?

3. To what extent are the motivational methods used by Valassis Communications transferable to other companies?

Case: Virtual Teamwork

Senad Hadzic is an IT project manager for Engelhard Corporation, a specialty chemical manufacturer. Hadzic supervises several teams of employees and suppliers located in different offices who are working on new software applications for Engelhard. Making sure team members communicated with each other and kept on top of deadlines used to be a never-ending struggle for Hadzic. "There was always a bottleneck," he says. "Every time someone on a team wanted to add a task or have somebody else do a task, it had to be centralized and go through a central approval process and that would be me."

Recently, Engelhard installed Inovie Software's TeamCenter software on the company's computers. Now, team members sign on to a centralized, interactive Web site to share up-to-date information, ideas, and documents; they also participate in real-time planning and problem solving. "TeamCenter has provided a way for our team members to see one another's work and to leave their knowledge in detail with their task," says Hadzic. "There's no longer a need for me to be directly involved and give assignments."

Like Hadzic, Carolyn Sechler, owner of a successful accounting firm in Phoenix, Arizona, must also manage a far-flung team of workers. All of her employees, and Sechler herself, work from home—some from as far away as Nebraska, Missouri, and Michigan. When it comes time to develop ideas or work on projects as a team, Sechler and her employees log on to the Internet for a virtual meeting using an Internet chat service. If employees need to check a file, or get information on a project's progress, they also sign on to the Internet. All of the company's files, including spreadsheets, correspondence, and accounting ledgers, are stored on a company server at an Internet service provider.

Matt Light, an analyst with research firm Gartner-Group, says Sechler and Hadzic are part of a growing trend using Internet technology to tie together workers and team members located in different places. "The knowledge base for today's fast-growing companies resides in virtual teams," he says. "Successful team collaboration and a new style of virtual management will be essential for these companies to compete."

Questions for Critical Thinking

1. What employee motivation challenges might managers face in managing employees located in far-off locations?
2. What problems might self-managed teams encounter when they need to rely on Internet technology to connect them? How could these problems be overcome?

SOURCES: Chris Sandlund, "Remote Control," *BusinessWeek* (March 27, 2000), downloaded from **http://www.businessweek.com**; Chris Sandlund, "Tools of the Remote Trade," *BusinessWeek* (March 27, 2000), downloaded from **http://www.businessweek.com**; Lisa Vaas, "Taming Rush-Hour Projects," *eWeek* (May 15, 2000), downloaded from **http://www.zdnet.com**; "Teaming is Fundamental to Ensuring E-Business Success," *PR Newswire* (March 29, 2000), downloaded from **http://www.prnewswire.com**.

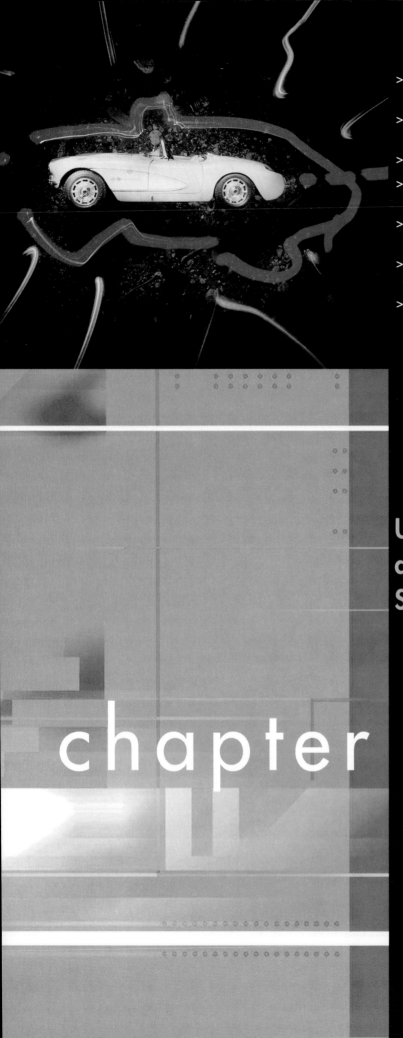

learning goals

>lg 1   What are the marketing concept and relationship building?

>lg 2   How do managers create a marketing strategy?

>lg 3   What is the marketing mix?

>lg 4   How do consumers and organizations make buying decisions?

>lg 5   What are the five basic forms of market segmentation?

>lg 6   How is marketing research used in marketing decision making?

>lg 7   What are the trends in understanding the consumer?

Understanding the Customer and Creating Goods and Services That Satisfy

chapter 11

Targeting Baby Boomers at DaimlerChrysler

In 1955, Chrysler needed an icon. It had no Corvette, no Thunderbird for crew cut young men in blue jeans to drool over. That year the company found its muscle car: the C-300. Touted as "America's most powerful car," the C-300 tore up the tracks at NASCAR and Daytona, positioning Chrysler as a leader in high-performance, upscale American automobiles. The company launched a new model in its "letter-car" series every year until 1965's 300L and then discontinued the line.

Now, 45 years later, Chrysler had merged with Germany's Daimler-Benz, and the new company, DaimlerChrysler (**http://www.daimlerchrysler.de/**) needed an icon to catch the attention of 40-something baby boomers. "Bringing a car to market is a $1 billion to $4 billion investment," says Steven Bruyn, large-car marketing executive at the Chrysler division of Daimler-Chrysler. "As a result, you like to be right." The company didn't have to go far for its concept: it resurrected the 300 letter series from the 1950s and 1960s, and simply picked up where it left off in the alphabet. After three years of development, engineering tinkering, and intense market research, the car maker launched the 300M in 1998. Sales have been booming since, and it was named the *Motor Trend* 1999 Car of the Year.

Steering the 300M from drafting table to dealer has been no easy task. At the start of the project, Bruyn and his team studied the potential of the near-luxury car market by looking at population trends and forecasts for its target customers. America's baby boomers were aging and well educated, and their personal income was growing, courtesy of a strong national economy. They wanted room for their expanding waistlines—and were willing to pay for it.

Factors like these indicated a robust future for near-luxury car sales, but how did the 300M fit into the picture? Through marketing research, DaimlerChrysler honed its profile of the car's typical driver. "To 300M drivers, the car is more than just something to get them from point A to point B," says Bruyn.

Target customers are real car enthusiasts. They read *Motor Trend* and other car magazines. And, says Paul Leinberger, senior vice president at Roper Starch Worldwide, they're looking for a product that represents who they are. "It's not about status, but their sense of identity," he says.

America's mood swing toward nostalgia also influenced the design of the 300M, both inside and out. The egg-crate grille harks back to earlier styles in the letter series, and simple analog dials dot the dashboard. Chrysler restored the series's vintage silver-winged badge, which now appears on the hood of all of the brand's cars and trucks. Of course, not everything about the 300M recalls the 1950s—standard features include leather seats, climate control, and a stereo system with nine speakers. "We marketed the 300M with an 'American heritage' wrapper," Bruyn says. "It differentiated us from the others in the market."[1]

Critical Thinking Questions

As you read this chapter, consider the following questions as they relate to DaimlerChrysler:

- Why do companies identify target customers for their products?
- Why is it important to differentiate a product?
- How does a company like DaimlerChrysler find out what customers and potential customers want in a car?

BUSINESS IN THE 21ˢᵀ CENTURY

marketing

The process of discovering the needs and wants of potential buyers and customers and then providing goods and services that meet or exceed their expectations.

exchange

The process in which two parties give something of value to each other to satisfy their respective needs.

In marketing its 300M model, DaimlerChrysler conducted research to find out what potential buyers wanted and needed and then designed the car to satisfy those wants and needs.

Marketing played an important role in DaimlerChrysler's successful launch of its 300M. Marketing is the process of getting the right goods or services to the right people at the right place, time, and price, using the right promotion techniques. This concept is referred to as the *"right" principle.* We can say that **marketing** is finding out the needs and wants of potential buyers and customers and then providing goods and services that meet or exceed their expectations. Marketing is about creating exchanges. An **exchange** takes place when two parties give something of value to each other to satisfy their respective needs. In a typical exchange, a consumer trades money for a good or service.

To encourage exchanges, marketers follow the "right" principle. If your local DaimlerChrysler dealer doesn't have the right car for you when you want it, at the right price, you will not exchange money or credit for a new car. Think about the last exchange (purchase) you made: What if the price had been 30 percent higher? What if the store or other source had been less accessible? Would you have bought anything? The "right" principle tells us that marketers control many factors that determine marketing success. In this chapter, you will learn about the marketing concept and how organizations create a marketing strategy. You will learn how the marketing mix is used to create sales opportunities. Next, we examine how and why consumers and organizations make purchase decisions. Then, we discuss the important concept of market segmentation, which helps marketing managers focus on the most likely purchasers of their wares. We conclude the chapter by examining how marketing research and decision support systems help guide marketing decision making.

THE MARKETING CONCEPT

>lg 1

marketing concept

Identifying consumer needs and then producing the goods or services that will satisfy them while making a profit for the organization.

If you study today's best organizations, you'll see that they have adopted the **marketing concept,** which involves identifying consumer needs and then producing the goods or services that will satisfy them while making a profit. The marketing concept is oriented toward pleasing consumers by offering value. Specifically, the marketing concept involves:

- Focusing on customer wants so the organization can distinguish its product(s) from competitors' offerings.
- Integrating all of the organization's activities, including production, to satisfy these wants.

• Achieving long-term goals for the organization by satisfying customer wants and needs legally and responsibly.

Today, companies of every size in all industries are applying the marketing concept. McDonald's, for example, found that burger eaters like to determine what's on their burger rather than buying a hamburger that is already dressed in a heated bin. Now, its restaurants deliver fresh sandwiches made to order. After McDonald's changed its procedures to satisfy this customer need, its sales rose 9 percent and profits increased 25 percent.[2]

production orientation

An approach in which a firm works to lower production costs without a strong desire to satisfy the needs of customers.

Firms have not always followed the marketing concept. Around the time of the Industrial Revolution in America (1860–1910), firms had a **production orientation,** which meant that they worked to lower production costs without a strong desire to satisfy the needs of their customers. To do this, organizations concentrated on mass production, focusing internally on maximizing the efficiency of operations, increasing output, and ensuring uniform quality. They also asked such questions as What can we do best? What can our engineers design? What is economical and easy to produce with our equipment?

There is nothing wrong with assessing a firm's capabilities. In fact, such assessments are necessary in planning. But the production orientation does not consider whether what the firm produces most efficiently also meets the needs of the marketplace. By implementing the marketing concept, an organization looks externally to the consumers in the marketplace and commits to customer value, customer satisfaction, and relationship marketing as explained in this section.

Customer Value

customer value

The ratio of benefits to the sacrifice necessary to obtain those benefits, as determined by the customer; reflects the willingness of customers to actually buy a product.

Customer value is the ratio of benefits to the sacrifice necessary to obtain those benefits. The customer determines the value of both the benefits and the sacrifices. Creating customer value is a core business strategy of many successful firms. Customer value is rooted in the belief that price is not the only thing that matters. A business that focuses on the cost of production and price to the customer will be managed as though it were providing a commodity differentiated only by price. In contrast, businesses that provide customer value believe that many customers will pay a premium for superior customer service. Sir Colin Marshall, chairman of the board of British Airways (BA), is explicit about his commitment to superior customer service, insisting that BA can succeed only by meeting all of its customers' value-driven needs, not just price. In a highly competitive industry, BA has used this customer-value-based strategy to become the world's most profitable airline.[3]

The automobile industry also illustrates the importance of creating customer value. To penetrate the fiercely competitive luxury automobile market, Lexus adopted a customer-driven approach, with particular emphasis on service. Lexus stresses product quality with a standard of zero defects in manufacturing. The service quality goal is to treat each customer as one would treat a guest in one's home, to pursue the perfect person-to-person relationship, and to strive to improve continually. This strategy has enabled Lexus to establish a clear quality image and capture a significant share of the luxury car market.

Customer Satisfaction

customer satisfaction

The customer's feeling that a product has met or exceeded expectations.

Customer satisfaction is the customer's feeling that a product has met or exceeded expectations. New York State Electric and Gas Corp. says that its top priority is customer satisfaction. "We're committed to providing superior customer service and earning our customers' business every day," said Ralph Tedesco, president of NYSEG. "We're very proud that our customers acknowledge our restoration efforts following devastating storms and give us high marks for customer service."[4]

Read Embassy Suites's Guest Guarantee at

http://www.embassysuites. com

At DoubleTree Hotels, guests are asked to fill out a CARE card several times during their stay to let staff know how they are doing. Managers check the cards daily to solve guests' problems before they check out. Guests can also use a CARE phone line to call in their complaints at the hotel. A CARE committee continually seeks ways to improve guest services. The goal is to offer a solution to a CARE call in 15 minutes. Embassy Suites goes one step further by offering a full refund to guests who are not satisfied with their stay.

Customer satisfaction may indicate how consumers feel about a product, but it may not indicate their willingness to actually purchase that product. General Motors' Cadillac Division, for example, was quite pleased that more than 90 percent of its customers reported that they were either "satisfied" or "highly satisfied" with their recent purchase of a new Cadillac, figures comparable with those reported by purchasers of Japanese automobiles. But Cadillac was quite dismayed to learn that only 30 to 40 percent of these new Cadillac owners would buy another Cadillac, compared with more than 80 percent of Japanese auto purchasers.[5] GM had been asking only about customer satisfaction, not customer value, the willingness of customers to actually buy a new Cadillac.

Building Relationships

relationship marketing

A strategy that focuses on forging long-term partnerships with customers by offering value and providing customer satisfaction.

Relationship marketing is a strategy that focuses on forging long-term partnerships with customers. Companies build relationships with customers by offering value and providing customer satisfaction. Companies benefit from repeat sales and referrals that lead to increases in sales, market share, and profits. Costs fall because it is less expensive to serve existing customers than to attract new ones. Keeping a customer costs about one-fourth of what it costs to attract a new customer, and the probability of retaining a customer is over 60 percent, whereas the probability of landing a new customer is less than 30 percent.[6]

Customers also benefit from stable relationships with suppliers. Business buyers have found that partnerships with their suppliers are essential to producing high-quality products while cutting costs. Customers remain loyal to firms that provide them greater value and satisfaction than they expect from competing firms.

Frequent buyer clubs are an excellent way to build long-term relationships. All major airlines including American and United have frequent flyer programs. After you fly a certain number of miles, you become eligible for a free ticket. Now, cruise lines, hotels, car rental agencies, credit card companies, and even mortgage companies give away "airline miles" with purchases. Consumers patronize the airline and its partners because they want the free tickets. Thus, the program helps to create a long-term relationship with the customer.[7]

If an organization is to build relationships with customers, its employees' attitudes and actions must be customer oriented. Any person, department, or division that is not customer oriented weakens the positive image of the entire organization. An employee may be the only contact a potential customer has with the firm. In that person's eyes, the employee is the firm. If greeted discourteously, the potential customer may well assume that the employee's attitude represents the whole firm.

Building long-term relationships with customers is an excellent way for small businesses to compete against the big chains. Some-

concept check

- What is marketing?
- Explain the marketing concept.
- Explain the difference between customer value and customer satisfaction.
- What is meant by relationship marketing?

IF YOU WANT TO BUY A CROCK-POT, TRY SOMEPLACE ELSE

With Wal-Marts and Home Depots overrunning the landscape, it looked as though Josh and Michael Bracken's small nursery in Dallas, Texas, would quickly wilt. So how is it that profit at the Brackens' Nicholson-Hardie Nursery & Garden Center rose 11 percent last year and the brothers are talking of expansion? Well, they make house calls, for one thing. One afternoon, 29-year-old Josh responds to a plea from retiree Jon Bauman, who is fretting over a bed of withering azaleas. "These are way dry," the nurseryman says, prodding the brittle plants and snapping off a twig. He advises Bauman to either water his shrubs more often or find a plant that is better suited to the dense clay soil. "At the Gap, anyone with a smile can sell a shirt," Josh boasts. "But it takes a couple of years to learn about plants."

In industry after industry, chain competitors have driven independents into the ground. The same thing almost happened in the nursery business, where big retailers now control two-thirds of the $71 billion lawn-and-garden market. But today, many of the nation's 10,000 independent nurseries are stubbornly holding their own by stocking plants suited for local conditions, pampering customers, and luring them with inventive promotions. Homestead Gardens in Davidsonville, Maryland, holds an herb festival, with local chefs demonstrating how to make herbal marinades and garnishes.

Because the Brackens can't buy in bulk as the chains do, they don't even attempt to match the chains' prices. Instead, they offer superior customer service by stocking more than 1,000 plant varieties, far more than the chains carry. Rare perennial flowers such as Tapien verbena and Mount Fuji phlox, which sell for between $3 and $6, can be found only at Nicholson-Hardie.

To distinguish themselves, the brothers aim for the sort of customer who "would buy a Land Rover versus a Chevrolet," says Josh. Thus, the stores stock top-of-the-line tools one might find in Martha Stewart's garden, including $35 British sheep shears for trimming grass and $45 Swiss pruners. There are dozens of brass and animal-shaped fountains, some selling for thousands of dollars. Nicholson-Hardie even carries a $20.95 imported British rosemary-scented herbal hand cream. It can't be found anywhere else in Dallas except at Neiman Marcus. Michael Bracken, who handles the company's finances, says he loves the association with the fancy retailer. "It adds to the aura."

Critical Thinking Questions

1. What else could the Brackens do to build long-term relationships with customers?
2. Would a frequent purchaser program work?
3. What about giving away airline miles with purchases?

times small firms, with few employees, are in a better position to "go the extra mile," as explained in the Focusing on Small Business box.

CREATING A MARKETING STRATEGY

>lg 2   There is no secret formula for creating goods and services that provide customer value and customer satisfaction. An organization that is committed to providing superior customer satisfaction puts customers at the very center of its marketing strategy. Creating a customer-focused marketing strategy involves four main steps: understanding the external environment, defining the target market, creating a competitive advantage, and developing a marketing mix. This section will examine the first three steps, and the next section will discuss how a company develops a marketing mix. The marketing mix is explained in detail in Chapter 12.

Understanding the External Environment

Unless marketing managers understand the external environment, a firm cannot intelligently plan for the future. Thus, many organizations assemble a team of specialists to continually collect and evaluate environmental information, a process called **environmental scanning.** The goal in gathering the environmental data is to identify future market opportunities and threats.

For example, as technology continues to blur the lines between personal computers, television, and compact disc players, a company like Sony may find itself competing against a company like Compaq. Research shows that children would like more games bundled with computer software, while adults desire various types of word-processing and business-related software. Is this information an opportunity or a threat to Compaq marketing managers?

In general, six categories of environmental data shape marketing decisions:

- *Social forces* such as the values of potential customers and the changing roles of families and women working outside the home.
- *Demographic forces* such as the ages, birth and death rates, and locations of various groups of people.
- *Economic forces* such as changing incomes, inflation, and recession.
- *Technological forces* such as advances in communications and data retrieval capabilities.
- *Political and legal forces* such as changes in laws and regulatory agency activities.
- *Competitive forces* from domestic and foreign-based firms.

Defining the Target Market

Managers and employees focus on providing value for a well-defined target market. The **target market** is the specific group of consumers toward which a firm directs its marketing efforts. It is selected from the larger overall market.

For instance, Carnival Cruise Lines says its main target market is "blue-collar entrepreneurs," people with an income of $25,000 to $50,000 a year who own auto supply shops, dry cleaners, and the like. Unlike other cruise lines, it does not seek affluent retirees. Quaker Oats targets its grits to blue-collar consumers in the South. Kodak targets Ektar color print film, designed for use only in rather sophisticated cameras, to advanced amateur photographers. The Limited, Inc. has several different types of stores, each for a distinct target market: Express for trendy younger women, Lerner New York for budget-conscious women, and Henri Bendel for upscale, high-fashion women. These target markets are all part of the overall market for women's clothes.

Identifying a target market helps a company focus its marketing efforts on those who are most likely to buy its products or services. Concentrating on potential customers lets the firm use its resources efficiently. The target markets for Marriott International's lodging alternatives are shown in Exhibit 11-1. The latest in the Marriott family is SpringHill Suites. The SpringHill idea came from another Marriott chain, Fairfield Suites, an offshoot of Marriott's Fairfield Inns. The suites, opened in 1997, were roomy but devoid of most frills: the closets didn't have doors, and the lobby floors were covered with linoleum. Some franchisees com-

environmental scanning
The process in which a firm continually collects and evaluates information about its external environment.

target market
The specific group of consumers toward which a firm directs its marketing efforts.

The National Fluid Milk Processor Promotion Board creates ads targeted at different market segments to promote the consumption of milk. It targets the youth market with ads featuring celebrities such as NASCAR driver Jeff Gordon.

	Price Range	Target Market
Fairfield Inn	$45–65	Economizing business and leisure travelers
TownePlace Suites	$55–70	Moderate-tier travelers who stay three to four weeks
SpringHill Suites	$75–95	Business and leisure travelers looking for more space and amenities
Courtyard	$75–105	Travelers seeking quality and affordable accommodations designed for the road warrior
Residence Inn	$85–110	Travelers seeking a residential-style hotel
Marriott Hotels, Resorts, and Suites	$90–235	Grounded achievers who desire consistent quality
Renaissance Hotels and Resorts	$90–235	Discerning business and leisure travelers who seek creative attention to detail
Ritz-Carlton	$175–300	Senior executives and entrepreneurs looking for a unique, luxury, personalized experience

SOURCE: Christina Binkley, "Marriott Outfits an Old Chain for New Market," *Wall Street Journal* (October 13, 1998), pp. B1, B3.

plained to Marriott that the suites were *under*priced: Fairfield Suites guests were saying they would pay a little more for a few more frills.

So Marriott began planning an upgrade. To create each of the first 20 or so SpringHill locations, Marriott spent $200,000 renovating an existing Fairfield Suites unit, adding ergonomic chairs, ironing boards, and other amenities. Lobbies at SpringHill hotels are fancier than the rooms themselves: the lobbies have fireplaces, breakfast rooms, crown moldings at the ceiling, and granite or ceramic tile floors.

Look for other ways Marriott builds customer relationships at
http://www.marriott.com

Creating a Competitive Advantage

competitive advantage

A set of unique features of a company and its products that are perceived by the target market as significant and superior to those of the competition; also called *differential advantage*.

A **competitive advantage**, also called a differential advantage, is a set of unique features of a company and its products that are perceived by the target market as significant and superior to those of the competition. As Andrew Grove, former CEO of Intel, says, "You have to understand what it is you are better at than anybody else and mercilessly focus your efforts on it." Competitive advantage is the factor or factors that cause customers to patronize a firm and not the competition. There are three types of competitive advantage: cost, product/service differential, and niche.

cost competitive advantage

A firm's ability to produce a product or service at a lower cost than all other competitors in an industry while maintaining satisfactory profit margins.

Cost Competitive Advantage A firm that has a **cost competitive advantage** can produce a product or service at a lower cost than all its competitors while maintaining satisfactory profit margins. Firms become cost leaders by obtaining inexpensive raw materials, making plant operations more efficient, designing products for ease of manufacture, controlling overhead costs, and avoiding marginal customers. DuPont, for example, has an exceptional cost competitive advantage in the production of titanium dioxide. Technicians created a production process using low-cost feedstock that gives DuPont a 20 percent cost advantage over its competitors. The cheaper feedstock technology is complex and can be accomplished only by investing about $100 million and several years of testing time.

A cost competitive advantage enables a firm to deliver superior customer value. Chaparral Steel, for example, is the leading low-cost U.S. steel producer because it uses only scrap iron and steel and a very efficient continuous-casting process to make new steel. In fact, Chaparral is so efficient that it is the only U.S. steel producer that ships to Japan.

differential competitive advantage

A firm's ability to provide a unique product or service that offers something of value to buyers besides simply a lower price.

Differential Competitive Advantage   A product/service **differential competitive advantage** exists when a firm provides something unique that is valuable to buyers beyond simply offering a low price. Differential competitive advantages tend to be longer lasting than cost competitive advantages because cost advantages are subject to continual erosion as competitors catch up. Cost advantages fail to last for two reasons. For one thing, technology is transferable. For example, Bell Labs invented fiber optic cable that reduced the cost of voice and data transmission by dramatically increasing the number of calls that could be transmitted simultaneously through a two-inch cable. Within five years, however, fiber optic technology had spread throughout the industry. Second, for most production processes or product categories (e.g., running shoes and laptop computers), there are alternative suppliers. Over time, high-cost producers tend to seek out lower-cost suppliers and they can compete more effectively with the industry's low-cost producers.

The durability of a differential competitive advantage tends to make this strategy more attractive to many top managers. Common differential advantages are brand names (Lexus), a strong dealer network (Caterpillar Tractor for construction work), product reliability (Maytag washers), image (Neiman Marcus in retailing), and service (Federal Express). Brand names such as Coca-Cola, BMW, and Cartier stand for quality the world over. Through continual product and marketing innovations and attention to quality and value, managers at these organizations have created enduring competitive advantages.

niche competitive advantage

A firm's ability to target and effectively serve a single segment of the market within a limited geographic area.

Niche Competitive Advantage   A company with a **niche competitive advantage** targets and effectively serves a single segment of the market within a limited geographic area. For small companies with limited resources that potentially face giant competitors, "niche-ing" may be the only viable option. A market segment that has good growth potential but is not crucial to the success of major competitors is a good candidate for a niche strategy. Once a potential segment has been identified, the firm needs to make certain it can defend against challengers through its superior ability to serve buyers in the segment. For example, A Pea in the Pod is a small chain of retail stores that sells maternity clothes. Its quality materials, innovative designs, and reasonable prices serve as a barrier against competition.

c o n c ə p t   c h ə c k

- What is environmental scanning?
- What is a target market, and why should a company have one?
- What is a competitive advantage?
- Explain the three types of competitive advantages.

DEVELOPING A MARKETING MIX

>lg 3

Once a firm has defined its target market and identified its competitive advantage, it can create the **marketing mix,** that is, the blend of product offering, pricing, promotional methods, and distribution system that brings a specific group

marketing mix

The blend of product offering, pricing, promotional methods, and distribution system that brings a specific group of consumers superior value.

four Ps

Product, price, promotion, and place (distribution), which together make up the marketing mix.

of consumers superior value. Distribution is sometimes referred to as place, so the marketing mix is based on the **four Ps:** product, price, promotion, and place. Every target market requires a unique marketing mix to satisfy the needs of the target consumers and meet the firm's goals. A strategy must be constructed for each of the four Ps and blended with the strategies for the other elements. Thus, the marketing mix is only as good as its weakest part. An excellent product with a poor distribution system could be doomed to failure.

Compare McDonald's and Wendy's marketing efforts by visiting their home pages at http://www.mcdonalds.com and http://www.wendys.com

A successful marketing mix requires careful tailoring. For instance, at first glance you might think that McDonald's and Wendy's have roughly the same marketing mix. After all, they are both in the fast-food business. But McDonald's targets parents with young children through Ronald McDonald, heavily promoted children's Happy Meals, and playgrounds. Wendy's is targeted to a more adult crowd. Wendy's has no playgrounds but it does have carpeting (a more adult atmosphere), and it pioneered fast-food salad bars.

Product Strategy

product strategy

The part of the marketing mix that involves choosing a brand name, packaging, colors, a warranty, accessories, and a service program for the product.

Marketing strategy typically starts with the product. You can't plan a distribution system or set a price if you don't know what you're going to market. Marketers use the term *product* to refer to both *goods,* such as tires, stereos, and clothing, and *services,* such as hotels, hair salons, and restaurants. Thus, the heart of the marketing mix is the good or service. Creating a **product strategy** involves choosing a brand name, packaging, colors, a warranty, accessories, and a service program.

Marketers view products in a much larger context than you might imagine. They include not only the item itself but also the brand name and the company image. The names Yves St. Laurent and Gucci, for instance, create extra value for everything from cosmetics to bath towels. That is, products with those names sell at higher prices than identical products without the names. We buy things not only for what they do, but also for what they mean.

Pricing Strategy

pricing strategy

The part of the marketing mix that involves establishing a price for the product based on the demand for the product and the cost of producing it.

Pricing strategy is based on demand for the product and the cost of producing it. Some special considerations can also influence the price. Sometimes, for instance, a special introductory price is used to get people to try a new product. Some firms enter the market with low prices and keep them low, such as Carnival Cruise Lines and Suzuki cars. Others enter a market with very high prices and then lower them over time, such as producers of high-definition televisions and personal computers.

Distribution Strategy

distribution strategy

The part of the marketing mix that involves deciding how many stores and which specific wholesalers and retailers will handle the product in a geographic area.

Distribution is the means (the channel) by which a product flows from the producer to the consumer. One aspect of **distribution strategy** is deciding how many stores and which specific wholesalers and retailers will handle the product in a geographic area. Cosmetics, for instance, are distributed in many different ways. Avon has a sales force of several hundred thousand representatives who call directly on consumers. Clinique and Estée Lauder are distributed through selected department stores. Cover Girl and Del Laboratories use mostly chain drugstores and other mass merchandisers. Redken sells through beauticians. Revlon uses several of these distribution channels.

Promotion Strategy

promotion strategy
The part of the marketing mix that involves personal selling, advertising, public relations, and sales promotion of the product.

Many people feel that promotion is the most exciting part of the marketing mix. **Promotion strategy** covers personal selling, advertising, public relations, and sales promotion. Each element is coordinated with the others to create a promotional blend. An advertisement, for instance, helps a buyer get to know the company and paves the way for a sales call. A good promotion strategy can dramatically increase a firm's sales.

Public relations plays a special role in promotion. It is used to create a good image of the company and its products. Bad publicity costs nothing to send out, but it can cost a firm a great deal in lost business. Good publicity, such as a television or magazine story about a firm's new product, may be the result of much time, money, and effort spent by a public relations department.

Sales promotion directly stimulates sales. It includes trade shows, catalogs, contests, games, premiums, coupons, and special offers. McDonald's contests offering money and food prizes are an example. The company also issues discount coupons from time to time.

Considering a career in marketing? Visit

http://www.marketingpower.com

MAKING ETHICAL CHOICES

OMNILIFE: THE STORY OF A CONTEMPORARY MEDICINE MAN?

Jorge Vergara got his start in the weight-loss and nutritional supplement business by working for Herbalife when it expanded into Mexico following investigations into its sales methods by the U.S. Food and Drug Administration and the California attorney general's office. To satisfy the investigating authorities, Herbalife agreed to stop making excessive product claims and engaging in questionable sales practices.

Thinking he could do better on his own, Vergara left Herbalife in 1991 and started his own business, Omnilife, geared to the Mexican market. Rather than selling diet pills and diet formulas, Vergara put vitamins and minerals in sweetened canned drinks, teas, coffees, and chewing gum. He focused on smaller communities where nutritional products are rare. Additionally, he used cash-and-carry distribution centers to supply the company's distributors, who operated in a multilevel marketing system similar to that used by Herbalife and Amway, among others.

Arturo Rodriguez, an Omnilife distributor, says the company is concerned about customers' health and consequently sells delicious products that make customers feel better. Another distributor, Pepe Vergara, who is also Jorge Vergara's cousin, provides a different perspective on Omnilife products. He says the company sells junk food—but that it is nutritional junk food!

Omnilife's sales pitches rely heavily on testimonials. They include claims that Omnilife products have helped customers "to avoid cancer operations or to walk again." Jorge Vergara admits "that he and his distributors sometimes make claims that wouldn't pass regulatory muster in the U.S." The spouse of an Omnilife distributor compares Vergara to the "medicine men who can still be found touting herbal potions in town squares throughout Latin America."

Critical Thinking Questions

1. How would you describe Omnilife's marketing mix?
2. Is Omnilife's marketing mix managed in an ethical fashion? Explain your answer.

Not-for-Profit Marketing

Profit-oriented companies are not the only ones that analyze the marketing environment, find a competitive advantage, and create a marketing mix. The application of marketing principles and techniques is also vital to not-for-profit organizations. Marketing helps not-for-profit groups identify target markets and develop effective marketing mixes. In some cases, marketing has kept symphonies, museums, and other cultural groups from having to close their doors. In other organizations, such as the American Heart Association and the U.S. Army, marketing ideas and techniques have helped managers do their jobs better. The army, for instance, has identified the most effective ways to get men and women between the ages of 18 and 24 to visit a recruiter.

In the private sector, the profit motive is both an objective for guiding decisions and a criterion for evaluating results. Not-for-profit organizations do not seek to make a profit for redistribution to owners or shareholders. Rather, their focus is often on generating enough funds to cover expenses. For example, the Methodist Church does not gauge its success by the amount of money left in offering plates. The Museum of Science and Industry does not base its performance evaluations on the dollar value of tokens put into the turnstile.

Not-for-profit marketing is also concerned with **social marketing,** that is, the application of marketing to social issues and causes. The goals of social marketing are to effect social change (for instance, by creating racial harmony), further social causes (for instance, by helping the homeless), and evaluate the relationship between marketing and society (for instance, by asking whether society should allow advertising on television shows for young children). Individual organizations also engage in social marketing. The Southern Baptist Radio and Television Convention promotes brotherhood and goodwill by promoting religion and good deeds. M.A.D.D. counsels against drunk driving, and the National Wildlife Federation asks your help in protecting endangered animals and birds.

social marketing
The application of marketing techniques to social issues and causes.

concept check

- What is meant by the marketing mix?
- What are the components of the marketing mix?
- How can marketing techniques help not-for-profit organizations?
- Define social marketing.

BUYER BEHAVIOR

buyer behavior
The actions people take in buying and using goods and services.

An organization cannot reach its goals without understanding buyer behavior. **Buyer behavior** is the actions people take in buying and using goods and services. Marketers who understand buyer behavior, such as how a price increase will affect a product's sales, can create a more effective marketing mix.

To understand buyer behavior, marketers must understand how consumers make buying decisions. The decision-making process has several steps, which are shown in Exhibit 11-2. The entire process is affected by a number of personal and social factors. A buying decision starts (step 1) with a stimulus. A *stimulus* is anything that affects one or more of our senses (sight, smell, taste, touch, or hearing). A stimulus might be the feel of a sweater, the sleek shape of a new-model car, the design on a package, or a brand name mentioned by a friend. The stimulus leads to problem recognition (step 2): "This sweater feels so soft and looks good on me. Should I buy it?" In other words, the consumer decides that there's a purchase need.

The consumer next gets information about the purchase (step 3). What other styles of sweaters are available? At what price? Can this sweater be bought at a lower price elsewhere? Next, the consumer weighs the options and decides whether to make the purchase (step 4). If the consumer buys the product (step

5), certain outcomes are expected. These outcomes may or may not become reality: the sweater may last for years, or the shoulder seams may pull out the first time it's worn. Finally, the consumer assesses the experience with the product (step 6) and uses this information to update expectations about future purchases (step 7).

Influences on Consumer Decision-Making

As Exhibit 11-2 shows, individual and social factors can influence the consumer decision-making process. *Individual factors* are within the consumer and are unique to each person. They include perception, beliefs and attitudes, values, learning, self-concept, and personality. Companies often conduct research to better understand individual factors that cause consumers to buy or not to buy. For instance, Hyatt Hotels found that people who stayed at Hyatt while on business chose other hotels when they traveled on vacation with their children.

e x h i b i t 1 1 - 2 | Consumer Decision-Making Process

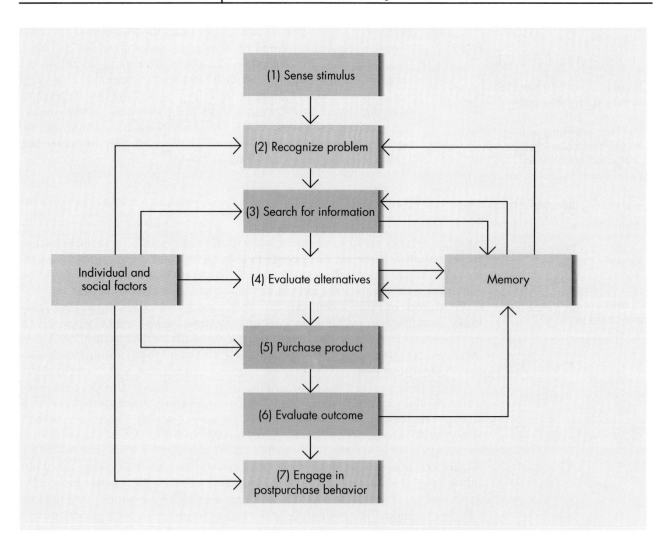

Hyatt was perceived as a businessperson's hotel. So Hyatt came up with a program called Camp Hyatt, which caters to children with a year-round program that varies by season. It combines attractive rates that appeal to parents with lots of activities for kids.

Social factors that affect the decision-making process include all interactions between a consumer and the external environment: family, opinion leaders, social class, and culture. Families may be the most important of these social factors. Yet families have limited resources, so many buying decisions are compromises. Since a number of decisions include input from several family members, marketing managers sometimes promote products using a family theme, such as Camp Hyatt.

Business-to-Business Purchase Decision-Making

Business buyer behavior and business markets are different from consumer markets. Business markets include institutions such as hospitals and schools, manufacturers, wholesalers and retailers, and various branches of government. The key difference between a consumer product and a business product is the intended use. If you purchase a certain model Dell computer for your home so you can surf the Internet, it is a consumer good. If a purchasing agent for MTV buys exactly the same computer for an MTV scriptwriter, it is a business good. Why? The reason is that MTV is a business, so the computer will be used in a business environment.

Characteristics of the Business-to-Business Market   The main differences between consumer markets and business markets are as follows:

1. *Purchase volume.* Business customers buy in much larger quantities than consumers. Think how many truckloads of sugar Mars must purchase to make one day's output of M&Ms.
2. *Number of customers.* Business marketers usually have far fewer customers than consumer marketers. As a result, it is much easier to identify prospective buyers and monitor current needs. Think about how few customers for airplanes or industrial cranes there are compared to the more than 70 million consumer households in the United States.
3. *Location of buyers.* Business customers tend to be much more geographically concentrated than consumers. Aircraft manufacturing is found in Seattle, St. Louis, and Dallas/Fort Worth. Suppliers to these manufacturers often locate close to the manufacturers to lower distribution costs and facilitate communication.
4. *Direct distribution.* Business sales tend to be made directly to the buyer because such sales frequently involve large quantities or custom-made items like heavy machinery. Consumer goods are more likely to be sold through intermediaries like wholesalers and retailers.
5. *Rational purchase decisions.* Unlike consumers, business buyers usually approach purchasing rather formally. Businesses use professionally trained purchasing agents or buyers who spend their entire career purchasing a limited number of items.

c o n c ə p t   c h ə c k

- Explain the consumer decision-making process.
- How do business markets differ from consumer markets?

MARKET SEGMENTATION

>lg 5

The study of buyer behavior helps marketing managers better understand why people make purchases. To identify the target markets that may be most

market segmentation

The process of separating, identifying, and evaluating the layers of a market in order to design a marketing mix.

proftable for the firm, managers use **market segmentation,** which is the process of separating, identifying, and evaluating the layers of a market to design a marketing mix. For instance, a target market might be segmented into two groups: families with children and families without children. Families with young children are likely to buy hot cereals and presweetened cereals. Families with no children are more likely to buy health-oriented cereals. You can be sure that cereal companies plan their marketing mixes with this difference in mind. A business market may be segmented by large customers and small customers or by geographic area.

The five basic forms of consumer market segmentation are demographic, geographic, psychographic, benefit, and volume. Their characteristics are summarized in Exhibit 11-3 and discussed in the following sections.

Demographic Segmentation

demographic segmentation

The differentiation of markets through the use of categories such as age, education, gender, income, and household size.

Demographic segmentation uses categories such as age, education, gender, income, and household size to differentiate among markets. This form of market segmentation is the most common. The U.S. Census Bureau provides a great deal of demographic data. For example, marketing researchers can use census data to find areas within cities that contain high concentrations of high-income consumers, singles, blue-collar workers, and so forth.

You don't have to be an adult to have market clout. One study found that aggregate spending by or on behalf of children ages 4 to 12 roughly doubled every decade in the 1960s, 1970s, and 1980s. It tripled in the 1990s to more than $24 billion.[8] And whereas children in the 1960s spent almost all their money on candy, today only one-third of the money goes to food and drink, with the balance spent on toys, clothes, movies, and games.

Mature Americans (those born before 1945), baby boomers (consumers born between 1946 and 1964), and Generation Xers (younger consumers born between 1965 and 1978) all have different needs, tastes, and consumption pat-

HOT links

Find a vast array of census data at

http://www.census.gov

e x h i b i t   1 1 - 3 | Forms of Consumer Market Segmentation

Form	General Characteristics
Demographic segmentation	Age, education, gender, income, race, social class, household size
Geographic segmentation	Regional location (e.g., New England, Mid-Atlantic, Southeast, Great Lakes, Plains States, Northwest, Southwest, Rocky Mountains, Far West); population density (urban, suburban, rural); city or county size; climate
Psychographic segmentation	Lifestyle, personality, interests, values, attitudes
Benefit segmentation	Benefits provided by the good or service
Volume segmentation	Amount of use (light versus heavy)

terns. Exhibit 11-4 shows some of these generational differences; note that baby boomers tend to be nostalgic and prefer the old to the new, whereas Generation Xers tend to be video oriented and would rather see the movie than read the book.

Certain markets are segmented by gender. These include clothing, cosmetics, personal care items, magazines, jewelry, and footwear. Gillette, for example, is one of the world's best-known marketers of personal care products and has historically targeted men for the most part. Yet women's products have generated most of Gillette's growth since 1992. Gillette's shaving line for women has expanded into a $400 million global business, growing nearly 20 percent annually.

Income is another popular way to segment markets. Income level influences consumers' wants and determines their buying power. Housing, clothing, automobiles, and alcoholic beverages are among the many markets segmented by income. Budget Gourmet frozen dinners are targeted to lower-income groups, whereas the Le Menu line is aimed at higher-income consumers.

Geographic Segmentation

geographic segmentation
The differentiation of markets by region of the country, city or county size, market density, or climate.

Geographic segmentation means segmenting markets by region of the country, city or county size, market density, or climate. *Market density* is the number of people or businesses within a certain area. Many companies segment their markets geographically to meet regional preferences and buying habits. Pizza Hut, for instance, gives easterners extra cheese, westerners more ingredients, and midwesterners both. Both Ford and Chevrolet sell more pickup trucks and

e x h i b i t   1 1 - 4 | Preferences of Mature Adults, Baby Boomers, and Generation Xers

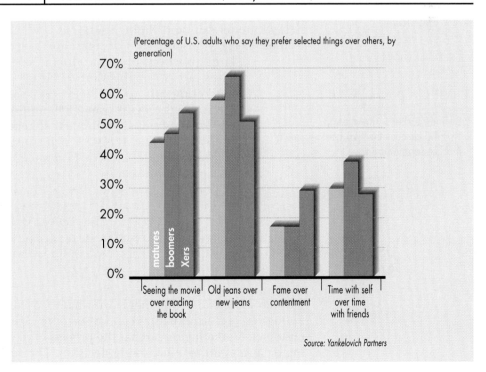

Source: Yankelovich Partners

truck parts in the middle of the country than on either coast. The well-defined "pickup truck belt" runs from the upper Midwest south through Texas and the Gulf states. Ford "owns" the northern half of this truck belt, and Chevrolet the southern half.

Psychographic Segmentation

psychographic segmentation

The differentiation of markets by personality or lifestyle.

Race, income, occupation, and other demographic variables help in developing strategies but often do not paint the entire picture of consumer needs. Demographics provide the skeleton, but psychographics add meat to the bones. **Psychographic segmentation** is market segmentation by personality or lifestyle. People with common activities, interests, and opinions are grouped together and given a "lifestyle name."

Benefit Segmentation

benefit segmentation

The differentiation of markets based on what a product will do rather than on customer characteristics.

Benefit segmentation is based on what a product will do rather than on consumer characteristics. For years Crest toothpaste was targeted toward consumers concerned with preventing cavities. Recently, Crest subdivided its market. It now offers regular Crest, Crest Tartar Control for people who want to prevent cavities and tartar buildup, Kid's Crest with sparkles that taste like bubble gum, and another Crest that prevents gum disease. Another toothpaste, Topol, targets people who want whiter teeth—teeth without coffee, tea, or tobacco stains. Sensodyne toothpaste is aimed at people with highly sensitive teeth.

Volume Segmentation

volume segmentation

The differentiation of markets based on the amount of the product purchased.

The fifth main type of segmentation is **volume segmentation**, which is based on the amount of the product purchased. Just about every product has heavy, moderate, and light users, as well as nonusers. Heavy users often account for a very large portion of a product's sales. Thus, a firm might want to target its marketing mix to the heavy-user segment. Kraft recently ran a $30 million advertising campaign directed at heavy users of Miracle Whip. A heavy user consumes 550 servings or 17 pounds of Miracle Whip a year.[9]

Links to major marketing research firms are available at http://www.quirks.com/source/links.htm

concept check

• Define market segmentation.
• List and discuss the five basic forms of market segmentation.

USING MARKETING RESEARCH TO SERVE EXISTING CUSTOMERS AND FIND NEW CUSTOMERS

>lg 6

How do successful companies learn what their customers value? Through marketing research, companies can be sure they are listening to the voice of the customer. **Marketing research** is the process of planning, collecting, and analyzing data relevant to a marketing decision. The results of this analysis are then communicated to management. The information collected through marketing

marketing research
The process of planning, collecting, and analyzing data relevant to a marketing decision.

research includes the preferences of customers, the perceived benefits of products, and consumer lifestyles. Research helps companies make better use of their marketing budgets. Marketing research has a range of uses from fine-tuning products to discovering whole new marketing concepts.

This section examines the marketing research process, which consists of the following steps:

1. Define the marketing problem.
2. Choose a method of research.
3. Collect the data.
4. Analyze the research data.
5. Make recommendations to management.

Define the Marketing Problem

The most critical step in the marketing research process is defining the marketing problem. This involves either writing a problem statement or a list of research objectives. If the problem is not defined properly, the remainder of the research will be a waste of time and money. Two key questions can help in defining the marketing problem correctly:

APPLYING TECHNOLOGY

USING THE WEB TO GATHER DECISION-MAKING INFORMATION

Web-based marketing research studies are changing the way marketing research will be conducted in the future. Web-based surveys have many advantages over traditional methods. For starters, no interviewers are involved, so interviewer errors are eliminated, as is interviewer bias. If the interviewer is in a bad mood or doesn't like certain types of people or subjects, then the data can be affected. In Web-based surveys, every respondent has exactly the same interviewer—one that is never tired, moody, prejudiced, impatient, or opinionated. Telephone interviews are limited to audio, but Web surveys can be truly multimedia. For example, a recent study of a new computer game showed respondents a variety of screen shots as well as a video clip of sample game play.

In contrast to traditional market research surveys, which can take six weeks to process, Web-based surveys are fast. Questionnaires are posted on a secure Web site, and respondents are directed to the site from banner ads or personal invitations issued by e-mail. Respondents drop by the survey site whenever they want to (even at 3 A.M.) and complete their surveys. Often, a sufficiently large sample, say, 300 or 400 respondents, can be completed over a weekend.

Any research project has two major cost components: data collection and analysis. Data collection costs for a Web-based survey are almost zero. With over 170 million Internet users worldwide in 2001, you can find just about any type of respondent on the Web. Analysis costs are also reduced because with advanced software programs data can be analyzed as quickly as consumers fill out a questionnaire online.

Overall, Web-based surveys offer tremendous potential to the marketing research industry because they are faster, generate more accurate information, and cost less than traditional surveys. Used properly, Web-based marketing research soon will vastly increase the amount of customer feedback on which managers base critical business decisions.

Critical Thinking Questions

1. Do you see any disadvantages of Internet surveys?
2. Would you participate in a Web survey? Why or why not?

Interviewing people in a shopping mall is a popular survey research method that allows firms to gather information about consumer opinions and attitudes.

survey research
A marketing research method in which an interviewer interacts with respondents, either in person, by mail, at a mall, or through the Internet to obtain facts, opinions, and attitudes.

observation research
A marketing research method in which the investigator monitors respondents' actions without interacting directly with the respondents; for example, by using cash registers with scanners.

experiment
A marketing research method in which the investigator changes one or more variables—price, packaging, design, shelf space, advertising theme, or advertising expenditures—while observing the effects of these changes on another variable (usually sales).

primary data
Information collected directly from the original source to solve a problem.

secondary data
Information that has already been collected for a project other than the current one, but which may be used to solve the current problem.

1. Why is the information being sought? By discussing with managers what the information is going to be used for and what decisions might be made as a result, the researcher can get a clearer grasp of the problem.
2. Does the information already exist? If so, money and time can be saved and a quick decision can be made.

Choose a Method of Research

After the problem is correctly defined, a research method is chosen. There are three basic research methods: survey, observation, and experiment.

With **survey research,** an interviewer interacts with respondents, either in person or by mail, to obtain facts, opinions, and attitudes. A questionnaire is used to provide an orderly and structured approach to data gathering. Face-to-face interviews may take place at the respondent's home, in a shopping mall, the Internet, or at a place of business.

Observation research is research that monitors respondents' actions without direct interaction. In the fastest grow-ing form of observation research, researchers use cash registers with scanners that read tags with bar codes to identify the item being purchased. Technological advances are rapidly expanding the future of observation research. For example, ACNielsen has been using black boxes for years on television sets to silently obtain information on a family's viewing habits. But what if the set is on and no one is in the room? To overcome that problem, researchers will soon rely on infrared passive "people meters" that will identify the faces of family members watching the television program. Thus, the meter will duly record when the set is on and no one is watching.

In the third research method, **experiment,** the investigator changes one or more variables—price, package, design, shelf space, advertising theme, or advertising expenditures—while observing the effects of those changes on another variable (usually sales). The objective of experiments is to measure causality. For example, an experiment may reveal the impact that a change in package design has on sales.

Collect the Data

Two types of data are used in marketing research: **primary data,** which are collected directly from the original source to solve a problem; and **secondary data,** which is information that has already been collected for a project other than the current one but may be used to help solve it. Secondary data can come from a number of sources, among them government agencies, trade associations, research bureaus, universities, the Internet, commercial publications, and internal company records. Company records include sales invoices, accounting records, data from previous research studies, and historical sales data.

See examples of the secondary research available from CACI at
http://demographics.caci.com

Primary data are usually gathered through some form of survey research. As described earlier, survey research often relies on interviews (see Exhibit 11-5 for the different types of interviews). Today, conducting surveys over the Internet is the fastest growing form of survey research, as the Applying Technology box on p. 329 describes.

Analyze the Data

After the data have been collected, the next step in the research process is data analysis. The purpose of this analysis is to interpret and draw conclusions from the mass of collected data. Many software statistical programs such as SAS and SPSS are available to make this task easier for the researcher.

Make Recommendations to Management

After completing the data analysis, the researcher must prepare the report and communicate the conclusions and recommendations to management. This is a key step in the process because marketing researchers who want their

---

e x h i b i t   1 1 - 5 | Types of Interviews Used in Survey Research

Type	Description
Door-to-door	Interviewer interviews consumer in consumer's home (this practice is almost extinct).
Executive interview	Interviewer interviews industrial product user (e.g., engineer, architect, doctor, executive) or decision maker at place of business regarding an industrial product.
Mall intercept	Interviewer interviews consumer in shopping mall or other high-traffic location. Interviews may be done in public areas of the mall, or the respondent may be taken to a private test area.
Central location telephone interview	Interviewing is conducted from a telephone facility set up for that purpose. These facilities typically have equipment that permits the supervisor to unobtrusively monitor the interview while it is taking place. Some facilities have Wide Area Telephone Service (WATS) to permit national sampling from a single location. The questionnaire is programmed into a computer. The interviewer enters responses directly.
Self-administered questionnaires	These are most frequently employed at high-traffic locations such as shopping malls or in captive audience situations such as classrooms and airplanes. Respondents are given general information on how to fill out the questionnaire and are left to complete it on their own.
Ad hoc (one-shot) mail surveys	Questionnaires are mailed to a sample of consumers or industrial users. Instructions are included. Respondents are asked to fill out the questionnaire and return it via mail. Sometimes a gift or monetary incentive is provided.
Mail panels	Several companies, including Market Facts, The NPD Group, and National Family Opinion, operate large (more than 100,000 households) consumer panels and ad hoc mail surveys. The company has contacted the people on the panel earlier and explained the panel concept to them. They have agreed to participate for a certain period of time. In addition, participants are offered gratuities to participate in mail panels.
Point-of-service touch-screen monitors	Kiosks, equipped with touch-screen monitors, provide a new way to capture information from individuals in stores, health clinics, and other shopping or service environments.
Internet surveys	This is the fastest growing form of survey research. As the number of individuals connected to the Internet increases, this approach will become increasingly attractive. Internet surveys are discussed in the Applying Technology box.

concept check

- Define marketing research.
- Explain the marketing research process.
- What are the three basic marketing research methods?

conclusions acted upon must convince the manager that the results are credible and justified by the data collected. Today, presentation software like PowerPoint and Astound provides easy-to-use tools for creating reports and presentations that are more interesting, compelling, and effective than was possible just a few years ago.

CAPITALIZING ON TRENDS IN BUSINESS

>lg 7

To discover exactly what customers value most, organizations are using innovative techniques for collecting customer information. Some of the more sophisticated marketing research techniques that are growing in popularity are advanced observation research methods, decision support systems (DDSs), and database marketing.

Advanced Observation Research Methods

All forms of observation research are increasingly using more sophisticated technology. The major television networks, for example, are supporting an advanced technology that provides highly accurate market data about television viewers' behavior. The networks have been discouraged by the data flowing from ACNielsen media research, which indicate that the networks are losing market share. The networks say that ACNielsen's research is faulty and are backing a new measurement system created by Statistical Research Inc. (SRI), which in 2001 merged with Knowledge Networks. The stakes are about $13 billion in advertising revenue generated annually by the major networks.[10] During the 1990s SRI developed Systems for Measuring And Reporting Television, or SMART, at a cost of $160 million. The SMART setup consists of meters with sensors that can pick up signals from the air. The meter looks like a VCR and sits on top of the television. Users log in and out before and after watching television by pressing a device similar to a TV remote control, which was designed for ease of use. The device accurately tracks which program is being watched and by whom.

Perhaps most astounding of all is the new technology that is allowing us to learn how the brain receives and processes information. Brain science has come so far that researchers are now able to routinely eavesdrop on brains while they think. The new technology offers insights about how we perceive, think, and make decisions. This information will enable researchers to uncover consumers' root motivations—or hot buttons. These come from the subliminal regions of our brains, where values, needs, and motivations originate.[11]

decision support system (DSS)

An interactive, flexible, computerized information system that allows managers to make decisions quickly and accurately; used to conduct sales analyses, forecast sales, evaluate advertising, analyze product lines, and keep tabs on market trends and competitors' actions.

Decision Support Systems

More and more managers are turning to another form of technology called a **decision support system (DSS),** an interactive, flexible computerized information system that allows managers to make decisions quickly and accurately. Managers use DSS to conduct sales analyses, forecast sales, evaluate advertising, analyze product lines, and keep tabs on market trends and competitors' actions. A DSS not only allows managers to ask "what if" questions, but enables them to slice the data any way they want. A DSS has the following characteristics:

1. *Interactive.* The manager gives simple instructions and sees results generated on the spot. The process is under the manager's direct control; no computer programmer is needed.
2. *Flexible.* It can sort, regroup, total, average, and manipulate the data in a variety of ways. It will shift gears as the user changes topics, matching information to the problem at hand. For example, the chief executive can see highly aggregated figures, while the marketing analyst views detailed breakouts.
3. *Discovery oriented.* It helps managers probe for trends, isolate problems, and ask new questions.
4. *Easy to learn and use.* Managers need not be particularly computer knowledgeable. Novice users can elect a standard, or "default," method of using the system that enables them to bypass optional features and work with the basic system while they gradually learn its possibilities. This minimizes the frustration that frequently accompanies new computer software.

Using Databases for Micromarketing

database marketing

The creation of a large computerized file of the profiles and purchase patterns of customers and potential customers; usually required for successful micromarketing.

Perhaps the fastest growing use of DSS is for **database marketing,** which is the creation of a large computerized file of the profiles and purchase patterns of customers and potential customers. Using the very specific information in the database, a company can, if it wishes, direct a different individualized message to every customer or potential customer.

Beginning in the 1950s, network television enabled advertisers to "get the same message to everyone simultaneously." Database marketing can get a customized, individual message to everyone simultaneously through direct mail. This is why database marketing is sometimes called *micromarketing.* Specifically, database marketing can:

- Identify the most profitable and least profitable customers.
- Identify the most profitable market segments or individuals and target efforts with greater efficiency and effectiveness.
- Aim marketing efforts to those goods, services, and market segments that require the most support.
- Increase revenue through repackaging and repricing products for various market segments.
- Evaluate opportunities for offering new products and services.
- Identify products and services that are best-sellers and most profitable.

Database marketing can create a computerized form of the old-fashioned relationship that people used to have with the corner grocer, butcher, or baker. "A database is sort of a collective memory," says Richard G. Barlow, president of Frequency Marketing, Inc., a Cincinnati-based consulting firm. "It deals with you in the same personalized way as a mom-and-pop grocery store, where they knew customers by name and stocked what they wanted."[12] American Express, for example, can pull from its database all cardholders who made purchases at golf pro-shops in the past six months, attended symphony concerts, or traveled to Europe more than once in the last year.

concept check

- How is technology being used in marketing research?
- What is a decision support system (DSS) and what is its purpose?
- Explain what database marketing is and describe some of its uses.

Applying This Chapter's Topics

APPLYING THIS CHAPTER'S TOPICS

As a consumer, you participate in shaping consumer products by the choices you make and the products and services you buy. You can become a better consumer by actively participating in marketing surveys and learning more about the products you buy.

Participate in Marketing Research Surveys

All of us get tired of telephone solicitations where people try to sell us everything from new carpet to chimney cleaning. Recognize that marketing research surveys are different. A true marketing research survey will *never* involve a sales pitch nor will the research firm sell your name to a database marketer. The purpose of marketing research is to build better goods and services for you and me. Help out the researchers and ultimately help yourself. The Council for Marketing and Opinion Research (CMOR) is an organization of hundreds of marketing research professionals that is dedicated to preserving the integrity of the research industry. If you receive a call from someone who tries to sell you something under the guise of marketing research, get the name and address of the organization. Call CMOR at 1-800-887-CMOR and report the abuse.

Understand Cognitive Dissonance

cognitive dissonance

The condition of having beliefs or knowledge that are internally inconsistent or that disagree with one's behavior.

When making a major purchase, particularly when the item is expensive and choices are similar, consumers typically experience **cognitive dissonance;** that is, they have beliefs or knowledge that are internally inconsistent or that disagree with their behavior. In other words, instead of feeling happy with their new purchase, they experience doubts, feel uneasy, and wonder if they have done the right thing. Understand that this feeling of uneasiness is perfectly normal and goes away over time. Perhaps the best way to avoid cognitive

TRY IT NOW!

1. **Stop junk mail** If you are upset about junk mail, contact the Direct Marketing Association and have your name removed from mailing lists. The email address is **http://www.the-dma.org/.** You can also join an umbrella organization dedicated to stopping the flood of junk email, intrusive telemarketing calls, and junk mail. One such organization is Junkbusters. It can be found at **http://www.junkbusters.com.**

2. **Know Your Profile** Do you wonder where marketers place you in their psychographic profiles? To find out, go to **http://www.future.sri.com/vals/ presurvey.shtml** and take the Values and Life-Styles self-test. Where do you fit in?

dissonance is to insist on a strong warranty or money-back guarantee. A second approach is to read everything you can find about your purchase. Go to the Internet and use the search engines to find articles relevant to your purchase. Find Internet chat rooms about your product and join in the discussion. And, before you buy, check out the *Consumer Reports* ratings on your product at **http://www.consumerreports.org.**

SUMMARY OF LEARNING GOALS

>lg 1   **What are the marketing concept and relationship building?**
Marketing includes those business activities that are designed to satisfy consumer needs and wants through the exchange process. Marketing managers use the "right" principle—getting the right goods or services to the right people at the right place, time, and price, using the right promotional techniques. Today, many firms have adopted the marketing concept. The marketing concept involves identifying consumer needs and wants and then producing goods or services that will satisfy them while making a profit. Relationship marketing entails forging long-term relationships with customers, which can lead to repeat sales, reduced costs, and stable relationships.

>lg 2   **How do managers create a marketing strategy?**
A firm creates a marketing strategy by understanding the external environment, defining the target market, determining a competitive advantage, and developing a marketing mix. Environmental scanning enables companies to understand the external environment. The target market is the specific group of consumers toward which a firm directs its marketing efforts. A competitive advantage is a set of unique features of a company and its products that are perceived by the target market as significant and superior to those of the competition.

>lg 3   **What is the marketing mix?**
To carry out the marketing strategy, firms create a marketing mix—a blend of products, distribution systems, prices, and promotion. Marketing managers use this mix to satisfy target consumers. The mix can be applied to nonbusiness as well as business situations.

>lg 4   **How do consumers and organizations make buying decisions?**
Buyer behavior is what people and businesses do in buying and using goods and services. The consumer decision-making process consists of the following steps: responding to a stimulus, recognizing a problem or opportunity, seeking information, evaluating alternatives, purchasing the product, judging the purchase outcome, and engaging in postpurchase behavior. A number of factors influence the process including individual and social factors. The main differences between consumer and business markets are purchase volume, number of customers, location of buyers, direct distribution, and rational purchase decisions.

>lg 5   **What are the five basic forms of market segmentation?**
Success in marketing depends on understanding the target market. One technique used to identify a target market is market segmentation. The five basic forms of segmentation are demographic (population statistics), geographic (location), psychographic (personality or lifestyle), benefit (product features), and volume (amount purchased).

>lg 6   **How is marketing research used in marketing decision-making?**
Much can be learned about consumers through marketing research, which involves collecting, recording, and analyzing data important in marketing goods and

services and communicating the results to management. Marketing researchers may use primary data, which are gathered through door-to-door, mall-intercept, telephone, the Internet, and mail interviews. Secondary data are available from a variety of sources including government, trade, and commercial associations. Both primary and secondary data give researchers a better idea of how the market will respond to the product. Thus, they reduce the risk of producing something the market doesn't want.

at DaimlerChrysler

Before a company can create a marketing mix, it must identify the target market for the product. Thus, DaimlerChrysler first had to identify the target market for the 300M. To be successful, the company had to identify one or more competitive advantages unique to the 300M. DaimlerChrysler used marketing research to identify the target market for the 300M and then determined the needs and desires of these potential buyers. With this information, the company could build customer value into the 300M. The automaker must continue to use marketing research to identify the ever-changing desires of the target market. DaimlerChrysler can retain its leadership position with the 300M by continuing to deliver value to target buyers.

>lg 7 What are the trends in understanding the consumer?

New technology has increased the sophistication of observation research techniques and improved the accuracy of data, such as measurements of the size of television audiences. Researchers are also analyzing the brain to better understand how people think. A second trend is the growing use of decision support systems. These enable managers to make decisions quickly and accurately. A third trend is the growing use of databases for micromarketing.

PREPARING FOR TOMORROW'S WORKPLACE

1. Can the marketing concept be applied effectively by a sole proprietorship, or is it more appropriate for larger businesses with more managers? Explain.
2. Write a memo to your manager explaining why it is important for his small business (a restaurant) to have a competitive advantage.
3. Divide the class into two groups. Debate the following propositions: (1) business buyer behavior can be just as emotional as consumer buyer behavior; (2) consumer buyer behavior can be just as rational as business buyer behavior.
4. "Market segmentation is the most important concept in marketing." Why do you think some marketing professionals make this statement? Give an example of each form of segmentation.
5. Write a paper explaining when a marketer would want to use primary data and when it would be better to use secondary data.
6. Divide the class into two teams. Debate the concept that marketing research is an invasion of privacy.
7. Can marketing research be carried out in the same manner all over the world? Why or why not?

WORKING THE NET

1. You've been hired by a snack food manufacturer that is interested in adding popcorn snacks to its product line. First, however, the company asks you to

KEY TERMS

benefit
segmentation
328

buyer behavior
323

cognitive
dissonance 334

competitive
advantage 319

cost competitive
advantage 319

customer
satisfaction 315

customer value
315

database marketing
333

decision support
system (DSS) 332

demographic
segmentation
326

differential
competitive
advantage 320

distribution strategy
321

environmental
scanning 318

exchange 314

experiment 330

four Ps 321

geographic
segmentation
327

market
segmentation
326

marketing 314

marketing concept
314

marketing mix 320

marketing research
328

niche competitive
advantage 320

observation
research 330

pricing strategy
321

primary data 330

product strategy
321

production
orientation 315

promotion strategy
322

psychographic
segmentation
328

relationship
marketing 316

find some secondary data on the current market for popcorn. Go to the Dogpile Search Engine (**http://www.dogpile.com**) and do a search for "popcorn consumption." Can you find how much popcorn is sold annually? The geographic locations with the highest popcorn sales? The time of the year when the most popcorn is sold? What are the limitations of doing research like this on the Internet?

2. You and a friend want to start a new magazine for people who work at home. Do a search of the U.S. Census database at **http://www.census.gov** to get information about the work-at-home market.

3. Take the VALS lifestyle survey at **http://www.future.sri.com/vals/presurvey. shtml** and find out which psychographic segment you're in. Do you agree or disagree with the results? Why or why not?

CREATIVE THINKING CASE

The American Automobile Association—Building Long-Term Relationships?

This case is built upon the experience of Don Schultz, a marketing professor at Northwestern University. He tells his story in the first person.

Almost every car owner knows about the American Automobile Association. They're the people who slog through rain and snow to rescue stranded motorists. Whether it's a flat tire on the expressway or a broken axle or keys locked in a car parked in a lot, the AAA professionals come running. And they do a good job. I've been a member of the Chicago Motor Club, a "Triple A" affiliate, for 20 years. They have given good service to me, my wife, my children, and my mother.

In recent months, my car has had a problem. For reasons known only to the car, the battery discharges at random. Sometimes it happens overnight, sometimes weeks go by without a problem. When the battery discharges itself, I call AAA. No matter where I am, they come out and give me a jump. Seemingly my problem is no problem for them. They provide cheerful, friendly service, day and night.

Until recently, that is, when apparently I triggered their brand relationship destroying mechanism. While other service suppliers were sending end-of-the-year calendars and thank-you letters, I got threats from AAA. In a letter, Gerald F. Svarz, manager of member relations, wrote:

> Our records indicate that you have requested Emergency Road Service four times during the past 12 months. As outlined in the Member's Handbook, the Club reserves the right to notify a member when they have used four or more service calls in the previous 12 months. Excessive use of Emergency Road Service can result in the nonrenewal or the cancellation of a membership. The nonrenewal or cancellation of membership is based solely on the number of calls in a membership year.

Wow, talk about *building* brand *relationships!* Here's an organization that's going to kick me out of its club, whose primary claim to fame and only reason for being—at least for most of its members—is emergency road service. Only don't use our service too much, they say, or we'll cancel your membership. We reserve that right.

Just to make sure I wasn't overlooking something, I checked out AAA in the Yellow Pages. "Emergency Road Service," the ad says. Same for the newspaper ads I found. And "Emergency Road Service" is splashed all over the relation-*building* magazine they send me every few months. Their promotional literature says "Emergency Road Service" in big bold letters.

secondary data
  330
social marketing
  323
survey research
  330
target market 318
volume
  segmentation
  328

The problem is, they reserve the right to limit the Emergency Road Service you need. Am I a better AAA *customer* if I don't ever use their services? It sure sounds like it. What about all those years I paid the membership fee and never used the service? They didn't write to thank me for that, nor did they adjust my membership fee the way auto insurance companies do for safe drivers.

Critical Thinking Questions

1. Is AAA following the marketing concept?
2. Doesn't it make economic sense to "weed out" people who use the service too much?
3. Insurance companies cancel people's auto insurance if they get too many speeding tickets. Isn't AAA's policy the same thing?
4. Would you make any changes in AAA's operations? If so, what?

VIDEO CASE

Burke Marketing Research

Burke Marketing Research (**http://www.burke.com**), with offices and affiliates in 40 countries throughout the world, provides marketing research services to a wide range of clients. They include companies in the following industries: agricultural/chemical; computer hardware and software; communications/technology; consumer goods and services; entertainment, television, and cable; insurance and financial; pharmaceutical and health care; consulting; and industrial/business-to-business. Across this broad spectrum of industries, Burke deals with both quantitative and qualitative marketing issues. Each project is customized to fit the specific client's marketing needs and decision-making requirements.

As a partly employee-owned firm, Burke has a special commitment to its clientele. "Every employee is personally committed to providing the best possible service" to clients. Clients work directly with an account team which is charged with ensuring that the client's "objectives are met efficiently, economically, and on time."

To generate information for its studies, Burke uses a variety of data collection methods including focus groups, mail surveys, Internet online surveys, phone surveys, and mall intercept interviews. From its experience in "dealing with recurrent marketing problems across many industry and product categories," the company has developed a variety of marketing research protocols for examining and diagnosing common marketing problems. These protocols include onsite vendor/customer focus groups, image and positioning analysis, advertising campaign evaluation, new product demand and pricing analysis, product testing analysis, brand equity analysis, marketing performance analysis, and an integrated concept evaluation system. Each account team shapes the protocols to deal with the client's unique issues. In using each protocol, Burke follows a generally accepted approach to marketing research: defining the marketing problem; selecting and adapting the appropriate protocol for collecting the data; collecting and analyzing the data; and, finally, generating a report for the client that contains useful results and recommendations.

Burke's executives believe that effective "marketing research consists of much more than telephone surveys." They say that good marketing research requires knowledgeable, experienced people who are familiar with the client's industry and the challenges the client faces every day. Good marketing research also requires "attention to detail and a commitment to finding . . . results."

Critical Thinking Questions

1. How would you describe Burke's competitive advantage in the marketing research marketplace?
2. How does Burke Marketing Research use market segmentation in its own business?
3. Do you think Burke's approach to marketing research is effective? Why or why not?

Case: Boo.com's Big Boo-Boo

When Ernst Malmsten and Kajsa Leander announced the launch of Boo.com, they promised that their online shopping site would be a "gateway to world cool." They planned to sell international sportswear brands to fashion-savvy customers in Europe and North America. The pair quickly lined up over $130 million in capital and opened offices in New York and London.

Malmsten and Leander seemed to epitomize their target market. Both Swedish, they were in their late 20s and dressed in stylish clothes. Making sure the site focused on the coolest fashions was a critical factor, they decided, so they designated employees as "cool hunters" who observed what hip consumer groups were wearing. For example, one group of "cool hunters" spent time watching what young, chic architects in New York were wearing.

Several months before the Boo.com site was launched, the firm's public relations team started publicizing its debut. A multimillion-dollar advertising campaign also began to generate interest in the site.

Products on the site were shown in three-dimensional pictures that could be rotated for a closer look. Virtual mannequins let shoppers mix and match outfits and accessories. Miss Boo, an animated personal shopping assistant, stood ready to help customers with shopping advice and witty banter. However, the site had problems. It was built for high-speed access and the most advanced browsers but few Internet users had those tools. Technological and design problems meant the site couldn't start taking orders until months after its launch was announced.

Although Boo.com seemed off to a promising start, the firm closed its doors just a year after it opened. Some business analysts said the firm had spent too much too quickly on advertising while ignoring issues like merchandise selection. Others blamed the site's technological glitches for turning off customers. At least one analyst noted that younger women shoppers enjoy the social process of going shopping with friends, something that an online store couldn't duplicate.

Two months later, Fashionmall.com, a six-year-old fashion Internet portal, purchased the rights to use Boo.com's name, Web design elements, and editorial concepts. Fashionmall.com eventually relaunched Boo.com as one of its "floors."

Questions for Critical Thinking

1. Analyze Boo.com's marketing strategy and explain possible reasons for its failure.
2. What additional marketing research would you have recommended Boo.com conduct?
3. What advice would you have given to Fashionmall.com before it relaunched the Boo.com Web site?

SOURCES: William Echikson, "Designers Climb on the Virtual Catwalk," *BusinessWeek Online* (September 27, 1999), downloaded from **http://www.businessweek.com**; Ellen Neuborne, "Why Boo Really Went Bust," *BusinessWeek Online* (June 12, 2000), downloaded from **http://www.businessweek.com**; Bernhard Warner, "Boo.com Scares Up a Buyer," *The Standard* (June 1, 2000), downloaded from **http://www.thestandard.com**.

learning goals

>lg 1   What is the role of the product in the market-
ing mix, and how are products classified
and developed?

>lg 2   What are the stages of the product life cycle?

>lg 3   What strategies are used for pricing products?

>lg 4   Describe the distribution channels and the
manner in which they are organized.

>lg 5   What are the functions of physical
distribution?

>lg 6   Explain the promotional mix and its primary
elements.

>lg 7   Describe the trends affecting elements of the
marketing mix.

Developing the Marketing Mix

chapter 12

Hot Air to Ride

Each May, an eclectic group of inventor-aeronauts from all over the country converges on a grass airstrip in central Vermont. Officially, the event is the Experimental Balloon and Airship Meet. Unofficially it's "Brian's parts," in honor of Brian Boland, the shaggy-haired, bushy-bearded 51-year-old who owns the property. The beer drinking starts early, and before long a replica Viking ship built on the chassis of an '86 Chevy Astro swoops on the grass in big, crazy circles with a crew of shirtless, whooping men hanging over the gunwales.

A little context. Commercial blimps, the kind that fly corporate logos over sporting arenas, float on helium. The gas is expensive, so the blimps have to stay inflated all the time. Starting at $2 million a pop, with as much again in yearly upkeep, helium blimps are wildly impractical for private owners.

But there's an alternative: hot air. It's cheap, and you don't have to worry about storage. The era of personal blimping dawned in 1973 when an Englishman named Don Cameron showed up at a balloon meet with a rumpled-looking hot-air dirigible powered by a Volkswagen engine. Zipping out from over the tree line, he astonished the crowd by actually being able to steer his craft.

On paper, personal blimps are a can't-miss proposition, combining the grace of hot-air ballooning with the control of powered flight. A new top-of-the-line model starts at $150,000, about the same as a new single-engine Cessna. The reality, however, is that in this country personal blimping hardly exists. There are 530,000 private airplane pilots in the United States. The number flying their own blimps is two.

Boland wants blimping to take off, but he's less hepped on creating a business plan. He just wants to have as much fun as possible, and hopes someone else out there has the same definition of fun that he does. His most practical contribution to the field is a craft he dubs the Pocket Blimp. Designed to break down into pieces small enough to bring on a plane as check-in baggage, the model is just 70 feet long—one-third as long as a Goodyear blimp. Unlike top-end hot-air airships, the Pocket Blimp is unpressurized, lending it a fairly baggy appearance and reducing its practical speed to about six mph, barely enough to handle even the lightest breezes. But the Pocket Blimp is cheap—$30,000—and so simple that the FAA doesn't require certification for would-be pilots.

Sales, though, have been lackluster. "It would be great if someone would buy one," sighs Boland.[1]

Critical Thinking Questions

As you read this chapter, consider these questions as they relate to the Pocket Blimp:

- Is the Pocket Blimp a consumer product or a business product?
- Where is the Pocket Blimp in the product life cycle?
- What price strategy should be used for the Pocket Blimp?

BUSINESS IN THE 21ST CENTURY

As discussed in Chapter 11, the marketing mix is the blend of product, pricing, distribution and promotion strategies designed to produce mutually satisfying exchanges with a target market. Each element of the marketing mix can be manipulated to fine-tune the customer offering and achieve competitive success. This chapter examines each element of the marketing mix.

THE ROLE OF THE PRODUCT IN THE MARKETING MIX

product

In marketing, any good or service, along with its perceived attributes and benefits, that creates value for the customer.

In marketing, a **product** is any good or service, along with its perceived attributes and benefits, that creates value for the customer. Attributes can be tangible or intangible. Among the tangible attributes are packaging and warranties as illustrated in Exhibit 12-1. Intangible attributes are symbolic, such as brand image. People make decisions about which products to buy after considering both tangible and intangible attributes of a product. For example, when you buy a pair of jeans, you consider price, brand, store image, and style before you buy. These factors are all part of the marketing mix.

Types of Consumer Products

Because most things sold are a blend of goods and services, the term *product* can be used to refer to both. After all, consumers are really buying packages of benefits that deliver value. The person who buys a plane ride on United

e x h i b i t   1 2 - 1 | Tangible and Intangible Attributes of a Product Create Value for the Buyer

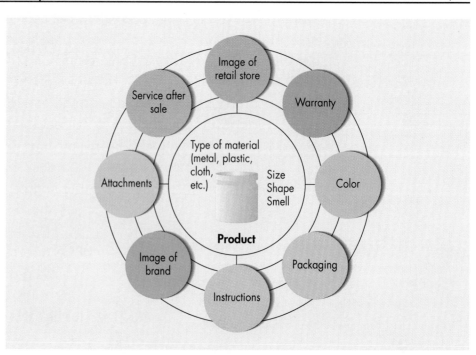

Airlines is looking for a quick way to get from one city to another (the benefit). Providing this benefit requires goods (a plane, food) and services (ticketing, maintenance, piloting).

Marketers must know how consumers view the types of products their companies sell so that they can design the marketing mix to appeal to the selected target market. To help them define target markets, marketers have devised product categories. Products that are bought by the end user are called *consumer products*. They include electric razors, sandwiches, cars, stereos, magazines, and houses. Consumer products that get used up, such as Breck hair mousse and Lays potato chips, are called *consumer nondurables*. Those that last for a long time, such as Whirlpool washing machines and Apple computers, are *consumer durables*.

Another way to classify consumer products is by the amount of effort consumers are willing to make to acquire them. The four major categories of consumer products are defined below:

unsought products

Products that either are unknown to the potential buyer or are known but the buyer does not actively seek them.

convenience products

Relatively inexpensive items that require little shopping effort and are purchased routinely without planning.

shopping products

Items that are bought after considerable planning, including brand-to-brand and store-to-store comparisons of price, suitability, and style.

specialty products

Items for which consumers search long and hard and for which they refuse to accept substitutes.

- **Unsought products** are products unknown to the potential buyer or known products that the buyer does not actively seek. New products fall into this category until advertising and distribution increase consumer awareness of them. Insurance, burial plots, encyclopedias, and similar items require agressive personal selling and highly persuasive advertising.
- **Convenience products** are relatively inexpensive items that require little shopping effort. Soft drinks, candy bars, milk, bread, and small hardware items are examples.
- **Shopping products** are bought only after a brand-to-brand and store-to-store comparison of price, suitability, and style. Examples are furniture, automobiles, a vacation in Europe, and some items of clothing.
- **Specialty products** are products for which consumers search long and hard for which they refuse to accept substitutes. Expensive jewelry, designer clothing, state-of-the-art stereo equipment, limited-production automobiles, and gourmet dinners fall into this category.

Types of Business Products

Products bought by businesses or institutions for use in making other products or in providing services are called *business* or *industrial products*. They are classified as either capital products or expense items. **Capital products** are usually large, expensive items with a long life span. Examples are buildings, large machines, and airplanes. **Expense items** are typically smaller, less expensive items that usually have a life span of less than a year. Examples are printer ribbons and paper. Industrial products are sometimes further classified in the following categories:

capital products

Large, expensive items with a long life span that are purchased by businesses for use in making other products or providing a service.

expense items

Items, purchased by businesses, that are smaller and less expensive than capital products and usually have a life span of less than one year.

1. *Installations.* These are large, expensive capital items that determine the nature, scope, and efficiency of a company. Capital products like General Motors' Saturn assembly plant in Tennessee represent a big commitment against future earnings and profitability.

2. *Accessories.* Accessories do not have the same long-run impact on the firm as installations, and they are less expensive and more standardized. But they are still capital products. Minolta copy machines, IBM personal computers (PCs), and smaller machines such as Black and Decker table drills and saws are typical accessories.

3. *Component parts and materials.* These are expense items that are built into the end product. Some component parts are custom-made, such as a drive shaft for an automobile, a case for a computer, or a special pigment for painting U.S. Navy harbor buoys; others are standardized for sale to many industrial

users. Intel's Pentium chip for PCs and cement for the construction trade are examples of standardized component parts and materials.

4. *Raw materials.* Raw materials are expense items that have undergone little or no processing and are used to create a final product. Examples include lumber, copper, and zinc.

5. *Supplies.* Supplies do not become part of the final product. They are bought routinely and in fairly large quantities. Supply items run the gamut from pencils and paper to paint and machine oil.

6. *Services.* These are expense items used to plan or support company operations; for example, janitorial cleaning and management consulting.

Branding

Most industrial and consumer products have a brand name. If everything came in a plain brown wrapper, life would be less colorful and competition would decrease. Companies would have less incentive to put out better products because consumers would be unable to tell one company's products from those of another.

The product identifier for a company is its **brand.** Brands appear in the form of words, names, symbols, or designs. They are used to distinguish a company's products from

Find out how to trademark a design, name or other identifying mark by visiting the U.S. Patent and Trademark Office at

http://www.uspto.gov

those of its competitors. Examples of well-known brands are Kleenex tissues, Jeep automobiles, and IBM computers. A **trademark** is the legally exclusive design, name, or other identifying mark associated with a company's brand. No other company can use that same trademark.

brand

A company's product identifier that distinguishes the company's products from those of its competitors.

trademark

The legally exclusive design, name, or other identifying mark associated with a company's brand.

brand equity

The value of company and brand names.

These brand names for laundry detergents are effective because they are short, distinctive, and easy to pronounce, recognize, and remember.

Benefits of Branding Branding has three main purposes: product identification, repeat sales, and new product sales. The most important purpose is *product identification.* Branding allows marketers to distinguish their products from all others. Many brand names are familiar to consumers and indicate quality. The term **brand equity** refers to the value of company and brand names. A brand that has high awareness, perceived quality, and brand loyalty among customers has high brand equity. Brand equity is more than awareness of a brand— it is the personality, soul, and emotion associated with the brand. Think of the feelings you have when you see the brand name Harley-Davidson, Nike, or even Microsoft. A brand with strong brand equity is a valuable asset. Some brands such as Coke, Kodak, Marlboro, and Chevrolet are worth millions of dollars.

FOCUSING ON SMALL BUSINESS

LITTLE GUYS CAN WIN THE BRANDING WAR

Small companies are embracing branding in part because they've seen the Fortune 500 corporations concentrating on building and leveraging their brands more than ever before. Coca-Cola Co. made the new Braves baseball stadium in Atlanta a shrine to Coke; giant Niketown stores extend the icon of the Nike Swoosh into the realm of "experiential" retailing.

Entrepreneurs thinking about creating their own brands should consider these suggestions:

1. *Establish your uniqueness.* That's what Cape Cod Potato Chips has done as it has battled with snack-industry giants for supermarket shelf space and a share of the dollars spent by potato chip lovers across the country. The company, which is based in Hyannis, Massachusetts, focuses on its self-developed "batch" processing of potatoes, which yields a distinctive taste and texture; extends its product line with chips made from different varieties of potatoes rather than just dusting on flavorings as some of its bigger competitors do; relies on product sampling instead of traditional advertising as its marketing workhorse; and supports its regional identity with everything from tours of its factory to its product packaging, which features a lighthouse.
2. *Stay within your core.* China Mist Tea Co. in Scottsdale, Arizona, has grown to a $5 million company in just a few years by providing only iced tea and selling only to restaurants and institutions. Along with that growth, however, has come the temptation to expand beyond its core business or to partner with a beverage giant such as Coca-Cola or PepsiCo. "We have such fanatically loyal customers that even Coke has noticed it and commented to us about it, and that's the key to our growth," says Dan Schweiker, co-owner of the company. "The reason is we know what our niche is and pay attention to it. We're not trying to become Lipton tea."
3. *Dominate a geographic or niche market.* Coke may have taught the world to sing, but a savvy small brander can dominate southwestern Mississippi or Schenectady, New York. Utz Quality Foods, Inc. of Hanover, Pennsylvania, for instance, has built a whole advertising campaign around the fact that people outside the mid-Atlantic region can't buy Utz products in stores. Small regional brewer Stevens Point Brewery stopped a five-year sales decline last year by paring back to the 12-county region around its headquarters in Stevens Point, Wisconsin.

Critical Thinking Questions

1. Should all small businesses try to build a brand? Why or why not?
2. What other suggestions do you have for an entrepreneur attempting to build a brand?

---

manufacturer brands

Brands that are owned by national or regional manufacturers and widely distributed; also call *national brands.*

dealer brands

Brands that are owned by the wholesaler or retailer rather than the name of the manufacturer.

generic products

Products that carry no brand name, come in plain containers, and sell for much less than brand-name products.

Types of Brands Brands owned by national or regional manufacturers and widely distributed are **manufacturer brands.** (These brands are sometimes called national brands, but since some of the brands are not owned by nationwide or international manufacturers, *manufacturer brands* is a more accurate term.) A few well-known manufacturer brands are Polaroid, Liz Claiborne, Nike, and Sony.

Brands that are owned by the wholesaler or retailer, rather than that of the manufacturer, are **dealer brands.** Sears has several well-known dealer (or private) brands, including Craftsman, DieHard, and Kenmore. The Independent Grocers Alliance (IGA), a large wholesale grocery organization, uses the brand name Shurfine on its goods. Dealer brands tie consumers to particular wholesalers or retailers. If you want a Kenmore washing machine, you must go to Sears.

Many consumers don't want to pay the costs of manufacturer or dealer brands. One popular way to save money is to buy **generic products.** These products carry no brand name, come in plain containers, and sell for much less than brand-name products. The most popular generic products are garbage bags, jelly, paper towels, coffee cream substitutes, cigarettes, and paper napkins.

Packaging

Curious about how generic and private label products are manufactured? Visit the Private Label Manufacturers Association at

http://www.plma.com

Just as a brand gives a product identity, its packaging also distinguishes it from competitors' products and increases its customer value. When you go to the store and reach for a bottle of dishwashing detergent, the package is the last chance a manufacturer has to convince you to buy its brand over a competitor's. A good package may cause you to reach for Joy rather than Palmolive.

The Functions of a Package   A basic function of packaging is to protect the product from breaking or spoiling and thus extend its life. A package should be easy to ship, store, and stack on a shelf and convenient for the consumer to buy. Many new packaging methods have been developed recently. Aseptic packages keep foods fresh for months without refrigeration. Examples are Borden's "sipp' packs" for juices, the Brik Pak for milk, and Hunt's and Del Monte's aseptic boxes for tomato sauce.

A second basic function of packaging is to help promote the product by providing clear brand identification and information about the product's features. For example, Ralston Purina Co.'s Dog Chow brand, the leading dog food, was losing market share. The company decided that the pictures of dog breeds on the package were too old-fashioned and rural. With a new package featuring a photo of a dog and a child, sales have increased.

Developing New Products

New products pump life into company sales, enabling the firm not only to survive but also to grow. Companies like Allegheny Ludlum (steel), Corning (fiber optics), Dow (chemicals), Hewlett-Packard (computers), Campbell Soup (foods), and Stryker (medical products) get most of their profits from new products. Companies that lead their industries in profitability and sales growth get 49 percent of their revenues from products developed within the last five years.

How New Products Are Developed

Developing products is both costly and risky. About two-thirds of all new products fail. To increase their chances for success, most firms use the following product development process, which is also summarized in Exhibit 12-2.

1. *Set new product goals.* New product goals are usually stated as financial objectives. For example, a company may want to recover its investment in three years or less. Or it may want to earn at least a 15 percent return on the investment. Nonfinancial goals may include using existing equipment or facilities.

2. *Develop new product ideas.* Smaller firms usually depend on employees, customers, investors, and distributors for new ideas. Larger companies use these sources and more structured marketing research techniques, such as focus groups and brainstorming. A **focus group** consists of 8 to 12 participants led by a moderator in an in-depth discussion on one particular topic or concept. The intent is to find out how they feel about a product, concept, idea, or organization, how it fits into their lives, and their emotional involvement

focus group
A group of 8 to 12 participants led by a moderator in an in-depth discussion on one particular topic or concept.

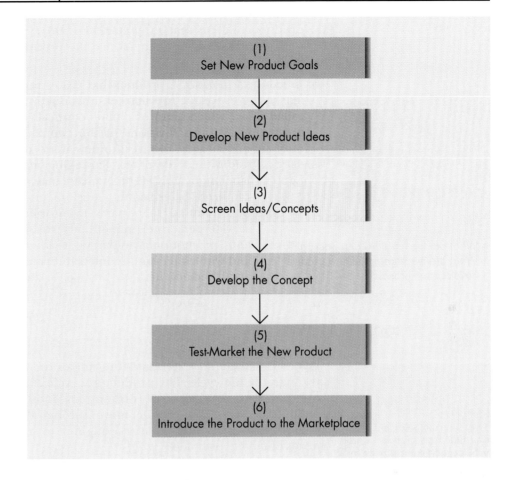

with it. Focus groups often generate excellent product ideas. A few examples are the interior design of the Ford Taurus, Stick-Up room deodorizers, Dustbusters, and Wendy's salad bar. In the industrial market, machine tools, keyboard designs, aircraft interiors, and backhoe accessories evolved from focus groups.

3. *Screen ideas and concepts.* As ideas emerge, they are checked against the firm's new product goals and its long-range strategies. Many product concepts are rejected because they don't fit well with existing products, needed technology is not available, the company doesn't have enough resources, or the sales potential is low.

4. *Develop the concept.* Developing the new product concept involves creating a prototype of the product, testing the prototype, and building the marketing strategy. The type and amount of product testing vary, depending on such factors as the company's experience with similar products, how easy it is to make the item, and how easy it will be for consumers to use it.

   As the marketing strategy and prototype tests mature, a communication strategy is developed. A logo and package wording are created. As part of the communication strategy, promotion themes are developed, and the product is introduced to the sales force.

test-marketing

The process of testing a new product among potential users.

5. *Test-market the new product.* **Test-marketing** is testing the product among potential users. It allows management to evaluate various strategies and to see how well the parts of the marketing mix fit together. Few new product concepts reach this stage. For those that pass this stage, the firm must decide whether to introduce the product on a regional or national basis.

6. *Introduce the product.* A product that passes test-marketing is ready for market introduction, called *rollout,* which requires a lot of logistical coordination. Various divisions of the company must be encouraged to give the new item the attention it deserves. Packaging and labeling in a different language may be required. Sales training sessions must be scheduled, spare parts inventoried, service personnel trained, advertising and promotion campaigns readied, and wholesalers and retailers informed about the new item.

concept check

- Explain how business products are classified?
- What are the functions of a package?
- What are the steps in the new product development process?

PRODUCT LIFE CYCLE

>lg 2

product life cycle

The pattern of sales and profits over time for a product or product category; consists of an introductory stage, growth stage, maturity, and decline (and death).

Product managers create marketing mixes for their products as they move through the life cycle. The **product life cycle** is a pattern of sales and profits over time for a product (Ivory dishwashing liquid) or a product category (liquid detergents). As the product moves through the stages of the life cycle, the firm must keep revising the marketing mix to stay competitive and meet the needs of target customers.

As illustrated in Exhibit 12-3, the product life cycle consists of the following stages:

1. *Introduction.* When a product enters the life cycle, it faces many obstacles. Although competition may be light, the *introductory stage* usually features frequent product modifications, limited distribution, and heavy promotion. The failure rate is high. Production and marketing costs are also high, and sales volume is low. Hence profits are usually small or negative.

2. *Growth.* If a product survives the introductory stage, it advances to the *growth stage* of the life cycle. In this stage, sales grow at an increasing rate, profits are healthy, and many competitors enter the market. Large companies may start to acquire small pioneering firms that have reached this stage. Distribution becomes a major key to success during the growth stage, as well as in later stages. Manufacturers scramble to acquire dealers and distributors and to build long-term relationships. Without adequate distribution, it is impossible to establish a strong market position.

   Toward the end of the growth phase, prices normally begin falling and profits peak. Price reductions result from increased competition and from cost reductions from producing larger quantities of items (economies of scale). Also, most firms have recovered their development costs by now, and their priority is in increasing or retaining market share and enhancing profits.

3. *Maturity.* After the growth stage, sales continue to mount—but at a decreasing rate. This is the *maturity stage.* Most products that have been on the market for a long time are in this stage. Thus, most marketing strategies are de-

exhibit 1 2 - 3 | Sales and Profits during the Product Life Cycle

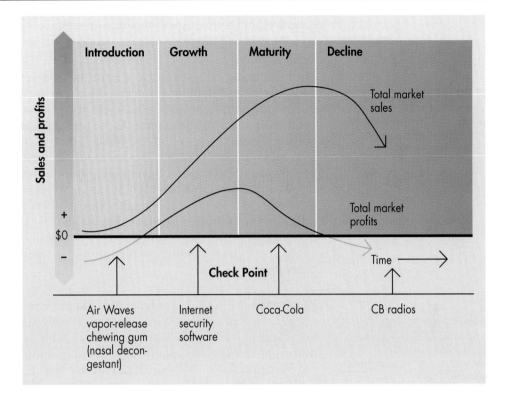

signed for mature products. One such strategy is to bring out several variations of a basic product (line extension). Kool-Aid, for instance, was originally offered in three flavors. Today there are twenty, as well as sweetened and unsweetened varieties.

4. *Decline (and death)*. When sales and profits fall, the product has reached the *decline stage*. The rate of decline is governed by two factors: the rate of change in consumer tastes and the rate at which new products enter the market. Sony turntables are an example of a product in the decline stage. The demand for turntables has now been surpassed by the demand for compact disc players and cassette players.

concept check

- What is the product life cycle?
- Describe each stage of the product life cycle.
- What are the marketing strategies for each stage of the product life cycle?

PRICING PRODUCTS RIGHT

>lg 3

Another component of the marketing mix is the price of the product. Price is the perceived value that is exchanged for something else. Value in our society is most commonly expressed in dollars and cents. Thus, price is typically the amount of money exchanged for a good or service. Note that *perceived value* refers to the time of the transaction. After you've used a product you've bought, you may decide that its actual value was less than its perceived value. Managers use various strategies when determining the price of a product, as this section explains.

Pricing Strategies

Price-skimming and penetration pricing are strategies used in pricing new products; other strategies such as odd-even pricing and prestige pricing and bundling may be used for established products as well.

Price Skimming   The practice of introducing a new product on the market with a high price and then lowering the price over time is called **price skimming.** As the product moves through its life cycle, the price usually is lowered because competitors are entering the market. As the price falls, more and more consumers can buy the product.

Price skimming has four important advantages. First, a high initial price can be a way to find out what buyers are willing to pay. Second, if consumers find the introductory price too high, it can be lowered. Third, a high introductory price can create an image of quality and prestige. Fourth, when the price is lowered later, consumers may think they are getting a bargain. The disadvantage is that high prices attract competition. Price skimming can be used to price virtually any new products such as high-definition televisions, PCs, and color computer printers.

Penetration Pricing   A company that doesn't use price skimming will probably use **penetration pricing.** With this strategy, the company offers new products at low prices in the hope of achieving a large sales volume. Penetration pricing requires more extensive planning than skimming does because the company must gear up for mass production and marketing. When Texas Instruments entered the digital-watch market, its facilities in Lubbock, Texas, could produce 6 million watches a year, enough to meet the entire world demand for low-priced watches. If the company had been wrong about demand, its losses would have been huge.

Penetration pricing has two advantages. First, the low initial price may induce consumers to switch brands or companies. Using penetration pricing on its jug wines, Gallo has lured customers away from Taylor California Cellars and Inglenook. Second, penetration pricing may discourage competitors from entering the market. Their costs would tend to be higher, so they would need to sell more at the same price to break even.

Odd-Even Pricing   Psychology often plays a big role in how consumers view prices and what prices they will pay. **Odd-even pricing** (or **psychological pricing**) is the strategy of setting a price at an odd number to connote a bargain and at an even number to imply quality. For years, many retailers have priced their products in odd numbers—for example, $99.95 or $49.95—to make consumers feel that they are paying a lower price for the product. Even-numbered pricing is sometimes used to denote quality. Examples include a fine perfume at $100 a bottle, a good watch at $500, or a mink coat at $3,000.

Prestige Pricing   The strategy of raising the price of a product so consumers will perceive it as being of higher quality, status, or value is called **prestige pricing.** This type of pricing is common where high prices indicate high status. In the specialty shops on Rodeo Drive in Beverly Hills, which cater to the super-rich of Hollywood, shirts that would sell for $15 elsewhere sell for at least $50. If the price were lower, customers would perceive them as being of low quality.

---

price skimming
The strategy of introducing a product with a high initial price and lowering the price over time as the product moves through its life cycle.

penetration pricing
The strategy of selling new products at low prices in the hope of achieving a large sales volume.

odd-even (psychological) pricing
The strategy of setting a price at an odd number to connote a bargain and at an even number to suggest quality.

prestige pricing
The strategy of increasing the price of a product so that consumers will perceive it as being of higher quality, status, or value.

concept check

- What is the difference between penetration pricing and price skimming?
- Describe odd-even pricing and prestige pricing.

THE ROLE OF DISTRIBUTION IN THE MARKETING MIX

distribution channel
The series of marketing entities through which goods and services pass on their way from producers to end users.

marketing intermediaries
Organizations that assist in moving goods and services from producers to end users.

agents
Sales representatives of manufacturers and wholesalers.

brokers
Go-betweens that bring buyers and sellers together.

industrial distributors
Independent wholesalers that buy related product lines from many manufacturers and sell them to industrial users.

wholesalers
Firms that sell finished goods to retailers, manufacturers, and institutions.

retailers
Firms that sell goods to consumers and to industrial users for their own consumption.

merchant wholesaler
An institution that buys goods from manufacturers (takes ownership) and resells them to businesses, government agencies, other wholesalers, or retailers.

A successful marketing mix includes a distribution strategy that defines how the product moves through the **distribution channel,** a series of marketing entities through which goods and services pass on their way to end users and consumers. This section will look first at the entities that make up a distribution channel and then will examine the functions that channels serve.

Marketing Intermediaries in the Distribution Channel

A distribution channel is made up of **marketing intermediaries,** or organizations that assist in moving goods and services from producers to end users and consumers. Marketing intermediaries are so called because they are in the middle of the distribution process between the producer and the end user. The following marketing intermediaries most often appear in the distribution channel:

- *Agents and brokers.* **Agents** are sales representatives of manufacturers and wholesalers, and **brokers** are entities that bring buyers and sellers together. Both agents and brokers are usually hired on commission basis by either a buyer or a seller. Agents and brokers are go-betweens whose job is to make deals. They do not own or take possession of goods.
- *Industrial distributors.* **Industrial distributors** are independent wholesalers that buy related product lines from many manufacturers and sell them to industrial users. They often have a sales force to call on purchasing agents, make deliveries, extend credit, and provide information. Industrial distributors are used in such industries as aircraft manufacturing, mining, and petroleum.
- *Wholesalers.* **Wholesalers** are firms that sell finished goods to retailers, manufacturers, and institutions (such as schools and hospitals). Historically, their function has been to buy from manufacturers and sell to retailers.
- *Retailers.* **Retailers** are firms that sell goods to consumers and to industrial users for their own consumption.

At the end of the distribution channel are final consumers, like you and me, and industrial users. Industrial users are firms that buy products for internal use or for producing other products or services. They include manufacturers, utilities, airlines, railroads, and service institutions, such as hotels, hospitals, and schools.

Exhibit 12-4 shows various ways marketing intermediaries can be linked. For instance, a manufacturer may sell to a wholesaler that sells to a retailer that in turn sells to a customer. In any of these distribution systems, goods and services are physically transferred from one organization to the next. As each takes possession of the products, it may take legal ownership of them. As the exhibit indicates, distribution channels can handle either consumer products or industrial products.

Wholesalers

As described earlier, wholesalers are channel members that buy finished products from manufacturers and sell them to retailers. Retailers in turn sell the products to consumers. Wholesalers also sell products to institutions, such as manufacturers, schools, and hospitals, for use in performing their own missions. A manufacturer, for instance, might buy typing paper from Nationwide Papers, a wholesaler. A hospital might buy its cleaning supplies from Lagasse Brothers, one of the nation's largest wholesalers of janitorial supplies.

Two main types of wholesalers are merchant wholesalers and agents and brokers. A **merchant wholesaler** is an institution that buys goods from manufacture x h i b i t   1 2 - 4 | Channels of Distribution for Industrial and Consumer Products

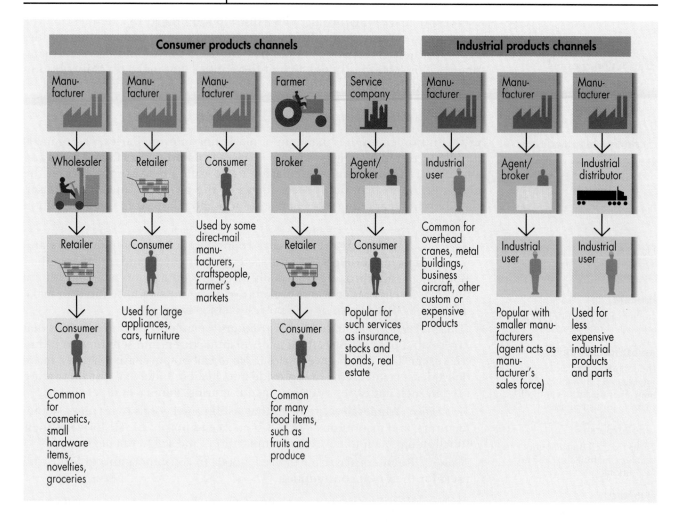

ers and resells them to businesses, government agencies, other wholesalers and retailers. Merchant wholesalers make up 80 percent of all wholesaling establishments and conduct slightly under 60 percent of all wholesale sales. All merchant wholesalers take title to the goods they sell.

Agents and brokers, as described earlier, are another type of wholesaler. **Manufacturers' representatives** (also called manufacturers' agents) represent noncompeting manufacturers. These salespeople function as independent agents, not salaried employees of the manufacturer. They do not take title to or possession of merchandise. They get commissions if they make sales—and nothing if they don't. Brokers bring buyers and sellers together. Like agents, brokers do not take title to merchandise, they receive commisions on sales, and they have little say over company sale policies. They are frequently found in real estate, agriculture, insurance, and commodities.

Retailers

The major types of retailers are described in Exhibit 12-5, which divides them into two main categories: in-store retailing and nonstore retailing. Examples of *in-store retailing* include Sears, Wal-Mart, and Saks. These retailers get most of their revenue from people who come to the store to make purchases. *Nonstore*

manufacturers' representatives

Salespeople who represent noncompeting manufacturers; function as independent agents rather than as salaried employees of the manufacturers.

efficient consumer response (ECR)

A method of managing inventory and streamlining the movement of products from supplier to distributor to retailer; relies on electronic data interchange to communicate information such as automatic shipping notifications, invoices, inventory data, and forecasts.

retailing involves selling products outside of the traditional bricks-and-mortar store. Nonstore retailing includes electronic retailing over the Internet (e-tailing), vending machines, direct selling (Mary Kay, Amway), home-shopping networks, and direct-response marketing (Land's End, Publisher's Weekly, J. Crew).

One of the challenges facing in-store and nonstore retailers is managing inventory. Managing inventory includes all aspects of moving goods from the seller to the retailer such as shipping, storing and stocking. The trick is to manage the inventory by cutting prices to move slow goods and by keeping adequate suppliers of hot-selling items in stock.

One of the more efifficient new methods of managing inventory and streamlining the way products are moved from supplier to distributor to retailer is **efficient consumer response (ECR).** At the heart of ECR is **electronic data**

e x h i b i t   1 2 - 5 | In-Store and Nonstore Retailing

Types of In-Store Retailing	Description	Examples
Department store	Houses many departments under one roof with each treated as a separate buying center to achieve economies of buying, promotion, and control	JCPenney, Saks, May Co., Rich's, Bloomingdale's
Specialty store	Specializes in a category of merchandise and carries a complete assortment	Toys "R" Us, RadioShack, Zales Jewelers
Variety store	Offers a variety of inexpensive goods	Ben Franklin
Convenience store	Offers convenience goods with long store hours and quick checkout	7-Eleven, Circle K
Supermarket	Specializes in a wide assortment of food, with self-service	Safeway, Kroger, Winn-Dixie
Discount store	Competes on the basis of low prices and high turnover; offers few services	Wal-Mart, Target, Kmart
Off-price retailer	Sells at prices 25% or more below traditional department store prices in spartan environment	Robs, T.J. Maxx, Clothestime
Factory outlet	Owned by manufacturer; sells close-outs, factory seconds, and canceled orders	Levi Strauss, Ship 'n Shore, Dansk
Catalog store	Sends catalogs to customers and displays merchandise in showrooms where customers can order from attached warehouse	Best, Service Merchandise, Lurias
Hypermart	Offers huge selection of food and general merchandise with very low prices; sometimes called "mall without a wall"	Hypermart USA, American Fare
Types of Nonstore Retailing	**Description**	**Examples**
Vending machine	Sells merchandise by machine	Canteen
Direct selling	Sells face-to-face, usually in the person's home	Fuller Brush, Avon, Amway
Direct-response marketing	Attempts to get immediate consumer sale through media advertising, catalogs, or direct mail	K-Tel, L.L. Bean, Ronco
Home shopping networks	Selling via cable television	Home Shopping Network, QVC
Internet retailing (e-commerce)	Selling over the Internet	Bluefly.com, CDnow, eToys, Amazon.com

electronic data interchange (EDI)

Computer-to-computer exchange of information, including automatic shipping notifications, invoices, inventory data, and forecasts; used in efficient consumer response systems.

interchange (EDI), the computer-to computer exchange of information, including automatic shipping notifications, invoices, inventory data, and forecasts. Many retailers have successfully implemented ECR and EDI. The pioneer and market leader in ECR system is Wal-Mart, discussed in the Applying Technology box on page 356.

How Channels Organize and Cover Markets

In an efficient distribution channel, all the channel members work smoothly together and do what they're expected to do. A manufacturer expects wholesalers to promote its products to retailers and to perform several other functions as well. Not all channels have a leader or a single firm that sets channel policies. But all channels have members who rely on one another.

vertical marketing system

An organized, formal distribution channel in which firms are aligned in a hierarchy from manufacturer to wholesaler to retailer.

corporate distribution system

A vertical marketing system in which one firm owns the entire distribution channel.

Vertical Marketing Systems   To increase the efficiency of distribution channels, many firms have turned to vertical marketing systems. In a **vertical marketing system,** firms are aligned in a hierarchy (manufacturer to wholesaler to retailer). Such systems are planned, organized, formalized versions of distribution channels. The three basic types of vertical marketing systems are corporate, administrative, and contractual.

In a **corporate distribution system,** one firm owns the entire channel of distribution. Corporate systems are tops in channel control. A single firm that owns the whole channel has no need to worry about channel members. The channel owner will always have supplies of raw materials and long-term contact with customers. It will have good distribution and product exposure in the marketplace. Examples of corporate distribution systems abound. Evans Products Co. (a manufacturer of plywood), for instance, bought wholesale lumber distributors to better market its products to retail dealers.

administrative distribution system

A vertical marketing system in which a strong organization takes over as leader and sets policies for the distribution channel.

In an **administrative distribution system,** a strong organization takes over as leader and sets channel policies. The leadership role is informal; it is not written into a contract. Companies such as Gillette, Hanes, Campbell's, and Westinghouse are administrative system leaders. They can often influence or control the policies of other channel members without the costs and expertise required to set up a corporate distribution system. They may be able to dictate how many wholesalers will be in the channel or require that the wholesalers offer 60-day credit to retail customers, among other things.

contractual distribution system

A vertical marketing system in which a network of independent firms at different levels (manufacturer, wholesaler, retailer) coordinate their distribution activities through a written contract.

The third form of vertical marketing is a **contractual distribution system.** It is a network of independent firms at different levels (manufacturer, wholesaler, retailer) that coordinate their distribution activities through a written contract. Franchises are a common form of the contractual system. The parent companies of McDonald's and ChemLawn, for instance, control distribution of their products through the franchise agreement each franchisee signs.

The Intensity of Market Coverage   All types of distribution systems must be concerned with market coverage. How many dealers will be used to distribute the product in a particular area? The three degrees of coverage are exclusive, selective, and intensive. The type of product determines the intensity of the market coverage.

exclusive distribution

A distribution system in which a manufacturer selects only one or two dealers in an area to market its products.

When a manufacturer selects one or two dealers in an area to market its products, it is using **exclusive distribution.** Only items that are in strong demand can be distributed exclusively because consumers must be willing to travel some distance to buy them. If Wrigley's chewing gum were sold in only one drugstore per city, Wrigley's would soon be out of business. However, Bang and Olufsen stereo components, Jaguar automobiles, and Adrienne Vittadini designer clothing are distributed exclusively with great success.

selective distribution

A distribution system in which a manufacturer selects a limited number of dealers in an area (but more than one or two) to market its products.

c o n c ə p t   c h ə c k

- What is meant by an efficient channel of distribution?
- What are the three types of vertical marketing systems?
- Name the three degrees of market coverage.

>lg 5

intensive distribution

A distribution system in which a manufacturer tries to sell its products wherever there are potential customers.

distribution centers

Warehouses that specialize in changing shipment sizes, rather than in storing goods.

c o n c ə p t   c h ə c k

- Discuss the functions of physical distribution.
- What is the goal of a materials-handling system?

A manufacturer that chooses a limited number of dealers in an area (but more than one or two) is using **selective distribution.** Since the number of retailers handling the product is limited, consumers must be willing to seek it out. Timberline boots, a high-quality line of footwear, are distributed selectively. So are Sony televisions, Maytag washers, Waterford crystal, and Tommy Hilfiger clothing.

A manufacturer that wants to sell its products everywhere there are potential customers is using **intensive distribution.** Such consumer goods as bread, tape, and lightbulbs are often distributed intensively. Usually, these products cost little and are bought frequently, which means that complex distribution channels are necessary. Coca-Cola is sold in just about every type of retail business, from gas stations to supermarkets.

Using Physical Distribution to Increase Efficiency and Customer Satisfaction

Physical distribution is an important part of the marketing mix. Retailers don't sell products they can't deliver, and salespeople don't (or shouldn't) promise deliveries they can't make. Late deliveries and broken promises may mean loss of a customer. Accurate order filling and billing, timely delivery, and arrival in good condition are important to the success of the product.

Distribution managers are responsible for making decisions that affect the successful delivery of a product to the end consumer. These decisions, presented in this section, include choosing a warehouse location and type, setting up a materials-handling system, and choosing among the available modes of transportation.

Choosing a Warehouse Location and Type Deciding where to put a warehouse is mostly a matter of deciding which markets will be served and where production facilities will be located. A *storage warehouse* is used to hold goods for a long time. For instance, Jantzen makes bathing suits at an even rate throughout the year to provide steady employment and hold down costs. It then stores them in a warehouse until the selling season.

Distribution centers are a special form of warehouse. They specialize in changing shipment sizes rather than storing goods. Such centers make bulk (put shipments together) or break bulk. They strive for rapid inventory turnover. When shipments arrive, the merchandise is quickly sorted into orders for various retail stores. As soon as the order is complete, it is delivered. Distribution centers are the wave of the future, replacing traditional warehouses. Companies simply can't afford to have a lot of money tied up in idle inventory.

Setting Up a Materials-Handling System A materials-handling system moves and handles inventory. The goal of such a system is to move items as quickly as possible while handling them as little as possible. When Kodak built a new plant for making photographic coated paper, for example, it designed a way to minimize materials handling. It built a 10-level concrete rack to hold the one-ton rolls of raw paper. A computer handles inventory control and commands machines that can retrieve and carry the rolls without damage and then load the paper onto the assembly line.

Making Transportation Decisions Transportation typically accounts for between 5 and 10 percent of the price of goods. Physical distribution managers must decide which mode of transportation to use to

WAL-MART KNOWS WHAT YOU LIKE

Many retailers talk a good game when it comes to mining data collected at cash registers as a way to build sales. Wal-Mart, the nation's largest retailer, has been doing it since about 1990. Now, it is sitting on a treasure trove of information so vast and detailed that it far exceeds what many manufacturers know about their own products.

Wal-Mart's database is second in size only to that of the U.S. government. Along with raw sales, profit margin, and inventory numbers, Wal-Mart also collects "market-basket data" from customer receipts at all its stores, so it knows what products are likely to be purchased together. The company receives about 100,000 queries a week from suppliers and its own buyers looking for purchase patterns or checking on a product.

At 192,000 square feet, Wal-Mart supercenters are about the size of four football fields. Wal-Mart quickly found customers were having trouble navigating them. To address customers' frustrations, Wal-Mart dug through heaps of purchase data from its supercenters and unearthed lots of ways to help people find things they didn't even know they needed. Kleenex tissues are in the paper-goods aisle and also mixed in with the cold medicine. Measuring spoons are in housewares and also hanging next to Crisco shortening. In October, flashlights are in the hardware aisle and also with the Halloween costumes.

To get real-time reports on sales, profitability, and inventory position, Wal-Mart managers can use a hand-held computer that scans bar codes on store shelves. The information is crucial for pricing and shipping decisions, but it doesn't leave much room for creativity: "Everybody thinks they have a feel for what people like, but we keep data," says Randy Mott, Wal-Mart's chief information officer.

The data also help Wal-Mart time merchandise deliveries so that its shelves stay stocked—but not overstocked. The supercenters have cut back on how high they stack merchandise, making stores feel less crowded. The data have also helped keep inventory levels leaner and turning faster—a must for a retailer of perishable produce as well as of perishable fashion.

Critical Thinking Questions

1. Do you think that Wal-Mart's database could help in creating displays?
2. How can Wal-Mart's database be used in stocking a new Wal-Mart?
3. Is it a good idea to continually change a store's merchandise layout?

---

promotion

The attempt by marketers to inform, persuade, or remind consumers and industrial users to engage in the exchange process.

move products from producer to buyer. This decision is, of course, related to all other physical distribution decisions. The five major modes of transportation are railroads, motor carriers, pipelines, water transportation, and airways.

CREATING AN EFFECTIVE PROMOTION STRATEGY

differential advantage

A set of unique features of a product that the target market perceives as important and better than the competition's features.

Very few goods or services can survive in the marketplace without good promotion. Marketers, such as those touting Levi's Dockers, promote their products to build consumer demand. **Promotion** is an attempt by marketers to inform, persuade, or remind consumers and industrial users to engage in the exchange process. Once the product has been created, promotion is often used to convince target customers that it has a **differential advantage** over the competition. A differential advantage is a set of unique features that the target market perceives as important and better than the competition's features. Such features may include high quality, fast delivery, low price, good service, and the like. Lexus, for example, is seen as having a quality differential advan-

Water is one of the five major modes of transportation that distribution managers can choose from in moving products from the producer to the buyer.

tage over other luxury cars. Therefore, promotion for Lexus stresses the quality of the vehicle.

The Promotional Mix

The combination of advertising, personal selling, sales promotion, and public relations used to promote a product is called the **promotional mix.** Each firm creates a unique mix for each product. But the goal is always to deliver the firm's message efficiently and effectively to the target audience. These are the elements of the promotional mix:

The Freight World Web site offers detailed information on various transportation modes and links to transportation companies. Visit it at
http://www.freightworld.com

- *Advertising.* Any paid form of nonpersonal promotion by an identified sponsor.
- *Personal selling.* A face-to-face presentation to a prospective buyer.
- *Sales promotion.* Marketing activities (other than personal selling, advertising, and public relations) that stimulate consumer buying, including coupons and samples, displays, shows and exhibitions, demonstrations, and other types of selling efforts.
- *Public relations.* The linking of organizational goals with key aspects of the public interest and the development of programs designed to earn public understanding and acceptance.

The sections that follow examine the elements of the promotional mix in more detail.

promotional mix

The combination of advertising, personal selling, sales promotion, and public relations used to promote a product.

Advertising

Most Americans are bombarded daily with advertisements to buy things. **Advertising** is any paid form of nonpersonal presentation by an identified sponsor. It may appear on television or radio; in newspapers, magazines, books, or direct mail; or on billboards or transit cards.

The money that big corporations spend on advertising is mind-boggling. Total advertising expenses in this country are estimated at more than $190 billion a year. The largest percentage of the money goes to network television, followed closely by newspapers.[2] Nearly 12¢ of every dollar spent on perfume and cosmetics goes to advertising, and 15¢ out of every dollar spent on dolls and stuffed toys goes for advertising.[3] Even the missile and space industry spends nearly 2¢ of every sales dollar on ads. Spending by companies such as Procter & Gamble, Kraft-General Foods, Philip Morris, and General Motors averages more than $100,000 an hour, 24 hours a day; much of it is used in the prime evening hours on network television.

The channels through which advertising is carried to prospective customers are the **advertising media.** Both product and institutional ads appear in all the

advertising

Any paid form of nonpersonal presentation by an identified sponsor.

advertising media

The channels through which advertising is carried to prospective customers; includes newspapers, magazines, radio, television, outdoor advertising, direct mail, and the Internet.

major advertising media: newspapers, magazines, radio, television, outdoor advertising, direct mail, and the Internet.

Media are evaluated on (1) **cost per thousand contacts (CPM)**; (2) **reach,** which is the number of different customers who are exposed to a commercial at least once per period of time (usually four weeks); and (3) **frequency,** which is the number of times an individual is exposed to a message.

Personal Selling

Advertising acquaints potential customers with a product and thereby makes personal selling easier. **Personal selling** is a face-to-face sales presentation to a prospective customer. Sales jobs range from salesclerks at clothing stores to engineers with MBAs who design large, complex systems for manufacturers. About 6.5 million people are engaged in personal selling in the United States. Slightly over 45 percent of them are women. The number of people who earn a living from sales is huge compared, for instance, with the half a million workers employed in the advertising industry.

Selling is a process that can be learned. The steps in the selling process are as follows:

1. *Prospecting.* To start the process, the salesperson looks for **sales prospects,** those companies and people who are most likely to buy the seller's offerings.
2. *Approaching customers.* After identifying a prospect, the salesperson explains the reason for wanting an appointment and sets a specific date and hour. At the same time, the salesperson tries to build interest in the coming meeting.
3. *Presenting and demonstrating the product.* The presentation and demonstration can be fully automated, completely unstructured, or somewhere in between.
4. *Handling objections.* Almost every sales presentation, structured or unstructured, meets with some objection. Rarely does a customer say "I'll buy it" without asking questions or voicing concerns. The professional salesperson tries to anticipate objections so they can be countered quickly and with assurance.
5. *Closing the sale.* Asking the prospect to buy the product.
6. *Following up on the sale.* After the product is delivered to the customer, the salesperson must make a routine visit to see that the customer is satisfied.

Sales Promotion

Sales promotion helps make personal selling and advertising more effective. **Sales promotions** are marketing events or sales efforts—not including advertising, personal selling, and public relations—that stimulate buying. Today, sales promotion is an $80 billion industry and growing. Couponing alone is a $6 billion industry with over 275 billion coupons being distributed annually.[4] Sales promotion is usually targeted toward either of two distinctly different markets. Consumer sales promotion is targeted to the ultimate consumer market. Trade sales promotion is directed to members of the marketing channel, such as wholesalers and retailers.

The objectives of a promotion depend on the general behavior of target consumers. For ex-

Entrepreneurs and small businesses don't always have big sales promotion budgets. For hundreds of low-cost promotion ideas, turn to the Guerrilla Marketing Web page at

http://www.gmarketing.com.

---

cost per thousand (CPM)
Cost per thousand contacts is a term used in expressing advertising costs; refers to the cost of reaching 1,000 members of the target market.

reach
The number of different target consumers who are exposed to a commercial at least once during a specific period, usually four weeks.

frequency
The number of times an individual is exposed to an advertising message.

personal selling
A face-to-face sales presentation to a prospective customer.

sales prospects
The companies and people who are most likely to buy a seller's offerings.

sales promotions
Marketing events or sales efforts—not including advertising, personal selling, and public relations—that stimulate buying.

concept check

- What are the elements of the promotional mix?
- How does sales promotion differ from advertising?
- Describe several types of sales promotion.

ample, marketers who are targeting loyal users of their product don't want to change behavior. Instead, they want to reinforce existing behavior or increase product usage. Frequent-buyer programs that reward consumers for repeat purchases can be effective in strengthening brand loyalty. Other types of promotions are more effective with customers prone to brand switching or with those who are loyal to a competitor's product. Cents-off coupons, free samples, or an eye-catching display in a store will often entice shoppers to try a different brand.

Sales promotion offers many opportunities for entrepreneurs. Entrepreneurs design contests and sweepstakes, fabricate displays, manufacture premiums, and deliver free samples, among other things.

Public Relations

public relations
Any communication or activity designed to win goodwill or prestige for a company or person.

publicity
Information about a company or product that appears in the news media and is not directly paid for by the company.

Like sales promotion, public relations can be a vital part of the promotional mix. **Public relations** is any communication or activity designed to win goodwill or prestige for a company or person. Its main form is **publicity,** information about a company or product that appears in the news media and is not directly paid for by the company. Publicity can be good or bad. Children dying from eating tainted Jack in the Box hamburgers is an example of negative publicity.

Naturally, firms' public relations departments try to create as much good publicity as possible. They furnish company speakers for business and civic clubs, write speeches for corporate officers, and encourage employees to take active roles in such civic groups as the United Way and the Chamber of Commerce. The main tool of the public relations department is the *press release*, a formal announcement of some newsworthy event connected with the company, such as the start of a new program, the introduction of a new product, or the opening of a new plant.

Learn how to write a press release at

http://www. publicrelationscentral.com/ article1002.html

CAPITALIZING ON TRENDS IN BUSINESS

>lg 7

As customer expectations increase and competition becomes fiercer, perceptive managers will find innovative strategies to satisfy demanding consumers and establish unique products in the market. The key to success is to build a marketing mix that delivers value to the target customer.

Mass Customization

mass customization
A flexible manufacturing technique in which mass-market goods and services are tailored to the unique needs of the individuals who buy them.

A silent revolution is changing the way many goods are made and services are delivered. Companies as diverse as BMW, Dell Computer, Levi Strauss, Mattel, McGraw-Hill, Wells Fargo, and many leading Web businesses are adopting mass customization to maintain or obtain a competitive edge. As we described in an earlier chapter, **mass customization** involves tailoring mass-market goods and services to the unique needs of the individuals who buy them.

Mass producers dictate a one-to-many relationship, whereas mass customizers engage in a continual dialogue with customers. Although production is cost-efficient, the flexibility of mass customization can cut inventory. And mass customization offers two other advantages over mass production: it provides superior customer service, and it makes full use of cutting-edge technology.

Services and Physical Distribution

The fastest-growing part of our economy is the service sector. Although distribution in the service sector is difficult to visualize, the same skills, techniques, and strategies used to manage goods inventory can also be used to manage service inventory, such as hospital beds, bank accounts, or airline seats. The quality of the planning and execution of distribution can have a major impact on costs and customer satisfaction. Because service industries are so customer oriented, customer service is a priority. Service distribution focuses on three main areas:

- *Minimizing wait times.* Minimizing the amount of time customers wait to deposit a check, obtain their food at a restaurant, or see a doctor for an appointment is a key factor in maintaining the quality of service. FedEx, for example, revolutionized the delivery market when it introduced guaranteed overnight delivery of packages and documents to commercial and residential customers.

- *Managing service capacity.* For a product manufacturer, inventory acts as a buffer, enabling it to provide the product during periods of peak demand without extraordinary efforts. Service firms don't have this luxury. If they don't have the capacity to meet demand, they must either turn down some prospective customers, let service levels slip, or expand capacity.

- *Improving delivery through new distribution channels.* Like manufacturers, service firms are now experimenting with different distribution channels for their services. These new channels can increase the time that services are available (like round-the-clock automated teller machines) or add to customer convenience (like pizza delivery or walk-in medical clinics).

Integrated Marketing Communications

Ideally, marketing communications from each promotional mix element (personal selling, advertising, sales promotion, and public relations) should be integrated. That is, the message reaching the consumer should be the same regardless of whether it comes from an advertisement, a salesperson in the field, a magazine article, or a coupon in a newspaper insert.

From the consumer's standpoint, a company's communications are already integrated. Typical consumers do not think in terms of advertising, sales promotion, public relations, or personal selling. To them, everything is an "ad." Unfortunately, many marketers neglect this fact when planning promotional messages and fail to integrate the various elements of their communication efforts. The most common rift typically arises between personal selling and the other elements of the promotional mix.

This unintegrated, disjointed approach to promotion has propelled many companies to adopt the concept of **integrated marketing communications (IMC)**. IMC involves carefully coordinating all promotional activities—media advertising, sales promotion, personal selling, and public relations, as well as direct marketing, packaging, and other forms of promotion—to produce a consistent, unified message that is customer focused. Following the concept of IMC, marketing managers carefully work out the roles the various promotional elements will play in the marketing mix. Timing of promotional activities is coordinated, and the results of each campaign are carefully monitored to improve future use of the promotional mix tools. Typically, a marketing communications director is appointed who has overall responsibility for integrating the company's marketing communications.

integrated marketing communications (IMC)

The careful coordination of all promotional activities—media advertising, sales promotion, personal selling, and public relations, as well as direct marketing, packaging, and other forms of promotion—to produce a consistent, unified message that is customer focused.

APPLYING THIS CHAPTER'S TOPICS

This chapter makes several important points that can affect your life right now. First, businesses are using mass customization to deliver low-cost, specialized products and services that meet the unique needs of individual customers. The Internet has helped usher in mass customization and has opened up vast sources of information on business and consumer products as explained in this section.

Custom Products and Services

Mass customization means that now, more than ever, you can get exactly the product that will fit your needs. A number of companies have adapted this strategy for competition, including AT&T, Coke and Pepsi, and fast-food companies such as McDonald's. The Internet is frequently the primary avenue for delivering customized products, giving you easy access to product and pricing information.

Looking for cheap airfares? Priceline.com lets consumers bid on air and hotel rates. Check out

http://www.priceline.com

Always Sell Yourself

If you stop and think about it, all of us must be salespeople. If you are going to be successful in business, and in life in general, you must be a salesperson. You must be able to effectively explain and sell your plans, ideas, and hopes. A straight "A" student who can't do this will not be successful. Conversely, a "C" student who can will be successful. *Always* be prepared to sell yourself and your ideas. It's the best way to get ahead in business and in life.

TRY IT NOW!

1. **Comparison Shop** A beauty of the Internet is the ability to comparison shop like never before. To compare brands, features, and prices of products, go to one of these sites: **http://www.bottomdollar. com, http://www.mysimon.com,** or **http://www. compare.net.**

2. **Kick the Tires Before You Buy** At some point you are going to buy a car. The Web can simplify the process, help you make an intelligent decision, and save you money. Start at **http://www. edmunds.com.** The online version of the respected car-buying guide is crammed with information about new and used cars. The site offers thousands of car reviews and current loan rates. Once you decide what you want, go to one or all of these sites to get the best price: **http://www.autobytel. com, http://www.autotrader.com,** or **http://www. autoweb.com.** If you decide to buy a used car but are not sure about the strange sound or unexplained dent, go to **http://www.carfax.com** and plug in the car's vehicle identification number. In return you will get an immediate report of the car's public history that will tell you such things as whether the car has been auctioned and its emission test results. The report costs $20, but if there are no data, you don't pay. Once you have found the car of your dreams, go to **http://www. carfinance.com** for a loan or a lease plan at no charge.

at the Pocket Blimp

The Pocket Blimp could be a consumer or business product depending on use. If a person bought one for personal enjoyment, it would be a consumer good. If a company bought a Pocket Blimp to be used as an advertising vehicle, then it would be a business good. The Pocket Blimp is in the early part of the introductory stage of the product life cycle. Since the Pocket Blimp is a specialty product, a skimming price strategy would probably be best.

SUMMARY OF LEARNING GOALS

>lg 1 **What is the role of the product in the marketing mix, and how are products classified and developed?**

A product is any good or service, along with its perceived attributes and benefits, that creates customer value. Tangible attributes include the good itself, packaging, and warranties. Intangible attributes are symbolic like a brand's image.

Most items are a combination of goods and services. Services and goods are often marketed differently. Products are categorized as either consumer products or industrial products. Consumer products are goods and services that are bought and used by the end users. They can be classified as unsought products, convenience products, shopping products, or specialty products, depending on how much effort consumers are willing to exert to get them.

Industrial products are those bought by organizations for use in making other products or in rendering services. Capital products are usually large, expensive items with a long life span. Expense items are typically smaller, less expensive items that usually have a life span of less than a year.

Products usually have brand names. Brands identify products by words, names, symbols, designs, or a combination of these things. The two major types of brands are manufacturer (national) brands and dealer (private) brands. Generic products carry no brand name. Branding has three main purposes: product identification, repeat sales, and new product sales.

Often the promotional claims of well-known brands are reinforced in the printing on the package. Packaging is an important way to promote sales and protect the product. A package should be easy to ship, store, and stack on a store shelf.

The steps in new product development are setting new product goals, exploring ideas, screening ideas, developing the concept (creating a prototype and building the marketing strategy), test-marketing, and introducing the product. When the product enters the marketplace, it is often managed by a product manager.

>lg 2 **What are the stages of the product life cycle?**

After a product reaches the marketplace, it enters the product life cycle. This cycle typically has four stages: introduction, growth, maturity, and decline (and possibly death). Profits usually are small in the introductory phase, reach a peak at the end of the growth phase, and then decline.

>lg 3 **What strategies are used for pricing products?**

Price indicates value, helps position a product in the marketplace, and is the means for earning a fair return on investment. If a price is too high, the product won't sell well, and the firm will lose money. If the price is too low, the firm may lose money even if the product sells well.

The two main strategies for pricing a new product are price skimming and penetration pricing. Price skimming involves charging a high introductory price and then, usually, lowering the price as the product moves through its life cycle. Penetration pricing involves selling a new product at a low price in the hope of achieving a large sales volume.

Pricing tactics are used to fine-tune the base prices of products. Among these tactics are odd-even pricing and prestige pricing. Setting a price at an odd number tends to create a perception that the item is cheaper than the actual price. Prices in even numbers denote quality or status. Raising the price so an item will be perceived as having high quality and status is called prestige pricing. Consumers pay more because of the perceived quality or status.

>lg 4   **Describe the distribution channels and the manner in which they are organized.**
Distribution channels are the series of marketing entities through which goods and services pass on their way from producers to end users. Distribution systems focus on the physical transfer of goods and services and on their legal ownership at each stage of the distribution process.

A vertical marketing system is a planned, hierarchically organized distribution channel. There are three types of vertical marketing systems: corporate, administrative, and contractual. In a corporate system, one firm owns the entire channel. In an administrative system, a strong organization takes over as leader and sets channel policies. In a contractual distribution system, the independent firms coordinate their distribution activities by written contract.

>lg 5   **What are the functions of physical distribution?**
The functions of physical distribution include choosing a warehouse location and type, setting up a materials-handling system, and choosing modes of transportation (air, highway, rail, water, or pipeline). Criteria for selecting a mode of transportation include cost, transit time, reliability, capability, accessibility, and traceability.

>lg 6   **Explain the promotional mix and its primary elements.**
The unique combination of advertising, personal selling, sales promotion, and public relations used to promote a product is the promotional mix. Advertising is any paid form of nonpersonal promotion by an identified sponsor. Personal selling consists of a face-to-face presentation in a conversation with a prospective purchaser. Sales promotion consists of marketing activities—other than personal selling, advertising, and public relations—that stimulate consumers to buy. These activities include coupons and samples, displays, shows and exhibitions, demonstrations, and other selling efforts. Public relations is the marketing function that links the policies of the organization with the public interest and develops programs designed to earn public understanding and acceptance.

The main types of advertising media are newspapers, magazines, radio, television, outdoor advertising, direct mail, and the Internet. Newspaper advertising delivers a local audience but has a short life span. Magazines deliver special-interest markets and offer good detail and color. Radio is an inexpensive and highly portable medium but has no visual capabilities. Television reaches huge audiences and offers visual and audio opportunities, but it can be very expensive. Outdoor advertising requires short messages but is only moderately expensive. Direct mail can reach targeted audiences, but it is only as good as the mailing list. The Internet is global in scope and can offer a personalized message response by email, but as yet not everyone is on the Net. Media are evaluated on a CPM (cost per thousand contacts) basis and by reach and frequency.

KEY TERMS

administrative
 distribution system
 354
advertising 357
advertising media
 357
agents 351
brand 344
brand equity 344
brokers 351
capital products
 343
contractual
 distribution system
 354
convenience
 products 343
corporate
 distribution system
 354
cost per thousand
 (CPM) 358
dealer brands 345
differential
 advantage 356
distribution centers
 351
distribution channel
 355
efficient consumer
 response (ECR)
 353
electronic data
 interchange (EDI)
 354
exclusive
 distribution 354
expense items 343
focus group 346
frequency 358
generic products
 345
industrial distributors
 351
integrated marketing
 communications
 (IMC) 360
intensive
 distribution 355
manufacturer
 brands 345
manufacturers'
 representatives
 352
marketing
 intermediaries
 351
mass customization
 359
merchant
 wholesaler 351
odd-even
 (psychological)
 pricing 350
penetration pricing
 350
personal selling
 358

About 6.5 million people in the United States are directly engaged in personal selling. Personal selling enables a salesperson to demonstrate a product and tailor the message to the prospect; it is effective in closing a sale.

Immediate purchase is the goal of sales promotion whether it is aimed at consumers or the trade (wholesalers and retailers). The most popular sales promotions are coupons, samples, premiums, contests, and sweepstakes. Public relations is mostly concerned with getting good publicity for companies. Public relations helps build a positive image for an organization, which is a good backdrop for selling its products.

>lg 7 **Describe the trends affecting the marketing mix.**
Mass customization, the growth of Internet auctions, improved techniques for managing service inventories, and integrated marketing communications are key trends in maximizing the effectiveness of the marketing mix.

PREPARING FOR TOMORROW'S WORKPLACE

1. Under what circumstances would a jeans maker market the product as a convenience product? A shopping product? A specialty product?
2. Go to the library and look through magazines and newspapers to find examples of price skimming and penetration pricing. Make copies and show them to the class.
3. Explain how something as obvious as a retail price can have a psychological dimension.
4. Divide the class into teams of four. Trace the channel for some familiar product. Each group should tell why they think the channel has evolved as it has and how it is likely to change.
5. Go to a successful, independent specialty store in your area that has been in business for quite a while. Interview the manager and try to determine how the store successfully competes with the national chains.
6. Choose a current advertising campaign, determine whether it is effective, and then explain why or why not. Present your results to the class.
7. How can advertising, sales promotion, and publicity work together? Give an example.

WORKING THE NET

1. Visit an online retailer such as Amazon.com (**http://www.amazon.com**) or eToys (**http://www.eToys.com**). At the site, try to identify examples of leader pricing, bundling, odd pricing, and other pricing strategies. Do online retailers have different pricing considerations than real-world retailers? Explain.
2. What are some of the logistics problems facing firms that operate internationally? Visit the *Logistics Management & Distribution Report* Web site at **http://www.manufacturing.net/lm** and see if you can find information about how firms manage global logistics.
3. The Zenith Media site at **http://www.zenithmedia.com** is a good place to find links to Internet resources on advertising. At the site, click on "category sites" and then click on one of the categories. Pick three of the company sites listed and review them, using the concepts in this chapter.

prestige pricing
  350
price skimming
  350
product 342
product life cycle
  348
promotion 356
promotional mix
  357
public relations 359
publicity 359
reach 358
retailers 351
sales promotions
  358
sales prospects
  358
selective
  distribution 355
shopping products
  343
specialty products
  343
test-marketing 348
trademark 344
unsought products
  343
vertical marketing
  system 354
wholesalers 351

INFOTRAC®
COLLEGE EDITION

CREATIVE THINKING CASE

Personality Puffs and Cardio Chips

There was a time when potato chips were just potato chips, their greasy crunch leaving the snacker with an aftertaste of delicious guilt. No more. A new kind of chip aims at tackling the psyche rather than tickling the taste bud, promising to turn Americans into kinder, happier, and gentler souls.

The secret? Herbs and plant extracts, such as St. John's wort, ginkgo biloba, and kava kava, are added to the chips along with essences of edible flowers—violet, chamomile, peppermint, and passion flower—to help combat depression, promote long life, and improve memory. "It's just one of those next steps in the evolution of snacks and food," said the chips' manufacturer, Robert Ehrlich. "There are definitely benefits from the product."

But not everyone is swallowing that claim. Some nutritionists have expressed concern that all the feel-good messages about the snacks are just advertising gimmicks to sell chips. "They're just ridiculous," said Norman Rosenthal, clinical professor of psychiatry and author of *St. John's Wort: The Herbal Way to Feeling Good*. "It would be like having a penicillin pie or an antibiotic apple strudel."

Ehrlich founded Robert's American Gourmet, which began making his mood-enhancing snacks four years ago. A group of herbalists, zen masters, a psychiatrist, and young consumers help put the products together. At 99 cents for a 2-ounce bag, the chips are sold in supermarkets—in the health food section—in the United States and in some parts of Europe, Asia, and South America.

Low-fat Cardio Chips containing a blend of natural herbs to improve cardiovascular health, metabolic conditions, the immune system, and aging are one of Ehrlich's products. His other herbal products include St. John's Wort Tortilla Chips to improve moods, Ginkgo Biloba Rings to enhance memory, and Kava Corn Chips to promote relaxation. Personality Puffs, which come in the shape of little people, are made up of a blend of flowers, St. John's wort, and ginkgo biloba.

Unlike other herbal products, Personality Puffs come with a set of printed rules that will "open you to the magic that is ready to happen in your life." Snackers are asked to buy at least two bags and give one away to a stranger within one hour of purchase. That, Ehrlich said, will create goodwill and kindness.

Critical Thinking Questions

1. How would you classify these consumer goods?
2. Describe the pricing strategy for the herbal chips.
3. What distribution channel should be used for the chips?
4. What media would you recommend and what would you suggest as a promotional theme?

VIDEO CASE

**The Internet and Burton Snowboards' Distribution System:
Reaching Out to Newbies**

Burton Snowboards (**http://www.burton.com**), a manufacturer of snowboards and outerwear for snowboard riders, is located in Burlington, Vermont. Burton Snowboards uses its Web site to promote the sport of snowboarding as well as to market its products to professionals and amateurs alike.

Selected retailers sell Burton Snowboards' products to newbies as well as to those with more snowboarding experience. The products are intended to appeal to the discriminating buyer regardless of experience or ability level. Burton's snowboards are premium products—"equipment that starts where many companies reach their 'high-end.'"

Burton's also produces clothing to wear while snowboarding or in the lodge afterward. Emphasizing a layered approach for maximum comfort and warmth, Burton's produces a first layer, a thermal layer, a heater layer, and an outer layer of snowboarding outerwear. Burton's sells gloves, hats, and lodge clothing as well.

Although Burton Snowboards maintains distribution relationships with selected retailers, it has discovered that the Internet can be an important vehicle for developing customer traffic to those retailers.

Critical Thinking Questions

1. What function does Burton Snowboards' Web site serve in its distribution channel?
2. What does the Learn to Ride (LTR) Guide, available by clicking *LTR* at the Burton Snowboard home page, accomplish in terms of servicing Burton's distribution channel?
3. Do you think using the Internet to reach prospective customers is a wise business decision?

Case: Video on Demand

Feel like renting a movie tonight? Don't hop in your car for a run to your local video store. Instead, turn on your computer, log onto the Internet, and download the latest hit flick.

MGM and Blockbuster Video hope that consumers will soon welcome "video on demand" delivered via the Internet. MGM owns the world's largest movie library with 4,100 titles. Blockbuster Video is one of the world's largest video rental chains with over 7,700 retail stores in 27 countries. Under an Internet movie distribution agreement recently signed by both companies, Blockbuster will charge a fee for films ordered and delivered to customers through digital streaming or downloads. The two companies will split profits from movies sold this way. The deal is nonexclusive, meaning either firm can form partnerships with other firms in addition to this one.

"This is an exciting announcement for movie lovers," says John Antioco, Blockbuster's chief executive officer. "It underscores our goal to provide quality, in-home entertainment, in whatever form our consumers want it delivered, whether through our stores or other channels such as electronic delivery."

MGM already offers video clips at its corporate Web site, but hasn't yet made full-length feature films available for download. MGM isn't the only major movie studio looking at Internet distribution. Miramax Films plans to offer 12 full-length films for downloading in an agreement with multimedia distribution company SightSound.com. Miramax will set up an individual Web site for each film.

Online movie distribution has been discussed in the entertainment industry for over a decade, but no movie studio has yet utilized the Internet as a major distribution channel. One problem is the lack of widespread availability of the high-speed, high-capacity Internet access necessary to download movies quickly. However, as more consumers get faster Internet access, studios are hopeful that Internet distribution will debut to consumer applause.

Questions for Critical Thinking

1. Analyze the risks and benefits of their Internet distribution agreement for both Blockbuster and MGM.
2. Explain how Miramax's decision to offer films directly to consumers over the Internet could affect its relationships with customers and other channel members.
3. Do you think Internet movie distribution will succeed? Why or why not?

SOURCES: Mary Hullebrand, "Miramax Films Inks Online Distribution Deal," *E-Commerce Times* (April 19, 2000), downloaded from **http://www.ecommercetimes.com**; Robert La Franco, "Hype on Demand," *Redherring.com* (August 1, 2000), downloaded from **http://www.redherring.com**; Ken Yamada, "Digital Entertainment's Growing Pains," *Redherring.com* (August 2, 2000), downloaded from **http://www.redherring.com**; "MGM.com and Microcast Lead the Way in the Convergence of Film and Internet," *PR Newswire* (August 14, 2000), downloaded from **http://www.prnewswire.com**; "MGM and Blockbuster Announce Agreement to Develop Digital Streaming Model for Selected MGM Film Library Titles," Blockbuster Inc. company press release (January 18, 2000), downloaded from **http://www.blockbuster.com**.

learning goals

>lg 1   Why are computer networks an important part of today's business information systems?

>lg 2   What is the structure of a typical information system?

>lg 3   How can companies manage information technology to their advantage?

>lg 4   What are the leading trends in information technology?

Using Technology to Manage Information

chapter 13

Unlocking KeyCorp's Customer Database for Greater Profits

Cleveland-based KeyCorp (**http://www.keybank. com**) wondered why its per-customer profitability was below average, even though it spent a considerable amount on marketing campaigns. The bank's executives knew that 18 percent of its customers generated 82 percent of bank revenue—but not which customers were the most profitable, the products they used, or which products to promote to different customer groups. Instead of targeting promotions effectively, salespeople based sales tactics on intuition, rather than hard data.

KeyCorp turned to a state-of-the-art data warehouse, a collection of data that supports management decision making, to solve these problems. Housed in its own IBM mainframe computer, the data warehouse consolidates all customer and prospect information from 40 separate databases. The data warehouse's customer profiles include 150 factors—from name and age to loan balances, services used, and frequency of automatic teller machine (ATM) usage. It is now the central information source for sales and marketing decisions throughout the bank.

With specialized software designed for financial services companies, KeyCorp marketing personnel look for hidden patterns and relationships in a group of data. They query the data warehouse to get answers to questions like:

- What kinds of customers purchase each KeyCorp product, when, and why?
- Who are the most profitable and least profitable customers?
- What distribution channels do different customers prefer?
- What would cause a customer to leave KeyCorp?

KeyCorp marketers work with technology personnel to get information to analyze consumer behavior and produce lists of customers most likely to respond to a product offer. The information is available in just a day or two, rather than the month it took with multiple databases.

Automated marketing campaign software identifies customers best suited to receive a particular offer, determines the best medium to reach them, and gathers data on campaign responses. By taking over much of the campaign execution, the software gives marketing managers more time for planning and evaluating campaigns and creating more effective strategies. They know what offers did well and the return on investment for the campaign and can allocate

Critical Thinking Questions

As you read this chapter, consider the following questions as they relate to KeyCorp:

- How does managing information give KeyCorp a competitive advantage?
- What problems might KeyCorp have while implementing the data warehouse?
- What steps could KeyCorp take to encourage acceptance of the new data warehouse and ensure that employees use it?

marketing dollars to the most profitable customer and prospect segments. "You set the rules and you take your hands off and measure results," says Todd Thompson, vice president of corporate marketing. "Once you set it up, the technology just makes it happen."

Since implementing the data warehouse and installing the market automation software, higher direct mail response rates—5 to 10 percent, versus 1 to 2 percent in the past—are the rule rather than the exception, says Jo Ann Boylan, executive vice president of Key Services Corp. Lower marketing costs are another benefit of targeted marketing campaigns. The bank reduced the number of total direct marketing messages by 20 percent yet increased the number of annual campaigns from seven major cross-selling programs to 45 smaller, targeted campaigns. The new marketing strategies have paid off: the number of people who buy the offered products is up 200 percent.[1]

BUSINESS IN THE 21ST CENTURY

information technology (IT)

The equipment and techniques used to manage and process information.

As KeyCorp's executives discovered, harnessing the power of **information technology (IT)** gives a company a significant competitive advantage. The data warehouse helped KeyCorp cut costs, increase profits, spot market trends faster, and communicate more effectively with customers. It also showed the bank where to invest more marketing dollars to build stronger customer relationships.

information system (IS)

The methods and equipment that provide information about all aspects of a firm's operations.

Information systems (IS) like KeyCorp's data warehouse and the computers that comprise them are so much a part of our lives that we almost take them for granted. In less than 60 years, we have shifted from an industrial society to a knowledge-based economy driven by information. Businesses depend on information technology for everything from running daily operations to making strategic decisions. Computers are the tools of this information age, performing extremely complex operations as well as everyday jobs like word processing and creating spreadsheets. Through networks of linked computers, one manager can share information with hundreds of thousands of people around the world almost as easily as with a colleague on another floor of the same office building. Many companies now have a **chief information officer (CIO),** an executive with responsibility for managing all information resources.

chief information officer (CIO)

An executive with responsibility for managing all information resources in an organization.

Because most jobs today depend on managing information, this chapter begins with a description

If you want to know more about a computer term or learn more about a topic, head to Webopaedia's online computer encyclopedia at

http://www.pcwebopaedia.com/

PEPSI-COLA BOTTLES A NEW PURCHASING SYSTEM

An IT manager's job is never done. As soon as Pepsi-Cola North America completed the redesign of its vendor processing system in 1995, it began a related project to use the purchasing information in its new data warehouse to identify cost savings. Both projects were so successful that Pepsi-Cola improved its materials management, purchasing processes, and customer service—and saved more than $100 million over a three-year period.

Before revamping its purchasing systems, Pepsi bought supplies from 300,000 vendors who submitted 1.5 million invoices each year. It took 200 employees to manage this flood of paper and pay suppliers, leaving little time to analyze purchasing trends. By replacing local agreements with national contracts, Pepsi was able to purchase 90 percent of its supplies from just 1,000 vendors, who submit about half as many invoices.

Next, Pepsi centralized and automated its labor-intensive system. Now purchasers search an online catalog of approved items. Clicking on the item automatically enters it on a purchase order that fills in price and other data. The system automatically submits the completed form to the appropriate vendor. Once an employee confirms receipt, the system automatically generates payment in 30 days and records the purchase in the appropriate accounting files. Processing time dropped to 15 minutes per order, errors from 10 percent to less than 1 percent, and the cost of processing each invoice by over 60 percent.

The new system does more than cut costs. Pepsi's national supplier development staff now analyzes the centralized database for purchasing patterns. "We've found the biggest savings in the peripheral items—office supplies, lubricants, tires, uniforms, you name it—that used to be purchased regionally or locally," says controller and vice president Peter Bridgman. "Using the data warehouse, we've been able to identify important items, find national suppliers for them, and leverage those relationships to reduce costs."

Not content to rest on his laurels, Bridgman put his team to work expanding the vendor processing system to inventory management and other stages of the supply chain. Company-wide, the beverage division is creating information system synergies with PepsiCo's Frito-Lay snack foods division. By consolidating IT across product lines, PepsiCo will be able to offer more merchandising incentives and improve customer service.

Critical Thinking Questions

1. Why should companies view information systems' design as a dynamic and evolving process?
2. What different departments were involved in planning Pepsi's new purchasing systems? Why is this joint effort an important part of designing IT systems?
3. Make a list of the types of questions the technology specialists should raise. What questions are important to other departments?

of computer networks and goes on to discuss business information systems and the management of information technology. Finally, we'll also look at the latest trends in information technology. Throughout the chapter, examples show how managers and their companies are using computers to make better decisions in a highly competitive world.

computer network

A group of two or more computer systems linked together by communications channels to share data and information.

COMPUTER NETWORKS

>lg 1

Today most businesses use networks to deliver information to employees, suppliers, and customers. A **computer network** is a group of two or more computer systems linked together by communications channels to share data and information.

Networks have been widely used for about 20 years, but microcomputers have made networking much more affordable and popular. Whereas early networks could connect about 20 users and share only data, today's networks link thousands of users and can transmit audio and video as well as data.

By making it easy and fast to share information, networks have created new ways to work and increase productivity. They provide more efficient use of resources, permitting communication and collaboration across distance and time. With file sharing, all employees, regardless of location, have access to the same information. Shared databases also eliminate duplication of effort. Employees at different sites can "screen share" computer files, working on data as if they were in the same room. Their computers are connected by phone or cable lines, they all see the same thing on their display, and anyone can make changes that are seen by the other participants. The employees can also use the networks for videoconferencing.

Networks make it possible for companies to run enterprise software, large programs with integrated modules that manage all of the corporation's internal operations. Enterprise resource planning (ERP) systems (first described in Chapter 8) run on networks. Typical subsystems include finance, human resources, engineering, sales and order distribution, and order management and procurement. These modules work independently and then automatically exchange information, creating a company-wide system that includes current delivery dates, inventory status, quality control, and other critical information. ERP applications can also be integrated with Web-based resources, as explained in Enrichment Chapter A, "Using the Internet for Business Success," on the CD that accompanies this textbook. Let's now look at the two basic types of networks companies use to transmit data: local area networks and wide area networks.

Can't tell a LAN from a WAN? Learn more about networking at About.com's Networking pages,

http://www.compnetworking.about.com/mbody.htm.

Local Area Networks

local area network (LAN)

A network that connects computers at one site, enabling the computer users to exchange data and share the use of hardware and software from a variety of computer manufacturers.

A **local area network (LAN)** lets people at one site exchange data and share the use of hardware and software from a variety of computer manufacturers. LANs offer companies a more cost-effective way to link computers than linking terminals to a mainframe computer. The most common uses of LANs at small businesses, for example, are office automation, accounting, and information management.[2]

LANs can help companies reduce staff, streamline operations, and cut processing costs. United Science Industries, a fast-growing general contractor in Woodlawn, Illinois, invested $76,000 in a LAN with 15 networked computers. Instead of using field managers' handwritten sheets to produce invoices, the accounting department can access field manager files through the network. Invoices go out in 10 to 12 days instead of two months, the company collects accounts receivable 5 to 10 days faster, and its monthly labor costs dropped $20,000. "With the network, people spend less time hunting for information and more time working on tasks crucial to operations," says CEO Jay Koch.[3]

Wide Area Networks

wide area network (WAN)

A network that connects computers at different sites via telecommunications media such as phone lines, satellites, and microwaves.

A **wide area network (WAN)** connects computers at different sites via telecommunications media such as phone lines, satellites, and microwaves. A modem connects the computer or a terminal to the telephone line and transmits data almost instantly, in less than a second. The Internet is essentially a worldwide WAN. Long-distance telephone companies, such as AT&T, MCI WorldCom, and Sprint, operate very large WANs. Companies also connect LANs at various locations into WANs. WANs make it possible for companies to work on critical projects around the clock by using teams in different time zones.

Two forms of WANs—intranets and extranets—use Internet technology. Here we'll look at intranets, internal corporate networks that are widely available in the corporate world. Extranets are discussed in Enrichment Chapter A, "Using the Internet for Business Success," on the CD that accompanies this textbook.

Intranets

intranet

An internal corporate-wide area network that uses Internet technology to link employees in many locations and with different types of computers.

Like LANs, **intranets** are private corporate networks. Many companies use both types of internal networks. However, because they use Internet technology to connect computers, intranets are WANs that link employees in many locations and with different types of computers. Essentially mini-Internets that serve only the company's employees, intranets operate behind a *firewall* that prevents unauthorized access. Employees navigate using a standard Web browser, which makes the intranet easier to use than a client/server system. They are also considerably less expensive to install and maintain and can take advantage of Internet interactive features such as chat rooms and team work spaces.

Until recently, intranets were too complicated and expensive for small businesses, but the cost has dropped as companies develop off-the-shelf programs. Children's Orchard, a franchiser whose stores sell new, secondhand, and manufacturers' overstock toys and children's clothing, uses an intranet to communicate with franchisees around the United States. It is the primary source of company news, corporate services, and peer support. Franchisees have a password to access the intranet through the company's regular Web site. There they can read newsletters, order supplies, and call up statistics on other stores to see how they compare. They can also chat with other franchisees to share ideas and solve problems. CEO Walter Hamilton estimates that the intranet saves the company at least $40,000 a year.[4]

concept check

- What is a computer network? How do a LAN and a WAN differ?
- What benefits do companies gain by using networks?
- You are an employee in the marketing department of a consumer products company. Make a list of the information you would expect to find on the company's intranet.

BUSINESS INFORMATION SYSTEMS

>lg 2

While individuals use business productivity software to accomplish a variety of tasks, the job of managing a company's information needs falls to information systems: users, hardware, and software that support decision making. Information systems collect and store the company's key data and produce the information needed by managers for analysis, control, and decision making.

As we learned in Chapter 8, factories use computer-based information systems to automate production processes and order and monitor inventory. Most companies use them to process customer orders and handle billing and vendor payments. Financial services companies like KeyCorp use a variety of information systems to process transactions such as deposits, ATM withdrawals, and loan payments. Most consumer transactions also involve information systems. When you check out at the supermarket, book a hotel room using a toll-free hotel reservations number, or buy CDs over the Internet, information systems record and track the transaction and transmit the data to the necessary places. Companies typically have several types of information systems:

- *Transaction processing systems* handle the daily business operations of the firm—for example, customer orders, pricing, employee payrolls, and inventory. These operational systems capture and organize raw data and convert these data into information.
- *Management support, or analytic, systems* are dynamic systems that help managers make decisions. These systems allow users to analyze data, including the transaction systems' operational data, to identify business trends, make forecasts, and model business strategies.

- *Office automation systems* use information technology tools such as e-mail, facsimile (fax) machines, and word processing to improve the flow of information throughout an organization. These systems support employees at all levels.

Each type of information system serves a particular level of decision making: operational, tactical, and strategic. Exhibit 13-1 shows the relationship between transaction processing and management support systems as well as the management levels they serve. Let's now take a more detailed look at how companies and managers use transaction processing and management support systems to manage information.

Transaction Processing Systems

transaction processing system (TPS)

An information system that handles the daily business operations of a firm. The system receives and organizes raw data from internal and external sources for storage in a database.

batch processing

A method of updating a database in which data are collected over some time period and processed together.

The firm's integrated information system starts with its **transaction processing system (TPS).** The TPS receives raw data from internal and external sources and prepares these data for storage in a database similar to a microcomputer database but vastly larger. In fact, all the company's key data are stored in a single huge database that becomes the company's central information resource. A *database management system* tracks the data and allows users to query the database for the information they need.

The database can be updated in two ways. With **batch processing,** data are collected over some time period and processed together. Batch processing uses

e x h i b i t   1 3 - 1 | A Company's Integrated Information System

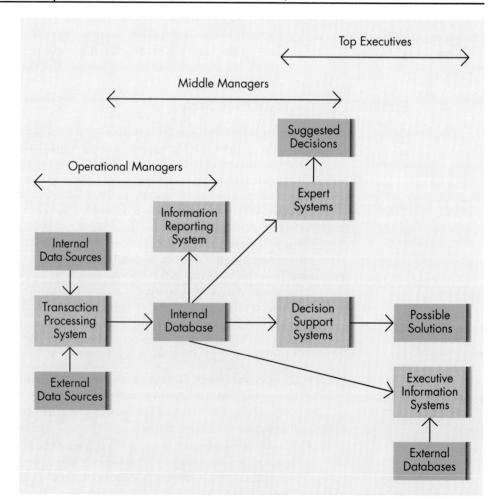

online (real-time) processing
A method of updating a database in which data are processed as they become available.

computer resources very efficiently and is well suited to applications such as payroll processing that require periodic rather than continuous processing. **Online,** or **real-time, processing** processes data as they become available. When you make an airline reservation, the agent enters your reservation directly into the airline's computer and quickly receives confirmation. Online processing keeps the company's data current. Because absolutely current data are needed for management decision making, many large companies use online processing systems.

The transaction processing systems of large companies are custom-designed to keep the records they need. But some applications in the areas of accounting and finance, human resource management, sales and marketing, and manufacturing are nearly universal. For example, the accounting information system diagrammed in Exhibit 13-2 is a typical TPS. It has subsystems for order entry, accounts receivable (for billing customers), accounts payable (for paying bills), payroll, inventory, and general ledger (for determining the financial status and profitability of the business). The accounting information system provides input to and receives input from the firm's other information systems, such as manufacturing (production planning data, for example) and human resources (data on hours worked and salary increases to generate paychecks).

Management Support Systems

Transaction processing systems were the first stage of information technology. By automating routine and tedious back-office processes such as accounting, order processing, and financial reporting, they reduced clerical expenses and provided basic operational information more quickly. As technology improved,

e x h i b i t   1 3 - 2 | Accounting Information System

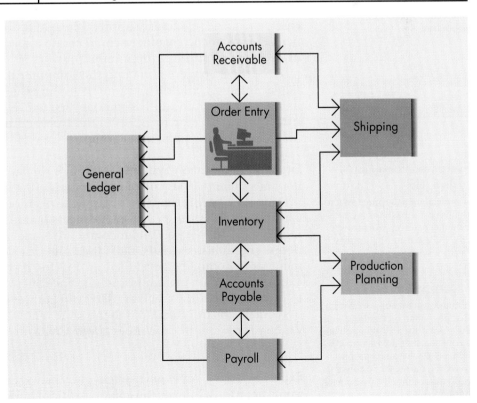

management support system (MSS)

A dynamic information system that helps managers make decisions by allowing them to analyze data, identify business trends, make forecasts, and model business strategies.

data warehouse

An information technology that combines many databases across a whole company into one central database that supports management decision making.

decision support system (DSS)

A management support system that helps managers make decisions using computer models that describe real-world processes.

executive information system (EIS)

A management support system that is customized for an individual executive; provides specific information for strategic decisions.

expert system

A management support system that gives managers advice similar to what they would get from a consultant; it uses artificial intelligence to enable computers to reason and learn to solve problems in much the same way humans do.

businesses realized that computers could do more than merely process data. Managers now have several types of **management support systems (MSSs)** that use the internal database to help them make better decisions.

As we saw in the KeyCorp opening vignette, information technologies such as data warehousing are part of more advanced MSSs. A **data warehouse** combines many databases across the whole company into one central database that supports management decision making. Data warehouses include software to extract data from operational databases, maintain the data in the warehouse, and provide data to users.

Information Reporting Systems   At the first level of an MSS is an *information reporting system,* which uses summary data collected by the TPS to produce reports with statistics that managers can use to make decisions. Some reports are scheduled and present information on a regular basis. For instance, payroll personnel at Homestyle Corp., a large furniture maker, get a weekly payroll report showing how each employee's paycheck was determined. The next level of report summarizes information. A payroll summary report might show higher-level managers total labor cost by department, overtime as a percentage of total payroll cost by department, and a comparison of current labor costs with those in the prior year. Exception reports help identify problems by telling about cases that fail to meet some standard. An accounts receivable exception report that lists all customers with overdue accounts would help collection personnel focus their work. Demand reports are special reports generated only when a manager requests them. The marketing manager for the Honey Wood furniture line might call for reports on sales by region and type of store to identify reasons for the sales decline.

Decision Support Systems   A **decision support system (DSS)** helps managers make decisions using computer models that describe real-world processes. The DSS also uses data from the internal database but looks for specific data that relate to the problems at hand. It is a tool for answering "what if" questions about what would happen if the manager made certain changes. In simple cases, a manager can create a spreadsheet and try changing some of the numbers. For instance, a manager could create a spreadsheet to show the amount of overtime required if the number of workers increases or decreases. With models, the manager enters into the computer the values that describe a particular situation, and the program computes the results. Homestyle's marketing executives could run DSS models that use sales data and demographic assumptions to develop forecasts of the types of furniture that would appeal to the fastest growing population groups.

Executive Information Systems   Although similar to a DSS, an **executive information system (EIS)** is customized for an individual executive. These systems provide specific information for strategic decisions. For example, Homestyle's CEO has an EIS with special spreadsheets that present financial data comparing Homestyle to its principal competitors and graphs showing current economic and industry trends. Belk, Inc., America's largest privately held department store company, developed an EIS for its buyers, assistant buyers, and executives. Its easy-to-understand interface allows users to quickly get answers to high-level questions such as, "How did last week's markdowns affect the sale of intimate apparel compared to the same time last year?" "Will our current inventory for Kenneth Cole shoes at our Charlotte store be sufficient, given the pending promotion?"[5]

Expert Systems   An **expert system** gives managers advice similar to what they would get from a human consultant. Artificial intelligence enables computers to

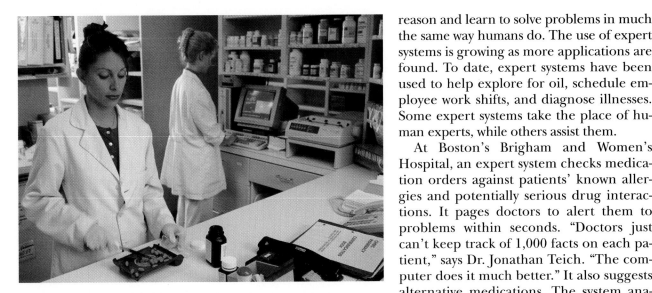

Medical professionals use expert systems to analyze patients' medications, ensuring that they do not cause allergic reactions and potentially dangerous interactions with patients' other prescriptions.

office automation system

An information system that uses information technology tools such as word processing systems, e-mail systems, cellular phones, pagers, and fax machines, to improve communications throughout an organization.

reason and learn to solve problems in much the same way humans do. The use of expert systems is growing as more applications are found. To date, expert systems have been used to help explore for oil, schedule employee work shifts, and diagnose illnesses. Some expert systems take the place of human experts, while others assist them.

At Boston's Brigham and Women's Hospital, an expert system checks medication orders against patients' known allergies and potentially serious drug interactions. It pages doctors to alert them to problems within seconds. "Doctors just can't keep track of 1,000 facts on each patient," says Dr. Jonathan Teich. "The computer does it much better." It also suggests alternative medications. The system analyzes about 13,000 orders per day. Its fast response time—no longer does a lab technician have to call the pharmacist, who then finds the doctor—prevents about 400 serious medication errors daily.[6]

Office Automation Systems

Today's **office automation systems** make good use of the computer networks in many companies to improve communications. Office automation systems assist all levels of employees and enable managers to handle most of their own communication. The key elements include:

- *Word processing systems* for producing written messages.
- *E-mail systems* for communicating directly with other employees and customers and transferring computer files.
- *Departmental scheduling systems* for planning meetings and other activities.
- *Cellular phones* for providing telephone service away from the office, as in cars.
- *Pagers* that notify employees of phone calls. Some pagers have the ability to display more extensive written messages sent from a computer network.
- *Voice mail systems* for recording, storing, and forwarding phone messages.
- *Facsimile (fax) systems* for delivering messages on paper within minutes.
- *Electronic bulletin boards* and *computer conferencing systems* for discussing issues with others who are not present.

Office automation systems also make telecommuting and home-based businesses possible. An estimated 8 million people work at home, using microcomputers and other high-tech equipment to keep in touch with the office. Instead of spending time on the road twice a day, telecommuters work at home two or more days a week. As we discussed in Chapter 5, home offices are a popular trend among small business owners.

c o n c ə p t   c h ə c k

- What are the main components of an information system, and what does each do?
- Differentiate between the types of management support systems, and give examples of how each is used.
- How can office automation systems help employees work more efficiently?

MANAGING INFORMATION TECHNOLOGY

>lg 3

With the help of computers, people have produced more data in the last 30 years than in the previous 5,000 years combined. Companies today make sizable investments in information technology to help them manage this overwhelming amount of data, convert the data into knowledge, and deliver it to the people who need it. In many cases, however, the companies do not reap the desired benefits from these expenditures. Among the typical complaints from senior executives are that the payoff from IT investments is inadequate, IT investments do not relate to business strategy, the firm seems to be buying the latest technology for technology's sake, and communications between IT specialists and IT users are poor.[7]

Managing a company's information resources requires a coordinated effort among a firm's top executives, IT managers, and business unit managers. The goal is to develop an integrated, company-wide technology plan that achieves a balance between business judgment and technology expertise. Protecting company information and privacy concerns are other important aspects of knowledge management.

Technology Planning

Like any other business activity that involves the entire company, IT requires coordinated strategies and planning that take into account the company's strategic objectives. Then managers can select the right technology to help them reach those goals.

The goal of technology planning is to provide employees with the tools they need to perform their jobs at the highest levels of efficiency. The first step is a general needs assessment, followed by ranking of projects and the specific choices of hardware and software. Some basic questions departmental managers and IT specialists should ask when planning technology purchases include:

- What are the company's overall objectives?
- What problems does the company want to solve?
- How can technology help meet those goals and solve the problems?
- What are the company's priorities, both short- and long-term?
- Which technologies meet the company's requirements?
- Are additional hardware and software required? If so, will they integrate with the company's existing systems?

Once managers identify the projects that make business sense, they can choose the best products for the company's needs. The final step is to evaluate the potential benefits of the technology, in terms of efficiency and effectiveness. This requires developing specific criteria—not only quantitative measures like cost savings and profit improvement, but also qualitative factors such as employee satisfaction. For example, how will the new technology increase revenues? Will it get products to market faster by shortening the product development cycle or streamlining the production process? Will it save employees time and cut labor costs? What other benchmarks does the company want to achieve? How can prevention strategies guard against information loss?

Plans will change over time in response to company needs. "Basically, business and technology plans should become living documents that drive the company forward," says Cheryl Currid, a technology analyst.[8] The planning process can even be a catalyst for growth, as the Focusing on Small Business box demonstrates.

Protecting Computers and Information

Protecting the information stored in computers is no easy task. With the ever-increasing dependence on computers, companies must develop plans to cover power outages, equipment failure, human error, and disasters such as major

ACI BENEFITS FROM IT PLANNING

Sales at Actuarial Consultants, Inc. (ACI), a 38-person employee benefits consulting firm in Torrance, California, had been flat for four years. But before CEO Pat Byrnes could implement any growth strategies, ACI needed to revamp its business procedures and install centralized computer systems.

The company's benefits consultants each kept their own customer files and used whatever software they liked to prepare benefit plans. ACI's computer systems were a mess because it had no technology plan. Low-level tech support personnel bought hardware and software to fill immediate needs, without regard to compatibility with existing products. In addition, ACI had no marketing database or client tracking system. Its information sources were spread out all over the company, often on handwritten forms, and its accounting and record-keeping systems could barely keep track of its current accounts. "We are in a business that needs to move information quickly," said Byrnes. "We just couldn't go on like this any longer."

To avoid past mistakes, Byrnes hired Howard Moore, an experienced IT executive, to serve as the chief information officer and to build a solid IT infrastructure to support ACI's marketing, sales, and accounting operations and future growth. Moore developed a comprehensive technology plan to help ACI reach its goals. He first standardized ACI's computer systems on one platform—the Windows operating system, Microsoft Office suite, and PCs from one manufac-

turer. Before installing additional applications such as e-mail and file sharing on the office's upgraded network, Moore had employees test them. If the employees weren't satisfied, he told the systems consultant to find something else.

Once the basics were in place, Moore began working on ACI's internal business processes. To improve customer acquisition methods, he created a prospect information form that could be shared over the network. For the first time, sales, marketing, and accounting personnel had access to information they needed. ACI could now forecast future staffing needs and do other long-range planning. Finally, Moore encouraged better communications through increased use of e-mail, instituted security and backup procedures, and developed a telecommuting program.

With the new IT systems in place, ACI was able to increase its client load without additional personnel.

Critical Thinking Questions

1. How did the absence of technology planning cause problems at ACI?
2. Why did hiring a chief information officer, something usually found only at large companies, make sense for ACI?
3. If you were Moore, how would you evaluate ACI's technology needs to develop a technology plan?

fires, earthquakes, or floods. Many companies install fault-tolerant computer systems designed to withstand such disasters. Preventing costly problems can be as simple as regularly backing up applications and data. Companies should have systems in place that automatically back up the company's data every day. In addition, employees should back up their own work regularly.

Disasters are not the only threat to data. A great deal of data, much of it confidential, can easily be tapped or destroyed by anyone who knows about computers.

Data Security Issues   Firms are taking steps to prevent computer crimes, which cost large companies hundreds of thousands of dollars every year. There are several major categories of computer crimes:

- *Unauthorized access and use.* This can create havoc with a company's systems. For example, employees at Bluebird Systems, a software company in Carlsbad, California, kept having unexplained system crashes and network slowdowns.

A consultant traced the problem to Bluebird's network administrator, who was also a Sierra Club member and claimed that he'd asked permission to create and maintain the Sierra Club Web site on a Bluebird server. As the site expanded from a few pages to over 2,000, the heavy traffic affected Bluebird's network operations. Hal Tilbury, Bluebird's CEO, estimates that the network crashes cost the company several million dollars from lost employee productivity and missed deadlines—not to mention the risk of unauthorized access to the company's files and research.[9]

- *Security breaches and unauthorized access.* Employees can copy confidential new product information and provide it to competitors. Networking links make it easier for someone outside the organization to gain access to a company's computers. Computer crooks are getting more sophisticated all the time and find new ways to get into ultrasecure sites. For example, a British hacker was able to break into the network of the highly secret Rome Laboratory in New York by using computers in Latvia, Colombia, and Chile. Then he attacked defense and government systems.[10]

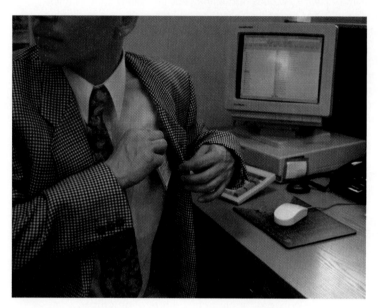

Employers can guard against employee theft of confidential information by installing special authorization systems that prevent unwanted access from inside their organization.

To protect data, companies can encode confidential information so only the recipient can decipher it. Special authorization systems can help stop unwanted access from inside or outside. These can be as simple as a password or as sophisticated as fingerprint or voice identification. Companies can also install intrusion-detection systems to monitor networks for activities that signal the possibility of unauthorized access and document suspicious events. Further discussion of protecting confidential data is covered in Enrichment Chapter A, "Using the Internet for Business Success," on the CD that accompanies this textbook.

- *Software piracy.* The copying of copyrighted software programs by people who haven't paid for them is another form of unauthorized use. Piracy takes revenue away from the company that developed the program—usually at great cost. Thus, software firms take piracy seriously and go after the offenders. Many also make special arrangements so that large companies can get multiple copies of programs at a lower cost rather than use illegal copies.

- *Deliberate damage to information.* For example, an unhappy employee in the purchasing department could get into the computer system and delete information on past orders and future inventory needs. The sabotage could severely disrupt production and the accounts payable system. Willful acts to destroy or change the data in computers are hard to prevent. To lessen the damage, companies should back up critical information.

computer virus

A computer program that copies itself into other software and can spread to other computer systems.

- *Computer viruses.* A computer program that copies itself into other software and can spread to other computer systems, a **computer virus** can destroy the contents of a computer's hard drive or damage files. Another form is called a "worm" be-

To find out if that e-mail alerting you to another virus threat is real or a hoax, check out the latest information at

http://www.sophos.com/virusinfo/analyses

MAKING ETHICAL CHOICES

THE PAIRGAIN HOAX

At 9:27 A.M. on April 7, 1999, investors were jolted by a posting on the Yahoo! finance message board. The posting indicated that PairGain Technologies, Inc. had been acquired, and that the information had been found on the Internet site run by Bloomberg—a provider of news and financial data. The posting also provided "an electronic link to what appeared to be a news article on a Web site identified as Bloomberg.com."

As a result of this posting, heavy trading of PairGain's stock ensued, with the per share price rising by 32 percent at one point. Unfortunately for the buyers, the news story turned out to be fictitious. When investors began to discover the hoax, the stock fell, but was still up 10 percent at the end of the day. In all, 13.7 million shares were traded—more than six times PairGain's daily trading average of 2.1 million shares.

The fake news story, described as a very sophisticated example of "investors being duped by false or misleading postings on the Internet," illustrates "how cheaply and easily programmers can pull off Internet hoaxes using widely available technology and the anonymity afforded by the online world." The fake Bloomberg.com Web page was posted on the free Angelfire service provided by Lycos. To sign up for this free service, a person need only fill out a brief form, including "such unverifiable information as a name and address." A workable e-mail address is also required, but someone can easily use another person's e-mail address.

Critical Thinking Questions

1. Do Internet services have a moral or ethical responsibility to ensure that information provided on their free sites is not false or misleading?
2. What would you do if you discovered false or misleading information on an Internet site?

cause it spreads itself automatically from computer to computer. Viruses can hide for weeks or months before starting to damage information. A virus that "infects" one computer or network can be spread to another computer by sharing disks or by downloading infected files over the Internet. To protect data from virus damage, software developers have created virus protection programs. This software automatically monitors computers to detect and remove viruses. Program developers make regular updates available to guard against newly created viruses. In addition, experts are becoming more proficient at tracking down virus authors, who are subject to criminal charges.

Preventing Problems   Firms that take a proactive approach can prevent security and technical problems before they start. Here are some ways to avoid an IT meltdown:

- Set up an IT management service that works closely with other employees to troubleshoot problems in advance rather than just react to them. Act on them *before* they affect the operation.

- Train IT managers to treat employees in other areas as customers.

- Establish a multimedia in-house help center to respond quickly and professionally to employee concerns. Use e-mail and the Web to minimize phone use for answers to nonurgent questions.

- Know your IT environment. Maintain a complete database of all IT hardware, software, and user details to give help-desk agents the information to

All organizations using computers were involved in the technology planning project of rewriting computer code instructions involving dates to accept the year 2000.

assist employees. This speeds up diagnosis of problems and improves management of software licenses and updates.

- Give IT support staff remote access to servers and PCs so they can use "remote diagnostics" to provide automatic updates of applications and services and to allow monitoring and fixing of problems.

- Help users help themselves. Establish a database of useful information and FAQs (frequently asked questions) for employees so they can solve problems themselves.

- Develop a healthy communications atmosphere.

- Secure data by making firewalls a priority.

- Invest in skills. Hold frequent staff training sessions to maintain skills and learn about new technology. Investing in adequate training now will save considerable time and money later.[11]

Privacy Concerns The very existence of huge electronic file cabinets full of personal information presents a threat to our personal privacy. Until recently, our financial, medical, tax, and other records were stored in separate computer systems. Computer networks make it easy to pool these data into data warehouses. Companies also sell the information they collect about you from sources like warranty registration cards, credit card records, registration at Web sites, and grocery store discount club cards. Telemarketers can combine data from different sources to create fairly detailed profiles of consumers.

Increasingly, consumers are fighting to regain control of personal data and how that information is used. Public outcry over a flaw in Microsoft's Windows 98 that allowed it to gather computer identification without the user's knowledge and electronic serial numbers in Intel's Pentium III chips resulted in changes to both products. Privacy advocates are working to block state governments from selling driver's license information. Legislation under discussion in California would restrict how businesses, nonprofit organizations, and government entities can collect and use personal information. For example, one proposal would prevent supermarkets from collecting and selling information gathered when shoppers use barcoded plastic discount cards. With information about their buying habits, advertisers can target consumers for specific marketing programs.[12]

The challenge to companies is to find a balance between collecting the information they need while at the same time protecting individual consumer rights. Most registration and warranty forms that ask questions about income and interests have a box for consumers to check to prevent the company from selling their names. Many companies now state their privacy policies to ensure consumers that they will not abuse the information they collect. Although supermarket chain Safeway records purchase data, it will not sell customer information to third parties like telemarketers and direct mail firms or manufacturers who want to send customers coupons. "What we're trying to assess is general shopping patterns," says Debra Lambert, Safeway's corporate director of public affairs.[13]

concept check

- Why is technology planning an essential element of information management? What are its benefits?
- Describe the different threats to data security and the ways companies can protect information from destruction and from unauthorized use.
- Why are privacy rights advocates alarmed over the use of techniques such as data warehouses?

CAPITALIZING ON TRENDS IN BUSINESS

Information technology is a continually evolving field. The fast pace and amount of change, coupled with IT's broad reach, make it especially challenging to isolate industry trends. From the time we write this chapter to the time you read it—as little as six months—new trends will appear and those that seemed important may fade. However, three trends that are reshaping the IT landscape at the beginning of the 21st century are knowledge management, the emergence of information appliances, and the shortage of qualified IT personnel.

Managing Knowledge Resources

Although companies may have procedures to manage information, they are now tackling the more difficult task of knowledge management (KM). *Information management* involves collecting, processing, and condensing information. *Knowledge management,* however, focuses on gathering and sharing an organization's collective knowledge to improve productivity and foster innovation. Some companies are even creating a new position, chief knowledge officer, to head up this effort.

We've already seen how companies like KeyCorp and Belk use software tools to comb through company databases seeking information. But better software is not the only answer to KM. Effective KM calls for a cultural change within the company. It's a whole new way of working and communicating that encourages departments and employees to share knowledge. This attitude can be difficult to promote among employees who are used to protecting their own turf. KM's benefits can be significant in terms of both time and money. Chevron Corp.'s individual oil refineries had their own methods to improve efficiency. By mounting a formal effort to collect the best refinery management practices and make them available to all locations, Chevron saved $170 million.[14]

End of the Personal Computer Era?

"Information appliances," easy-to-use, inexpensive, consumer-oriented products that perform only one or two tasks, may soon replace the PC as our most popular information tool. In addition to simplicity and convenience, many of these appliances use wireless technology to make computing more portable.

These devices run counter to the recent trend to make PCs increasingly complex and powerful. Though businesses may need these PCs, most personal users don't. "The PC is so general purpose that very few of us use more than 5 percent of its capability," says former Hewlett-Packard CEO Lewis Platt. And for users who only want to do one thing—access the Internet, for example—a PC is more than they need. PCs won't disappear, however. They will coexist with other alternatives, but will no longer dominate to the degree that they do now.

Handheld personal digital assistants are getting more powerful all the time. Find out what they can do at 3Com's Palm site,

www.palm.com/

Searching for Information Technology Talent

The good news: the rapidly growing IT industry has led the way among all industries in new job creation. The bad news: there aren't enough qualified IT personnel to fill those jobs. The Information Technology Association of America estimates that over 840,000 positions—more than half the 1.6 million new jobs created in 2000—are likely to go unfilled. One of every 12 IT jobs in the total U.S. IT workforce of 10 million will be vacant. In fact, IT companies rank the shortage of skilled workers their most significant barrier to growth.

If the shortage of IT talent continues, companies will be hard-pressed to keep up with the latest IT developments. According to Commerce Department predictions, information systems analysts, computer engineers, and computer scientists will be the fastest-growing groups in terms of job demand through 2008. Yet the number of new college graduates with computer science degrees or programming skills has dropped in recent years. To attract and retain IT talent, companies are implementing new recruitment programs, partnering with educational institutions, increasing in-house training programs for individuals with no previous IT skills, and developing programs to improve employee satisfaction.

concept check

- Differentiate between information management and knowledge management. What steps can companies take to manage knowledge?
- What benefits do information appliances offer? Do you think they will diminish the importance of PCs?
- Why is the shortage of qualified IT personnel a serious problem?

APPLYING THIS CHAPTER'S TOPICS

Computer literacy is no longer a luxury. To succeed in business today, almost everyone must develop technological competence. Whether you have a part-time job in a fast-food restaurant that uses computerized ordering systems or

TRY IT NOW!

1. Stay Current Keeping up with the fast pace of technology change is a real challenge, but it is necessary if you wish to remain up-to-date on the latest IT developments. The Internet has simplified this task, however. Get into the habit of visiting news sites such as ZDNet (**http://www.zdnet.com**). Its Anchor Desk is updated daily with current news. You can also link to Ziff Davis publications such as *PC Magazine* and find on-line classes. Another excellent site is CNet's News.com (**http://www.news.com**), which updates the technology news headlines throughout the day. It has sections on enterprise computing, the Internet, IT services, telecommunications, and personal technology.

2. Know Who's Hiring You can benefit from the severe shortage of technology personnel—even if you don't think you want a job in IT. Read the classified employment ads in your local newspaper and *The Wall Street Journal*. Go online to browse the employment ads from almost any major newspaper and surf through the Web sites with job listings. Many technology company Web sites also post job openings. Make a list of jobs that interest you. In addition, read the general job listings to see how many require computer skills.

Unlike about one-third of all banking data warehouse projects, KeyCorp's data warehouse project was a big success. A major factor was the support of top management, who involved managers in the design process, emphasized the importance of the data warehouse to the bank's ability to compete in the financial services marketplace, and provided compensation incentives to use the data warehouse.

KeyCorp's data warehouse not only drives its customer focus but also improves profitability. The monthly and annual customer profit reports allow the bank to maximize account profitability and quickly spot changing customer needs. Information from the data warehouse shows sales reps what services a customer is likely to buy next—or avoid—so they can cross-sell. For example, customers who don't use ATMs aren't likely to try on-line banking. By removing those customers from prospect lists, KeyCorp saved money on mailings.[16]

perform financial analyses that guide the future of your own company, you will depend on computers. The more you increase your knowledge of technology, the more valuable you will be as an employee in today's information-driven businesses. In addition, the shortage of qualified IT personnel opens up new career avenues to those that enjoy working with technology. You can also take steps to protect your privacy.

Preparation Pays Off

Whether you are an employee or a business owner, you need to be aware of how technology affects the way your firm operates. New applications can change fundamental company operations and employees' roles. For example, companies that install ERP systems want individual employees to make more strategic, far-reaching decisions than before. This requires a dramatic shift in employee's roles and the way they should view their jobs. For example, an accountant's responsibilities might now include analyzing budgets, not just auditing expenses. A salesperson's role might expand to include more strategic decision making about customer issues. Your company will see the business benefits sooner if you prepare for these changing roles. A manager should begin teaching employees operational procedures before implementing the new system and help them acquire the necessary analytical skills. As an employee, you can take the initiative to learn as much as possible about the new technology and how it operates.

Keeping Secrets

By understanding how companies collect and use information, you can protect your personal data from being mined. The first step is simply saying no. You can usually get a store's discounts and products even if you withhold some personal information, explains Beth Givens of the Privacy Rights Clearinghouse in San Diego. "You don't have to give your name when you get a supermarket card. Safeway says you can register as an anonymous shopper." Also have your name removed from direct market lists to curb unwanted mail and data exchange.

Next, check your credit report for unfamiliar accounts and monthly charge card statements for fraudulent charges that signal that someone may have stolen your personal information. Then contact the creditors and let them know the information is not accurate. Major credit reporting agencies must correct the information. Finally, contact the major credit reporting agencies, Equifax, Experian, and TransUnion, and forbid prescreening credit rating checks. This puts a stop to unsolicited credit card offers, which can fall into the wrong hands.[15]

SUMMARY OF LEARNING GOALS

>lg 1   **Why are computer networks an important part of today's business information systems?**

Local area networks (LANs) and wide area networks (WANs) are used to link computers so they can share data and expensive hardware. Today companies use networks extensively to improve operating efficiency. Networking techniques like e-mail allow employees to communicate with each other quickly, regardless of their location.

>lg 2   **What is the structure of a typical information system?**

An information system consists of a transaction processing system, management support systems, and an office automation system. The transaction processing system collects and organizes operational data on the firm's activities. Management support systems help managers make better decisions. They include an information reporting system that provides information based on the data to the managers who need it; decision support systems that use models to assist in answering "what if" types of questions; and expert systems that give managers advice similar to what they would get from a human consultant. Executive information systems are customized to the needs of top management. All employees benefit from office automation systems that facilitate communication by using word processing, e-mail, fax machines, and similar technologies.

>lg 3   **How can companies manage information technology to their advantage?**

To get the most value from information technology (IT), companies must go beyond simply collecting and summarizing information. Technology planning involves evaluating the company's goals and objectives and using the right technology to reach them. Because companies are more dependent on computers than ever before, they need to protect data and equipment from natural disasters and computer crime such as unauthorized access and use and malicious damage. They must also take steps to protect customers' personal privacy rights.

>lg 4   **What are the leading trends in information technology?**

Knowledge management focuses on sharing an organization's collective knowledge to improve productivity and foster innovation. The CIO plays a pivotal role in knowledge management. The emergence of simpler information appliances may make the PC a less important information tool. Consumers may prefer these easy-to-use devices to multifunction PCs. The shortage of qualified IT personnel is making it harder for companies to stay current with the latest IT developments.

PREPARING FOR TOMORROW'S WORKPLACE

1. Some people view the spread of computers with alarm, worrying that computers pose a threat to the job security of such workers as secretaries and factory workers and can lead to invasions of privacy, both in the workplace and at home. Others believe that computers bring benefits that far outweigh any of these concerns. Divide the class in half to debate these conflicting views.

2. Visit or conduct a phone interview with a local small business owner about the different ways her or his firm uses information technology. Prepare a brief report on your findings that includes the hardware and software used, benefits of technology for the company, and any problems in implementing or using it.

KEY TERMS

batch processing
  374
chief information
  officer (CIO) 370
computer network
  371
computer virus 380
data warehouse
  376
decision support
  system (DSS) 376
executive
  information
  system (EIS) 376
expert system 376
information system
  (IS) 370
information tech-
  nology (IT) 370
intranet 373
local area network
  (LAN) 372
management
  support system
  (MSS) 376
office automation
  system 377
online (real-time)
  processing 375
transaction
  processing system
  (TPS) 374
wide area network
  (WAN) 372

3. Your school wants to automate the class registration process. Prepare a memo to the Dean of Information Systems describing an integrated information system that would help a student choose and register for courses. Include a graphic representation of the system similar to Exhibit 13-2 that shows how the data become useful information. Indicate the information a student needs to choose courses and its sources. Explain how several types of management support systems could help students make better course decisions. How could the school use the information it collects from this system?

WORKING THE NET

1. One of the fastest growing areas of business software is enterprise resource planning (ERP) applications. Visit the site of one of the following companies: SAP (**http://www.sap.com**); PeopleSoft (**http://www.peoplesoft.com**); Oracle (**http://www.oracle.com**); or Baan (**http://www.baan.com**). Prepare a short presentation for the class about the company's ERP product offerings and capabilities. Include examples of how companies use the ERP software.
2. What can an intranet accomplish for a company? Find out by exploring the Intranet.com Web site (**http://www.intranet.com**). Read the case studies. Summarize the different features an intranet provides.

CREATIVE THINKING CASE

IT Energizes La-Z-Boy

During 2001, declining sales and an uncertain economic future required companies to take a hard look at their spending for information technology (IT), typically one of a company's largest capital expense categories. Companies like La-Z-Boy, the leading U.S. manufacturer of upholstered furniture, had to implement major cost-cutting programs. One of the biggest dilemmas it faced was deciding where to trim the IT budget, no easy task. In addition to hard costs and quantifiable dollar benefits—for example, transactional systems where order volume provides an objective measure—companies must attempt to quantify indirect and qualitative benefits. How does a company place a dollar amount on increased customer satisfaction generated by new, easier-to-use interface for its customer information system?

La-Z-Boy looked for projects that provided the highest return on dollars invested or the greatest strategic advantage. Gary Clark, La-Z-Boy director of corporate IT services, said, "Previously, we would look primarily at high-level issues. Now, we're not only examining the details of a project but also the underlying assumptions and the business case. It's all about cost and results." La-Z-Boy decided to postpone information security and general business systems projects. It also curtailed use of outside consultants. However, it kept several strategic technology initiatives moving forward. For example, analysis of a new payroll and human resources system showed that it should lower costs for the entire organization. The benefits would increase further when La-Z-Boy's company-wide shared services system comes online.

Critical Thinking Questions

1. If you were Gary Clark, how would you evaluate La-Z-Boy's information security, general business, and payroll/human resources projects? Prepare a list of questions you would ask managers to justify their projects.

2. What steps can La-Z-Boy take to protect information until it can implement its security project? What types of trade-offs may be required when funds are tight?

3. Why is it important to have a technology plan and to evaluate IT projects in terms of the company's overall strategy and objectives?

Sources: Russ Banham and Hillary Rosenberg, "ROI: Mad to Measure," *eCFO*, September 26, 2001, downloaded from http://www.ecfo.com; and Sam Greengard, "IT: Luxury or Necessity?" *Industry Week*, December 1, 2001, downloaded from http://www.industryweek.com.

VIDEO CASE

Information Management Challenges and Solutions at Archway Cookies

Archway Cookies (**http://www.archwaycookies.com** and **http://www.intermec.com/solutions/archway.htm**), family owned and headquartered in Battle Creek, Michigan, is the third largest cookie manufacturer in the United States and has a 5 percent share of the American cookie market. With two company-owned and four licensed bakeries in the United States and Canada, Archway produces more than one billion cookies annually.

Founding the company in 1936, Harold and Ruth Swanson "set the standard for what would become a one-of-a-kind cookie." The Swansons baked cookies that used only the finest quality ingredients and then delivered them fresh to the stores where they were sold. "This commitment to traditional quality and guaranteed freshness is the foundation of Archway Cookies."

Archway Cookies is a bake-to-order company. With over 60 different varieties of Home Style, Gourmet, Fat Free, Sugar Free, Bag, and Holiday cookies, Archway is a "bake today, ship tomorrow" manufacturing operation. Cookies are ordered by distributors, baked by the company, and shipped to distributors within 48 hours.

To "bake today" and "ship tomorrow," Archway must have accurate and timely information. Prior to 1991, the company managed its information using paper-based sales and tracking systems that were introduced in the 1930s. These systems did not provide for the fastest, most effective, and most efficient flow and use of data.

Archway's management recognized the need to automate data collection, improve data flow, and create a single database. Without these information management changes, achieving the company's sales growth goals would be difficult. So in 1991 Archway Cookies began using a system of hardware and software from Intermec Technologies Corp. Key components of the system were Intermec's Norand Base Bakery database software and Norand 4410 handheld computers.

Before 1991, distributors wrote everything down in route books, and Archway employed people to perform manual data entry. As a result, managers had difficulty understanding, comprehending, and analyzing data on a timely basis. This changed drastically when Archway supplied its distributors with the handheld computers and began using the route accounting software designed specifically for the baking industry. With the new management information system, Archway was able to track, analyze, and adjust sales to customers at the distributor level.

According to Gene H. McKay III, Archway's chief of finance and operations, the use of information technology has produced considerable benefits. He says that "implementing this technology has saved the distributors an enormous amount of time on their routes, so the distributors have additional time for call-backs and for soliciting new sales." In turn, this has contributed to a 3 to 4 percent sales increase for Archway every year since the system was installed. The system has also provided better information access and information sharing throughout the company.

Critical Thinking Questions

1. Why is timely and accurate information essential for Archway's manufacturing operations?
2. How does Archway Cookies manage information technology to its advantage?
3. Do you think Archway Cookies would be able to achieve its sales growth goals without the use of computerized information technology?

Case: Opening the Bottleneck in Online Wine Sales

E-commerce wine sites appeal to connoisseurs and novices alike. The wealth of information and search features available online make it easy for wine lovers to get helpful advice and product information; consumers can find a large selection of wines—from rare vintages to moderately priced bottles—and then conveniently order them. Thanks to wine's growing popularity, the U.S. market boasts about $19 billion in sales annually. Plus, margins of about 30 percent are well above the 9 to 14 percent for most consumer items such as books, music, videos, and electronics.

Despite the obvious potential for online wine sales, Internet wine vendors sell less than $100 million per year. The problem is largely legal: archaic liquor laws dating back to Prohibition allow each state to determine who can sell alcohol directly to residents. Most retailers can't ship across state lines and some states prohibit direct shipping to customers' homes. Even counties within a state may have special laws. Wine e-tailers face a logistical tangle in trying to keep track of each jurisdiction. In fact, no one can sell wine nationally; the largest wine wholesaler operates in just eight states.

Wineshopper.com tried to solve the problem by creating an automated nationwide database that joined wine wholesalers and retailers into one large online store. Wineshopper.com could then offer wine for sale online from any distributor's or retailer's inventory. Many frustrating months and $20 million later, the project was still incomplete. In addition to the legal hassles, Wineshopper.com faced another problem.

Just as each state had its own liquor laws, each distributor used a different inventory tracking and coding system. The lack of standards made it impossible to create a national distribution system. In August 2000 Wineshopper.com merged with Wine.com, another leading online wine merchant.

Just as its predecessor companies did, Wine.com (the merged entity) operates as a "buyer's agent" so it can make multi-state sales. It arranges order delivery or pickup with a wholesaler and retailer located in a jurisdiction that can legally sell to the customer. Its Web site's customer information system has specific screens and ordering forms based on where the customer lives. Other databases and site links provide extensive reviews and recommendations as well as searches by region and type of wine.

Critical Thinking Questions

1. Although it failed, why was Wineshopper.com's plan to develop a national database of distributors and retailers a good strategy? Would you have recommended that it continue to work on this information systems project?
2. Assume that Wineshopper.com/Wine.com continues to work on this information systems project. Prepare a list of the types of information Wine.com should include in its distributor database.
3. How can Wine.com/Wineshopper.com use the information in its customer and distributor databases to increase sales?

learning goals

>lg 1 Why are financial reports and accounting information important, and who uses them?

>lg 2 What are the differences between public and private accountants?

>lg 3 What are the six steps in the accounting cycle?

>lg 4 In what terms does the balance sheet describe the financial condition of an organization?

>lg 5 How does the income statement report a firm's profitability?

>lg 6 Why is the statement of cash flows an important source of information?

>lg 7 How can ratio analysis be used to identify a firm's financial strengths and weaknesses?

>lg 8 What major trends are affecting the accounting industry today?

Using Financial Information and Accounting

chapter 14

Testing 1, 2, 3

"My first accounting system—if you could call it that!—was a handheld electronic personal organizer to track tutoring appointments," says Jared Wells, owner of Wells Test Preparation Center in San Diego, California. When he opened a permanent location offering tutoring plus courses for SAT preparation, writing, and study skills, Wells wanted a better system to track revenues and expenses.

"When I started, I didn't even know what I wanted to get from my accounting system," he says. "That was probably one of my biggest problems. Unless you know the purpose of your system, you can't develop the right structure. It took me two years to find out that, as a sole proprietor, tax reporting was my primary need. I also wanted to have the information to make better business decisions."

With a friend's help he developed a client information system using Microsoft Access, a database program, to record client information, post transactions, and generate invoices and simple financial reports. Wells soon recognized that he needed specialized software for accurate tax reporting and professional assistance with bookkeeping and accounting. The firm he hired recommended QuickBooks Pro, popular small business accounting software that is easy to use—even for people who don't know much about accounting.

The transition to QuickBooks was anything but smooth, however. Wells still didn't understand the purpose of accounting other than tracking revenues and expenses. In addition, the basic format was geared to companies that made or sold goods, rather than service businesses. "That's what got me into trouble in the first place," Wells recalls. "The general chart of accounts didn't fit my business." In addition, his first accounting firm worked mostly with larger companies with full-time controllers. Instead of advising him on the right way to proceed, the accountants let him make decisions and take shortcuts. "They set up more accounts and expense categories than we really needed, and because they didn't correspond to those on tax forms, we had a terrible time preparing our 1998 tax forms."

In early 1999 Wells started from scratch to create an entirely new QuickBooks accounting system. "I had learned enough accounting over two years to dive in and figure out the system myself," he says. "I now understood *why* I needed an accounting system—for tax reporting and to manage the business more efficiently—and *what* information I needed to accomplish these goals." Rather than using the program's standard account system, he set up the appropriate accounts for his firm. Expense records now have both a main category that relates to a line on the tax form and subcategories as needed for internal purposes. This makes tax filing easier and provides backup records in case of an audit.

Wells learned about accounting by trial and error. "I don't recommend this," he says. "If I'd had it to

Critical Thinking Questions

As you read this chapter, consider the following questions as they relate to Wells Test Preparation Center:

- If you were starting a new company, what planning steps would you take to avoid the difficulties Wells encountered?

- Jared Wells went through several different accounting firms before he found the right one. How could he have avoided these difficulties? Develop a questionnaire that he could have used to interview potential accountants.

- What factors should a company consider when selecting accounting software?

do over, I'd have taken business and accounting courses." Instead, he had to juggle financial reporting systems along with the other demands of a new company. "I went through three bookkeeping/accounting firms because of my naïveté," says Wells. "If I'd had some basic accounting background, I would have saved several thousand dollars in actual cash expenditures, plus who knows how much in lost time and wasted productivity."[1]

Understanding financial accounting information such as sales and inventory helps managers in all types of organizations make decisions that enhance operational effectiveness and efficiency.

BUSINESS IN THE 21ST CENTURY

As Jared Wells learned when he started his own company, accounting is the backbone of any business. He attributes many of his early problems to his lack of accounting knowledge. Because he was unable to evaluate the advice of his accounting firm, his first QuickBooks system did not meet his company's needs. Once he understood the basics of accounting, he could decide which financial information was important for his company, what those numbers meant, and how he could use them to make decisions.

Financial information is central to every organization. To operate effectively, businesses must have a way to track income, expenses, assets, and liabilities in an organized manner. Financial information is also essential for decision making. Managers prepare financial reports using *accounting,* a set of procedures and guidelines for companies to follow when preparing financial reports. Unless you understand basic accounting concepts, you will not be able to "speak" the standard financial language of businesses.

This chapter starts by discussing why accounting is important for businesses and for users of financial information and then presents an overview of accounting procedures. Next the three main financial statements—the balance sheet, the income statement, and the statement of cash flows—are described. The chapter then discusses how to analyze financial statements using ratio analysis. Finally, it explores some of the trends affecting accounting.

THE PURPOSE OF ACCOUNTING

accounting
The process of collecting, recording, classifying, summarizing, reporting, and analyzing financial activities.

Accounting is the process of collecting, recording, classifying, summarizing, reporting, and analyzing financial activities. It results in reports that describe the financial condition of an organization. All types of organizations—businesses, hospitals, schools, government agencies, civic groups—use accounting procedures. Accounting provides a framework for looking at past performance, current financial health, and possible future performance. It also provides a frame-

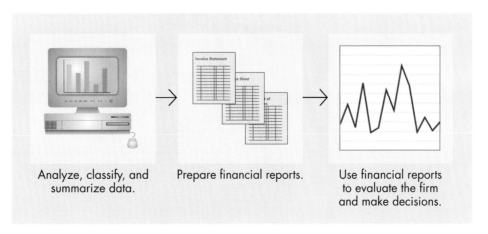

work for comparing the financial positions and financial performances of different firms. Understanding how to prepare and interpret financial reports will enable you to evaluate two computer companies and choose the one that is more likely to be a good investment.

As Exhibit 14-1 shows, the accounting system converts the details of financial transactions (sales, payments, and so on) into a form that people can use to evaluate the firm and make decisions. Data become information, which in turn becomes reports. These reports describe a firm's financial position at one point in time and its financial performance during a specified period. Financial reports include *financial statements,* such as balance sheets and income statements, and special reports, such as sales and expense breakdowns by product line.

In managerial accounting, internal reports detailing financial information such as the costs of labor and material in production are shared with other managers to assess the organization's performance.

managerial accounting

Accounting that provides financial information that managers inside the organization can use to evaluate and make decisions about current and future operations.

financial accounting

Accounting that focuses on preparing external financial reports that are used by outsiders such as lenders, suppliers, investors, and government agencies to assess the financial strength of a business.

Who Uses Financial Reports?

The accounting system generates two types of financial reports, as shown in Exhibit 14-2: internal and external. Internal reports are used within the organization. As the term implies, **managerial accounting** provides financial information that managers inside the organization can use to evaluate and make decisions about current and future operations. For instance, the sales reports prepared by managerial accountants show how well marketing strategies are working. Production cost reports help departments track and control costs. Managers may prepare very detailed financial reports for their own use and provide summary reports to top management.

Financial accounting focuses on preparing external financial reports that are used by outsiders, that is, people who have an interest in the business but are not part of management. Although these reports also provide useful information for managers, they are primarily used by lenders, suppliers, investors, and government agencies to assess the financial strength of a business.

To ensure accuracy and consistency in the way financial information is reported, accountants in the United States follow **generally accepted accounting principles (GAAP)** when preparing financial statements. The **Financial**

---

e x h i b i t   1 4 - 1 | The Accounting System

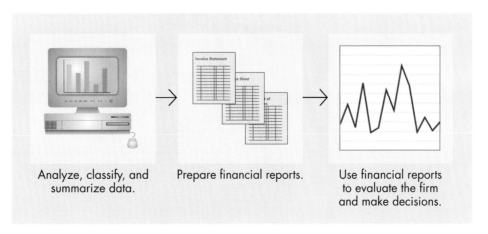

Analyze, classify, and summarize data. → Prepare financial reports. → Use financial reports to evaluate the firm and make decisions.

generally accepted accounting principles (GAAP)

The financial accounting standards followed by accountants in the United States in preparing financial statements.

Financial Accounting Standards Board (FASB)

The private organization that is responsible for establishing financial accounting standards in the United States.

annual report

A yearly document that describes a firm's financial status and usually discusses the firm's activities during the past year and its prospects for the future.

What issues is the FASB working on now? Check out the news section of

www.accountingnet.com

Accounting Standards Board (**FASB**) is a private organization that is responsible for establishing financial accounting standards in the United States.

At the present time, there are no international accounting standards, although the International Accounting Standards Committee is trying to develop them. Because accounting practices vary from country to country, a multinational company must make sure that its financial statements conform to both its own country's accounting standards and those of the parent company's country.

Financial statements are the chief element of the **annual report,** a yearly document that describes a firm's financial status. Annual reports usually discuss the firm's activities during the past year and its prospects for the future. Three primary financial statements included in the annual report are discussed and illustrated later in this chapter:

1. The balance sheet
2. The income statement
3. The statement of cash flows

The Accounting Profession

>lg 2

The accounting profession has grown rapidly due to the increased complexity, size, and number of businesses and the frequent changes in the tax laws. Accounting is now an over $40 billion industry. The more than 1 million accountants in the United States are classified as either public accountants or private (corporate) accountants.

public accountants

Independent accountants who serve organizations and individuals on a fee basis.

Public Accountants   Independent accountants who serve organizations and individuals on a fee basis are called **public accountants.** Public accountants

e x h i b i t   1 4 - 2 | Reports Provided by the Accounting System

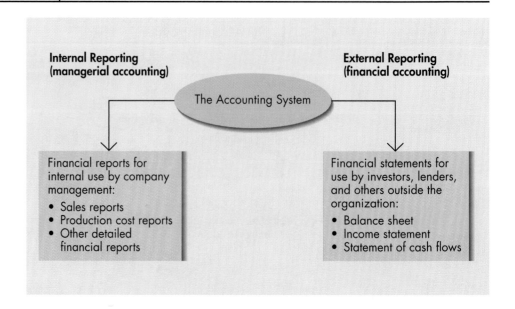

auditing

The process of reviewing the records used to prepare financial statements and issuing a formal *auditor's opinion* indicating whether the statements have been prepared in accordance with accepted accounting rules.

certified public accountant (CPA)

An accountant who has completed an approved bachelor's degree program, passed a test prepared by the American Institute of Certified Public Accountants, and met state requirements. Only a CPA can issue an auditor's opinion on a firm's financial statements.

private accountants

Accountants who are employed to serve one particular organization.

offer a wide range of services, including preparation of financial statements and tax returns, independent auditing of financial records and accounting methods, and management consulting. **Auditing,** the process of reviewing the records used to prepare financial statements, is an important responsibility of public accountants. They provide a formal *auditor's opinion* indicating whether the statements have been prepared in accordance with accepted accounting rules. This written opinion is an important part of the annual report.

The largest public accounting firms, called the Big Five, operate worldwide and offer a variety of business consulting services in addition to accounting services. In order of size, they are Pricewaterhouse-Coopers, Andersen Worldwide, KPMG International, Ernst & Young, and Deloitte & Touche Tohmatsu International.

To become a **certified public accountant (CPA),** an accountant must complete an approved bachelor's degree program and pass a test prepared by the American Institute of Certified Public Accountants. Each state also has requirements for CPAs such as several years' on-the-job experience and continuing education. Only CPAs can provide the auditor's opinion on a firm's financial statements. Most CPAs first work for public accounting firms and later become private accountants or financial managers.

To find out more about the accounting profession and becoming a CPA, visit the American Institute of Certified Public Accountants' Web site at **http://www. aicpa.org/** and click on "Students."

concept check

- Explain who uses financial information.
- Differentiate between financial accounting and managerial accounting.
- Compare the responsibilities of public and private accountants. How are they certified?

Private Accountants Accountants employed to serve one particular organization are **private accountants.** Their activities include preparing financial statements, auditing company records to be sure employees follow accounting policies and procedures, developing accounting systems, preparing tax returns, and providing financial information for management decision making. Managerial accountants also have a professional certification program. Requirements to become a **certified management accountant (CMA)** include passing an examination.

BASIC ACCOUNTING PROCEDURES

certified management accountant (CMA)

A managerial accountant who has completed a professional certification program, including passing an examination.

Using generally accepted accounting principles, accountants record and report financial data in similar ways for all firms. They report their findings in financial statements that summarize a company's business transactions over a specified time period. As mentioned earlier, the three major financial statements are the balance sheet, income statement, and statement of cash flows.

People sometimes confuse accounting with bookkeeping. Accounting is a much broader concept. *Bookkeeping,* the system used to record a firm's financial transactions, is a routine, clerical process. Accountants take bookkeepers' transactions, classify and summarize the financial information, and then prepare and analyze financial reports. Accountants also develop and manage financial systems and help plan the firm's financial strategy.

The Accounting Equation

assets

Things of value owned by a firm.

The accounting procedures used today are based on those developed in the late fifteenth century by an Italian monk, Brother Luca Pacioli. He defined the three main accounting elements as assets, liabilities, and owners' equity. **Assets** are things of value owned by a firm. They may be *tangible,* such as cash, equipment, and buildings, or *intangible,* such as a patent or trademarked name.

liabilities

What a firm owes to its creditors; also called *debts*.

owners' equity

The total amount of investment in the firm minus any liabilities; also called *net worth*.

Liabilities—also called *debts*—are what a firm owes to its creditors. **Owners' equity** is the total amount of investment in the firm minus any liabilities. Another term for owners' equity is *net worth*.

The relationship among these three elements is expressed in the accounting equation:

$$Assets = Liabilities + Owners'\ equity$$

The accounting equation must always be in balance (that is, the total of the elements on one side of the equals sign must equal the total on the other side).

Suppose you start a bookstore and put $10,000 in cash into the business. At that point, the business has assets of $10,000 and no liabilities. This would be the accounting equation:

$$
\begin{array}{ccccc}
Assets & = & Liabilities & + & Owners'\ equity \\
\$10,000 & = & \$0 & + & \$10,000
\end{array}
$$

The liabilities are zero and owner's equity (the amount of your investment in the business) is $10,000. The equation balances.

To keep the accounting equation in balance, every transaction must be recorded as two entries. As each transaction is recorded, there is an equal and opposite event so that two accounts or records are changed. This method is called **double-entry bookkeeping.**

Suppose that after starting your bookstore with $10,000 cash, you borrow another $10,000 from the bank. The accounting equation will change as follows:

double-entry bookkeeping

A method of accounting in which each transaction is recorded as two entries so that two accounts or records are changed.

Assets		Liabilities		Owners' equity	
$10,000	=	$0	+	$10,000	Initial equation
$10,000	=	$10,000	+	$0	Borrowing transaction
$20,000	=	$10,000	+	$10,000	Equation after borrowing

Now you have $20,000 in assets—your $10,000 in cash and the $10,000 loan proceeds from the bank. The bank loan is also recorded as a liability of $10,000 because it's a debt you must repay. Making two entries keeps the equation in balance.

The Accounting Cycle

>lg 3

The *accounting cycle* refers to the process of generating financial statements, beginning with a business transaction and ending with the preparation of the report. Exhibit 14-3 shows the six steps in the accounting cycle. The first step in the cycle is to analyze the data collected from many sources. All transactions that have a financial impact on the firm—sales, payments to employees and suppliers, interest and tax payments, purchases of inventory, and the like—must be documented. The accountant must review the documents to make sure they're complete.

Next each transaction is recorded in a *journal,* a listing of financial transactions in chronological order. Then the journal entries are recorded in *ledgers,* which show increases and decreases in specific asset, liability, and owners' equity accounts. The ledger totals for each account are summarized in a *trial balance,* which is used to confirm the accuracy of the figures. These values are used to prepare financial statements and management reports. Finally, individuals analyze these reports and make decisions based on the information in them.

Computers in Accounting

Computerized accounting programs do many different things. Most accounting packages offer six basic modules that handle general ledger, sales order,

e x h i b i t   1 4 - 3 | The Accounting Cycle

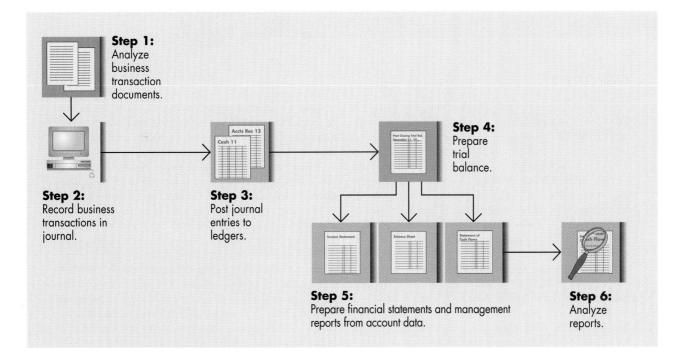

Step 1: Analyze business transaction documents.

Step 2: Record business transactions in journal.

Step 3: Post journal entries to ledgers.

Step 4: Prepare trial balance.

Step 5: Prepare financial statements and management reports from account data.

Step 6: Analyze reports.

accounts receivable, purchase order, accounts payable, and inventory control functions. Tax programs use accounting data to prepare tax returns and tax plans. Computerized point-of-sale terminals used by many retail firms automatically record sales and do some of the bookkeeping. The Big Five and many other large public accounting firms develop accounting software for themselves and for clients.

As the Applying Technology box explains, companies need to upgrade and reconfigure these critical computer systems regularly. Accounting and financial applications typically represent one of the largest portions of a company's software budget. Accounting software ranges from off-the-shelf programs for small businesses to full-scale customized enterprise resource planning systems for major corporations.

The Accounting Library site has a virtual consultant to help companies choose the best accounting applications for their needs. Check it out at

http://ww.excelco.com/

c o n c ə p t   c h ə c k

- Explain the accounting equation.
- Describe the six-step accounting cycle.
- What role do computers play in accounting?

THE BALANCE SHEET

>lg 4

balance sheet

A financial statement that summarizes a firm's financial position at a specific point in time.

The **balance sheet,** one of three financial statements generated from the accounting system, summarizes a firm's financial position at a specific point in time. It reports the resources of a company (assets), the company's obligations (liabilities), and the difference between what is owned (assets) and what is owed (liabilities), or owners' equity.

CASE CLOSED

You'd think that Fortune 500 companies like $6.1 billion Case Corp. of Racine, Wisconsin, would be masters at designing corporate accounting systems. Yet when Case gained its independence from Tenneco in 1994, the manufacturer of farming and construction equipment had a hodgepodge of systems in its operating units around the world: 15 general ledger systems, 25 accounts payable systems, and 17 accounts receivable systems. In 1994, Case's financial managers began revamping its accounting systems to make them consistent throughout the company. Its overall financial reengineering was so successful that Case won *CFO* magazine's REACH awards for excellence in financial process reengineering in 1996, 1997, and 1998.

The first step was to benchmark other companies like Toyota and GM. "We took a serious look at what we were doing and how our competition was doing it," says Blaine Metzger, director of financial planning and analysis. "We unearthed some faults, to be frank, but these led us to improve our functional capabilities rather than outsource them."

Case began to consolidate, standardize, and automate its accounting systems. Representatives from payables, receivables, payroll, and ledger formed teams to develop standard processes for each accounting function. The result was three regional centers—in Racine, Paris, and Sydney—using the same system, standards, and processes. Each center handled all transaction processing in its region. "Our goal has been to eliminate the processing we don't need to do, automate those processes we do need, and standardize everything throughout the company," says Metzger.

Instead of multiple general ledger systems, for example, Case implemented Geac's SmartStream as its standard worldwide integrated client/server finance and accounting system. The need to make journal entries manually dropped 40 percent, reducing errors and providing faster and less costly financial closings. By 1998, Case had reduced the number of computer applications from 20 to 9, the error rate from 7.7 percent to 4.6 percent, and saved over $11 million a year. The cost of general accounting as a percentage of revenues dropped from 3.9 percent to 2.6 percent. Perhaps the most important benefit, however, was reducing the time employees spent on transaction processing from 70 percent to 30 percent so that they had significantly more time for business analysis.

Critical Thinking Questions

1. Why did the existence of many different computerized accounting systems create problems for Case Corp.?
2. What are the benefits of an integrated financial reporting system for a company? How does it help areas other than accounting and finance?

---

liquidity

The speed with which an asset can be converted to cash.

The assets are listed in order of their **liquidity,** the speed with which they can be converted to cash. The most liquid assets come first, and the least liquid are last. Because cash is the most liquid asset, it is listed first. Buildings, on the other hand, have to be sold to be converted to cash, so they are listed after cash. Liabilities are arranged similarly: liabilities due in the short term are listed before those due in the long term.

The balance sheet at December 31, 2003 for Delicious Desserts, Inc., an imaginary bakery, is illustrated in Exhibit 14-4. The basic accounting equation is reflected in the three totals highlighted on the balance sheet: assets of $148,900 equal the sum of liabilities and owners' equity ($70,150 + $78,750). The three main categories of accounts on the balance sheet are explained below.

Assets

current assets

Assets that can or will be converted to cash within the next 12 months.

Assets can be divided into three broad categories: current assets, fixed assets, and intangible assets. **Current assets** are assets that can or will be converted to cash within the next 12 months. They are important because they provide the funds

Delicious Desserts, Inc.
Balance Sheet as of December 31, 2003

Assets

Current assets:

Cash		$15,000
Marketable securities		4,500
Accounts receivable	$45,000	
Less: Allowance for doubtful accounts	1,300	43,700
Notes receivable		5,000
Inventory		15,000
Total current assets		$83,200

Fixed assets:

Bakery equipment	$56,000	
Less: Accumulated depreciation	16,000	$40,000
Furniture and fixtures	$18,450	
Less: Accumulated depreciation	4,250	14,200
Total fixed assets		54,200

Intangible assets:

Trademark		$4,500
Goodwill		7,000
Total intangible assets		11,500
Total assets		**$148,900**

Liabilities and Owners' Equity

Current liabilities:

Accounts payable	$30,650	
Notes payable	15,000	
Accrued expenses	4,500	
Income taxes payable	5,000	
Current portion of long-term debt	5,000	
Total current liabilities		$60,150

Long-term liabilities:

Bank loan for bakery equipment	$10,000	
Total long-term liabilities		10,000
Total liabilities		**$70,150**

Owners' equity

Common stock (10,000 shares outstanding)		$30,000
Retained earnings		48,750
Total owners' equity		**78,750**
Total liabilities and owners' equity		**$148,900**

fixed assets

Long-term assets used by a firm for more than a year, such as land, buildings, and machinery.

depreciation

The allocation of an asset's original cost to the years in which it is expected to produce revenues.

On its balance sheet, this paper mill and wood processing plant would list long-term resources such as land, buildings, machinery, furniture, and fixtures as fixed assets.

intangible assets

Long-term assets with no physical existence, such as patents, copyrights, trademarks, and goodwill.

current liabilities

Short-term claims that are due within a year of the date of the balance sheet.

used to pay the firm's current bills. They also represent the amount of money the firm can quickly raise. Current assets include:

- *Cash.* Funds on hand or in a bank
- *Marketable securities.* Temporary investments of excess cash that can readily be converted to cash
- *Accounts receivable.* Amounts owed to the firm by customers who bought goods or services on credit
- *Inventory.* Stock of goods being held for production or for sale to customers

Fixed assets are long-term assets used by the firm for more than a year. They tend to be used in production and include land, buildings, machinery, equipment, furniture, and fixtures. Except for land, fixed assets wear out and become outdated over time. Thus, they decrease in value every year. This declining value is accounted for through depreciation. **Depreciation** is the allocation of the asset's original cost to the years in which it is expected to produce revenues. A portion of the cost of a depreciable asset—a building or piece of equipment, for instance—is charged to each of the years it is expected to provide benefits. This practice helps match the asset's cost against the revenues it provides. Since it is impossible to know exactly how long an asset will last, estimates are used. They are based on past experience with similar items or IRS guidelines for assets of that type. Notice that, through 2003, Delicious Desserts has taken a total of $16,000 in depreciation on its bakery equipment.

Intangible assets are long-term assets with no physical existence. Common examples are patents, copyrights, trademarks, and goodwill. *Patents* and *copyrights* shield the firm from direct competition, so their benefits are more protective than productive. For instance, no one can use more than a small amount of copyrighted material without permission from the copyright holder. *Trademarks* are registered names that can be sold or licensed to others. Delicious Desserts' intangible asset is a trademark valued at $4,500. *Goodwill* occurs when a company pays more for an acquired firm than the value of its tangible assets.

Liabilities

Liabilities are the amounts a firm owes to creditors. Those liabilities coming due sooner—current liabilities—are listed first on the balance sheet, followed by long-term liabilities.

Current liabilities are those due within a year of the date of the balance sheet. These short-term claims may strain the firm's current assets because they must be paid in the near future. Current liabilities include:

- *Accounts payable.* Amounts the firm owes for credit purchases due within a year. This account is the liability counterpart of accounts receivable.
- *Notes payable.* Short-term loans from banks, suppliers, or others that must be repaid within a year. For example, Delicious Desserts has a six-month, $15,000 loan from its bank that is a note payable.
- *Income taxes payable.* Taxes owed for the current operating period but not yet paid. Taxes are often shown separately when they are a large amount.
- *Current portion of long-term debt.* Any repayment on long-term debt due within the year. Delicious Desserts is scheduled to repay $5,000 on its equipment loan in the coming year.

long-term liabilities

Claims that come due more than one year after the date of the balance sheet.

Long-term liabilities come due more than one year after the date of the balance sheet. They include bank loans (such as Delicious Desserts' $10,000 loan for bakery equipment), mortgages on buildings, and the company's bonds sold to others.

Owners' Equity

Owners' equity is the owners' total investment in the business after all liabilities have been paid. For sole proprietorships and partnerships, amounts put in by the owners are recorded as capital. In a corporation, the owners provide capital by buying the firm's common stock. For Delicious Desserts, the total common stock investment is $30,000. **Retained earnings** are the amounts left over from profitable operations since the firm's beginning. They are total profits minus all dividends (distributions of profits) paid to stockholders. Delicious Desserts has $48,750 in retained earnings.

c o n c ə p t   c h ɔ c k

- What is a balance sheet?
- What are the three main categories of accounts on the balance sheet, and how do they relate to the accounting equation?
- How do retained earnings relate to owners' equity?

THE INCOME STATEMENT

>lg 5

retained earnings

The amounts left over from profitable operations since the firm's beginning; equal to total profits minus all dividends paid to stockholders.

income statement

A financial statement that summarizes a firm's revenues and expenses and shows its total profit or loss over a period of time.

revenues

The dollar amount of a firm's sales plus any other income it received from sources such as interest, dividends, and rents.

gross sales

The total dollar amount of a company's sales.

net sales

The amount left after deducting sales discounts and returns and allowances from gross sales.

expenses

The costs of generating revenues.

cost of goods sold

The total expense of buying or producing a firm's goods or services.

The balance sheet shows the firm's financial position at a certain point in time. The **income statement** summarizes the firm's revenues and expenses and shows its total profit or loss over a period of time. Most companies prepare monthly income statements for management and quarterly and annual statements for use by investors, creditors, and other outsiders. The primary elements of the income statement are revenues, expenses, and net income (or net loss). The income statement for Delicious Desserts for the year ended December 31, 2003, is shown in Exhibit 14-5.

Revenues

Revenues are the dollar amount of sales plus any other income received from sources such as interest, dividends, and rents. The revenues of Delicious Desserts arise from sales of its bakery products. Revenues are determined starting with **gross sales,** the total dollar amount of a company's sales. Delicious Desserts had two deductions from gross sales. *Sales discounts* are price reductions given to customers that pay their bills early. For example, Delicious Desserts gives sales discounts to restaurants that buy in bulk and pay at delivery. *Returns and allowances* is the dollar amount of merchandise returned by customers because they didn't like a product or because it was damaged or defective. **Net sales** is the amount left after deducting sales discounts and returns and allowances from gross sales. Delicious Desserts' gross sales were reduced by $4,500, leaving net sales of $270,500.

Expenses

Expenses are the costs of generating revenues. Two types are recorded on the income statement: cost of goods sold and operating expenses.

The **cost of goods sold** is the total expense of buying or producing the firm's goods or services. For manufacturers, cost of goods sold includes all costs directly related to production: purchases of raw materials and parts, labor, and factory overhead (utilities, factory maintenance, machinery repair). For wholesalers and retailers, it is the cost of goods bought for resale. For all sellers, cost of goods sold includes all the expenses of preparing the goods for sale, such as shipping and packaging.

Delicious Desserts' cost of goods sold is based on the value of inventory on hand at the beginning of the accounting period, $18,000. During the year, the

Delicious Desserts, Inc.
Income Statement for the Year Ended December 31, 2003

Revenues		
Gross sales	$275,000	
Less: Sales discounts	2,500	
Less: Returns and allowances	2,000	
Net Sales		$270,500
Cost of Goods Sold		
Beginning inventory, January 1	$ 18,000	
Cost of goods manufactured	109,500	
Total cost of goods available for sale	$127,500	
Less: Ending inventory December 31	15,000	
Cost of goods sold		112,500
Gross profit		**$158,000**
Operating Expenses		
Selling expenses		
Sales salaries	$31,000	
Advertising	16,000	
Other selling expense	18,000	
Total selling expenses	$65,000	
General and administrative expenses		
Professional and office salaries	$20,500	
Utilities	5,000	
Office supplies	1,500	
Interest	3,600	
Insurance	2,500	
Rent	17,000	
Total general and administrative expenses	50,100	
Total operating expenses		115,100
Net profit before taxes		**$42,900**
Less: Income taxes		10,725
Net profit		**$32,175**

company spent $109,500 to produce its baked goods. This figure includes the cost of raw materials, labor costs for bakery workers, and the cost of operating the bakery area. Adding the cost of goods manufactured to the value of beginning inventory, we get the total cost of goods available for sale, $127,500. To determine the cost of goods sold for the year, we subtract the cost of inventory at the end of the period:

$$\$127,500 - \$15,000 = \$112,500$$

gross profit

The amount a company earns after paying to produce or buy its products but before deducting operating expenses.

The amount a company earns after paying to produce or buy its products but before deducting operating expenses is the **gross profit.** It is the difference between net sales and cost of goods sold. Since service firms do not produce goods, their gross profit equals net sales. Gross profit is a critical number for a company because it is the source of funds to cover all the firm's other expenses. Analyzing gross profits by product can translate into higher profits, as the Focusing on Small Business box demonstrates.

operating expenses

The expenses of running a business that are not directly related to producing or buying its products.

The other major expense category is **operating expenses.** These are the expenses of running the business that are not related directly to producing or buying its products. The two main types of operating expenses are selling expenses and general and administrative expenses. *Selling expenses* are those related to marketing and distributing the company's products. They include salaries and commissions paid to salespeople and the costs of advertising, sales supplies, delivery, and other items that can be linked to sales activity, such as insurance, telephone and other utilities, and postage. *General and administrative expenses* are the business expenses that cannot be linked to either cost of goods sold or sales. Examples of general and administrative expenses are salaries of top managers and office support staff; office supplies; fees for accounting, consulting, and legal services; insurance; rent; and utilities. Delicious Desserts' operating expenses totaled $115,100.

Net Profit or Loss

net profit (net income)

The amount obtained by subtracting all of a firm's expenses from its revenues, when the revenues are more than the expenses.

net loss

The amount obtained by subtracting all of a firm's expenses from its revenues, when the expenses are more than the revenues.

The final figure—or bottom line—on an income statement is the **net profit** (or **net income**) or **net loss.** It is calculated by subtracting all expenses from revenues. If revenues are more than expenses, the result is a net profit. If expenses exceed revenues, a net loss results.

Several steps are involved in finding net profit or loss. (These are shown in the right-hand column of Exhibit 14-5.) First, cost of goods sold is deducted from net sales to get the gross profit. Then total operating expenses are subtracted from gross profit to get the net profit before taxes. Finally, income taxes are deducted to get the net profit. As shown in Exhibit 14-5, Delicious Desserts earned a net profit of $32,175 in 2003.

It is very important to recognize that profit does not represent cash. The income statement is a summary of the firm's operating results during some time period. It does not present the firm's actual cash flows during the period. Those are summarized in the statement of cash flows, which is discussed briefly in the next section.

c o n c e p t   c h e c k

- What is an income statement? How does it differ from the balance sheet?
- Describe the key parts of the income statement. Distinguish between gross sales and net sales.
- How is cost of goods sold calculated?

THE STATEMENT OF CASH FLOWS

>lg 6

statement of cash flows

A financial statement that provides a summary of the money flowing into and out of a firm.

Net profit or loss is one measure of a company's financial performance. However, creditors and investors are also keenly interested in how much cash a business generates and how it is used. The **statement of cash flows,** a summary of the money flowing into and out of a firm, is the financial statement used to assess the sources and uses of cash during a certain period, typically one year. All publicly traded firms must include a statement of cash flows in their financial reports to stockholders. The statement of cash flows tracks the firm's cash receipts and cash payments. It gives financial managers and analysts a way to identify cash flow problems and assess the firm's financial viability.

Using income statement and balance sheet data, the statement of cash flows divides the firm's cash flows into three groups:

- *Cash flow from operating activities.* Those related to the production of the firm's goods or services
- *Cash flow from investment activities.* Those related to the purchase and sale of fixed assets
- *Cash flow from financing activities.* Those related to debt and equity financing

GROSS PROFITS SOLVE THE PROFITABILITY AND CASH FLOW MYSTERY

The owner of a small cosmetics accessories business should have been very pleased with herself. Just four years after starting her business, sales reached $1.5 million. But the fast sales growth did not translate into fatter profits, and the company had problems paying its bills each month. She suspected that she needed more sales volume and better marketing and sales promotions. However, small business consultant Norm Brodsky recognized that the problems were financial in origin.

Brodsky narrowed the trouble spots to two areas: either her gross profit was not high enough, or she didn't know where cash was going. Because the company sent orders to manufacturers who then shipped directly to retailers, it didn't carry inventory. Accounts receivable and accounts payable were at low levels. So Brodsky suspected they'd find the answer by analyzing the company's sales and cost of goods sold to see if gross profits were too low on some products. A quick review of the past three months' sales by customer proved him right.

Because the owner had no records of gross profit by product line and customer, Brodsky provided a form to record monthly sales, cost of goods sold, gross profit, and gross margin (gross profit as a percentage of sales) by product line. The owner also prepared a report by customer.

The analysis showed that in some areas gross profits were extremely low. The owner had set low profit goals when starting the business to help build sales, but she did not know how to increase profitability once she had a relationship with her customers. She was able to change her profit picture considerably by focusing on four areas: pricing, manufacturing costs, turning down low-profit customers, and adding products that sell at higher profits. For example, she now sells imported furniture, which has 38 percent gross margins versus 15 percent for her cosmetics lines.

Although compiling these reports took less than an hour a month using pencil and paper, they were an eye-opener for the owner. These numbers made it crystal clear that she had no idea where she generated profits and how her decisions affected profits. As she admitted, like many inexperienced small business owners she was "winging it," basing decisions on guesswork because she did not have the right information. The tracking system to analyze gross profit provided the clues to unravel her cash flow mystery.

Critical Thinking Questions

1. Why is it important to analyze the details of a company's financial statements once they are prepared?
2. Suggest other ways that a small business owner can delve into the numbers on the income statement to make better operating decisions.
3. Brodsky recommends tracking gross margins by hand rather than using a computer spreadsheet because calculating the percentages yourself makes the numbers more real. He says it's easy to overlook numbers on a printout because they all blend together. Do you agree? Why or why not?

concept check

• What is the purpose of the statement of cash flows?

Delicious Desserts' statement of cash flows for 2003 is presented in Exhibit 14-6. It shows that the company's cash and marketable securities have increased over the last year. And during the year the company generated enough cash flow to increase inventory and fixed assets and to reduce accounts payable, accruals, notes payable, and long-term debt.

ANALYZING FINANCIAL STATEMENTS

>lg 7

Individually, the balance sheet, income statement, and statement of cash flows provide insight into the firm's operations, profitability, and overall financial condition. By studying the relationships among the financial statements, however, one can gain even more insight into a firm's financial condition and performance.

e x h i b i t   1 4 - 6 | Statement of Cash Flows for Delicious Desserts

Delicious Desserts, Inc.
Statement of Cash Flows for 2003

Cash Flow from Operating Activities		
Net profit after taxes	$27,175	
Depreciation	1,500	
Decrease in accounts receivable	3,140	
Increase in inventory	(4,500)	
Decrease in accounts payable	(2,065)	
Decrease in accruals	(1,035)	
Cash provided by operating activities		$24,215
Cash Flow from Investment Activities		
Increase in gross fixed assets	($5,000)	
Cash used in investment activities		($5,000)
Cash Flow from Financing Activities		
Decrease in notes payable	($3,000)	
Decrease in long-term debt	(1,000)	
Cash used by financing activities		($4,000)
Net increase in cash and marketable securities		**$15,215**

ratio analysis

The calculation and interpretation of financial ratios taken from the firm's financial statements in order to assess its condition and performance.

Ratio analysis involves calculating and interpreting financial ratios taken from the firm's financial statements to assess its condition and performance. A financial ratio states the relationship between amounts as a percentage. For instance, current assets might be viewed relative to current liabilities or sales relative to assets. The ratios can then be compared over time, typically three to five years. A firm's ratios can also be compared to industry averages or to those of another company in the same industry.

It's important to remember that ratio analysis is based on historical data and may not indicate future financial performance. Ratio analysis merely highlights potential problems; it does not prove that they exist. However, ratios can help managers understand operations better and identify trouble spots.

Ratios can be classified by what they measure: liquidity, profitability, activity, and debt. Using Delicious Desserts' 2003 balance sheet and income statement (Exhibits 14-4 and 14-5), we can calculate and interpret the key ratios in each group. Exhibit 14-7 summarizes the calculations of these ratios for Delicious Desserts.

Liquidity Ratios

liquidity ratios

Ratios that measure a firm's ability to pay its short-term debts as they come due.

Liquidity ratios measure the firm's ability to pay its short-term debts as they come due. These ratios are of special interest to the firm's creditors. The three main measures of liquidity are the current ratio, the acid-test (quick) ratio, and net working capital.

current ratio

The ratio of total current assets to total current liabilities; used to measure a firm's liquidity.

The **current ratio** is the ratio of total current assets to total current liabilities. Traditionally, a current ratio of 2 ($2 of current assets for every $1 of current liabilities) has been considered good. Whether it is sufficient depends on the industry in which the firm operates. Public utilities, which have

e x h i b i t   1 4 - 7 | Ratio Analysis for Delicious Desserts at Year-End 2003

Ratio	Formula	Calculation	Result
Liquidity Ratios			
Current ratio	Total current assets / Total current liabilities	$83,200 / $60,150	1.4
Acid-test (quick) ratio	Total current assets − inventory / Total current liabilities	$83,200 − $15,000 / $60,150	1.1
Net working capital	Total current assets − Total current liabilities	$83,200 − $60,150	$23,050
Profitability Ratios			
Net profit margin	Net profit / Net sales	$ 32,175 / $270,500	11.9%
Return on equity	Net profit / Total owners' equity	$32,175 / $78,750	40.9%
Earnings per share	Net profit / Number of shares of common stock outstanding	$32,175 / 10,000	$3.22
Activity Ratio			
Inventory turnover	Cost of goods sold / Average inventory		
	Cost of goods sold / (Beginning inventory + Ending inventory)/2	$112,500 / ($18,000 + $15,000)/2	
		$112,500 / $16,500	6.8 times
Debt Ratio			
Debt-to-equity ratio	Total liabilities / Owners' equity	$70,150 / $78,750	89.1%

a very steady cash flow, operate quite well with a current ratio below 2. A current ratio of 2 might not be adequate for manufacturers and merchandisers that carry high inventories and have lots of receivables. The current ratio for Delicious Desserts for 2003, as shown in Exhibit 14-7, is 1.4. This means little without a basis for comparison. If the analyst found that the industry average for small bakeries was 2.4, Delicious Desserts would appear to have low liquidity.

The **acid-test (quick) ratio** is like the current ratio except that it excludes inventory, which is the least liquid current asset. The acid-test ratio is used to measure the firm's ability to pay its current liabilities without selling inventory. The name *acid-test* implies that this ratio is a crucial test of the firm's liquidity. An acid-test ratio of at least 1 is preferred. But again, what is an acceptable value varies by industry. The acid-test ratio is a good measure of liquidity when inventory cannot easily be converted to cash (for instance, if it consists of very specialized goods with a limited market). If inventory is liquid, the current ratio is better. Delicious Desserts' acid-test ratio for 2003 is 1.1. Because the bak-

acid-test (quick) ratio

The ratio of total current assets excluding inventory to total current liabilities; used to measure a firm's liquidity.

COOKING THE BOOKS

Cendant Corp. was created through the merger of HFS, Inc., a franchisor of lodging, real estate, and rental cars, and CUC, a conglomerate whose businesses included software, advertising publications, and an online venture. CUC's main revenue source, however, was from memberships in discount shopping, entertainment, and travel clubs.

In early April of 1998, Casper Sabatino and Steven Sparks, two CUC managers who stayed on after the merger, informed Michael Monaco, Cendant Corp.'s chief financial officer (CFO), that they had been ordered to "cook the books" at CUC by recording millions of dollars of fake orders and "arbitrarily adjust[ing] revenue up or expenses down." Sabatino and Sparks signed sworn affidavits a few days later, specifically naming Cosmo Corigliano, formerly CUC's CFO, and Anne Pember, CUC's former senior vice president of finance and controller, as the executives who ordered them to falsify accounting records. Subsequently, Cendant officials announced that the company had uncovered evidence of wide-ranging fraud. According to Cendant's announcement, "people just made things up." The following day Cendant's stock price fell by 46.5 percent.

Further investigation led Cendant officials to conclude that Corigliano and Pember falsified accounting records by using "consolidation entries" to increase revenues or cut expenses a few hundred thousand dollars at a time. Cendant officials also concluded that Corigliano and Pember ordered about half of CUC's divisional controllers to create fictitious consolidation entries.

As of mid-August 1998, investors had filed at least 71 lawsuits against Cendant Corp.

Critical Thinking Questions

1. What moral issues does this case raise?
2. Why is accurate information important in the operation of a business?
3. Suppose that you are working for someone who asks you to falsify information. What would you do? Why?

---

ery's products are perishable, it does not carry large inventories. Thus, the values of its acid-test and current ratios are fairly close. At a manufacturing company, however, inventory typically makes up a large portion of current assets, so the acid-test ratio will be lower than the current ratio.

net working capital

The amount obtained by subtracting total current liabilities from total current assets; used to measure a firm's liquidity.

Net working capital, though not really a ratio, is often used to measure a firm's overall liquidity. It is calculated by subtracting total current liabilities from total current assets. Delicious Desserts' net working capital for 2003 is $23,050. Comparisons of net working capital over time often help in assessing a firm's liquidity.

Profitability Ratios

profitability ratios

Ratios that measure how well a firm is using its resources to generate profit and how efficiently it is being managed.

To measure profitability, a firm's profits can be related to its sales, equity, or stock value. **Profitability ratios** measure how well the firm is using its resources to generate profit and how efficiently it is being managed. The main profitability ratios are net profit margin, return on equity, and earnings per share.

net profit margin

The ratio of net profit to net sales; also called *return on sales*. It measures the percentage of each sales dollar remaining after all expenses, including taxes, have been deducted.

The ratio of net profit to net sales is the **net profit margin,** also called *return on sales*. It measures the percentage of each sales dollar remaining after all expenses, including taxes, have been deducted. Higher net profit margins are better than lower ones. The net profit margin is often used to measure the firm's earning power. "Good" net profit margins differ quite a bit from industry to industry. A grocery store usually has a very low net profit margin, perhaps below 1 percent, while a jewelry store's net profit margin would probably exceed 10 percent. Delicious Desserts' net profit margin for 2003 is 11.9 percent. In other words, Delicious Desserts is earning 11.9 cents on each dollar of sales.

return on equity (ROE)

The ratio of net profit to total owners' equity; measures the return that owners receive on their investment in the firm.

The ratio of net profit to total owners' equity is called **return on equity (ROE).** It measures the return that owners receive on their investment in the firm, a major reason for investing in a company's stock. Delicious Desserts has a 40.9 percent ROE for 2003. On the surface, a 40.9 percent ROE seems quite good. But the level of risk in the business and the ROE of other firms in the same industry must also be considered. The higher the risk, the greater the ROE investors look for. A firm's ROE can also be compared to past values to see how the company is performing over time.

earnings per share (EPS)

The ratio of net profit to the number of shares of common stock outstanding; measures the number of dollars earned by each share of stock.

Earnings per share (EPS) is the ratio of net profit to the number of shares of common stock outstanding. It measures the number of dollars earned by each share of stock. EPS values are closely watched by investors and are considered an important sign of success. EPS also indicates a firm's ability to pay dividends. Note that EPS is the dollar amount earned by each share, not the actual amount given to stockholders in the form of dividends. Some earnings may be put back into the firm. Delicious Desserts' EPS for 2003 is $3.22.

Activity Ratios

activity ratios

Ratios that measure how well a firm uses its assets.

Activity ratios measure how well a firm uses its assets. They reflect the speed with which resources are converted to cash or sales. A frequently used activity ratio is inventory turnover.

inventory turnover ratio

The ratio of cost of goods sold to average inventory; measures the speed with which inventory moves through a firm and is turned into sales.

The **inventory turnover ratio** measures the speed with which inventory moves through the firm and is turned into sales. It is calculated by dividing cost of goods sold by the average inventory. (Average inventory is estimated by adding the beginning and ending inventories for the year and dividing by 2.) On average, Delicious Desserts' inventory is turned into sales 6.8 times each year, or about once every 54 days (365 days ÷ 6.8). The acceptable turnover ratio depends on the line of business. A grocery store would have a high turnover ratio, maybe 20 times a year, whereas the turnover for a heavy equipment manufacturer might be only 3 times a year.

Debt Ratios

debt ratios

Ratios that measure the degree and effect of a firm's use of borrowed funds (debt) to finance its operations.

Debt ratios measure the degree and effect of the firm's use of borrowed funds (debt) to finance its operations. These ratios are especially important to lenders and investors. They want to make sure the firm has a healthy mix of debt and equity. If the firm relies too much on debt, it may have trouble meeting interest payments and repaying loans. The most important debt ratio is the debt-to-equity ratio.

The **debt-to-equity ratio** measures the relationship between the amount of debt financing (borrowing) and the amount of equity financing (owners' funds). It is calculated by dividing total liabilities by owners' equity. In general, the lower the ratio, the better. But it is important to assess the debt-to-equity ratio against both past values and industry averages. Delicious Desserts' ratio for 2003 is 89.1 percent. The ratio indicates that the company has 89 cents of debt for every dollar the owners have provided. A ratio above 100 percent means the firm has more debt than equity. In such a case, the lenders are providing more financing than the owners.

c o n c ə p t c h ə c k

- How can ratio analysis be used to interpret financial statements?
- Name the two main liquidity ratios and explain what they indicate.
- Describe the main profitability ratios and the aspect of profitability measured by each.

CAPITALIZING ON TRENDS IN BUSINESS

>lg 8

debt-to-equity ratio
The ratio of total liabilities to owners' equity; measures the relationship between the amount of debt financing and the amount of equity financing.

In the past, accountants were portrayed primarily as "bean-counters" who over-analyzed financial data and were of little help to the managers and employees who produced the numbers the auditors examined. Although accountants still perform the important task of assuring that a company's financial reporting conforms to GAAP, they have become a valuable part of the financial team and consult with clients on information technology and other areas as well.

The increasing complexity of today's business environment creates additional challenges for the accounting profession. The information explosion means that the FASB must consider a greater number of new regulations and develop more position statements to keep up with the pace of change. The FASB also has an emerging issues task force that studies ways to make accounting standards more relevant for today's companies.

No longer can a company's assets be measured solely in terms of its bricks and mortar. Knowledge assets—brand names, patents, research and development (R&D) costs, and similar expenses—make up a large portion of the value of many information technology companies. As yet, however, there is no accepted way to value those assets; indeed, there is disagreement over whether companies should even try. In other areas GAAP is either unclear or subject to different interpretations.

Accountants Expand Their Role

Moving beyond their traditional task of validating a company's financial information, accountants now take an active role advising their clients on systems and procedures, accounting software, and changes in accounting regulations. They also delve into operating information to discover what's behind the numbers. By examining the risks and weaknesses in a company, they can help managers develop financial controls and procedures to prevent future trouble spots. For example, auditors in a manufacturing company may spend more time on inventory, a likely problem area.

At their Web sites, you can learn about the types of consulting projects Big Five accounting firms handle. Go to About.com's business majors page and click on Accounting for the links

http://businessmajors.about.com

Honeywell, Inc., the $8 billion building-controls company headquartered in Minneapolis, formed a collaborative relationship with Deloitte & Touche, its audit firm (Honeywell and Allied Signal merged in fall 1999). Instead of being a once-a-year event, Honeywell's audit included quarterly meetings to discuss changes in company operations and accounting regulations. In this way Honeywell learned about upcoming changes in accounting regulations and avoided potential reporting problems before they happened. Thus, the company knew in advance how forthcoming changes would affect its financial statements, both at the operating division level and for the company as a whole. As a result, management avoided last-minute surprises in reported earnings.

Accounting firms have greatly expanded the consulting services they provide clients. As a result, accountants—especially the Big Five firms—have become more involved in the operations of their clients. This raises the question of potential conflicts of interest. Can auditors serve both the public and the client? Auditors' main purpose is to certify financial statements. Will they maintain sufficient objectivity to raise questions while auditing a client that provides significant consulting revenues? Can they review systems and methods that they recommended? Paul Danos, dean of Dartmouth's Amos Tuck School of Business Administration, believes that audit firms will act ethically to maintain their reputations. "If the financial markets don't believe in a firm's audit, the firm has nothing," he says.[2]

Valuing Knowledge Assets

As the world's economy becomes knowledge-based rather than industrial-based, more of a company's value may come from internally generated intangible intellectual assets such as R&D, brands, trademarks, and employee talent than from traditional tangible assets. Consider, for example, Dell Computer's direct marketing strategy, Gap's brand image, and AOL's subscriber base. How should these be valued? Today's accounting system is based on historical costs of physical assets. GAAP has no rules for estimating or reporting the value of investments in intangibles. The stock market, on the other hand, places a value on them. In fact, the value of knowledge assets now approaches or even exceeds the value of reported book assets. This is what creates the huge discrepancy between book value and market value.[3] Clearly, there are no quick and easy solutions to this issue, which will continue to be studied in the coming years.

Tightening the GAAP

Although GAAP is supposed to ensure uniformity of U.S. companies' financial reporting, in reality companies have some discretion in how they interpret certain accounting standards. Companies appear to be taking advantage of loopholes in GAAP to manipulate numbers. Cendant, for example, was accused of fraudulently inflating income by booking $500 million in fictitious revenues. Many companies are pushing accounting to the edge—and over it—to keep earnings rising to meet the expectations of investment analysts, who project earnings, and investors, who panic when a company misses the analysts' forecasts. This has raised serious concerns about the quality of earnings and questions about the validity of financial reports.

concept check

- What new roles are accountants playing? Do you see any potential problems from these new roles?
- What are knowledge assets, and why have they become so important?
- How can large one-time write-offs distort a company's financial results?

APPLYING THIS CHAPTER'S TOPICS

By now it should be very clear that basic accounting knowledge is a valuable skill to have, whether you start your own company or work for someone else. Analyzing a company's financial statements before you take a job there can tell you quite a bit about its financial health. Once you are on the job, you need to understand how to read financial statements and how to develop financial information for business operations. It's almost impossible to operate effectively in a business environment otherwise. Especially in a small company, you will

1. **Learn to Read Financial Statements** To become more familiar with annual reports and key financial statements, head for IBM's Guide to Understanding Financials at **http://www.ibm.com/investor/financialguide/**. The material offers a good overview of financial reporting and shows you what to look for when you read these documents.

2. **Prepare Personal Financial Statements** One of the best ways to learn about financial statements is to prepare them. Put together your personal balance sheet and income statement, using Exhibits 14-4 and 14-5 as samples.

You will have to adjust the account categories to fit your needs. Here are some suggestions:

- Current assets—cash on hand, balances in savings and checking accounts
- Investments—stocks and bonds, retirement funds
- Fixed assets—real estate, personal property (cars, furniture, jewelry, etc.)

- Current liabilities—charge card balances, loan payments due in one year
- Long-term liabilities—mortgage on real estate, loan balances that will not come due until after one year
- Income—employment income, investment income (interest, dividends)
- Expenses—housing, utilities, food, transportation, medical, clothing, insurance, loan payments, taxes, personal care, recreation and entertainment, and miscellaneous expenses

After you complete your personal financial statements, use them to see how well you are managing your finances. Consider the following questions:

- Should you be concerned about your debt ratio?
- Would a potential creditor conclude that it is safe or risky to lend you money?
- If you were a company, would people want to invest in you? Why or why not? What could you do to improve your financial condition?

wear many hats, and having accounting skills may help you get the job. In addition, accounting will help you manage your personal finances.

If you own your own firm, you can't rely on someone else to take charge of your accounting system. You must decide what financial information you need to manage your company better and to track its progress. If you can't understand the reports your accountant prepares, you will have no idea whether they are accurate.

Managing your personal finances is also a lot easier if you understand accounting. Suppose your Great-Aunt Helen wants to buy you a few shares of stock to encourage your interest in business. Her stockbroker suggests two computer companies, and Aunt Helen asks you to choose one of them. The product lines of the companies are nearly identical. Where can you get more information to help you make your choice? Someone suggests that you should study their financial statements. The companies send you their financial statements upon request. Now that you have a basic understanding of accounting, you have an idea of what all those numbers mean and how you can use them to make your decision.

As you will see in Question 2 in the Try It Now box, accounting can also help you create personal financial statements. Budgeting, a key part of personal finance discussed in Enrichment Chapter B, "Managing Your Personal Finances," on the CD that accompanies this textbook, also uses accounting concepts. And as noted above, financial statements are at the core of investment analysis.

SUMMARY OF LEARNING GOALS

>lg 1 **Why are financial reports and accounting information important, and who uses them?**

Accounting involves collecting, recording, classifying, summarizing, and reporting a firm's financial activities according to a standard set of procedures. The financial reports resulting from the accounting process give managers, employees, investors, customers, suppliers, creditors, and government agencies a way to analyze a company's past, current, and future performance. Financial accounting is concerned with the preparation of financial reports using generally accepted accounting principles. Managerial accounting provides financial information that management can use to make decisions about the firm's operations.

>lg 2 **What are the differences between public and private accountants?**

Public accountants work for independent firms that provide accounting services—such as financial report preparation and auditing, tax return preparation, and management consulting—to other organizations on a fee basis. Private accountants are employed to serve one particular organization and may prepare financial statements, tax returns, and management reports.

>lg 3 **What are the six steps in the accounting cycle?**

The accounting cycle refers to the process of generating financial statements. It begins with analyzing business transactions, recording them in journals, and posting them to ledgers. Ledger totals are then summarized in a trial balance that confirms the accuracy of the figures. Next the accountant prepares the financial statements and reports. The final step involves analyzing these reports and making decisions.

>lg 4 **In what terms does the balance sheet describe the financial condition of an organization?**

The balance sheet represents the financial condition of a firm at one moment in time, in terms of assets, liabilities, and owners' equity. The key categories of assets are current assets, fixed assets, and intangible assets. Liabilities are divided into current and long-term liabilities. Owners' equity, the amount of the owners' investment in the firm after all liabilities have been paid, is the third major category.

>lg 5 **How does the income statement report a firm's profitability?**

The income statement is a summary of the firm's operations over some period. The main parts of the statement are revenues (gross and net sales), cost of

>looking ahead
at Wells Test Preparation Center

Wells Test Preparation Center now has an accounting system that works smoothly. Jared Wells can generate financial statements and quickly get tax-related data. He also has the financial information he needs to make wise business decisions, such as whether he can afford to take on another instructor or rent more space. With his knowledge of accounting, he was able to analyze his products to see how much each service contributed to the center's overall profit picture. "It turned out to be very different than I thought it would be," Wells says. "I learned that the SAT preparation course has the highest profit margin." The center's primary growth was coming from referrals for tutoring for individual classes like math and science. Wells decided to market the SAT course more heavily in the future. He also began looking for ways to lower some of the costs of services with lower margins, thereby increasing profit margins.

In addition, Wells can now develop realistic forecasts, something that was impossible without basic accounting knowledge. "Now I not only have an accurate picture of where my firm is now but can also see where it could be down the road if I make certain decisions. This provides a reality check."[4]

KEY TERMS

accounting 392
acid-test (quick)
   ratio 406
activity ratios 408
annual report 394
assets 395
auditing 395
balance sheet 397
certified
   management
   accountant (CMA)
   395
certified public
   accountant (CPA)
   395
cost of goods sold
   401
current assets 398
current liabilities
   400
current ratio 405
debt ratios 408
debt-to-equity ratio
   408
depreciation 400
double-entry
   bookkeeping 396
earnings per share
   (EPS) 408
expenses 401
financial
   accounting 393
Financial
   Accounting
   Standards Board
   (FASB) 394
fixed assets 400
generally accepted
   accounting
   principles (GAAP)
   393
gross profit 402
gross sales 401
income statement
   401
intangible assets
   400
inventory turnover
   ratio 408
liabilities 396
liquidity 398
liquidity ratios 405
long-term liabilities
   401
managerial
   accounting 393
net loss 403
net profit margin
   407
net profit (net
   income) 403
net sales 401
net working capital
   407

goods sold, operating expenses (selling and general and administrative expenses), taxes, and net profit or loss.

>lg 6 **Why is the statement of cash flows an important source of information?**
The statement of cash flows summarizes the firm's sources and uses of cash during a financial reporting period. It breaks the firm's cash flows into those from operating, investment, and financing activities. It shows the net change during the period in the firm's cash and marketable securities.

>lg 7 **How can ratio analysis be used to identify a firm's financial strengths and weaknesses?**
Ratio analysis is a way to use financial statements to gain insight into a firm's operations, profitability, and overall financial condition. The four main types of ratios are liquidity ratios, profitability ratios, activity ratios, and debt ratios. Comparing a firm's ratios over several years and comparing them to ratios of other firms in the same industry or to industry averages can indicate trends and highlight financial strengths and weaknesses.

>lg 8 **What major trends are affecting the accounting industry today?**
The accounting industry is responding to the rise in information technology in several ways. The role of accountants has expanded beyond the traditional audit and tax functions and now includes management consulting in areas such as computer systems, human resources, and electronic commerce. A major issue facing the industry is how to treat key intangible assets—knowledge assets such as patents, brands, research and development—and whether they should be valued and included on a company's balance sheet. In addition, both the FASB and the SEC have raised concerns about the quality of reported earnings. Loose interpretation of GAAP has given companies leeway in how they deal with items like restructuring charges and write-offs resulting from acquisitions.

PREPARING FOR TOMORROW'S WORKPLACE

1. Two years ago, Rebecca Mardon started a computer consulting business, Mardon Consulting Associates. Until now, she has been the only employee, but business has grown enough to support an administrative assistant and another consultant this year. Before she adds staff, however, she wants to hire an accountant and computerize her financial record keeping. Divide the class into small groups, assigning one person to be Rebecca and the others to represent members of a medium-size accounting firm. Rebecca should think about the type of financial information systems her firm requires and develop a list of questions for the firm. The accountants will prepare a presentation making recommendations to her as well as explaining why their firm should win the account.

2. Divide the class into small groups that represent accounting firms. Your firm has been hired to help several small businesses with their year-end financial statements.
   a. Based on the following account balances, prepare the Marbella Enterprise Co.'s balance sheet as of December 31, 2003:

Cash	$30,250
Accounts payable	28,500
Fixtures and furnishings	85,000
Notes payable	15,000

operating expenses
  403
owners' equity 396
private accountants
  395
profitability ratios
  407
public accountants
  394
ratio analysis 405
retained earnings
  401
return on equity
  (ROE) 408
revenues 401
statement of cash
  flows 403

Retained earnings	64,450
Accounts receivable	24,050
Inventory	15,600
Equipment	42,750
Accumulated depreciation on fixtures and furnishings	12,500
Common shares (50,000 shares at $1)	50,000
Long-term debt	25,000
Accumulated depreciation on equipment	7,800
Marketable securities	13,000
Income taxes payable	7,500

b. The following are the account balances for the revenues and expenses of the Windsor Gift Shop for the year ending December 31, 2003. Prepare the income statement for the shop.

Rent	$ 15,000
Salaries	23,500
Cost of goods sold	98,000
Utilities	8,000
Supplies	3,500
Sales	195,000
Advertising	3,600
Interest	3,000
Taxes	12,120

3. During the year ended December 31, 2003, Lawrence Industries sold $2 million worth of merchandise on credit. A total of $1.4 million was collected during the year. The cost of this merchandise was $1.3 million. Of this amount, $1 million has been paid, and $300,000 is not yet due. Operating expenses and income taxes totaling $500,000 were paid in cash during the year. Assume that all accounts had a zero balance at the beginning of the year (January 1, 2003). Write a brief report for the company controller that includes calculation of the firm's (a) net profit and (b) cash flow during the year. Explain why there is a difference between net profit and cash flow.

4. A friend has been offered a sales representative position at Draper Publications, Inc., a small publisher of computer-related books, but wants to know more about the company. Because of your expertise in financial analysis, you offer to help analyze Draper's financial health. Draper has provided the following selected financial information:

Account balances on December 31, 2003:

Inventory	$ 72,000
Net sales	450,000
Current assets	150,000
Cost of goods sold	290,000
Total liabilities	180,000
Net profit	35,400
Total assets	385,000
Current liabilities	75,000

Other information

Number of common shares outstanding	25,000
Inventory at January 1, 2003	$ 48,000

Calculate the following ratios for 2003: acid-test (quick) ratio, inventory turnover ratio, net profit margin, return on equity (ROE), debt-to-equity ratio, and earnings per share (EPS). Summarize your assessment of the company's financial performance, based on these ratios, in a report for your friend. What other information would you like to have to complete your evaluation?

WORKING THE NET

1. Do annual reports confuse you? ABC News' Business Section is one of many Web sites that can take the mystery out of this important document. "Secrets of the Annual Report" has advice on analyzing the CEO's message and financial statements. Check it out at **http://abcnews.go.com/sections/business/dailynews/startstocks4/**.
2. Corporate reports filed with the SEC are now available on the Web at the EDGAR (Electronic Data Gathering, Analysis, and Retrieval system) Web site, **http://www.sec.gov/edgar.shtml**. First, read about the EDGAR system; then go to the search page **http://www.sec.gov/edgar/searchedgar/webusers.htm**. To see the type of information that companies must file with the SEC, use the search feature to locate a recent filing by a well-known company. What types of reports did you find, and what was the purpose of each report?
3. Can you judge an annual report by its cover? What are the most important elements of a top annual report? Go to Sid Cato's Official Annual Report Web site, **http://www.sidcato.com**/, to find his 15 standards for annual reports and read about the reports that receive his honors. Then get a copy of an annual report and evaluate it using Cato's 135-point scale. How well does it compare to his top picks?
4. Go to the Web site of the company whose annual report you evaluated in Question 3. Find the Web version of its annual report and compare it to the print version. What differences do you find, if any? Do you think companies should put their financial information online? Why or why not?

CREATIVE THINKING CASE

Wrong Numbers Mean Wrong Decisions

R.S. Bacon Veneer Co. was selling $4 million in wood veneer products annually. Its accounting firm, one of the Big Five, produced reports that Bacon's president, Jim McCracken, couldn't understand: "We'd get this set of financial documents each month that would have made better sense for General Motors. We wanted to know if we were making money or losing money. But instead, we got all these numbers that were impossible for us to use." When McCracken forwarded these monthly reports to Bacon's bankers, he would include a letter explaining what he thought had actually happened during the month.

Using these financial reports, the accounting firm decided that Bacon was on the verge of financial disaster. It advised the company to sell everything and close up shop. McCracken shakes his head: "I'm still amazed that we had the courage to throw them and their reports out the door." Bacon switched to another, smaller accounting firm on the advice of its bankers.

The new firm found Bacon basically sound. One of the partners quizzed McCracken about the types of information he needed for management decisions. The result was a report of no more than 10 pages. McCracken could now see what each product cost. He used this information to plan ways to diversify. The clear, concise, informative reports convinced Bacon's bankers to increase the company's credit lines so it could expand. In the next five years, sales went up 300 percent. Profit margins remained more than adequate.

Critical Thinking Questions

1. If you were the president of R.S. Bacon Veneer, what financial data would you want from the new accounting system?

2. Why might the two accounting firms have come up with such different conclusions about Bacon's health? Why might a Big Five firm not be a good choice for a small business?

3. What role should a small company's banker play in choosing the right accounting firm?

VIDEO CASE

The Weathervane Terrace Inn and Suites

Charlevoix is a northern Michigan resort community located in a valley between Lake Charlevoix and Lake Michigan. With its majestic maple trees, picket fences, Victorian homes, three-masted schooners and gleaming yachts, blue water, and white sand beaches, Charlevoix is reminiscent of a summer resort town from the 1800s. In the winter, it offers scenic cross-country ski trails and snowmobiling trails. In short, Charlevoix is a year-round tourist destination.

One of Charlevoix's premier lodging facilities is the Weathervane Terrace Inn and Suites (**http://www.weathervane-chx.com**/). The Weathervane Inn, housed in an "architectural and historic masterpiece," provides "a special and unique lodging experience" for guests. The inn has special guest packages such as the Charlevoix Sampler and several different golf packages. The Weathervane's staff readily accommodates guests' special requests whether they involve organizing special outings, making reservations with other hotels on a guest's itinerary, arranging a charter fishing expedition, or renting a sailboat.

The Weathervane Inn has an interesting, if not unique, ownership structure. The rooms and suites are essentially condominium units that are owned by individual investors. A management team operates the inn for the owners. The managers' duties include promoting the inn, renting units to guests when they are not being used by the owners, cleaning and maintaining the rental units, and regularly reporting operating results to the owners. The managers strive to equitably allocate rentals across all the units. By doing this, they assure that all owners receive reasonable rental income from their condominium properties.

Essentially, the Weathervane's staff are sales and management agents for the condominium owners. As agents, they have a stewardship responsibility with regard to the investors' assets. This agency relationship also imposes important financial reporting requirements on the managers.

To enable them to do an effective and efficient job of financial reporting, the Weathervane Inn's managers use a computerized accounting information system. This system tracks all the accounting and financial data for each condominium unit, including rental activity and income, operating expenses, and maintenance expenses. This information is used to generate monthly accounting reports for each condominium owner. Thus, the owners are able to monitor and evaluate the management of their investment properties.

Critical Thinking Questions

1. Why is it important for the Weathervane Inn to have an effective and efficient accounting information system?

2. What types of accounting reports are likely to be most useful to the condominium owners? Explain your answer.

3. How can the condominium owners make use of financial accounting? How can they make use of managerial accounting?

Case: Dot-com Accounting: Is It Revenue, or Isn't It?

What constitutes revenue for an e-commerce company? Executives of dot-coms ask themselves that question frequently these days. Because most of these companies do not have any profits, standard performance and valuation measures, such as earnings per share, don't apply. Instead, many investors judge dot-coms on revenue-based measures, such as revenue growth, revenue per user, and revenue per 1,000 Web page views. "Investors haven't been caring about the quality of revenues—just whether revenues are going up," says Jack Ciesielski, editor of the newsletter *Analyst's Accounting Observer*. As a result, e-commerce companies have resorted to aggressive accounting practices as a way to report the highest revenue possible.

For example, online broker Priceline.com allows customers to name their own price for items ranging from airline tickets and other travel arrangements to cars, long-distance service, and even life insurance. The company books as net revenue the *full* price of the item sold, not just the commission earned. So if it bought a luxury hotel room for $175 and resold it for $225, it would include the full $225 as net revenue, which artificially boosts its revenue line. Yet in reality it only has the commission amount to cover expenses. Priceline.com considers this accounting practice acceptable because it claims to takes ownership of the ticket for a brief time during the transaction. Traditional travel agents, however, only book as revenue their commissions.

Another area under scrutiny is expense accounting. Amazon.com allocates warehousing, customer service, and shipping costs to sales and marketing expenses, which investors expect to be high, rather than to cost of goods sold. This practice boosts gross margins.

In December 1999 the SEC issued guidelines that allow an Internet company that acts as a sales agent to book as revenues only the commission earned. The SEC also instructed the Financial Accounting Standards Board to review other Internet company accounting practices that could boost revenues or reduce costs unfairly. The goal is to create new accounting guidelines to eliminate the current diversity of practice among Internet companies.

Critical Thinking Questions

1. Why is it important to investors that e-commerce companies report revenue in a consistent manner?
2. Do you think Priceline.com is justified in claiming the full price of what it sells, or is it indeed just a broker between the service providers—airlines, hotels, car rental agencies—and the consumer?

SOURCES: Marlene Bellamy, "Is It Revenue or Isn't It?" *Technology Times*, a Deloitte and Touche Newsletter (Winter 2000) p. 5; Microstrategy's Saylor: "We have been caught in That Gray Zone," *Business Week Online* (April 13, 2000), downloaded from **http://www.businessweek.com**; and Catherine Yang, "Earth to Dot-Com Accountants", *Business Week* (April 3, 2000), pp. 40–41.

learning goals

>lg 1   What is money, what are its characteristics,
         and functions, and what are the three parts
         of the U.S. money supply?

>lg 2   What are the basic functions of the Federal
         Reserve, and what tools does it use to man-
         age the money supply?

>lg 3   What are the key financial institutions, and
         what role do they play in the process of
         financial intermediation?

>lg 4   How does the Federal Deposit Insurance
         Corporation protect depositors' funds?

>lg 5   What trends are reshaping the banking
         industry?

Understanding Money
and Financial Institutions

chapter 15

One-Stop Shopping at Citigroup

If you need a car loan, want to open a checking account, or decide to buy life insurance or invest some money, you might consider doing business with Citigroup (http://www.citi.com). Citigroup is the world's largest financial services firm, with almost $800 billion in assets and more than 100 million business and consumer customers worldwide. It was formed in April 1998 by the merger of Citicorp, a world banking powerhouse, and Travelers Group, an insurance and brokerage firm.

The Citicorp/Travelers merger represents a new era in banking. During the past decade, mergers between banks have increased steadily. But the marriage of Citicorp and Travelers combines two very different financial institutions. With passage of the Financial Services Modernization Act, which repealed the Glass-Steagall Act, in November 1999, banks can now offer insurance and investment products. Citigroup expects that repeal of the law will cause it and other banks to integrate bank, insurance, and investment products.

Some industry experts say that the survival of banks depends on their ability to offer nonbanking financial services. Banks have lost a lot of commercial business as companies have turned to other institutions to finance their growth. Banks have also lost consumer business. In 1975, the typical American household had 36 percent of its financial assets at a bank. Today, that percentage has dropped to 17 percent. Rather than putting money in a bank for retirement or to save for college, Americans have shifted to money market funds, which pay higher interest rates than bank accounts, and the stock market. "What people want—and what they're going to continue to want—is investment vehicles," says bank consultant Edward Furash. He believes the Citicorp/Travelers merger "makes banking relevant again."

Citigroup expects to generate substantial earnings and cost savings from the cross-selling opportunities created by the merger. Citicorp and Travelers market products and services that can be sold in each other's distribution system. For example, Travelers can sell its investment and insurance products via Citicorp's vast global distribution system, which includes private bankers in 32 countries and some 1,100 Citibank branches. Citicorp gains access to Travelers' 20 million customers in the United States and can expand the sale of its bank products through the thousands of Travelers' financial consultants and salespeople.

Citigroup wants to expand its current customer base to 1 billion by 2012. It plans to use technology—primarily the Internet—to reach its goal. In addition to offering products online, it launched Finance.com, an online financial and investment

Critical Thinking Questions

As you read this chapter, consider the following questions as they relate to Citigroup:

- How is technology changing the way financial institutions interact with business and consumer customers?
- What are the benefits of banks merging with other banks and other financial services firms? What are the disadvantages?
- How does government regulation affect the financial services industry?

advisory service. It's also exploring the use of other technologies to broaden its distribution channels. In Singapore, for example, Citigroup formed a partnership with Mobile One that allows customers to open accounts and transfer money by using cell phones equipped with screens. A company goal is to let people use their cell phones as virtual credit cards to do banking, sell stocks, and buy insurance—the ultimate convenience in one-stop shopping.[1]

BUSINESS IN THE 21ST CENTURY

Imagine using your cell phone to open a bank account! The financial services industry is indeed moving in new directions, as demonstrated by Citigroup. Advanced technology, globalization of markets, and the relaxation of regulatory restrictions are accelerating the pace of change in financial services. The changes are giving businesses and consumers new options for conducting their financial transactions. The competitive landscape for financial institutions is also changing as they develop new ways to increase their market share and boost profits.

Because financial institutions connect people with money, this chapter begins with a discussion of money, its characteristics and functions, and the components of the U.S. money supply. Next it explains the role of the Federal Reserve System in managing the money supply. Then it describes different types of financial institutions and their services and the organizations that insure customer deposits. The chapter ends with a discussion of trends in the banking industry.

MONEY

>lg 1

money
Anything that is acceptable as payment for goods and services.

Money is anything that is acceptable as payment for goods and services. It affects our lives in many ways. We earn it, spend it, save it, invest it—and often wish we had more of it. Business and government use money in similar ways. Both require money to finance their operations. By controlling the amount of money in circulation, the federal government can promote economic growth and stability. For this reason, money has been called the lubricant for the machinery of our economic system. Our banking system was developed to ease the handling of money.

Characteristics of Money

For money to be a suitable means of exchange, it should have these key characteristics:

- *Scarcity.* Money should be scarce enough to have some value but not so scarce as to be unavailable. Pebbles, which meet some of the other criteria, would not work well as money because they are widely available. Too much money in circulation increases prices (inflation, as discussed in Chapter 1).

Governments control the scarcity of money by limiting the quantity of money produced.

- *Durability.* Any item used as money must be durable. A perishable item such as a banana becomes useless as money when it spoils. Even early societies used durable forms of money, such as metal coins and paper money, that lasted for a long time.

- *Portability.* Money must be easily moved around. Large or bulky items, such as boulders or heavy gold bars, cannot be transported easily from place to place.

- *Divisibility.* Money must be capable of being divided into smaller parts. Divisible forms of money help make possible transactions of all sizes and amounts.

Tour the American Currency Exhibit to learn the history of our nation's money.
http://www.frbsf.org/currency/

Functions of Money

Using several types of goods as money would be confusing. Thus, societies develop a uniform money system to measure the value of goods and services. For money to be acceptable, it must function as a medium of exchange, as a standard of value, and as a store of value.

As a *medium of exchange,* money makes transactions easier. Having a common form of payment in each country is much less complicated than having a barter system—where goods and services are exchanged for other goods and services. Money allows the exchange of products to be a simple process.

Money also serves as a *standard of value.* With a form of money whose value is accepted by all, goods and services can be priced in standard units. This makes it easy to measure the value of products and allows transactions to be recorded in consistent terms.

As a *store of value,* money is used to hold wealth. It retains its value over time. Someone who owns money can keep it for future use rather than exchange it today for other types of assets.

The U.S. Money Supply

The U.S. money supply has three parts: currency, demand deposits, and time deposits. *Currency* is cash held in the form of coins and paper money. Other forms of currency are traveler's checks, cashier's checks, and money orders. As of October 2000, the United States had about $524 billion of currency in circulation.

Demand deposits consist of money kept in checking accounts that can be withdrawn by depositors on demand. As of October 2000, U.S. demand deposits totaled $324 billion. Demand deposits include regular checking accounts as well as interest-bearing and other special types of checking accounts.

Time deposits are deposits at a bank or other financial institution that pay interest but cannot be withdrawn on demand. Examples are savings accounts, money market deposit accounts, and certificates of deposit. Time deposits totaled about $3.8 trillion as of October 2000.

Credit cards, sometimes referred to as "plastic money," are used as a substitute for cash and checks. Credit cards are simply a form of borrowing. When Citigroup issues a credit card to a small business owner, it gives a short-term loan to the business by directly paying the seller for the business's purchases. The business pays Citigroup when it receives its monthly statement.

Credit cards do not replace money; they simply defer payment.

demand deposits

Money kept in checking accounts that can be withdrawn by depositors on demand.

time deposits

Deposits at a bank or other financial institution that pay interest but cannot be withdrawn on demand.

concept check

- What is money, and what are its characteristics?
- What are the main functions of money?
- What are the components of the U.S. money supply?

THE FEDERAL RESERVE SYSTEM

>lg 2

Before the twentieth century, there was very little government regulation of the U.S. financial system. For most of its history, the country's banking system was decentralized because the public was afraid that a large central bank would negatively affect the financial system.

To learn more about how the Federal Reserve System works, visit the Web site of the Federal Reserve Bank of St. Louis at

http://www.stls.frb.org/ publications/pleng

In 1907 several large banks failed. These failures caused a public panic that resulted in a run on other banks by depositors who wanted to withdraw their money. This caused cash shortages and resulted in the failure of many other banks. The Panic of 1907 was so severe that Congress had to act. In 1913 it created the Federal Reserve System (commonly called the Fed) to correct weaknesses of the U.S. financial system.

The **Federal Reserve System** is the central bank of the United States. It consists of 12 district banks, each located in a major U.S. city. Originally, the Federal Reserve System was created to control the money supply, act as a borrowing source for banks, hold the deposits of member banks, and supervise banking practices. Its activities have since been broadened, making it the most powerful financial institution in the United States. Today, four of the Federal Reserve System's major activities are carrying out monetary policy, setting rules on credit, distributing currency, and making check clearing easier.

Federal Reserve System

The central bank of the United States; it consists of 12 district banks, each located in a major U.S. city.

Carrying Out Monetary Policy

The most important function of the Federal Reserve System is carrying out monetary policy. It uses its power to change the money supply in order to control inflation and interest rates, increase employment, and influence economic activity. Three tools used by the Federal Reserve System in managing the money supply are open market operations, reserve requirements, and the discount rate. Exhibit 15-1 summarizes the short-term effects of these tools on the economy.

Open market operations—the tool most frequently used by the Federal Reserve—involve the purchase or sale of U.S. government bonds. The U.S. Treasury issues bonds to obtain the extra money needed to run the government (if taxes and other revenues aren't enough). In effect, Treasury bonds are long-term loans (five years or longer) made by businesses and individuals

open market operations

The purchase or sale of U.S. government bonds by the Federal Reserve to stimulate or slow down the economy.

e x h i b i t   1 5 - 1 | The Federal Reserve System's Monetary Tools and Their Effects

Tool	Action	Effect on Money Supply	Effect on Interest Rates	Effect on Economic Activity
Open market operations	Buy government bonds	Increases	Lowers	Stimulates
	Sell government bonds	Decreases	Raises	Slows Down
Reserve requirements	Raise reserve requirements	Decreases	Raises	Slows Down
	Lower reserve requirements	Increases	Lowers	Stimulates
Discount rate	Raise discount rate	Decreases	Raises	Slows Down
	Lower discount rate	Increases	Lowers	Stimulates

to the government. The Federal Reserve buys and sells these bonds for the Treasury. When the Federal Reserve buys bonds, it puts money into the economy. Banks have more money to lend so they reduce interest rates, and lower rates generally stimulate economic activity. The opposite occurs when the Federal Reserve sells government bonds.

reserve requirement

Requires banks that are members of the Federal Reserve System to hold some of their deposits in cash in their vaults or in an account at a district bank.

Banks that are members of the Federal Reserve System must hold some of their deposits in cash in their vaults or in an account at a district bank. This **reserve requirement** ranges from 3 to 10 percent on different types of deposits. When the Federal Reserve raises the reserve requirement, banks must hold larger reserves and thus have less money to lend. As a result, interest rates rise and economic activity slows down. Lowering the reserve requirement increases loanable funds, causes banks to lower interest rates, and stimulates the economy. The Federal Reserve seldom changes reserve requirements, however.

discount rate

The interest rate that the Federal Reserve charges its member banks.

The Federal Reserve is called "the banker's bank" because it lends money to banks that need it. The interest rate that the Federal Reserve charges its member banks is called the **discount rate.** When the discount rate is less than the cost of other sources of funds (such as certificates of deposit), commercial banks borrow from the Federal Reserve and then lend the funds at a higher rate to customers. The banks profit from the *spread,* or difference, between the rate they charge their customers and the rate paid to the Federal Reserve. Changes in the discount rate usually produce changes in the interest rate that banks charge their customers. The Federal Reserve raises the discount rate to slow down economic growth and lowers it to stimulate growth.

Setting Rules on Credit

selective credit controls

The power of the Federal Reserve to control *consumer credit rules* and *margin requirements.*

Another activity of the Federal Reserve System is setting rules on credit. It controls the credit terms on some loans made by banks and other lending institutions. This power, called **selective credit controls,** includes consumer credit rules and margin requirements. *Consumer credit rules* establish the minimum down payments and maximum repayment periods for consumer loans. The Federal Reserve uses credit rules to slow or stimulate consumer credit purchases. *Margin requirements* specify the minimum amount of cash an investor must put up to buy securities—investment certificates issued by corporations or governments. The balance of the purchase cost can be financed through borrowing from a bank or brokerage firm. By lowering the margin requirement, the Federal Reserve stimulates securities trading. Raising the margin requirement slows the trading. Margin requirements are discussed further in Chapter 16.

Distributing Currency

The Federal Reserve is distributing new paper currency that features larger and more detailed portraits, making the new notes harder to counterfeit than older currency.

The Federal Reserve distributes to banks the coins minted and the paper money printed by the U.S. Treasury. Most paper money is in the form of Federal Reserve notes. Look at a dollar bill and you'll see "Federal Reserve Note" at the top. The large letter seal on the left indicates which Federal Reserve Bank issued it. For example, bills bearing a D seal are issued by the Federal Reserve Bank of Cleveland, and those with an L seal are issued by the San Francisco district bank.

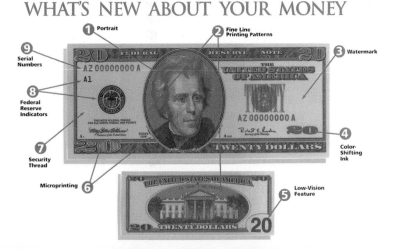

WHAT'S NEW ABOUT YOUR MONEY

Making Check Clearing Easier

Another important activity of the Federal Reserve is helping banks and other financial institutions clear checks. It handles about 18 billion checks a year. Its check-clearing system lets banks quickly convert

MAKING ETHICAL CHOICES

ARE BANKS TAKING ADVANTAGE OF BOUNCED CHECKS?

What happens when a checking account contains $1,000 and checks for $980, $30, $20, and $10 arrive at the bank for processing on the same day? The account is overdrawn by $40, but the customer may have to pay bounced-check fees amounting to as much as $120. With high-to-low check processing, which is used by six of the nine largest banks in the United States in at least some of their banks, when several checks arrive for processing on the same day, the bank processes the largest one first, thereby increasing the possibility that at least some checks will bounce.

High-to-low check processing can significantly increase a bank's profit because of the charges that are applied to bounced checks. Processing a bad check costs a bank between 50 cents and $1.50, yet most banks charge customers who write bad checks up to $30 per bad check processed. With high-to-low check processing, a bank is able to bounce as many checks as possible—and the fees paid by the customer are nearly all profit for the bank.

Increasingly, bank customers are beginning to protest high-to-low processing. One lawsuit accuses First Security Bank of New Mexico of "unfairly impos-

ing unreasonable and excessive fees" and of adopting "high-to-low check processing without adequately notifying customers."

Banks defend high-to-low processing by pointing out that federal and state laws permit them to process checks in any order. A spokesperson for the American Bankers Association says, "If you want to avoid paying a fee, just don't write a bad check" or alternatively get overdraft protection.

Critical Thinking Questions

1. The practice of high-to-low check processing results in bouncing as many checks as possible. In your opinion, is this a fair banking practice?
2. Is it ethical for a bank to charge up to $30 for processing a customer's bad check when the bank's cost of processing is between 50 cents and $1.50?
3. Should a bank have an ethical responsibility to inform customers in advance that it uses high-to-low processing?

checks drawn on other banks—even distant ones—into cash. Checks drawn on banks within the same Federal Reserve district are handled locally and reported to the Federal Reserve, which uses a series of bookkeeping entries to transfer funds between the banks. The process is more complex for checks drawn on banks outside a bank's Federal Reserve district.

The time between when the check is written and when the funds are deducted from the check writer's account provides float. *Float* benefits the check writer by allowing it to retain the funds until the check clears, i.e., the funds are actually withdrawn from its accounts. Businesses open accounts at banks throughout the country that are known to have long check-clearing times. By "playing the float," firms can keep their funds invested for several extra days, thus earning more money. To reduce this practice, in 1988 the Fed established maximum check-clearing times.

concept check

- What are the four key functions of the Federal Reserve System?
- What three tools does the Federal Reserve System use in managing the money supply, and how does each affect economic activity?

THE U.S. FINANCIAL SYSTEM

>lg 3

The well-developed financial system in the United States supports our high standard of living. The system allows those who wish to borrow money to do so with relative ease. It also gives savers a variety of ways to earn interest on their savings. For example, a computer company that wants to build a new headquarters in Atlanta might be financed partly with the savings of families in California. The Californians deposit their money in a local financial institution. That institution looks for a profitable and safe way to use the money and decides to make a real estate loan to the computer company. The transfer of funds from savers to investors enables businesses to expand and the economy to grow.

Households are important participants in the U.S. financial system. Although many households borrow money to finance purchases, they supply funds to the financial system through their purchases and savings. Overall, businesses and governments are users of funds. They borrow more money than they save.

Sometimes those who have funds deal directly with those who want them. A wealthy realtor, for example, may lend money to a client to buy a house. But most often, financial institutions act as intermediaries—or go-betweens—between the suppliers and demanders of funds. The institutions accept savers' deposits and invest them in financial products (such as loans) that are expected to produce a return. This process, called **financial intermediation,** is shown in Exhibit 15-2. Households are shown as suppliers of funds, and businesses and governments are shown as demanders. But a single household, business, or government can be either a supplier or a demander, depending on the circumstances.

Financial institutions are the heart of the financial system. They are a convenient vehicle for financial intermediation. They can be divided into two broad groups: depository institutions (those that accept deposits) and nondepository institutions (those that do not accept deposits).

financial intermediation

The process in which financial institutions act as intermediaries between the suppliers and demanders of funds.

e x h i b i t   1 5 - 2 | The Financial Intermediation Process

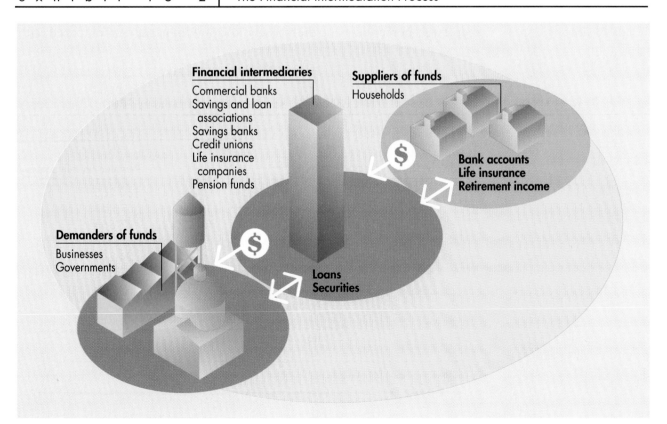

Depository Financial Institutions

Not all depository financial institutions are alike. Most people call the place where they save their money a "bank." Some of those places are indeed banks, but other depository institutions include thrift institutions and credit unions.

commercial banks

Profit-oriented financial institutions that accept deposits, make business and consumer loans, invest in government and corporate securities, and provide other financial services.

Commercial Banks   A **commercial bank** is a profit-oriented financial institution that accepts deposits, makes business and consumer loans, invests in government and corporate securities, and provides other financial services. There are about 8,500 commercial banks in the United States accounting for $6 trillion in loans and investments (a bank's assets) and $3.8 trillion in deposits. Exhibit 15-3 lists the top 10 U.S. commercial banks.

Customers' deposits are a commercial bank's main source of funds; the main use of those funds is loans. The difference between the interest earned on loans and the interest paid on deposits, plus fees earned from other financial services, pays the bank's costs and provides a profit. Commercial banks are corporations owned and operated by individuals or other corporations. To do business, they must get a **bank charter**—an operating license—from either the federal government or a state government. Thus U.S. commercial banks can be either national or state banks.

bank charter

An operating license issued to a bank by the federal government or a state government; required for a commercial bank to do business.

National banks are chartered by the Comptroller of the Currency, who is part of the U.S. Treasury Department. These banks must belong to the Federal Reserve System and must carry insurance on their deposits from the Federal Deposit Insurance Corporation. *State banks* are chartered by the state in which they are based. Generally, state banks are smaller than national banks, are less closely regulated than national banks, and are not required to belong to the Federal Reserve System.

thrift institutions

Depository institutions formed specifically to encourage household saving and to make home mortgage loans.

Thrift Institutions   A **thrift institution** is a depository institution formed specifically to encourage household saving and to make home mortgage loans. Thrift institutions include *savings and loan associations (S&Ls)* and *savings banks*. S&Ls keep large percentages of their assets in home mortgages. Compared with

credit unions

Not-for-profit, member-owned financial cooperatives.

---

e x h i b i t   1 5 - 3 | Top 10 U.S. Commercial Banks Based on Revenues, 2000

Rank by Revenue	Bank	Revenue (in Millions)
1	JP Morgan Chase	$60,065
2	Bank of America Corp.	57,747
3	Wells Fargo	27,568
4	Bank One Corp.	25,168
5	First Union Corp.	24,246
6	FleetBoston Financial	22,608
7	U.S. Bancorp	9,966
8	National City Corp.	9,051
9	SunTrust Banks	8,619
10	KeyCorp	8,471

SOURCE: "Fortune 1,000 Ranked within Industries," *Fortune*, April 16, 2001, pp. F-47–48.

S&Ls, savings banks focus less on mortgage loans and more on stock and bond investments. The 1,630 thrift institutions in the United States have about $1.1 trillion in assets and $712 billion in deposits.

Credit Unions   A **credit union** is a not-for-profit, member-owned financial cooperative. Credit union members typically have something in common—their employer, union, professional group, or church, for example. The not-for-profit status of credit unions makes them tax-exempt, so they can pay good interest rates on deposits and offer loans at favorable interest rates. The approximately 12,000 credit unions in the United States have more than 75 million members. Credit union assets total almost $400 billion.

Commercial banks, thrift institutions, and credit unions offer a wide range of financial services for businesses and consumers. Typical services offered by depository institutions are listed in Exhibit 15-4. These services play an important role in helping to fuel the U.S. economy and foster individual financial security. One of the newest bank services is online banking. The Applying Technology box describes a bank that operates exclusively on the Internet.

One of the most popular services offered by depository institutions is the automated teller machine. ATMs on college campuses make it easy for students to deposit and withdraw money.

e x h i b i t   1 5 - 4 | Services Offered by Depository Institutions

Service	Description
Savings accounts	Pay interest on deposits
Checking accounts	Allow depositors to withdraw any amount of funds at any time up to the amount on deposit
Money market deposit accounts	Savings accounts on which the interest rate is set at market rates
Certificates of deposit (CDs)	Pay a higher interest rate than regular savings accounts, provided that the deposit remains for a specified period
Consumer loans	Loans to individuals to finance the purchase of a home, car, or other expensive items
Business loans	Loans to businesses and other organizations to finance their operations
Money transfer	Transfer of funds to other banks
Electronic funds transfer	Use of telephone lines and computers to conduct financial transactions
Automated teller machine (ATM)	Allows bank customers to make deposits and withdrawals from their accounts 24 hours a day
Debit cards	Allow customers to transfer money from their bank account directly to a merchant's account to pay for purchases
Smart card	Card that stores monetary value and can be used to buy goods and services instead of using cash, checks, and credit and debit cards
Online banking	Allows customers to conduct financial transactions via the Internet or through a dial-in line that operates with a bank's software

NETBANK OPENS ITS VIRTUAL DOORS

Many banks offer online banking services. But NetBank is different. It's a virtual bank with no physical location, no branches, and no tellers. It operates exclusively on the Internet yet offers all the services of brick-and-mortar banks. NetBank customers can open checking accounts, pay their bills, get a mortgage loan, and use their debit and credit cards online. And they can do all these things at any time because they have access to their accounts 24 hours a day, seven days a week. They also get *BankNotes*, an online newsletter, that keeps them informed about new products and services.

Many banks offer customers the convenience of banking at home via their computers. But NetBank gives its customers more than convenience. Because it has no tellers or physical locations, NetBank saves on overhead costs and passes the savings on to customers with lower service fees and higher interest rates on deposit accounts.

High rates and low fees are attracting people to NetBank. Since its opening in 1996, NetBank has amassed more than 17,000 customers. NetBank's CEO Danner Grimes plans to broaden the bank's line of products and services to attract more customers. But a major hurdle is convincing people that Internet-only

banking is safe. Grimes says that the two questions he is asked most frequently by potential customers are "Are my deposits safe?" and "How secure is banking on the Internet?"

NetBank assures customers that their deposits are safe because they are insured by the Federal Deposit Insurance Corporation for up to $100,000. And all online transactions are encrypted, which means that information customers give the bank is not available on the Internet in a form that can be read.

Still, customer doubts about security persist. One customer admits that as much as he loves to bank at NetBank, he still keeps half of his cash at a traditional bank and half at NetBank. "It's psychological," he explains.

Critical Thinking Questions

1. What can NetBank do to ease customers' concerns about the security of their deposits?
2. Do you think NetBank's strategy of targeting Internet users only is a sound business plan?
3. What business trends support NetBank's focus on technology as a competitive tool?

Nondepository Financial Institutions

Some financial institutions provide a few banking services but do not accept deposits. These nondepository financial institutions include insurance companies, pension funds, brokerage firms, and finance companies. They serve both individuals and businesses.

Insurance Companies   Insurance companies are major suppliers of funds. Policyholders make payments (called *premiums*) to buy financial protection from the insurance company. Insurance companies invest the premiums in stocks, bonds, real estate, business loans, and real estate loans for large projects. The insurance industry is discussed in detail in Appendix B, Managing Risk and Insurance.

pension funds

Large pools of money set aside by corporations, unions, and governments for later use in paying retirement benefits to their employees or members.

Pension Funds   Corporations, unions, and governments set aside large pools of money for later use in paying retirement benefits to their employees or members. These **pension funds** are managed by the employers or unions themselves or by outside managers, such as life insurance firms, commercial banks, and private investment firms. Pension plan members receive a specified monthly payment when they reach a given age. After setting aside enough money to pay near-term benefits, pension funds invest the rest in business loans, stock, bonds, or real estate. They often invest large sums in the stock of the employer. Pension fund assets total almost $4 trillion.

Brokerage Firms   A *brokerage firm* buys and sells securities (stocks and bonds) for its clients and gives them related advice. Many brokerage firms offer some banking services. They may offer clients a combined checking and savings account with a high interest rate and also make loans, backed by securities, to them.

Finance Companies   A *finance company* makes short-term loans for which the borrower puts up tangible assets (such as an automobile, inventory, machinery, or property) as security. Finance companies often make loans to individuals or businesses that cannot get credit elsewhere. To compensate for the extra risk, finance companies usually charge higher interest rates than banks do. *Consumer finance companies* make loans to individuals. Beneficial Corp. and Household International, which recently merged, are two of the largest consumer finance companies. Together, they have more than 30 million customers. Promising new businesses with no track record and firms that can't get more credit from a bank often obtain loans from *commercial finance companies*. AT&T Capital Business Finance, GE Capital Small Business Finance, and The Money Store Commercial Lending are examples of commercial finance companies.

c o n c ə p t   c h ə c k

- What is the financial intermediation process?
- What are the three types of depository institutions and what services do they offer?
- What are the four main types of nondepository institution?

INSURING BANK DEPOSITS

>lg 4

The U.S. banking system worked fairly well from the establishment of the Federal Reserve System in 1913 until the 1929 stock market crash and the Great Depression that followed. Business failures caused by these events resulted in major cash shortages as people rushed to withdraw their money from banks. Many cash-starved banks failed because the Federal Reserve did not, as expected, lend money to them. The government's efforts to prevent bank failures were ineffective. In the next two years, 5,000 banks—about 20 percent of the total number—failed.

President Franklin D. Roosevelt made strengthening the banking system his first priority. After taking office in 1933, Roosevelt declared a bank holiday, closing all banks for a week so he could take corrective actions. Congress passed the Banking Act of 1933, which gave the Federal Reserve System power to regulate banks and reform the banking system. The act's most important provision was the creation of the **Federal Deposit Insurance Corporation (FDIC)** to insure deposits in commercial banks. The 1933 act also gave the Federal Reserve authority to set reserve requirements, ban interest on demand deposits, regulate the interest rates on time deposits, and prohibit banks from investing in specified types of securities. In 1934 the Federal Savings and Loan Insurance Corporation (FSLIC) was formed to insure deposits at S&Ls. When the FSLIC went bankrupt in the 1980s, the FDIC took responsibility for administering the fund that insures deposits at thrift institutions. Today, the major deposit insurance funds include the following:

Federal Deposit Insurance Corporation (FDIC)

An independent, quasi-public corporation backed by the full faith and credit of the U.S. government that insures deposits in commercial banks and thrift institutions for up to a ceiling of $100,000 per account.

- *The Bank Insurance Fund (BIF)*. Administered by the FDIC, this fund provides deposit insurance to commercial banks.
- *The Savings Association Insurance Fund (SAIF)*. Administered by the FDIC, this fund provides deposit insurance to thrift institutions.

• *The National Credit Union Share Insurance Fund.* Administered by the National Credit Union Administration, this fund provides deposit insurance to credit unions.

Role of the FDIC

The FDIC is an independent, quasi-public corporation backed by the full faith and credit of the U.S. government. It insures about 314 million deposit accounts in commercial banks and 79 million accounts in thrift institutions against loss if the financial institution fails. All member banks in the Federal Reserve System must be insured by the FDIC.

The FDIC gets so many requests about banks' insurance status that it added an option to determine "Is my bank insured?" on its Web site. Visit

http://www.fdic.gov

The ceiling on insured deposits is $100,000 per account. Each insured bank pays the insurance premiums, which are a fixed percentage of the bank's domestic deposits. The FDIC charged a flat rate for deposit insurance until 1993. Then, due to the large number of bank and thrift failures during the 1980s and early 1990s, it implemented a risk-based premium system that bases each bank's premium on the risk the bank poses to the insurance fund. Some experts argue that certain banks take too much risk because they view deposit insurance as a safety net for their depositors—a view many believe contributed to earlier bank failures.

Enforcement by the FDIC

To ensure that banks operate fairly and profitably, the FDIC sets guidelines for banks and then reviews the financial records and management practices of member banks at least once a year. These reviews are performed by bank examiners, whose visits are unannounced. Bank examiners rate banks on their compliance with banking regulations. For example, banks must comply with the Equal Credit Opportunity Act, which states that a bank cannot refuse to lend money to people because of their color, religion, or national origin. Examiners also rate a bank's overall financial condition. They focus on loan quality, management practices, earnings, liquidity, and whether the bank has enough capital (equity) to safely support its activities.

c o n c ə p t   c h ə c k

• What is the FDIC, and what are its responsibilities?
• What are the major deposit insurance funds?
• What can the FDIC do to help financially troubled banks?

When bank examiners conclude that a bank has serious financial problems, the FDIC can take several actions. It can lend money to the bank, recommend that the bank merge with a stronger bank, require the bank to use new management practices or replace its managers, buy loans from the bank, or provide extra equity capital to the bank. The FDIC may even cover all deposits at a troubled bank, including those over $100,000, to restore the public's confidence in the financial system.

CAPITALIZING ON TRENDS IN BUSINESS

>lg 5

Once a highly regulated industry offering limited services, the banking industry continues to change. Trends influencing the direction of banking are online banking, consolidation, and the integration of banking with brokerage and insurance services.

Online Banking

Banks are using Internet technology to expand their services. A research study from International Data Corp. predicts that about 23 million U.S. households will bank online by 2004, up from 10.5 million households in 1999. "Online banking may be the critical service that enables banks to maintain their role as the dominant provider of financial services," says Paul Johnson, an analyst with International Data.[2]

One service that offers banks tremendous profit potential is online bill presentment and payment. Although only 1 million households currently use electronic bill payment, the number is expected to surge to 40 million households by 2005.[3] Three large U.S banks—Chase Manhattan, First Union, and Wells Fargo—have formed a joint venture to create an online network for delivering consumers' monthly bills to the Web site that handles their checking account. The service will benefit many businesses, such as utility firms, because it will eliminate the time-consuming and costly process of printing bills, mailing them to customers, and waiting for the checks to arrive and clear.[4]

Consolidation

The number of depository institutions declined more than 40 percent over the past 25 years, falling from almost 19,000 in 1975 to less than 9,000 today. Although part of the decline can be attributed to the failure of banks and thrift institutions, most of it was due to consolidation through mergers and acquisitions. Mergers increased substantially during the 1990s, with many banks acquiring local competitors to increase their market share within a region. In 1996 alone, more than 360 banks merged. Some banks, such as Bank of America and NationsBank, merged to create a nationwide customer base.

Proponents of bank consolidation believe that it will strengthen the U.S. banking system. They contend that a national banking system would reduce costs, improve operating efficiency, and increase customer convenience. Mergers can also help banks reduce the risks inherent in depending on one region's economy.

Opponents of consolidation fear that it will concentrate power in large financial institutions. They worry that small banks' personal service and knowledge of the local economy will disappear. But, in a countertrend to consolidating, small banks are not only surviving, they are actually increasing in number. According to the Independent Bankers Association of America, there's been a resurgence in the creation of small banks because many people still prefer the personal service provided by the nation's 8,000 community banks. Other small banks are being formed to target niche markets. The Focusing on Small Business box shows how a community start-up plans to compete against larger banks by targeting a specific customer segment.

The Integration of Banking, Brokerage, and Insurance Services

As mentioned in the opening vignette, The Financial Services Modernization Act passed in November 1999 repealed the Glass-Steagall Act of 1933, which prohibited banks from selling securities and insurance. Glass-Steagall was passed after federal investigations of bank failures following the 1929 stock market crash indicated that banks' practice of buying stock in their customers' firms had contributed to the failures. Banks argued that the law was outdated and put them at a disadvantage in competing with security and investment firms, which were not bound by the same laws that regulated banks.

The Financial Services Modernization Act now allows banks, such as Citigroup, to sell securities and insurance products. Industry experts at the

Applying This Chapter's Topics

time of its passage correctly predicted that the Act would result in a new wave of mergers and acquisitions between commercial banks and brokerage and insurance firms.

APPLYING THIS CHAPTER'S TOPICS

The bank you use today is vastly different from the bank your parents used 30 years ago. And the bank you will use in 2030 will be far different from your bank today. Because technology is driving many of the changes in banking, expect to use your computer and innovations like smart cards to conduct your financial transactions. Soon you may be getting your telephone bill via your computer rather than in the mailbox. Because technology-based banking options are cheaper for banks, you'll see more promotions like the Citigroup ad whose headline proclaims "Pay 2 bills online. Get $25." As banks introduce new ways to deliver their products and services, the prediction of a cashless, checkless society is becoming a reality.

New bank products and services mean consumers have many more choices. You can choose the convenience of online banking or opt for a more personal

FOCUSING ON SMALL BUSINESS

A LITTLE BANK THAT CARES

Emma Chappell is the founder and chief executive of United Bank of Philadelphia. United Bank is an African American-owned community bank providing financial services to unserved and underserved communities, especially to African Americans, Hispanics, Asians, and women.

Chappell viewed the trend of bank mergers as an opportunity to start a community bank. "There are still a lot of people out there who want the specialized attention" that a small bank can offer, says Chappell.

United Bank focuses on the needs of entrepreneurs and small businesses—groups that have been hurt by the trend of mergers. For example, Lea Argiris, president of a small manufacturing firm, found that her line of credit was reduced and her loan payback period was shortened when her bank was acquired by a large bank. She learned that her six-employee firm was considered too small for the takeover bank.

United Bank offers special accounts for small businesses. Its Entrepreneurial-25 Business Checking targets firms that write 25 checks or less each month. It offers

a business money market deposit account, a business interest-bearing checking account, and customized loans and lines of credit. It also provides traveler's checks, wire transfers, safe deposit boxes, direct deposit, bank by mail, domestic and international collections, and international money transfers.

Chappell says mergers benefit small banks in other ways. For example, mergers eliminate the need for many employees and branches, leaving many bank professionals out of work. "The small community banks then have a pool by which they can acquire better-trained employees," says Chappell.

Critical Thinking Questions

1. What is United Bank of Philadelphia's advantage in competing against larger banks?
2. In what ways can Chappell help her bank's business customers beyond offering them banking products?

banking relationship at a community bank. Especially if you are an entrepreneur or a small business owner, you'll want to build a personal relationship with your banker.

Getting Connected

Here's what you'll need to bank online. If you're going online through the World Wide Web, you'll need a computer with Internet capability—one with a 56.6 bps modem or high-speed Web access, a Web browser, and service from an Internet or online service provider. Most providers charge about $20 per month for unlimited use. If you don't want to pay for Internet access or are concerned about the security of your transactions, you can get special software from your bank that connects you to the bank through a dial-in line. Most banks don't charge customers for the software. But online service fees vary among banks, so visit the Web sites of several banks to compare their fees and the services they offer.

Finding Financing

Entrepreneurs and small businesses have a more difficult time obtaining credit from a bank than do large firms that have proven track records and larger asset bases. The best way to improve your chances of getting a business loan is to give the bank information that can help it understand the strengths of your business. Prospective bankers are impressed by well-prepared presentations that include your business plan, financial history, and a management team that is committed to helping you achieve your goals.

When investigating banks, entrepreneurs and small business owners need to look at banks as more than just lending institutions. They need to ask what bank services and products can help them improve their efficiency and profitability. They should describe the type of relationship they want with their banker and the kinds of loans they'll need and the terms of payment they expect.

T R Y   I T   N O W !

1. **Stay Informed** To keep current with the changing trends and new products in the financial services industry, arm yourself with information. A banking Web site that will help you make informed decisions is **http://www.bankrate.com**. It has a How-to section that teaches the basics of banking and helps you calculate your payment on loans. The site's collection of interest rate information covers everything from car loans to money market accounts and enables you to compare rates from financial institutions in all 50 states. You can also check the fees different banks charge for their services and compare them to online banking service charges.

2. **Locate Lenders** More and more financial institutions are expanding their lending to entrepreneurs and small business owners. The following Web sites help start-ups and small businesses find financing:

   • **http://www.icba.org** The Web site of the Independent Community Bankers of America provides leads to all U.S. community banks.

>looking ahead

at Citigroup

Like its peers, Citigroup has had to move quickly to keep up with the pace of change in the financial services industry. Citigroup continues to expand its global businesses; its acquisition of Schroders, an investment bank, increases its investment and corporate banking presence throughout Europe. In addition to building its Asian operations, it has acquired banks and finance companies in emerging countries such as Poland and Chile.

On the home front, Citigroup has been no less acquisitive. In September 2000 it acquired Associates First Capital Corporation, the largest publicly traded finance company in the United States. To increase its technology capabilities, Citigroup formed an alliance with America Online (AOL). AOL, CompuServe, Netscape Netcenter, and other AOL brand members will be able to easily and securely purchase goods and services, send money, complete auction transactions, and eventually transfer money between accounts. Citigroup will become a preferred provider of financial products and services such as banking, mortgages, loans and credit cards, brokerage and investment, and insurance. It also was the first global financial services firm to launch a personal Web site where customers can aggregate all their accounts in one place.[5]

SUMMARY OF LEARNING GOALS

>lg 1   What is money, what are its characteristics and functions, and what are the three parts of the U.S. money supply?
Money is anything accepted as payment for goods and services. For money to be a suitable means of exchange, it should be scarce, durable, portable, and divisible. Money functions as a medium of exchange, a standard of value, and a store of value. The U.S. money supply consists of currency (coins and paper money), demand deposits (checking accounts), and time deposits (interest-bearing deposits that cannot be withdrawn on demand).

>lg 2   What are the basic functions of the Federal Reserve System, and what tools does it use to manage the money supply?
The Federal Reserve System (the Fed) is an independent government agency that performs four main functions: carrying out monetary policy, setting rules on credit, distributing currency, and making check clearing easier. The three tools it uses in managing the money supply are open market operations, reserve requirements, and the discount rate.

>lg 3   What are the key financial institutions, and what role do they play in the process of financial intermediation?
Financial institutions can be divided into two main groups: depository institutions and nondepository institutions. Depository institutions include commercial banks, thrift institutions, and credit unions. Nondepository institutions include insurance companies, pension funds, brokerage firms, and finance companies. Financial institutions ease the transfer of funds between suppliers and demanders.

>lg 4   How does the Federal Deposit Insurance Corporation protect depositors' funds?
The Federal Deposit Insurance Corporation insures deposits in commercial banks through the Bank Insurance Fund and deposits in thrift institutions through the Savings Association Insurance Fund. The FDIC sets banking policies and practices and reviews banks annually to ensure that they operate fairly and profitably.

>lg 5   What trends are reshaping the banking industry?
By using Internet technology, banks are delivering more services online. Bank mergers and acquisitions continue to consolidate the banking industry, helping banks to improve their operating efficiency, reduce costs, and extend their geographic reach. Recent passage of bank reform legislation that allows banks to market securities and insurance products will help banks compete with nondepository institutions and with banks in other countries.

KEY TERMS

bank charter 426
commercial banks 426
credit unions 426
demand deposits 421
discount rate 423
Federal Deposit Insurance Corporation (FDIC) 429
Federal Reserve System 422
financial intermediation 425
money 420
open market operations 422
pension funds 428
reserve requirement 423
selective credit controls 423
thrift institutions 426
time deposits 421

PREPARING FOR TOMORROW'S WORKPLACE

1. According to bank regulators, about 80 percent of U.S. bank customers prefer the convenience of banking with a large bank while 20 percent prefer the personalized service of a small bank. Interview 10 people, asking them their preference and the reasons for it.

2. In 1983 the Federal Reserve Bank of Atlanta published a report predicting that check writing would almost disappear in the United States by 2000. The bank based its prediction on the spread of technology in the banking industry. Consumers, the report said, would prefer using debit cards and paying their bills via computer rather than writing checks. But Americans are writing more checks each year—twice the number they wrote 20 years ago and eight times more than the average European. Find articles in the business press to discover why Americans are reluctant to change their check-writing habits and why banks want customers to write fewer checks.

3. Interview a local small business owner about his or her relationship with a bank. What services does the bank provide for the owner? Why did the owner choose that particular bank over other banks?

WORKING THE NET

1. Make a virtual visit to the Federal Reserve Bank at **http://www.federalreserve.gov**. What are its four primary functions? Click on *Monetary Policy* and then *Federal Open Market Committee* (FOMC). When does this group meet? Click on the most recent Statement and summarize what the Committee decided. Return to the FOMC page and click on *Beige Book*. What information does the Beige Book provide? Click on the link for the most recent report and describe the economic condition of the various districts. Explore the Press Release section and report on several recent actions the Board took.

2. The convenience of online banking is appealing to you, but you're not sure if you should bank with an Internet-only bank like NetBank or an online service of a traditional bank. Use the Electronic Banking Association's Web site, **http://ww.e-banking.org,** to find financial institutions online. Compare the services offered by Internet-only and traditional banks and their service fees. Which offers the best deal?

CREATIVE THINKING CASE

Starting a Niche Bank

Nat Padget worked in the banking industry for 21 years as a bank examiner, loan officer, and top manager. But he wanted a bank of his own. Padget knew that starting a traditional full-service bank was an enormous and expensive undertaking, so he decided to start a bank that targets a niche market. In 1998 Padget opened the Chattahoochee National Bank in Alpharetta, Georgia. The bank serves professional service firms such as insurance brokers and computer and engineering consulting firms that generate revenues ranging from $3 million to $30 million.

Chattahoochee is a no-frills bank. Padget leases space in an office building, but he doesn't have tellers or drive-up windows. Instead, he has six loan officers who visit customers and conduct transactions using laptop computers. He also provides a courier service that customers can use to deposit their checks. Padget charges his customers a slightly higher loan rate than that charged by competing banks. Since its opening, Chattahoochee has amassed assets of $23 million.

Critical Thinking Questions

1. Why do you think Chattahoochee's customers are willing to pay a higher rate on loans than they could get at competing banks?
2. What is Padget's strategy of operating a profitable bank?

VIDEO CASE

Roney & Co. and Firstbank Corp.

Founded in 1925 by William C. Roney, Sr., Roney & Co., headquartered in Michigan, grew into the state's largest investment securities and investment banking firm. In November 1997, Roney & Co. announced that it had been purchased by First Chicago NBD Corp., the region's banking leader. On October 2, 1998, First Chicago NBD and Banc One Corp. merged to form Bank One Corp; eight months later, on May 28, 1999, Bank One divested Roney & Co. Roney then became a wholly owned subsidiary of Raymond James Financial Inc. (**http://www.raymondjames.com**)

As a regional full-service investment firm, Roney & Co. strives "to build and preserve wealth for . . . clients." The firm does this by meeting virtually any investment need that its clients have "from stocks and bonds to mutual funds, options, unit investment trusts, money market funds, and insurance, along with investment management services, pension . . . [and] retirement plan services, plus complete investment banking capabilities." Roney's professional, knowledgeable, and ethical employees work as a team to provide outstanding service to all clients.

Firstbank Corp. (**www.firstbank-alma.com**) is a bank holding company consisting of a small network of affiliated community banks located in Michigan. The affiliated banks are the Bank of Alma, Firstbank of Mt. Pleasant, First Bank of West Branch, and the Bank of Lakeview. Offering a full range of deposit and loan products, Firstbank's affiliates seek to differentiate themselves from their banking competition by continuously focusing on exceptional customer service. The banks believe that integrity, customer satisfaction, and trust are the key elements of solid community banking.

Firstbank of Mt. Pleasant, for instance, is headed by Thomas Sullivan. He emphasizes that Firstbank customers will have a more personal and flexible banking experience because the bank strives to tailor its services to individual customer needs. The bank offers "a wide variety of checking and savings accounts to fit . . . [customer's] individual or corporate needs, and all types of consumer, mortgage, and commercial loans." The bank also has an affiliation with SII Investments, Inc. to provide customers with access to stocks, bonds, mutual funds, annuities, and insurance products.

The Bank of Alma, another affiliate, is headed by John McCormack, who is also president and CEO of Firstbank Corp. As the head of the Bank of Alma, McCormack emphasizes making banking convenient for customers and knowing customers well so that the bank can recommend appropriate financial solutions, whatever a customer's banking needs happen to be.

Another unit of Firstbank Corp. is 1st Armored, Inc., which provides several armored courier services for financial institutions in Michigan. These services include Federal Reserve shipping, individual bank deliveries, coin wrapping, and automated teller machine servicing.

Critical Thinking Questions

1. What roles do Roney & Co. and Firstbank Corp. play in the U.S. financial system?
2. What similarities do you see in how Roney & Co. and Firstbank Corp. conduct their respective businesses?
3. What differences do you see in how Roney & Co. and Firstbank Corp. conduct their respective businesses?

Case: Salem Five Cents Savings Bank Casts a Cyber-Spell

Despite its traditional name and location in a Massachusetts town best known for its 17th century witchcraft trials, tiny Salem Five Cents Savings Bank is a pioneer in online banking services. Where many large banks looked at Web banking as a defensive move to keep customers, the bank's management recognized an opportunity to use Internet technology to its advantage. In 1995 the community bank hired a group of young programmers to develop its online banking presence. As word of its low-fee, high-interest-rate accounts spread, customers from around the country and overseas flocked to the bank's Web site, **http://www. directbanking.com**.

As the bank's visionary CEO William Mitchelson saw other community institutions losing ground to national chains, he understood that price and distribution, not personal service, was the key to long-term survival. Online banking saves labor costs, so in exchange for use of a physical banking facility, Salem Five's online customers earn higher interest rates on checking and other services and receive better account terms, such as no minimum balance or monthly fees. The profitable Internet subsidiary's division has proven Mitchelson right, contributing about 15 percent of both total deposits and earnings.

Salem Five Cents Savings Bank is proof indeed that the Internet can level the playing field for small insitutions. Directbanking.com consistently receives high marks for its Web site's ease of use, customer confidence, account fees, and interest rates from research firm Gomez Advisors' listings of online banks—often above some major money center banks.

It ranked #1 saver in the Summer 2000 Internet Bank category for its high yields, low fees, and the best deposit rates. The bank continues to break new ground—literally and figuratively—with the opening of interactive branches that offer ATMs and Video Banker Internet kiosks for personalized customer support via live video conferences. It was also the first bank in New England and the second bank in the country to offer an account consolidation service, OneView, that allows users to gather all their online financial relationships on a personalized directbanking.com home page.

Critical Thinking Questions

1. Why does an Internet strategy make sense for a small bank like Salem Five Cents Savings Bank? Compare its strategy to the online-only approach taken by Netbank, described in the "Applying Technology" box on page 428.
2. Explore the Directbanking.com Web site, **http://www.directbanking.com**. What banking and other financial services does it offer? What features do you especially like? How would you rank it for ease of use and other features?

SOURCES: "Another First for Directbanking.Com: Oneview Service Goes Live on Award-Winning Website," Directbanking.com press release (September 21, 2000), downloaded from **http://www.directbanking.com**; John Hechinger, "A Tiny Bank Turns Big Player on the Internet," *The Wall Street Journal* (July 20, 2000), downloaded from **http://www.wsj.com**; "Virtual Bank Gets Physical," Directbanking.com press release (October 18, 2000), downloaded from **http://www.directbanking.com**.

learning goals

>lg 1   How do finance and the financial manager affect the firm's overall strategy?

>lg 2   What types of short-term and long-term expenditures does a firm make?

>lg 3   What are the main sources and costs of unsecured and secured short-term financing?

>lg 4   What are the key differences between debt and equity, and the major types and features of long-term debt?

>lg 5   When and how do firms issue equity, and what are the costs?

>lg 6   How do securities markets help firms raise funding, and what securities trade in the capital markets?

>lg 7   What are the major U.S. securities exchanges and how are they regulated?

>lg 8   What are the current developments in financial management and the securities markets?

Financial Management and Securities Markets

chapter 16

Continental Airlines' New Routes to Profitability

What does it take to be a successful chief financial officer (CFO) today? CFOs are no longer behind-the-scenes players but key members of the executive team, setting the firm's overall strategy and participating in managerial activities that go well beyond traditional areas. Team building, strategic and operational planning, managing risks, selling and acquiring companies—it's all in a day's work for financial managers like Larry Kellner, executive vice president and CFO of Continental Airlines.

When Kellner took over the financial pilot's seat in 1995, the airline was about to crash into bankruptcy for the third time. At the end of 1994, Continental reported a net loss of $613 million, and its stock price was a mere $4.63 per share. The airline had very little credibility with investors and lenders: its debt amounted to more than $500 million, it owed $1 billion in overdue payments on leases from aircraft manufacturers, and it needed billions of dollars in additional financing to survive. "We had basically run out of cash," says Kellner.

Kellner and his financial staff set out to rebuild Continental's relationships with investors, analysts, banks, and trade creditors. They had to convince these key groups that the airline would not only take off but keep on flying this time.

The first step was to make sure Continental had the financial resources it needed to operate. Navigating through turbulent financial skies, Kellner negotiated with lenders and aircraft manufacturers to restructure high-interest debt on more favorable terms. From 1994 to 1998, annual interest expense dropped from $204 million to $64 million.

Kellner also tapped the securities markets to raise over $6 billion in new financing at advantageous rates and increase cash reserves to over $1 billion. As a result, Continental operated more efficiently and had the resources to weather a future economic downturn. By the end of 1999, the company's net income was $485 million, earnings per share were $6.66, and its stock was selling for about $44 in October 2000—quite a change from the situation when Kellner came on board.

Once the airline's financial house was in order, operational performance and customer service also improved. The airline had the resources to upgrade and expand its fleet, add services, and enter more international markets through partnerships with other airlines. Continental's reputation within the airline industry and the investment community soared. So did Kellner's; he was awarded a CFO Excellence Award from *CFO* magazine in 1998, 1999, and 2000.[1]

Critical Thinking Questions

As you read this chapter, consider the following questions as they relate to Continental Airlines:

- In addition to raising funds for Continental Airlines, what other types of financial activities would Larry Kellner oversee?
- Did Kellner's actions help to achieve the financial manager's primary goal of maximizing the value of the firm to its owners?
- Why is it important for financial managers to understand how securities markets operate?

BUSINESS IN THE 21ˢᵀ CENTURY

In today's fast-paced global economy, managing a firm's finances is more complex than ever. For managers like Larry Kellner, a thorough command of traditional finance activities—financial planning, investing money, and raising funds—is only part of the job. Financial managers are more than number crunchers. As part of the top management team, chief financial officers (CFOs) need a broad understanding of their firm's business and industry, as well as leadership ability and creativity. They must never lose sight of the primary goal of the financial manager: to maximize the value of the firm to its owners.

Financial management—raising and spending a firm's money—is both a science and an art. The science part is analyzing numbers and flows of cash through the firm. The art is answering questions like these: Is the firm using its financial resources in the best way? Aside from costs, why choose a particular form of financing? How risky is each option?

This chapter focuses on the financial management of a firm and the securities markets in which firms raise funds. We'll start with an overview of the role of finance and of the financial manager in the firm's overall business strategy. Discussions of investment decisions and sources of short- and long-term financing follow. Next we'll examine the function, operation, and regulation of securities markets. Finally, we'll look at key trends affecting financial management and securities markets in the 21st century.

THE ROLE OF FINANCE AND THE FINANCIAL MANAGER

financial management

The art and science of managing a firm's money so that it can meet its goals.

Finance is critical to the success of all companies. It may not be as visible as marketing or production, but management of a firm's finances is just as much a key to its success.

Financial management—the art and science of managing a firm's money so it can meet its goals—is not just the responsibility of the finance department. All business decisions have financial consequences. Managers in all departments must work closely with financial personnel. If you are a sales representative, for example, the company's credit and collection policies will affect your ability to make sales.

Any company, whether it's a two-attorney law partnership or General Motors, needs money to operate. To make money, it must first spend money—on inventory and supplies, equipment and facilities, and employee wages and salaries.

When you come across a finance term you don't understand, visit the Hypertextual Finance Glossary at

http://www.duke.edu/ ~charvey/Classes/wpg/ glossary.htm.

Revenues from sales of the firm's products should be the chief source of funding. But money from sales doesn't always come in when it's needed to pay the bills. Financial managers must track how money is flowing into and out of the firm (see Exhibit 16-1). They work with the firm's other department managers to determine how available funds will be used and how much money is needed. Then they choose the best sources to obtain the required funding.

For example, a financial manager will track day-to-day operational data such as cash collec-

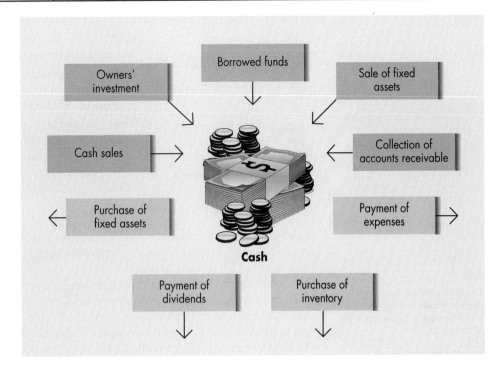

cash flows

The inflow and outflow of cash for a firm.

Financial managers at Ford Motor Company plan and monitor cash flow to ensure that funds are available to finance the labor and material costs of producing vehicles.

tions and disbursements to ensure that the company has enough cash to meet its obligations. Over a longer time horizon, the manager will thoroughly study whether and when the company should open a new manufacturing facility. The manager will also suggest the most appropriate way to finance the project, raise the funds, and then monitor the project's implementation and operation.

Financial management is closely related to accounting. In most firms both areas are the responsibility of the vice president of finance or the CFO. But accountants' main function is to collect and present financial data. Financial managers use financial statements and other information prepared by accountants to make financial decisions. Financial managers focus on **cash flows,** the inflow and outflow of cash. They plan and monitor the firm's cash flows to ensure that cash is available when needed.

The Financial Manager's Responsibilities and Activities

Financial managers have a complex and challenging job. They analyze financial data prepared by accountants, monitor the firm's financial status, and prepare and implement financial plans. One day they may be developing a better way to automate cash collections,

the next they may be analyzing a proposed acquisition. The key activities of the financial manager are:

- *Financial planning.* Preparing the financial plan, which projects revenues, expenditures, and financing needs over a given period.
- *Investment (spending money).* Investing the firm's funds in projects and securities that provide high returns in relation to the risks.
- *Financing (raising money).* Obtaining funding for the firm's operations and investments and seeking the best balance between debt (borrowed funds) and equity (funds raised through the sale of ownership shares in the business).

The Goal of the Financial Manager

How can financial managers make wise planning, investment, and financing decisions? The main goal of the financial manager is *to maximize the value of the firm to its owners.* The value of a publicly owned corporation is measured by the share price of its stock. A private company's value is the price at which it could be sold.

To maximize the firm's value, the financial manager has to consider both short- and long-term consequences of the firm's actions. Maximizing profits is one approach, but it should not be the only one. Such an approach favors making short-term gains over achieving long-term goals. What if a firm in a highly technical and competitive industry did no research and development? In the short run, profits would be high because research and development is very expensive. But in the long run, the firm might lose its ability to compete because of its lack of new products.

Financial managers constantly strive for a balance between the opportunity for profit and the potential for loss. In finance, the opportunity for profit is termed **return;** the potential for loss, or the chance that an investment will not achieve the expected level of return, is **risk.** A basic principle in finance is that the higher the risk, the greater the return that is required. This widely accepted concept is called the **risk-return trade-off.** Financial managers consider many risk and return factors when making investment and financing decisions. Among them are changing patterns of market demand, interest rates, general economic conditions, market conditions, and social issues (such as environmental effects and equal employment opportunity policies).

return

The opportunity for profit.

risk

The potential for loss or the chance that an investment will not achieve the expected level of return.

risk-return trade-off

A basic principle in finance that holds that the higher the risk, the greater the return that is required.

c o n c e p t c h e c k

- What is the role of financial management in a firm?
- How do the three key activities of the financial manager relate?
- What is the main goal of the financial manager? How does the risk-return trade-off relate to the financial manager's main goal?

HOW ORGANIZATIONS USE FUNDS

>lg 2

To grow and prosper, a firm must keep investing money in its operations. The financial manager decides how best to use the firm's money. Short-term expenses support the firm's day-to-day activities. For instance, athletic apparel maker Nike regularly spends money to buy such raw materials as leather and fabric and to pay employee salaries. Long-term expenses are typically for fixed assets. For Nike, these would include outlays to build a new factory, buy automated manufacturing equipment, or acquire a small manufacturer of sports apparel.

Short-Term Expenses

Short-term expenses, often called *operating expenses,* are outlays used to support current production and selling activities. They typically result in current assets, which include cash and any other assets (accounts receivable and inventory) that can be converted to cash within a year. The financial manager's goal is to manage current assets so the firm has enough cash to pay its bills and to support its accounts receivable and inventory.

Cash Management: Assuring Liquidity Cash is the lifeblood of business. Without it, a firm could not operate. An important duty of the financial manager is **cash management,** or making sure that enough cash is on hand to pay bills as they come due and to meet unexpected expenses.

Businesses estimate the cash requirements for a specific period. Many companies keep a minimum cash balance to cover unexpected expenses or changes in projected cash flows. The financial manager arranges loans to cover any shortfalls. If the size and timing of cash inflows closely match the size and timing of cash outflows, the company needs to keep only a small amount of cash on hand. A company whose sales and receipts are fairly predictable and regular throughout the year needs less cash than a company with a seasonal pattern of sales and receipts. A toy company, for instance, whose sales are concentrated in the fall, spends a great deal of cash during the spring and summer to build inventory. It has excess cash during the winter and early spring, when it collects on sales from its peak selling season.

Because cash held in checking accounts earns little, if any, interest, the financial manager tries to keep cash balances low and to invest the surplus cash. Surpluses are invested temporarily in **marketable securities,** short-term investments that are easily converted into cash. The financial manager looks for low-risk investments that offer high returns. Three of the most popular marketable securities are Treasury bills, certificates of deposit, and commercial paper. (**Commercial paper** is unsecured short-term debt— an IOU—issued by a financially strong corporation.)

In addition to seeking the right balance between cash and marketable securities, the financial manager tries to shorten the time between the purchase of inventory or services (cash outflows) and the collection of cash from sales (cash inflows). The three key strategies are to collect money owed to the firm (accounts receivable) as quickly as possible, to pay money owed to others (accounts payable) as late as possible without damaging the firm's credit reputation, and to minimize the funds tied up in inventory.

Find an introduction to the types of cash management services banks offer their customers at Centura Bank's site

http://www.centura.com/ business/cash_management/ indx.cfm

cash management
The process of making sure that a firm has enough cash on hand to pay bills as they come due and to meet unexpected expenses.

marketable securities
Short-term investments that are easily converted into cash.

commercial paper
Unsecured short-term debt (an IOU) issued by a financially strong corporation.

accounts receivable
Sales for which a firm has not yet been paid.

Managing Accounts Receivable **Accounts receivable** represent sales for which the firm has not yet been paid. Because the product has been sold but cash has not yet been received, an account receivable amounts to a use of funds. For the average manufacturing firm, accounts receivable represent about 15 to 20 percent of total assets.

The financial manager's goal is to collect money owed to the firm as quickly as possible—while offering customers credit terms attractive enough to increase sales. Accounts receivable management involves setting *credit policies,* guidelines on offering credit, and *credit terms,* specific repayment conditions, including how long customers have to pay their bills and whether a cash discount is given for quicker payment. Another aspect of accounts receivable management is deciding on *collection policies,* the procedures for collecting overdue accounts.

Setting up credit and collection policies is a balancing act for financial managers. On the one hand, easier credit policies or generous credit terms (a longer repayment period or larger cash discount) result in increased sales. On the other hand, the firm has to finance more accounts receivable. The risk of uncollectible accounts receivable also rises.

Technology can also help firms speed up collections. To cope with the meteoric rise in sales and, hence, accounts receivable, Dell Computer implemented an automated receivables collection system. Customized software improved order processing and collection methods. The new system also took over labor-intensive tasks such as sending letters to overdue accounts at specified times and creating activity reports with current account status. Dell's days receivables outstanding dropped from 50 to 37 days, freeing up a significant amount of cash.[2]

Inventory In a typical manufacturing firm, inventory is nearly 20 percent of total assets. The cost of inventory includes not only its purchase price, but also ordering, handling, storage, interest, and insurance costs. Financial managers must work closely with production and marketing managers to minimize the amount of inventory the firm carries without harming production efficiency or sales. Techniques for reducing the investment in inventory—efficient order quantities, the just-in-time system, and materials requirement planning—were described in Chapter 8.

Long-Term Expenditures

capital expenditures

Investments in long-lived assets, such as land, buildings, machinery, and equipment, that are expected to provide benefits over a period longer than one year.

capital budgeting

The process of analyzing long-term projects and selecting those that offer the best returns while maximizing the firm's value.

A firm also uses funds for its investments in long-lived assets, such items as land, buildings, machinery, and equipment. These are called **capital expenditures.** Unlike operating expenses, which produce benefits within a year, the benefits from capital expenditures extend beyond one year. For instance, a printer's purchase of a new printing press with a usable life of seven years is a capital expenditure. It appears as a fixed asset on the firm's balance sheet. Paper, ink, and other supplies, however, are expenses. Mergers and acquisitions, discussed in Chapter 4, are also considered capital expenditures.

Firms make capital expenditures for many reasons. The most common are to expand and to replace or renew fixed assets. Another reason is to develop new products. Most manufacturing firms have a big investment in long-term assets. Boeing Co., for instance, puts millions of dollars a year into airplane-manufacturing facilities.

Because capital expenditures tend to be costly and have a major effect on the firm's future, the financial manager must analyze long-term projects and select those that offer the best returns while maximizing the firm's value. This process is called **capital budgeting.** Decisions involving new products or the acquisition of another business are especially important. Another challenge managers face is assessing the value of proposed information technology expenditures, as the Applying Technology box demonstrates.

concept check

- Distinguish between short- and long-term expenses.
- What is the financial manager's goal in cash management? List the three key cash management strategies.
- Describe the firm's main motives in making capital expenditures.

OBTAINING SHORT-TERM FINANCING

>lg 3

How do firms raise the funding they need? They borrow money (debt), sell ownership shares (equity), and retain earnings (profits). The financial manager must assess all these sources and choose the one most likely to help maximize the firm's value.

Like expenses, borrowed funds can be divided into short- and long-term loans. A short-term loan comes due within one year; a long-term loan has a maturity greater than a year. Short-term financing is shown as a current liability on the balance sheet. It is used to finance current assets and support operations. Short-term loans can be unsecured or secured.

NET PAYOFFS

Do investments in the latest technology pay off? So far, the results are mixed. According to International Data Corp., a major information technology research firm, through 1998 companies received only $1.00 back for every $1.50 they invested.

One exception to this rule is Loanshop.com, the first online mortgage company. Profitability in this high-volume business depends on a company's ability to generate high-quality loan transactions at the lowest possible cost.

The company gets over half of its customer communications via e-mail, and quick response was the key to converting leads to sales. The conversion rate was greatest for replies within an hour of receipt and then dropped quickly, to less than 1 percent after 24 hours. Unless Loanshop could quickly separate incoming e-mail according to priority, it would miss promising sales opportunities.

Loanshop.com had two options to speed up the process of separating serious leads from routine questions: hire more staff or invest in special software to filter e-mail and route high-priority inquiries to mortgage counselors. But what were the relevant financial, operating, or process measurements that showed whether the new technology added value? While many of its rivals focused on the number of visitors to the Web site, Loanshop.com president Jack Rodgers disagreed: "It's a meaningless number if no one buys our product."

Loanshop.com's managers knew that one person could process 100 e-mail messages in an eight-hour day. The e-mail automation system could perform this task in just 15 minutes—a 96 percent reduction. Armed with these data, managers performed a capital budgeting analysis and determined that the technology solution was the better choice.

The new software acts as the company's inbound e-mail telemarketing agent. It filters e-mail, answers routine inquiries, and sends loan requests directly to loan counselors. It also can forward completed loan applications to the Federal National Mortgage Association's automated underwriting system. The results speak for themselves: Loanshop.com doubled its mortgage counselors' sales, reduced the number of employees handling e-mail by over one-third, and earned a 40 percent return on investment in 14 months. Customers are happy, too: they learn whether they qualify for a loan in five minutes and save an average of $1,500 in administrative costs.

Critical Thinking Questions

1. Describe the steps a company should take to evaluate a proposed investment in new information technology equipment.
2. What measures and performance outcomes were relevant for Loanshop.com's capital budgeting decision?
3. What mistakes could a company make by investing in new technology? How did Loanshop.com avoid them?

Unsecured Short-Term Loans

unsecured loans

Short-term loans for which the borrower does not have to pledge specific assets as security.

Unsecured loans are made on the basis of the firm's creditworthiness and the lender's previous experience with the firm. An unsecured borrower does not have to pledge specific assets as security. The three main types of unsecured short-term loans are trade credit, bank loans, and commercial paper.

trade credit

The extension of credit by the seller to the buyer between the time the buyer receives the goods or services and when it pays for them.

accounts payable

Purchase for which a buyer has not yet paid the seller.

Trade Credit: Accounts Payable When Goodyear sells tires to General Motors, GM does not have to pay cash on delivery. Instead, Goodyear regularly bills GM for its tire purchases, and GM pays at a later date. This is an example of **trade credit**—the seller extends credit to the buyer between the time the buyer receives the goods or services and when it pays for them. Trade credit is a major source of short-term business financing. The buyer enters the credit on its books as an **account payable.** In effect, the credit is a short-term loan from the seller to the buyer of the goods and services. Until GM pays

Goodyear, Goodyear has an account receivable from GM—and GM has an account payable to Goodyear.

Bank Loans   Unsecured bank loans are another source of short-term business financing. Companies often use these loans to finance seasonal (cyclical) businesses. Unsecured bank loans include lines of credit and revolving credit agreements. A **line of credit** specifies the maximum amount of unsecured short-term borrowing the bank will allow the firm over a given period, typically one year. The firm either pays a fee or keeps a certain percentage of the loan amount (10 to 20 percent) in a checking account at the bank. Another bank loan, the **revolving credit agreement,** is basically a guaranteed line of credit that carries an extra fee in addition to interest. Revolving credit agreements are often arranged for a two- to five-year period.

Commercial Paper   Financially strong major corporations issue commercial paper in multiples of $100,000 for periods ranging from 30 to 270 days. Many big companies use commercial paper instead of short-term bank loans because the interest rate on commercial paper is usually 1 to 3 percent below bank rates.

BetzDearborn, a Pennsylvania manufacturer of water treatment chemicals, saved $800,000 a year by replacing a portion of its short-term financing with a $500 million commercial paper program.[3]

Secured Short-Term Loans

Secured loans require the borrower to pledge specific assets as *collateral,* or security. The secured lender can legally take the collateral if the borrower doesn't repay the loan. Commercial banks and commercial finance companies are the main sources of secured short-term loans to business. Borrowers whose credit is not strong enough to qualify for unsecured loans use these loans.

Typically, the collateral for secured short-term loans is accounts receivable or inventory. Because accounts receivable are normally quite liquid (easily converted to cash), they are an attractive form of collateral. The appeal of inventory—raw materials or finished goods—as collateral depends on how easily it can be sold at a fair price.

Another form of short-term financing using accounts receivable is **factoring.** A firm sells its accounts receivable outright to a *factor,* a financial institution (usually a commercial bank or commercial finance company) that buys accounts receivable at a discount. Factoring is widely used in the clothing, furniture, and appliance industries. Factoring is more expensive than a bank loan, however, because the factor buys the receivables at a discount from their actual value.

Learn about the services and current rates offered by 21st Capital Corp., a factoring firm, at

http://www.21stcapital.com.

line of credit
An agreement between a bank and a business that specifies the maximum amount of unsecured short-term borrowing the bank will allow the firm over a given period, typically one year.

revolving credit agreement
A guaranteed line of credit whereby a bank agrees that a certain amount of funds will be available for a business to borrow over a given period.

secured loans
Loans for which the borrower is required to pledge specific assets as collateral, or security.

factoring
A form of short-term financing in which a firm sells its accounts receivable outright at a discount to a *factor.*

concept check

- Distinguish between unsecured and secured short-term loans.
- Briefly describe the three main types of unsecured short-term loans.
- Discuss the two ways that accounts receivable can be used to obtain short-term financing.

RAISING LONG-TERM FINANCING

>lg 4

A basic principle of finance is to match the term of the financing to the period over which benefits are expected to be received from the associated outlay. Short-term expenses should be financed with short-term funds, and long-term expenses should be financed with long-term funds. Long-term financing sources include both debt (borrowing) and equity (ownership). Equity financing comes either from selling new ownership interests or from retaining earnings.

SHAKY FINANCIAL MANAGEMENT

Paul Nussbaum assembled a $7 billion hotel empire in less than three years when he was CEO of Patriot American Hospitality, Inc. Patriot acquired a 450-hotel portfolio that included boutique hotels in England and the Wyndham Hotels chain in the United States, among others.

Patriot's buying spree was financed with large amounts of short-term debt and financial instruments called equity forward contracts, which were to be re-paid in the future with Patriot stock. "The contracts were, in essence, a huge bet that Patriot's stock price would climb." If the stock price rose, Patriot would be able to pay off the equity forward contracts with fewer shares. If the stock price fell, more shares would be re-quired to pay off the contracts.

Patriot's stock price declined during most of 1998, compromising the company's financial stability. More-over, the company was forced to issue additional shares of common stock to cover its equity forward contracts, thereby "diluting its existing pool of stock and pushing its share price into a potentially fatal nose dive."

Patriot's financial position was further compromised by its load of short-term debt. Hundreds of millions of dollars of short-term debt were due in the first quarter of 1999. Nussbaum had planned to pay off that debt by selling long-term debt to investors, but because of the credit crunch set off by Russia's debt default, Patriot was unable to float its bond offering.

Patriot was hurt by other events as well. Nussbaum never established effective financial controls. Appropriate financial oversight was lacking for several months due to conflicts among the firm's key financial managers and the voluntary departure of the person who shared the chief fi-nancial officer's duties. Nussbaum also "lost credibility on Wall Street when the company repeatedly failed to meet earnings targets."

Critical Thinking Questions

1. Does Patriot's financial situation reflect question-able business ethics, or is it simply a case of poor management or unfortunate circumstances?
2. Is it unethical for a business firm to assume a high level of risk in its financial management?
3. Do publicly traded business firms have an ethical responsibility to their investors? Why or why not?

Debt versus Equity Financing

Say that the Boeing Co. plans to spend $2 billion over the next four years to build and equip new factories to make jet aircraft. Boeing's top management will assess the pros and cons of both debt and equity and then consider several possible sources of the desired form of long-term financing. The overall goal is to choose the mix of debt and equity to balance cost and risk.

The major advantage of debt financing is the deductibility of interest ex-pense for income tax purposes, which lowers its overall cost. In addition, there is no loss of ownership. The major drawback is **financial risk**—the chance that the firm will be unable to make scheduled interest and principal payments. The lender can force a borrower that fails to make scheduled debt payments into bankruptcy. Most loan agreements have restrictions to ensure that the bor-rower operates efficiently.

Equity, on the other hand, is a form of permanent financing that places few restrictions on the firm. The firm is not required to pay dividends or repay the investment. However, equity financing gives common stockholders voting rights that provide them with a voice in management. Equity is more costly than debt. Unlike the interest on debt, dividends to owners are not tax-deductible expenses.

financial risk

The chance that a firm will be unable to make scheduled inter-est and principal payments on its debt.

Debt Financing

Long-term debt is used to finance long-term (capital) expenditures. The maturities of long-term debt typically range between 5 and 20 years. Three important forms of long-term debt are term loans, bonds, and mortgage loans.

A **term loan** is a business loan with a maturity of more than one year. Term loans generally have 5- to 12-year maturities and can be unsecured or secured. They are available from commercial banks, insurance companies, pension funds, commercial finance companies, and manufacturers' financing subsidiaries. A contract between the borrower and the lender spells out the amount and maturity of the loan, the interest rate, payment dates, the purpose of the loan, and other provisions such as operating and financial restrictions on the borrower to control the risk of default. The payments include both interest and principal, so the loan balance declines over time. Borrowers try to arrange a repayment schedule that matches the forecast cash flow from the project being financed.

Bonds are long-term debt obligations (liabilities) of corporations and governments. A bond certificate is issued as proof of the obligation. The issuer of a bond must pay the buyer a fixed amount of money—called **interest,** stated as the *coupon rate*—on a regular schedule, typically every six months. The issuer must also pay the bondholder the amount borrowed—called the **principal,** or *par value*—at the bond's maturity date (due date). Bonds are usually issued in units of $1,000—for instance, $1,000, $5,000, or $10,000. They may be secured or unsecured, include special provisions for early retirement, or be convertible to common stock. Exhibit 16-2 summarizes the features of some popular types of corporate bonds.

A **mortgage loan** is a long-term loan made against real estate as collateral. The lender takes a mortgage on the property, which lets the lender seize the property, sell it, and use the proceeds to pay off the loan if the borrower fails to make the scheduled payments. Long-term mortgage loans are often used to finance office buildings, factories, and warehouses. Life insurance companies

---

term loan

A business loan with a maturity of more than one year; can be unsecured or secured.

bonds

Long-term debt obligations (liabilities) issued by corporations and governments.

interest

A fixed amount of money paid by the issuer of a bond to the bondholder on a regular schedule, typically every six months; stated as the *coupon rate*.

principal

The amount borrowed by the issuer of a bond; also called *par value*.

mortgage loan

A long-term loan made against real estate as collateral.

---

e x h i b i t   1 6 - 2 | Popular Types of Corporate Bonds

Bond Type	Characteristics
Collateral trust bonds	Secured by securities (stocks and bonds) owned by the issuer. Value of collateral is generally 25 to 35 percent higher than the bond's par value.
Convertible bonds	Unsecured bonds that can be exchanged for a specified number of shares of common stock.
Debenture	Unsecured bonds typically issued by creditworthy firms.
Equipment trust certificates	Used to finance "rolling stock"—airplanes, ships, trucks, railroad cars. Secured by the assets financed.
Floating-rate bonds	Bonds whose interest rate is adjusted periodically in response to changes in specified market interest rates. Popular when future inflation and interest rates are uncertain.
High-yield (junk) bonds	Bonds rated Ba or lower by Moody's or BB or lower by Standard & Poor's. High-risk bonds with high returns to investors. Frequently used to finance mergers and takeovers.
Mortgage bonds	Secured by property, such as land, equipment, or buildings.
Zero-coupon bonds	Issued with no coupon rate and sold at a large discount from par value. "Zeros" pay no interest prior to maturity. Investor's return comes from the gain in value (par value minus purchase price).

are an important source of these loans. They make billions of dollars' worth of mortgage loans to businesses each year.

Bond Ratings

Bonds vary in quality, depending on the financial strength of the issuer.

Bond ratings are letter grades assigned to bond issues to evaluate their quality or level of risk. Higher ratings indicate lower risk of *default*—the failure of a company to make scheduled principal or interest payments. Ratings for corporate bonds are easy to find. The two largest and best-known rating agencies are Moody's and Standard & Poor's (S&P), whose publications are in most libraries and in stock brokerages. Exhibit 16-3 lists the letter grades assigned by Moody's and S&P. A bond's rating may change with events.

bond ratings

Letter grades assigned to bond issues to indicate their quality, or level of risk; assigned by rating agencies such as Moody's and Standard & Poor's.

For the latest news about bond rating upgrades and downgrades, visit Moody's Investor Services at

http://www.moodys.com/

Equity Financing

>lg 5

Equity is the owners' investment in the business. In corporations, the preferred and common stockholders are the owners. A firm obtains equity financing by selling new ownership shares (external financing) or by retaining earnings (internal financing).

common stock

A security that represents an ownership interest in a corporation.

Selling New Issues of Common Stock **Common stock** is a security that represents an ownership interest in a corporation.

When a high-growth company *goes public*, it has an *initial public offering (IPO)* to raise more funds to finance continuing growth. (Companies that are already public can issue and sell additional shares of common stock to raise equity funds.) An IPO often enables existing stockholders, usually employees, family, and friends who bought the stock privately, to earn big profits on their investment.

e x h i b i t   1 6 - 3 | Moody's and Standard & Poor's Bond Ratings

Moody's Ratings	S & P Ratings	Description
Aaa	AAA	**Prime-quality investment bonds:** Highest rating assigned; indicates extremely strong capacity to pay.
Aa A	AA A	**High-grade investment bonds:** Also considered very safe bonds, although not quite as safe as Aaa/AAA issues; Aa/AA bonds are safer (have less risk of default) than single As.
Baa	BBB	**Medium-grade investment bonds:** Lowest of investment-grade issues; seen as lacking protection against adverse economic conditions.
Ba B	BB B	**Junk bonds:** Provide little protection against default; viewed as highly speculative.
Caa	CCC	**Poor-quality bonds:** Either in default or very close to it.
Ca	CC	
C	C	
	D	

Yahoo co-founder Jerry Yang held a press conference to announce that his Internet search engine firm was going public to finance the expansion of Yahoo's online services.

dividends
Payments to stockholders from a corporation's profits.

stock dividends
Payments to stockholders in the form of more stock; may replace or supplement cash dividends.

retained earnings
Profits that have been reinvested in a firm.

preferred stock
An equity security for which the dividend amount is set at the time the stock is issued.

But going public has some drawbacks. For one thing, there is no guarantee an IPO will sell. It is also expensive. Big fees must be paid to investment bankers, brokers, attorneys, accountants, and printers. Once the company is public, it is closely watched by regulators, stockholders, and securities analysts. The firm must reveal such information as operating and financial data, product details, financing plans, and operating strategies. Providing this information is often costly.

Going public can be successful when a company is well established and market conditions are right. Strong equity markets in the late 1990s prompted many companies to go public, especially very young Internet-related companies. Frequently companies that were only a year or two old rushed to go public to take advantage of market conditions. Online toy retailer eToys went public in May 1999 at $20 a share. Its shares soared to $76.56 the first day of trading—even though the company was less than two years old and had not shown any profits. However, by October 2000, the stock had plunged to about $3.50 as e-commerce stocks fell from investor favor.[4] The company filed for bankruptcy in March 2001.

Dividends and Retained Earnings **Dividends** are payments to stockholders from a corporation's profits. A company does not have to pay dividends to stockholders. But if investors buy the stock expecting to get dividends and the firm does not pay them, the investors may sell their stock. If too many sell, the value of the stock decreases. Dividends can be paid in cash or in stock. **Stock dividends** are payments in the form of more stock. Stock dividends may replace or supplement cash dividends. After a stock dividend has been paid, more shares have a claim on the same company, so the value of each share often declines.

At their quarterly meetings, the company's board of directors (with the advice of its financial managers) decides how much of the profits to distribute as dividends and how much to reinvest. A firm's basic approach to paying dividends can greatly affect its share price. A stable history of dividend payments indicates good financial health. If a firm that has been making regular dividend payments cuts or skips a dividend, investors start thinking it has serious financial problems. The increased uncertainty often results in lower stock prices. Thus, most firms set dividends at a level they can keep paying.

Retained earnings, profits that have been reinvested in the firm, have a big advantage over other sources of equity capital: they do not incur underwriting costs. Financial managers strive to balance dividends and retained earnings to maximize the value of the firm. Often the balance reflects the nature of the firm and its industry. Well-established firms and those that expect only modest growth, like public utilities, typically pay out much of their earnings in dividends. High-growth companies, like those in the computer and biotechnology fields, finance most of their growth through retained earnings and pay little or no dividends to stockholders.

Preferred Stock Another form of equity is **preferred stock.** Unlike common stock, preferred stock usually has a dividend amount that is set at the time the stock is issued. These dividends must be paid before the company can pay any dividends to common stockholders. Also, if the firm goes bankrupt and sells its assets, preferred stockholders get their money back before common stockholders do.

Like debt, preferred stock increases the firm's financial risk because it obligates the firm to make a fixed payment. But preferred stock is more flexible. The firm can miss a dividend payment without suffering the serious results of failing to pay back a debt. Most preferred stock is *cumulative preferred stock* that requires issuers to repay all unpaid dividends before any dividends can be paid to the holders of common stock.

Preferred stock is more expensive than debt financing, however, because preferred dividends are not tax-deductible. Also, because the claims of preferred stockholders on income and assets are second to those of debt holders, preferred stockholders require higher returns to compensate for the greater risk.

Venture Capital As we learned in Chapter 5, *venture capital* is another source of equity capital often used by small and growing firms that aren't big enough to sell securities to the public. This type of financing is especially popular among high-tech companies that need large sums of money.

Venture capitalists invest in new businesses in return for part of the ownership, sometimes as much as 60 percent. They look for new businesses with high growth potential, and they expect a high investment return within 5 to 10 years. By getting in on the ground floor, venture capitalists buy stock at a very low price. They earn profits by selling the stock at a much higher price when the company goes public. Venture capitalists generally get a voice in management through a seat on the board of directors. For example, in October 2000 two-year-old Thoughtworks, which develops customized business-to-business systems, raised $28 million from two venture capital firms. Representatives of the investing firms joined Thoughtworks' board and are using their expertise and industry contacts to help the company expand.[5]

Getting venture capital is difficult, even though there are hundreds of private venture capital firms in this country. Most venture capitalists finance only about 1 to 5 percent of the companies that apply.

concept check

- Compare the advantages and disadvantages of debt and equity to the issuer.
- Discuss the costs involved in issuing common stock.
- Briefly describe these sources of equity: retained earnings, preferred stock, venture capital.

SECURITIES MARKETS

>lg 6

securities

Investment certificates issued by corporations or governments that represent either equity or debt.

Securities markets facilitate the transfer of funds from lenders and investors to corporate and governmental borrowers. Stocks, bonds, and other securities trade in securities markets. These markets streamline the purchase and sales activities of investors by allowing transactions to be made quickly and at a fair price from lenders to borrowers much easier. **Securities**—investment certificates issued by corporations or governments—represent either equity (ownership in the issuer) or debt (a loan to the issuer).

Securities markets are busy places. On an average day, individual and institutional investors trade more than 1.8 billion shares of stock in over 10,000 companies. They also trade bonds, mutual funds, futures contracts, and options. *Individual investors* invest their own money to achieve their personal financial goals. About 70 million individual investors (representing about 50 percent of U.S. households) hold about 64 percent of the more than $5 trillion total U.S. equities outstanding, either directly or through mutual funds.

institutional investors

Investment professionals who are paid to manage other people's money.

Institutional investors are investment professionals who are paid to manage other people's money. Most of these professional money managers work for financial institutions, such as banks, mutual funds, insurance companies, and pension funds. Institutional investors control very large sums of money,

primary market

The securities market where *new* securities are sold to the public.

secondary market

The securities market where (already issued) old securities are traded among investors; includes the organized stock exchanges, the over-the-counter market, and the commodities exchanges.

investment bankers

Firms that act as underwriters, buying securities from corporations and governments and reselling them to the public.

underwriting

The process of buying securities from corporations and governments and reselling them to the public; the main activity of investment bankers.

stockbroker

A person who is licensed to buy and sell securities on behalf of clients.

concept check

- How do securities markets help businesses and investors?
- Distinguish between primary and secondary securities markets.
- How does an investment banker work with companies to issue securities?

Most securities transactions take place in secondary markets such as on the trading floor of the New York Stock Exchange, shown here.

often buying stock in 10,000-share blocks. They aim to meet the investment goals of their clients. Institutional investors are a major force in the securities markets, accounting for about half of the dollar volume of equities traded.

Businesses and governments also take part in the securities markets. Corporations issue bonds and stocks to raise funds to finance their operations. They are also among the institutional investors that purchase corporate and government securities. Federal, state, and local governments sell securities to finance specific projects and cover budget deficits.

Types of Markets

Securities markets can be divided into primary and secondary markets. The **primary market** is where *new* securities are sold to the public, usually with the help of investment bankers. In the primary market, the issuer of the security gets the proceeds from the transaction. A security is sold in the primary market just once—when it is first issued by the corporation or government.

Later transactions take place in the **secondary market,** where *old* (already issued) securities are bought and sold, or traded, among investors. The issuers generally are not involved in these transactions. The vast majority of securities transactions take place in secondary markets, which include the organized stock exchanges, the over-the-counter securities market, and the commodities exchanges.

The Role of Investment Bankers and Stockbrokers

Two types of investment specialists play key roles in the functioning of the securities markets. **Investment bankers** help companies raise long-term financing. These firms act as intermediaries, buying securities from corporations and governments and reselling them to the public. This process, called **underwriting,** is the main activity of the investment banker, which acquires the security for an agreed-upon price and hopes to be able to resell it at a higher price to make a profit. Investment bankers advise clients on the pricing and structure of new securities offerings, as well as on mergers, acquisitions, and other types of financing. Well-known investment banking firms include Goldman Sachs Group, Merrill Lynch & Co., Morgan Stanley Dean Witter, First Boston, UBS PaineWebber, and Salomon Smith Barney (a division of Citigroup).

A **stockbroker** is a person who is licensed to buy and sell securities on behalf of clients. Also called *account executives,* these investment professionals work for brokerage firms and execute the orders customers place for stocks, bonds, mutual funds, and other securities. We'll discuss the different types of brokers later in this chapter.

Other Popular Securities

In addition to corporate issues of equity and debt, securities markets trade several other types of securities. These include Treasury securities, municipal bonds, mutual funds, futures contracts, and options. The first three appeal to a wide range of investors. Futures contracts and options are more complex investments for experienced investors.

U.S. Government Securities and Municipal Bonds   The U.S. Treasury sells three major types of debt securities, commonly called "governments": Treasury bills, Treasury notes, and Treasury bonds. All three are viewed as risk-free because they are backed by the U.S. government. *Treasury bills* mature in less than a year and are issued with a minimum par value of $1,000. *Treasury notes* have maturities of 10 years or less, and *Treasury bonds* have maturities as long as 25 years or more. Both notes and bonds are sold in denominations of $1,000 and $5,000. The interest earned on government securities is subject to federal income tax but is free from state and local income taxes.

municipal bonds

Bonds issued by states, cities, counties, and other state and local government agencies.

Municipal bonds are issued by states, cities, counties, and other state and local government agencies. These bonds typically have a par value of $5,000 and are either general obligation or revenue bonds. *General obligation bonds* are backed by the full faith and credit (and taxing power) of the issuing government. *Revenue bonds*, on the other hand, are repaid only from income generated by the specific project being financed. Examples of revenue bond projects include toll highways and bridges, power plants, and parking structures. Because the issuer of revenue bonds has no legal obligation to back the bonds if the project's revenues are inadequate, they are considered more risky and therefore have higher interest rates than general obligation bonds.

You'll find a minicourse on municipal bonds when you click on municipal bonds at the top of the page at http://www.investingbonds.com

Municipal bonds are attractive to investors because interest earned on them is exempt from federal income tax. For the same reason, the coupon interest rate for a municipal bond is lower than for a similar-quality corporate bond. In addition, interest earned on municipal bonds issued by governments within the taxpayer's home state is exempt from state income tax as well. In contrast, all interest earned on corporate bonds is fully taxable.

Mutual Funds   Suppose that you have $1,000 to invest but don't know which stocks or bonds to buy, when to buy them, or when to sell them. By investing in a mutual fund, you can buy shares in a large, professionally managed *portfolio*, or group, of stocks and bonds. A **mutual fund** is a financial service company

mutual fund

A financial service company that pools investors' funds to buy a selection of securities that meet its stated investment goals.

that pools its investors' funds to buy a selection of securities—marketable securities, stocks, bonds, or a combination of securities—that meet its stated investment goals.

Each mutual fund focuses on one of a wide variety of possible investment goals, such as growth or income. Many large financial service companies, like Fidelity Investments and Vanguard, sell a wide variety of mutual funds, each with a different investment goal. Investors can pick and choose funds that match their particular interests. Some specialized funds invest in a particular type of company or asset—in one industry such as health care or technology, a geographical region such as Asia, or an asset such as precious metals. To help investors find the right fund for their needs, many mutual fund companies are using the Internet to good advantage.

futures contracts

Legally binding obligations to buy or sell specified quantities of commodities or financial instruments at an agreed-on price at a future date.

Futures and Options   **Futures contracts** are legally binding obligations to buy or sell specified quantities of commodities (agricultural or mining products) or financial instruments (securities or currencies) at an agreed-on price at a future date. An investor can buy commodity futures contracts in cattle, pork bellies (large slabs of bacon), eggs, frozen orange juice concentrate, gasoline, heating oil, lumber, wheat, gold, and silver. Financial futures include Treasury securities and foreign currencies, such as the euro or Japanese yen.

Futures contracts do not pay interest or dividends. The return depends solely on favorable price changes. These are very risky investments because the prices can vary a great deal.

Options are contracts that entitle holders to buy or sell specified quantities of common stocks or other financial instruments at a set price during a specified time. As with futures contracts, investors must correctly guess future price movements in the underlying financial instrument to earn a positive return. Unlike futures contracts, options do not legally obligate the holder to buy or sell and the price paid for an option is the maximum amount that can be lost. But because options have very short maturities, it is easy to quickly lose a lot of money with them.

concept check

- Who issues municipal bonds and why?
- Why do mutual funds appeal to investors? Discuss some of the investment goals pursued by mutual funds.
- What are futures contracts? Why are they risky investments? How do options differ from futures contracts?

SECURITIES EXCHANGES

>lg 7

options

Contracts that entitle holders to buy or sell specified quantities of common stocks or other financial instruments at a set price during a specified time.

organized stock exchanges

Organizations on whose premises securities are resold using an auction-style trading system.

The two key types of securities exchanges are organized stock exchanges and the over-the-counter market. **Organized stock exchanges** are organizations on whose premises securities are resold. They operate using an auction-style trading system. All other securities are traded in the over-the-counter market.

To make transactions in an organized stock exchange, an individual or firm must be a member and own a "seat" on that exchange. Owners of the limited number of seats must meet certain financial requirements and agree to observe a broad set of rules when trading securities.

U.S. Stock Exchanges

The oldest and most prestigious U.S. stock exchange is the *New York Stock Exchange (NYSE)*, which has existed since 1792. Often called the Big Board, it is located on Wall Street in downtown New York City. The NYSE, which lists the securities of about 2,800 corporations, handles most of the shares traded on organized stock exchanges in the United States. Major companies like IBM, Coca-Cola, AT&T, Procter & Gamble, Ford Motor Co., and Chevron list their shares on the NYSE. In 1999, 204 billion shares were traded on the NYSE, with a total dollar value of over $8.9 trillion. The NYSE is also popular with non-U.S. companies. About 400 foreign companies now list their securities on the NYSE.

How many shares traded hands today? Find out at the New York Stock Exchange site

http://www.nyse.com/floor/floor.html

Another national stock exchange, the American Stock Exchange (AMEX), lists the securities of about 700 corporations. With 1999 trading volume of just over 7 billion shares, it is dwarfed by the NYSE. Because the AMEX's rules are less strict than those of the NYSE, most firms traded on the AMEX are smaller and less well known than NYSE-listed corporations.

In addition to the NYSE and AMEX, several regional exchanges list about 100 to 500 securities of firms located in their area. Regional exchange membership rules are much less strict than for the NYSE. The top regional exchanges are the Boston, Cincinnati, Chicago, and Pacific exchanges. An electronic network linking the NYSE and many of the regional exchanges allows

Many U.S. and other firms outside of Japan list their stock on the Tokyo Stock Exchange, one of the world's largest foreign exchanges.

brokers to make securities transactions at the best prices.

Global Trading and Foreign Exchanges

Improved communications and the elimination of many legal barriers are helping the securities markets go global. The number of securities listed on exchanges in more than one country is growing. Foreign securities are now traded in the United States. Likewise, foreign investors can easily buy U.S. securities.

Stock exchanges also exist in foreign countries. The London and Tokyo Stock Exchanges rank behind the NYSE and Nasdaq (described below). Other important foreign stock exchanges include those in Toronto, Montreal, Buenos Aires, Zurich, Sydney, Paris, Frankfurt, Hong Kong, and Taiwan. The number of big U.S. corporations with listings on foreign exchanges is growing steadily, especially in Europe. For example, over 10 percent of the daily activity in NYSE-listed stocks is due to trades on the London Stock Exchange.

The Over-the-Counter Market

over-the-counter (OTC) market

A sophisticated telecommunications network that links dealers throughout the United States and enables them to trade securities.

National Association of Securities Dealers Automated Quotation (Nasdaq) system

The first electronic-based stock market and the fastest-growing part of the stock market.

Unlike the organized stock exchanges, the **over-the-counter (OTC) market** is not a specific institution with a trading floor. It is a sophisticated telecommunications network that links dealers throughout the United States. The **National Association of Securities Dealers Automated Quotation (Nasdaq) system,** the first electronic-based stock market, is the fastest-growing part of the stock market. It provides up-to-date bid and ask prices on about 4,100 of the most active OTC securities, with a 1999 market value totaling $5.2 trillion. Its sophisticated electronic communication system is the main reason for the popularity and growth of the OTC market. In 1999, 270 billion shares with a value of $10.8 trillion exchanged hands, gains of 34 percent and 88 percent, respectively, over the preceding year.

The securities of many well-known companies, some of which could be listed on the organized exchanges, trade on the OTC market. Examples include Apple Computer, Coors, Dell Computer, Intel, MCI WorldCom, Microsoft, Nordstrom Department Stores, Qualcomm, and Starbucks. The stocks of most commercial banks and insurance companies also trade in this market, as do most government and corporate bonds. About 440 foreign companies also trade OTC.

What makes the Nasdaq different from an organized exchange? On the NYSE, one specialist handles all transactions in a particular stock, but on the Nasdaq system, a number of dealers handle ("make a market in") a security. For instance, about 40 dealers make a market in Apple Computer stock. Thus, dealers compete, improving investors' ability to get a good price.

Regulation of Securities Markets

The securities markets are regulated by both state and federal governments. The states were the first to pass laws aimed at preventing securities fraud. But most securities transactions occur across state lines, so federal securities laws are more effective. In addition to legislation, the industry has self-regulatory groups and measures.

Securities Legislation   The *Securities Act of 1933* was passed by Congress in response to the 1929 stock market crash and subsequent problems during the Great Depression. It protects investors by requiring full disclosure of information about new securities issues. The issuer must file a *registration statement* with the Securities and Exchange Commission (SEC), which must be approved by the SEC before the security can be sold.

The *Securities Exchange Act of 1934* formally gave the SEC power to control the organized securities exchanges. The act was amended in 1964 to give the SEC authority over the OTC market as well. The amendment included rules for operating the stock exchanges and granted the SEC control over all participants (exchange members, brokers, dealers) and the securities traded in these markets.

The 1934 act also banned **insider trading,** the use of information that is not available to the general public to make profits on securities transactions. Because of lax enforcement, however, several big insider trading scandals occurred during the late 1980s. The *Insider Trading and Fraud Act of 1988* greatly increased the penalties for illegal insider trading and gave the SEC more power to investigate and prosecute claims of illegal actions. The meaning of insider was expanded beyond a company's directors, employees, and their relatives to include anyone who gets private information about a company.

Other important legislation includes the *Investment Company Act of 1940,* which gives the SEC the right to regulate the practices of investment companies (such as mutual funds), and the *Investment Advisers Act of 1940,* which requires investment advisers to disclose information about their background. The *Securities Investor Protection Corporation (SIPC)* was established in 1970 to protect customers if a brokerage firm fails by insuring each customer's account for up to $500,000.

Self-Regulation   The investment community also regulates itself, developing and enforcing ethical standards to reduce the potential for abuses in the financial marketplace. The National Association of Securities Dealers (NASD), the parent organization of the Nasdaq-Amex Market Group, oversees the nation's 5,600 brokerage firms and more than half a million registered brokers. It develops rules and regulations, provides a dispute resolution forum, and conducts regulatory reviews of member activities for the protection and benefit of investors.

In response to "Black Monday"—October 19, 1987, when the Dow Jones Industrial Average plunged 508 points and the trading activity severely overloaded the exchange's computers—the securities markets instituted corrective measures to prevent a repeat of the crisis. Now, under certain conditions, **circuit breakers** stop trading for a short cooling-off period to limit the amount the market can drop in one day. The NYSE circuit breaker levels are set quarterly based on the Dow Jones Industrial Average closing values of the previous month, rounded to the nearest 50 points.

insider trading
The use of information that is not available to the general public to make profits on securities transactions.

circuit breakers
Measures that, under certain conditions, stop trading in the securities markets for a short cooling-off period to limit the amount the market can drop in one day.

concept check

- Describe the organized stock exchanges. How does the OTC market differ from them? What role does each type of market play?
- What is insider trading, and how can it be harmful?
- Briefly describe the key provisions of the main federal laws designed to protect securities investors. How does the securities industry regulate itself?

CAPITALIZING ON TRENDS IN BUSINESS

>lg 8

Many of the key trends shaping financial management as we enter the new millennium echo those in other disciplines. For example, technology is improving the efficiency with which financial managers run their operations and securities markets operate. As in other areas, the increasing interdependence of the world's economies requires an international approach to finance. One different note, however, is the expanding role of the financial manager in risk management.

Just as venturing overseas affects marketing, production, and general management practices, globalization brings additional complexity to financial management. Today's financial managers can make investments and raise financing both in the United States and overseas. They may have to compare the costs, risks, and benefits of relocating manufacturing facilities to another country versus expanding at home. And they must pay attention not only to the U.S. economy, but to economic developments in Japan, Russia, Germany, and other nations as well.

Risk Management

risk management
The process of identifying and evaluating risks and selecting and managing techniques to adapt to risk exposures.

The 1998 turmoil in Asian and Russian financial markets proved that going global increases a company's risk, whether or not the company has operations in those regions. As a result, financial managers are spending more time on **risk management,** the process of identifying and evaluating risks and selecting and managing techniques to adapt to risk exposures. Companies face a wide range of risks, including:

- *Credit risk.* Exposure to loss as a result of default on a financial transaction or a reduction in a security's market value due to decline in the credit quality of the debt issuer.
- *Market risk.* Risk resulting from adverse movements in the level or volatility of market prices of securities, commodities, and currencies.
- *Operational risk.* The risk of unexpected losses arising from deficiencies in a firm's management information, support, and control systems and procedures.

The job of Microsoft's financial managers is complex as they manage the company's global manufacturing, licensing, and wholesale and retail distribution of more than 200 products, such as the software sold by the retailer in Hong Kong shown here.

A failure in a company's risk control procedures can lead to substantial financial losses. Major financial institutions like Daiwa and Sumitomo Corp. lost huge amounts of money because their control systems collapsed. A breakdown in risk control eventually costs the shareholders money. They may have to invest more capital to bail out the troubled firm. Otherwise their equity investment will decline in value when the company's problems become known to the public.[6]

Recently, some insurance companies have entered the risk management arena. They offer new types of policies to protect companies against disappointing financial results. Reliance Group, a New York insurer, introduced Enterprise Earnings Protection Insurance. This policy reimburses a company for any operating earnings shortfall that is due to forces beyond management's control, such as drought, floods, or the Asian

GOING DIRECT WITH NIPHIX

Companies that are too small to trade in the OTC market no longer have to wait to qualify for Wall Street to tap the equity markets. Electronic trading networks like Niphix Investments provide an alternate route to the capital markets.

Niphix—itself a small company—is the first Internet-based direct stock market. "We cater to companies that are too small for Nasdaq, but we hope they can grow at Niphix," says Nimish Ghandi, Niphix's founder. At Niphix, microcap companies (with a market capitalization—the value of their equity—under $50 million) find services designed for their needs. Niphix helps small companies market and sell their stock without using an underwriter. Such issues are called direct public offerings (DPOs). Niphix's goal is to be a starting point for high-growth companies that will eventually move up to the more established exchanges.

To be listed on Niphix, a company must agree to full disclosure, including quarterly and annual audited reports using GAAP (generally accepted accounting principles) accounting. Standard & Poor's has agreed to cover all companies listed with Niphix.

Investors who want to buy and sell shares in Niphix-listed companies simply open a standard brokerage account with Niphix. Unlike similar trading systems, Niphix operates a matching system rather than acting as an intermediary. Buyers and sellers conduct their own online negotiations until they agree on a price. Then Niphix immediately executes the trade using its staff of registered brokers. Niphix also offers low transaction fees, ranging from $24 to $44.

Niphix is still young, and it is too soon to know if it will improve the liquidity of shares of companies going the DPO route. Thus far, the number of companies and investors using Niphix remains small. Tom Stewart-Gordon, editor of a DPO report, believes that investors who buy DPO shares focus on the company's products or philosophy rather than its liquidity. Supporters of exchanges like Niphix think that having a place to sell their securities will encourage more investors to consider DPOs.

Critical Thinking Questions

1. What advantages does Niphix offer a small company?
2. If you were a company owner planning to go public, would you consider Niphix? Justify your answer.
3. How does the availability of research reports for Niphix companies from a major firm like Standard & Poor's help both Niphix and the companies?

economic crisis. Reliance is hoping that CFOs will buy its policies to prevent earnings surprises. Guaranteeing results is likely to be an expensive proposition, however. And predicting the volatility of a client's earnings is a new area for insurers.[7]

Market Competition Heats Up

Whereas the NYSE was once the undisputed leader among stock exchanges, the Nasdaq has successfully challenged its position. The largest electronic exchange in the world, Nasdaq captures about 54 percent of total U.S. trading volume compared to the NYSE's 43 percent—reversing their positions of five years earlier. The Nasdaq lists 4,100 companies versus 2,800 on the NYSE.

As a result, the competition between the two institutions is intense. Each promotes itself as the best place for a major corporation to list its securities. The NYSE touts its prestige to convince Nasdaq and AMEX companies to switch their listings to the NYSE. Even though it spent millions on new information technology and uses order-matching technology for almost half its trades, the NYSE still lags behind the Nasdaq and major foreign exchanges technologically, however.[8]

The Nasdaq, calling itself "The market for the next 100 years" due to its emphasis on technology, merged with the AMEX in early 1999 to create what it termed a "market of markets." They operate as separate markets under the management of the Nasdaq-Amex Market Group, a subsidiary of the National Association of Securities Dealers, Inc. (NASD). This merger could pressure the remaining regional exchanges to find partners.

Threatening both the NYSE and the Nasdaq is the emergence of other electronic exchanges called *electronic communications networks (ECNs)*. ECNs allow institutional traders and some individuals to make direct transactions, without using brokers, securities exchanges, or the Nasdaq, in what is called the *fourth market*. Because they deal mostly in Nasdaq stocks, ECNs are taking trading volume away from the Nasdaq. ECNs are most effective for high-volume, actively traded stocks. Money managers and institutions such as pension funds and mutual funds with large amounts of money to invest like ECNs because they cost less than other trading venues.[9]

Starting in April 1999, the SEC allowed ECNs to register as exchanges. Orders could bypass members of the NYSE entirely. Discount brokerage firm Datek Online was the first to petition the SEC to turn its ECN, Island, into a self-regulated stock exchange. Niphix Investments, the ECN described in the Focusing on Small Business box, specializes in helping small companies go public.

APPLYING THIS CHAPTER'S TOPICS

Whether you are a marketing manager, purchasing agent, or systems analyst, knowledge of finance will help you to do your job better. You'll be able to understand your company's financial statements, its financial condition, and management's investment and financing decisions. Financial information also provides feedback on how well you are doing and identifies problems. On a more practical note, you may be asked to prepare a budget for your department or unit. Employees who understand the financial decision-making process will be able to prepare proposals that address financial concerns. As a result, they will be more likely to get the resources they require to accomplish the firm's goals.

If you own a business, you must pay close attention to financial management. Without financial plans you may find yourself running out of cash. It's easy to get so caught up in growing sales that you neglect your billing and collection methods. In fact, managing accounts receivable is often one of the more challenging aspects of running a young company. But you can't rely on revenue increases to solve your cash flow problems. Good receivables practices start with credit policies. Be choosy when it comes to offering trade credit and check customers' credit references and payment history thoroughly. Set the initial credit limit fairly low until the customer establishes a prompt payment history. Here are some other ways to improve collections:

- Bill frequently, not just at the end of the month, so that money flows in throughout the month.
- Clearly state payment terms.
- Establish regular and frequent follow-up procedures. Some companies call to notify the customer that the bill has been sent and to make sure the customer is satisfied. Weekly calls are in order for late payments.
- Monitor results of outstanding receivables collection.
- Don't fill new orders from customers who are continually delinquent.[10]

1. Small Business Loans, **http://www.smallbusinessloans. com,** offers a wide range of loans for small businesses. Choose five types of loans and describe the reasons businesses choose each type. Look at the application and summarize the type of information required to start the loan process. What other information do you think the lender will require before granting a loan?

2. The MaxFunds University, **http://www.maxfunds. com/content/university.html,** offers a course on investing in mutual funds: Maxuniversity–Part II. Use it to learn about the basics of mutual funds. Prepare a presentation for the class based on the materials.

SUMMARY OF LEARNING GOALS

>lg 1   **How do finance and the financial manager affect the firm's overall strategy?**
Finance involves managing the firm's money. The financial manager must decide how much money is needed and when, how best to use the available funds, and how to get the required financing. The financial manager's responsibilities include financial planning, investing (spending money), and financing (raising money). Maximizing the value of the firm is the main goal of the financial manager, whose decisions often have long-term effects.

>lg 2   **What types of short-term and long-term expenditures does a firm make?**
A firm invests in short-term expenses—supplies, inventory, and wages—to support current production, marketing, and sales activities. The financial manager manages the firm's investment in current assets so that the company has enough cash to pay its bills and support accounts receivable and inventory. Long-term expenditures (capital expenditures) are made for fixed assets such as land, buildings, and equipment. Because of the large outlays required for capital expenditures, financial managers carefully analyze proposed projects to determine which offer the best returns.

>lg 3   **What are the main sources and costs of unsecured and secured short-term financing?**
Short-term financing comes due within one year. The main sources of unsecured short-term financing are trade credit, bank loans, and commercial paper. Secured loans require a pledge of certain assets, such as accounts receivable or inventory, as security for the loan. Factoring, or selling accounts receivable outright at a discount, is another form of short-term financing.

>lg 4   **What are the key differences between debt and equity and the major types and features of long-term debt?**
Financial managers must choose the best mix of debt and equity for their firm. The main advantage of debt financing is the tax-deductibility of interest. But debt involves financial risk because it requires the payment of interest and principal on specified dates. Equity—common and preferred stock—is considered a permanent form of financing on which the firm may or may not pay dividends. Dividends are not tax-deductible.

The main types of long-term debt are term loans, bonds, and mortgage loans. Term loans can be secured or unsecured and generally have 5- to 12-year maturities. Bonds usually have maturities of 10 to 30 years. Mortgage loans are secured by real estate. Long-term debt usually costs more than

>looking ahead

at Continental Airlines

After years of shaky financial skies, Continental Airlines is flying high. Its solid financial condition has paid off in many areas. With improved access to the financial markets, the airline has been able to finance the acquisition of new aircraft and retire old ones, giving Continental one of the youngest fleets in the industry. Newer planes appeal to business travelers and allow Continental to offer higher quality service and comfort. Airlines are now eager to form alliances with the revitalized Continental. Recently, Continental expanded its domestic and international route networks through a strategic partnership with Northwest and marketing alliances with Alaska, Air France, British Midland, Virgin, and other airlines.

Employees and passengers like the new Continental as well. In 2001, *Fortune* magazine named Continental one of its "100 Best Companies to Work for in America," and Continental was also on *Fortune*'s "World's Most Admired Companies" list. It has been praised for it its innovative use of information technology among airlines, thanks in large part to Larry Kellner's emphasis on upgrading Continental's communication and information systems. Gordon Bethune, Continental's chairman and chief executive officer, praised employees' efforts to focus on eliminating non-value-added costs.[11]

short-term financing because of the greater uncertainty that the borrower will be able to make the scheduled loan payments.

>lg 5   When and how do firms issue equity, and what are the costs?
The chief sources of equity financing are common stock, retained earnings, and preferred stock. The cost of selling stock includes issuing costs and potential dividend payments. Retained earnings are profits reinvested in the firm. For the issuing firm, preferred stock is more expensive than debt because its dividends are not tax-deductible and its claims are secondary to those of debtholders, but less expensive than common stock. Venture capital is often a source of equity financing for young companies.

>lg 6   How do securities markets help firms raise funding, and what securities trade in the capital markets?
Securities markets allow stocks, bonds, and other securities to be bought and sold quickly and at a fair price. New issues are sold in the primary market. After that, securities are traded in the secondary market. Investment bankers specialize in issuing and selling new security issues. Stockbrokers are licensed professionals who buy and sell securities on behalf of their clients.

In addition to corporate securities, investors can trade U.S. government Treasury securities and municipal bonds, mutual funds, futures, and options. Mutual funds are financial service companies that pool the funds of many investors to buy a diversified portfolio of securities. Investors choose mutual funds because they offer a convenient way to diversify and are professionally managed. Futures contracts are legally binding obligations to buy or sell specified quantities of commodities or financial instruments at an agreed-on price at a future date. They are very risky investments because the price of the commodity or financial instrument may change drastically. Options are contracts that entitle the holder the right to buy or sell specified quantities of common stock or other financial instruments at a set price during a specified time. They, too, are high-risk investments.

>lg 7   What are the major U.S. securities exchanges and how are they regulated?
Securities are resold on organized stock exchanges, like the New York Stock Exchange and regional stock exchanges, and in the over-the-counter market, a telecommunications network linking dealers throughout the United States. The most actively traded securities are listed on the Nasdaq system, so dealers and brokers can perform trades quickly and efficiently.

The Securities Act of 1933 requires disclosure of important information regarding new securities issues. The Securities Exchange Act of 1934 and its 1964

KEY TERMS

accounts payable 445

accounts receivable 443

bond ratings 449

bonds 448

capital budgeting 444

capital expenditures 444

cash flows 441

cash management 443

circuit breakers 456

commercial paper 443

common stock 449

dividends 450

factoring 446

financial management 440

financial risk 447

futures contracts 453

insider trading 456

institutional investors 451

interest 448

investment banker 452

line of credit 446

marketable securities 443

mortgage loan 448

municipal bonds 453

mutual fund 453

National Association of Securities Dealers Automated Quotation (Nasdaq) system 455

options 454

organized stock exchanges 454

over-the-counter (OTC) market 455

preferred stock 450

primary market 451

principal 448

retained earnings 450

return 442

revolving credit agreement 446

risk 442

risk management 457

risk-return trade-off 442

secondary market 452

secured loans 446

amendment formally empowered the Securities and Exchange Commission and granted it broad powers to regulate the organized securities exchanges and the over-the-counter market. The Investment Company Act of 1940 places investment companies such as mutual funds under SEC control. The securities markets also have self-regulatory groups like the NASD and measures such as "circuit breakers" to halt trading if the Dow Jones Industrial Average drops rapidly.

>lg 8   **What are the current developments in financial management and the securities markets?**

Globalization brings additional complexity to financial management. Financial managers must be prepared to invest and raise funds overseas and make transactions in multiple currencies. Financial managers are spending more time on risk management, identifying and evaluating risks, and selecting techniques to control and reduce risk. Companies face a wide range of risks, including credit risk, market risk, and operational risk.

The securities markets and investment industry are in the midst of considerable change. No longer does the New York Stock Exchange dominate equity market activity. The Nasdaq is challenging the Big Board, and the emergence of electronic exchanges could further alter the market positions of these two securities marketplaces.

PREPARING FOR TOMORROW'S WORKPLACE

1. The head of your school's finance department has asked you to address a group of incoming business students about the importance of finance to their overall business education. Develop an outline with the key points you would cover in your speech.

2. Edward M. Kerschner, a securities analyst at Wall Street's UBS PaineWebber, considers dividends a terribly tax-inefficient way of delivering returns to investors, because they are taxed twice, at the corporate and individual level. Many industries that traditionally pay large dividends—telecommunications and utilities, for example—are allocating funds to acquisitions, debt paydown, and other uses, and raising dividends more slowly as they face intensified competition. Divide the class into two teams to debate Kerschner's statement that dividends no longer add value.

3. You are the chief financial officer of Discovery Labs, a privately held, five-year-old biotechnology company that needs to raise $3 million to fund the development of a new drug. Prepare a report for the board of directors that discusses the types of long-term financing available to the firm, their pros and cons, and the key factors to consider in choosing a financing strategy.

4. Research the trends in the IPO marketplace from 1995 to 2000. Then select two IPO success stories and two failures. Prepare a report for the class on their performance. What lessons about the securities markets can you learn from their stories? Is it better to wait longer to go public or to use one of the alternative exchanges like Niphix to go public while the firm is still fairly small?

5. While having dinner at a Manhattan restaurant, you overhear two investment bankers at the next table. They are discussing the takeover of Bellamco Industries by Gildmart Corp., a deal that has not yet been announced. You have been thinking about buying Bellamco stock for a while, so the next day you buy 500 shares for $30 each. Two weeks later, Gildmart announces its acquisition of Bellamco at a price of $45 per share. Have you fairly earned a profit, or are you guilty of insider trading? What's wrong with insider trading?

securities 451
stockbroker 452
stock dividends
 450
term loan 448
trade credit 445
underwriting 452
unsecured loans
 445

WORKING THE NET

1. If factorig accounts receivable is still a mystery to you, visit the Global Financial Group site, **http://www.global-factoring.com.** Click on the top buttons to get information on "What is Factoring?", "Reasons to Factor," "How Does it Work?" "Factoring Terminology," "FAQs," and "How Do I Qualify?" Summarize your findings.

2. Go to vFinance.com, **http://www.vfinance.com,** and link to three different venture capital firms. Compare the firms' investment strategies (industry specialization, age of companies in which they invest, etc.).

3. The International Finance and Commodities Institute (IFCI) Financial Risk Site, **http://riskinstitute.ch**, offers an excellent introduction to risk management concepts. Explore the site, especially the Key Concepts page, develop a list of sources and types of financial risks, and give an example of each. Discuss briefly the consequences of not controlling these risks. How can companies implement sound risk management procedures?

4. Compare the listing requirements of the NYSE, Nasdaq, and AMEX using the information at their Web sites: **http://www.nyse.com** and **http://www. nasdaq.com-amex.com.** Search the sites for listing requirements. What types of companies qualify for listing on each exchange? Why do the Nasdaq and AMEX offer alternative listing standards?

5. Become a pro at researching companies on the Web. Take the tutorial on Researching Companies Online at **http://home.sprintmail.com/ ~debflanagan/index.html**. Put your newfound skills to use by researching the investment potential of a company of your choice.

CREATIVE THINKING CASE

Nonstop Trading

For many do-it-yourself investors, the normal trading day—9:30 A.M. to 4:00 P.M. Eastern time for the NYSE and Nasdaq—is not long enough. Now that they can research companies online at all hours, they want to manage their portfolios when they get home from work or react to late-breaking news outside normal trading hours. West Coast investors, for whom regular trading ends at 1:00 P.M. Pacific time, have long been unhappy about losing afternoon trading hours. Day traders, who buy and sell stocks the same day to capture tiny differences in stock prices, also want longer hours.

In 1999, brokers rushed to respond to the demand for longer trading hours by tapping into the resources of electronic stock trading systems. Datek was one of the first, extending its trading day with a 4:00 P.M. to 5:15 P.M. Eastern time session. Discover Brokerage and Dreyfus Brokerage Services added a session from 6:00 P.M. to 8:00 P.M. Eastern time. E*Trade allowed individual investors to join major traders such as mutual fund managers and institutional investors and trade from 4:00 P.M. to 6:30 P.M. through Instinet, a major ECN. "What our customers want is access to opportunity and a level playing field with larger institutional investors," says Christos Cotsakos, chairman of E*Trade. "It's all part of democratizing personal investing."

Following suit, the NYSE and Nasdaq announced plans for longer hours as well. Starting in fall 1999, investors could trade 100 of the largest Nasdaq stocks during a 5:30 P.M. to 10:00 P.M. after-hours session. The NYSE delayed the introduction of after-hours trading for about 500 of its stocks until 2000. By limiting trading to major companies, these exchanges hope to generate sufficient demand to avoid sharp price swings.

Not everyone is in favor of after-hours trading sessions, however. Conditions in after-hours trading could be different from regular daytime trading sessions. Prices could be more volatile, increasing the risk for small investors. As Alan Davidson, president of the Independent Broker-Dealer Association, says, "It extends the stock market into a casino . . . and emphasizes short-term over long-term investment."

Critical Thinking Questions

1. What are some of the advantages and disadvantages of extended trading hours?
2. Do you think it's important to have a "resting period" to allow investors to reflect on the day's market activity?
3. Why are smaller online brokerages and ECNs in the forefront of the push toward longer trading hours, while the NYSE and Nasdaq are following a more conservative approach?

VIDEO CASE

Growth through Acquisitions

Scotsman Industries (**http://www.scotsman-ice.com**) manufactures and markets refrigerated display cases, food preparation and storage equipment, beverage systems, ice machines, and walk-in coolers and freezers. Its primary customers are supermarkets, restaurants, lodging and health care facilities, and convenience stores. The company's goals include increasing sales and earnings by 15 to 20 percent annually. Internal growth should account for about 6 to 8 percent of the increase, with the rest from acquisitions.

The company's acquisition strategy targets companies that either strengthen existing product lines or add new but related areas. Since 1990 Scotsman has used acquisitions to transform itself from a company highly dependent on one product line to a more diversified company with product lines marketed to similar customer groups worldwide. In 1994 Scotsman acquired commercial food-service equipment manufacturer Delfield Co. (**http://www.delfield.com**). With the 1997 acquisition of Kysor Industrial Corp., Scotsman entered the markets for walk-in coolers and freezers and supermarket and convenience store environmental control systems. Other acquisitions expanded Scotsman's global reach. Its Whitlenge and Homark subsidiaries in the United Kingdom and Hartek unit in Germany and Austria produce and sell beverage systems in Europe.

These acquisitions fueled Scotsman's growth as sales and earnings tripled during the 1990s. According to Richard Osborne, Scotsman's chairman, president, and CEO, the company will continue to acquire companies with strong fundamentals and complementary products, using these acquisitions to improve the strategic positions of current business lines.

Critical Thinking Questions

1. What are the financial management implications of growing the company through acquisitions?
2. Should a company finance acquisitions with debt or equity? Explain your answer.
3. What does Osborne mean when he says future acquisitions will focus on companies with strong fundamentals and complementary products?

Case: Pets.com Ends Up in the Doghouse

Pets.com was the cat's meow of online pet stores. Founded in February 1999, it caught the fancy of investors who were looking to grab some dot.com riches for themselves. Money flowed in from major venture capital firms and partners like Amazon.com. By December 1999, Pets.com raised $110 million in four financing rounds and seemed destined for Internet stardom. It scheduled its initial public offering (IPO) for its first birthday in February 2000.

With a lavish $27 million advertising campaign featuring their Sock Puppet mascot, Pets.com courted pet lovers who spared no expense on their pets, dressing them in diamond-studded collars, special coats, and other pricey accessories. However, the business model for pet e-tailers was not sustainable. "Pet products simply do not lend themselves very well to online purchases," says Andrew Bartels of Giga Information Group. "You can certainly order a 50-pound bag of dry dog food online, but think about the overnight shipping costs." To counter high shipping costs, Pets.com offered discounts to attract customers. As a result, it sold most products below cost, losing as much as $5 for every $1 of merchandise sold in the first quarter of 2000 alone.

"It was astounding to see how few pure dot.com e-tailers had a grasp of their gross margins," says Jim Breyer, managing partner at Accel Partners, a venture capital firm. They assumed that building sales to a high enough level would bring profits. Instead they discovered that expenses like marketing and personnel rose along with sales. At Pets.com, overall sales volume was slow to build; customers never returned to buy the higher-margin pet toys. The company quickly ran through their cash on hand.

By the time Pets.com went public, investors shunned Internet companies with small revenues, heavy losses, and no profits in sight. The stock never sold above the $11 offering price as the once-hot market for dot-coms fizzled. From there it was all downhill. Pets.com launched a private-label food line, started selling sock-puppet merchandise, and built a second distribution center to improve profitability and develop brand awareness. However, these strategies failed to interest new investors in providing the additional $20 million necessary for Pets.com to continue operations. On November 7, 2000, Pets.com stock closed its doors.

Questions for Critical Thinking

1. In an interview just after the company's demise, Pets.com chairman and chief executive Julie Wainwright said, "In the end, we thought [closing the company] was the best thing for our shareholders, who are our primary concern, since we're a public company." Do you agree with Wainwright, and why? How does being a public company change the picture for Pets.com? What additional responsibilities and risks does it involve?

2. How could better financial planning have helped Pets.com in the early stages of its life?

3. Assume you were Pets.com's chief financial officer in early 2000. What steps could you have taken to possibly avoid the company's downfall?

SOURCES: Timothy Hanrahan, Danielle Sessa, et. al, "Dot-Com Dominoes," *The Wall Street Journal Interactive Edition* (November 7, 2000), downloaded from **www.wsj.com**; Suzanne Koudsi, "Dot-Com Deathwatch: Why Is This Sock Puppet Still Smiling?" *Fortune* (June 26, 2000), p. 54; Pui-Wing Tam and Mylene Mangalindan, "Pets.com Will Shut Down, Citing Insufficient Funding," *The Wall Street Journal Interactive Edition*, November 8, 2000, downloaded from **www.wsj.com**; Fred Vogelstein, Janet Rae-Dupree, Paul Sloan, and William J. Holstein; "Easy Dot Com, Easy Dot Go," *U.S. News & World Report*, May 1, 2000, p. 42; Jerry Useem, "Dot-coms: What Have We Learned?" *Fortune* (October 30, 2000), pp. 82–104.

APPENDIX A: UNDERSTANDING THE LEGAL AND TAX ENVIRONMENT

laws

The rules of conduct in a society, created and enforced by a controlling authority, usually the government.

common law

The body of unwritten law that has evolved out of judicial (court) decisions rather than being enacted by a legislature; also called *case law.*

statutory law

Written law enacted by a legislature (local, state, or federal).

administrative law

The rules, regulations, and orders passed by boards, commissions, and agencies of government (local, state, and federal).

business law

The body of law that governs commercial dealings.

Our legal system affects everyone who lives and does business in the United States. The smooth functioning of society depends on the law, which protects the rights of people and businesses. The purpose of law is to keep the system stable while allowing orderly change. The law defines which actions are allowed or banned and regulates some practices. It also helps settle disputes. The legal system both shapes and is shaped by political, economic, and social systems. As Judge Learned Hand wrote in *The Spirit of Liberty,* "Without [the law] we cannot live; only with it can we insure the future which by right is ours."

In any society **laws** are the rules of conduct created and enforced by a controlling authority, usually the government. They develop over time in response to the changing needs of people, property, and business. The legal system of the United States is thus the result of a long and continuing process. In each generation new social problems occur, and new laws are created to solve them. For instance, in the late 1800s corporations in certain industries, such as steel and oil, merged and became dominant. The Sherman Antitrust Act was passed in 1890 to control these powerful firms. Eighty years later, in 1970, Congress passed the National Environmental Policy Act. This law dealt with pollution problems, which no one had thought about in 1890. Today new areas of law are developing to deal with the Internet.

The Main Sources of Law

Common law is the body of unwritten law that has evolved out of judicial (court) decisions rather than being enacted by legislatures. It is also called case law. It developed in England and came to America with the colonists. All states except Louisiana, which follows the Napoleonic Code inherited from French settlers, follow the English system. Common law is based on community customs that were recognized and enforced by the courts.

Statutory law is written law enacted by legislatures at all levels, from city and state governments to the federal government. Examples of statutory law are the federal and state constitutions, bills passed by Congress, and *ordinances,* which are laws enacted by local governments. Statutory law is the chief source of new laws in the United States. Among the business activities governed by statutory law are securities regulation, incorporation, sales, bankruptcy, and antitrust.

Related to statutory law is **administrative law,** or the rules, regulations, and orders passed by boards, commissions, and agencies of federal, state, and local governments. The scope and influence of administrative law have expanded as the number of these government bodies has grown. Federal agencies issue more rulings and settle more disputes than all the courts and legislatures combined. Some federal agencies that issue rules are the Civil Aeronautics Board, the Internal Revenue Service, the Securities and Exchange Commission, the Federal Trade Commission, and the National Labor Relations Board.

Business Law

Business law is the body of law that governs commercial dealings. These laws provide a protective environment within which businesses can operate. They serve as guidelines for business decisions. Every businessperson should be familiar with the laws governing his or her field. Some laws, such as the Internal Revenue Code, apply to all businesses. Other types of business laws may apply to a specific industry, such as Federal Communications Commission laws that regulate radio and TV stations.

In 1952 the United States grouped many business laws into a model that could be used by all the states. The **Uniform Commercial Code (UCC)** sets

Uniform Commercial Code (UCC)

A model set of rules that apply to commercial transactions between businesses and between businesses and individuals; has been adopted by all states except Louisiana, which uses only part of it.

judiciary

The branch of government that is responsible for settling disputes by applying and interpreting points of law; consists of the court system.

trial courts

The lowest level of courts, where most cases begin; also called *courts of general jurisdiction*.

appellate courts (courts of appeals)

The level of courts above the trial courts; the losing party in a civil case and the defendant in a criminal case may appeal the trial court's decision to an appellate court.

forth the rules that apply to commercial transactions between businesses and between individuals and businesses. It has been adopted by 49 states; Louisiana uses only part of it. By standardizing laws, the UCC simplifies the process of doing business across state lines. It covers the sale of goods, bank deposits and collections, letters of credit, documents of title, and investment securities. Many articles of the UCC are covered later in this appendix.

The Court System

The United States has a highly developed court system. This branch of government, the **judiciary,** is responsible for settling disputes by applying and interpreting points of law. Although court decisions are the basis for common law, the courts also answer questions left unanswered by statutes and administrative rulings. They have the power to assure that these laws do not violate the federal or state constitutions.

Trial Courts Most court cases start in the **trial courts,** also called courts of general jurisdiction. The main federal trial courts are the U.S. district courts. There is at least one federal district court in each state. These courts hear cases involving serious federal crimes, immigration, postal regulations, disputes between citizens of different states, patents, copyrights, and bankruptcy. Specialized federal courts handle tax matters, international trade, and claims against the United States.

Appellate Courts The losing party in a civil (noncriminal) case and a losing defendant in a criminal case may appeal the trial court's decision to the next level in the judicial system, the **appellate courts (courts of appeals).** There are 12 U.S. circuit courts of appeals. Cases that begin in a federal district court are appealed to the court of appeals for that district. These courts may also review orders from administrative agencies. Likewise, the states have appellate courts and supreme courts for cases tried in state district or superior courts.

No cases start in appellate courts. Their purpose is to review decisions of the lower courts and affirm, reverse, or modify the rulings.

The Supreme Court The U.S. Supreme Court is the highest court in the nation. It is the only court specifically established by the U.S. Constitution. Any cases involving a state or in which an ambassador, public minister, or consul is a party are heard directly by the Supreme Court. Its main function is to review decisions by the U.S. circuit courts of appeals. Parties not satisfied with a decision of a state supreme court can appeal to the U.S. Supreme Court. But the Supreme Court accepts only those cases that it believes will have the greatest effect on the country, only about 200 of the thousands of appeals it gets each year.

Administrative Agencies Administrative agencies have limited judicial powers to regulate their special areas. These agencies exist at the federal, state, and local levels. For example, in 1998 the Federal Trade Commission enacted the "Federal Universal Service Fund," which subjects each pager phone to an $0.18 fee. This fund was created by the Federal Trade Commission to ensure that all citizens, schools, libraries, and hospitals in rural areas have access to telecommunications service (like the Internet) at prices comparable to those charged in urban and suburban areas. A list of selected federal agencies is shown in Exhibit A-1.

Nonjudicial Methods of Settling Disputes

Settling disputes by going to court is both expensive and time-consuming. Even if the case is settled prior to the actual trial, sizable legal expenses can be incurred in preparing for trial. Therefore, many companies now use private arbitration and mediation firms as alternatives to litigation. Private firms offer these services, which are a high growth area within the legal tax profession.

exhibit A - 1 | Federal Regulatory Agencies

Agency	Function
Federal Trade Commission (FTC)	Enforces laws and guidelines regarding unfair business practices and acts to stop false and deceptive advertising and labeling.
Food and Drug Administration (FDA)	Enforces laws and regulations to prevent distribution of adulterated or misbranded foods, drugs, medical devices, cosmetics, veterinary products, and hazardous consumer products.
Consumer Product Safety Commission	Ensures compliance with the Consumer Product Safety Act and seeks to protect the public from unreasonable risk of injury from any consumer product not covered by other regulatory agencies.
Federal Communications Commission (FCC)	Regulates wire, radio, and TV communication in interstate and foreign commerce.
Environmental Protection Agency (EPA)	Develops and enforces environmental protection standards and researches the effects of pollution.

arbitration

A method of settling disputes in which the parties agree to present their case to an impartial third party and are required to accept the arbitrator's decision.

mediation

A method of settling disputes in which the parties submit their case to an impartial third party but are not required to accept the mediator's decision.

contract

An agreement that sets forth the relationship between parties regarding the performance of a specified action; creates a legal obligation and is enforceable in a court of law.

express contract

A contract in which the terms are specified in either written or spoken words.

implied contract

A contract that depends on the acts and conduct of the parties to show agreement; the terms are not specified in writing or orally.

With **arbitration,** the parties agree to present their case to an impartial third party and are required to accept the arbitrator's decision. **Mediation** is similar, but the parties are not bound by the mediator's decision. The mediator suggests alternative solutions and helps the parties negotiate a settlement. Mediation is more flexible than arbitration and allows for compromise. If the parties cannot reach a settlement, they can then go to court, an option not available in most arbitration cases.

In addition to saving time and money, corporations like the confidentiality of testimony and settlement terms in these proceedings. Arbitration and mediation also allow businesses and medical professionals to avoid jury trials, which can result in large settlements in certain types of lawsuits, such as personal injury, discrimination, medical malpractice, and product liability.

Contract Law
Linda Price, a 22-year-old college student, is looking at a car with a sticker price of $12,000. After some negotiating, she and the salesperson agree on a price of $11,000, and the salesperson writes up a contract, which they both sign. Has Linda legally bought the car for $11,000? The answer is yes, because the transaction meets all the requirements for a valid contract.

A **contract** is an agreement that sets forth the relationship between parties regarding the performance of a specified action. The contract creates a legal obligation and is enforceable in a court of law. Contracts are an important part of business law. Contract law is also incorporated into other fields of business law, such as property and agency law (discussed later in this appendix). Some of the business transactions that involve contracts are buying materials and property, selling goods, leasing equipment, and hiring consultants.

A contract can be an **express contract,** which specifies the terms of the agreement in either written or spoken words, or an **implied contract,** which depends on the acts and conduct of the parties to show agreement. An example of an express contract is the written sales contract for Linda Price's new car. An implied contract exists when you order and receive a sandwich at Jason's Grill. You and the restaurant have an implied contract that you will pay the price shown on the restaurant's menu in exchange for an edible sandwich.

Contract Requirements   Businesses deal with contracts all the time, so it's important to know the requirements of a valid contract. For a contract to be legally enforceable, all of the following elements must be present:

- *Mutual assent.* Voluntary agreement by both parties to the terms of the contract. Each party to the contract must have entered into it freely, without duress. Using physical or economic harm to force the signing of the contract—threatening injury or refusing to place another large order, for instance—invalidates a contract. Likewise, fraud—misrepresenting the facts of a transaction—makes a contract unenforceable. Telling a prospective used-car buyer that the brakes are new when in fact they have not been replaced makes the contract of sale invalid.

- *Capacity.* Legal ability of a party to enter into contracts. Under the law, minors (those under 18), mental incompetents, drug and alcohol addicts, and convicts cannot enter into contracts.

- *Consideration.* Exchange of some legal value or benefit between the parties. Consideration can be in the form of money, goods, or a legal right given up. Suppose that an electronics manufacturer agrees to rent an industrial building for a year at a monthly rent of $1,500. Its consideration is the rent payment of $1,500, and the building owner's consideration is permission to occupy the space. But if you offer to type a term paper for a friend for free and your offer is accepted, there is no contract. Your friend has not given up anything, so you are not legally bound to honor the deal.

- *Legal purpose.* Absence of illegality. The purpose of the contract must be legal for it to be valid. A contract cannot require performance of an illegal act. A contract to smuggle drugs into a state for a specified amount of money would not be legally enforceable.

- *Legal form.* Oral or written form, as required. Many contracts can be oral. For instance, an oral contract exists when Bridge Corp. orders office supplies by phone from Ace Stationery Store and Ace delivers the requested goods. Written contracts include leases, sales contracts, and property deeds. Some types of contracts must be in writing to be legally binding. In most states, written contracts are required for the sale of goods costing more than $500, for the sale of land, for contract performance that cannot be carried out within a year, and for guarantees to pay the debts of someone else.

As you can see, Linda Price's car purchase meets all the requirements for a valid contract. Both parties have freely agreed to the terms of the contract. Linda is not a minor and presumably does not fit any of the other categories of incapacity. Both parties are giving consideration, Linda by paying the money and the salesperson by turning over the car to her. The purchase of the car is a legal activity. And the written contract is the correct form because the cost of the car is over $500.

breach of contract

The failure by one party to a contract to fulfill the terms of the agreement without a legal excuse.

Breach of Contract   A **breach of contract** occurs when one party to a contract fails (without legal excuse) to fulfill the terms of the agreement. The other party then has the right to seek a remedy in the courts. There are three legal remedies for breach of contract:

- *Payment of damages.* Money awarded to the party who was harmed by the breach of contract, to cover losses incurred because the contract wasn't fulfilled. Suppose that Ajax Roofing contracts with Fred Wellman to fix the large hole in the roof of his factory within three days. But the roofing crew doesn't show up as promised. When a thunderstorm four days later causes $45,000 in damage to Wellman's machinery, Wellman can sue for damages to cover the costs of the water damage because Ajax breached the contract.

- *Specific performance of the contract.* A court order requiring the breaching party to perform the duties under the terms of the contract. Specific performance is the most common method of settling a breach of contract. Wellman might ask the court to direct Ajax to fix the roof at the price and conditions in the contract.

- *Restitution.* Canceling the contract and returning to the situation that existed before the contract. If one party fails to perform under the contract, neither party has any further obligation to the other. Because Ajax failed to fix Wellman's roof under the terms of the contract, Wellman does not owe Ajax any money. Ajax must return the 50 percent deposit it received when Wellman signed the contract.

Warranties

Express warranties are specific statements of fact or promises about a product by the seller. This form of warranty is considered part of the sales transaction that influences the buyer. Express warranties appear in the form of statements that can be interpreted as fact. The statement "This machine will process 1,000 gallons of paint per hour" is an express warranty, as is the printed warranty that comes with a computer or a telephone answering machine.

Implied warranties are neither written nor oral. These guarantees are imposed on sales transactions by statute or court decision. They promise that the product will perform up to expected standards. For instance, a man bought a used car from a dealer, and the next day the transmission fell out as he was driving on the highway. The dealer fixed the car, but a week later the brakes failed. The man sued the car dealer. The court ruled in favor of the car owner because any car without a working transmission or brakes is not fit for the ordinary purpose of driving. Similarly, if a customer asks to buy a copier to handle 5,000 copies per month, she relies on the salesperson to sell her a copier that meets those needs. The salesperson implicitly warrants that the copier purchased is appropriate for that volume.

Patents, Copyrights, and Trademarks

The U.S. Constitution protects authors, inventors, and creators of other intellectual property by giving them the rights to their creative works. Patents, copyrights, and registration of trademarks and servicemarks are legal protection for key business assets.

A **patent** gives an inventor the exclusive right to manufacture, use, and sell an invention for 20 years. The U.S. Patent and Trademark Office, a government agency, grants patents for ideas that meet its requirements of being new, unique, and useful. The physical process, machine, or formula is what is patented. Patent rights—pharmaceutical companies' rights to produce drugs they discover, for example—are considered intangible personal property.

The government also grants copyrights. A **copyright** is an exclusive right, shown by the symbol ©, given to a writer, artist, composer, or playwright to use, produce, and sell her or his creation. Works protected by copyright include printed materials (books, magazine articles, lectures), works of art, photographs, and movies. Under current copyright law, the copyright is issued for the life of the creator plus 70 years after the creator's death. Patents and copyrights, which are considered intellectual property, are the subject of many lawsuits today.

patent
A form of protection established by the government for inventors; gives an inventor the exclusive right to manufacture, use, and sell an invention for 20 years.

copyright
A form of protection established by the government for creators of works of art, music, literature, or other intellectual property; gives the creator the exclusive right to use, produce, and sell the creation during the lifetime of the creator and for 70 years thereafter.

trademark
A design, name, or other distinctive mark that a manufacturer uses to identify its goods in the marketplace.

servicemark
A symbol, name, or design that identifies a service rather than a tangible object.

A **trademark** is a design, name, or other distinctive mark that a manufacturer uses to identify its goods in the marketplace. Apple Computer's multicolored apple logo (symbol) is an example of a trademark. A **servicemark** is a symbol, name, or design that identifies a *service* rather than a tangible object. The Travelers Insurance umbrella logo is an example of a servicemark.

Most companies identify their trademark with the ® symbol in company ads. This symbol shows that the trademark is registered with the Register of Copyrights, Copyright Office, Library of Congress. The trademark is followed by a generic description: Fritos corn chips, Xerox copiers, Scotch brand cellophane tape, Kleenex tissues.

Trademarks are valuable because they create uniqueness in the minds of customers. At the same time, companies don't want a trademark to become so well known that it is used to describe all similar types of products. For instance, *Coke* is often used to refer to any cola soft drink, not just those produced by the Coca-Cola Company. Companies spend millions of dollars each year to keep their trademarks from becoming *generic words,* terms used to identify a product class rather than the specific product. Coca-Cola employs many investigators and files 70 to 80 lawsuits each year to prevent its trademarks from becoming generic words.

Once a trademark becomes generic (which a court decides), it is public property and can be used by any person or company. Names that were once trademarked but are now generic include *aspirin, thermos, linoleum,* and *toll house cookies.*

Tort Law

tort
A civil, or private, act that harms other people or their property.

A **tort** is a civil, or private, act that harms other people or their property. The harm may involve physical injury, emotional distress, invasion of privacy, or *defamation* (injuring a person's character by publication of false statements). The injured party may sue the wrongdoer to recover damages for the harm or loss. A tort is not the result of a breach of contract, which would be settled under contract law. Torts are part of common law. Examples of tort cases are medical malpractice, *slander* (an untrue oral statement that damages a person's reputation), *libel* (an untrue written statement that damages a person's reputation), product liability (discussed in the next section), and fraud.

A tort is generally not a crime, although some acts can be both torts and crimes. (Assault and battery, for instance, is a criminal act that would be prosecuted by the state and also a tort because of the injury to the person.) Torts are private wrongs and are settled in civil courts. *Crimes* are violations of public law punishable by the state or county in the criminal courts. The purpose of criminal law is to punish the person who committed the crime. The purpose of tort law is to provide remedies to the injured party.

For a tort to exist and damages to be recovered, the harm must be done through either negligence or deliberate intent. *Negligence* occurs when reasonable care is not taken for the safety of others. For instance, a woman attending a New York Mets baseball game was struck on the head by a foul ball that came through a hole in the screen behind home plate. The court ruled that a sports team charging admission has an obligation to provide structures free from defects and seating that protects spectators from danger. The Mets were found negligent. Negligence does not apply when an injury is caused by an unavoidable accident, an event that was not intended and could not have been prevented even if the person used reasonable care. This area of tort law is quite controversial, because the definition of negligence leaves much room for interpretation.

Product-Liability Law

product liability
The responsibility of manufacturers and sellers for defects in the products they make and sell.

Product liability refers to manufacturers' and sellers' responsibility for defects in the products they make and sell. It has become a specialized area of law combining aspects of contracts, warranties, torts, and statutory law (at both the state and federal levels). A product-liability suit may be based on negligence or strict liability (both of which are torts) or misrepresentation or breach of warranty (part of contract law).

An important concept in product-liability law is **strict liability.** A manufacturer or seller is liable for any personal injury or property damage caused by defective products or packaging—even if all possible care was used to prevent such defects. The definition of *defective* is quite broad. It includes manufacturing and design defects and inadequate instructions on product use or warnings of danger.

Product-liability suits are very costly. More than 100,000 product-liability suits were filed against hundreds of companies that made or used asbestos, a substance that causes lung disease and cancer but was once used widely in insulation, brake linings, textiles, and other products. Eighteen companies were forced into bankruptcy as a result of asbestos-related lawsuits, and the total cost of asbestos cases to defendants and their insurers exceeds $10 billion (most of which was paid not to the victims but to lawyers and experts).

Bankruptcy Law

Congress has given financially distressed firms and individuals a way to make a fresh start. **Bankruptcy** is the legal procedure by which individuals or businesses that cannot meet their financial obligations are relieved of their debts. A bankruptcy court distributes any assets to the creditors.

Bankruptcy can be either voluntary or involuntary. In a *voluntary bankruptcy,* the debtor files a petition with the court, stating that debts exceed assets and asking the court to declare the debtor bankrupt. In an *involuntary bankruptcy,* the creditors file the bankruptcy petition.

The Bankruptcy Reform Act of 1978, amended in 1984 and 1986, provides for the quick and efficient resolution of bankruptcy cases. Under this act, two types of bankruptcy proceedings are available to businesses: *Chapter 7* (liquidation) and *Chapter 11* (reorganization). Most bankruptcies, an estimated 70 percent, use Chapter 7. After the sale of any assets, the cash proceeds are given first to secured creditors and then to unsecured creditors. A firm that opts to reorganize under Chapter 11 works with its creditors to develop a plan for paying part of its debts and writing off the rest.

Laws to Promote Fair Competition

Many measures have been taken to try to keep the marketplace free from influences that would restrict competition. These efforts include **antitrust regulation,** laws that prevent companies from entering into agreements to control trade through a monopoly. The first act regulating competition was the Sherman Antitrust Act, passed in 1890 to prevent large companies from dominating an industry and making it hard for smaller firms to compete. This broad act banned monopolies and contracts, mergers, or conspiracies in restraint of trade. In 1914 the Clayton Act added to the more general provisions of the Sherman Antitrust Act. It outlawed the following:

- *Price discrimination.* Offering a customer discounts that are not offered to all other purchasers buying on similar terms.
- *Exclusive dealing.* Refusing to let the buyer purchase a competitor's products for resale.
- *Tying contracts.* Requiring buyers to purchase merchandise they may not want in order to get the products they do want.
- *Purchase of stock in competing corporations so as to lessen competition.* Buying competitors' stock in such quantity that competition is reduced.

The 1950 *Celler-Kefauver Act* amended the Clayton Act. It bans the purchase of one firm by another if the resulting merger decreases competition within

strict liability

A concept in product-liability law under which a manufacturer or seller is liable for any personal injury or property damage caused by defective products or packaging even though all possible care was used to prevent such defects.

bankruptcy

The legal procedure by which individuals or businesses that cannot meet their financial obligations are relieved of their debt.

antitrust regulation

Laws that prevent companies from entering into agreements to control trade through a monopoly.

the industry. As a result, all corporate acquisitions are subject to regulatory approval before they can be finalized.

Most antitrust actions are taken by the U.S. Department of Justice, based on federal law. Violations of the antitrust acts are punishable by fines, imprisonment, or civil damage payments that can be as high as three times the actual damage amount. These outcomes give defendants an incentive to resolve cases.

The *Federal Trade Commission Act,* also passed in 1914, bans unfair trade practices. This act created the Federal Trade Commission (FTC), an independent five-member board with the power to define and monitor unfair trade practices, such as those prohibited by the Sherman and Clayton Acts. The FTC investigates complaints and can issue rulings called *cease-and-desist orders* to force companies to stop unfair business practices. Its powers have grown over the years. Today the FTC is one of the most important agencies regulating the competitive practices of business.

Regulation of Advertising and Pricing A number of federal laws directly affect the promotion and pricing of products. The *Wheeler-Lea Act* of 1938 amended the Federal Trade Commission Act and gave the FTC authority to regulate advertising. The FTC monitors companies' advertisements for false or misleading claims.

The most important law in the area of pricing is the *Robinson-Patman Act,* a federal law passed in 1936 that tightened the Clayton Act's prohibitions against price discrimination. An exception is made for circumstances like discounts for quantity purchases, as long as the discounts do not lessen competition. But a manufacturer cannot sell at a lower price to one company just because that company buys all its merchandise from the manufacturer. Also, if one firm is offered quantity discounts, all firms buying that quantity of goods must get the discounts. The FTC and the antitrust division of the Justice Department monitor pricing.

consumerism

A social movement that seeks to increase the rights and powers of buyers vis-à-vis sellers.

Consumer Protection Laws **Consumerism** reflects the struggle for power between buyers and sellers. Specifically, it is a social movement seeking to increase the rights and powers of buyers vis-à-vis sellers. Sellers' rights and powers include the following:

- To introduce into the marketplace any product, in any size and style, that is not hazardous to personal health or safety, or if it is hazardous, to introduce it with the proper warnings and controls.
- To price the product at any level they wish, provided they do not discriminate among similar classes of buyers.
- To spend any amount of money they wish to promote the product, so long as the promotion does not constitute unfair competition.
- To formulate any message they wish about the product, provided that it is not misleading or dishonest in content or execution.
- To introduce any buying incentives they wish.

Meanwhile, buyers have the following rights and powers:

- To refuse to buy any product that is offered to them.
- To expect products to be safe.
- To expect a product to be essentially as the seller represents it.
- To receive adequate information about the product.

Many laws have been passed to protect consumer rights. Exhibit A-2 lists the major consumer protection laws.

deregulation

The removal of rules and regulations governing business competition.

Deregulation of Industries During the 1980s and 1990s, the U.S. government has actively promoted **deregulation,** the removal of rules and regulations governing business competition. Deregulation has drastically changed some once-regulated industries (especially the transportation, telecommunications, and

exhibit A - 2 | Key Consumer Protection Laws

Mail Fraud Act (1872)	Makes it a federal crime to defraud consumers through use of the mail.
Pure Food and Drug Act (1906)	Created the Food and Drug Administration (FDA); protects consumers against the interstate sale of unsafe and adulterated foods and drugs.
Food, Drug, and Cosmetic Act (1938)	Expanded the power of the FDA to cover cosmetics and therapeutic devices and to establish standards for food products.
Flammable Fabrics Act (1953)	Prohibits sale or manufacture of clothing made of dangerously flammable fabric.
Child Protection Act (1966)	Prohibits sale of harmful toys and gives the FDA the right to remove dangerous products from the marketplace.
Cigarette Labeling Act (1965)	Requires cigarette manufacturers to put labels warning consumers about health hazards on cigarette packages.
Fair Packaging and Labeling Act (1966)	Regulates labeling and packaging of consumer products.
Consumer Credit Protection Act (Truth-in-Lending Act) (1968)	Requires lenders to fully disclose to borrowers the loan terms and the costs of borrowing (interest rate, application fees, etc.).
Fair Credit Reporting Act (1971)	Requires consumers denied credit on the basis of reports from credit agencies to be given access to their reports and to be allowed to correct inaccurate information.
Consumer Product Safety Act (1972)	Created the Consumer Product Safety Commission, an independent federal agency, to establish and enforce consumer product safety standards.
Equal Credit Opportunity Act (1975)	Prohibits denial of credit on the basis of gender, marital status, race, religion, age, or national origin.
Magnuson-Moss Warranty Act (1975)	Requires that warranties be written in clear language and that terms be fully disclosed.
Fair Debt Collection Practice Act (1978)	Makes it illegal to harass or abuse any person, to make false statements, or to use unfair methods when collecting a debt.
Alcohol Labeling Legislation (1988)	Provides for warning labels on liquor saying that women shouldn't drink when pregnant and that alcohol impairs our abilities.
Nutrition Labeling and Education Act (1990)	Requires truthful and uniform nutritional labeling on every food the FDA regulates.
Children's Television Act (1990)	Limits the amount of advertising to be shown during children's television programs to not more than 10.5 minutes per hour on weekends and not more than 12.0 minutes per hour on weekdays.
Americans with Disabilities Act (ADA) (1990)	Protects the rights of people with disabilities; makes discrimination against the disabled illegal in public accommodations, transportation, and telecommunications.
Brady Law (1998)	Imposes a 5-day waiting period and a background check before a gun purchaser can take possession of the gun.

financial services industries) and created many new competitors. The result has been entries into and exits from some industries. One of the latest industries to deregulate is the electric power industry. With almost 200 investor-owned electric utilities, it is the largest industry to be deregulated so far. California became the first state to deregulate electricity. Consumers can now buy electricity from several different suppliers, either local utilities or those in other states. In some parts of California, electric rates have risen rather than fallen, however. As a result, there is a movement to re-regulate electricity in California.

Despite the California experience, consumers typically benefit from deregulation. Increased competition often means lower prices. Businesses also benefit because they have more freedom to operate and can avoid the costs associated with government regulations. But more competition can also make it hard for small or weak firms to survive.

Regulation of the Internet   Although 70 million Americans are signing onto the Web regularly, only a minority do so to purchase products. The majority of electronic commerce remains business-to-business transactions. Americans are still far more likely to get the latest news, rather than the latest fashions, in cyberspace. Yet there are clear successes: Amazon.com is America's biggest bookstore. Egghead.com holds hyperauctions in cyberspace to sell off surplus items. Loyal Wal-Mart shoppers can browse for discounts at the retail giant's Web site.

Many states would like to tax commerce on the Internet. Washington, however, has promised to stop any such activity. In June 1997, the White House released "A Framework for Global Electronic Commerce," which advocated a minimalist approach to government intervention in electronic commerce. After providing a Universal Commercial Code for Electronic Commerce and protecting intellectual property, there's not much more for the government to do, according to the framework. And in November 1997, the TransAtlantic Business Dialogue, an international group composed of executives from such giants as Coca-Cola, Erickson, Ford, France Telecom, Goodyear, Pfizer, and Time Warner, released a report that called for governments to sit back and let markets evolve standards for privacy protection and encryption. Governments, the report asserted, should refrain from levying special taxes on electronic transactions, while working with the private sector to harmonize international legal standards and protecting intellectual property.

Taxation of Business

Taxes are sometimes seen as the price we pay to live in this country. Taxes are assessed by all levels of government on both business and individuals, and they are used to pay for the services provided by government. The federal government is the largest collector of taxes, accounting for 54 percent of all tax dollars. States are next, followed closely by local government taxes. The average American family pays about 37 percent of its income for taxes, 28 percent to the federal government and 9 percent to state and local governments.

income taxes
Taxes that are based on the income received by businesses and individuals.

Income Taxes   **Income taxes** are based on the income received by businesses and individuals. The income taxes paid to the federal government are set by Congress, regulated by the Internal Revenue Code, and collected by the Internal Revenue Service. These taxes are *progressive*, meaning that rates increase as income increases. Most of the states and some large cities also collect income taxes from individuals and businesses. The state and local governments establish their own rules and tax rates.

Other Types of Taxes   Besides income taxes, individuals and businesses pay a number of other taxes. The four main types are property taxes, payroll taxes, sales taxes, and excise taxes.

property taxes
Taxes that are imposed on real and personal property based on the assessed value of the property.

Property taxes are assessed on real and personal property, based on the assessed value of the property. They raise quite a bit of revenue for state and local governments. Most states tax land and buildings. Property taxes may be based on fair market value (what a buyer would pay), a percentage of fair market value, or replacement value (what it would cost today to rebuild or buy something like the original). The value on which the taxes are based is the assessed value.

payroll taxes
The employer's share of Social Security taxes and federal and state unemployment taxes.

Any business that has employees and meets a payroll must pay **payroll taxes,** the employer's share of Social Security taxes and federal and state unemployment taxes. These taxes must be paid on wages, salaries, and commissions. State unemployment taxes are based on the number of employees in a firm

sales taxes

Taxes that are levied on goods when they are sold; calculated as a percentage of the price.

who have become eligible for unemployment benefits. A firm that has never had an employee become eligible for unemployment will pay a low rate of state unemployment taxes. The firm's experience with employment benefits does not affect federal unemployment tax rates.

Sales taxes are levied on goods when they are sold and are a percentage of the sales price. These taxes are imposed by states, counties, and cities. They vary in amount and in what is considered taxable. Some states have no sales tax. Others tax some categories (such as appliances) but not others (such as clothes). Still others tax all retail products except food, magazines, and prescription drugs. Sales taxes increase the cost of goods to the consumer. Businesses bear the burden of collecting sales taxes and sending them to the government.

excise taxes

Taxes that are imposed on specific items such as gasoline, alcoholic beverages, airline tickets, and guns.

Excise taxes are placed on specific items, such as gasoline, alcoholic beverages, cigarettes, airline tickets, cars, and guns. They can be assessed by federal, state, and local governments. In many cases, these taxes help pay for services related to the item taxed. For instance, gasoline excise taxes are often used to build and repair highways. Other excise taxes—like those on alcoholic beverages, cigarettes, and guns—are used to control practices that may cause harm.

KEY TERMS

administrative law
  466
antitrust regulation
  472
appellate courts
  467
arbitration 468
bankruptcy 472
breach of contract
  469
business law 466
common law 466
consumerism 473
contract 468
copyright 470
deregulation 473
express 468
implied contract
  468
income taxes 475
judiciary 467
laws 466
mediation 468
patent 470
payroll taxes 475
product liability
  471
property taxes 475
strict liability 472
trademark 471
trial courts 467
Uniform
  Commercial Code
  (UCC) 466

APPENDIX B: MANAGING RISK AND INSURANCE

Overview

Every day, businesses and individuals are exposed to many different kinds of risk. Investors who buy stocks or speculate in commodities may earn a profit, but they also take the risk of losing all or part of their money. Illness is another type of risk, involving financial loss from not only the cost of medical care but also the loss of income.

Businesses, too, are exposed to many types of risk. Market risks, such as lower demand for a product or worsening economic conditions, can hurt a firm. Other risks involve customers, who could be injured on a company's premises or by a company's product. Like homes and cars owned by individuals, business property can be damaged or lost through fire, floods, and theft. Businesses must also protect themselves against losses from theft by dishonest employees. The loss of a key employee is another risk, especially for small firms.

It is impossible to avoid all risks, but individuals and businesses can minimize risks or buy protection—called insurance—against them. Although some risks are uninsurable, many others are insurable. Let's now look at basic risk concepts and the types of insurance available to cover them.

Risk Management

risk management

Involves analyzing the firm's operations, evaluating potential risks, and figuring out how to minimize losses in a cost-effective manner.

Every business faces risks like the ones listed above. **Risk management** involves analyzing the firm's operations, evaluating the potential risks, and figuring out how to minimize losses in a cost-efficient manner. In today's complex business environment, the concern for public and employee welfare and the potential for lawsuits have both increased. Risk management thus plays a vital role in the overall management of a business.

Types of Risk

risk

The chance of financial loss due to a peril.

speculative risk

The chance of either a loss or a gain.

Individuals and firms need to protect themselves against the economic effects of certain types of risk. In an insurance sense, **risk** (sometimes called *pure risk*) is the chance of financial loss due to a peril. Insurable risks include fire, theft, auto accident, injury or illness, a lawsuit, or death. **Speculative risk** is the chance of either loss or gain. Someone who buys stock in the hope of later selling it at a profit is taking a speculative risk and cannot be insured against it.

Strategies to Manage Risk

risk avoidance

Staying away from the situations that can lead to loss.

Risk is part of life. Nevertheless, people have four major ways to deal with it:

- **Risk avoidance.** Staying away from situations that can lead to loss. A person can avoid the risk of a serious injury by choosing not to go skydiving. Kinder-Care, a nationwide day-care chain, could avoid risk by not transporting children to and from school or taking them on field trips. Manufacturers who wish to avoid risks could produce only goods that have a proven track record. But these risk-avoidance strategies could stifle growth in the long run. Thus risk avoidance is not good for all risks.

self-insurance

The willingness to bear risk without insurance.

- **Self-insurance.** The willingness to bear a risk without insurance, also called *risk assumption*. This offers a more practical way to handle many types of risks. Many large firms with warehouses or stores spread out over the United States—Sears or Kmart, for instance—may choose not to insure them. They assume that, even if disaster strikes one location,

the others won't be harmed. The losses will probably be less than the insurance premiums for all the locations. Many companies self-insure because it is cheaper to assume some risks than to insure against them. Some choose to pay small claims themselves and insure only for catastrophic losses. Others "go naked," paying for all claims from company funds. This is clearly the most risky strategy. A big claim could cripple the firm or lead to bankruptcy.

risk reduction

Adopting techniques to prevent financial losses.

- **Risk reduction.** Adopting techniques to prevent financial losses. For example, companies adopt safety measures to reduce accidents. Construction workers are required to wear hard hats and safety glasses. Airlines keep their aircraft in good condition and require thorough training programs for pilots and flight attendants. Hotels install smoke alarms, sprinkler systems, and firewalls to protect guests and minimize fire damage.

risk transference

Paying someone else to bear some or all of the risk of financial loss for certain risks that can't be avoided, assumed, or reduced to acceptable levels.

- **Risk transference.** Paying someone else to bear some or all of the risk of financial loss for certain risks that can't be avoided, assumed, or reduced to acceptable levels. The way to transfer risk is through **insurance.** Individuals and organizations can pay a fee (a *premium*) and get the promise of compensation for certain financial losses. The companies that take on the risks are called *insurance companies.*

Insurance Concepts

insurance

A promise of compensation for certain financial losses.

Companies purchase insurance to cover insurable risks. An **insurance policy** is the written agreement that defines what the insurance covers and the risks that the insurance company will bear for the insured party. It also outlines the policy's benefits (the maximum amount that it will pay in the event of a loss), and the premium (the cost to the insured for coverage). Any demand for payment for losses covered by the policy is a *claim.*

insurance policies

A written agreement that defines what the insurance covers and the risks that the insurance company will bear for the insured party.

Before issuing a policy, an insurance company reviews the applications of those who want a policy and selects those that meet its standards. This **underwriting** process also determines the level of coverage and the premiums. Each company sets its own underwriting standards based on its experience. For instance, a life insurance company may decide not to accept an applicant who has had a heart attack within five years (or to charge a 50 to 75 percent higher premium). A property insurer may refuse to issue a policy on homes near brush-filled canyons, which present above-average fire hazards.

underwriting

A review process of all insurance applications and the selection of those who meet the standards.

insurable interest

An insurance applicant's chance of loss if a particular peril occurs.

To get insurance, the applicant must have an **insurable interest**—the chance of suffering a loss if a particular peril occurs. In most cases, a person cannot insure the life of a friend, because the friend's death would not be considered a financial loss. But business partners can get life insurance on each other's lives because the death of one of them would have a financial impact on their firm.

Insurable Risks

Insurance companies are professional risk takers, but they won't provide coverage against all types of risk. Some risks are insurable, some are not. For instance, changes in political or economic conditions are not insurable. An **insurable risk** is one that an insurance company will cover. For a risk to be insurable, it must meet these criteria:

insurable risk

A risk that an insurance company will cover. It must meet certain criteria.

- *The loss must not be under the control of the insured.* The loss must be accidental—that is, unexpected and occurring by chance. Insurance companies do not cover losses purposely caused by the insured party. No insurance company will pay for the loss of a clothing store that the insured set on fire. Nor will most companies pay life insurance benefits for a suicide.

law of large numbers

Insurance companies' predictions of the likelihood that a peril will occur in order to calculate premiums.

- *There must be many similar exposures to that peril.* Insurance companies study the rates of deaths, auto accidents, fires, floods, and many other perils. They know about how many of these perils will occur each year. The **law of large numbers** lets them predict the likelihood that the peril will occur and then calculate premiums.

Suppose that an insurance company has 150 policies in Morton, Iowa. The company knows from past experience that these policyholders are likely to have 12 car accidents a year and that the average payment for a claim in Morton has been $1,000. The total claims for one year's car accidents in Morton would be $12,000 (12 accidents × $1,000). Thus the company would charge each policyholder a premium of at least $80 ($12,000 ÷ 150). Profits and administrative expenses would make the premium somewhat higher.

- *Losses must be financially measurable.* The dollar amount of potential losses must be known so the insurance company can figure the premiums. Life insurance is for a fixed amount specified at the time the policy is bought. Otherwise, the company and the *beneficiary* (the one who gets the funds) would have to agree on the value of the deceased's life at the time of death. Premiums have to be calculated before then, however.

- *The peril must not be likely to affect all the insured parties at the same time.* Insurance companies must spread out their risks by insuring many people and businesses in many locations. This strategy helps minimize the chance that a single calamity will wipe out the insurance company.

- *The potential loss must be significant.* Insurance companies cannot afford to insure trivial things for small amounts. Many policies have **deductibles,** amounts that the insured must pay before insurance benefits begin.

- *The company must have the right to set standards for insurance coverage.* Insurance companies can refuse to cover people with health problems like AIDS, cancer or heart trouble, a poor driving record, or a dangerous job or hobby. They can also charge higher premiums because of the higher risks they are covering.

deductibles
The amounts that the insured must pay before insurance benefits begin.

Premium Costs

Insurance policies must be economical—relatively low in cost compared to the benefits—so people will want to buy them. Yet the premiums must also cover the risks that the insurance company faces. Insurance companies collect statistics on many perils. Then specially trained mathematicians called *actuaries* use the law of large numbers to develop actuarial tables. These tables show how likely each peril is. Actuarial tables are the basis for calculating premiums. For example, actuaries use a mortality table showing average life expectancy and the expected number of deaths per 1,000 people at given ages to set life insurance premiums.

Almost every homeowner buys insurance to cover the perils of fire, theft, vandalism, and other home-related risks. With such a large pool of policyholders, homeowners' policies are usually inexpensive. Annual premiums are about 0.5 percent (or less) of the value of the home. This low cost encourages people to buy policies and thereby helps spread the insurance companies' risk over many homes throughout the country.

When setting premiums, insurers also look at the risk characteristics of certain groups, to assess the probability of loss for those groups. For instance, smokers tend to die younger than nonsmokers do and thus pay higher life insurance premiums. Female drivers under the age of 25 have a lower rate of accidents than male drivers, so their car insurance premiums are lower.

Insurance Providers

Insurers can be either public or private. Public insurance coverage is offered by specialized government agencies. The federal government is in fact the largest single insurer in the United States. Private insurance coverage is provided by privately organized (nongovernment) companies.

Public Insurance   Government-sponsored insurance falls into two general categories: social insurance programs and other programs. Social insurance provides protection for problems beyond the scope of private insurers. These programs include:

unemployment insurance
Pays laid-off workers weekly benefits while they seek new jobs.

- *Unemployment insurance.* Every state has an **unemployment insurance** program that pays laid-off workers weekly benefits while they seek new jobs. Persons who terminate their employment voluntarily or are fired for cause are not eligible for unemployment insurance. These programs also provide job counseling and placement services. The benefits usually start a week after a person has lost a job and continue for 26 to 39 weeks, depending on the state. The size of the weekly benefit depends on the workers' previous income and varies from state to state. Unemployment insurance is funded by payroll taxes levied on employers.

workers' compensation
Covers the expenses of job-related injuries and diseases, including medical costs, rehabilitation, and job retraining if necessary.

- *Workers' compensation.* Every state has laws requiring employers to fund **workers' compensation** insurance to cover the expenses of job-related injuries and diseases, including medical costs, rehabilitation, and job retraining if necessary. It also provides disability income benefits (salary and wage payments) for workers who can't perform their job. Employers can buy workers' compensation policies or self-insure. A company's premium is based on the amount of its payroll and the types of risks present in the workplace. For instance, a construction company would pay a higher premium for workers' compensation insurance than would a jewelry store.

Social Security
Insurance that provides retirement, disability, death, and health benefits.

- *Social Security.* **Social Security** insurance provides retirement, disability, death, and health insurance benefits. Social Security is funded by equal contributions from workers and employers. These benefits go mostly to people over 65, although they are available to younger people who are disabled. More than 90 percent of all U.S. workers and their families are eligible to qualify for Social Security benefits.

Medicare
A health insurance program for those over 65.

- *Medicare.* A health insurance program for those over 65, **Medicare** was added to Social Security in 1965 and has two parts: hospital insurance, financed through the Social Security tax, and medical insurance, financed through government contributions and monthly premiums paid by those who want this coverage. Because Medicare pays only part of the insured's medical expenses, many people buy *supplemental insurance* from private insurance companies.

Private Insurance Companies Private insurance companies sell property and liability insurance, health insurance, and life insurance. Life and health insurance companies dominate the industry, accounting for about 70 percent of total assets. Regulation of private insurance companies is under the control of the states and thus varies from state to state.

There are two basic ownership structures for private insurance companies: stockholder and mutual. Just like other publicly owned corporations, *stock insurance companies* are profit-oriented companies owned by stockholders. The stockholders do not have to be policyholders, and the policyholders do not have to be stockholders. Their profits come from insurance premiums in excess of claim payments and operating expenses and from investments in securities and real estate. CIGNA Corporation is the largest stockholder-owned insurance company in the United States, with assets of about $114 billion. Other major stock insurance companies are Aetna, Allstate Insurance, Continental Insurance, Fireman's Fund Insurance, and Metropolitan Life. Of about 5,000 insurance companies in the United States, most are stock insurance companies.

The rest are *mutual insurance companies,* which are not-for-profit organizations owned by their policyholders and chartered by each state. Any excess income is returned to the policyholder-owners as dividends, used to reduce premiums, or retained to finance future operations. The policyholders elect the board of directors, who manage the company. Most of the large life insurance companies in the United States are mutuals, including John Hancock, New York Life, and Northwestern Mutual Life. State Farm, the largest auto insurer, is also a mutual insurance company.

Types of Insurance

Several types of personal insurance coverage exist: property, liability, health, and life. Businesses also purchase insurance for these risks, but with some differences. Most companies offer group health and life insurance plans for their employees as a fringe benefit. Employers typically pay some of the health insurance premiums, and employees pay the rest. The cost is usually considerably less than for individual policies, although it pays to check before signing up. For example, companies may pay for the entire cost of life insurance equal to one or two times the employee's annual salary, with an option to purchase more under the group plan, but the premiums may be more expensive than buying an individual policy.

Businesses often insure the lives of key employees, such as top executives, salespeople, inventors, and researchers, whose death could seriously limit the income or value of a firm. To protect themselves, businesses buy **key-person life insurance**, a term insurance policy that names the company as beneficiary. In the case of a partnership, which is dissolved when a partner dies, key-person insurance is often bought for each partner, with the other partner named as the beneficiary, so that the surviving partner can buy the partnership interest from the estate of the deceased and continue operating.

key-person life insurance
A term insurance policy that names the company as beneficiary.

Property and Liability Insurance

Over 3,500 companies offer property and liability policies. This type of insurance is important for businesses, which wish to protect against losses of property and lawsuits arising from harm to other people.

Property insurance covers financial losses from damage to or destruction of the insured's assets as a result of specified perils, while *liability insurance* covers financial losses from injuries to others and damage to or destruction of others' property when the insured is considered to be the cause. It also covers the insured's legal defense fees up to the maximum amount stated in the policy. Automobile liability insurance is an example. It would pay for a fence damaged when the insured person lost control of his or her car. Commercial and product liability insurance also fall into this category.

Commercial liability insurance covers a variety of damage claims, including harm to the environment from pollution. In the case of *product liability*, if a defective furnace exploded and damaged a home, the manufacturer would be liable for the damages. If the manufacturer were insured, the insurance company would cover the losses or pay to dispute the claim in court.

Property and liability insurance is a broad category. Businesses buy many types of property and liability insurance. These protect against loss of property due to fire, theft, accidents, or employee dishonesty and financial losses arising from liability cases. Landlords and owners of business property buy *building insurance*, a type of property coverage, for protection against both property damage and liability losses. For instance, if a person broke an arm slipping on a wet floor in a hardware store, the business's insurance policy would cover any claim.

Property insurance policies usually include a coinsurance clause. **Coinsurance** requires the property owner to buy insurance coverage equal to a certain percentage of the property's value. To cut premium costs, policyholders often insure buildings for less than their full value, in the hope that a fire or other disaster will damage only part of the property. But insurers limit the payout if the property is underinsured. They use coinsurance clauses as an incentive for businesses to maintain full insurance on their buildings. For instance, some fire insurance policies have an 80 percent coinsurance clause. If the owner of a building valued at $400,000 buys a policy with coverage equal to at least $320,000 (80% × $400,000), he or she will collect the full amount of any partial loss. If the owner buys a policy for less coverage, the insurance company will pay for only part of the partial loss.

coinsurance
Property insurance coverage that is equal to a certain percentage of the property's value.

business interruption insurance

Covers such costs as rental of temporary facilities, wage and salary payments to employees, payments for leased equipment, fixed payments, and profits that would have been earned during that period.

theft insurance

A broad insurance coverage that protects business against losses for an act of stealing.

professional liability insurance

Insurance designed to protect top corporate management, who have been the target of malpractice lawsuits.

KEY TERMS

business interruption insurance 482
coinsurance 481
deductibles 479
insurable interest 478
insurable risk 478
insurance 478
insurance policies 478
key-person life insurance 481
law of large numbers 478
Medicare 480
professional liability insurance 482
risk 477
risk avoidance 477
risk management 477
risk reduction 478
risk transference 478
self-insurance 477
Social Security 480
speculative risk 477
theft insurance 482
underwriting 478
unemployment insurance 480
workers' compensation 480

Special Types of Business Liability Insurance

Businesses also purchase several other types of insurance policies, depending on their particular needs:

- *Business interruption insurance.* This optional coverage is often offered with fire insurance. It protects business owners from losses occurring when the business must be closed temporarily after property damage. **Business interruption insurance** may cover such costs as rental of temporary facilities, wage and salary payments to employees, payments for leased equipment, fixed payments (for instance, rent and loans), and profits that would have been earned during the period. *Contingent business interruption insurance* covers losses to the insured in the event of property damage to a major supplier or customer.

- *Theft insurance.* Businesses also want to protect their property against financial losses due to crime. **Theft insurance** is the broadest coverage and protects businesses against losses from an act of stealing. Businesses can also buy more limited types of theft insurance.

- *Fidelity and surety bonds.* What if a firm has a dishonest employee? This situation is covered by a *fidelity bond,* an agreement that insures a company against theft committed by an employee who handles company money. If a restaurant manager is bonded for $50,000 and steals $60,000, the restaurant will recover all but $10,000 of the loss. Banks, loan companies, and retail businesses that employ cashiers typically buy fidelity bonds.

  A *surety bond,* also called a *performance bond,* is an agreement to reimburse a firm for nonperformance of acts specified in a contract. This form of insurance is most common in the construction industry. Contractors buy surety bonds to cover themselves in case the project they are working on is not completed by the specified date or does not meet specified standards. In practice, the insurance company often pays another contractor to finish the job or to redo shoddy work when the bonded contractor fails to perform.

- *Title insurance.* A title policy protects the buyer of real estate against losses caused by a defect in the title—that is, a claim against the property that prevents the transfer of ownership from seller to purchaser. It eliminates the need to search legal records to be sure that the seller was actually the owner of (had clear title to) the property.

- *Professional liability insurance.* This form of insurance covers financial losses (legal fees and court-awarded damages up to specific limits) resulting from alleged malpractice by professionals in fields like medicine, law, architecture, and dentistry. *Directors and officers insurance* is a type of **professional liability insurance** designed to protect top corporate management, who have also been the target of malpractice lawsuits. It pays for legal fees and court-awarded damages up to specific limits.

absolute advantage The situation when a country can produce and sell a product at a lower cost than any other country or when it is the only country that can provide the product.

accounting The process of collecting, recording, classifying, summarizing, reporting, and analyzing financial activities.

accounts payable Purchase for which a buyer has not yet paid the seller.

accounts receivable Sales for which a firm has not yet been paid.

acid-test (quick) ratio The ratio of total current assets excluding inventory to total current liabilities; used to measure a firm's liquidity.

acquisition The purchase of a corporation by another corporation or by an investor group; the identity of the acquired company may be lost.

activity ratios Ratios that measure how well a firm uses its assets.

administrative distribution system A vertical marketing system in which a strong organization takes over as leader and sets policies for the distribution channel.

administrative law The rules, regulations, and orders passed by boards, commissions, and agencies of government (local, state, and federal).

advertising Any paid form of nonpersonal presentation by an identified sponsor.

advertising media The channels through which advertising is carried to prospective customers; includes newspapers, magazines, radio, television, outdoor advertising, direct mail, and the Internet.

affirmative action programs Programs established by organizations to expand job opportunities for women and minorities.

agents Sales representatives of manufacturers and wholesalers.

angel investors Individual investors or groups of experienced investors who provide funding for start-up businesses.

annual report A yearly document that describes a firm's financial status and usually discusses the firm's activities during the past year and its prospects for the future.

antitrust regulation Laws that prevent companies from entering into agreements to control trade through a monopoly.

appellate courts (courts of appeals) The level of courts above the trial courts; the losing party in a civil case and the defendant in a criminal case may appeal the trial court's decision to an appellate court.

apprenticeship A form of on-the-job training that combines specific job instruction with classroom instruction.

arbitration A method of settling disputes in which the parties agree to present their case to an impartial third party and are required to accept the arbitrator's decision.

assembly process A production process in which the basic inputs are either *combined* to create the output or *transformed* into the output.

assets Things of value owned by a firm.

auditing The process of reviewing the records used to prepare financial statements and issuing a formal *auditor's opinion* indicating whether the statements have been prepared in accordance with accepted accounting rules.

authority Legitimate power, granted by the organization and acknowledged by employees, that allows an individual to request action and expect compliance.

autocratic leaders Directive leaders who prefer to make decisions and solve problems on their own with little input from subordinates.

baby boomers Americans born between 1946 and 1964.

balance of payments A summary of a country's international financial transactions showing the difference between the country's total payments to and its total receipts from other countries.

balance of trade The difference between the value of a country's exports and the value of its imports during a certain time.

balance sheet A financial statement that summarizes a firm's financial position at a specific point in time.

bank charter An operating license issued to a bank by the federal government or a state government; required for a commercial bank to do business.

bankruptcy The legal procedure by which individuals or businesses that cannot meet their financial obligations are relieved of their debt.

barriers to entry Factors, such as technological or legal conditions, that prevent new firms from competing equally with a monopoly.

batch processing A method of updating a database in which data are collected over some time period and processed together.

benefit segmentation The differentiation of markets based on what a product will do rather than on customer characteristics.

bill of material A list of the items and the number of each required to make a given product.

board of directors A group of people elected by the stockholders to handle the overall management of a corporation, such as setting corporate goals and policies, hiring cor-porate officers, and overseeing the firm's operations and finances.

bond ratings Letter grades assigned to bond issues to indicate their quality, or level of risk; assigned by rating agencies such as Moody's and Standard & Poor's.

bonds Long-term debt obligations (liabilities) issued by corporations and governments.

brand A company's product identifier that distinguishes the company's products from those of its competitors.

brand equity The value of company and brand names.

breach of contract The failure by one party to a contract to fulfill the terms of the agreement without a legal excuse.

brokers Go-betweens that bring buyers and sellers together.

business An organization that strives for a profit by providing goods and services desired by its customers.

business cycles Upward and downward changes in the level of economic activity.

business interruption insurance Covers such costs as rental of temporary facilities, wage and salary payments to employees, payments for leased equipment, fixed payments, and profits that would have been earned during that period.

business law The body of law that governs commercial dealings.

business plan A formal written statement that describes in detail the idea for a new business and how it will be carried out; includes a general description of the company, the qualifications of the owner(s), a description of the product or service, an analysis of the market, and a financial plan.

buyer behavior The actions people take in buying and using goods and services.

CAD/CAM systems Linked computer systems that combine the advantages of computer-aided design and computer-aided manufacturing. The system helps design the product, control the flow of resources, and operate the production process.

capital The inputs, such as tools, machinery, equipment, and buildings, used to produce goods and services and get them to the customer.

capital budgeting The process of analyzing long-term projects and selecting those that offer the best returns while maximizing the firm's value.

capital expenditures Investments in long-lived assets, such as land, buildings, machinery, and equipment, that are expected to provide benefits over a period longer than one year.

capital products Large, expensive items with a long life span that are purchased by businesses for use in making other products or providing a service.

capitalism An economic system based on competition in the marketplace and private ownership of the factors of production (resources); also known as the *private enterprise system*.

cash flows The inflow and outflow of cash for a firm.

cash management The process of making sure that a firm has enough cash on hand to pay bills as they come due and to meet unexpected expenses.

centralization The degree to which formal authority is concentrated in one area or level of an organization.

certified management accountant (CMA) A managerial accountant who has completed a professional certification program, including passing an examination.

certified public accountant (CPA) An accountant who has completed an approved bachelor's degree program, passed a test prepared by the American Institute of Certified Public Accountants, and met state requirements. Only a CPA can issue an auditor's opinion on a firm's financial statements.

chain of command The line of authority that extends from one level of an organization's hierarchy to the next, from top to bottom, and makes clear who reports to whom.

chief information officer (CIO) An executive with responsibility for managing all information resources in an organization.

circuit breakers Measures that, under certain conditions, stop trading in the securities markets for a short cooling-off period to limit the amount the market can drop in one day.

circular flow The movement of inputs and outputs among households, businesses, and governments; a way of showing how the sectors of the economy interact.

code of ethics A set of guidelines prepared by a firm to provide its employees with the knowledge of what the firm expects in terms of their responsibilities and behavior toward fellow employees, customers, and suppliers.

coercive power Power that is derived from an individual's ability to threaten negative outcomes.

cognitive dissonance The condition of having beliefs or knowledge that are internally inconsistent or that disagree with one's behavior.

coinsurance Property insurance coverage that is equal to a certain percentage of the property's value.

command economy An economic system characterized by government ownership of virtually all resources and economic decision making by central government planning; also known as *communism*.

commercial banks Profit-oriented financial institutions that accept deposits, make business and consumer loans, invest in government and corporate securities, and provide other financial services.

commercial paper Unsecured short-term debt (an IOU) issued by a financially strong corporation.

committee structure An organizational structure in which authority and responsibility are held by a group rather than an individual.

common law The body of unwritten law that has evolved out of judicial (court) decisions rather than being enacted by a legislature; also called *case law*.

common stock A security that represents an ownership interest in a corporation.

competitive advantage A set of unique features of a company and its products that are perceived by the target market as significant and superior to those of the competition; also called differential advantage.

component lifestyle A lifestyle made up of a complex set of interests and choices.

computer network A group of two or more computer systems linked together by communications channels to share data and information.

computer virus A computer program that copies itself into other software and can spread to other computer systems.

computer-aided design (CAD) The use of computers to design and test new products and modify existing ones.

computer-aided manufacturing (CAM) The use of computers to develop and control the production process.

computer-integrated manufacturing (CIM) The combination of computerized manufacturing processes (like robots and flexible manufacturing systems) with other computerized systems that control design, inventory, production, and purchasing.

conceptual skills A manager's ability to view the organization as a whole, understand how the various parts are interdependent, and assess how the organization relates to its external environment.

conglomerate merger A merger of companies in unrelated businesses; done to reduce risk.

consensual leaders Leaders who encourage discussion about issues and then require that all parties involved agree to the final decision.

consultative leaders Leaders who confer with subordinates before making a decision, but who retain the final decision-making authority.

consumer fraud The practice of deceiving customers by such means as failing to honor warranties or other promises or selling goods or services that do not meet advertised claims.

consumer price index (CPI) An index of the prices of a market basket of goods and services purchased by typical urban consumers.

consumerism A social movement that seeks to increase the rights and powers of buyers vis-à-vis sellers.

contingency plans Plans that identify alternative courses of action for very unusual or crisis situations; typically stipulate the chain of command, standard operating procedures, and communication channels the organization will use during an emergency.

contingent workers Persons who prefer temporary employment, either part-time or full-time.

continuous process A production process that uses long production runs lasting days, weeks, or months without equipment shutdowns; generally used for high-volume, low-variety products with standardized parts.

contract An agreement that sets forth the relationship between parties regarding the performance of a specified action; creates a legal obligation and is enforceable in a court of law.

contract manufacturing The practice in which a foreign firm manufactures private-label goods under a domestic firm's brand name.

contractionary policy The use of monetary policy by the Fed to tighten the money supply by selling government securities or raising interest rates.

contractual distribution system A vertical marketing system in which a network of independ-ent firms at different levels (manufacturer, wholesaler, retailer) coordinate their distribution activities through a written contract.

controlling The process of assessing the organization's progress toward accomplishing its goals; includes monitoring the implementation of a plan and correcting deviations from the plan.

convenience products Relatively inexpensive items that require little shopping effort and are purchased routinely without planning.

conventional ethics The second stage in the ethical development of individuals in which people move from an egocentric viewpoint to consider the expectations of an organization of society.

cooperatives Legal entities typically formed by people with similar interests, such as customers or suppliers, to reduce costs and gain economic power. A cooperative has limited liability, an unlimited life span, an elected board of directors, and an administrative staff; all profits are distributed to the member-owners in proportion to their contributions.

copyright A form of protection established by the government for creators of works of art, music, literature, or other intellectual property; gives the creator the exclusive right to use, produce, and sell the creation during the lifetime of the creator and for 70 years thereafter.

corporate culture The set of attitudes, values, and standards that distinguishes one organization from another.

corporate distribution system A vertical marketing system in which one firm owns the entire distribution channel.

corporate philanthropy The practice of charitable giving by corporations; includes contributing cash, donating equipment and products, and supporting the volunteer efforts of company employees.

corporation A legal entity with an existence and life separate from its owners, who therefore are not personally liable for the entity's debts. A corporation is chartered by the state in which it is formed and can own property, enter into contracts, sue and be sued, and engage in business operations under the terms of its charter.

cost competitive advantage A firm's ability to produce a product or service at a lower cost than all other competitors in an industry while maintaining satisfactory profit margins.

cost of goods sold The total expense of buying or producing a firm's goods or services.

cost per thousand (CPM) Cost per thousand contacts is a term used in expressing advertising costs; refers to the cost of reaching 1,000 members of the target market.

cost-push inflation Inflation that occurs when increases in production costs push up the prices of final goods and services.

costs Expenses incurred in creating and selling goods and services.

countertrade A form of international trade in which part or all of the payment for goods or services is in the form of other goods and services.

credit unions Not-for-profit, member-owned financial cooperatives.

critical path In a critical path method network, the longest path through the linked activities.

critical path method (CPM) A scheduling tool that enables a manager to determine the critical path of activities for a project—the activities that will cause the entire project to fall behind schedule if they are not completed on time.

cross-functional teams Teams of employees who are from about the same level in the organizational hierarchy but from different functional areas; for example, task forces, organizational committees, and project teams.

current assets Assets that can or will be converted to cash within the next 12 months.

current liabilities Short-term claims that are due within a year of the date of the balance sheet.

current ratio The ratio of total current assets to total current liabilities; used to measure a firm's liquidity.

customer departmentalization Departmentalization that is based on the primary type of customer served by the organizational unit.

customer satisfaction The customer's feeling that a product has met or exceeded expectations.

customer value The ratio of benefits to the sacrifice necessary to obtain those benefits, as determined by the customer; reflects the willingness of customers to actually buy a product.

customization The production of goods or services one at a time according to the specific needs or wants of individual customers.

cyclical unemployment Unemployment that occurs when a downturn in the business cycle reduces the demand for labor throughout the economy.

data warehouse An information technology that combines many databases across a whole company into one central database that supports management decision making.

database marketing The creation of a large computerized file of the profiles and purchase patterns of customers and potential customers; usually required for successful micromarketing.

dealer brands Brands that are owned by the wholesaler or retailer rather than the name of the manufacturer.

debt A form of business financing consisting of borrowed funds that must be repaid with interest over a stated time period.

debt ratios Ratios that measure the degree and effect of a firm's use of borrowed funds (debt) to finance its operations.

debt-to-equity ratio The ratio of total liabilities to owners' equity; measures the relationship between the amount of debt financing and the amount of equity financing.

decentralization The process of pushing decision-making authority down the organizational hierarchy.

decision support system (DSS) An interactive, flexible, computerized information system that allows managers to make decisions quickly and accurately; used to conduct sales analyses, forecast sales, evaluate advertising, analyze product lines, and keep tabs on market trends and competitors' actions.

decisional roles A manager's activities as an entrepreneur, resource allocator, conflict resolver, or negotiator.

deductibles The amounts that the insured must pay before insurance benefits begin.

delegation of authority The assignment of some degree of authority and responsibility to persons lower in the chain of command.

demand The quantity of a good or service that people are willing to buy at various prices.

demand curve A graph showing the quantity of a good or service that people are willing to buy at various prices.

demand deposits Money kept in checking accounts that can be withdrawn by depositors on demand.

demand-pull inflation Inflation that occurs when the demand for goods and services is greater than the supply.

democratic leaders Leaders who solicit input from all members of the group and then allow the members to make the final decision through a vote.

demographic segmentation The differentiation of markets through the use of categories such as age, education, gender, income, and household size.

demography The study of people's vital statistics, such as their age, race and ethnicity, and location.

demotion The downgrading or reassignment of an employee to a position with less responsibility.

departmentalization The process of grouping jobs together so that similar or associated tasks and activities can be coordinated.

depreciation The allocation of an asset's original cost to the years in which it is expected to produce revenues.

deregulation The removal of rules and regulations governing business competition.

devaluation A lowering of the value of a nation's currency relative to other currencies.

differential advantage A set of unique features of a product that the target market perceives as important and better than the competition's features.

differential competitive advantage A firm's ability to provide a unique product or service that offers something of value to buyers besides simply a lower price.

direct foreign investment Active ownership of a foreign company or of manufacturing or marketing facilities in a foreign country.

discount rate The interest rate that the Federal Reserve charges its member banks.

distribution centers Warehouses that specialize in changing shipment sizes, rather than in storing goods.

distribution channel The series of marketing entities through which goods and services pass on their way from producers to end users.

distribution strategy The part of the marketing mix that involves deciding how many stores and which specific wholesalers and retailers will handle the product in a geographic area.

diversity Employee differences in age, race and ethnicity, gender, educational background, and work experience.

dividends Payments to stockholders from a corporation's profits.

division of labor The process of dividing work into separate jobs and assigning tasks to workers.

double-entry bookkeeping A method of accounting in which each transaction is recorded as two entries so that two accounts or records are changed.

dumping The practice of charging a lower price for a product in foreign markets than in the firm's home market.

earnings per share (EPS) The ratio of net profit to the number of shares of common stock outstanding; measures the number of dollars earned by each share of stock.

economic growth An increase in a nation's output of goods and services.

economic system The combination of policies, laws, and choices made by a nation's government to establish the systems that determine what goods and services are produced and how they are allocated.

economics The study of how a society uses scarce resources to produce and distribute goods and services.

efficient consumer response (ECR) A method of managing inventory and streamlining the movement of products from supplier to distributor to retailer; relies on electronic data interchange to communicate information such as automatic shipping notifications, invoices, inventory data, and forecasts.

electronic data interchange (EDI) Computer-to-computer exchange of information, including automatic shipping notifications, invoices, inventory data and forecasts; used in efficient consumer response systems.

embargo A total ban on imports or exports of a product.

employee orientation Training that prepares a new employee to perform on the job; includes information about job assignments, work rules, equipment, and performance expectations, as well as about company policies, salary and benefits, and parking.

empowerment The process of giving employees increased autonomy and discretion to make decisions, as well as control over the resources needed to implement those decisions.

enterprise resource planning (ERP) A computerized resource planning system that includes information about the firm's suppliers and customers as well as data generated internally.

entrepreneurs People with vision, drive, and creativity who are willing to take the risk of starting and managing a new business to make a profit or of greatly changing the scope and direction of an existing firm.

environmental scanning The process in which a firm continually collects and evaluates information about its external environment.

equilibrium The point at which quantity demanded equals quantity supplied.

equity A form of business financing consisting of funds raised through the sale of stock in a business.

equity theory A theory of motivation that holds that worker satisfaction is influenced by employees' perceptions about how fairly they are treated compared with their coworkers.

ethics A set of moral standards for judging whether something is right or wrong.

European Union (EU) An organization of 15 European nations (as of 1999) that works to foster political and economic integration in Europe; formerly called the European Community.

exchange The process in which two parties give something of value to each other to satisfy their respective needs.

exchange controls Laws that require a company earning foreign exchange (foreign currency) from its exports to sell the foreign exchange to a control agency, such as a central bank.

excise taxes Taxes that are imposed on specific items such as gasoline, alcoholic beverages, airline tickets, and guns.

exclusive distribution A distribution system in which a manufacturer selects only one or two dealers in an area to market its products.

executive information system (EIS) A management support system that is customized for an individual executive; provides specific information for strategic decisions.

expansionary policy The use of monetary policy by the Fed to increase the growth of the money supply.

expectancy theory A theory of motivation that holds that the probability of an individual acting in a particular way depends on the strength of that individual's belief that the act will have a particular outcome and on whether the individual values that outcome.

expense items Items, purchased by businesses, that are smaller and less expensive than capital products and usually have a life span of less than one year.

expenses The costs of generating revenues.

experiment A marketing research method in which the investigator changes one or more variables—price, packaging, design, shelf space, advertising theme, or advertising expenditures—while observing the effects of these changes on another variable (usually sales).

expert power Power that is derived from an individual's extensive knowledge in one or more areas.

expert system A management support system that gives managers advice similar to what they would get from a consultant; it uses artificial intelligence to enable computers to reason and learn to solve problems in much the same way humans do.

exporting The practice of selling domestically produced goods to buyers in another country.

exports Goods and services sold outside a firm's domestic market.

express contract A contract in which the terms are specified in either written or spoken words.

factoring A form of short-term financing in which a firm sells its accounts receivable outright at a discount to a *factor*.

factors of production The resources used to create goods and services.

federal budget deficit The condition that occurs when the federal government spends more for programs than it collects in taxes.

Federal Deposit Insurance Corporation (FDIC) An independent, quasi-public corporation backed by the full faith and credit of the U.S. government that insures deposits in commercial banks and thrift institutions for up to a ceiling of $100,000 per account.

Federal Reserve System (the Fed) The central banking system of the United States.

financial accounting Accounting that focuses on preparing external financial reports that are used by outsiders such as lenders, suppliers, investors, and government agencies to assess the financial strength of a business.

Financial Accounting Standards Board (FASB) The private organization that is responsible for establishing financial accounting standards in the United States.

financial intermediation The process in which financial institutions act as intermediaries between the suppliers and demanders of funds.

financial management The art and science of managing a firm's money so that it can meet its goals.

financial risk The chance that a firm will be unable to make scheduled interest and principal payments on its debt.

fiscal policy The government's use of taxation and spending to affect the economy.

fixed assets Long-term assets used by a firm for more than a year, such as land, buildings, and machinery.

fixed-position layout A facility arrangement in which the product stays in one place and workers and machinery move to it as needed.

flexible manufacturing system (FMS) A system that combines automated workstations with computer-controlled transportation devices—automatic guided vehicles (AGVs)—that move materials between workstations and into and out of the system.

floating exchange rates A system in which prices of currencies move up and down based upon the demand for and supply of the various currencies.

focus group A group of 8 to 12 participants led by a moderator in an in-depth discussion on one particular topic or concept.

formal organization The order and design of relationships within a firm; consists of two or more people working together with a common objective and clarity of purpose.

four Ps Product, price, promotion, and place (distribution), which together make up the marketing mix.

franchise agreement A contract setting out the terms of a franchising arrangement, including the rules for running the franchise, the services provided by the franchisor, and the financial terms. Under the contract, the franchisee is allowed to use the franchisor's business name, trademark, and logo.

franchisee In a franchising arrangement, the individual or company that sells the goods or services of the franchisor in a certain geographic area.

franchising A form of business organization based on a business arrangement between a *franchisor*, which supplies the product concept, and the *franchisee*, who sells the goods or services of the franchisor in a certain geographic area.

franchisor In a franchising arrangement, the company that supplies the product concept to the franchisee.

free trade The policy of permitting the people of a country to buy and sell where they please without restrictions.

free-rein (laissez-faire) leadership A leadership style in which the leader turns over all authority and control to subordinates.

free-trade zone An area where the nations allow free, or almost free, trade among each other while imposing tariffs on goods of nations outside the zone.

frequency The number of times an individual is exposed to an advertising message.

frictional unemployment Short-term unemployment that is not related to the business cycle.

fringe benefits Indirect compensation such as pensions, health insurance, and vacations.

full employment The condition when all people who want to work and can work have jobs.

functional departmentalization Departmentalization that is based on the primary functions performed within an organizational unit.

futures contracts Legally binding obligations to buy or sell specified quantities of commodities or financial instruments at an agreed-on price at a future date.

Gantt charts Bar graphs plotted on a time line that show the relationship between scheduled and actual production.

general partners Partners who have unlimited liability for all of the firm's business obligations and who control its operations.

general partnership A partnership in which all partners share in the management and profits. Each partner can act on behalf of the firm and has unlimited liability for all its business obligations.

generally accepted accounting principles (GAAP) The financial accounting standards followed by accountants in the United States in preparing financial statements.

Generation X Americans born between 1965 and 1978.

Generation Y Americans born after 1978.

generic products Products that carry no brand name, come in plain containers, and sell for much less than brand-name products.

geographic departmentalization Departmentalization that is based on the geographic segmentation of the organizational units.

geographic segmentation The differentiation of markets by region of the country, city or county size, market density, or climate.

global management skills A manager's ability to operate in diverse cultural environments.

global vision The ability to recognize and react to international business opportunities, be aware of threats from foreign competition, and effectively use international distribution networks to obtain raw materials and move finished products to customers.

goal-setting theory A theory of motivation based on the premise that an individual's intention to work toward a goal is a primary source of motivation.

goods Tangible items manufactured by businesses.

gross domestic product (GDP) The total market value of all final goods and services produced within a nation's borders in a year.

gross profit The amount a company earns after paying to produce or buy its products but before deducting operating expenses.

gross sales The total dollar amount of a company's sales.

group cohesiveness The degree to which group members want to stay in the group and tend to resist outside influences.

Hawthorne effect The phenomenon that employees perform better when they feel singled out for attention or feel that management is concerned about their welfare.

horizontal merger A merger of companies at the same stage in the same industry; done to reduce costs, expand product offerings, or reduce competition.

human relations skills A manager's interpersonal skills that are used to accomplish goals through the use of human resources.

human resource (HR) planning Creating a strategy for meeting future human resource needs.

human resource management The process of hiring, developing, motivating, and evaluating employees to achieve organizational goals.

hygiene factors Extrinsic elements of the work environment that do not serve as a source of employee satisfaction or motivation.

implied contract A contract that depends on the acts and conduct of the parties to show agreement; the terms are not specified in writing or orally.

import quota A limit on the quantity of a certain good that can be imported.

imports Goods and services that are bought from other countries.

income statement A financial statement that summarizes a firm's revenues and expenses and shows its total profit or loss over a period of time.

income taxes Taxes that are based on the income received by businesses and individuals.

industrial distributors Independent wholesalers that buy related product lines from many manufacturers and sell them to industrial users.

inflation The situation in which the average of all prices of goods and services is rising.

informal organization The network of connections and channels of communication based on the informal relationships of individuals inside an organization.

information system (IS) The methods and equipment that provide information about all aspects of a firm's operations.

information technology (IT) The equipment and techniques used to manage and process information.

informational roles A manager's activities as an information gatherer, an information disseminator, or a spokesperson for the company.

infrastructure The basic institutions and public facilities upon which an economy's development depends.

insider trading The use of information that is not available to the general public to make profits on securities transactions.

institutional investors Investment professionals who are paid to manage other people's money.

insurable interest An insurance applicant's chance of loss if a particular peril occurs.

insurable risk A risk that an insurance company will cover. It must meet certain criteria.

insurance A promise of compensation for certain financial losses.

insurance policies A written agreement that defines what the insurance covers and the risks that the insurance company will bear for the insured party.

intangible assets Long-term assets with no physical existence, such as patents, copyrights, trademarks, and goodwill.

integrated marketing communications (IMC) The careful coordination of all promotional activities—media advertising, sales promotion, personal selling, and public relations, as well as direct marketing, packaging, and other forms of promotion—to produce a consistent, unified message that is customer focused.

intensive distribution A distribution system in which a manufacturer tries to sell its products wherever there are potential customers.

interest A fixed amount of money paid by the issuer of a bond to the bondholder on a regular schedule, typically every six months; stated as the *coupon rate*.

intermittent process A production process that uses short production runs to make batches of different products; generally used for low-volume, high-variety products.

International Monetary Fund (IMF) An international organization, founded in 1945, that promotes trade, makes short-term loans to member nations, and acts as a lender of last resort for troubled nations.

interpersonal roles A manager's activities as a figurehead, company leader, or liaison.

intranet An internal corporate-wide area network that uses Internet technology to link employees in many locations and with different types of computers.

intrapreneurs Entrepreneurs who apply their creativity, vision, and risk taking within a large corporation, rather than starting a company of their own.

inventory The supply of goods that a firm holds for use in production or for sale to customers.

inventory management The determination of how much of each type of inventory a firm will keep on hand and the ordering, receiving, storing, and tracking of inventory.

inventory turnover ratio The ratio of cost of goods sold to average inventory; measures the speed with which inventory moves through a firm and is turned into sales.

investment bankers Firms that act as underwriters, buying securities from corporations and governments and reselling them to the public.

job analysis A study of the tasks required to do a particular job well.

job description The tasks and responsibilities of a job.

job enlargement The horizontal expansion of a job by increasing the number and variety of tasks that a person performs.

job enrichment The vertical expansion of a job by increasing the employee's autonomy, responsibility, and decision-making authority.

job fair An event, typically one day, held at a convention center to bring together thousands of job seekers and hundreds of firms searching for employees.

job rotation The shifting of workers from one job to another; also called *cross-training*.

job sharing A scheduling option that allows two individuals to split the tasks, responsibilities, and work hours of one 40-hour-per-week job.

job shop A manufacturing firm that produces goods in response to customer orders.

job specification A list of the skills, knowledge, and abilities a person must have to fill a job.

joint venture An agreement in which a domestic firm buys part of a foreign firm or joins with a foreign firm to create a new entity.

judiciary The branch of government that is responsible for settling disputes by applying and interpreting points of law; consists of the court system.

justice What is considered fair according to the prevailing standards of society; in the twentieth century, an equitable distribution of the burdens and rewards that society has to offer.

just-in-time (JIT) A system in which materials arrive exactly when they are needed for production, rather than being stored on site.

key-person life insurance A term insurance policy that names the company as beneficiary.

knowledge The combined talents and skills of the workforce.

law of large numbers Insurance companies predictions of the likelihood that a peril will occur in order to calculate premiums.

laws The rules of conduct in a society, created and enforced by a controlling authority, usually the government.

layoff A temporary separation of an employee from the organization; arranged by the employer, usually because business is slow.

leadership The process of guiding and motivating others toward the achievement of organizational goals.

leadership style The relatively consistent way that individuals in leadership positions attempt to influence the behavior of others.

lean manufacturing Streamlining production by eliminating steps in the production process that do not add benefits that customers are willing to pay for.

legitimate power Power that is derived from an individual's position in an organization.

leveraged buyout (LBO) A corporate takeover financed by large amounts of borrowed money; can be done by outside investors or by a company's own management.

liabilities What a firm owes to its creditors; also called *debts*.

licensing The legal process whereby a firm agrees to allow another firm to use a manufacturing process, trademark, patent, trade secret, or other proprietary knowledge in exchange for the payment of a royalty.

limited liability company (LLC) A hybrid organization that offers the same liability protection as a corporation but may be taxed as either a partnership or a corporation.

limited partners Partners whose liability for the firm's business obligations is limited to the amount of their investment. They help to finance the business, but do not participate in the firm's operations.

limited partnership A partnership with one or more *general partners*, who have unlimited liability, and one or more *limited partners*, whose liability is limited to the amount of their investment.

line of credit An agreement between a bank and a business that specifies the maximum amount of unsecured short-term borrowing the bank will allow the firm over a given period, typically one year.

line organization An organizational structure with direct, clear lines of authority and communication flowing from the top managers downward.

line positions All positions in the organization directly concerned with producing goods and services and which are directly connected from top to bottom.

line-and-staff organization An organizational structure that includes both line and staff positions.

liquidity The speed with which an asset can be converted to cash.

liquidity ratios Ratios that measure a firm's ability to pay its short-term debts as they come due.

local area network (LAN) A network that connects computers at one site, enabling the computer users to exchange data and share the use of hardware and software from a variety of computer manufacturers.

long-term liabilities Claims that come due more than one year after the date of the balance sheet.

Maastricht Treaty A 1993 treaty concluded by the members of the European Community (now the European Union) that outlines plans for tightening bonds among the members and creating a single market; officially called the Treaty on European Union.

macroeconomics The subarea of economics that focuses on the economy as a whole by looking at aggregate data for large groups of people, companies, or products.

make-or-buy decision The determination by a firm of whether to make its own production materials or buy them from outside sources.

management The process of guiding the development, maintenance, and allocation of resources to attain organizational goals.

management support system (MSS) A dynamic information system that helps managers make decisions by allowing them to analyze data, identify business trends, make forecasts, and model business strategies.

managerial accounting Accounting that provides financial information that managers inside the organization can use to evaluate and make decisions about current and future operations.

managerial hierarchy The levels of management within an organization; typically, includes top, middle, and supervisory management.

manufacturer brands Brands that are owned by national or regional manufacturers and widely distributed; also call *national brands*.

manufacturers' representatives Salespeople who represent noncompeting manufacturers; function as independent agents rather than as salaried employees of the manufacturers.

manufacturing resource planning II (MRPII) A complex computerized system that integrates data from many departments to control the flow of resources and inventory.

market segmentation The process of separating, identifying, and evaluating the layers of a market in order to design a marketing mix.

market structure The number of suppliers in a market.

marketable securities Short-term investments that are easily converted into cash.

marketing The process of discovering the needs and wants of potential buyers and customers and then providing goods and services that meet or exceed their expectations.

marketing concept Identifying consumer needs and then producing the goods or services that will satisfy them while making a profit for the organization.

marketing intermediaries Organizations that assist in moving goods and services from producers to end users.

marketing mix The blend of product offering, pricing, promotional methods, and distribution system that brings a specific group of consumers superior value.

marketing research The process of planning, collecting, and analyzing data relevant to a marketing decision.

Maslow's hierarchy of needs A theory of motivation developed by Abraham Maslow; holds that humans have five levels of needs and act to satisfy their unmet needs. At the base of the hierarchy are fundamental physiological needs, followed in order by safety, social, esteem, and self-actualization needs.

mass customization A manufacturing process in which goods are mass-produced up to a point and then custom tailored to the needs or desires of individual customers.

mass production The ability to manufacture many identical goods at once.

materials requirement planning (MRP) A computerized system of controlling the flow of resources and inventory. A master schedule is used to ensure that the materials, labor, and equipment needed for production are at the right places in the right amounts at the right times.

matrix structure (project management) An organizational structure that combines functional and product departmentalization by bringing together people from different functional areas of the organization to work on a special project.

mechanistic organization An organizational structure that is characterized by a relatively high degree of job specialization, rigid departmentalization, many layers of management, narrow spans of control, centralized decision making, and a long chain of command.

mediation A method of settling disputes in which the parties submit their case to an impartial third party but are not required to accept the mediator's decision.

Medicare A health insurance program for those over 65.

mentoring A form of on-the-job training in which a senior manager or other experienced employee provides job- and career-related information to a protégé.

merchant wholesaler An institution that buys goods from manufacturers (takes ownership) and resells them to businesses, government agencies, other wholesalers, or retailers.

Mercosur A trade agreement among Argentina, Brazil, Paraguay, and Uruguay that eliminates most tariffs among the member nations.

merger The combination of two or more firms to form a new company, which often takes on a new corporate identity.

microeconomics The subarea of economics that focuses on individual parts of the economy such as households or firms.

middle management Managers who design and carry out tactical plans in specific areas of the company.

mission An organization's purpose and reason for existing; its long-term goals.

mission statement A formal document that states an organization's purpose and reason for existing and describes its basic philosophy.

mixed economies Economies that combine several economic systems; for example, an economy where the government owns certain industries but others are owned by the private sector.

monetary policy A government's programs for controlling the amount of money circulating in the economy and interest rates.

money Anything that is acceptable as payment for goods and services.

monopolistic competition A market structure in which many firms offer products that are close substitutes and in which entry is relatively easy.

mortgage loan A long-term loan made against real estate as collateral.

motivating factors Intrinsic job elements that lead to worker satisfaction.

multiculturalism The condition when all major ethnic groups in an area, such as a city, county, or census tract, are about equally represented.

multinational corporations Corporations that move resources, goods, services, and skills across national boundaries without regard to the country in which their headquarters are located.

municipal bonds Bonds issued by states, cities, counties, and other state and local government agencies.

mutual fund A financial service company that pools investors' funds to buy a selection of securities that meet its stated investment goals.

National Association of Securities Dealers Automated Quotation (Nasdaq) system The first electronic-based stock market and the fastest-growing part of the stock market.

national debt The accumulated total of all of the federal government's annual budget deficits.

nationalism A sense of national consciousness that boosts the culture and interests of one country over those of all other countries.

net loss The amount obtained by subtracting all of a firm's expenses from its revenues, when the expenses are more than the revenues.

net profit (net income) The amount obtained by subtracting all of a firm's expenses from its revenues, when the revenues are more than the expenses.

net profit margin The ratio of net profit to net sales; also called *return on sales*. It measures the percentage of each sales dollar remaining after all expenses, including taxes, have been deducted.

net sales The amount left after deducting sales discounts and returns and allowances from gross sales.

net working capital The amount obtained by subtracting total current liabilities from total current assets; used to measure a firm's liquidity.

niche competitive advantage A firm's ability to target and effectively serve a single segment of the market within a limited geographic area.

nonprogrammed decisions Responses to infrequent, unforeseen, or very unusual problems and opportunities where the manager does not have a precedent to follow in decision making.

North American Free Trade Agreement (NAFTA) A 1993 agreement creating a free-trade zone including Canada, Mexico, and the United States.

observation research A marketing research method in which the investigator monitors respondents' actions without interacting directly with the respondents; for example, by using cash registers with scanners.

odd-even (psychological) pricing The strategy of setting a price at an odd number to connote a bargain and at an even number to suggest quality.

office automation system An information system that uses information technology tools such as word processing systems, e-mail systems, cellular phones, pagers, and fax machines, to improve communications throughout an organization.

oligopoly A market structure in which a few firms produce most or all of the output and in which large capital requirements or other factors limit the number of firms.

online (real-time) processing A method of updating a database in which data are processed as they become available.

on-the-job training Training in which the employee learns the job by doing it with guidance from a supervisor or experienced coworker.

open market operations The purchase or sale of U.S. government bonds by the Federal Reserve to stimulate or slow down the economy.

operating expenses The expenses of running a business that are not directly relat-ed to producing or buying its products.

operational planning The process of creating specific standards, methods, policies, and procedures that are used in specific functional ar-

eas of the organization; helps guide and control the implementation of tactical plans.

operations management Management of the production process.

options Contracts that entitle holders to buy or sell specified quantities of common stocks or other financial instruments at a set price during a specified time.

organic organization An organizational structure that is characterized by a relatively low degree of job specialization, loose departmentalization, few levels of management, wide spans of control, decentralized decision making, and a short chain of command.

organization chart A visual representation of the structured relationships among tasks and the people given the authority to do those tasks.

organized stock exchanges Organizations on whose premises securities are resold using an auction-style trading system.

organizing The process of coordinating and allocating a firm's resources in order to carry out its plans.

outsourcing The purchase of items from an outside source rather than making them internally; the assignment of various functions, such as human resources, accounting, or legal work, to outside organizations.

over-the-counter (OTC) market A sophisticated telecommunications network that links dealers throughout the United States and enables them to trade securities.

owners' equity The total amount of investment in the firm minus any liabilities; also called *net worth*.

participative leadership A leadership style in which the leader shares decision making with group members and encourages discussion of issues and alternatives; includes democratic, consensual, and consultative styles.

partnership An association of two or more persons who agree to operate a business together for profit.

patent A form of protection established by the government for inventors; gives an inventor the exclusive right to manufacture, use, and sell an invention for 20 years.

payroll taxes The employer's share of Social Security taxes and federal and state unemployment taxes.

penetration pricing The strategy of selling new products at low prices in the hope of achieving a large sales volume.

pension funds Large pools of money set aside by corporations, unions, and governments for later use in paying retirement benefits to their employees or members.

perfect (pure) competition A market structure in which a large number of small firms sell similar products, buyers and sellers have good information, and businesses can be easily opened or closed.

performance appraisal A comparison of actual performance with expected performance to assess an employee's contributions to the organization.

perpetual inventory A continuously updated list of inventory levels, orders, sales, and receipts.

personal selling A face-to-face sales presentation to a prospective customer.

planning The process of deciding what needs to be done to achieve organizational objectives; identifying when and how it will be done; and determining by whom it should be done.

postconventional ethics The third stage in the ethical development of individuals in which people adhere to the ethical standards of a mature adult and are less concerned about how others view their behavior than about how they will judge themselves in the long run.

power The ability to influence others to behave in a particular way.

preconventional ethics A stage in the ethical development of individuals in which people behave in a childlike manner and make ethical decisions in a calculating, self-centered, selfish way, based on the possibility of immediate punishment or reward.

preferential tariff A tariff that is lower for some nations than for others.

preferred stock An equity security for which the dividend amount is set at the time the stock is issued.

prestige pricing The strategy of increasing the price of a product so that consumers will perceive it as being of higher quality, status, or value.

price skimming The strategy of introducing a product with a high initial price and lowering the price over time as the product moves through its life cycle.

pricing strategy The part of the marketing mix that involves establishing a price for the product based on the demand for the product and the cost of producing it.

primary data Information collected directly from the original source to solve a problem.

primary market The securities market where *new* securities are sold to the public.

principal The amount borrowed by the issuer of a bond; also called *par value*.

principle of comparative advantage The concept that each country should specialize in the products that it can produce most readily and cheaply and trade those products for those that other countries can produce more readily and cheaply.

private accountants Accountants who are employed to serve one particular organization.

problem-solving teams Teams of employees from the same department or area of expertise and from the same level of the organizational hierarchy who meet regularly to share information and discuss ways to improve processes and procedures in specific functional areas.

process departmentalization Departmentalization that is based on the production process used by the organizational unit.

process layout A facility arrangement in which work flows according to the production process. All workers performing similar tasks are grouped together, and products pass from one workstation to another.

process manufacturing A production process in which the basic input is *broken down* into one or more outputs (products).

producer price index (PPI) An index of the prices paid by producers and wholesalers for various commodities such as raw materials, partially finished goods, and finished products.

product In marketing, any good or service, along with its perceived attributes and benefits, that creates value for the customer.

product (assembly-line) layout A facility arrangement in which workstations or departments are arranged in a line with products moving along the line.

product departmentalization Departmentalization that is based on the goods or services produced or sold by the organizational unit.

product liability The responsibility of manufacturers and sellers for defects in the products they make and sell.

product life cycle The pattern of sales and profits over time for a product or product category; consists of an introductory stage, growth stage, maturity, and decline (and death).

product strategy The part of the marketing mix that involves choosing a brand name, packaging, colors, a warranty, accessories, and a service program for the product.

production The creation of products and services by turning inputs, such as natural resources, raw materials, human resources, and capital, into outputs, products and services.

production orientation An approach in which a firm works to lower production costs without a strong desire to satisfy the needs of customers.

production planning The aspect of operations management in which the firm considers the competitive environment and its own strategic goals in an effort to find the best production methods.

production process The way a good is made.

productivity The amount of goods and services one worker can produce.

professional liability insurance Insurance designed to protect top corporate management, who have been the target of malpractice lawsuits.

profit The money left over after all expenses are paid.

profitability ratios Ratios that measure how well a firm is using its resources to generate profit and how efficiently it is being managed.

program evaluation and review technique (PERT) A scheduling tool that is similar to the CPM method but assigns three time estimates for each activity (optimistic, most probable, and pessimistic); allows managers to anticipate delays and potential problems and schedule accordingly.

programmed instruction A form of computer-assisted off-the-job training.

promotion strategy The part of the marketing mix that involves personal selling, advertising, public relations, and sales promotion of the product.

promotion An upward move in an organization to a position with more authority, responsibility, and pay; the attempt by marketers to inform, persuade, or remind consumers and industrial users to engage in the exchange process.

promotional mix The combination of advertising, personal selling, sales promotion, and public relations used to promote a product.

property taxes Taxes that are imposed on real and personal property based on the assessed value of the property.

protected classes The specific groups who have legal protection against employment discrimination; include women, African Americans, Native Americans, and others.

protectionism The policy of protecting home industries from outside competition by establishing artificial barriers such as tariffs and quotas.

protective tariffs Tariffs that are imposed in order to make imports less attractive to buyers than domestic products are.

psychographic segmentation The differentiation of markets by personality or lifestyle.

public accountants Independent accountants who serve organizations and individuals on a fee basis.

public relations Any communication or activity designed to win goodwill or prestige for a company or person.

publicity Information about a company or product that appears in the news media and is not directly paid for by the company.

purchasing The process of buying production inputs from various sources; also called *procurement*.

purchasing power The value of what money can buy.

pure monopoly A market structure in which a single firm accounts for all industry sales and in which there are barriers to entry.

quality control The process of creating standards for quality and then measuring finished products and services against them.

quality of life The general level of human happiness based on such things as life expectancy, educational standards, health, sanitation, and leisure time.

ratio analysis The calculation and interpretation of financial ratios taken from the firm's financial statements in order to assess its condition and performance.

reach The number of different target consumers who are exposed to a commercial at least once during a specific period, usually four weeks.

recession A decline in GDP that lasts for at least two consecutive quarters.

recruitment The attempt to find and attract qualified applicants in the external labor market.

reengineering The complete redesign of business structures and processes in order to improve operations.

referent power Power that is derived from an individual's personal charisma and the respect and/or admiration the individual inspires.

relationship management The practice of building, maintaining, and enhancing interactions with customers and other parties in order to develop long-term satisfaction through mutually beneficial partnerships.

relationship marketing A strategy that focuses on forging long-term partnerships with customers by offering value and providing customer satisfaction.

reserve requirement Requires banks that are members of the Federal Reserve System to hold some of their deposits in cash in their vaults or in an account at a district bank.

resignation A permanent separation of an employee from the organization, done voluntarily by the employee.

retailers Firms that sell goods to consumers and to industrial users for their own consumption.

retained earnings The amounts left over from profitable operations since the firm's beginning; equal to total profits minus all dividends paid to stockholders; profits that have been reinvested in a firm.

retirement The separation of an employee from the organization at the end of his or her career.

return The opportunity for profit.

return on equity (ROE) The ratio of net profit to total owners' equity; measures the return that owners receive on their investment in the firm.

revenue The money a company earns from providing services or selling goods to customers.

revenues The dollar amount of a firm's sales plus any other income it received from sources such as interest, dividends, and rents.

revolving credit agreement A guaranteed line of credit whereby a bank agrees that a certain amount of funds will be available for a business to borrow over a given period.

reward power Power that is derived from an individual's control over rewards.

risk The potential to lose time and money or otherwise not be able to accomplish an organization's goals; the chance that an investment will not achieve the expected level of return.

risk avoidance Staying away from the situations that can lead to loss.

risk management The process of identifying and evaluating risks and selecting and managing techniques to adapt to risk exposures.

risk reduction Adopting techniques to prevent financial losses.

risk transference Paying someone else to bear some or all of the risk of financial loss for certain risks that can't be avoided, assumed, or reduced to acceptable levels.

risk-return trade-off A basic principle in finance that holds that the higher the risk, the greater the return that is required.

robotics The technology involved in designing, constructing, and operating (computer-controlled machines that can perform tasks independently).

routing The aspect of production control that involves setting out the work flow—the sequence of machines and operations through which the product or service progresses from start to finish.

S corporation A hybrid entity that is organized like a corporation, with stockholders, directors, and officers, but taxed like a partnership, with income and losses flowing through to the stockholders and taxed as their personal income.

sales promotions Marketing events or sales efforts—not including advertising, personal selling, and public relations—that stimulate buying.

sales prospects The companies and people who are most likely to buy a seller's offerings.

sales taxes Taxes that are levied on goods when they are sold; calculated as a percentage of the price.

savings bonds Government bonds of relatively small denominations.

scheduling The aspect of production control that involves specifying and controlling the time required for each step in the production process.

scientific management A system of management developed by Frederick W. Taylor and based on four principles: developing a scientific approach for each element of a job, scientifically selecting and training workers, encouraging cooperation between workers and managers, and dividing work and responsibility between management and workers according to who can better perform a particular task.

seasonal unemployment Unemployment that occurs during specific seasons in certain industries.

secondary data Information that has already been collected for a project other than the current one, but which may be used to solve the current problem.

secondary market The securities market where (already issued) old securities are traded among investors; includes the organized stock exchanges, the over-the-counter market, and the commodities exchanges.

secured loans Loans for which the borrower is required to pledge specific assets as collateral, or security.

securities Investment certificates issued by corporations or governments that represent either equity or debt.

selection The process of determining which persons in the applicant pool possess the qualifications necessary to be successful on the job.

selection interview An in-depth discussion of an applicant's work experience, skills and abilities, education, and career interests.

selective credit controls The power of the Federal Reserve to control *consumer credit rules* and *margin requirements*.

selective distribution A distribution system in which a manufacturer selects a limited number of dealers in an area (but more than one or two) to market its products.

self-insurance The willingness to bear risk without insurance.

self-managed work teams Highly autonomous teams of employees who manage themselves without any formal supervision and take responsibility for setting goals, planning and scheduling work activities, selecting team members, and evaluating team performance.

separation The departure of an employee from the organization; can be a layoff, termination, resignation, or retirement.

servicemark A symbol, name, or design that identifies a service rather than a tangible object.

services Intangible offerings of businesses that can't be held, touched, or stored.

shopping products Items that are bought after considerable planning, including brand-to-brand and store-to-store comparisons of price, suitability, and style.

small business A business that is independently owned, is owned by an individual or a small group of investors, is based locally, and is not a dominant company in its industry.

Small Business Administration (SBA) A government agency that helps people start and manage small businesses, helps small business owners win federal contracts, and speaks on behalf of small business.

Small Business Investment Company (SBIC) Privately owned and managed investment companies that are licensed by the Small Business Administration and provide long-term financing for small businesses.

social investing The practice of limiting investments to securities of companies that behave in accordance with the investor's beliefs about ethical and social responsibility.

social marketing The application of marketing techniques to social issues and causes.

social responsibility The concern of businesses for the welfare of society as a whole; consists of obligations beyond those required by law or contracts.

Social Security Insurance that provides retirement, disability, death, and health benefits.

socialism An economic system in which the basic industries are owned either by the government itself or by the private sector under strong government control.

sole proprietorship A business that is established, owned, operated, and often financed by one person.

span of control The number of employees a manager directly supervises; also called *span of management*.

specialization The degree to which tasks are subdivided into smaller jobs.

specialty products Items for which consumers search long and hard and for which they refuse to accept substitutes.

speculative risk The chance of either a loss or a gain.

staff positions Positions in an organization held by individuals who provide the administrative and support services that line employees need to achieve the firm's goals.

stakeholders Individuals or groups to whom a business has a responsibility; include employees, customers, the general public, and investors.

standard of living A country's output of goods and services that people can buy with the money they have.

statement of cash flows A financial statement that provides a summary of the money flowing into and out of a firm.

statutory law Written law enacted by a legislature (local, state, or federal).

stock dividends Payments to stockholders in the form of more stock; may replace or supplement cash dividends.

stockbroker A person who is licensed to buy and sell securities on behalf of clients.

stockholders The owners of a corporation, who hold shares of stock that provide certain rights; also known as *shareholders*.

strategic alliance A cooperative agreement between business firms; sometimes called a strategic partnership.

strategic giving The practice of tying philanthropy closely to the corporate mission or goals and targeting donations to regions where a company operates.

strategic planning The process of creating long-range (one to five years), broad goals for the organization and determining what resources will be needed to accomplish those goals.

strict liability A concept in product-liability law under which a manufacturer or seller is liable for any personal injury or property damage caused by defective products or packaging even though all possible care was used to prevent such defects.

structural unemployment Unemployment that is caused by a mismatch between available jobs and the skills of available workers in an industry or region; not related to the business cycle.

supervisory management Managers who design and carry out operation plans for the ongoing daily activities of the firm.

supply The quantity of a good or service that businesses will make available at various prices.

supply chain The entire sequence of securing inputs, producing goods, and delivering goods to customers.

supply chain management The process of smoothing transitions along the supply chain so that the firm can satisfy its customers with quality products and services; focuses on developing tighter bonds with suppliers.

supply curve A graph showing the quantity of a good or service that a business will make available at various prices.

survey research A marketing research method in which an interviewer interacts with respondents, either in person, by mail, at a mall, or through the Internet to obtain facts, opinions, and attitudes.

tactical planning The process of beginning to implement a strategic plan by addressing issues of coordination and allocating resources to different parts of the organization; has a shorter time frame (less than one year) and more specific objectives than strategic planning.

target market The specific group of consumers toward which a firm directs its marketing efforts.

tariff A tax imposed on imported goods.

technical skills A manager's specialized areas of knowledge and expertise, as well as the ability to apply that knowledge.

technology The application of science and engineering skills and knowledge to solve production and organizational problems.

telecommuting An arrangement in which employees work at home and are linked to the office by phone, fax, and computer.

term loan A business loan with a maturity of more than one year; can be unsecured or secured.

termination A permanent separation of an employee from the organization, arranged by the employer.

test-marketing The process of testing a new product among potential users.

theft insurance A broad insurance coverage that protects business against losses for an act of stealing.

Theory X A management style, formulated by Douglas McGregor, that is based on a pessimistic view of human nature and assumes that the average person dislikes work, will avoid it if possible, prefers to be directed, avoids responsibility, and wants security above all.

Theory Y A management style, formulated by Douglas McGregor, that is based on a relatively optimistic view of human nature; assumes that the average person wants to work, accepts responsibility, is willing to help solve problems, and can be self-directed and self-controlled.

thrift institutions Depository institutions formed specifically to encourage household saving and to make home mortgage loans.

time deposits Deposits at a bank or other financial institution that pay interest but cannot be withdrawn on demand.

top management The highest level of managers; includes CEOs, presidents, and vice-presidents, who develop strategic plans and address long-range issues.

tort A civil, or private, act that harms other people or their property.

total quality management (TQM) The use of quality principles in all aspects of a company's production and operations.

trade credit The extension of credit by the seller to the buyer between the time the buyer receives the goods or services and when it pays for them.

trade deficit An unfavorable balance of trade that occurs when a country imports more than it exports.

trade surplus A favorable balance of trade that occurs when a country exports more than it imports.

trademark The legally exclusive design, name, or other identifying mark associated with a company's brand.

training and development Activities that provide learning situations in which an employee acquires additional knowledge or skills to increase job performance.

transaction processing system (TPS) An information system that handles the daily business operations of a firm. The system receives and organizes raw data from internal and external sources for storage in a database.

transfer A horizontal move in an organization to a position with about the same salary and at about the same organizational level.

trial courts The lowest level of courts, where most cases begin; also called *courts of general jurisdiction*.

underwriting The process of buying securities from corporations and governments and reselling them to the public; the main activity of investment bankers; a review process of all insurance applications and the selection of those who meet the standards.

unemployment insurance Pays laid-off workers weekly benefits while they seek new jobs.

unemployment rate The percentage of the total labor force that is actively looking for work but is not actually working.

Uniform Commercial Code (UCC) A model set of rules that apply to commercial transactions between businesses and between businesses and individuals; has been adopted by all states except Louisiana, which uses only part of it.

unsecured loans Short-term loans for which the borrower does not have to pledge specific assets as security.

unsought products Products that either are unknown to the potential buyer or are known but the buyer does not actively seek them.

Uruguay Round A 1994 agreement by 117 nations to lower trade barriers worldwide.

utilitarianism A philosophy that focuses on the consequences of an action to determine whether it is right or wrong; holds that an action that affects the majority adversely is morally wrong.

variable pay A system of paying employees in which a portion of an employee's pay is directly linked to an individual or organizational performance measure.

venture capital Financing obtained from investment firms that specialize in financing small, high-growth companies and receive an ownership interest and a voice in management in return for their money.

vertical marketing system An organized, formal distribution channel in which firms are aligned in a hierarchy from manufacturer to wholesaler to retailer.

vertical merger A merger of companies at different stages in the same industry; done to gain control over supplies of resources or to gain access to different markets.

vestibule training A form of off-the-job training in which trainees learn in a scaled-down version or simulated work environment.

virtual corporation A network of independent companies linked by information technology to share skills, costs, and access to one another's markets; allows the companies to come together quickly to exploit rapidly changing opportunities.

volume segmentation The differentiation of markets based on the amount of the product purchased.

wholesalers Firms that sell finished goods to retailers, manufacturers, and institutions.

wide area network (WAN) A network that connects computers at different sites via telecommunications media such as phone lines, satellites, and microwaves.

work groups Groups of employees who share resources and coordinate efforts so as to help members better perform their individual duties and responsibilities. The performance of the group can be evaluated by adding up the contributions of the individual group members.

work teams Groups of employees who not only coordinate their efforts, but also collaborate by pooling their knowledge, skills, abilities, and resources in a collective effort to attain a common goal; causing the performance of the team to be greater than the sum of the members' individual efforts.

workers' compensation Covers the expenses of job-related injuries and diseases, including medical costs, rehabilitation, and job retraining if necessary.

World Bank An international bank that offers low-interest loans, as well as advice and information, to developing nations.

World Trade Organization (WTO) An organization established by the Uruguay Round in 1994 to oversee international trade, reduce trade barriers, and resolve disputes among member nations.

PROLOGUE NOTES

1. "2 Dockers Away," *The Globe and Mail* (April 23, 1998), p. C9.
2. "Wives Earn More of Family Income, Stay Home Less," *Fort Worth Star Telegram* (September 30, 1998), p. A5.
3. "Retooling for Buying Power of '90s Women," *The Plain Dealer* (August 18, 1998), p. 3C.
4. Ibid.
5. Melinda Beck, "Next Population Bulge Shows Its Might," *Wall Street Journal* (February 2, 1997), pp. B1, B6.
6. J. Walker Smith, "Beyond Rocking the Ages," *American Demographics* (May 1998), pp. 45–50.
7. "Influx of Immigrants Benefits American Economy Overall," *Fort Worth Star Telegram* (May 18, 1997), p. A18.
8. "The Next Wave," *Business Week* (August 31, 1998), pp. 80–83.
9. "Two Steps Forward, One Step Back," *Business Week* (August 31, 1998), p. 116.
10. "It Was a Hit in Buenos Aires—So Why Not Boise?" *Business Week* (September 7, 1998), pp. 56–58.
11. Ibid.

CHAPTER 1 NOTES

1. Brandon Mitchener, "Can Daimler's Tiny Swatchmobile Sweep Europe?" *Wall Street Journal* (October 2, 1998), pp. B1, B4.
2. John Daniels and Lee Radebaugh, *International Business*, 8th ed. (Reading, Mass.: Addison-Wesley, 1998), p. 153.
3. Jennifer Kushnell, "Minding Their Own Business," *Brandweek* (February 9, 1998), pp. 28–32.
4. Ibid.
5. Lester Thurow, "Changing the Nature of Capitalism," in *Rethinking the Future*, ed. Rowan Gibson (London: Nicholas Brealey, 1997), p. 228; also see Thomas Stewart, "Knowledge, the Appreciating Commodity," *Fortune* (October 12, 1998), pp. 199–200.
6. "Unemployment Rate Breaks 4 percent Barrier for the First Time in Over Three Decades," *White House Press Release* (May 5, 2000).
7. "Unemployment Held Down Despite Layoffs," *South China Morning Post* (June 6, 1998), p. 4.
8. "Governor's Task Force Recommends High-Tech Tools in Employee Training and Education to Meet 21st Century Demands," *Business Week* (March 11, 1998), pp. 1–2.

9. Louis Tong, "Consumerism Sweeps the Mainland," *Marketing Management* (Winter 1998), pp. 32–36.
10. "The Amazing Mr. Kuok," *Forbes* (July 28, 1998), pp. 90–98.
11. Ibid.
12. "Revolution in Reverse," *Sydney Morning Herald* (September 27, 1997), p. 6.
13. "Russia's 'Peoples Capitalism' Benefiting Only the Elite; Big Tycoons Squeeze Out Small Business," *Washington Post* (December 28, 1997), p. AO1.

Making Ethical Choices sources: Adapted from P. Dodson, "Prices Show Dramatic Rise," *South Bend Tribune*, March 20, 1999 pp. A1, A10; and B. Stanley, "Pump Prices Up; Supply Cuts Anticipated," *South Bend Tribune*, (March 23, 1999) pp. A1, A8.

Focusing on Small Business source: Republished with permission of the *Wall Street Journal*, from "Microcredit Arrives in Africa, But Can It Match Asian Success," by Ken Wells, September 29, 1998, pp. A1, A15; permission conveyed through Copyright Clearance Center.

Creative Thinking Case source: Glen R. Simpson and John Simons, "A Little Internet Firm Got a Big Monopoly; Is That Such a Bad Thing?" *Wall Street Journal*, (October 8, 1998), pp. A1, A6.

Video Case sources: Adapted from material contained on the following Internet sites: "Awards & Sponsorships," **http://www.mercedescenter.com/black/information-awards.html;** "Meet Our Departments," **http://www.mercedescenter.com/black/information-departments.html;** and "Our History," **http://www.mercedecenter.com/black/information-history.html;** and from material in the video: *A Case Study in Customer Value and Satisfaction: Mercedes-Benz.*

CHAPTER 2 NOTES

1. Anne Swardson, "Wal-Mart Off to a Slow Start in Germany," *Washington Post* (March 25, 2000).
2. "Gillette Won't Meet Profit-Growth Goal While Emerging Markets Face Turmoil," *Wall Street Journal* (September 30, 1998), pp. A3, A8.
3. "Salty Snack Attack on Europe," *Financial Times* (February 2, 1998), p. 13.
4. Charles Lamb, Joe Hair, and Carl McDaniel, *Essentials of Marketing* (Cincinnati: South-Western Publishing Company 1999), p. 55.
5. "Secretary of Commerce William Daley Recognizes U.S. Companies

for Excellence in Exporting," *U.S. Department of Commerce Press Release* (December 17, 1997).
6. Figure projected by authors from **www.gov/foreign-trade/Press-Release/current_press_release/exhl.txt** on August 22, 2000.
7. "Overview of the Economy," *Bureau of Economic Analysis* from **www.bea.doc.gov** (August 22, 2000).
8. "Russian Devaluation a High Stakes Gamble," *The Financial Post* (August 18, 1998), p. 9.
9. "Clinton Signs Africa-Caribbean Trade Benefits into Law," Dow Jones Newswire (May 18, 2000).
10. "United States Anti-Dumping Laws Hook Many Countries," *Miami Herald* (July 27, 1998), p. 3–19.
11. "World Band Report: Focus on Acquiring Knowledge: Information Gaps Help Cause Crisis," *Bangkok Post* (October 13, 1998), p. A1.
12. "Ambassador: NAFTA Works, We Just Need to Tell People," *Orlando Sentinel* (October 2, 1998), p. A14.
13. See Kent Granzin, John Painter, Jeffrey Brazell, and Janeen Olsen, "Public Support for Free Trade Agreements," *Journal of Macromarketing* (Spring 1998), pp. 11–23.
14. Masuaki Kotabe and Maria de Arruda, "South America's Free Trade Gambit," *Marketing Management* (Spring 1998), pp. 38–46.
15. *Opportunities in Exporting* (Washington, D.C.: Small Business Administration Office of International Trade, 1998) p. 2.
16. "International Trading Partners Help Small Wisconsin Firms Grow," *Knight Ridder Tribune Business News* (March 23, 1998), p. 15.
17. "Trouble Underneath the Arches," *Australian Financial Review* (March 9, 1998), p. 14.
18. "E*Trade Signs Second International Joint Venture Agreement in Seven Days; U.K. Joint Venture Follows Entry into Japanese Market," *PR Newswire* (June 11, 1998).
19. "Kodak Quickly Develops Deal to Purchase State-Owned Firms," *Journal of Commerce* (October 1, 1998), pp. 1C–3C.
20. "Barter Grows as Trade Deals Hit Problems," *Financial Times* (September 17, 1998), p. O7.
21. "France Rejects Coca-Cola's Purchase of Orangina," *Wall Street Journal* (September 18, 1998), p. A3.
22. "The Stateless Corporation," *Business Week* (May 14, 1990), p. 99.
23. Hal Lancaster, "Global Managers Need Boundless Sensitivity, Rugged

Constitutions," *Wall Street Journal* (October 13, 1998), p. B1.

Focusing on Small Business source: Michael White, "Small American Business Scrambles for Success in China," Associated Press Business News (on-line), September 10, 1998 at 17:53 EDT.

Making Ethical Choices sources: C. Adams, "Trade Secrets; Steelmakers Complain about Foreign Steel; They Also Import It," *Wall Street Journal* (March 22, 1999): pp. A1 & A11.

Creative Thinking Case source: Gautam Naik, "Inventor's Adjustable Glasses Could Spark Global Correction," *Wall Street Journal* (October 14, 1998), pp. B1, B4.

Video Case source: Adapted from material contained on the following Internet sites: **www.autocite.com/;** **http://208.240.91.101/main/conference/** or **199/exh_99.htm;** and from material in the video: *Global Strategy: A Study of ETEC.*

CHAPTER 3 NOTES

1. Greg Jaffe, "Miami Airport's Lack of Luggage Carts Is Cause for Carrying On," *Wall Street Journal* (November 2, 1998), pp. A1, A22; and "Lobbyists Play a Key Role in Operation of Miami International Airport," *The Miami Herald* (October 17, 1999).
2. The section "Individual Rights" is from John Jackson, Roger Leroy Miller, and Shawn Miller, *Business and Society Today* (Cincinnati: International Thomson Publishing Company, 1997), pp. 92–93.
3. The concept of "Justice" is from John Jackson et al. pp. 89–90.
4. Milton Borden, "The Three R's of Ethics," *Management Review* (June 1998), pp. 59–61.
5. Marianne Moody Jennings, *Case Studies in Business Ethics,* 2d. ed. (St. Paul: West Publishing Company, 1997), pp. xx–xxiii.
6. Ibid.
7. L. S. Berger, "Train All Employees to Solve Ethical Dilemmas," *Life-Health Insurance Edition* (March 1, 1998), p. 70.
8. Jennings, *Case Studies,* p. 11.
9. Margaret Ann Cleek and Sherry Lynn Leonard, "Can Corporate Codes of Ethics Influence Behavior?" *Journal of Business Ethics* (April 1998), pp. 619–630.
10. "3 Out of 4 Say They Have Not Faced Ethical Dilemma at Work," *New York Times* (October 26, 1998), p. 10D.
11. Charles Lamb, Joe Hair, Carl McDaniel, *Essentials of Marketing* (Cincinnati: South-Western College Publishing Co., 1999), pp. 46–47.
12. "Pollution Fine Hits Cruise Line," *Orlando Sentinel* (September 17, 1998), p. B1.
13. "Louisiana-Pacific To Pay Pollution Fines," *Los Angeles Times* (May 28, 1998), p. D3.
14. "Effect of Tobacco Maker's $60 Million Effort Lingers On," *Advertising Age* (September 21, 1998), p. 18.
15. "Third Annual Lucent Technologies 'Global Days of Caring' Set," *PR Newswire* (September 24, 1998), pp. 1–4.
16. "IOMEGA Agrees to Improve Customer Support," *Business* (March 4, 1998), pp. 1–2.
17. Karen Krouse, "Computer School Hit With State Fraud Suit; Students Accuse of Unrealistic Claims," *Chicago Tribune* (March 11, 1998), p. 1.
18. Curt Weeden, "Corporate Social Investing," *Journal of Commerce* (September 23, 1998), p. 6A.
19. "Bittersweet Charity," *Industry Week* (September 7, 1998), pp. 16–20.
20. "The Only Way to Stay Ahead," *Industry Week* (August 17, 1998), pp. 98–102.
21. "Bittersweet," . . . . p. 19.
22. Ibid.
23. Karl Schoenberger, "Human Rights: The Firm Should Clarify Its Reentry Into the Nation and Set a Code of Conduct for Multinationals," *Los Angeles Times* (April 20, 1998), p. B5.

Applying Technology source: "Hey, You! Back to Work," *Seattle Times* (October 17, 1998), p. A15.

Focusing on Small Business source: Thomas Love, "Taking the Ethical Temperature of Entrepreneurs and Managers," *Nations Business* (September 1998), p. 12.

Making Ethical Choices sources: J. Versau, "At Costas, Profits Drive the Bottom Line, But Values Start at the Top," *The Times* (December 25, 1997), pp. D1, D2; J. Versau, "Being Good for Goodness' Sake: Striking a Balance between Value-Free Management and Paying Heed to Ethics Is a Challenge to Businesses Worldwide," *The Times* (December 25, 1997), pp. D1, D5.

Creative Thinking Case source: Yumiko Ono, "Seeking Adventure, Girl Scouts Hike to the Mall," *Wall Street Journal* (August 17, 1998), pp. B1, B4.

Video Case source: Adapted from material contained on the following Internet sites: "Bank of Alma Mission," "CEO's Message," "History and Over-view," "and Products & Services," links at **www.firstbank-alma.com/ban...**/; and from material in the video: *Business Environment: A Study of Healthcare and Central Michigan Community Hospital.*

CHAPTER 4 NOTES

1. David D'Addio, "Job Search Ends Up Creating New Jobs," Pittsburgh Post-Direct (July 15, 1998), downloaded from **www.post-gazette.com;** Carlye Adler, "Have Resumes, Will Travel," *Business Week, Enterprise* section (May 25, 1998), p. ENT 18; Robert E. Ford, President, Job-Direct, telephone interview, January 6, 1999; JobDirect Web site, **www.jobdirect.com.**
2. Carreen Maloney-Monro, "For Starters, Small Firms Don't Need Big Problems," *San Diego Union-Tribune* (April 19, 1998), Electric Library, Business Edition, downloaded from **business.elibrary.com;** and personal interview with Gail Cecil, January 1, 1999.
3. Jerry Useem, "Partners on the Edge," *Inc.* (August 1998), pp. 52–64.
4. Ibid.
5. "National Cooperative Bank Releases NCB Co-op 100," National Cooperative Bank press release (October 5, 1998), downloaded from **www.ncb.com;** and "The Coop Home Page—Coop Primer," downloaded January 13, 1999, from **www.ncba.org/primer.htm.**
6. Jane Seccombe, "Doing It Best Independent Store Holds Its Own," *Greensboro News & Record* (December 30, 1998), Electric Library, Business Edition, downloaded from **business.elibrary.com.**
7. Chieh Chieng, "Do You Want to Know a Secret?" *Entrepreneur* (January 1999), pp. 177–178.
8. Mark Hamstra, "Diedrich Coffee Inks Franchisee Deal with Taco Bell," *Nation's Restaurant News* (September 28, 1998), Electric Library, Business Edition, downloaded from **business.elibrary.com;** and Greg Hardesty, "Diedrich Inks Deal to Open on East Coast," *The Orange County Register* (September 17, 1998), Electric Library, Business Edition, downloaded from **business.elibrary.com.**
9. *Profile of Franchising:* vol. 1—*Fact Sheet,* press release from the IFA Educational Foundation (November 9, 1998).
10. Alf Nucifora, "Franchising Stays Hot as Millennium Approaches,"

Jacksonville Business Journal (June 26, 1998), Electric Library, Business Edition, downloaded from **business.elibrary.com.**

11. "Worldwide Refinishing Announces Expansion into Korea," Franchise Handbook Online NewsBytes, downloaded January 7, 1999, from **www.franchise1.com/articles/newsbyte.html**

12. Peter Coy, "Tremors from Cheap Oil," *Business Week* (December 12, 1998), pp. 34-37; and Sallie L. Grimes, "Appetite for Cost Cutting Keeps Mergers on Menu," *San Diego Union-Tribune* (January 1, 1999), p. C-3.

13. Ira Sager, "A New Cyber Order," *Business Week* (December 7, 1998, pp. 27-31.

14. Christopher Rhoads, "Low Key GE Capital Expands in Europe," *Wall Street Journal,* (September 17, 1998), p. A18; Bill Shepherd, "GE Capital's M&A Strategy," *Global Finance,* (November 1, 1998), Electric Library, Business Edition, downloaded from **www.business.elibrary.com.**

15. Julie Bennett, "Franchising: New Companies Take Offbeat Path to Profits," *Wall Street Journal* (December 13, 1998), p. B13 (special advertising section)

16. Ibid.

17. Echo Montgomery Garrett, "The Changing World of Franchising," (special advertising section), *Inc.* (November 1998), pp. 120-123.

18. Geoffrey Colvin, "The Year of the Mega-Merger," *Fortune* (January 11, 1999), pp. 62-64; and "So How Big Was It?" *Fortune* (January 11, 1999), pp. 65-71.

19. "So How Big Was It?" pp. 65-71.

20. "Mergers Weren't Job-Friendly," *San Diego Union-Tribune* (January 25, 1999), p. C-1.

21. Robert E. Ford, President, Job-Direct, telephone interview, January 13, 1999; "JobDirect Partners with Barnes and Noble College Bookstores to Launch JobDirect's Job-Drive for the 1998–99 Academic Year," press release downloaded from **www.jobdirect.com/pr-barnesnoble.html;** and JobDirect Web site, **www.jobdirect.com.**

Focusing on Small Business sources:
Carol Dannhauser, "How One Couple Parlayed Their Differences into a Thriving PR Company, *Business Week Online* (December 9, 1998), downloaded from **www.businessweek.com/smallbiz;** and Alison Bass, "Home Sweet Home Away from Home:

Couples Find Work is a Labor of Love," *San Diego Union-Tribune* (January 2, 1999), pp. E-1, E-3.

Making Ethical Choices source:
Adapted from D. Morse, "Just Sell It: Where Gang Members Are Shoe Salesmen: A Novel Franchise," *Wall Street Journal* (February 19, 1999), pp. A1, A6.

Applying Technology sources:
"Franchising Meets the Internet," Intel E-Business Web site, downloaded January 5, 1999, from **www.intel.com/businesscomputing/ebusiness/biz-biz/franchise.htm;** Tricon Global Web site, **www.triconglobal.com;** and "Tricon's KFC Brands Itself," Intel E-Business Web site, downloaded January 5, 1999, from **www.intel.com/businesscomputing/ebusiness/biz-biz/kfc.htm.**

Creative Thinking Case sources:
Richard Behar, "Franchises: Why Subway Is "The Biggest Problem in Franchising,.." *Fortune* (March 16, 1998) p. 126; "Subway Sandwich Shops Inc.," *Hoover's Company Capsules* (December 1, 1998), downloaded from Electric Library, Business Edition, **business.elibrary.com;** Subway corporate Internet site, **www.Subway.com;** Dan Uhlinger, "Let the Sandwich Wars Begin: Rival Shops to Fight for Fast-Food Business," *Hartford Courant* (June 29, 1998), downloaded from Electric Library, Business Edition, **business.elibrary.com.**

Video Case source: Adapted from material contained on the following Internet site: "Second Chance Body Armor," **www.sruniforms.com/fsecond.html;** and from material in the video *Second Chance Body Armor: A Study of Entrepreneurship.*

CHAPTER 5 NOTES

1. Nick Charles and Tom Duffy, "Not Pulp Fiction: 'Juice Guys' Tom Scott and Tom First Built an Empire out of Fresh Fruit," *People* (November 10, 1997), downloaded from Electric Library, Business Edition, **business.elibrary.com;** Paul Tanklefsky, "Future Is Looking Sweet for Juice Guys," *Boston Herald* (November 9, 1998), downloaded from Electric Library Business Edition, **business.elibrary.com;** and "Two Men and a Bottle," *Inc. State of Small Business* (May 19, 1998), pp. 60-63.

2. Edith Updike, "A Green Thumb for Startups," *Business Week* (October 12, 1998), p. ENT 26.

3. "American Small Business in Numbers," National Federation of

Independent Businesses, downloaded April 1, 2002 from **www.nfib.org.**

4. Ibid

5. Edith Updike, "A Green Thumb for Startups," *Business Week* (October 12, 1998), p. ENT 26.

6. Nora Caley, "Batter Up! Colorado Pines Recycled into Treebats," *Denver Rocky Mountain News* (March 1, 1998), downloaded from Electric Library, Business Edition, **business.elibrary.com.**

7. Robert D. Hof, "The Wild World of Amazon.com," *Business Week* (December 14, 1998), pp. 106–108.

8. Steve Hamm, "Jim Clark Is Off and Running Again," *Business Week* (October 12, 1998), pp. 64–69.

9. Marshall Goldsmith, "Retain Your Top Performers," *Executive Excellence* (November 1, 1997), downloaded from Electric Library Business Edition, **business.elibrary.com;** Jan Norman, "Intrapreneurs Keep Creativity In-House," *Austin-American Statesman* (November 17, 1997), downloaded from Electric Library, Business Edition, **business.elibrary.com;** and Robert G. Stein and Gifford Pinchot, "Are You Innovative?" *Association Management* (February 1, 1998), downloaded from Electric Library, Business Edition, **business.elibrary.com.**

10. Steve Ginsberg, "Xerox Makes New Attempt to Duplicate Research Triumphs," *San Francisco Business Times* (March 28, 1997), downloaded from Electric Library, Business Edition, **business.elibrary.com;** and "Stimulating Creativity and Innovation," *Research-Technology Management* (March 1, 1997), downloaded from Electric Library, Business Edition, **business.elibrary.com.**

11. Gina M. Larson, "Once Is Not Enough," *Entrepreneurial Edge* (Winter 1998), downloaded from **www.edgeonline.com.**

12. Daile Tucker, "Are You an Entrepreneur?" *Home Business* (April 1998), downloaded from **www.homebusinessmag.com;** and "Do You Act Like an Entrepreneur?" *Entrepreneur Magazine's Small Business Square* (September 30, 1998), downloaded from **www.entrepreneurmag.com.**

13. "CEO's Notebook," *Inc.* (December 1998), p. 123.

14. Hamm, "Jim Clark Is Off and Running Again."

15. Elaine W. Teague, "Designing Woman," *Entrepreneur* (January 1999), pp. 112–115.

496/**end notes**

16. Gina M. Larson, "Judy Estrin Spots Trends before They Emerge," *Entre-prenuerial Edge* (Winter 1998), downloaded from **www.edgeonline.com.**

17. "Do You Act like an Entrepreneur?" *Entrepreneur Magazine's Small Business Square.*

18. Tom Richman, "The Eight Books to Read before You Start Your Business," *Inc. State of Small Business* (May 19, 1998), p. 114.

19. Robert McGarvey, "Words from the Wise," *Entrepreneur* (May 1997), pp. 152–155.

20. "Small Business: An Economic Powerhouse," National Federation of Independent Businesses (1998), downloaded from **www.nfibonline.com.**

21. "U.S. Economic Census, 1998," U.S. Census Bureau, downloaded from **www.census.gov.**

22. "Small Business Answer Card, 1998," Office of Advocacy, Small Business Administration, downloaded from **www.sba.gov/ADVO.**

23. Michael Barrier, "Raking in the Blue Chips," *Nation's Business* (April 1, 1998), downloaded from **www.nbmag.com.**

24. All information for the SBA section is from the Small Business Administration Web site, **www.sba.gov/.**

25. "Senate Hearing Assesses SBA Performance: A Decade of Small Business Success," Small Business Administration press release (July 20, 2000), downloaded from **www.sba.gov/news.**

26. "SBIC Overview," *SBIC Venture Capital-SBIC Program,* **www.sba.gov/INV/overview.html**, and "What Is ACE-Net?" Ace-Net Web pages, **ace-net.sr.unh.edu/pub/**, both downloaded April 1, 2002.

27. Jerry Useem, "Ideas by the Gross," *Inc.* (February 1997), p. 50.

28. Don Debelak, "Where's the Big Idea?" *Business StartUps* (March 1998), downloaded from **www.entrepreneurmag.com.**

29. Carrie Mason-Draffen, "Business Plan Is a Tool No Company Should Be Without," *Newsday* (October 12, 1998), downloaded from Electric Library, Business Edition, **business.elibrary.com.**

30. Ibid.

31. "Inc. 500 Almanac," *Inc. 500* (October 20, 1998), p.18; and "Small Business: An Economic Powerhouse," National Federation of Independent Businesses (1998).

32. "Small Business Answer Card, 1998," Office of Advocacy, Small Business Administration.

33. "Outsourcing Tech Services Costs Less, but Comes with Risks," *Electronic Commerce News,* March 12, 2001, downloaded from eLibirary, **ask.elibrary.com.**

34. Anne Zeiger, "The Many Virtues of 'Virtual Services,'" *Business Week Enterprise* (September 14, 1998), p. ENT 20.

35. Gary Andrew Poole, "Help Wanted: Desperately: Horizon Communications," *Business Week Enterprise* (May 25, 1998), p. ENT 8.

36. Joanne H. Pratt, "Homebased Business: The Hidden Economy," SBA Office of Advocacy (March 2000), downloaded from **www.sba.gov.**

37. John Grossman, "Meeting's at 9. I'll Be the One in Slippers," *Inc. State of Small Business* (May 19, 1998), pp. 47–48.

38. Debra Phillips et al., "Quick Guide for Women Entrepreneurs," *Entrepreneur* (January 1999), pp. 23–26.

39. "Women's World," *Entrepreneur* (January 1999), p. 24–25.

40. "News Report on Growth of Minority-Owned Businesses," U.S. SBA Office of Advocacy press release (April 15, 1999), downloaded from **www.sba.gov.**

41. Cynthia E. Griffin, "Quick Guide for Minorities," *Entrepreneur* (February 1999), p. 24.

42. Lee Romney, "Latino Entrepreneurs Looking to Mexico," *Los Angeles Times* (September 30, 1998), downloaded from Electric Library Business Edition, **business.elibrary.com.**

43. Griffin, "Quick Guide for Minorities"; Gene Koretz, "Wanted: Black Entrepreneurs," *Business Week* (December 14, 1998), p. 26; and Julianne Malveaux, "Banking on Us: The State of Black Wealth," *Essence* (October 1, 1998), p. 100.

44. "D&B Study Shows that 7 out of 10 Small Businesses Now Have Internet Access," Dun & Bradstreet company press release (May 25, 2000), downloaded from **www.dnb.com.**

45. Quentin Hardy, "Think Big," *Wall Street Journal Interactive Edition* (December 7, 1998), downloaded from **interactive.wsj.com.**

46. John J. O'Callaghan, "Ten Tips for Would-Be Entrepreneurs," downloaded from Home Business Magazine Web site, **www.homebusinessmag.com,** February 12, 1999; and Bob Weinstein, "What's the Big Idea?" *Entrepreneur* (February 1999), pp. 184A–184C.

47. Charles and Duffy, "Not Pulp Fiction: 'Juice Guys' Tom Scott and Tom First Built an Empire out of Fresh Fruit"; Gerry Khermouch, "Nantucket Resets 'Super' Nectars in Push for Broader Herbal Appeal," *BrandWeek* (March 22, 1999), p. 6; Jennie Leszkiewisz, "Drinking Is Their Life: Tom and Tom Return to Brown," *Brown Daily Herald* (October 23, 1997), downloaded from Electric Library, Business Edition, **business.elibrary.com,** and Tanklefsky, "Future Is Looking Sweet for Juice Guys."

Making Ethical Choices source: Adapted from: J.G. Auerbach, M. Maremont, and G. Putka, "Prying Eyes: With These Operators, Your Bank Account Is Now an Open Book," *Wall Street Journal* (November 5, 1998), pp. A1, A3.

Focusing on Small Business sources: Marc Ballon , MIT Springboard Sends Internet Company Aloft," *Inc.* (December 1998), pp. 23–25; Marc Ballon, "Spawning Start-Ups at San Diego State," *Inc.* (December 1998), p. 24; and Marc Ballon, "Texas Super Bowl," *Inc.* (March 1998), p. 39–41.

Applying Technology sources: Melanie Trottman, "The Web @ Work: Hotel Reservations Network," *Wall Street Journal* (September 17, 2001), p. B6; Wendy Zellner, "Where the Net Delivers: Travel," *Business Week* (June 11, 2001), p. 142.

Creative Thinking Case sources: "For the Two Biggest Failures of All Time, Life Couldn't Be Better," *Inc.* (May 1, 1998), downloaded from Electric Library, Business Edition, **business.elibrary.com;** Gina M. Larson, "Once Is Not Enough," *Entrepreneurial Edge* (Winter 1998), downloaded from **www.edgeonline.com;** Susan Moran, "Life after Death," *Business 2.0* (January 1999), pp. 72–73; and "Onsale CEO Reports High Growth in Sales and Customer Registrations," *PR Newswire* (February 24, 1998), downloaded from Electric Library, Business Edition, **business.elibrary.com.**

Video Case source: Adapted from material contained on the following Internet sites: "Yahoo! Home Page," **http://www.yahoo.com/;** "Yahoo! – Company History," **http://www.docs.yahoo.com/info/misc/history.html;** "Yahoo! Introduces Expanded Suite of Services for Small Businesses," **http://www.yahoo.com/docs/pr/;** "Yahoo! Reports Fourth Quarter and 1998 Fiscal Year End Financial Results," **http://www.yahoo.com/docs/pr/;**

and from material in the video: *Entrepreneur-ship and Innovation: A Study of Yahoo!*

CHAPTER 6 NOTES

1. Alex Taylor III, "Rally of the Dolls: It Worked for Toyota. Can It Work for Toys?" *Fortune* (January 11, 1999), p. 36.
2. "Inside Hewlett-Packard Carly Fiorina Combines Discipline, New-Age Talk," *Wall Street Journal* (August 22, 2000), pp. A-1, A-18.
3. Nina Munk, "Gap Gets It," *Fortune* (August 2, 1998), pp. 68–82.
4. Scott Wilson, "From Ice Storm to Fire Storm, Did Pepco Slip?" *Washington Post* (January 31, 1999) pp. A1, A6.
5. Leslie Walker, "Business at Cyber-speed," © 1999, *The Washington Post*. Reprinted with permission.
6. Peter Elkind, "A Merger Made in Hell," *Fortune* (November 9, 1998).
7. John Huey and Geoffery Colvin, "The Jack and Herb Show," *Fortune* (January 1, 1999), p. 163.
8. Tara Parker-Pope, "New CEO Preaches Rebellion for P&G's Cult," *Wall Street Journal* (January 11, 1998), p. B1.
9. Jeffrey Ball, "DaimlerChrysler's Renschler Holds Job of Melding Officieal Into Cohesive Team," *Wall Street Journal* (January 12, 1999).
10. Scott Thurm, "A Blitz of Fixes Helps Factories Prepare for 2000," *Wall Street Journal* (January 5, 1999).
11. Dana Fields, "Teamwork Powers Harley Bike Factory," *Fort Worth Star-Telegram* (June 16, 1998), Section C, p. 3.
12. Richard Pascale, "Grassroots Leadership—Royal Dutch Shell," *Fast Company*, (April 1998), p. 110.
13. "Humane Technology—PeopleSoft," Paul Roberts, *Fast Company* (April 1998), p. 122.
14. Anna Muoio, "Decisions, Decisions," *Fast Company* (October 1998), pp. 93–106.
15. Danielle Sessa, "For College Students, Web Offers a Lesson in Discounts," *Wall Street Journal* (January, 21, 1999), p. B7.

Focusing on Small Business source: Carol Hymowitz, "CEO's Set the Tone for How to Handle Questions of Ethics," *Wall Street Journal* (December 22, 1998).

Making Ethical Choices source: Adapted from R. Wartzman, "Trade Patterns: In the Wake of Nafta, a Family Firm Sees Business Go South," *Wall Street Journal* (February 23, 1999), pp. A1, A10.

Applying Technology source: J. William Gurley, "A Dell for Every Industry," *Fortune* (October 12, 1998), pp. 167–172.

Creative Thinking Case source: Leigh Buchanan, "The Smartest Little Company in America," *Inc.* (January 1999), pp. 43–54.

Video Case source: Adapted from material contained on the following Internet sites: **www.dhc.com; http**: and //**www.corporate-ir.com**; and from material in the video: *Planning and Implementing: A Study of Hudson's.*

CHAPTER 7 NOTES

1. Tara Parker-Pope, "P&G, in Effort to Give Sales a Boost, Plans to Revamp Corporate Structure," *Wall Street Journal* (September 2, 1998), pp. B1, B6.
2. "Warm and Fuzzy Won't Save Procter and Gamble," *Business Week* (June 26, 2000), p. 46.
3. Dana Fields, "Teamwork Powers Harley Bike Factory," *Fort Worth Star-Telegram* (June 16, 1998), Section C, p. 3.
4. Roy S. Johnson, "Home Depot Renovates," *Fortune* (November 23, 1998), pp. 201–219.
5. Carol Hymowitz, "More Top Executives Used to the Single Life, Are Cohabiting Now," *Wall Street Journal* (January 5, 1999), p. B1.
6. Roger O. Crockett, "Motorola: Slow and Steady Isn't Winning Any Races," *Business Week* (August 10, 1998), pp. 62–64.
7. Cathy Olofson, "Stairway to Information Heaven," *Fast Company* (April 1999), p. 68.
8. Gina Imperato, "He's Become BankAmerica's 'Mr. Project,'" *Fast Company* (June 1998; first appeared in *Fast Company* issue 15, p. 42).
9. John A. Byrne, "The Corporation of the Future," *Business Week* (August 31, 1998), pp. 102–106.
10. "How New Chief Forged One Company from Two While Boosting Profit," Carol Hymowitz, *Wall Street Journal,* February 2, 1999, p. B1.
11. Ram Charon, "Stand By Your CEO (Sometimes) Fumbling or Failure," *Fortune* (August 14, 2000), pp. 296–304.

Applying Technology source: Nellie Andreeva, "Do the Math–It is a Small World," *Business Week* (August 17, 1998), pp. 54–55.

Focusing on Small Business source: Cathy Olofson, "Stairway to Information Heaven," *Fast Company* (April 1999), p. 68.

Making Ethical Choices source: Adapted from L. Cohen, "U.S. Organizers of Olympics Control Damage," *Wall Street Journal* (March 22, 1999), pp. B1, B4; S. Fatsis, "Olympic Sponsors Study Their Options amid Scandal," *Wall Street Journal* (March 10, 1999), p. B2; S. Fatsis, "IOC Tries to Sell Reforms to Corporate Sponsors," *Wall Street Journal* (March 19, 1999), p. B2; S. Fatsis, "Olympic Scandal Is Result of Culture of Corruption, U.S. Panel Concludes," *Wall Street Journal* (March 22, 1999), p. A4.

Creative Thinking Case source: Lisa Chadderdon, "Monster World," *Fast Company* (January 1999), pp. 112–117.

Video Case source: Adapted from material contained on the following Internet sites: "About JIAN," **www. jian.com/ab_jian.asp;** and "Powerful Software to Build Your Business," **www.jian.com/prod.asp;** and from material in the video: *Organizational Design: A Study of JIAN.*

CHAPTER 8 NOTES

1. Cindy Eberting, "The Harley Mystique Comes to Kansas City," *Kansas City Star* (January 6, 1998); Randolph Heaster and Cindy Eberting, "Harley Celebrates Start of Production," *Kansas City Star* (January 7, 1998); Geeta Shjarma Jensen and Dyan Machan, "Is Hog Going Soft?" *Forbes* (March 10, 1997), p. 114; Rick Romell, "With $517.2 Million in Revenue, Harley Sets Another Record," *Milwaukee Journal Sentinel* (July 14, 1998); Stephen Roth, "New Harley Plant Spotlights Training and Empowerment," *Kansas City Business Journal* (January 9, 1998), all articles except Jensen/Machan were downloaded from Electric Library, Business Edition, **business.elibrary.com.**
2. "Golf-equipment Manufacturer Cuts Strokes off Its Process," *Industry Week* (September 21, 1998): downloaded from **www.industryweek. com.**
3. Charles W. Thurston, "Branded Offshore Manufacturing Finds a Home in Ireland and Singapore," *Chemical Market Reporter* (June 8, 1998), downloaded from Electric Library, Business Edition, **business. elibrary.com.**
4. Keith E. Gottschalk, "Bloomington OKs Tax Extension," *Peoria Journal Star* (December 15, 1998), downloaded from Electric Library, Business Edition, **business.elibrary.com.**
5. Louis Uchitelle, "Not Too Big, Not Too Small, Midsize Cities Proving to

Be a Profitable Lure to Corporate America," *San Diego Union Tribune* (January 9, 1999), downloaded from Electric Library, Business Edition, **business.elibrary.com.**

6. "Cabot's Microelectronics Materials Division Opens New Slurry Manufacturing Facility in Geino, Japan, to Meet Increasing Customer Demand," company press release (January 10, 1999).

7. Emily R. Sendler and Gregory L. White, "Auto Makers Battle Y2K Bug in Vast Supplier Network," *Wall Street Journal* (November 30, 1998), p. B4.

8. "World Class Supplier Process," from AMD corporate Web page, **www.amd.com,** downloaded February 5, 1999.

9. "We're Not There Yet," downloaded from National Association of Purchasing Managers Web site, **www.napm.org,** February 12, 1999.

10. Kimberly Koster, "What's Cooking? *Quick Service Restaurant* (September/October 1998), p. 47.

11. "Winnebago Revs Up Quality," *Providence Journal-Bulletin* (July 2, 1997), downloaded from Electric Library, Business Edition, **business.elibrary.com.**

12. Lawrence Gould, "What Makes Automotive CAD/CAM Systems So Special?" *Automotive Manufacturing & Production* (October 1, 1998), downloaded from Electric Library, Business Edition, **business.elibrary.com.**

13. Jon Van, "Automation Making Inroads at Hospitals: Robots Free Medical Personnel from Repetitive Tasks," *Cincinnati Enquirer* (September 13, 1998), downloaded from Electric Library, Business Edition, **business.elibrary.com.**

14. Glenn Hasek and Weld Royal, "Measuring Industry's Might," *Industry Week* (June 8, 1998), downloaded from Industry Week Web site, **www.industryweek.com.**

15. Bill Vlasic, "Imitation is Sincere Form of Productivity: Lean Manufacturing System Focuses on Team Production, *Detroit News* (December 21, 1998), p. F9.

16. Charles Gilbert, "Did Modules Fail Levi's or Did Levi's Fail Modules?" *Apparel Industry Magazine* (September 1, 1998), downloaded from Electric Library, Business Edition, **business.elibrary.com.**

17. Bruce Caldwell, "Harley Shifts into High Gear," *Information Week* (November 30, 1998), downloaded from **www.informationweek.com.**

Focusing on Small Business sources: Jeffrey Zygmont, "Does Size Really Matter?" and "The Ties That Bind," *Inc. Technology No. 3* (September 15, 1998) downloaded from Electric Library, Business Edition, **business.elibrary.com.**

Making Ethical Choices source: Adapted from R. L. Simison, "Buyer's Market: General Motors Drives Some Hard Bargains with Asian Suppliers," *Wall Street Journal* (April 2, 1999), pp. A1, A6.

Applying Technology sources: Kimberly Koster, "What's Cooking?" "Speedy Delivery," and "Bringing 'Em Back," *Quick Service Restaurant* (September/October 1998), pp. 46, 49, 53; Alan Liddle, "The Millennium: A Food-service Odyssey," *Nation's Restaurant News* (September 14, 1998), downloaded from Electric Library, Business Edition, **business.elibrary.com.**

Creative Thinking Case sources: Marla Dickerson, "Tailored for Efficiency: Apparel Makers Respond to Need to Automate, " *Los Angeles Times* (April 8, 1998), downloaded from Electric Library, Business Edition, **business.elibrary.com;** Clay Parnell, "Supply Chain Management in the Soft Goods Industry," *Apparel Industry Magazine* (June 1, 1998), downloaded from Apparel Industry Magazine Online, **www.aimmagazine.com.**

Video Case source: Adapted from material contained on the following Internet site: The Vermont Teddy Bear Company!® **www.vermontteddybear.com;** and from material in the video *A Case Study in Manufacturing Operations: The Vermont Teddy Bear Company.*

CHAPTER 9 NOTES

1. Joanne Lee-Young, "Starbucks' Expansion in China Is Slated," *Wall Street Journal* (October 5, 1998), p. A27c.

2. Ellen Joan Pollock, "Sir: Your Application for a Job Is Rejected; Sincerely, Hall 9000," *Wall Street Journal* (July 30, 1998), pp. A1, A12.

3. Eileen P. Gunn, "How Mirage Resorts Sifted 75,000 Applicants to Hire 9,600 in 24 Weeks," *Fortune* (October 12, 1998), p. 195.

4. "Work Week," *Wall Street Journal* (December 22, 1998), p. A1.

5. "Gore-Text," *Fast Company* (January 1999), p. 160.

6. "Study May Spur Job-Applicant Drug Screening," *Wall Street Journal* (November 28, 1998), pp. B1, B7.

7. "Companies Are Finding It Really Pays to Be Nice to Employees," *Wall Street Journal* (July 22, 1998), p. B1.

8. Joann S. Lubin, "New Hires Win Fast Raises in Accelerated Job Reviews," *Wall Street Journal* (October 6, 1998), pp. B1, B16.

9. "It's Not a Job, It's an Adventure," *Fast Company* (January 1999), pp. 52–54.

10. "Eight Years Later, Many Still Unaware of Disabilities Act," *Dallas Morning News* (September 26, 1998), p. 7C.

11. Sandra Baker, "Service Helps Employees Manage Challenges of Their Private Lives," *Fort Worth Star-Telegram Tarrant Business* (October 26, 1998), p. 17.

12. Patricia Sellers, "The 50 Most Powerful Women in American Business," *Fortune* (October 12, 1998), pp. 76–98.

13. Michael J. Flynn, "Crystal Vision," *Telecommute* (January 1999), pp. 14–19.

14. "Making Stay-at-Homes Feel Welcome," *Business Week* (October 12, 1998), pp. 155–156.

15. "Saying Adios to the Office," *Business Week* (October 12, 1998), pp. 152–154.

16. Sherry E. Sullivan, William A. Carden, and David F. Martin, "Careers in the Next Millennium: Directions for Future Research," *Human Resource Management Review* (Summer 1998), pp. 165–185.

Focusing on Small Business source: Robert Reich, "The Company of the Future," *Fast Company* (November 1998), pp. 124–148.

Creative Thinking Case source: Christopher Cuggiano, "Worker, Rule Thyself," *Inc.* (February 1999), pp. 89–90.

Making Ethical Choices source: Adapted from: Siconolfi, M. "Lynched? Merrill Broker Protests Policies, Is Fired, Finds His Clients Divvied Up," *Wall Street Journal* (February 27, 1998): pp. A1, A8.

Video Case source: Adapted from material contained on the following Internet sites: **www.valassis.com:** and **www.pathfinder.com/fortune/;** and from material in the video: *Employee Recruitment and Selection: A Study of Valassis Communications, Inc.*

CHAPTER 10 NOTES

1. Charles Fishman, "Sanity Inc.," *Fast Company,* (January 1999), p. 85.

2. Timothy D. Schellhardt, "An Idyllic Workplace under a Tycoon's Thumb," *Wall Street Journal* (November 23, 1998), p. B1.

3. Shelly Branch, "The 100 Best Companies to Work for in America," *Fortune* (January 11, 1999), pp. 118–144.

4. Ibid.
5. De'Ann Weimer, "I Want to Lead with Love not Fear," *Business Week* (August 17, 1998), pp. 52–53
6. David A. Nadler and Edward E. Lawler III, "Motivation—A Diagnostic Approach," in William Hackman, Edward E. Lawler III, and Michael Porter (Eds.), *Perspectives on Behavior in Organizations* (New York, McGraw-Hill, 1977).
7. Bruce Tulgan, *FAST Feedback,* (HRD Press, 1998).
8. Gina Imperato, "How to Give Good Feedback," *Fast Company* (September 1998), pp. 144–156.
9. G. Fuchsberg, "Four-Day Workweek Has Become a Stretch for Some Employees," *Wall Street Journal* (August 2, 1994), pp. B1, B4.
10. John R. Katzenbach and Douglas K. Smith, *The Wisdom of Teams: Creating the High-Performance Organization,* (Boston: Harvard Business School Press, 1993).
11. Ibid.
12. Shari Caudron, "The Only Way to Stay Ahead," *Industry Week* (August 17, 1998).
13. Robert Levering and Milton Moskowitz, "The 100 Best Companies to Work for in America," *Fortune* (January 10, 2000).
14. Ibid.
15. Ibid.
16. "Culture Watch," *Fortune* (November 9, 1998), p. 67.

Focusing on Small Business sources: Chuck Salter, "Insanity Inc.," *Fast Company* (January 1999), p. 106;

Evan Ramstad "High Rollers: How Trilogy Software Trains Its Raw Recruits to be Risk Takers," *Wall Street Journal* (September 21, 1998), p. B1.

Applying Technology source: Anthony M. Townsend, Samuel M. DeMarie, and Anthony R. Hendrickson, "Virtual Teams: Technology and the Workplace of the Future," *Academy of Management Executive,* 13 no. 3 (August 1998), p. 17(13).

Making Ethical Choices source: Adapted from: T. Appeal, "Missing the Boss: Not All Workers Find Idea of Empowerment as Neat as It Sounds," *Wall Street Journal* (September 8, 1997), pp. A1, A13; R.Y. Bergstrom, "Be Prepared to Be Involved," *Automotive Manufacturing & Production* (February 1997); pp. 66+.

Creative Thinking Case source: Almar Latour, "Detroit Meets a Worker Paradise," *Wall Street Journal* (March 3, 1999), pp. B1, B4.

Video Case source: Adapted from material contained on the following Internet sites: **http://www.valassis. com**: and **http://www.pathfinder. com/fortune/**; and from material in the video: *Motivating for Performance: A Study of Valassis Communications, Inc.*

CHAPTER 11 NOTES

1. Jennifer Lach, "Boomers on the Drawing Board," *American Demographics* (November 1998), pp. 48–49.
2. "The New Chief Is Ordering Up Changes at McDonald's," *Wall Street Journal* (August 24, 1998), p. B1.
3. Leonard Goodstein and Howard Butz, "Customer Value: The Linchpin of Organizational Change," *ASAP* (June 22, 1998), p. 22.
4. "NYSEG Highlighting Superior Customer Satisfaction," *PR Newswire* (October 6, 1998), p. 1.
5. Goodstein and Butz, "Customer Value," p. 24.
6. Kevin Clancy and Robert Shulman, "Marketing—Toss Fatal Flaws," *The Retailing Issues Letter* (November 1998), p. 4.
7. "Frequent Perks Keep Travelers Loyal," *American Demographics* (September 1998), pp. 32–35.
8. "As Children Become More Sophisticated, Marketers Think Older," *Wall Street Journal* (October 13, 1998), pp. A1, A6.
9. "Kraft's Miracle Whip Targets Core Consumers," *Advertising Age* (February 3, 1998), p. 12.
10. "Rating Wars," *American Demographics* (October 1998), pp. 31–33.
11. David Wolfe, "What Your Customers Can't Say," *American Demographics* (February 1998), pp. 24–29.
12. "A Potent New Tool for Selling—Database Marketing," *Business Week* (September 5, 1997), pp. 56–62.

Creative Thinking Case source: Don Schultz, "AAA Gets an 'F' in Building Relationships with Customers," *Marketing News* (March 30, 1998), pp. 5–6.

Focusing on Small Business source: Louise Lee, "If You Also Want to Buy a Crock-Pot, This Isn't the Place," *Wall Street Journal* (August 26, 1997), pp. A1, A11.

Applying Technology source: Dick McCullough, "Web-Based Market Research Ushers In New Age," *Marketing News* (September 14, 1998), pp. 27–28.

Video Case source: Adapted from material contained on the following Internet site: **www.burke.com**; and from material in the video: *A Case Study in Decision Support Systems and Marketing Research: Burke Inc.*

Making Ethical Choices source: Adapted from: Friedland, J. "Sweet Solution: Mexican Mogul Offers Omnilife as the Answer to Poor Diet, Poverty," *Wall Street Journal* (March 2, 1999); pp. A1, A8.

CHAPTER 12 NOTES

1. Jeff Wise, "A Lot of Hot Air," *Fortune* (August 14, 2000), pp. 308–322.
2. "Total Measured Media Spending 1998," *Advertising Age* (November 9, 1998), p. 50.
3. "1998 Advertising-to-Sales Ratios," *Advertising Age* (June 29, 1998), p. 22.
4. Letter to the authors from Suzanne Gornowicz, Valassis Communications Inc., dated September 4, 1998.

Focusing on Small Business source: Dale Buss, "Making Your Mark through Branding," *Nation's Business* (October 1998), pp. 27–31.

Applying Technology source: Emily Nelson, "Why Wal-Mart Sings, Yes, We Have Bananas!" *Wall Street Journal* (October 6, 1998), pp. B1, B4.

Creative Thinking Case source: 1 "Makers of Herb-Dusted Chips Tout Mood-Altering Effects, But Some Are Skeptical," *Dallas Morning News* (September 27, 1998), p. 9A.

Video Case source: Adapted from material contained on the following Internet site: **www.burton.com/main. asp**; and from material in the video: *A Case Study in Distribution Strategy: Burton Snowboards.*

CHAPTER 13 NOTES

1. Ann B. Graham, "All for One and One for All," *Executive Edge* (Special Gartner Group/Forbes Magazine supplement) (September 1998), pp. 24–28; "IBM Bolsters Business Intelligence Solutions with Exchange Applications' Software for Managing Marketing Campaigns," *Business Wire* (July 21, 1998); Carol Power, "Key-Corp Touts Payoff from Data Warehouse In Marketing Efforts," *American Banker* (March 12, 1999). The latter two articles were downloaded from Electric Library, Business Edition, **business.elibrary.com.**
2. "LANs of Opportunity," *Inc. Technology* 1998, No. 2 (June 16, 1998), p. 20.
3. "Let a LAN Leverage Productivity," *Inc.'s 301 Great Ideas for Using Technology,* downloaded May 5, 1999, from **www.inc.com/301/ideas.**

4. Emily Esterson, "Inner Beauties," *Inc. Technology 1998*, No. 4 (December 15, 1998), pp. 79–90.
5. "Largest Privately Held Department Store Chain Implements Microstrategy Decision Support Tech," *M2 PressWIRE* (November 16, 1998), downloaded from Electric Library, Business Edition, **business.elibrary.com.**
6. Michael Menduno, "Software That Plays Hardball," *Hospitals & Health Networks* (May 20, 1998), downloaded from Electric Library, Business Edition, **business. elibrary.com.**
7. M. Bensaou and Michael Earl, "The Right Mind Set for Managing Iinformation Technology," *Harvard Business Review* (September 1, 1998), downloaded from Electric Library, Business Edition, **business. elibrary.com.**
8. Bronwyn Fryer, "No False Moves," *Inc. Technology 1998*, No. 4 (November 17, 1998), pp. 48–58.
9. Emily Esterson, "Bluebird's Unhappiness," *Inc. Technology 1998*, No. 1 (March 16, 1998), p. 20.
10. John Omicinski, "Internet Explosion Has Given Hackers Thousands of New Entry Points," Gannett News Service (February 27, 1998), downloaded from Electric Library, Business Edition, **business. elibrary.com**.
11. Marcia Stepanek, "Y2K Is Worse Than Anyone Thought," *Business Week* (December 14, 1998), pp. 38–40; Scott Thurm, "A Blitz of Fixes Helps Factories Prepare for 2000," *Wall Street Journal* (January 5, 1999, pp. B1, B6.
12. Denise Caruso, "Long Running Fight over Data Privacy Has Been Heating Up," *San Diego Union-Tribune ComputerLink* (March 9, 1999), p. 2; Michael Gardner, "Shopper Privacy Bill Goes to Assembly," *San Diego Union-Tribune* (April 27, 1999), pp. A3–A4.
13. Teena Massingill, "Privacy Lost," The San Diego Union-Tribune (April 4, 1999), pp. I3, I6.
14. Gary McWilliams, "Taming the Info Monster," *Business Week* (June 22, 1998), pp. 171–172; and "Surfing the Hype Curve," *Executive Edge* (September 1998), pp. 16–17.
15. Teena Massingill, "Privacy Lost."
16. Graham, "All for One and One for All"; Power, "KeyCorp Touts Payoff."

Applying Technology sources: Frank Gibney, Jr., "Pepsi Gets Back in the Game," *Time* (April 26, 1999), downloaded from Electric Library, Business Edition, **business.elibrary.com**; Julia King and Thomas Hoffman, "The Next IT Generation," *Computerworld* (April 6, 1998), p. 1; Ian Springsteel, "Pepsi's Next Generation of Purchasing," *CFO* (December 1997), downloaded from **www.cfonet.com.**

Focusing on Small Business sources: Leigh Buchanan, "The Buying Game," *Inc. Tech 1998*, No. 2 (June 16, 1998), p. 11; Emily Esterson, "Hail to the Chiefs," *Inc. Tech 1998*, No. 2 (June 16, 1998), pp. 65–78; and Tim McCollum, "Computer Systems According to Plan," *Nation's Business* (August 1, 1998), downloaded from Electric Library, Business Edition, **business.elibrary.com**.

Video Case source: Adapted from material contained on the following Internet sites: "Archway (r) News," **www.archwaycookies.com**; "Archway Cookies: Solutions & Success Stories," **www.intermec.com/solutions/archway. htm**; and from material in the video *Management Information Systems: A Study of Archway Cookies.*

Making Ethical Choices source: Adapted from M. Maremont, "Extra! Extra! Internet Hoax, Get the Details," *Wall Street Journal* (April 8, 1999), pp. C1, C18; M., Maremont, and W. M. Bulkeley, "Who Did the Hoax? SEC Seeks Answers a Day after PairGain's Stock Rockets," *Wall Street Journal* (April 9, 1999), p. C22.

CHAPTER 14 NOTES

1. Based on personal interview with Jared Wells, Wells Test Preparation Center, La Jolla, CA, April 8, 1999.
2. Karen M. Kroll, "Auditors: No Longer Shooting the Wounded?" *Industry Week* (April 20, 1998), downloaded from **www.industryweek. com**; Melody Petersen, "When Watchdog, Watched Become Business Partners," *Minneapolis Star Tribune* (July 26, 1998), downloaded from Electric Library Business Edition, **business.elibrary.com.**
3. Bernard Condon, "Gaps in GAAP," *Forbes* (January 25, 1999), pp. 76–80; S. L. Mintz, "Seeing Is Believing," *CFO* (February 1999), downloaded from **www.cfonet.com.**
4. Telephone interview, Jared Wells, April 15, 1999.

Applying Technology sources: Russ Banham, "A New Beginning for Case," *CFO* (December 1997); Russ Banham, "Case Conquers All," *CFO* (January 1999), and "Best at the Basics," *CFO* (January 1999). All articles were downloaded from **www.cfonet.com.**

Focusing on Small Business source: Norm Brodsky and Bo Burlingham, "Forget Spreadsheets," *Inc.* (November 1997), pp. 27–28.

Creative Thinking Case source: Jill Andresky Fraser, "Straight Talk," *Inc.* (March 1990), p. 97.

Making Ethical Choices source: Adapted from E. Nelson, and J. S. Lublin, "Buy the Numbers? How Whistle-Blowers Set Off a Fraud Probe That Crushed Cendant," *Wall Street Journal* (August 13, 1998), pp. A1, A8.

Video Case source: Adapted from material contained on the following Internet sites: **www.charlevoix.org/ cvb/;** and **www.weathervane-chx.com/ main.htm;** from the promotional brochure, *Weathervane Terrace Hotel;* and from material in the video: *Accounting Information Systems: A Study of the Weathervane Terrace Inn and Suites.*

CHAPTER 15 NOTES

1. Bob Violino, "Banking on E-Business—Citigroup Is Dramatically Expanding Its Internet Presence in an Effort to Approach Its Target of 1 Billion Customers," Information Week (May 3, 1999), downloaded from Electric Library, Business Edition, **www.business.elibrary. com;** Joseph Nocera, "Banking Is Necessary—Banks Are Not," *Fortune,* (May 11, 1998), pp. 82–84; Kevin Maney, "Citigroup's Billion-Customer Plan Relies on High Tech," *USA Today,* (April 16, 1998), downloaded from **www.usatoday. com;** "Citigroup and Travelers Group to Merge, Creating Citigroup: The Global Leader in Financial Services," press release (April 6, 1998), downloaded from **www.citi.com/citigroup/.**
2. "Online Banking Booming, Says IDC," downloaded from **www. electronicbanker.com,** (June 2, 1999).
3. "Banking Technologies," downloaded from **www.electronicbanker. com,** (June 4, 1999).
4. "Top Banks Plan Online Billing Network," (Reuters), The Sheboygan Press, June 24, 1999, p. C5.
5. James Kraus, "Citigroup Said to Plan Opening 25 Branches in Poland," *American Banker* (April 22, 1999), downloaded from **www. americanbanker.com;** "Citigroup Strengthens Core Consumer Business with Three Acquisitions," press release (March 23, 1999), downloaded from **www.citi.com/ citigroup/pr/news.**

Applying Technology sources: Scott Woolley, "Virtual Banker," Forbes, June 15, 1998, pp. 127-128; "About NetBank" and "NetBank FAQ," **www.netbank.com/** and NetBank 1998 Annual Report, downloaded from **www.netbank.com/ annlrpt98.**

Focusing on Small Business sources: Sharon Nelton, "Sizing Up Megabanks," Nation's Business, November 1998, pp. 14–21; and **www.unitedbankofphila.com.**

Creative Thinking Case source: Joshua Macht, "Niche Bank Targets White-Collar Market, Inc., March 1999, pp. 23–24.

Making Ethical Choices source: Adapted from: R. Brooks, "How Banks Make the Most of Bounced Checks," *Wall Street Journal* (February 25, 1999), pp. B1, B8.

Video Case source: Adapted from material contained on the following Internet sites: **www.roney.com;** and **www.firstbank-alma.com;** and from material in the video *Financial Statement Analysis/Creditor and Investor Decisions: Firstbank and Roney & Co.*

CHAPTER 16 NOTES

1. Russ Banham, "Larry Kellner—Continental Airlines: Managing External Stakeholders," *CFO* (September 1998), downloaded from **www.cfonet.com;** "Continental Airlines, Inc.," *Hoover's Company Profiles* (May 1, 1999); "Continental Airlines Reports 15th Consecutive Profitable Quarter, Ends Year on High Note," *PR Newswire* (January 21, 1999). The latter two articles were downloaded from Electric Library, Business Edition, **business.elibrary.com.**

2. Richard Gamble, "No More Dunning Days," *Treasury & Risk Management* (September 1998), downloaded from **www.cfonet.com.**

3. John F. Greer, Jr., "Commercial Paper Redux," *Treasury & Risk Management* (October 1998), downloaded from **www.cfonet.com.**

4. "eToys IPO Takes a Rocket Ride," *Bloomberg News* (May 20, 1999): Dawn Kawamoto, "eToys Prices IPO at $20 per Share," *CNET News.com* (May 19, 1999), both downloaded from CNET News.com, **www.news.com.**

5. "Lara Technology, Inc. Completes $13.8 Million Second Round Funding," *Business Wire* (June 24, 1999), downloaded from Electric Library, Business Edition, **business.elibrary.com.**

6. Information downloaded July 1, 1999, from the International Finance and Commodities Institute (IFCI) Risk Watch site, **risk.if.ci.ch/ index.htm.**

7. Diane Brady, "Is Your Bottom Line Covered?" *Business Week* (February 8, 1999), pp. 85–86.

8. Terzah Ewig, "How Electronic Networks Snag Trades," *Wall Street Journal* (March 1, 1999), pp. C1, C26.

9. "Rising Tide Economics," *Research Reports,* American Institute for Economic Research (June 14, 1999), pp. 61–62.

10. Jill Andresky Fraser, "Riding the Economic Roller Coaster," *Inc.* (December 1998), pp. 126–129.

11. "Continental Airlines Receives No. 1 Spot for Long Flights in Frequent Flyer Magazine/J.D. Power and Associates Study," *PR Newswire* (May 11, 1999); "Continental Airlines Reports 15th Consecutive Profitable Quarter, Ends Year on High Note," *PR Newswire* (January 21, 1999); "Continental Airlines Retires Its Last Boeing 747 and 737-200; Launches 777 Service between London and Houston," *PR Newswire* (March 2, 1999), all downloaded from Electric Library, Business Edition, **business.elibrary.com.**

Applying Technology sources: Mary Addonizio, "Loanshop.com Measures Productivity in Terms of Leads and Sales," *Mainspring ProofPoint*

(November 1998), downloaded from **www.mainspring.com/BaseAll/;** and Beth Lipton, "Net Investment Still Exceeds Return," *CNET News.com* (August 31, 1998), downloaded from **www.news.com.**

Making Ethical Choices source: Adapted from: N. Templin, "Inn Trouble: Hurricane Georges Was Just One of the Blows That Battered Patriot," *Wall Street Journal* (March 4, 1999), pp. A1, A16.

Focusing on Small Business sources: "An Internet Stock Exchange? Not Quite Yet," *Investor Relations Business* (November 23, 1998);"Beacon Light Announces Entrance Into the Internet Stock Exchange," *Business Wire* (May 28, 1999); Kimberly Weisul, "New Web-Based Exchange Is Tailored to 'Nanocap' Companies," *Investor Relations Business* (September 28, 1998); all downloaded from Electric Library, Business Edition, **business.elibrary. com;** and Niphix Investments Web site, **www.niphix.com.**

Creative Thinking Case sources: "After-hours Trading Debuts in New Venue," *Washington Times* (August 26, 1999), p. B8; James Bernstein, "ETrade to Expand Trading, *Newsday* (August 18, 1999), p. A51; ileen Glanton, "Not All Take Stock in Extended Trading Days," *San Diego Union-Tribune* (June 5, 1999), pp. C-1, C-3; Greg Ip and Terzah Ewing, "NASD Prepares for Late Hours; Date Isn't Set," *Wall Street Journal* (May 28, 1999), pp. C1, C18.

Video Case source: Adapted from material contained on the following Internet sites: **www.delfield.com;** and **www.scotsman-ind.com;** and from material in the video *Capital Structure and Dividend Policy: Scotsman Industries.*

A

Absolute advantage, 52
Accessories, 343
Accountants, 394–395, 412, 441
  expanding role of, 409–410
Account executives. *See* Stockbrokers
Accounting, 441
  computers in, 396–397
  corporate, 398
  definition of, 392
  dot-com, 417
  equation, 395–396
  financial, 393
  importance of, 410–411, 412
  industry, major trends affecting, 413
  managerial, 393
  procedures, basic, 395–397
  profession, 394–395
  purpose of, 392–393
  records, falsifying, 407
  software, 397
Accounting cycle, 396
  steps in, 412
Accounts payable, 400, 445–446
Accounts receivable, 400
  managing, 443–444
Acid-test (quick) ratio, 406–407
Acquisitions, 47, 444, 452
  in banking industry, 431, 432
  changes brought about by, 132
  corporate growth through, 125–128, 134
  definition of, 126
  employee resistance during, 212
  motives for, 127
  regulatory approval for, 473
  strategies, 464
Activity ratios, 408
Actuarial tables, 479
Actuaries, 479
Adams, Phyllis, 159–160
Administrative agencies, 467
Administrative distribution systems, 354
Administrative law, 466
Advantage, 52. *See also* Absolute advantage; Comparative advantage; Competitive advantage
  size as an, 129
  taking unfair, 86. *See also* Ethics
Adverse impact, 274–275. *See also* Affirmative action
Advertising, 357–358
  regulation of, 473
Advertising campaigns
  controversial, 93
  use of personal information in, 382
Advertising media, 357–358
  main types of, 363
Affirmative action, 274–275. *See also* Minorities; Women
Affirmative action programs, 274
Age Discrimination in Employment Act (1967), 271, 273
Agents, 351
Aggregate data, 19
Agile manufacturing, 246
AIDS testing, 272
Albo, Lazaro, 82, 101
American Association of Home-Based Businesses, 158, 163
American Bar Association, 115
American Institute of Certified Public Accountants, 395
American Stock Exchange (AMEX), 454–455, 458–459
Americans with Disabilities Act (1990), 273, 281

Amos Tuck School of Business Administration (Dartmouth), 410
Analysis, investment, 411
Analysts, financial, 410
Analytic systems, 373
Andersson, Claes, 309
Andreeson, Marc, 144
Angel Capital Electronic Network (ACE-Net), 150. *See also* Small Business Administration (SBA)
Angel investors, 154
Annual reports, 394
Antidumping laws, 56
Antioco, John, 367
Antitrust cases, 34
Antitrust regulation, 472
Appellate courts, 467
Appreciation, 51
Apprenticeship, 265
Arbitration, 468
Argiris, Lea, 432
Arthur, W. Brian, 190
Articles of incorporation, 115, 116. *See also* Corporations
Ashbrook, Tom, 169
Assembly-line
  employees, 224
  layout, 234. *See also* Facility layouts
  production, 289
Assembly-line layout, 234. *See also* Facility layouts
Assembly process, 228. *See also* Production process
Assets, 395, 397
  American household financial, 419
  categories of, 398, 400
  current, 442–443. *See also* Current assets
  difficulty of evaluating certain, 409
  listing of, 398
  long-term, 444
Asset utilization, 187
Auditing, 395
Auditors, 410
Auditor's opinion, 395
Authority, 202
Autocratic leaders, 178–179
Automated teller machines (ATMs), 225, 244, 310, 360, 369, 385, 427
Automatic guided vehicles (AGVs), 243
Automation, 242–243
  in restaurants, 244
  role of, in operations management, 249
  and technology in nonmanufacturing operations, 244

B

Babcock, Lewis, 92–93
Baby boomers, 5–6, 326
  preferences of, 327
  targeting, 313
Background check, 263–264
Balance of payments, 50–51
Balance of trade, 50, 51
Balance sheet, 397, 412
  sample, 399
Bank charters, 426
Bank holding companies, 436
Banking
  consolidation in, 431
  early decentralized, 422
  integration of brokerage and insurance services with, 431–432
  new era in, 419
  online. *See* Online banking
  trends reshaping, 434
Bank Insurance Fund (BIF), 429, 434

Bankruptcy, 439
  resulting from asbestos-related lawsuits, 472
Bankruptcy law, 472
Bankruptcy Reform Act (1978), 472
Banks. *See also* Financial institutions
  commercial, 426
  community-oriented, 104–105
  failure of, 422, 429, 430, 431
  high-to-low check processing by, 424
  insuring deposits of, 429–430
  no-frills, 435
  resurgence of small, 431, 432
  types of, 426
  use of technology by, 224–225
  virtual, 428. *See also* Online banking
Barlow, Richard G., 333
Barriers to entry, 32–33
Bartels, Andrew, 465
Barter, 66, 421. *See also* Countertrade
Batch processing, 374–375
Batson, Hayes, 153
Beebe, Andrew, 195
Behavior
  ethical. See Ethics
  illegal and irresponsible, 92–93
  irresponsible but legal, 93
  legal and responsible, 93–94
  of target consumers, and promotions, 358–359
  views on unethical, 91
Beige Book, 25. *See also* Federal Reserve Board
Beijing Youth Daily, 260
Bell, Rachel, 107–108, 132
Beneficiary, 479
Benefits, 267, 308–309, 310
  fringe, 268–269
  required by law, 280
  work-life, 303
Benefit segmentation, 328
Bezos, Jeff, 141, 142
Big Board. *See* New York Stock Exchange (NYSE)
Big Five, 395, 397, 409, 410, 415. *See also* Accounting
Bill of material, 234
Blair, Tony, 9
Bleustein, Jeffrey, 223–224
Blimps, commercial, 341
Board of directors, 116–117. *See also* Corporations
Boland, Brian, 341
Bond ratings, 449
Bonds, 448–449, 453
  corporate, 27
    popular types of, 448
    ratings for, 449
  savings, 27
  U.S. government, 422–423
Bonuses, 268, 297
Bookkeeping, 395, 396
Borovoi, Konstantin, 38–39
Boston Globe, 260
Boylan, Jo Ann, 370
Bracken, Josh, 317
Bracken, Michael, 317
Braden, Jason, 135–136
Brady Law (1998), 474
Brand equity, 344
Branding, 344–346
  benefits of, 344
  suggestions for small companies embracing, 345
Brands, 344
  types of, 345–346
Branson, Jody, 251

Breach of contract, 469
  legal remedies for, 469–470
Breyer, Jim, 465
Bridgman, Peter, 371
Brinkman, Andrea, 121
Brodsky, Norm, 404
Brokerage firms, 429. See also
  Stockbrokers
Brokers, 351
Brown, Herbert, 171
Bruyn, Steven, 313
Bryant, Robin, 120–121
Budgeting, 459. See also Capital
  budgeting
Building insurance, 481
Bureau of Labor Statistics, 22, 146
Business. See also Business organization;
  Entrepreneurs; Small business
  building blocks of, 17–18
  building Web sites for, 195
  environment, changes in, 2–3
  ethics, liabilities caused by poor, 84. See
    also Ethics
  financing for, 153–154
  home-based, 158
    reasons for starting, 158
    using Internet to research, 164
  insurance, 481
    special types of liability, 482
  ownership trends, 158–160
  people starting, by age, 159
  plan, development of, 151–153
  recognizing unethical actions in, 85–86.
    See also Ethics
  resolving ethical problems in, 86–87. See
    also Ethics
  risks, 477. See also Risk
  starting your own, 150–151, 165
  strategies, coordinating global, 72
  taxation of, 475–476
  workings of economies and, 18–19. See
    also Economics; Economy
Business cycles, 21
Business interruption insurance,
  482
Business law, 466–467
Business organization. See also Business
  control activities of, 182
  forms of
    choosing, 151
    comparing, 109
    specialized, 120–121. See also
      Cooperatives; Franchising
  philosophy of, 180. See also Corporate
    culture
  types of, 109, 132–133. See also specific
    categories
    advantages and disadvantages of
      major, 119
Business plan, 165
  competitions, 153
  development of, 151–152
  outline for, 152
  use of, 152–153
Business products, 343–344
Business-to-business market, 325. See also
  E-commerce
  characteristics of, 325
  purchase decision making,
    325
  transactions, 475
Buyer behavior, 323, 335
  business, 325
Buyer cooperatives, 79, 120. See also
  Cooperatives
Buy-national regulations, 55
Byrnes, Pat, 379

C
CAD/CAM systems, 242–243
Cameron, Don, 341
Capacity, for contracts, 469
Capital
  ability of corporations to raise, 118
  availability of, for partnerships, 112
  difficulty in raising, for sole proprietor-
    ships, 110. See also Sole
    proprietorships
  to produce goods and services, 17
Capital budgeting, 444
Capital expenditures, 444, 448, 460
Capitalism, 7–8
Capital products, 343, 362
Career, planning, 278–279
Carpenter, Jim, 127
Case, Steve, 137
Cash, 400
Cash flows, 441
Cash management, 443
Cassidy, Mike, 181
Cazalet, Edward, 45
C corporations, 107. See also Corporations
Cease-and-desist orders, 473
Cecil, Gail, 109–110
Celler-Kefauver Act (1950), 472–473
Cellular manufacturing, 246
Cellular phones, 377
  use of, for banking, 420
Center for Entrepreneurship (Nassau
  Community College), 151
Centralization, 203–205, 217
Certificates of deposit, 443
Certified management accountants (CMAs),
  395
Certified public accountants (CPAs), 395
Chain of command, 202
  dual, 208. See also Matrix structure
Chamber of Commerce, 267, 359
Chambers, John, 215
Channels, 321
  distribution. See Distribution channels
  organization of, 354
Chappell, Emma, 432
Charren, Peggy, 104
Chicago Tribune, 260
Chief financial officer (CFO), 439, 440,
  441
Chief information officer (CIO), 370
Child Protection Act (1966), 474
Children's Television Act (1990), 474
Cigarette Labeling Act (1965), 474
Circuit breakers, 456, 462
Circular flow, 19–20, 52
Civil Aeronautics Board, 466
Civil Rights Act (1964), 273, 274
Claims, insurance, 478
Clark, Gary, 387
Clark, Jim, 142, 145, 291–292
Classic entrepreneurs, 142
Clayton Act (1914), 472
Clean Air Act, 277
Code of ethics, 89. See also Ethics
  example of, 90
Coercive power, 177
Cognitive dissonance, 334–335
Cohen, Ben, 87
Coinsurance, 481. See also Property
  insurance
Collaboration, 299, 307
Collaborative software systems, 302
Collection policies, 443. See also Collections
Collections, 440
  use of technology for, 444
  ways to improve, 459

Command economies, 8–9
  entrepreneurial spirit in former, 37–39
Commercial banks, 426
Commercial finance companies, 429
Commercial liability insurance, 481
Commercial paper, 443, 446
Commission, 268
Committee meetings, 208. See also
  Committee structure
  creative, 209
Committee structure, 207–208
Common law, 466. See also Tort law
Common market, 59
Common stock, 460, 461
  selling new issues of, 449–450
Communications
  advances in, 12
  electronic, 210. See also E-mail
  employee, 310
  face-to-face, importance of, 210
  improving supplier, 237–238
  informal channels of, 212
  between purchasers and suppliers, 237
  use of computers in restaurants to
    improve, 238
Communism. See Command economies
Comparative advantage, 52
Compensation, 280
  and benefits, 267–269
  types of, 268
Competition, 34
  effect of deregulation on, 45, 474
  foreign, in domestic market, 48–49
  in global marketplace, 47, 72, 277
  trends in, 11–13
  laws to promote fair, 472–473
  monopolistic, 33–34
  perfect (pure), 32
  price, 129
Competitive advantage, 172, 216, 226
  cost, 319–320
  creating, 319–320
  differential, 320
  employees as, 288
  niche, 320
  sustainable, 304
  use of internal production, to maintain,
    234
  use of virtual teams to create, 302
Component parts, and materials, 343–344
Compressed workweek, 297
Comptroller of the Currency, 426
Computer-aided design (CAD), 242, 243
Computer-aided manufacturing (CAM), 242
Computer conferencing systems, 377
Computer-integrated manufacturing (CIM),
  243
Computerized resource planning, 235–236
Computer networks, 371–372
  importance of, 386
Computers
  in accounting, 396–397
  categories of crimes involving, 379–381
  handheld, 388
  industrial use of, 242–243
  in information age, 370
  for job training and development, 266
  personal, 13, 386. See also Internet
    alternatives to, 383
  protecting information in, 378–382
  in restaurants, 238
  Washington state law regarding use of
    public, 85
Computer viruses, 380–381. See also
  Computers
Conceptual skills, 187–188
Confiscation, 67

Conflict of interest, 86
Conglomerate mergers, 127–128. See also Mergers
Congress. See U.S. Congress
Consensual leaders, 179
Consideration, for contracts, 469
Consolidations, 129. See also Mergers
    trends of, 132
Consultative leaders, 179
Consumer credit rules, 423
Consumer finance companies, 429
Consumer fraud, 95–96
Consumerism, 473
Consumer price index (CPI), 24
Consumer products, 342–343, 362
Consumer Product Safety Act (1972), 474
Consumer Product Safety Commission, 468, 474
Consumer protection laws, 473
Consumers, 343. See also Consumer products; Customers
    benefit of Internet commerce to, 216. See also E-commerce; Internet
    benefits of deregulation to, 474
    at end of distribution channels, 351
    expectations of, 224
    frequent-buyer programs for, 359
    increased banking choices for, 432–433
    influences on decision making of, 324
    older, 6. See also Mature market
    protecting rights of, 382
    quality demands of, 224
    understanding, 336
Contingency plans, 175–176
Contingent business interruption insurance, 482
Continuous process, 228–229. See also Production timing
Contractionary policy, 25
Contract law, 468–470
Contract manufacturing, 65
Contracts, 468–469
    breach of, 469–470
    requirements of valid, 469
    tying, 472
Contractual distribution systems, 354. See also Franchises
Controlling, 181–183, 192
    stages of, 181, 182
Convenience products, 343
Conventional ethics, 84. See also Ethics
Cooperatives, 79, 120–121
    definition of, 120
Copyright Office, 471
Copyrights, 400, 470
Core values, 195
Corigliano, Cosmo, 407
Corporate bonds, 27
Corporate culture, 180
    formal organizational groups and, 298
    influence of leadership style on, 192. See also Leadership style
Corporate distribution systems, 354
Corporate philanthropy, 97
    trends in, 98–99
Corporations, 114–119. See also Acquisitions; Mergers
    advantages of, 117–118
    C corporations, 107
    definition of, 114
    disadvantages of, 118
    mega-, 137
    multinational, 69–71. See also Multinational corporations
    philanthropy of, 97, 98–99
    process of setting up, 115–116
    S corporations, 118

structure of, 116–117, 133
    ten largest U.S., 115
    types of, 107, 118–119
Cosor, Brett, 111, 112–113
Costas, Bill, 94
Cost competitive advantage, 319–320
Cost of goods sold, 401–402
Cost per thousand contacts (CPM), 358
Cost-push inflation, 23–24
Costs, 16
Countertrade, 66
Coupon rate, 448
Court system, 467
Credit, 423, 433
    trade. See Trade credit
Credit cards, 421
    cell phones as virtual, 420
    unsolicited offers for, 385
Credit policies, 443, 459
Credit risk, 457. See also Risk
Credit terms, 443
Credit unions, 427
Crimes, 471
Critical path, 240
Critical path method (CPM), 240–241
Cross-branding, 129
Cross-functional teams, 300, 307
Cross-training, 224, 296
Crowding out, 26
    negative effect of, 27
Crum, Lorrie, 4
Culliss, Gary, 181
Culture
    clashes, 308–309
    differences in global marketplace, 67, 75
        examples of, 68, 79
        mergers and, 129
        need for managerial skills regarding, 188
Cumulative preferred stock, 451
Currency, 51, 421. See also Money
    changing value of. See also Exchange rates
    displaced, due to euro, 63
    distributing, in United States, 423. See also Federal Reserve System
    tips on exchanging, 74. See also Exchange rates
Current assets, 398, 400, 442–443
Current liabilities, 400
Current portion of long-term debt, 400
Current ratio, 405–406
Currid, Cheryl, 378
Customer departmentalization, 200
Customer expectations, 216, 245
Customers, 35. See also Consumers
    demands of, 241
    long-term, 36
        parnerships with, 316
    profiles and purchase patterns of, 333. See also Database marketing
    responsibility to, 95–96
    supply chain and, 237
Customer satisfaction, 36, 315–316
    companies and products that deliver, 35
    goal of, 225–226
    using physical distribution to increase efficiency and, 355–356
Customer service, 44, 436
    commitment to, 104–105
    main areas of service distribution for, 360
Customer value, 35, 315, 362
Customization, 227–228
    reducing cost of, 187
Custom regulations, 55
Customs union, 59

Cutler, Alexander, 301
Cyclical unemployment, 22. See also Unemployment

D

Danos, Paul, 410
Data
    analysis, 331
    collection, 330, 338
    security issues, 379–381, 385
Database management system, 374–375
Database marketing, 333. See also Micromarketing
Databases, 356, 388, 389
Data warehouses, 369–370, 371, 376, 382, 385
Davidson, Alan, 463–464
Davis, Richard, 136
Dealer brands, 345
Debt, 396. See also Debt financing; Debt ratios
    long-term, 448, 460–461
        current portion of, 400
    obligations, foreign, 51
    short-term, 446
    use of, for business financing, 154
Debt financing, 447, 448–449
Debt ratios, 408
Debt-to-equity ratio, 408
Decentralization, 204, 217
Decisional roles, 183, 184. See also Managers
Decision making
    business-to-business purchase, 325
    centralization of, 203–205
    empowering employees to share in, 171, 188–189. See also Employee empowerment
    family, 4
    group, 299. See also Work groups
    human resources, 279
    individual factors affecting, 324
    influences on consumer, 324, 335
    involving stakeholders in, 103
    lowering level of, 103
    managerial, 183–185
        steps in process of, 185
    marketing, 335–336
    questions related to better, 186
    sharing authority of, 179–180. See also Employee empowerment
    skills, 190
    social factors affecting, 325
Decision support system (DSS), 332–333, 376. See also Database marketing
    characteristics of, 333
Deductibles, insurance, 479
Defamation, 471
Delegation, 176
Delegation of authority, 202
Demand
    changes in, 30–31
    keeping up with, 223
    nature of, 28–29
    price determination, and interaction of supply and, 29–31
Demand curve, 28
Demand deposits, 421
Demand forecast, 259. See also Human resource planning
Demand-pull inflation, 23
Deming, W. Edwards, 241
Democratic leaders, 179
Demographics, 275–276, 328. See also Demographic segmentation
    trends in, 4–7

Demographic segmentation, 326–327
Demography, defined, 4
Demotions, 270
Dennis, William J., 159
Departmentalization, 176, 199–200, 201
    customer, 200
    functional, 200
    geographic, 197, 200
    process, 200
    product, 200
    types of, 217
Departmental scheduling systems, 377
Department of Commerce (DOC), 157
Department of Labor, 22, 24, 267
    Wage and Hour Division, 274, 281
Depository financial institutions, 426–428
Depreciation, 51, 400
Deregulation
    energy, 45, 474
    of industries, 473–474
Desktop videoconferencing system (DVCS), 302
Devaluation, 51
Developed nations, 49
Differential advantage, 356–357
Differential competitive advantage, 320
Direct foreign investment, 65–66
Directors and officers insurance, 482. See also Insurance
Direct public offerings (DPOs), 458
Discount rate, 423
Discounts, 473
Discount supermarkets, 47
Dismissals. See Terminations
Distribution
    centers, 355
    networks, international, 48
    physcial, 355–356, 363
    role of, in marketing mix, 351
    in the service sector, 360
    types of, 354–355
Distribution centers, 355
Distribution channels
    for industrial and consumer products, 352
    marketing intermediaries in, 351
    organization of, 363
    wholesalers and retailers in, 351–352
Distribution strategy, 321
    centralized, 47
    in international trade, challenges of, 78
Diversification, 464
Diversity, 7, 275–276
    of American labor force, 276
Dividends, 447, 450, 460, 461
Division of labor, 176, 198–199
Dorchak, Glenda, 285
Double-entry bookkeeping, 396
Dow Jones Industrial Average, 456, 462
Downsizing, 13, 302
    creation of small businesses due to, 145, 146
Drexler, Mickey, 174–175
Drug testing, 264, 272
Dumping, 56
    accusations of steel, 57
    predatory, 56
Durables, consumer, 343
Dwyer, Doug, 125

E

Earnings per share (EPS), 408
Eaton, Robert, 180
Eberle, Karl, 187
E-commerce, 105, 161, 169, 195. See also Internet; World Wide Web (WWW)
    marketplace for airline industry, 253

measuring revenue for, 417
    wine sites, 389
Economic communities, international, 59–62, 75
Economic growth, 21
    Federal Reserve System and, 423
    relation of exports to, 49
Economics, 18–19
    as circular flow, 19–20
    importance of understanding, 39–40
    subareas of, 19. See also Macro-economics; Microeconomics
Economic systems, 7–9
    of world, 10
Economic union, 59
Economies of scale, 47
    consolidation to achieve, 129
Economy. See also Command economies
    benefits of immigration to U.S., 6
    "click here," 11. See also Internet
    contribution of small businesses to, 165. See also Small business
    effect of Federal Reserve System on, 422–423
    factors in national, 41
    linkage between sectors of, 40–41
    role of corporations in U.S., 114–115. See also Corporations
    role of manufacturing in U.S., 245. See also Manufacturing
    Russian, 39
    shift to knowledge-based, 370
Edenborg, Mats, 309
Efficient consumer response (ECR) systems, 353
Egan, Michael, 139
Ehrlich, Robert, 365
Elahan, Kamran, 143
Electronic bulletin boards, 377
Electronic commerce. See E-commerce
Electronic communications networks (ECNs), 458, 459
    competition from, 462, 463
Electronic data interchange (EDI), 238, 354
Ellison, Larry, 221
E-mail
    importance to business of, 72
    servers, knowledge of, 84
    systems, 377
Embargoes, 55
Employee empowerment, 179–180, 187, 188–189, 296
Employee orientation, 265
Employee Retirement Income Security Act (1974), 273
Employees. See also Feedback; Jobs; Workforce
    absenteeism of, 296, 298, 303
    accommodating needs of disabled, 273. See also Americans with Disabilities Act
    compensation and benefits of, 267–269
    contingent workers, 260
    creating ethical awareness among, 102. See also Ethics
    decision to hire, 264
    difficulty of finding, for sole proprietor-ships, 111. See also Sole proprietorships
    education and training of, 303
    effect of mergers on, 132
    empowerment of. See Employee empowerment
    hiring and retaining, 156–157
    ideas generated by, 224
    initiatives to motivate and retain, 307
    new social contract trend between employers and, 99

orientation of, 265
    on overseas assignments, 277
    performance planning and evaluation of, 266–267
    recruitment of, 260–261, 280. See also Jobs
    responsibility to, 94–95
    selection of, 262–264, 280
        process, 262, 284
    sense of ownership by, 303
    and separations, 270–271
    in small businesses, advantages and dis-advantages of, 164
    training, 194, 280
        and development of, 264–265, 280
    turnover of, 287, 296, 298, 303
Employment
    effects of NAFTA, 60
    full, 22
Employment testing, 262–263
E-Myth Revisited, The (Gerber), 145
Enterprise resource planning (ERP), 236, 242, 372, 385
Entrepreneurs, 17–18, 164, 345. See also Branding; Brands
    characteristics of successful, 143–145, 165
    classic, 142
    definition of, 141
    development of business plan for, 151–153
    difficulty of obtaining credit for, 433
    effect of NAFTA on Hispanic, 160
    idea sources for, 150–151
    learning from, 163
    managerial ability and technical knowl-edge of, 144–145
    minority, 160
    reasons for becoming, 143
    sales promotion opportunities for, 359
    struggling South African, 38
    types of, 141–142
    U.S., in China, 53
    and views on ethical behavior, 91. See also Ethics
    women, 159, 160. See also Women
    young, 105, 139–140, 141, 159, 181
Entrepreneurship Competition, 181
Environmental protection, 88
    responsibility of business to, 97
Environmental Protection Agency (EPA), 468
Environmental scanning, 318
    data categories in, 318
Equal Credit Opportunity Act (1975), 430, 474
Equal Employment Opportunity Commission (EEOC), 274, 281
Equal Pay Act (1963), 273
Equilibrium, 30
Equity, 154
Equity financing, 446, 447, 449
Equity forward contracts, 446
Equity theory, 294, 306
Estrin, Judy, 144
Ethics
    choices involving, 33
    company, defined by managers, 177
    conventional, 84
    definition of, 82, 102
    dilemmas involving, 87, 89
    used for employee training, 88
    establishing formal code of, 89
    global and domestic trends in, 102–103
    individual business, 82–84
    influence of organizations on, 84–85
    as part of everyday life, 100–101
    postconventional, 84

Ethics *(continued)*
preconventional, 83–84
resolving problems regarding, 86–87
stages in development of, 83–84
training, 88
trends in global, and social resonsibility, 99–100
Euro, 62
Eurodollar, 62. *See also* Euro
countries converted to, 63
European Community (EC), 60
European Union (EU), 60–62, 72
member countries of, 61
Exchange, 314
Exchange controls, 56
Exchange rates, 51
importance of knowledge of, 74
Excise taxes, 476
Exclusive dealing, 472
Exclusive distribution, 354
Executive information system (EIS), 376
Expansionary policy, 25
Expectancy theory, 293–294, 306
Expense items, 343
Expenses, 401–403
long-term, 444, 460
short-term, 442–443, 460
Experiment, 330
Experimental Balloon and Airship Meet, 341
Expert power, 177
Expert systems, 376–377
Exporting, 63
Internet resources for, 64
Export management companies (EMCs), 157
Exports, 49–50
world, 11
Export Working Capital Program, 63
Express contracts, 468
Express warranties, 470
Expropriation, 67
External environment
social factors in, 325
understanding, 318
Extranets, 373

F

Facility layouts, 232, 233
trends in, 246
Facsimile (fax) systems, 377, 384
Factor, 446
Factoring, 446, 460
Factors of production, 17
Fair Credit Reporting Act (1971), 474
Fair Debt Collection Practice Act (1978), 474
Fair Labor Standards Act (1938), 272, 273
Fair Packaging and Labeling Act (Truth-in-Lending Act) (1968), 474
Families
average incomes of, worldwide differences in, 67, 69
buying decisions of, 325
changing role of, 4
dual-income, 4, 134, 281. *See also* Women
taxes paid by American, 475
Family and Medical Leave Act (1993), 273–274, 281
FAST Feedback (Tulgan), 296
Federal budget deficit, 27
Federal budget surplus, 27
Federal Communications Commission (FCC), 466–467, 468
Federal Deposit Insurance Corporation (FDIC), 426, 434
creation of, 429

enforcement by, 430
role of, 430
Federal Reserve Banks, 423
Federal Reserve Board, 25
Federal Reserve notes, 423
Federal Reserve System (the Fed), 25, 422–424
basic functions of, 434
check-clearing system of, 423–424
distribution of currency by, 423
insurance under, 430. *See also* Federal Deposit Insurance Corporation (FDIC)
setting of credit rules by, 423
Federal Savings and Loan Insurance Corporation (FSLIC), 429
Federal Trade Commission (FTC), 130, 466, 467, 468, 473
Federal Trade Commission Act (1914), 473
Federal Universal Service Fund, 467
Feedback
from employees, 310
giving positive, 187
performance and, 295
relation of control to, 182
Fidelity bond, 482
Filo, David, 168
Finance, 440–442, 460
Finance companies, 429
Financial accounting, 393
Financial Accounting Standards Board (FASB), 393–394, 409, 417
Financial institutions, 425–429
depository, 426–428
nondepository, 428–429
types of, 434
Financial intermediation, 425, 434
Financial management, 440–441. *See also* Financial managers
importance of, 459
trends in, 457–459
Financial managers, 440–441
goals of, 442, 443, 460
responsibilities and activities of, 441–442
Financial reports, 393–394, 415
questions regarding validity of, 410
use of, 412
Financial risk, 447
Financial services, 427
changing trends and new products in, 433
deregulation of, 474
pace of change in, 420
Financial Services Modernization Act (1999), 419, 431
Financial statements, 393, 394, 397, 441.
See also Annual reports
analyzing, 404–408
learning to read, 411
Financial system, U.S., 424–429
Financing. *See also* Bonds; Venture capital
debt, 448–449, 460
equity, 446, 447, 449, 461
debt versus, 447
raising long-term, 446–451
short-term, 44–446, 460
Fiorina, Carly, 173
Firewall, 373
First, Tom, 139, 144, 149, 164
Fiscal policy, 25
Fisher, Alan, 167
Fixed assets, 400
Fixed-position layout, 234. *See also* Facility layouts
Flammable Fabrics Act (1953), 474
Flexible manufacturing system (FMS), 243
Flextime, 297
Float, in banking, 424

Floating exchange rates, 51
Focus groups, 346–347
Food and Drug Administration (FDA), 468, 474
Food, Drug, and Cosmetic Act (1938), 474
Forbes, Walter, 179
Ford, Henry, 227
Ford, Robert, 107–108
Ford, William, Jr., 202
Formal organization, 198
Four Ps, 320. *See also* Marketing mix
Fourth market, 459. *See also* Electronic communications networks (ECNs)
Framework for Global Electronic Commerce, 475
Franchise agreement, 121
Franchisees, 121
benefits to, 122, 123
with franchisors in foreign countries, 125
traits for prospective, 131
use of intranets by, 373
Franchising, 121–125, 354, 373
advantages of, 122–123
cost comparison, 123
disadvantages of, 123–124
educating oneself about, 130–131
growing importance of, 133–134
growth of, 64, 124
international, 125
new twists for, 128–129
population by industry, 124
Franchisors, 121
ability for expansion of, 122, 123
in foreign countries, 125
Franklin, Burke, 220
Free market, competing in, 31–34
Free-rein (laissez-faire) leadership, 179
Free trade, 52, 75
Free-trade zone, 59
Frequency, as media evaluation, 358
Frictional unemployment, 22
Fringe benefits, 268–269, 481
Front page of newspaper test, 87
Full employment, 22. *See also* Employment
Functional departmentalization, 200
Funds, organizational use of, 442–444
Furash, Edward, 419
Futures contracts, 452, 453–454, 461

G

Gage, Kevin, 132
Gain-sharing plans, 297
Gallagher, Debbie, 151
Gallup survey, on franchising, 123
Gantt charts, 239
Gantt, Henry, 239
Gates, Bill, 18, 141, 177–178
GEC (goods for EC), 61. *See also* European Union
General Agreement on Tariffs and Trade (GATT), 58
Generally accepted accounting principles (GAAP), 393–394, 409, 458
tightening, 410
General obligation bonds, 453
General partners, 112. *See also* Partnerships
General partnerships, 112. *See also* Partnerships
General public, responsibility to, 96–97
Generation X, 5, 326–327
as entrepreneurs, 159. *See also* Entrepreneurs
mentality, 195
preferences of, 327
Generation Y, 4–5
Generic names, 471

Generic products, 345–346, 362
Geographic departmentalization, 197, 200
Geographic segmentation, 327–328
Gerber, Michael, 145
Ghandi, Nimish, 458
Givens, Beth, 385
Glass ceiling, 276
Glass-Steagall Act, 419, 431
Global competition, 72
   trends in, 11–13
Global management skills, 188
Global marketplace, 47
   banking in, 419–420
   competition in, 42, 72, 277
   cultural differences in, 47, 67, 75
      examples of, 68, 79
   difficulties of, 75
   economic environment in, 67–68. See
      also Multinational corporations
   effect of government actions on, 72
   financial management in, 457
   franchising in, 125
   gaining entry to, 75–76
   managing in, 189
   and need for market expansion, 71–72
   opportunities for small businesses in, 157
   participating in, 62–66
   political considerations in, 66–67
   resource acquisition in, 72
   securities in, 455. See also Securities;
      Stock exchanges
   technological change in, 72
   threats and opportunities in, 66–69, 76
   trends in, 76
   using Internet for, 63. See also Business-to-
      business market; Internet
Global vision, 48
Goal-setting theory, 295–296, 306
Goizueta, Roberto, 265
Gonzalez, José, 135
Goodnight, James H., 287
Goods, 16
   finding effective methods of producing,
      224
   increase in, 21. See also Economic
      growth
Goodwill, 400
Gordon, Jeff, 318
Grapevine, 212. See also Informal
   organization
Grassroots leadership, 189
Gray, Irwin, 113
Great Depression, 429
Greenfield, Hank, 4
Greenfield, Jerry, 87
Green movement, 70
Grimes, Danner, 428
Gross, Bill, 150–151
Gross domestic product (GDP), 11, 21
   contribution of manufacturing to, 245
   European Union (EU) and world, 62
   rate of growth in real, 21
Gross profit, 402–403
   analyzing, 404
Gross sales, 401
Group cohesiveness, 298
Group norms, 212
Grove, Andrew, 180, 319
Growth-oriented entrepreneurs, 142. See
   also Entrepreneurs

H

Hadzic, Senad, 311
Hamilton, Walter, 373
Hamm, Elle, 144
Hand, Learned, 466

Harper, Allen, 81
Harper, Kathy, 148
Hassan, Fred, 215
Hawthorne effect, 290, 304
Hawthorne studies, 289–290
   worker motivation and, 304
Henley, Jeff, 221
Herrera, George, 160
Herzberg, Frederick, 292–293, 306
Higgins, Chris, 210
Highsmith, Duncan, 193–194
Hills, Eric, 153
Hirshon, Jonathan, 156
Hobold, Jim, 129
Home Office Association of America
   (HOAA), 163
Horizontal mergers, 127. See also Mergers
Horton, Mark, 161
Hotchkiss, John, 276
Hourly wages, 268
Howitt, Heather, 160
Hughes, Christine, 73
Human relations skills, 187
Human resource management, 281
   definition of, 256
   laws affecting, 271–275, 281
      purpose and agencies of enforcement
         for, 273
   process, 256–257, 279
   role of government agencies in, 274–275,
      281
   trends affecting, 281
Human resource planning, 257–258,
   279–280
   and forecasting, 259–260
   job analysis and design, 258
   process, 259
Human resources
   accomplishing goals through use of, 187
   costs, overseas assignments and increase
      in, 277
   decision making, 279
   as underutilized asset, 297
Human rights, 83
   corporate dilemmas involving, 100
   violations, avoiding, of multinational
      suppliers, 103
Hyde, Matt, 79
Hygiene factors, 292. See also Job
   dissatisfiers
Hyman, Jeff, 261
Hyman, Richard, 47

I

Ilaw, Marianne, 104
Immigration, 6
Immigration Reform and Control Act (1986),
   273
Implied contracts, 468–469
Implied warranties, 470
Import quotas, 55
Imports, 49–50
Incentives, 230–231, 287, 303
   economic, 297
Income statement
   primary elements of, 401–403
   relation of profitability to, 412–413
   sample, 402
Income taxes, 475
Income taxes payable, 400
Independent Bankers Association of America,
   431
Individual rights, 83
Industrial distributors, 351
Industrial products, 343, 362. See also
   Business products

Industrial Revolution, 227, 315. See also
   Production orientation
Industrial users, 351
Infant-industry argument, for tariffs, 54. See
   also Tariffs
Inflation, 23
   causes of, 41
   impact of, 24
   measuring, 24
   types of, 23–24
Informal organization, 212
   functions of, 212
Informational roles, 183, 184. See also
   Managers
Information brokers, 148
Information, hiding or divulging, 86
Information management, 383
Information reporting systems, 376
Information systems
   business, 373–377
   structure of, 386
Information technology (IT), 370
   components of, 371–377
   managers and, 189
   managing, 187, 377–378, 386
   personnel, shortage of, 384
   planning, 378
      benefits from, 379
   preventing problems related to, 381–382
   privacy concerns regarding, 382
   trends in, 386
   and virtual corporations, 214–215. See
      also Virtual corporations
Infrastructure, 67–68
Initial public offerings (IPOs), 449–450, 465
Inputs
   availability of production, 230
   converting, into outputs, 225, 228, 229
      processes for, 228
   employee, 294. See also Equity theory
   process of buying production, 234. See
      also Procurement; Purchasing
Insourcing, 234
Insider trading, 456
Insider Trading and Fraud Act (1988), 456
Installations, 343
Institutional investors, 451–452
Insurable interest, 478
Insurable risk, 478
   criteria for, 478–479
Insurance, 477
   concepts, 478
   deductibles, 478, 479
   liability, 481
   premiums, 428, 478
      costs of, 479
   property, 481
   providers, 479
   public, 479–480
   risk transference through, 478
   theft, 482
   types of, 481–482
Insurance companies, 428, 478
   entry into risk management arena of,
      457–458. See also Risk management
   life, 448–449
   mutual, 480
   private, 480
   stock, 480
Insurance policies, 478, 479
Intangible assets, 395, 400
Integrated marketing communications (IMC),
   360
Intelligence network, 212. See also Informal
   organization
Intensive distribution, 355
Interest, 448

Intermittent process, 229. *See also* Production timing
Internal Revenue Code, 466, 475
Internal Revenue Service, 466, 475
Internal supply forecast, 259, 280. *See also* Human resource planning
International Accounting Standards Committee, 394
International location considerations, 231–232
International Monetary Fund (IMF), 58–59
International trade
　barriers to, 75
　challenges of distribution strategies in, 78
　fostering, 75
Internet. *See also* World Wide Web (WWW)
　bank use of, 431. *See also* Online banking-based business systems, 221
　career information on, 278–279
　checking applicant backgrounds on, 264
　commerce, benefit to consumers of, 216
　companies
　　IPOs and, 450
　　need for accounting guidelines for, 417
　comparison shopping on, 361
　courses for employees, 37
　delivery of customized products through, 361
　downloading films from, 367
　entrepreneurs, 141, 142
　ethics violations, attempts to stem, 84, 85. *See also* Ethics
　explosion, 161–162
　fueling growth of small businesses, 166
　hoaxes, 381
　impact of, 11
　increase in home-based businesses due to, 158
　increase in small businesses due to, 145. *See also* Small business
　Japanese consumers' use of, 79
　new areas of law developing regarding, 466
　regulation of, 475
　removal of geographic boundaries by, 72
　resources for small-business exporting, 64
　"root servers" of, 43
　search engines, 168, 279
　software, 181
　technology, 11
　use of
　　to attract new employees, 261
　　to enter global marketplace, 63
　　by manufacturing firms, 237–238
　virtual meetings on, 311
　as worldwide wide area network (WAN), 372–373
　young people starting businesses due to, 159
Internet service providers (ISPs), 311
Interpersonal roles, 183, 184. *See also* Managers
Intranets, 302, 373
Intrapreneurs, 142. *See also* Entrepreneurs
Inventory, 235, 400, 444
　just-in-time (JIT) system and, 242
Inventory management, 235, 236
Inventory turnover ratio, 408
Investment Advisers Act (1940), 456
Investment bankers, 452, 461
Investment Company Act (1940), 456, 462
Investments. *See also* Bonds; Securities; Stock
　high-risk, 461
Investors, 416
　angel, 154
　do-it-yourself, 463
　in Internet companies, 417

responsibilities to, 97–98
　risk of, 477
Involuntary bankruptcy, 472
Ivester, Douglas, 265

J

Jager, Durk, 197, 216
Jinks, Barry, 283
Job analysis, 258
Job description, 258
Job dissatisfiers, 292
Job enlargement, 296
Job enrichment, 296
Job fairs, 261
Job-protection argument, for tariffs, 54. *See also* Tariffs
Job rotation, 265, 296. *See also* Cross-training
Jobs. *See also* Compensation; Salaries
　changes within the organization, 269–271
　disappearance of low-skilled, in United States, 73
　loss of U.S., 54
　off-the-job training, 265–266
　on-the-job training, 265
　redesigning, to increase motivation and performance, 306–307
　search services for, 261
　sources of applicants for, 260–261
Job satisfiers, 292
Job sharing, 297
Job shops, 227, 229
Job specification, 258
Jobs, Steve, 206
Johnson, Paul, 431
Joint ventures, 65, 121
Jospin, Lionel, 9
Journal, accounting, 396. *See also* Accountants; Accounting
Judiciary, 467
Junk mail, stopping, 334
Justice, 83
Just-in-time (JIT), 242

K

Kaplan, Jerry, 167–168
Keller, Jesse, 107–108
Kellner, Larry, 439, 440
Key-person life insurance, 481
Kleinman, Jerry, 152–153
Knight, Phil, 100
Knowledge, 4
Knowledge management (KM), 383
Knowledge resources, managing, 383
Koch, Ed, 190
Koch, Jay, 372
Kryshtanovska, Olga, 39
Kuok, Robert, 38
Kutner, Harold, 234

L

Labor, 17. *See also* Workforce
　competition from foreign, 54
　costs, 230
　markets, internal and external, 260, 280
　need for cheap, 73
Labor Department, 60
Labour Party, 9
Lagman, Randy, 269–270
Lambert, Debra, 382
Lambros, Alex, Jr., 272
Lane, Ray, 221
Law of large numbers, 478–479

Laws, 466
　main sources of, 466–467
Layoffs, 270
Leadership, 177–178
　grassroots, 189
　styles of, 178–179
Leadership style, 178–179
　influence on corporate culture of, 192. *See also* Corporate culture
Leander, Kajsa, 339
Lean manufacturing, 241–242
Ledgers, accounting, 396. *See also* Accountants; Accounting
Legal form, for contracts, 469
Legal purpose, for contracts, 469
Legal rights, 83
Legitimate power, 177
Leinberger, Paul, 313
Lender of last resort, 58
Leshabane, Nurse, 38
Leveraged buyout (LBO), 127
Levin, Gerald, 137
Liabilities, 396, 397, 398, 448
　categories of, 400–401
Liability
　claims, due to poor business ethics, 84. *See also* Ethics
　insurance, 481. *See also* Insurance
　　special types of business, 482
　limited, for corporations, 117, 118–119
　unlimited
　　in partnerships, 112
　　in sole proprietorships, 110
Liability insurance, 481
　professional, 482
Libel, 471
Licensing, 63–64
Liemandt, Joe, 271, 295
Lifestyles, 328
　growth of component, 3–4
Light, Matt, 311
Limited liability companies (LLCs), 119
Limited liability partnerships (LLPs), 112. *See also* Partnerships
Limited partners, 112. *See also* Partnerships
Limited partnerships, 112. *See also* Partnerships
Line-and-staff organization, 207
Line of credit, 446
Line organization, 207
Line positions, 207
　difference between staff positions and, 217
Lin, Jian, 53
Liquidity, 398
　assuring, 443
Liquidity ratios, 405–407
Litow, Stanley, 98
Loans, 426, 427
　backed by securities, 429
　bank, 446
　business, 433
　mortgage, 448–449
　secured, 460
　short-term, 429, 444
　　secured, 446
　　unsecured, 445–446
Local area network (LAN), 372
Logos, 347
London Stock Exchange, 455
Long-term debt, 448–449
Long-term expenditures, 444, 460
Long-term liabilities, 401
Long-term relationships
　creating, 36
　with customers, 36, 316

M

Lopker, Pamela, 190
Los Angeles Times, 260

Maastricht Treaty, 60–61
McCabe, Danielle, 219
McConnell, Martin, 282–283
McCormack, John, 104–105, 436
McCracken, Jim, 415
McGinn, Richard, 93
McGregor, Douglas, 291, 305–306
McKay, Gene H., III, 389
McKinnel, Neil, 161
Macroeconomics, 19
  effect of entrepreneurs on, 42
  goals of, 20–24
    achieving, 24–27
McVey, Michael, 142
Magnuson-Moss Warranty Act (1975), 474
Mail Fraud Act (1872), 474
Make-or-buy decision, 234
Malmsten, Ernst, 339
Management. *See also* Managers
  classical era of, 288–289
  components of good, 173
  controlling, in, 181–183
  decision making, 183–185
  human relations era of, 289–290
  leading, in, 177–179. *See also*
    Leadership
  levels of, 177
    importance of skills at, 186
  marketing research recommendations to,
    331. *See also* Marketing research
  organizing function of, 176
  planning, 172–176
  role of, 172, 191
  roles in, 183
  skills, 185–188
    conceptual, 187–188
    global, 188
    human relations, 187
    technical, 185–186
  trends in, 188–189, 192
Management pyramid. *See* Managerial
  hierarchy
Management support system (MSS), 373,
  375–377
Managerial accounting, 393
Managerial hierarchy, 200–202
Managers. *See also* Management
  decision making of, 183–185
  empowering employees, 188–189. *See
    also* Employee empowerment
  establishment of behavior patterns by,
    87–88
  global, 73–74
    challenges for, 189
  influence of, on organizational ethics,
    102, 177. *See also* Ethics
  and information technology, 189
  leadership styles of, 178
  pyramid structure of, 176
  roles of, 183, 184, 192
  skills for successful, 185–188, 190, 192
  use of equity theory by, 294
Mannes, Alexis, 15
Manufacturer brands, 345
Manufacturers, 224
  production processes used by, 248
  use of lean manufacturing techniques by,
    241–242
Manufacturers' representatives, 352
Manufacturing. *See also* Inventory
  agile, 246
  cellular, 246

cities, top ten world-class, 231
  small businesses involved in, 147
Manufacturing environment, 231
Manufacturing resource planning II (MRPII),
  235, 242
Maquiladora plants, 160, 183. *See also*
  North American Free Trade Alliance
  (NAFTA)
Margaret, Julie, 151
Margin requirements, 423
Marketable securities, 400, 443
Market coverage, intensity of, 354–355
Market density, 327
Marketing
  campaign software, 369–370
  definition of, 314
  not-for-profit, 323
  problem, defining, 329
  strategy, creating, 370
  value, 35
Marketing concept, 314–317, 335
  components of, 314–315
  customer satisfaction, 315–316
  customer value, 315
  relationship marketing, 316
Marketing factors, 230
Marketing intermediaries, 351
Marketing mix, 335. *See also* Buyer
    behavior
  definition of, 342
  distribution strategy, 324
  heart of, 321
  physical distribution, as part of, 355–356
  pricing strategy, 324
  product strategy, 324
  promotion strategy, 324–325
  role of distribution in, 351
  role of product in, 342–348
  trends affecting, 364
Marketing research, 338–339
  analysis, 331
  data collection, 330
  definition of, 328
  methods of, 330
  process, 329–332
  recommendations to management, 331
  studies, Web-based, 329
  surveys, participating in, 334
  used in marketing decision making,
    335–336
Marketing strategy, creating, 317–320, 335
Market risk, 457. *See also* Risk
Markets
  difference between consumer and
    business, 325
  growing ethnic, 7
  segmented by gender, 327
Market segmentation, 325–328, 335
  benefit, 328
  demographic, 326–327
  forms of consumer, 326
  geographic, 327–328
  psychographic, 328
  volume, 328
Market structures, 31, 41–42
  types of, 31–33, 34
Marshall, Colin, 315
Maslow, Abraham, 290–292
Maslow's hierarchy of needs, 290–292
  relationship of motivation to, 304–305
Mass customization, 187, 227, 228, 359,
  361
Mass market, 5–6. *See also* Baby boomers
Mass production, 227, 228
Material requirement planning (MRO), 235,
  242
Materials-handling system, 355

Matrix structure, 208–210
  advantages of, 209
  disadvantages of, 210
Mature market, 6, 326
  preferences of, 327
Maude, Dan, 261
Mayo, Elton, 289–290, 304
Mechanistic organization, 205, 217
Mediation, 468
Medicaid, 269
Medicare, 269
  supplemental insurance and, 480
Megamergers, 202. *See also* Mergers
Mehserjian family, 183
Mentoring, 265, 276
Merchant wholesaler, 351
Mercosur, 60, 72
Mergers, 137, 202, 419, 444, 452
  in banking industry, 431, 432
  conglomerate, 127–128
  corporate growth through, 125–128
  cross-border, 129
  definition of, 126
  effect of, 132
  employee resistance during, 212
  global, 218
    structuring for, 215
  horizontal, 127
  motives for, 126–127
  recent, 125
  regulatory approval for, 472–473
  types of, 127–128
  use of, for growth, 134
  vertical, 127
Messmer, Jennifer, 285
Messmer, Shawn, 285
Metzger, Blaine, 398
Microeconomics, 19
  components of, 28–31
  key trend in, 37–39
  trends shaping, 42
Microelectromechanical systems (MEMS), 11
Micromarketing, 333. *See also* Database
  marketing
Micropreneurs, 142. *See also* Entrepreneurs
Middle management, 176, 177. *See also*
  Management
Migration, 6
Milgram, Stanley, 213
Miller, Mitch, 6
Miller, Steve, 188–189
Minnesota Clerical Test, 262
Minorities. *See also* Affirmative action
  appeal of business ownership to, 159
  businesses owned by, 160
  help from SBA to, 150, 160. *See also*
    Small Business Administration (SBA)
  mentoring of, 276
  small businesses and, 165–166
Minority Business Development Agency, 161
Mission, 173
Mission statement, 104, 174, 195
  example, 175
Mitchelson, William, 437
Mitterrand, François, 9
Mixed economies, 9
Model Business Corporation Act, 115
Modular production, 245
Module design, 246
Monaco, Michael, 407
Monetary policy, 24–25, 422–423
Money, 420, 434
  characteristics of, 420–421
  functions of, 421
  supply, United States, 421. *See also*
    Federal Reserve System
Monopolistic competition, 33–34

Monopoly, 43–44, 472. *See also* Antitrust regulation
  pure, 32–33
Moore, Darla, 276
Moore, Howard, 379
Moritz, Michael, 167
Mortgage loans, 448–449
Motivating factors, 292
Motivation, 287
  how expectations can lead to, 294
  McGregor's Theories X and Y related to, 305–306
  programs to foster employee, 310
  relation of job design to, 296–298
  use of teams to enhance, 298–302
Motivation theory, evolution of, 288–294
Motivator-hygiene theory, 292–293
  basic components of, 306
Mott, Randy, 356
Multiculturalism, 7
Multinational corporations
  advantages of, 70–71, 76
  competition among, 72
  impact of, 69
  issues of organizational abuse attributed to, 86, 103. *See also* Ethics
  responsibilities of, 99–100
  world's largest, 70
Multipreneurs, 142, 167. *See also* Entrepreneurs
Municipal bonds, 452, 453
Murray, Carolyn, 263
Mutual assent, for contracts, 469
Mutual funds, 452, 453, 461
Mutual insurance companies, 480
Myers-Briggs Type Indicator, 262–263

N

Nanotechnology, 11
Napoleonic Code, 466
Nasdaq-Amex Market Group, 456, 459
Nasser, Jacques, 202, 309
National Academy of Sciences, 272
National Association of Securities Dealers (NASD), 456, 459, 462
National Association of Securities Dealers Automated Quotation (Nasdaq) system, 455, 461
  challenge to NYSE by, 462
  extension of trading day by, 463
National banks, 426
National Credit Union Administration, 430
National Credit Union Share Insurance Fund, 430
National debt, 27
National Environmental Policy Act (1970), 466
National Federation of Independent Business (NFIB), 159
Nationalism, 66–67
National Labor Relations Board (NLRB), 466
Natural resources, 17
Negligence, 471
Nelson, Marilyn, 292
Net income, 403
Net loss, 403
Net profit, 403
Net profit margin, 407–408
Net sales, 401
Net working capital, 407
Newell, Chris, 190
New York Stock Exchange (NYSE), 272, 454–455, 461
  challenges to, 458–459
  circuit breakers of, 456
  extension of trading day by, 463

New York Times, 260
Niche competitive advantage, 320. *See also* Niche markets
Niche markets, 127, 132, 163, 345
  in banking industry, 431, 435
Nkuna, Ben, 38
Noble, Alex de, 153
Nondepository institutions, 428–429
Nondurables, consumer, 343
Nonprogrammed decisions, 184–185. *See also* Decision making
North American Free Trade Agreement (NAFTA), 59–60, 72
  as boon to Hispanic entrepreneurs, 160
Notes payable, 400
Not-for-profit organizations, 17
  marketing for, 323
Noto, Lucio, 127
Nussbaum, Paul, 446
Nutrition Labeling and Education Act (1990), 474

O

Observation research, 330
  advanced methods of, 332
Occupational Safety and Health Act (1970), 272, 273
Occupational Safety and Health Administration (OSHA), 272, 274, 281
Odd-even pricing, 350, 363
Office automation systems, 374, 377
Office of Federal Contract Compliance Programs (OFCCP), 274, 281
Office of Minority Enterprise Development, 150. *See also* Small Business Administration (SBA)
Off-the-job training, 265–266
Oligopoly, 34
Online banking, 427, 428, 431, 437
  physcial requirements necessary for, 433
Online (real-time) processing, 375
On-the-job training, 265
Open market operations, 422–423
Operating expenses, 403, 442–443. *See also* Short-term expenditures
Operating margin, 187
Operational planning, 174–175
Operational plans, 177. *See also* Operational planning
Operational risk, 457. *See also* Risk
Operations
  control, 238–241
  improving, 241–244
  trends affecting management of, 249
Operations management
  importance of, 247–248
  importance of production planning in, 226. *See also* Production planning
  main types of decisions in, 226
  and production, 225–226
  role of, 225–226
  techniques for improving, 249
  use of automation in, 242–244
Operations managers, 226, 248. *See also* Operations management
  scheduling and controlling production by, 249
Options, 452, 454, 461
Organic organization, 205, 217
Organizational career management, 269–271, 280
Organizational structure
  building blocks in, 198–205, 216, 217
  centralization of decision making, 203–205
  challenge of team-based, 302

  committee structure, 207–208
  common, 206–210
  departmentalization, 199–200, 201
  division of labor, 198–199
  effect on consumer of changes in, 215–216
  flat, 205. *See also* Organic organization
  tall versus, 206
  line-and-staff organization, 207
  line organization, 207
  managerial hierarchy, 200–202
  matrix structure, 208–210
  mechanistic versus organic, 205
  rebuilding, 198
  reengineering, 210–211
  span of control, 202–203
  streamlining, 221
  tall, 205. *See also* Mechanistic organization
Organization chart, 199
Organization of Petroleum Exporting Countries (OPEC), 33
Organized stock exchanges, 454–455
Organizing, 176, 192
  five ways of, 201
  process, 198. *See also* Organizational structure
Osborne, Richard, 464
Outcomes, 294, 295
  employee self-evaluation of, 294
Outputs
  converting inputs into, 225, 228, 229
  processes for, 228
Outsourcing, 145–146, 234–235, 276
  use of, by small businesses, 156
  of Web site management, 161
Over-the-counter (OTC) market, 454, 455
Owners' equity, 396, 397, 401

P

Pacheco, Javier, 160
Pacioli, Luca, 395–396
Packaging, 346, 348
Padget, Nat, 435
Panic of 1907, 422
Park, John, 122
Participative leadership, 179
Partnerships, 111–114
  advantages of, 112, 133
  between buyers and suppliers, 316
  choosing the right person in, 113
  combining marriage and, 114
  definition of, 111
  disadvantages of, 112–113, 133
  general, 112
  life insurance for, 478
    key-person, 481
  limited, 112
Par value, 448
Pate, John, 263
Patents, 395, 400, 470
Payne, Allison, 275
Payroll taxes, 475
PCs. *See* Computers, personal
Peabody, Bo, 105
Pember, Anne, 407
Penetration pricing, 350, 363
Pension funds, 428–429
Pension Reform Act (1974), 272, 273
Perceived value, 349
Perfect (pure) competition, 32
Performance, 295. *See also* Performance appraisal; Performance standards
  and feedback, 295
  group, 298
  use of teams to enhance, 298–302

Performance appraisal, 266–267, 280
Performance bond, 482
Performance standards, 181, 182
Perils of Partners, The (Gray), 113
Perks. *See also* Benefits
  health-related, 310
  as issue for workers, 308–309
Perpetual inventory, 235
Personal selling, 357, 358, 364
Pfeffer, Jeffrey, 287
Physical exams, 264
Piece-rate pay plans, 297
Piecework, 268
Piech, Ferdinand, 16
Pinchot, Gifford, 142
Planning, 172–176
  operational, 174–175
  strategic, 173–174
  tactical, 174
  types of, 173–176, 191–192
Platt, Lewis, 383
Pohn, Michael, 47
Point-of-sale (POS) terminals, 244, 397
Pomije, David, 204
Porter, Jim, 303
Portfolio, 453
Postconventional ethics, 84. *See also* Ethics
Power, primary sources of, 177
Preconventional ethics, 83–84. *See also* Ethics
Predatory dumping, 56. *See also* Dumping
Preferential tariffs, 59. *See also* Tariffs
Preferred stock, 450–451, 460, 461
Pregnancy Discrimination Act (1978), 273
Premiums, insurance, 428, 478
  costs of, 479
Preparedness argument, for tariffs, 54–55. *See also* Tariffs
Press releases, 359
Prestige pricing, 350, 363
Price discrimination, 472
Prices. *See also* Pricing
  demand for reasonable, 224
  establishing, 41
  interaction of demand and supply, to determine, 29–31
  steady, keeping, 23–24
Price skimming, 350, 362–363
Pricing, 349–350. *See also* Prices
  penetration, 350, 363
  prestige, 350, 363
  regulation of, 473
  relation of transportation to, 355–356
Pricing strategies, 321, 350, 362–363
Primary market, 452, 461
Principal, 448
Principles of Scientific Management, The (Taylor), 289
Privacy
  concerns, 382, 385, 386
  protection, report on evolving standards for, 475
Private accountants, 395, 412
Private enterprise system, 8. *See also* Capitalism
Problem-solving teams, 301–302, 307
Process departmentalization, 200. *See also* Departmentalization
Process layout, 234. *See also* Facility layouts
Process manufacturing, 228. *See also* Production process
Procurement, 234. *See also* Purchasing
Producer price index (PPI), 24
Product, 321
  definition of, 362
  departmentalization, 200. *See also* Departmentalization

differentiation, 33–34
  identification, 344
  offering, developing, 353–354
Product departmentalization, 200
Product identification, 344
Production, 246–247
  classification of types of, 228
  importance of, 247–248
  improving operations and, 241–244
  increased, 248
  inputs, availability of, 230
  modular, 245
  and operations control, 238–241
  and operations management, 225–226
  process for products and services, 225
  routing, 238
  streamlining, 241–242
  techniques for improving, 249
  timing, 228–229
  trends affecting management of, 249
  use of automation in, 242–243
Production orientation, 315
Production planning, 226
  facility layouts, 232, 233
  process, 227–229
  and resource planning, 232, 234
  site selection, 229
Production process
  considerations in choosing, 228–229
  types of, 228–229. *See also* Customization; Mass customization; Mass production
Production timing, 228–229
Productivity, 10
  improvements in, 13
Product layout, 234. *See also* Facility layouts
Product liability, 471–472
  insurance, 481
  suits, 472
Product liability law, 471–472
Product life cycle
  definition of, 348
  sales and profits during, 349
  stages, 348–349, 362
Products
  business, 343–344
  consumer, 342–343
  federal laws affecting promotion and pricing of, 473
  generic, 345–346
  process for developing new, 346–348
  role of, in marketing mix, 342–348
  tangible and intangible attributes of, 342
Product strategy, 321
Professional employer organization (PEO), 260
Professional liability insurance, 482. *See also* Insurance
Profitability ratios, 407–408
Profits, 16, 403
  maximizing, 442
  sharing of, in partnerships, 113. *See also* Partnerships
  of sole proprietorships, 110. *See also* Sole proprietorships
  taxation on corporate, 118
Profit sharing, 268
  plans, 297
Program evaluation and review technique (PERT), 240–241
Programmed instruction, 266
Prohibition, 389
Project management approach. *See* Matrix structure
Promotional mix, 357
  elements of, 357–359

Promotions, 269, 356
  sales. *See* Sales promotions
Promotion strategies, 322
  creating effective, 356–359
Property insurance, 481. *See also* Insurance
Property taxes, 475
Protected classes, 274–275. *See also* Affirmative action
Protectionism, 52, 62. *See also* Protective tariffs; Quotas, import
Protective tariffs, 54, 55
Psychographic segmentation, 328
Psychological pricing, 350
Public accountants, 394–395, 412
Public insurance, 479–480
Publicity, 359
Public relations, 322, 339, 357, 359
Purchasers, relationship between suppliers and, 237
Purchasing, 234
Purchasing power, 23
Pure Food and Drug Act (1906), 474
Pure monopoly, 32–33. *See also* Monopoly
Pure risk. *See* Risk

Q
Quality
  delivering value and, 34–35
  demand for high, 224, 241. *See also* Quality control; Total quality management (TQM)
  focus on, 225
Quality control, 241
Quality of life, 16, 309
Quotas, import, 55

R
Raiffa, Howard, 190
Rainbow, Roger, 190
Ratio analysis, 405
  sample, 406
  use of, 413
Raw materials, 344
Rayden, Michael, 104
Raymond, Lee, 127
Reach, as media evaluation, 358
Recession, 21
  in developing world, 51, 59
Recognition, 297–298, 310
Recruitment, 260
Reed, John, 202
Reengineering, 210–211
  goal of, 218
Reference check, 263–264
Referent power, 177
Regulations, trade, 55
Reid, Lucy, 195
Relationship management, 36
Relationship marketing, 316, 335
Renschler, Andreas, 180
Reserve requirements, 423, 429
Resignations, 270
Resource planning, 232, 234
  importance of, to production, 248–249
Restitution, 470
Restructuring, 197, 215. *See also* Reengineering
Résumés, 262, 280
Retailers, 351, 356
  in distribution channels, 352
  in-store and nonstore, 353
  small businesses as, 146. *See also* Small business
Retained earnings, 401, 450, 461
Retirement, 271

Return, 442
Return on equity (ROE), 408
Return on investment capital (ROIC), 187
Return on sales, 407–408
Returns and allowances, 401
Revenue, 16, 401
Revenue bonds, 453
Revolving credit agreement, 446
Reward power, 177
Richards, Stan, 209
Right principle, 314
Rings of defense approach, 270. See also
    Layoffs
Rios, Danielle, 271
Risk, 16, 442. See also Risk management
    assessment of, 479
    avoidance, 477
    bank, 430
    high, 429
    insurable, 478–479
    reduction, 478
    return on equity and level of, 408
    speculative, 477
    strategies to manage, 477–478
    takers, 17. See also Entrepreneurs
    transference, 478
    types of, 457, 477
    of uncollected accounts receivable, 443
Risk assumption. See Self-insurance
Risk management, 457–458, 477. See also
    Insurance companies
Risk-return trade-off, 442
Robinson-Patman Act (1936), 473
Robotics, 243
Robots, 223, 243
Rocca, Mike, 277
Rodriguez, Arturo, 322
Rogers, Fran, 114
Rollout, 348
Roney, William C., Sr., 436
Roosevelt, Franklin D., 429
Rosenthal, Norman, 365
Rouse, Rolly, 169
Routing, 238
Rowe, Derek, 47
Rumor mill, 212. See also Informal
    organization
Russian Commodities and Raw Materials
    Exchange, 38–39
Ryan, Tim, 122

S

Saarelainen, Jari, 309
Sabatino, Casper, 407
St. John's Wort: The Herbal Way to Feeling
    Good (Rosenthal), 365
Salaries, 267, 268
Salazar, Elaine, 153
Sales discounts, 401
Sales promotions, 357, 358–359
Sales prospects, 358
Sales taxes, 476
Salzman, Barry, 73
Samaranch, Juan Antonio, 211
San Jose Mercury News, 260
Savings and loan associations (S&Ls),
    426–427, 429
Savings Association Insurance Fund (SAIF),
    429, 434
Savings banks, 426–427
Savings bonds, 27
Scheduling, 238–239
    tools, 239–241
Schrempp, Jurgen, 180
Schroder, Henrik, 253
Schultz, Don, 337–338

Schulz, Carol, 283
Schutz, Jared, 141
Schwartz, Paula Mae, 114
Schwartz, Steve, 114
Scientific management, 288–289
    basic principles of, 289, 304
SCORE. See Service Corps of Retired
    Executives (SCORE)
S corporations, 118. See also Corporations
Scott, Tom, 139, 144, 149, 164
Seasonal unemployment, 23. See also
    Unemployment
Sechler, Carolyn, 311
Secondary market, 452, 461
Secured loans, 446, 460
Securities, 451, 461
    loans backed by, 429
    popular types of, 452
    selling of, by banks, 431
    trading, effect of Federal Reserve actions
        on, 423
    U.S. government, 453. See also specific
        types
Securities Act (1933), 456, 461
Securities and Exchange Commission (SEC),
    413, 417, 456, 459, 462, 466
Securities Exchange Act (1934), 456, 461
    amendment (1964), 462
Securities exchanges, 454–455
    major U.S., 461
Securities Investor Protection Corporation
    (SIPC), 456
Securities markets, 439, 451–454, 461
    regulation of, 456
        self-, 456
    role of investment bankers and
        stockbrokers in, 452
    types of, 452
Security, data, 379–381, 385
Selection
    interview, 263
    process of employee, 262–264
Selective credit controls, 423
Selective distribution, 354–355
Self-employment. See also Entrepreneurs;
    Small business
    as advancement for minority groups, 160.
        See also Minorities
    home-based, 158, 164
Self-insurance, 477–478
Self-managed work teams, 300, 307
Seller cooperatives, 120. See also
    Cooperatives
Selling process, steps in, 358
Separations, employee, 270–271. See also
    specific categories
Service Corps of Retired Executives (SCORE),
    150, 195
Servicemarks, 471
Services, 16, 344
    customized, 227–228
    delivery of, to customers, 224–225
    finding effective methods of producing,
        224
    growth of, 21, 245. See also Economic
        growth
    personalized, 251–252
    and physical distribution, 360
    small businesses engaged in, 146. See
        also Small business
    use of robots in, 243
Service sector, 134
Shareholders, 116. See also Stockholders
Sherman Antitrust Act (1890), 466, 472
Shopping products, 343
Short-term expenditures, 442–443, 460
Silver, Joshua, 77

Silverman, Henry, 179
Site selection, 229
    availability of production inputs related to,
        230
    consideration of manufacturing environ-
        ment for, 231
    importance of, 248
    influence of incentives on, 230–231
    international location considerations
        regarding, 231–232
    marketing factors related to, 230
"Six degrees of separation" concept, 213
Skills inventory, 260
Slander, 471
Small business, 140–141. See also
    Entrepreneurs
    advantages of, 147–148, 165
    buying, 154
    categories, 146–147
    challenges of, 165
    characteristics of, 146
    difficulty of obtaining credit for, 433
    disadvantages of, 148–149, 165
    environment, trends in, 165–166
    generating ideas for, 162–163
    global opportunities for, 157
    hiring and retaining employees, 156–157
    managing, 155–157
    minorities and, 165–166
    ownership, risks of, 154–155
    reasons for forming, 145–146
    start-up funding for, 153–154
        sources of, 155
    types of, by industry, 147
    typical American, 146
    use of outside consultants by, 156
    working for, advantages and disadvan-
        tages of, 163–164
Small Business Administration (SBA), 63,
    141, 146, 147, 154, 165
    financial assistance programs, 149–150
    help provided by, 165
    loan guarantees for African Americans,
        160. See also Minorities
    management assistance programs, 150
    Office of Advocacy, 159
Small Business Development Centers, 150.
    See also Small Business Administration
    (SBA)
Small Business Investment Companies
    (SBICs), 149–150
Small Enterprise Foundation, 38
Small-world model, 213
Smart car, 15–16, 19, 40
Smart cards, 432
Smith, Fred, 285
Social change, 275
Social investing, 98
Socialism, 9
Socialization, work, 298
Social marketing, 323
Social responsibility, 89, 91–94, 101
    of businesses, 102
    components of, 89, 92
    definition of, 102
    displayed through corporate philanthropy,
        97
    to environment, 97
    firms embracing, 87–88, 89, 91
    global and domestic trends in, 102–103
    pyramid of corporate, 92
    trends in global ethics and, 99–100
    understanding, 92–94
Social Security, 269
    benefits under, 480
    taxes, 475
Social Security Act (1935), 273

Software
  accounting, 397
  banking, 433
  customized, 444
  enterprise, 372
  industry-specific, 388
  marketing campaign, 369–370
  piracy, 380
  specialized, 391–392
Sole proprietorships, 109–111
  advantages of, 110, 133
  definition of, 110
  disadvantages of, 110–111, 133
Soliman, Peter, 15
Span of control, 202–203
Span of management. See Span of control
Sparks, Steven, 407
Specialization, 198–199
Specialty products, 343
Specific performance, of contract, 470
Speculative risk, 477
Spirit of Liberty, The (Hand), 466
Staff positions, 207
  difference between line positions and, 217
Stakeholders
  definition of, 94
  responsibilities to, 94–98, 102
Standard of living, 16
  factors in creating, 40
  in Korea, 125
Stanius, Brad, 81
Startup: A Silicon Valley Adventure (Kaplan), 167
State banks, 426
Statement of cash flows, 403–404
  importance of, 413
  sample, 405
Statutory law, 466
Stewart-Gordon, Tom, 458
Stock, 118, 442, 460
  common, 449–450, 460, 461
  preferred, 450–451, 460, 461
  purchase of, in competing corporations to lessen competition, outlawing of, 472
Stockbrokers, 452, 461
Stock dividends, 450. See also Dividends
Stock exchanges
  foreign, 455
  major U.S., 454–455
Stockholders, 116
  IPOs and, 449–450
Stock insurance companies, 480
Stock market. See also Bonds; Securities exchanges; Securities markets; Stock
  "Black Monday" of 1987, 456
  circuit breakers, 456
  crash of 1929, 429, 431, 456
Storage warehouses, 355
Stovall, Jim, 148
Strategic alliances, 36
Strategic giving, 98–99
Strategic partnerships. See Strategic alliances
Strategic planning, 173–174
Strategic plans, 177. See also Strategic planning
Strict liability, 472
Structural unemployment, 22. See also Unemployment
Studley, Jeff, 111, 112–113
Sullivan, Thomas, 436
Supervisory management, 176, 177. See also Management
Supplemental insurance, 480
Suppliers
  building relationships with quality, 235
  cost concessions from, 234

improving communications with, 237–238
  relationship between purchasers and, 237
Supplies, 344
Supply
  changes in, 31
  and demand, interaction to determine prices, 29–31
  nature of, 29
Supply chain, 237
Supply chain management, 237
Supply curve, 29
Surety bond. See Performance bond
Survey research, 330
  Internet, 329, 331
  types of interviews used in, 331
Sutton, Sara, 107–108, 132
Swanson, Harold, 388
Swanson, Ruth, 388
Synergy, 299, 307

T

Tactical planning, 174
Tactical plans, 177. See also Tactical planning
Tan, Chung-Jen, 190
Tangible assets, 395
Tareen, Shoaib, 236
Target markets, 313
  in banking industry, 431
  defining, 318
  dependence of retailers on, 353–354
  identifying, 336
  use of market segmentation to identify, 325–326. See also Market segmentation
Tariffs, 54
  arguments for and against, 54–55
  elimination of most, under Mercosur, 60
  preferential, 59
  protective, 54, 55
Taxes, 25, 475–476. See also Income taxes
  affecting employee compensation, 272
  business, 475–476
  for corporations, 117–118
  by country, 26
  European, 47
  excise, 476
  for partnerships, 112
  payroll, 475, 480
  progressive, 475
  property, 475
  reduction of, as incentives, 230–231
  sales, 476
  for sole proprietorships, 110
  unemployment, 475
Taylor, Frederick W., 288–289
Taylor, Jeffrey, 219
Teams
  cross-functional, 283, 300
  problem-solving, 300
  types of, 299–300. See also Work groups
  use of, to enhance motivation and performance, 298–302
  virtual, 302
Technical skills, 185–186
Technology, 9. See also Telecommuting
  advances in, 12
  advancing, 276–277
  and automation in nonmanufacturing operations, 244
  CAD/CAM, 242–243
  collections and, 444
  cutting-edge, for mass customization, 359
  effect on businesses of, 385
  growth of international trade fostered by new, 72

increase in home-based businesses due to, 158
  job searches using, 261
  in restaurants, 244
  role of, in operations management, 249
  secure Internet, 161
  sophisticated, for observation research, 332
  training workers for new, 303
  trends in, 10–11
  use of, by banks, 224–225
Tedesco, Ralph, 315–316
Teich, Jonathan, 377
Telecommuting, 276–277, 278, 297
  -friendly employers, 277
Telemarketers, 382
Terminations, 270, 272
Term loans, 448
Test-marketing, 348
Theft insurance, 482
Theory X, 291, 306
Theory Y, 292, 305–306
Thompson, Todd, 370
Three-questions test, 87
Thrift institutions, 426–427
  failure of, 430
Thurow, Lester, 4
Thylefors, Bjorn, 77
Tie, Liu, 53
Tilbury, Hal, 380
Time deposits, 421
Time management, 190
Title insurance, 482. See also Insurance
Tokyo Stock Exchange, 454, 455
Top management, 176, 177. See also Management
Tort law, 471
Torts, 471
Total quality management (TQM), 241
Toyoda, Shuhei, 16
Trade, 52
  barriers
    international, 52–56
    natural, 53–54
    nontariff, 55–56
    tariff, 54–55
  effect of Uruguay Round on, 56–58
  global, 62–66
    fostering, 56–59
    measurements of, 74–75
  international, 75
  regulations, 55
Trade and Development Act (2000), 55
Trade credit, 445–446
Trade deficit, 50
Trademarks, 344, 395, 400, 471
Trade shows, 78
Trade surplus, 50, 51
Training and development, 264–265
  process, 264
Transaction processing system (TPS), 373, 374–375
Transfers, 269
Transportation, 355–356, 357
  criteria for selecting mode of, 363
Treasury bills, 27, 443, 453
Treasury bonds, 27, 422–423, 453
Treasury Department, 56, 422–423, 426
Treasury notes, 27, 453
Treasury securities, 452
Treaty on European Union. See European Union (EU)
Trends, 1
  affecting marketing mix, 364
  banking, 430–431, 434

Trends *(continued)*
  business, 2–3, 34–39, 71–72, 98–100,
    128–129, 157–161, 188–189, 214–
    215, 245–246, 275–277, 302, 332–
    333, 359–360, 383–384, 409–410
  consolidation, 132. *See also* Acquisitions;
    Mergers
  in corporate philanthropy, 98–99
  demographic, 4–7
  in ethics, 99–100, 102–103
  in financial management, 457–459
  in financial services, 433
  in global competition, 11–13
  in global marketplace, 76
  in information technology, 386
  key, in microeconomics, 37–39
  major, affecting accounting industry, 413
  in management, 188–189, 192, 249
  merger, 134
  microeconomic, 34–35, 42
  new social contract, 99
  in small business environment, 165–166
  social, 3–4
  technological, 9–11
  in understanding consumers, 336
Trial balance, 396
Trial courts, 467
Triant, Deborah, 190
Tulgan, Bruce, 296
Tying contracts, 472

U

Underwriting, 452, 478
Unemployment
  rate, 22
  taxes, 475–476
  types of, 22–23
Unemployment compensation, 269
Unemployment Compensation Commission,
  269
Unemployment insurance, 480
Unemployment rate, 22
Unethical actions
  condoning, 86
  recognizing, 86–87
Uniform Commercial Code (UCC), 466–467
Uniform Franchise Offering Circular (UFOC),
  130
Unions, seniority system in, 269
United States
  absolute advantage of, 52
  economy. *See* Economy
  entrepreneurs. *See also* Entrepreneurs
  entrepreneurs in, 141
  federal government, as largest single
    insurer, 479
  federal regulatory agencies, 468
  financial system, 422, 424–429
  Fortune's list of best places to work in, 96
  importance of global trade to, 49, 74
  infrastructure of, 68
  as largest exporter, 63
  legal system, 466–467
  major stock exchanges, 454–455
  mixed economy of, 9
  money supply, 421, 434. *See also*
    Federal Reserve System (the Fed)
  small businesses in, 145, 146. *See also*
    Small business
  taxes in, 25. *See also* Taxes
  use of monetary policy and fiscal policy
    by, 41. *See also* Fiscal policy;
    Monetary policy
Unity of command principle, 202. *See also*
  Chain of command

Unsecured loans, 445–446
Unsought products, 343
Uruguay Round, 56–58
U.S. Army, 323
U.S. Bureau of Economic Analysis, 21
U.S. Census Bureau, 326
U.S. Commerce Department, 56, 66, 384
U.S. Congress
  creation of Federal Reserve System by,
    422. *See also* Federal Reserve System
  issue of tariffs and, 54–55
  lobbying of, by American steel producers,
    57
  passage of antidumping laws by, 56. *See
    also* Dumping
  ratification of NAFTA by, 59. *See also*
    North American Free Trade Agreement
    (NAFTA)
  setting of income taxes by, 475
U.S. Constitution, 83, 467, 470
U.S. Department of Energy, 45
U.S. Food and Drug Administration, 322
U.S. International Trade Administration (ITA),
  49
U.S. Patent and Trademark Office, 344, 470
U.S. Postal Service, 33
U.S. Supreme Court, 467
U.S. Treasury Department. *See* Treasury
  Department
Utilitarianism, 82–83

V

Value
  brand names and, 321
  customer, 35, 315
  delivering quality and, 34–35
  marketing, 35
  perceived, 349
Van Wezel, John, 81
Variable pay, 297
Venture capital, 154, 167, 451, 461, 465
Vergara, Jorge, 322
Vergara, Pepe, 322
Vernon, Lillian, 145
Verrochi, Paul M., 144
Vertical marketing systems, 354
Vertical mergers, 127. *See also* Mergers
Vestibule training, 265–266
Videoconferencing, 303
Vietnam Veterans Readjustment Act (1974),
  273
Virtual corporations, 214–215, 218
  key attributes of, 214
Virtual organizations, 220. *See also* Virtual
  corporations
Virtual teams, 302, 307, 311
Voice mail systems, 377
Volume segmentation, 328
Voluntary bankruptcy, 472
Voluntary reduction in pay, 270. *See also*
  Layoffs
Voluntary time off, 270. *See also* Layoffs

W

Wagenhals, Fred, 8
Wall Street, 19, 178, 446, 458
Wall Street Journal, 263, 384
Warehouses, 355
Warranties, 470
Washington Post, 260
Web. *See* World Wide Web (WWW)
Web sites. *See also* Business-to-business
    market; Internet; World Wide Web
    (WWW)

bargains on, 191
calculating popularity of, 181
creating, 168, 195, 216
for developing customer traffic to retailers,
  366
job announcements on, 261
job search, 219
for online marketing, 161. *See also*
  E-commerce
selling marketing space on, 169
for suppliers, 237–238
Weill, Sandy, 202
Weinberg, Sandy, 158
Welch, Jack, 94, 180
Wells, Jared, 391–392, 412
Wheeler-Lea Act (1938), 473
Wholesalers, 351
  in distribution channels, 351–352
  small businesses as, 146. *See also* Small
    business
Wickham, Dave, 85
Wide area network (WAN), 372–373. *See
  also* Extranets; Internet; Intranets
Williams, Julie, 148
Williams, Tom, 161
Winn, Craig, 285
Women. *See also* Affirmative action
  appeal of entrepreneurship to, 159
  business owners, 159
  mentoring of, 276
  small businesses and, 165–166
  working, 4, 134
Wonderlic Personnel Test, 262
Word processing systems, 377
Work cell design, 246
Workers' compensation, 269, 480
Workforce. *See also* Employees
  as competitive advantage, 304
  creating a competitive, 37
  employed in small businesses, 140. *See
    also* Small business
  knowledge of, 18
  women in, 4. *See also* Women
Work groups
  formal and informal, 298
  versus work teams, 299
Work-life benefits, 303
Work-scheduling options, 297
Work teams. *See also* Teams
  building high-performance,
    300–301
  self-managed, 300
  types of, 307
  virtual, 311
  versus work groups, 299
World Bank, 58
  official poverty line of, 38
World Health Organization, 77
World Trade Organization (WTO), 58, 72
World Wide Web (WWW). *See also* Internet
  increase in small businesses due to, 145.
    See also Small business
  potential of marketing surveys conducted
    on, 329
  registering addresses for, 43–44
  virtual stores on, 161, 162

Y

Yang, Jerry, 168

Z

Zagat, Nina, 162
Zagat, Tim, 162
Zarate, Steve, 189

A

Accel Partners, 465
Ace, 120
ACNielsen, 330, 332
Action for Children's Television, 104
Actuarial Consultants, Inc. (ACI), 379
ACT-UP, 99
Adaptive Eyecare Ltd., 77
Adrienne Vittadini, 354
Aetna, 480
AIDS Rides, 97
Airbus, 253
Air Canada, 259
Air France, 461
AirTouch Communications, 129
Alamo Rent a Car, 139
Alaska Airlines, 461
Alexander Doll Co., 171, 172, 191
Allegheny Ludlum, 346
Allied Signal, 303, 409
Allstate Insurance, 480
Amazon.com, 141, 142, 216, 417, 465, 475
AMD, 237
American Airlines, 17, 263, 264, 266, 275, 316
American Automobile Association (AAA), 337–338
American Bankers Association, 424
American Building Restoration Products, 63
American Cancer Society, 17
American Express, 74, 88, 333
American Heart Association, 323
American Information Systems, Inc. (AIS), 141
American Management Association, 187
American Society for Quality, 13
America Online (AOL), Inc., 127, 136, 161, 181, 195, 410, 434
Ampersand Art Supply, 153
Amway, 322
Analyst's Accounting Observer, 417
Andersen Worldwide, 395
Angelfire, 381
Anheuser-Busch, 99
Anthro Corp., 236
Apple Computer, Inc., 91, 98, 181, 191, 206, 343, 455, 471
APV, 69
Arby's, 244
Archway Cookies, 388-389
Argent Trading, 66
Ariel, 71
Associates First Capital Corporation, 434
Astound, 332
AT&T, 13, 62, 99, 274, 278, 361, 372, 429, 454
Athlete's Foot, 122
AutoCITE, 78
Automated Power Exchange (APX), 45
AutoPARK, 78
Avado Brands, 279
Avalon, 246
AviationX, 253
Avon, 321

B

Baan Co., 271
Banc One Corp., 436
Bang and Olufsen, 354
BankAmerica, 210
BankNotes, 428
Bank of Alma, 104–105, 436
Bank of America, 265, 431

Bank of Lakeview, 436
Bank of New York, 72
Barnes and Noble, 132
BASF, 70
Beacon Application Services Corp., 261
Beecham, 70
Beijing Dazhong Trading Group, 53
Belk, Inc., 376, 383
Bell Atlantic, 202
Bell Labs, 320
Ben & Jerry's, 87–88, 91, 174, 175, 188
Beneficial Corp., 429
Berne Apparel, 246
Bestfoods, 129
Bethlehem Steel, 288
BetzDearborn, 446
Be Your Own Boss magazine, 130
Bigstep.com, 195
BigWords.com, 191
BINDCO, 220
BizPlan*Builder*, 220
Black & Decker, 171, 343
Black Forest Motors, 44
Blockbuster Video, 367
Bloomberg, 381
Bluebird Systems, 379–380
Blue Diamond, 120
BMW, 3, 320, 359
Boeing Co., 11–12, 13, 34, 50, 66, 234, 236, 253, 260, 444, 447
Boo.com, 339
Booz-Allen Hamilton, 15, 177
Borden's, 346
Boys and Girls Clubs of America, 97
Boy Scouts of America, 16
Breck, 343
Brigham and Women's Hospital, 377
Brik Pak, 346
Bristol-Myers, 94
British Airways, 315
British Midland, 461
Broadview Associates, 127
Brooks Brothers, 353
BT: Employee Screening Services, 263
Budget Gourmet, 327
Budweiser, 93
Burger King, 129, 244
Burke Marketing Research, 338–339
Burlington Northern Santa Fe Railway, 264, 274
Burton Snowboards, 366

C

Cabot Corporation, 232
Cacharel, 65
Cadaco, 6
Cadillac, 3, 316
Calavo, 120
CAMI Automotive, 65
Campbell Soup, 88, 346, 354
Camp DaKaNi, 93
Camp Fire Boys and Girls, 93
Camry, 246
Canyon Cafe, 279
Cape Cod Potato Chips, 345
Capital Business Finance, 429
Capital Corp., 53
Capital Research Center, 99
Cardio Chips, 365
Career Central, 261
CareerPath, 260
Carlson Co., 292
Carlson Wagonlit Travel, 292
Carnival Cruise Lines, 318, 321
Cartier, 320

Case Corp., 398
Catera, 3
Caterpillar, 277, 320
CDNow, 162
Cendant Corp., 407, 410
Centura Bank, 443
Cessna, 341
CFO magazine, 398, 439, 442
Challenger, Gray & Christmas, 132
Chaparral Steel, 320
Charles Schwab, 3, 132
Chase Manhattan, 132, 431
Chattahoochee National Bank, 435
Check Point Software Technologies, Inc., 190
Cheer, 71
ChemLawn, 354
Chevrolet, 327, 341, 344
Chevron Corp., 383, 454
Children's Orchard, 121, 373
China Mist Tea Co., 345
Chrysler Corp., 15, 129, 180, 218, 313
CIGNA Corporation, 480
Cisco Systems, Inc., 214–215, 276
Citibank, 121
Citicorp, 419
Citigroup, 72, 88, 94, 190, 202, 419–420, 421, 431, 432, 434, 452
Clinique, 321
Club Med, 4
CMP Media, 95
CNet, 384
Coca-Cola, 18, 37, 38, 62, 67, 94, 97, 99, 174, 262, 265, 274, 320, 344, 345, 355, 361, 454, 471, 475
Colby Care Nurses, Inc., 89, 91
Cold Fusion Sports, 161, 162
Colorado Rules, 142
Colorado Wild Birds Unlimited, Inc., 128
Company Corporation, The, 116
Compaq Computer, 16, 195, 257–258, 266, 318
CompuServe, 434
Computer Learning Centers, 95–96
Consumer Reports, 335
Continental Airlines, 439, 461
Continental Insurance, 480
Contingency Planning & Management magazine, 175
Control Data Corp., 270
Coors, 455
Corning, Inc., 96–97, 346
Costas Foods, 94
Costco Wholesale, 89, 90
Council for Marketing and Opinion Research (CMOR), 334
Cover Girl, 321
CPR MultiMedia Solutions, 111, 112–113
Craftsman, 345
Crest, 197, 328
Crisco, 356
CUC International, 179, 407
Cyprus Amax Mineral Co., 10

D

Daimler-Benz, 15, 40, 129, 180, 218, 313
DaimlerChrysler, 3, 19, 180, 202, 215, 218, 313, 314, 336
Daiwa, 457
Dana Corp., 95
Datek Online, 459, 463
DeBeers Consolidated Mines Ltd., 33
DejaNews, 85
Delfield Co., 464

Del Laboratories, 321
Dell Computer, 62, 187, 325, 359, 410, 444, 455
Del Monte, 346
Deloitte & Touche Tohmatsu, 395, 409
Denny's, 97
Deutsche Genossenschaftsbank, 47
Dewar's, 105
Diedrich Coffee, Inc., 122, 129
DieHard, 345
Digital Equipment Corp. (DEC), 257–258
Directbanking.com, 437
Direct Hit Technologies, 153, 181
Direct Marketing Association, 334
Discover Brokerage, 463
Disneyland, 213
Disney World, 23
Dockers, 3, 356
Dog Chow, 346
Doing It Best, 120
Don Pablo's, 255, 256, 279
DoubleClick International, 73, 132, 189
DoubleTree Hotels, 316
Dow Chemical, 69, 71, 346
Dreyfus Brokerage Services, 463
Dun & Bradstreet, 149
DuPont, 136, 273, 319
Duracell International, Inc., 48
Dustbusters, 347

E

E*Trade, 65, 463
Eastman Kodak, 98, 99
Eaton Corp., 301
E-Bay, 11, 216
Edward Lowe Foundation, 144
Egghead.com, 168, 475
Ektar, 318
Electronic Share Information (ESI), 65
Elevonic 411, 71
Embassy Suites, 316
Employease, 156
Enforcement Technology, Inc. (ETEC), 78
Engelhard Corporation, 311
Enterprise Earnings Protection Insurance, 457–458
Entrepreneur magazine, 124, 130, 151, 180
Equifax, 385
Erickson, 475
Ernst & Young, 395
Esprit, 86
Estée Lauder, 321
eToys, 450
Evans Products Co., 354
Excite, 279
EXECUSTAFF, 220
Expedia Travel, 191
Experian, 385
Express, 318
Exxon, 127
Exxon Mobil, 69, 94, 127, 202, 204, 215

F

Farmland Industries, 120
Fashion Adventure program, 104
Fashionmall.com, 339
FAST, Inc., 244
FastWeb.com, 191
Federal Express, 1, 69, 72, 95, 256, 265, 277, 285, 291, 320, 360
Fiat, 55
Fidelity Mutual, 231
Finance.com, 419–420
Fireman's Fund Insurance, 480
1st Armored, Inc., 436

Firstbank Corporation, 104, 436
Firstbank of Mt. Pleasant, 436
First Bank of West Branch, 436
First Boston, 452
First Chicago NBD Corp., 436
First Security Bank of New Mexico, 424
First Union, 431
Ford Motor Company, 3, 5, 6, 15, 19, 50, 62, 94, 202, 303, 308–309, 327, 347, 441, 454, 475
Fortune 500, 115, 345, 398
Fortune magazine, 95, 96, 101, 115, 287, 291, 302, 310, 461
France Telecom, 475
Franchise 500, 124
Franchise World magazine, 130
Free-Standing Insert (FSI), 283, 310
Freight World, 357
Frequency Marketing, Inc., 333
Frito-Lay, 48, 343, 371, 471
Fruit-of-the-Loom, 64
Frullati Cafe and Bakery, 129
Fuji Film, 58, 66
Fuji Xerox, 71
FuncoLand, 204

G

Gallo, 350
Gap, Inc., 86, 174, 317, 410
GapKids, 175
GartnerGroup, 311
Geac, 398
GE Capital Corp., 127–128
GE Capital Small Business Finance, 429
Geekcorps, 105
General Dynamics, 258
General Electric Co., 18, 50, 62, 66, 69, 94, 99, 114, 127, 180, 188, 204, 260, 264
GeneraLife, 214
General Motors (GM), 3, 8, 13, 19, 50, 62, 63, 65, 66, 69, 94, 98, 99, 213, 230, 234, 235, 236, 243, 271, 316, 343, 357, 398, 415, 440, 445–446
General Motors Foundation, 98
GetSmart, 460
Giga Information Group, 465
Gillette, 12, 48, 69, 174, 327, 354
Ginkgo Biloba Rings, 365
Girl Scouts of America, 103
Global Days of Caring, 93
Go Corporation, 167
Goldman Sachs Group, 452
Gomez Advisors, 437
Goodyear, 341, 445–446, 475
Gore-Tex, 263
Greater Miami Chamber of Commerce, 81
Greenpeace, 17
GrowBiz, 128
GTE, 202
Gucci, 321
Guerrilla Marketing, 358
Guns 'n' Roses, 6

H

Häagen-Dazs, 12
Hagberg Consulting Group, 144
Hanes, 354
Hardee's, 244
Harley-Davidson, 54, 187, 188, 199, 223, 228, 234, 243, 248, 291, 300, 344
Hartek, 464
Hawthorne Western Electric, 289, 304
HCA–The Health Care Company, 228
Healtheon Corp., 142

Henri Bendel, 318
Herbalife, 322
Hertz, 122
Hewlett-Packard, 69, 99, 173, 271, 300, 346, 383
HFS, Inc., 178–179, 407
Highsmith, Inc., 193–194
Hilton Hotels, 274
Hoechst AG, 129
Holiday Inn, 122
Homark, 464
Home Depot, 84, 121, 200–201
HomePortfolio.com, 169
Homestead Gardens, 317
Homestyle Corp., 376
Honda, 62, 69, 70, 72, 265
Honeywell, Inc., 230, 277, 303, 409
Honey Wood, 376
Hops, 279
Horizon Communications, 156
Hot Pots, 109–110
Household International, 429
Houston Astros, 270
Hugo Boss, 197
Hunt's, 346
Hyatt Hotels, 324
Hypermart, 162

I

IBM, 50, 62, 63, 66, 97, 98–99, 114, 132, 271, 277, 343, 344, 369, 411, 454
IDC/LINK Resources Corp., 5
Idealab, 151
iMac, 206
Inc. 500, 142, 150, 157
Inc. magazine, 139
Inca Kola, 67
Independent Broker-Dealer Association, 463
Independent Grocers Alliance (IGA), 345
Industry Week, 231, 302
Information Technology Association of America, 384
InfoSpace, 162
Inglenook, 350
Inovie Software, 311
Instinet, 463
Intel, 180, 237, 263, 319, 344, 382, 455
Intermec Technologies Corp., 388
International Data Corp., 431, 445
International Franchise Association, 130
International Olympic Committee (IOC), 211
International Parking Conference and Exposition, 78
InterSpar, 47
IOMEGA Corp., 95
Island, 459

J

Jack in the Box, 359
Jaguar, 354
Jamba Juice, 121, 129
Jantzen, 91, 355
JCPenney, 6, 93, 204, 264, 352
Jeep, 344
JIAN, 220
Jiffy Lube, 121
JobDirect, Inc., 107–108, 132
Jody B Fashions, 251
Joe Camel, 93
John Hancock, 480
Joy, 346
JP Morgan, 94

K

Kava Corn Chips, 365
Keep America Beautiful, 17
Kellogg's, 35, 62
Kenmore, 345
Kenneth Cole, 376
Kentucky Fried Chicken, 124
KeyCorp, 369–370, 373, 376, 383, 385
Kinder-Care, 477
Kinko's, 121
Kleenex, 136, 344, 356, 471
Kmart, 251, 477
Knowledge Networks, 332
Kodak, 33, 58, 66, 318, 344, 355
Kool-Aid, 349
Korn/Ferry International, 132, 261
KPMG International, 395
Kraft-General Foods, 328, 357
Kroger, 265
Kysor Industrial Corp., 464

L

Labatt Brewing Company, 64
Lagasse Brothers, 351
Land O' Lakes, 120
Lands' End, 269
La-Z-Boy, 387
Le Menu, 327
Lerner New York, 318
Levi Strauss and Co., 3, 13, 36, 37, 65, 86, 88, 95, 100, 356, 359
Lexus, 3, 35, 315, 320, 356–357
Lillian Vernon, 145
Limited, Inc., 318
Limited Too, 104
Liz Claiborne, 345
Loanshop.com, 445
Lockheed Martin, 236
Lotus Institute, 190
Louisiana-Pacific Corp., 92–93
Lowe's, 121
Loyola University Medical Center, 243
Lucent Technologies, 93, 97
Lufthansa, 259
Lycos, 105, 279, 381

M

M.A.D.D., 323
M&Ms, 325
McDonald's, 16, 64, 69, 87, 121, 124, 238, 244, 268, 273, 315, 321, 322, 354, 361
McDonnell Douglas, 34
McGraw-Hill, 359
Macintosh, 220
MCI WorldCom, 265, 372, 455
Macy's, 132
Mail Boxes Etc., 129
Marlboro, 344
Marriott, 87, 318
Mars Corp., 21, 325
Marshall Field's, 194
Mattel, 359
Maytag, 320, 355
Mazda, 72
MBE Business Express, 129
Men's Warehouse, 264
Mercantile Transport, Inc., 160
Mercedes-Benz, 44
Merck, 97, 263
Merrill Lynch & Co., 265, 272, 452
Methodist Church, 323

Metropolitan Life, 480
MGM, 367
Miami Airport Authority, 101
Miami Baggage Cart, Inc., 82
Miami International Airport, 81–82, 101
Micro Compact Car, 15
Microsoft Corp., 8, 18, 53, 114, 121, 177–178, 221, 263, 266, 277, 344, 379, 382, 391, 455, 457
Midvale Steel, 288
Miller Brewing Co., 64, 268
Mimics, 151
Minolta, 343
Miracle Restoration Kit, 4
Miracle Whip, 328
Miramax Films, 367
Mitsubishi Motors, 67, 230
Mobil, 127
Mobile One, 420
Money Store Commercial Lending, The, 429
Monster.com, 157, 219
Moody's Investor Services, 449
Moore School of Business (University of South Carolina), 276
Morgan Stanley Dean Witter, 452
Moto Photo, 121
Motorola, 22, 53, 204–205, 274
Motor Trend magazine, 313
MTV, 325
Museum of Science and Industry, 323
Music Go Round, 128

N

Nantucket Allserve, 139, 164
Nantucket Nectars, Inc., 139, 149, 164
Narrative Television Network (NTN), 148
National Black MBA Association, 94
National Cooperative Business Association, 120
National Fluid Milk Processor Promotion Board, 318
National Geographic Society, 276
National Retail Federation, 353
National SemiConductor, 261
National Wildlife Federation, 323
NationsBank, 262, 431
Nation's Business magazine, 131
Nationwide Papers, 351
Neiman Marcus, 317, 320
Nestlé, 66, 71–72
NetBank, 428
Netscape Communications Corp., 127, 141, 142, 144, 267, 434
Network Solutions, Inc., 43–44
New York Life, 480
New York Mets, 471
New York State Electric and Gas Corp., 315–316
Nicholson-Hardie Nursery & Garden Center, 317
Nike, 34, 72, 100, 180, 345
Niphix Investments, 458, 459
Nissan, 72
Nordstrom Department Stores, 455
Northwest Airlines, 461
Northwestern Mutual Life, 480

O

Ocean Spray Cranberries, Inc., 120, 140
Old Navy, 175
Omnilife, 322
Once Upon a Child, 128
1-800 Contacts, 153
One Plus Financial, 259
Online Journal of Ethics, 85

Onsale.com, 167–168
Optimal Resolutions, Inc., 153
Oracle, 132, 221
Orangina, 67
Oregon Chai Tea Company, 160
OS/2 Warp, 63
Otis Elevator, 71

P

Pacific Bell, 292
PairGain Technologies, Inc., 381
Palm Computing, 245
Palmolive, 346
Palm Pilot, 245
Pandesic LLC, 161
Parker Brothers, 6
Partnerware Technologies, 153
Patriot American Hospitality, Inc., 447
PC Magazine, 384
Peace Corps, 132
Pea in the Pod, A, 320
Pentium, 344, 382
PeopleSoft, Inc., 189, 271
PepsiCo, 48, 300, 345, 361, 371
Personality Puffs, 365
Pets.com, 465
Peugeot, 62
Pfizer, 98, 126, 475
Pharmacia & Upjohn, 215
Pharmacia AB, 215
Philip Morris, 64, 99, 357
Phillips Petroleum, 271
Phylway Construction, 160
Pizza Hut, 122, 327
Planned Parenthood, 99
Play It Again Sports, 128
Pocket Blimp, 341, 362
Polaroid, 32–33, 345
Potomac Electric Power Co. (Pepco), 175–176
PowerPoint, 332
Precision Tune Auto Care, 128–129
Priceline.com, 361, 417
PricewaterhouseCoopers, 395
Pringles, 197
Privacy Rights Clearinghouse, 385
Private Label Manufacturers Association, 346
Procter & Gamble, 70, 71, 114, 180, 197, 198, 200, 204, 213, 216, 277, 348, 357, 454
Proflowers.com, 141
Provant, 144
Publix Super Markets, 84

Q

QAD, Inc., 190
Quaker Oats, 318
Qualcomm, 455
QuickBooks Pro, 391, 392
Qwest, 127

R

R.S. Bacon Veneer Co., 415–416
Race for the Cure, 93
RadioShack, 264
Radisson Hotels, 292
Rainmaker Thinking, 296
Rainwater, Inc., 276
Ralston Purina Co., 346
Raymond James Financial Inc., 436
Recreation Equipment Inc. (REI), 79
Redken, 321
Reengineering Resource Center, 210
Reliance Group, 457–458

Restrac, 262
Resume Exchange, 132
Resumix, 262
ReTool, 128
Revlon, 321
Rhone-Poulenc SA, 129
Richards Group, 208, 209
Ricoh, 91
Ritz Carlton, 95
Robert's American Gourmet, 365
Rocket Electric Co., 48
Rolex, 56
Rolls-Royce, 35
Rome Laboratory, 380
Roney & Co., 436
Roper Starch Worldwide, 313
Royal Caribbean Cruise Lines, 92
Royal Dutch/Shell Group, 188
Rubbermaid, Inc., 4
Rudwear Collection, 144

S

Safeway, 382
St. John's Wort Tortilla Chips, 365
Salem Five Cents Savings Bank, 437
Salomon Brothers, 87
Salomon Smith Barney, 452
Santa Cruz Amusement Park, 200
SAP, 236, 271
SAS Airlines, 259
SAS Institute, Inc., 287, 306
Saturn, 343
Save the Children, 97
Schroders, 434
Schwartz Communications, 114
Scotch, 471
Scotsman Industries, 464
Sears, 132, 265, 274, 345, 352, 477
Second Chance Body Armor, 136
Secure Computing, 73
Sensodyne, 328
Sequoia Capital, 167
Service Master, 69
Shell International Ltd., 190
Sherwin Williams, 66
SH Investments, Inc., 436
Showscan Entertainment, 53
Siemens A.G., 69
Siena, 246
Sierra Club, 17, 380
SightSound.com, 367
Silicon Graphics, Inc., 142
Silicon Valley Manufacturing Group, 45
SMART Commercial Kitchen system, 244
Smarte Carte, Inc., 81–82
SmartStream, 398
SmithKline, 70
Snap-on Tools, 274
Société Cease de Microelectronic et
    d'Horlogerie SA (SMH), 15
Society for Human Resource Management,
    275
Softbank Corp., 65
Sony, 318, 345, 349, 355
Southern Baptist Radio and Television
    Convention, 323
Southwest Airlines, 87, 260, 291
Spectrum Signal Processing, Inc., 282–283
Sportscape.com, 141
Sprint, 372
Spuds McKenzie, 93
Standard & Poor's (S&P), 449, 458

Star Alliance, 259
Starbucks, 72, 128, 260, 455
Stardot Consulting, 141
State Farm, 480
Statistical Research Inc. (SRI), 332
Steelcase, 95
Stevens Paint Brewery, 345
Stick-Up, 347
Stryker, 346
Student Advantage, 191
Stylus Innovation, Inc., 181
Subway, 135
Sumitomo Corp., 457
Summer Associates Information Services,
    148
Sunkist, 120
Susan G. Komen Breast Cancer Foundation,
    93
Suzuki, 65, 321
Systems for Measuring And Reporting
    Television (SMART), 332

T

Tacala, Inc., 122
Taco Bell, 121, 122
Tanqueray, 97
Target Corp., 194, 352
Taurus, 347
Taylor California Cellars, 350
Taylor Made Golf, 227
TBM Consulting, 171
TD Industries, 264
Teach for America, 132
TeamStaff, 259
Tenneco, 398
Texaco, 84, 265
Texas Instruments, 87, 88, 260–261, 350
TGI Friday, 292
Thai Airlines, 259
Thoughtworks, 451
3 Com, 383
Tide, 71
Time Warner, 136, 475
TMP Worldwide, 219
Tommy Hilfiger, 355
Topol, 328
Toyota Motor Corp., 16, 35, 62, 67, 72,
    97, 171, 182, 207–208, 242, 246,
    398
TransAtlantic Business Dialogue, 475
TransPoint, 121
TransUnion, 385
Travelers Group, 419, 471
Travelocity, 191
Travelodge, 36
Treebats, 142
Trilogy Software, Inc., 270, 271, 295
Tripod, 105
Trivial Pursuit, 6
TrueValue, 120
21st Capital Corp., 446
Tylenol, 34
Tyson, 35

U

UBS PaineWebber, 132, 262, 452
Unilever, 129
United Airlines, 17, 259, 263, 316,
    342–343
United Bank of Philadelphia, 432
United College Plus, 191

United Parcel Service (UPS), 260, 289
United Sciences Industries, 372
United States Olympic Committee (USOC),
    211
United Way, 17, 359
Upjohn Co., 215
UPR, Inc., 270
U.S. Hispanic Chamber of Commerce, 160
U.S. Steel. See USX
U.S. West, 127
USX, 34
Utz Quality Foods, 345

V

Valassis Communications, Inc., 283–284,
    309–310
Value America, 285
Vanguard Group, 460
Varig, 259
VarsityBooks.com, 191
Verdict Research Ltd., 47
Vermont Teddy Bear Co., 251–252
VF Corp., 211
Virgin Airlines, 461
Vodafone Group, 129
Volkswagen, 1, 15, 16, 341
Volvo, 308–309

W

Wal-Mart Stores Inc., 47, 75, 244, 260,
    317, 352, 355, 356, 475
Walt Disney Co., 4, 174, 263
Warner-Lambert, 126
Waterford, 355
Weathervane Terrace Inn and Suites, 416
Wells Fargo, 159, 195, 359, 431
Wells Test Preparation Center, 391–392,
    412
Wendy's, 321, 347
Wertkauf, 47
Westinghouse, 62, 63, 354
Whirlpool, 343
Whitlenge, 464
Wicks 'n' Sticks, 121
Windows, 220, 382
Wine.com, 389
Wineshopper.com, 389
Winnebago, 242
Wired Digital, Inc., 181
W.L. Gore and Associates, 263
Work Ethic, The, 88
Work/Family Directions, 114
Workforce Solutions, 276
Worldwide Refinishing Systems, 125
Wrigley, 91, 354

X

Xerox, 36, 69, 71, 132, 271, 300, 471
Xerox Technology Ventures (XTV), 142

Y

Yahoo!, 132, 161, 168, 381, 450
Yves St. Laurent, 321

Z

Zales Jewelers, 56
ZDNet, 384